1990 International Conference on Computer Languages

Proceedings

1990 International Conference on Computer Languages

March 12-15, 1990   New Orleans, Louisiana

Sponsored by The Computer Society
    Computer Languages Technical Committee

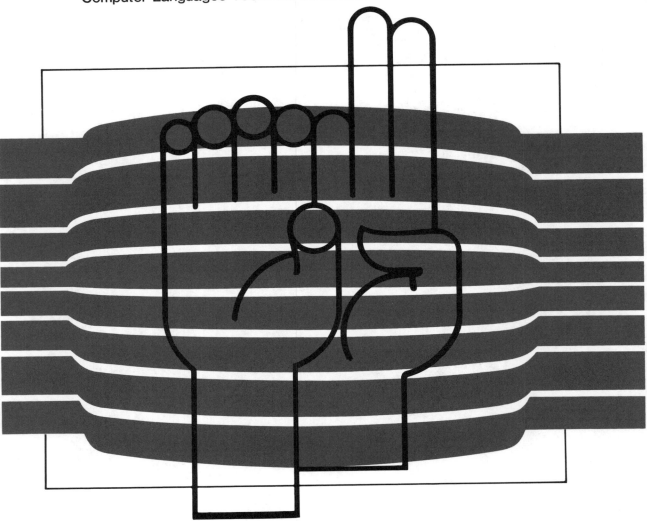

IEEE Computer Society Press   The Institute of Electrical and Electronics Engineerings, Inc.

1990 International Conference on Computer Languages

March 12-15, 1990   New Orleans, Louisiana

IEEE Computer Society Press
Los Alamitos, California

Washington   ●   Brussels   ●   Tokyo

Published by

IEEE Computer Society Press
10662 Los Vaqueros Circle
P.O. Box 3014
Los Alamitos, CA 90720-1264

Cover designed by Jack I. Ballestero

Printed in United States of America

IEEE Computer Society Press Order Number 2036
Library of Congress Number 89-82432
IEEE Catalog Number 90CH2854-8
ISBN 0-8186-2036-6 (paper)
ISBN 0-8186-6036-8 (microfiche)
ISBN 0-8186-9036-4 (case)
SAN 264-620X

Additional copies may be ordered from:

IEEE Computer Society
10662 Los Vaqueros Circle
P.O. Box 3014
Los Alamitos CA 90720-1264

IEEE Service Center
445 Hoes Lane
P.O. Box 1331
Piscataway, NJ 08855-1331

IEEE Computer Society
13, Avenue de l'Aquilon
B-1200 Brussels
BELGIUM

IEEE Computer Society
Ooshima Building
2-19-1 Minami-Aoyama,
Minato-Ku
Tokyo 107 JAPAN

 THE INSTITUTE OF ELECTRICAL AND ELECTRONICS ENGINEERS, INC.

IEEE

Message from the Conference Chair

ICCL is the flagship conference of the IEEE Computer Society Technical Committee on Computer Languages. ICCL '90 is the third of the series. Despite its youth, ICCL is asserting itself as a high-quality conference on computer languages. A look at the papers in these proceedings confirms the technical strength and international character of ICCL. The organizing committee is dedicated to maintain this level of technical quality.

The purpose of ICCL is to provide a forum for language designers, implementors, and users without being confined to one given category of languages. ICCL seeks to address issues of computer languages that encompass a wide spectrum of paradigms, computational models, and abstractions levels. Thus, we hope to provide a complete service to the computer languages community.

The organization of ICCL '90 spans over two years during which volunteers and Computer Society staff devoted part of their time to make the conference successful. I would like to thank everybody who was involved. Specifically, I would like to thank the program committee co-chairs, K.C. Tai and Alex Wolf, for selecting a strong program committee, for defining a rigorous refereeing process, and for making all the deadlines. I would like also to thank the other members of the organizing committee. These are: Mark Benard (treasurer), David Langan (publicity chair), Margaret Montehnyol (tutorial chair), Marguerite Saacks (publications chair), Joan Coats (local arrangements), and Pei Hsia and Joe Urban (steering committee). I would like also to thank the Conference and Tutorials staff and the Computer Society Press staff.

Boumediene Belkhouche, Tulane University

Message from the Program Co-Chairs

Throughout the brief history of computer science, a central theme has been communication with the computer. A cynic might say that computer science research ultimately amounts to the invention of one language after another. Whether or not you agree, it is certainly true that we computer scientists spend a lot of our time on issues of language. And we do this in a surprisingly wide variety of areas of computer science, not just the most obvious one of programming the computer to perform some task; consider, for example, requirements languages, design languages, hardware description languages, protocol languages, and input/output languages.

The purpose of this series of conferences is to bring together people broadly interested in all aspects of machine processable descriptions—i.e., *computer languages.* By "machine processable" we do not exclusively mean "machine executable". Rather we mean simply that the computer is in some way involved in the manipulation of the description, such as performing consistency analysis of a hardware description. It is our belief that there is a vast amount of common ground to be explored and that this, the third in the series of Computer Languages conferences, represents a uniquely thorough and extremely high quality examination of that terrain.

We received 132 submissions to the conference. Each submission was carefully reviewed by at least three people, of which at least two (and often all three) were program committee members. The submissions were reviewed on the basis of their relevance, significance, originality, correctness, and clarity. Our aim was to accept only top-quality submissions, no matter how many or few that may have been. The result of the review process was acceptance of only 32 of the submissions. We note that those 32 represent a truly international interest and participation in the conference, with authors from eight different countries.

Credit for such a strong technical program must go in large measure to a program committee that attacts strong submissions. We thank the members of the program committee for agreeing to serve and for the enormous effort and time they put into reviewing the submissions. We also thank the additional reviewers, whose help allowed us to more carefully review each submission. Finally, we thank Rick Greer of AT&T for his help in automating the record keeping and other administrative aspects of putting a conference program together through his DataShare database management system.

K.C. Tai, National Science Foundation
Alexander L. Wolf, AT&T Bell Laboratories

Organizing Committee

Program Committee Co-chairs
K.C. Tai, National Science Foundation
Alexander L. Wolf, AT&T Bell Laboratories

Program Committee
Mario Barbacci, *CMU–Software Eng. Inst.*
O. Peter Buneman, *Univ. of Pennsylvania*
S.K. Chang, *Univ. of Pittsburgh*
David Gelernter, *Yale University*
Donald Good, *Computational Logic, Inc.*
John Goodenough, *CMU–Software Eng. Inst.*
Carlo Ghezzi, *Politecnico di Milano*
Richard LeBlanc, *Georgia Tech*
Gary Lindstrom, *Univ. of Utah*
Al Mok, *Univ. of Texas, Austin*
Steven Reiss, *Brown University*
William Scherlis, *DARPA*
Alan Snyder, *Hewlett–Packard Laboratories*
Donald Stanat, *Univ. of N. Carolina, Chapel Hill*

Conference Chair
Boumediene Belkhouche, Tulane Univ.

Steering Committee
Pei Hsia, *Univ. of Texas, Arlington*
Joseph Urban, *Arizona State Univ.*

Treasurer
Mark Benard, *Tulane Univ.*

Tutorials
Margaret Montenyohl,
      Univ. of SW Louisiana

Publications
Marguerite Saacks, *Tulane Univ.*

Publicity
David Langan, *Univ. of S. Alabama*

Additional Reviewers

William Appelbe
Boumediene Belkhouche
Manuel Bermudez
Roberto Bisiani
Guy Blelloch
James Bowen
Val Breazu-Tannen
J. Dean Brock
Ugo Buy
Richard Carver
C.Y. Roger Chen
Shiu-Kai Chin
Jan Chomicki
Eric Cooper
James Coplien
Daniel Corkill
Akshay Despande
David Dettlefs
Laurie Dillon
Alan Fisher
Glenn Fowler
Phyllis Frankl
Anthony Gadient
Jean Gallier

Emden Gasner
Narain Gehani
Lal George
Judy Grass
Arun Gupta
John Hagerman
Philip Hatcher
Dennis Heimbigner
Pei Hsia
Gail Kaiser
Krishna Kavi
Eduardo Krell
Bala Krishnamurthy
Beth Lagnese
Kwei-Jay Lin
Gyula Mago
Dale Miller
J. Eliot B. Moss
Tim Muths
Stephen North
Evelyn Obaid
Atsuhi Ohori
Will Partain
Frank Pfenning

David Plaisted
H. Andy Podgurski
Jan Prins
Suresh Rajgopal
Krithi Ramamritham
Robert Rodman
David Rosenblum
Teo Rus
Barbara Ryder
Marguerite Saacks
Robert Schwanke
John Shilling
Bruce Smith
Richard Snodgrass
Stan Sutton
James Symon
Philip Thrift
Joseph Urban
Richard Waters
Jon Webb
Jack Wileden
Michal Young
Pamela Zave
Steven Zeil

Table of Contents

Visual Languages

Functional Language Implementation

Distributed Languages I

Language Design I

Object-Oriented Models

Distributed Language II

Language Design II

Logic Programming

Parallel Languages

Language Implementation

A Practical Animation Language for Software Development

John T. Stasko

School of Information and Computer Science

Georgia Institute of Technology

Atlanta, GA 30332-0280

stasko@prism.gatech.edu

Abstract

In this paper we describe a practical language for creating real-time, two-dimensional, smooth, color animations. Animation can be an valuable component in a variety of domains such as user interface design, on-line help information, and computer aided instruction. Unfortunately, current methods for creating animations tend to be ad-hoc, varying widely from application to application. Another weakness of current methods is that relatively little work has been done on the formal specification and semantics of graphics, especially animation.

Our animation language produces aesthetically pleasing, smooth imagery and is easy to learn and use. The language is based on four abstract data types: locations, images, paths, and transitions; animation designers create and modify objects of these types in order to produce animation sequences. In addition, we provide a precise specification and semantics for all the data type operations. This rigorous definition helps simplify animation design by formalizing the actions resulting from the operations. We have implemented a prototype algorithm animation system that utilizes our design language as its basis.

1 Introduction

The increasing availability and sophistication of workstations has made programmers come to expect more advanced imagery in user interfaces. With improvements in display hardware, animation is now a viable part of those interfaces. Unfortunately, animation design methods are usually ad-hoc, lacking conceptual support, and peculiar to the particular application. Often, such animations only consist of a repeated shuffle through slightly altered sequences of precomputed bitmaps.

What is needed is a practical graphics language containing primitives specifically tailored for animation. The language should be as simple as possible in order to encourage its use, and it should be general purpose, capable of displaying a wide variety of imagery. Another requirement for the language is that it have a precise semantics with formal specification. Although the merits of specification are universally acknowledged, relatively little work has occurred concerning specification of picture images, especially animated images.

We have developed a language for producing color, two-dimensional animation sequences. Our language supports aesthetically pleasing, smooth image changes, and

includes animation primitives specifically created to simplify animation design and implementation. We also provide formal models and precise semantics to insure the consistency of design sequences. Our approach is object based: by creating and manipulating objects of four simple data types, programmers produce their desired animation actions.

The specific application area that our work addresses is *algorithm animation*, the production of animated visualizations of the abstractions, data, and operations in executing computer programs. Algorithm animations occur in real-time, without delays from image rendering. As a program runs, it provides information to its accompanying animation view and thus controls the imagery and display. Algorithm animation is particularly difficult because animations cannot be totally predefined—run-time data dictates how the animation must appear.

The application of our animation language need not be restricted to algorithm animation, however. Animation is currently becoming more evident in a variety of areas such as computer-aided design, user interfaces, and online help information. The advantages of a formal design paradigm over ad-hoc methods are clear; our language provides a practical example that can be used in these and other areas.

2 The Path-Transition Paradigm

A computer animation consists of a collection of graphical objects to which a collection of modifications such as movement, changes in color or size, and so forth, occur over time. We have identified a set of four abstract data types that encapsulate the constituents of an animation. These animation data types serve as the basis for what we term our "animation framework." They include the graphical *images* on the screen, the *locations* they occupy, the *transitions* the images make, and the *paths* that modify the image transitions. Our animation design method is called the *path-transition* paradigm, based on the two data types that drive the animation actions. As part of each data type, we also provide a set of constituent operations. Defining an animation involves creating and manipulating specific instances of the data types using these operations.

To examine in more detail the way that the image, location, path, and transition data types are utilized, we will consider, as an example, a specific activity that might occur in an animation. Suppose that we have a rectangle and a line in the animation viewing area as in Figure 1.

Figure 1: A simple animation in which the rectangle moves up to the top of the line.

We would like to design an animation that consists of the rectangle moving in a straight path over to the top of the line.

The rectangle and line pictures are instances of the image data type. We will assume that some form of image creation operation put them in their current positions. Because we would like the rectangle to move to the top of the line, we will inquire the current positions of the center of the rectangle's lower edge and the top endpoint of the line. These coordinate positions are examples of the location data type. We can utilize the two locations as endpoints in a path that consists of a sequence of interpolated points between the two path endpoints; this path is an example of the path data type. The motion of the rectangle along the path provides an instance of the final data type, the transition. This is a very simple example of an animation activity and the way that the path-transition paradigm applies to it.

Our images and animations are laid out in a real-valued, infinite *animation coordinate system*. By designing in terms of real values instead of integer values representing pixels, animations can be designed to function regardless of the animation window size. In practice, our framework is designed to assist the production of animated views in windows on a bit-mapped graphics workstation. We will refer to such windows as *animation windows*. Therefore, the particular animation system implementation of the framework is responsible for mapping the animation coordinate system onto an actual animation window. One common example mapping is to create a square viewing area in the window with coordinate (0.0, 0.0) at the upper left corner and the coordinate (1.0, 1.0) at the lower right corner of the viewing area.

In the remainder of this section we will discuss each of the four animation data types in more detail. We also will list some of the operations that we have identified as being useful for creating the styles of animations we desire. To conclude the section, we will discuss our mapping mechanism from a computer process into the animation framework.

2.1 Abstract Data Types

2.1.1 Locations

A *location* is a position of interest within the animation coordinate system and is identified by an (x, y) coordinate pair. The ability to save and reference particular locations is an important tool for animation design because geometric positioning of the animation entities is one of the most valuable methods to convey information from a program.

We define the following operations on the location data type. The location creation operation *LocCreate* takes x

and y coordinate values and returns a location object. To determine if two particular location instances reference the same coordinate values, we provide a location equivalence inquiry operation, *LocEqual*. For calculations involving particular location coordinates, we provide the *LocX* and *LocY* operations to reference the individual x and y coordinates of a location. Coordinates within a location can be changed through the use of the *LocModify* operation. This operation provides a general modification scheme as the two real values are simply added to the x and y coordinates of the given location.

2.1.2 Images

Animation is the process of giving movement and action to objects. In computer animation these objects are static pictures that undergo changes in location, size, color, and so forth, throughout frames of the animation to simulate action. In our animation framework, two types of picture objects called *images*, exist: *primary images* and *composite images*.

Primary Images

Primary images are the most basic types of images manipulated in the framework. Some common examples are lines, circles, rectangles and text. Restricting primary images to a specific format or a given set of primary image types would greatly restrict the animation framework. Consequently, we define a primary image by a set of parameters and a set of methods. Formally, we define a primary image as a 6-tuple (t, o, v, P, R, d) where t is the primary image type, o is the image's position, v is the image's visibility, P is a set of parameters local to the image type, R is a set of transition methods, and d is a drawing method. The use of the local parameters P is necessary because specific types of primary images differ. For example, a line may have *size*, *thickness*, and *color* local parameters, whereas a circle may have *radius*, *fill*, and *color* parameters.

Images are modified by framework objects called transitions acting upon them. As part of a primary image definition, each image type must have a method in which the particular transitions affect the image parameters. Movement and visibility transitions affect each primary image type in the same manner: the position and visibility fields are modified. Primary images also must handle all the other types of framework transitions in a well-defined manner. For example, a circle may have its *radius* parameter modified by a *resize* transition, whereas a line may simply ignore a *fill* transition. The final component of the primary image definition is a draw method. This component translates a primary image from its parametric definition to a static, graphical picture image.

In an object-oriented sense, specific types of primary images are subtypes of a general primary image supertype. The primary image supertype consists of *position* and *visibility* parameters along with movement and visibility transition method handlers. Each type of image added to the framework inherits these fields from the supertype and also defines its own set of local parameters and methods. This object-oriented view of images is convenient for system designers implementing the animation framework.

Composite Images

Composite images create a new type of image that is a

```
rect 0.00 0.00 0.10 0.20 black unfilled
rect 0.01 0.01 0.08 0.08 black unfilled
rect 0.01 0.11 0.08 0.08 black unfilled
circ 0.09 0.10 0.005 black unfilled
```

Figure 2: A composite image definition representing a door and the resulting image object.

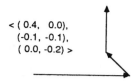

Figure 3: A sample path with length 3.

collection of primary images usually having some geometric relationship to one another. The ability to coalesce a set of primary images into one new image type and repeatedly create instances of the image greatly extends the graphical display of the framework. Composite images are defined as a list of primary images in a local coordinate system. Positions of the primary images are all relative to the position parameter provided as the location of the composite image. For example, suppose we wish to repeatedly create an instance of a door in an animation. The definition in Figure 2 produces the accompanying composite image. Each line of the definition identifies a new primary image. The first two real numbers on a line indicate the location of the image; the next numbers indicate widths and heights for the rectangles or a radius for the circle.

Both primary and composite images are created via the image creation operation, *ImageCreate*. We also provide a bounding box oriented image location query operation called *ImageLoc*. Given an image and a compass position such as *NorthWest* or *East* or the special *Center* position, the operation returns a location object that corresponds to that current position of the image. This operation is useful as illustrated by the following example. Suppose two rectangle images exist, and we want to create an animation in which the first rectangle moves over on top of the second rectangle, like boxes stacked up, with their left edges aligned. To do this, we would identify the *SouthWest* part of the first rectangle and the *NorthWest* part of the second rectangle. Then, to carry out the desired animation, we would create a movement path for the first rectangle to traverse with endpoints at these two locations.

Another issue involving images is their relative layering in the animation coordinate system. If two rectangles of differing colors occupy the same location, we must determine which one will be considered to be on a plane closer to the viewer, and hence be visible. To establish consistency in the framework, we set up a relative ordering of images in order to handle this problem. When a new image is added, it is always placed in the top-most relative plane (closest to the viewer). We also include transition actions in the framework that place images in the top-most and bottom-most planes. We will discuss these types of consistency issues in more detail in Section 3.

2.1.3 Paths

Images that undergo changes throughout time produce animation. In our framework *paths* are the only parameters to changes (called transitions) other than the affected image; paths serve as the primary definitional aspect of the actions occurring in a transition. Using paths as directional routes for images in movement transitions is a nat-

ural, well-accepted notion. An important concept within our framework, however, is the fact paths are the only modifiers used for all types of transitions, including those such as changes in color, visibility, and size. By establishing a consistent model for transitions, each takes an image and a path parameter, but nothing else, we have simplified the components necessary for designing animations. Animation designers need not worry about remembering the exact set of parameters that a particular transition type uses.

Formally, a path is defined to be a finite, ordered sequence of real-valued (x, y) coordinate pairs, where each pair designates a relative offset from the previous position. The initial coordinate pair of a path is offset from the path's starting position. The *length* of a path p is the number of coordinate pairs it includes. This concept of a path is a direct descendant of the *p-curve* structure of Baecker[2]. A pictorial view of a sample path of length 3 is given in Figure 3.

Paths designate two-dimensional routes in an abstract coordinate system. For actions such as movement, we can think of the coordinate system as our animation framework coordinate system. It is important to understand, however, that paths traverse purely relative coordinate values. Once a path is created, it is used in a transition to apply to an image that has an absolute position. Particular relative offsets of the path then define how the image will change in the animation. Notice that a path also contains a time component in some sense. Each subsequent offset determines the location and appearance of an image in the next frame or time unit of the animation. Consequently, paths actually define three-dimensional modifiers of images in animations: the x and y dimensions of the coordinate system and the time scale of the animation itself.

Animation designers maintain control of the relative spacing between offsets in a path. In a graphical environment that supports fast image updates, utilizing paths with very small changes in x and y from offset to offset produces smooth, visually pleasing animation effects. Removing intermediate offsets speeds up a motion; adding offsets slows it down. We believe this explicit mechanism of describing the path of an image's movement is a much more natural way to design animations than requiring repeated "image draw" calls on an implicit path.

The basic operation for creating paths, *PathCreate*, receives an ordered list of locations; each location defines the x and y relative offsets. Frequently, it is necessary to know the length of a path. The *PathLength* operation returns the number of offsets contained in a path. The *PathDx* and *PathDy* operations return the net change in x and y, respectively, that the path traverses from start to finish in the animation coordinate system. For the path in Figure 3, *PathDx* would return 0.3 and *PathDy* would

straight clockwise counterclockwise

Figure 4: The movements of the three basic path types. Each is defined to have length 20.

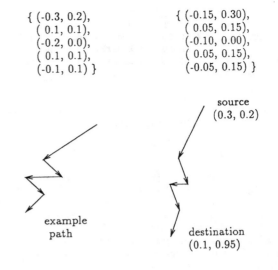

{ (-0.3, 0.2),
(0.1, 0.1),
(-0.2, 0.0),
(0.1, 0.1),
(-0.1, 0.1) }

{ (-0.15, 0.30),
(0.05, 0.15),
(-0.10, 0.00),
(0.05, 0.15),
(-0.05, 0.15) }

source
(0.3, 0.2)

example
path

destination
(0.1, 0.95)

Figure 5: An example path and the resultant produced by the PathExample operation, given the indicated source and destination locations.

return -0.3.

Although the *PathCreate* operation can produce every possible path, it is an inconvenient format for creating paths that will actually be used in the animation framework. For additional utility, we provide operations that create some basic types of paths by introducing other, more pragmatic, path creation operations below.

Because most image movements follow simple routes such as straight lines or simple arcs, we introduce three basic path types into the animation framework: *straight*, *clockwise*, and *counterclockwise*. Visualizations of the three path types are presented in Figure 4. We define a standard for these basic types so that each has length 20 and moves 0.2 distance units in x from the starting location to the ending location of the path. These values are somewhat arbitrary—they produce aesthetically pleasing motions in simple animations we designed to run in square animation windows with a side measuring 1.0 units. The *PathMakeType* operation creates a path in one of these types. Although the paths created by this operation can be used directly in a transition, most often the paths will be edited in some way by a path modification operation before actually being used.

The method for specifying arcs in the Metafont system[9] using intermediate points as well as enter and exit angles presents another possibility that we are considering for path creation in the future. The method would have to be supplemented with a technique for specifying the number of offsets in the arc, however.

In the framework we provide operations that copy, rotate, scale, and extend paths. The *PathInterpolate* operation adds or removes offsets from a path while maintaining its overall change in x and y. This operation can be used to control the relative speed of an action. Changes occur more quickly along a path with fewer offsets. We also provide operations to add or delete offsets from the head or tail of paths. The *PathColor* operation returns a path, which when used in a *color* transition, will change an image to a specified color.

One key issue in using paths in an animation occurs when using paths as routes for image movement. Image movement often takes the form of moving an image from its current location to some new location that depends upon particular run-time data. These two locations, the starting and ending points, typically cannot be determined until that particular instant before the movement transition occurs. Consequently, compiled paths defined at animation design time such as those from the *PathMakeType* operation, may not move the image to the desired position. Therefore, the framework must include operations that receive two locations and create a path that begins at the one location and ends at the other.

PathDistance is such an operation. In addition to two locations, it takes a distance parameter in order to define a path containing relative offsets spread apart by the given animation coordinate system distance and that moves in a straight line from source to destination. The *PathExample* operation also uses source and destination locations like *PathDistance*, but its parameter used for creating a new path is an example path. The new path is designed to "look like" the example path as closely as possible; this involves maintaining the same path length and the same geometric characteristics while still moving from the source to the destination location. An example of the use of this operation is given in Figure 5. The left path is the example path, and the right path is produced by *PathExample* given the indicated source and destination locations.

We define three operators, *concatenation*, *iteration*, and *composition*,[1] on paths. Concatenation and iteration append copies of paths together in the manner suggested by their names, and composition combines paths on an offset by offset basis, much like vector addition.

2.1.4 Transitions

Locations, images, and paths have set the foundation for the animation framework. All that is missing is the final component, action. The logical units of action or change in the animation framework, called *transitions*, utilize a path to affect an image by modifying its position or appearance. Moving a line in a wavy path, altering the fill style of a circle, or shrinking a rectangle as it changes color are all examples of transitions. Additionally, we can think of the simultaneous occurrence of all three of these actions as a new, albeit more complex, transition.

A *simple* transition is defined by the 3-tuple (t, i, p), where t is the transition type, i is the image being al-

---

[1] Our use of the word "composition" refers to a specific type of combination, not the formal mathematical definition of composition.

tered, and p is a path argument modifier. Some common examples of simple transition types are *move*, *resize*, *fill*, *color*, and *alter visibility*. Like that done for primary images, we do not restrict simple transitions to a specific set of transition types, however. The general model of a simple transition allows the framework implementation to be extended when a new type of transition is needed. Note that simple transitions correspond roughly to *methods* in a strict object-oriented sense. We can think of sending a *resize* method to a particular image object.

The path data type plays an important role in the definition of a transition. As discussed earlier, the coordinate pairs making up a path correspond to the individual frames of an animation. In essence, the path argument defines the duration of a transition. Nevertheless, different types of transitions utilize path arguments in different ways. *Move* transitions use paths as routes for images to follow. Each coordinate pair of the path specifies the distance and direction that the image should move for the next animation frame. *Visibility* transitions disregard the specific x and y values of the coordinate pairs of a path; each coordinate pair is simply interpreted by toggling the image's visibility in the next animation frame. *Fill* transitions utilize the x component of a coordinate pair by adding its value to an image's fill value, which ranges between 0.0 (outline) and 1.0 (completely filled).

If we decompose a path into its individual relative offsets and consider each along with the transition type and primary image components, we encounter the substructure that makes up a simple transition. This structure primitive, called a *transition unit*, is the atomic level action that occurs in an animation. Each transition unit defines the action to occur in order to generate the next frame of the animation. More formally, a transition unit is defined as a quadruple (t, i, x, y), where t is the transition type, i is the image affected, and x and y are the particular offset arguments. Simple transitions are nothing more than ordered lists of transition units.

Three important transition types, *delay*, *raise*, and *lower* are always included in the framework. The *delay* transition type creates transitions with "empty" transition units in which no change occurs. The length of the path argument denotes the number of empty transition units to create. This transition provides an animation designer with a method for delaying and coordinating the relative times of animation actions. The transition type *raise* forces an image to the top-most layer of the animation coordinate system. Each transition unit in a *raise* transition will bring the image argument of the transition unit to the viewing plane closest to that of the user. The image does not change its location in the animation coordinate system. The *lower* transition works in the expected, opposite manner. Semantics of these operations will be discussed in Section 3.

The *TransCreate* operation creates simple transitions for subsequent use. Three transition operators then combine transitions to form new, more complex transitions. The *concatenation* operator binds two transitions together into a single, new transition which corresponds to the latter transition argument commencing immediately after the initial transition argument is complete. That is, the two lists of transition units are appended to form one longer list. The *iteration* operator performs repeated concatenation of a transition with itself. The third transition operator, *composition*, is more complex.

Composition introduces a form of concurrent execution of transitions. When two transitions are composed, the animation actions they denote occur simultaneously. Consider two separate *move* transitions defined upon a circle and a line respectively, that each utilize the same path argument. Composing these transitions creates a new transition that exhibits each of the images moving by the same relative offset, as defined by the path, between each frame of the animation. In essence, between each animation frame two transition units will occur—one for the circle image and one for the line image. Let us define a transition *moment* as a list of transition units that occur "simultaneously" in one time unit, in order to generate a new frame of an animation. This allows us to formally define a general transition in the framework as on ordered list of moments. Notice that a simple transition contains moments with only one transition unit. Figure 6 provides examples of these different types of transitions.

The concurrency exhibited by *TransCompose* is accomplished by combining corresponding moments in the two transition arguments into a new, larger moment in the resulting transition. The two lists of transition units making up the first moment of each transition being composed are appended to form a longer transition unit list that is the first moment of the resulting composition transition. The process is repeated for all moments in the transitions. If two transitions containing an unequal number of moments are composed, the shorter transition is implicitly padded at the end with empty moments to make the composition one-to-one. A good way to intuitively think about these operations is that concatenation combines lists of transition moments end-to-end, whereas composition combines them side-to-side.

Composition provides a natural way to perform an animation where more than one object changes. For example, consider the exchange of the positions of two rectangles. In order to design this animation, first we create two *move* transitions, each corresponding to one of the rectangles moving to the other's position. Then we compose the two transitions into a single, new transition that denotes their concurrent movements.

As a more sophisticated example, suppose we wish to define a transition that moves an image i along a path p_1 that has length 20. We also would like the image's visibility to toggle during the middle 10 movements in the path. We shall use the following notation for the transition operators:

$t_1 \cdot t_2 \equiv$ concatenate transitions t_1 and t_2 (t_1 first),

$t^{num} \equiv$ iterate the transition t *num* times,

$t_1 \odot t_2 \equiv$ compose transitions t_1 and t_2.

If we create the paths

$p_2 = \text{PathNull}(5),$

$p_3 = \text{PathNull}(1),$

and the transitions

$t_1 = \text{TransCreate}(delay, i, p_2),$

$t_2 = \text{TransCreate}(visible, i, p_3),$

$t_3 = \text{TransCreate}(move, i, p_1),$

$$\langle \langle (move, i_1, 0.2, 0.4) \rangle, \qquad\qquad \langle \langle (resize, i_1, 0.1, 0.0), (fill, i_2, 0.1, 0.1) \rangle,$$
$$\langle (move, i_1, -0.1, -0.3) \rangle, \qquad moments \qquad \langle (delay, i_3, 0.0, 0.0) \rangle,$$
$$\langle (move, i_1, -0.4, 0.1) \rangle \rangle \qquad\qquad \langle (move, i_3, -0.5, 0.0), (color, i_3, 0.2, -0.04) \rangle,$$
$$\langle (visibility, i_2, 0.0, 0.0) \rangle \rangle$$

Figure 6: The left transition is simple; the general transition on the right has been built up using the *TransCompose* operation. The notation $\langle\rangle$ denotes a list.

the desired animation is simply the following expression:

$$(t_1 \cdot t_2^{10} \cdot t_1) \odot t_3.$$

Once a transition has been defined, the *TransPerform* operation actually executes it. Intuitively, this command works by sequentially examining the moments making up a transition; the changes denoted by the particular transition unit lists in a moment all occur "simultaneously" between the frames of the animation. By processing moments, one transition unit list after another, the frames of the animation are generated.

2.2 Mapping Component

Usually, an animation is a representation of a process, a mapping from the programming world into a visual world. For example, a direct manipulation user interface represents objects and data in an application. In algorithm animation the animated view is a simulation of the abstract processes of a computer program.

In our animation framework we provide the connection facility from program objects to animation objects through *associations*. Associations allow designers to connect data objects such as a framework image, location, or data value of importance to a set of parameters received from a driving program or process. An association between a framework object and another framework object can also be created. Associations are identified by unique names, and they can utilize zero or more parameters.

More formally, an association is a method to store a data object such as an animation data type object or a data value. A typical implementation uses hashing. The hash key for the data object is the name of the association and a list of parameters. The number of parameters to each association is fixed. Typically, the parameters are the data values being mapped from a program. For example, to associate an integer array a of length 10 with ten rectangle images, we could create an association with name "IMAGE", first parameter the initial memory address of a, and second parameter the particular array index position.

Animation designers are free to create new association names as needed. We also provide a small set of predefined associations: The "ID" association with two parameters is usually used as a general purpose data mapping facility. The "IMAGE_AT" association takes one parameter, typically a location object, and stores the image object currently associated with that location.

Three functions perform all of the association duties within the framework. The Create function defines an association and the number of parameters it utilizes. An association must be defined with this function before it can be utilized. The Store function associates a data object with a key—the association's name and a list of parameters. Attempts to store a data object in an association with the incorrect number of parameters will be considered an error; no data will be stored. The Retrieve function returns the data object associated with a given key. If no data object has been stored with the given key, a null value is returned.

2.3 Animation Scenes

For manageability reasons, in the framework we decompose an animation into a set of smaller logical components called *animation scenes*. The creation and breakdown of an animation into scenes is purely determined by the animation's designer; there is no "correct" decomposition. Quite often, however, a logical separation of important actions presents itself, not unlike the breakdown of a large computer program into subroutines.

In the framework we model an animation scene informally as a parameterized procedure. The procedure body consists primarily of the animation data type operations and association mapping calls described in this section. Animation scenes also often require mathematical and control flow facilities. Parameters to scenes are received by value; they consist of integer, real and string values.

As a first implementation, rather than creating a new stand-alone language, we utilized a host language for our framework. We implemented the four abstract data types in the framework as user-defined types in the C programming language. We also implemented the operations upon the types as a package of calls available to animation designers. This allows us to utilize C procedures as our animation scenes; the mathematical and control flow facilities provided by C are sufficient for designing sophisticated animation actions.

Figure 7 provides an example of an animation scene as it appears under our implementation. The scene's purpose is to retrieve two rectangles that were created and stored in a prior scene, and then exchange their positions in a smooth, continuous looping motion. We assume that the rectangles have been stored under an association "RECT" taking an ID and an index as parameters. This scene is often utilized in algorithm animations when illustrating the exchange of values in a sorting program.

3 Semantics of Animation Operations

As discussed earlier, the animation component of our framework includes the visual images presented in the display and the transformations they undergo as time passes. We model the animation component through an *animation state* defined by the 4-tuple (L, I, P, T), where L is a set of locations, I is a set of images, P is a set of paths,

```
Exchange(id1, n1, id2, n2)
    int id1, n1, id2, n2;
{
    Location      loc1, loc2;
    Image         rect1, rect2;
    Path          looper, expath, rotpath;
    Transition    move1, move2, composer;

    rect1 = AssocRetrieve("RECT", id1, n1);
    rect2 = AssocRetrieve("RECT", id2, n2);

    loc1 = ImageLoc(rect1, SouthWest);
    loc2 = ImageLoc(rect2, SouthWest);

        /* Create two semicircular movement paths */
    looper = PathMakeType(Clockwise);
    expath = PathExample(loc1, loc2, looper);
    rotpath = PathRotate(expath, 180);

        /* Do simultaneous rectangle movements */
    move1 = TransCreate(Move, rect1, expath);
    move2 = TransCreate(Move, rect2, rotpath);
    composer = TransCompose(2, move1, move2);
    TransPerform(composer);

        /* Reset associations due to exchange */
    AssocStore("RECT", id1, n1, rect2);
    AssocStore("RECT", id2, n2, rect1);
}
```

Figure 7: An *Exchange* animation scene in which two rectangles switch positions.

and T is a set of transitions. These four sets represent the active, available objects during an animation.

Note that at any particular point in time, the set of active images, I, does not uniquely determine the appearance of images existing in the animation coordinate system. For example, the set of images could include two rectangles, one green and one yellow, each with the same location and size. Depending upon the relative ordering or layering of the rectangles, we could see green or yellow at their location. Consequently, we will introduce the notion of the *configuration* of images, C, which is an ordered list of all the active images in the set I. Given two images, i_1 and i_2, if i_1 precedes i_2 in the configuration list, then i_1 is considered to be on a viewing plane closer to the animation viewer than i_2. That is, if i_1 and i_2 occupy the same location in the animation coordinate system, i_1 will obscure i_2 if i_1 it is earlier in the configuration list.

Transitions that are performed in the animation framework provide the intermediate points in time for identifying a particular configuration as a frame in the animation. The lists of transition units that occur "simultaneously" between frames generate a new configuration from the current one.[2] Within the framework we define the formal notion of an *animation* as an ordered list of configurations. Therefore, we capture the essence of an entire animation by this simple concept, a list of image lists.

[2] Recall that we defined a moment in a transition is as the list of transition units that correspond to the changes that occur between frames of an animation.

The sole semantic purpose of each of the animation framework operations except for *ImageCreate* and *TransPerform* is to modify the animation state. Most operations add a new location, image, path, or transition object to the corresponding field in the animation state. Some simply return a parameter value about a framework object and make no change to the animation state. The *ImageCreate* function, in addition to modifying the animation state, adds images to the front of the image configuration list. The *TransPerform* operation is even more complex, however, as it can modify the animation state, reorder the image configuration list, and add one or more of these new configurations to the animation list. The number of new configurations generated corresponds directly to the length of the path(s) that serves as an argument to the transition being performed.

Two related, primary semantic issues that arise in the framework are the ordering of transition units within a moment of a transition, and the ordering of images within the configuration. These issues are important because we want to provide consistency throughout the framework and its operations.

Because of the *TransCompose* operation, many transition unit actions can occur "simultaneously" in one moment of a transition between the frames of an animation. The appearance of simultaneity is given by displaying the images in the current configuration, modifying the images' parameters as dictated by the transition units in that moment, then redisplaying the images in the resulting configuration. The difficulty occurs in that at some level we must still apply the transition units in a serial manner within the moment. Two *move* transition units defined upon one image offer no problem. Either application ordering of the two results in the image ending up at the same location. But if two *color* transition units defined upon the same image, one red and one blue, exist in a moment, their application ordering is critical. Whichever one is applied last will determine the image's color in the subsequent configuration.

Fortunately, because the only method for combining transition units into a moment is the *TransCompose* operation, we can deal with this issue by defining the way *TransCompose* generates transition unit lists. This is done by simply declaring that when composing two transitions, those transition units in the first transition parameter precede those of the second parameter when forming transition unit lists. That is, given the operation *TransCompose*(tr_1, tr_2) where tr_1 changes an image to red and tr_2 changes an image to blue, following the performance of this composition transition, the image will be blue.

The second important semantic issue concerns the ordering of images in a configuration and subsequently in the viewing window. As noted previously, images at the beginning of the configuration list will appear to be closer to the viewer. But how do images establish positions within the configuration list? We solve this problem through two simple rules.

1. Whenever an image is created, it is added to the front of the configuration list.

2. Whenever a transition unit of type *raise* is applied to an image, the image is brought to the front of the configuration list.

Hence, barring any use of the *raise* transition, the initial creation order of images defines their relative ordering in viewing planes of the animation coordinate system.

Below we provide a look at the semantic formalisms we use to specify our design language. Due to space limitations, we include only a brief example. For the complete definitions, see [13].

The four animation data types are specified as follows:

Location	*lo*	*x*:Real, *y*:Real
Image	*im*	*type*:ImageType, *pos*:Location,
		vis:Boolean, {*local parameters*}
Path	*pa*	*offsets*:list(Location)
TransUnit	*tu*	*type*:TransType, *image*:Image,
		x:Real, *y*:Real
Transition	*tr*	*moment*:list(list(TransUnit))

The symbols $\langle \rangle$ denote a list of some object, and the symbol $\emptyset$ denotes an empty list.

Our definitions provide a means for a better understanding of the animation generation process. As stated earlier, previous animation work is often void of such analysis. We desired to describe the framework operations in detail, yet remain true to the framework goal of a straightforward design process. We chose techniques similar to those of Mallgren[10] to accomplish this.

Following Mallgren's axiomatic designations for describing operations upon graphic data types, we divide operations upon the animation data types into three categories. *Generators* produce objects of the type of the operation (location objects for location operations, etc.). *Inquiry* operations return objects of some type other than that of the operation. Typically, they examine an object of the type of interest and return some parameter about it. Finally, *basic generators* are subsets of the generators, and are a sufficient set of operations within a type to generate any object of the type.

Operations are denoted and defined in the following manner: Basic generator operations are identified by the "o" symbol preceding the operation name. Generator operations are defined by expressions consisting only of basic generators and simple algebraic manipulations, along with basic constructs such as *if-then-else* and *while-do*. For manipulations of objects such as paths and transitions consisting primarily of lists, we also utilize the list operations *car*, *cdr*, *cons*, *append*, and *reverse*. Inquiry operations are defined by providing their result upon objects generated by all of the basic generators of that data type.

As an example, consider the path data type. Its basic generator operation is *PathCreate*. All generator operations such as *PathNull*, *PathColor*, and *PathExample*, therefore, must be defined in terms of *PathCreate*.

Both generators and basic generators affect the animation state by adding a new object to a field in the animation state as discussed earlier. These manipulations can be defined as in the location example

$$LocCreate(x, y) \rightarrow lo[x, y] : (lo \in L) \cup S,$$

where L is the location component of the animation state S. The equation merely defines that the *LocCreate* operation adds a new location object with the given x and y values to the location component of the animation state. All generator operations within the framework function

similarly, so we will omit these manipulations from the operation definitions. Note that inquiry operations do not modify the animation state at all.

We believe that the descriptive methods we have chosen are rigorous enough to fully detail framework operations, and are informal enough so as not to obscure what is really going on. The conditional

$$if (x)$$

where x is a list of a given type of object, returns true except when x is the null list. We will focus on the transition data type here to illustrate these methods.

Data type Transition

Operations

oTransCreate:	transtype × image × path
	$\rightarrow$ transition;
TransConcatenate:	transition × transition
	$\rightarrow$ transition;
TransIterate:	transition × integer
	$\rightarrow$ transition;
TransCompose:	transition × transition
	$\rightarrow$ transition;
TransPerform:	transition
	$\rightarrow \langle\langle$ image $\rangle\rangle$.

Preliminaries

Below we define how a transition is generated by the *TransCreate* operation. The operation produces a list of moments, which in this case, are each only one transition unit. Assume $im = ImageCreate(imtype, bool, lo, \{params\})$, and $pa = PathCreate(\langle lo \rangle)$.

```
TransCreate(trtype, im, pa)
    → if (pa) then
        cons( cons( (ttype, im, LocX(car(pa)),
                              LocY(car(pa))), ∅ ),
              TransCreate(ttype, im, cdr(pa)) )
      else
        ∅.
```

Example Definition

Once a transition has been created via any of the first four transition operations in order to produce a desired animation, it is carried out with the special *TransPerform* operation. As discussed earlier, *TransPerform* may modify the animation state and rearrange the configuration. Additionally, it is the only operation that adds configurations to the animation list. This functionality of *TransPerform* is detailed below. The symbol C refers to the current configuration.

```
TransPerform(tr)
    → if (tr) then
        moment = car(tr)
        while (moment) do
            { trans_unit = car(moment)
              apply(trans_unit, C)
              moment = cdr(moment)
            }
        return( cons( C, TransPerform(cdr(tr)) ) )
      else
        return ∅.
```

The *apply* operation receives a transition unit which we denote as (*transtype, image, x, y*). It performs two main functions.

First, it affects the animation state by modifying the image's parameters (the image is a member of the I field of the animation state) as dictated by the transition type and the image type. For instance, given that *im* is a circle,

apply((*move, im, x', y'*), C)
$$\Rightarrow im:[\text{circle, (loc.x+}x', \text{loc.y+}y'), \text{vis, radius,}$$
$$\text{color, fill}] \in I,$$

apply((*resize, im, x', y'*), C)
$$\Rightarrow im:[\text{circle, loc, vis, radius+}x', \text{color, fill}] \in I.$$

Second, when given a transition unit of type *raise*, the *apply* operation removes the image from its current location in the configuration and brings it to the front of the list. The *lower* transition works similarly.

apply((*raise, im, x', y'*), C) $\Rightarrow$ $C - im$; cons(*im, C*).

All operations and manipulations within the framework occur in order to produce animation. We introduced the concept of a configuration, an ordered list of the active images, in order to characterize the relative ordering of image objects. It allows us to formally define an animation as a list of configurations.

The animation process begins with an empty list of configurations. As animation scenes are activated, individual framework operations modify the animation state and the current configuration as described in this section. The special *TransPerform* operation adds configurations as elements in the animation list as follows:

$AnimList$ = append($AnimList$, TransPerform(*tr*)).

$AnimList$ begins as a null list, and it grows each time *TransPerform* is called. After the final animation scene is processed, we are left with the list of configurations characterizing the particular animation that has occurred.

4 Prototype Implementation

The initial testing ground for our animation framework is an implementation of an algorithm animation system. Algorithm animation is the process of abstracting the data, operations, and semantics of computer programs, and then creating animated graphical views of those abstractions. Algorithm animation encompasses what has been known traditionally as *program animation* and *data structure rendering*. These two areas typically involve one-to-one mappings between program data and the images in the program's animation. Algorithm animation, however, is a broader term and involves program views that represent abstractions we would visualize when considering the semantics of the program. Although a strict definition of algorithm animation would not include what we would consider to be animated simulations, in practice we frequently can produce animated simulations using algorithm animation techniques. Some of the better known algorithm animation systems are Balsa[3], Animus[4], and Aladdin[8].

The system we have developed is called TANGO (Transition-based ANimation GeneratiOn). TANGO supports two-dimensional color animations in a window-based workstation environment. It includes line, rectangle, circle, ellipse, polyline, polygon, spline, and text

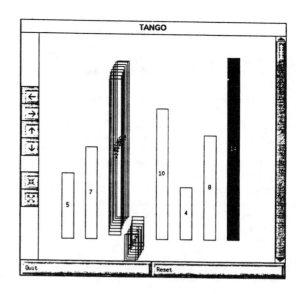

Figure 8: Sample TANGO sort animation.

image types, as well as move, resize, color, fill, visibility, raise, lower, and delay transitions. To drive TANGO animations, programmers supplement their programs with events that we call algorithm operations. As program execution occurs, events are sent out as interprocess messages to a central message server that passes the messages on to TANGO animation windows. Individual messages generate state transitions within TANGO and activate the appropriate animation routines. These animation routines are user-written animation scenes that use the data types and operations of our animation design language. Figure 8 shows an example of a TANGO animation of a bubblesort. We have superimposed a series of frames to illustrate the animation.

TANGO currently runs on a network of workstations and uses tools from the Brown Workstation Environment[11], an application interface toolkit built on top of the X11 window system[12]. We have used TANGO to animate programs from a wide variety of domains such as sorting, searching, hashing, and graph and tree manipulations, and we have designed animated simulations of a producer-consumer ring buffer, the Towers of Hanoi problem, and the post office queuing problem. TANGO also is being incorporated into computer science courses as an aid for understanding algorithms. The system is available for distribution.

5 Related Work

Our work touches on a variety of related areas such as graphical specification techniques and animation languages. With regard to graphical specification, previous work has focused primarily on static imagery. As mentioned earlier, Mallgren provided one of the earliest efforts toward formal specification of graphic objects by introducing special *graphic data types* such as points, regions, geometric functions, and graphic transformations[10]. Using algebraic axioms, Mallgren formally defined all operations on the data types. Fiume utilized a somewhat different approach to formal specifications for a non-trivial graphical object by attempting to specify formally a *bitmap* object and its relationship to an *image* object[6]. In his approach, bitmaps and images were modeled as abstract data types with lists of mathematically and set-defined operations.

The Dial animation language by Feiner, Salesin, and Banchoff utilized a simple, two–dimensional notation to let animators express parallelism[5]. Animators expressed the coordination of object's motions using a chart-like syntax in which the horizontal dimension representing time and the vertical dimension specifying individual animation actions. Taking an object-oriented approach to animation, Fiume, Tsichritzis, and Dami presented a language for expressing the temporal coordination of animated objects[7]. In their system, designers created animated objects that had special temporal behaviors with well defined semantics and that used a library of available motions. Arya employed a functional approach to designing animations in which simple keyframe animations were designed using the functional programming language ML[1]. The system provided pictures as an atomic data type, a compact set of primitive operations on the *picture* data type, and higher-order functions to provide more sophisticated operations for specific applications.

6 Future Work

The TANGO system provides a working prototype for the concepts in our animation paradigm. As touched upon earlier, we would like to produce further implementations and extensions of these ideas also.

One future direction may be to cast our framework in a more rigorous object-oriented environment such as C++. In TANGO we chose not to utilize the object-based appearance of the framework for local, pragmatic reasons: very few of our potential animation designers had experience with C++.

A possible object-oriented implementation might make transitions the methods that are sent to image objects. For example, we could send the *move* method to a particular image. Another possibility might create objects such as an "image exchange." This object would inherit default attributes such as the images' exchange motions that could be overridden as desired. Yet a further possibility is a Lisp implementation, simply due to the dynamic nature of the system and the prevalence of list structures throughout the path and transition data types.

Another future direction we plan to pursue is a definition of a formal, stand-alone animation language with its own specialized syntax. Choosing C as a backbone environment was a practical decision influenced by our goal of producing a quality algorithm animation system. This initial experience now lays the foundation for creating a comprehensive desktop animation language definition.

Acknowledgments
I would like to thank Steve Reiss, my thesis advisor, for all his help throughout the development of this animation framework. Jeff Vitter, Paris Kanellakis, Andy van Dam, Marc Brown, and Rob Rubin also have supplied insightful comments and suggestions. Scott Meyers read an early draft of this paper and provided helpful feedback.

References

[1] Kavi Arya. A functional approach to animation. *Computer Graphics Forum*, 5:297–312, 1986.

[2] Ronald M. Baecker. Picture-driven animation. In *Spring Joint Computer Conference*, volume 34, pages 273–288. AFIPS Press, 1969.

[3] Marc H. Brown. Exploring algorithms using Balsa-II. *IEEE Computer*, 21(5):14–36, May 1988.

[4] Robert A. Duisberg. Animated graphical interfaces using temporal constraints. In *Proceedings of the ACM SIGCHI '86 Conference on Human Factors in Computing Systems*, pages 131–136, Boston, MA, April 1986.

[5] Steven Feiner, David Salesin, and Thomas Banchoff. Dial: A diagrammatic animation language. *IEEE Computer Graphics and Applications*, 2(7):43—54, September 1982.

[6] E. Fiume. An attempt at formal specifications for a non-trivial object. In D. Tsichritzis, editor, *Objects and Things*, pages 149–164. Universite De Genève, 1987.

[7] E. Fiume, D. Tsichritzis, and L. Dami. A temporal scripting language for object-oriented animation. In D. Tsichritzis, editor, *Objects and Things*, pages 129–141. Universite De Genève, 1987.

[8] Esa Helttula, Aulikki Hyrskykari, and Kari-Jouko Räihä. Graphical specification of algorithm animations with Aladdin. In *Proceedings of the 22nd Hawaii International Conference on System Sciences*, pages 892–901, Kailua-Kona, HI, January 1989.

[9] Donald E. Knuth. $\TeX$ and METAFONT. *New Directions in Typesetting*. Digital Press, Bedford, MA, 1979.

[10] William R. Mallgren. Formal specification of graphic data types. *ACM Transactions on Programming Languages and Systems*, 4(4):687–710, October 1982.

[11] Steven P. Reiss and John T. Stasko. The Brown Workstation Environment: A user interface design toolkit. In *IFIP Working Conference on Engineering for Human Computer Communication*, Napa Valley, CA, August 1989. North Holland.

[12] Robert W. Schiefler and Jim Gettys. The X window system. *ACM Transactions on Graphics*, 5(2):79–109, April 1986.

[13] John T. Stasko. *TANGO: A Framework and System for Algorithm Animation*. PhD thesis, Brown University, Providence, RI, May 1989. Available as Technical Report No. CS-89-30.

GVL: A Graphical, Functional Language
For the Specification of Output in Programming Languages*

James R. Cordy

T.C. Nicholas Graham†

Department of Computing and Information Science
Queen's University at Kingston
Kingston, Canada K7L 3N6

Abstract

The conceptual view model of output is based on the complete separation of the output specification of a program from the program itself, and the use of implicit synchronization to allow the data state of the program to be continuously mapped to a display view. An output specification language called GVL is used to specify the mapping from the program's data state to the display. GVL is a functional language explicitly designed for specifying output. Building from a small number of basic primitives, it provides sufficient power to describe complex graphical output. Examples shown in the paper include GVL specifications for linked list diagrams, bar charts and an address card file. In keeping with its intended application, GVL is also a graphical language, in which the user draws output specifications directly on the display. It is shown how problems often associated with imperative graphical languages are avoided by using the functional paradigm. A prototype implementation of GVL was used to produce all examples of graphical output in the paper.

Introduction

The model of input/output used by most modern programming languages is based on streams. A stream is a one dimensional I/O channel: input characters are taken from the front of the input stream and output characters are appended to the end of the output stream. Output occurs only from specific points in the program where output statements have been inserted. This stream model most easily supports the glass teletype model of user interaction, where input and output take place on the bottom line of the screen, and earlier interactions are scrolled up onto the remaining screen lines. This glass teletype interaction leads to a prompt and respond program interface, where the program prompts for the required input in some order, and the user is obliged to respond in that order.

Sufficient diversity in interface and hardware design has occurred that this view is no longer adequately representative [1]. For example, sophisticated user interfaces are two dimensional, using the full display for interaction. Often the user is permitted to direct the interaction, filling in inputs in whatever order is convenient. This style of direct manipulation interface is difficult to implement when the programming language provides only stream level communication.

In recent years, considerable work has gone into developing high level constructs in programming languages to better support abstract data types. In modern application programs, between 29 and 88 percent of the program code is required to implement the user interface [2]. It is therefore appropriate to develop similar high level abstractions for program input and output.

This paper describes GVL (Graphical View Language), a graphical, functional language used to specify output. GVL is used to specify conceptual views of output, which map the data state of an application program to a display view. Following a brief overview of the conceptual view model, the paper describes GVL, the language on which

* This work was supported in part by the Natural Sciences and Engineering Research Council of Canada, and by the Information Technology Research Centre.

† Author's present address: GMD Karlsruhe, Haid-und-Neu Str. 7, D-7500 Karlsruhe, West Germany

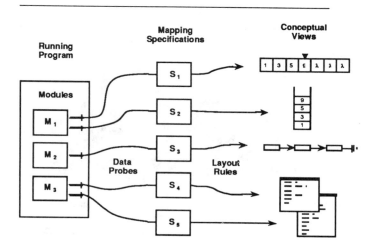

Figure 1. Typical Program Organization under the Conceptual View Model

the model is based. (Earlier papers describe the conceptual view model in more detail [3] [4].) Weasel, a prototype implementation of the conceptual view model, was used to produce the output shown in this paper.

The Conceptual View Model

The conceptual view model is based on a separation of a program's output from the program itself. Figure 1 shows a typical program organization under the conceptual view model. The program consists of a set of modules, encoded in the language of choice of the application programmer (e.g. C, Turing, Ada, etc.) The program contains no output statements, therefore containing only data structures and algorithms to manipulate the data structures.

A separate output specification maps the contents of a data structure to a display view. As the data structure is modified, the display view is automatically updated. Conceptual views can be thought of as a data probe, the software equivalent of a logic probe. Each probe continuously senses the data state of the program and maps it to a display view. The display view is an abstraction of the data structure, representing some facet of the data structure that is of interest to the programmer; the name conceptual view comes from this idea of abstraction.

A data structure can be mapped to multiple different output views. For example, in figure 1, the specification S1 maps the data structure implemented in module M1 to an array diagram with a cursor, while specification S2 shows the same data structure as a stack.

As the data structure is modified throughout the execution of the program, the display is implicitly updated. These updates are based on the invariant assertion of the module being displayed: when the invariant is false (i.e., an update is taking place), it is illegal to update the display. When the invariant is true, the module's data

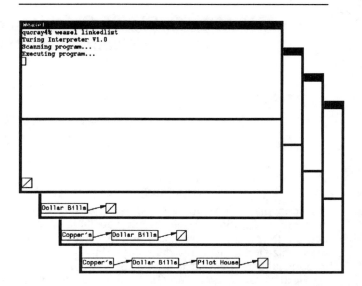

Figure 3. A series of snapshots over time of a linked list data structure as it is being constructed.

structure is guaranteed to be in a consistent state, and the display can be updated. Therefore, it is sufficient to update the display every time the module's invariant changes from false to true, which corresponds to the module being exited.

Conceptual view specifications are expressed in two parts. First a specification written in GVL expresses how the current state of the data structure is to be mapped to a set of display primitives such as boxes, lines and text. The mapping specification does not necessarily constrain the location or sizes of these primitives. Then a set of layout rules are applied to this form to determine the actual display. Layout rules determine any unconstrained sizes and positions, and resolve how to fit large displays when the physical display device is too small.

Figures 2, 3 and 4 show examples of conceptual views generated by the Weasel prototype. Figure 2 shows a bar graph as the output of a list of real numbers. Figure 3 is a series of snapshots over time as a linked list is constructed. Figure 4 shows three snapshots of an interface implementing a card-file address book. This paper describes how GVL can be used to specify these conceptual views.

A Simple Example

This section gives a brief example of a GVL output specification. This example is only an overview of how such a specification is constructed; more detailed examples are given later in the paper.

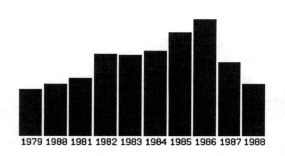

Figure 2. Bar graph output generated as a conceptual view of a list of real numbers.

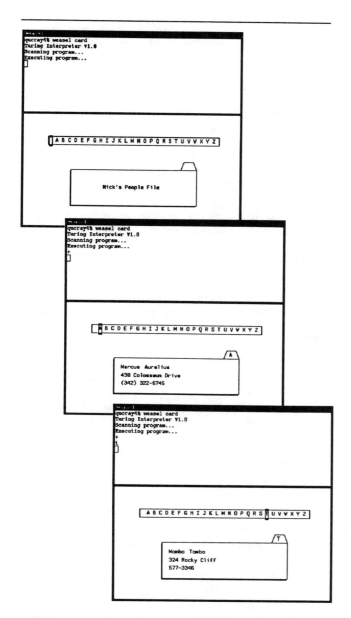

Figure 4. A card-file name and address interface implemented as a conceptual view.

CardFile (firstName, lastName, address, phoneNumber)

δ firstName : DisplayString   δ lastName : DisplayString

δ address : DisplayString

δ phoneNumber : DisplayString

Apply :

δ ("people (currentPerson).firstName :: string",
  "people (currentPerson).lastName :: string",
  "people (currentPerson).address :: string",
  "people (currentPerson).phoneNumber :: string") : CardFile

Mimi Feret
24 Avenue de Verdun, France
642-6852

Figure 5. GVL function to implement part of the card file output shown in figure 5, an application of this function, and the resulting output.

Consider that a programmer wishes to implement a data base for names and addresses. The user interface is modeled after a card file index, where the user can move back and forth within the card file, and the current card is displayed on the screen. The base program will contain the data structure to represent the card file, and will encode the algorithms for traversing the file. Separately, a conceptual view is to be specified to map the card file data structure to a screen view of the current card.

Figure 5 shows the GVL function to map from the card file data structure to a display view of the card. The programmer has drawn the card as he/she intends it to be seen. The card frame itself is drawn as a box, with a filled border to create the illusion of a shadow. Within the box, applications of additional display functions are used to indicate where the name, address and phone number information is to be placed on the card. Each application is of the form `δ p : f`, where p is one of the parameters to the CardFile function, and f is the name of the display function to be applied. For example, `δ firstName : displayString` indicates the first name is to appear in the upper-left corner of the card. (DisplayString is a predefined function that displays a character string.) A more traditional notation for `δ p : f` might be `f (p)`.

The CardFile function has four parameters, *firstName, lastName, address,* and *phoneNumber.* These four functions are to be bound to source expressions written in the application programming language that refer to the data structure to be viewed. Figure 6 shows a data structure encoded in the Turing language [5] that could be used to implement the card file. The data structure

```
type person :
    record
        lastName : string
        firstName : string
        address : string
        phoneNumber : string
    end record
...
var people :
    array nullPerson .. numberOfPeople of person
var currentPerson := nullPerson
```

Figure 6. A Turing language data structure to implement the card file data base.

consists of an array of records, one record per card. The *currentPerson* variable indicates which card is currently selected.

To display the card file, the programmer can use the following application of the CardFile function:

δ ("people (currentPerson).firstName :: string",
  "people (currentPerson).lastName :: string",
  "people (currentPerson).address :: string",
  "people (currentPerson).phoneNumber :: string")
 : *CardFile*

This means, for example, that whenever the *firstName* parameter is to be displayed, the expression "people (currentPerson).firstName" is evaluated to produce a character string to be displayed on the output device.

The remainder of this paper describes GVL, a graphical functional language used to specify conceptual view mappings.

GVL: A Graphical, Functional Language

A conceptual view mapping m is a mapping from the current state of a data structure to a display view; i.e.,

$$m : programState \times layoutRuleSet \rightarrow display$$

where a *programState* is the state of the application program at some instance, and a *layoutRuleSet* is a set of rules to guide the exact placement and sizing of the primitive elements of the display. We have found it convenient to describe these view specifications graphically using GVL.

GVL functions take a list of parameters and yield a conceptual view mapping. In particular, a GVL function is a function f such that

$f : parameterList \rightarrow$
    $(programState \times layoutRuleSet \rightarrow display)$

where each parameter in a parameter list can be a source expression encoded in the application programming language, a list of such expressions, or another GVL function.

The application of a GVL function results in a conceptual view, which in turn can be applied to the program state to produce a display. Figure 5 showed the application of the *CardFile* function to a list of expressions to produce a conceptual view that maintains a display of the current state of a card file data base.

Why A Language?

A notation used to express conceptual view mappings requires at least some of the features normally associated with a programming language. It is therefore desirable to define the notation as a language, and to attribute to it a well defined syntax and semantics. To be a programming language, features equivalent to abstraction, repetition and selection must be provided. The following paragraphs show why these features are required in the conceptual view specification language.

Abstraction

In specifying output, many displays are used over and over again. For example, a programmer would wish to reuse the same style of menus and dialogue boxes from program to program. Similarly, when developing a complicated interface, a programmer would wish to be able to develop different parts of the interface in isolation, and combine them later. Shaw et al. [1] discuss the need for hierarchies of predefined abstractions to aid in the development of program interactions. GVL provides function definitions as an abstraction mechanism.

Repetition

A bar graph display (figure 2) requires a sequence of bars to be drawn, each one beside the previous. A display of a linked list (figure 3) requires a sequence of list elements to be drawn. Each of these examples shows the necessity of including a mechanism for repeating the same action an arbitrary number of times. GVL allows the use of recursion for repetition.

Selection

In the example of the bar graph or linked list above, it is necessary to be able to test when to stop repeating. In other cases, a display may be tailored to be of a different form depending on the user's request. These examples show the need to be able to specify some form of conditions in output specifications; GVL provides a cond primitive for selection.

The need for mechanisms for abstraction, repetition and selection imply that the mapping specification language should be a full programming language.

Why Graphical?

The traditional approach has been to use a linear notation (i.e. text) to specify graphical output. Rather than a user having to define a coordinate space and specify the locations and sizes of objects in terms of numerical coordinates, a graphical notation allows direct manipulation of a two-dimensional display to specify where the various elements of a display are to be located and what size they are meant to be. To specify graphical output, a graphical language is less clumsy, more direct, and therefore less prone to error.

Why Functional?

Given the decision to use a graphical language, the functional paradigm presents some strong advantages. In GVL, a small, powerful language was sufficient to achieve the goals of combining flexibility with convenience. As examples will show, the high-level nature of the functional language simplifies specifications over imperative styles. For example, infinite recursion is used in some GVL functions to simplify the expression of the required output.

The functional style is appropriate to a graphical representation. Earlier graphical languages have been mainly general purpose languages, as opposed to special- purpose output languages, and have tended to follow the imperative paradigm. Imperative graphical languages tend to look like flow-charts, and inherit their tangled control flow. Graphically representing variables can be a problem; the Pict system [6], for example, uses colours to differentiate between variables. This not only loses the mnemonic nature of the variable name, but also limits the number of variables to four (i.e., the number of colours supported by the display.)

Another approach is to use graphics only to display templates for the control constructs of the imperative language [7]. It is not clear how this approach is an improvement over textual template-based systems such as the Cornell Program Synthesizer [8].

In a functional style these difficulties are avoided. Since the only control construct is function application, spaghetti-coding is avoided. Functional languages do not have variables or assignment, eliminating the problems of how to represent state manipulations.

A functional language also supports the building of programs from separate components. When programming with a graphical language, it is common to wish to draw two different programs and then combine them into one. In a functional style, there is no danger that one of the displays will have a side-effect that causes it to interfere with the other.

Finally, there is a wide class of known optimizations for functional languages. By restricting the language to being purely functional, optimizations such as tail-recursion elimination, inlining of functions, and memoization (removal of duplicate calls) are available.

In summary, the need for abstraction, selection and repetition imply that we should design a language for output specification. Graphical specifications are more convenient than textual ones for this purpose. Finally, a functional language appears to be appropriate for graphical programming.

Language Constructs

Figure 7 shows the GVL primitives. In general, primitives must appear exactly as they are drawn: if a line is 2 cm long in the specification, it must be 2 cm long in the displayed output. This constraint on the location and size of a primitive is expressed by placing an `×' symbol on a vertex to be constrained. This symbol indicates the vertex is to be drawn exactly where it is shown in the current definition. If a coordinate is not constrained with an `×' symbol, its location is chosen according to a set of layout rules.

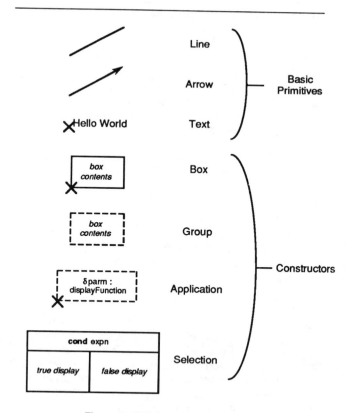

Figure 7. GVL Language Primitives.

GVL uses the concept of a *coordinate space* in a way analogous to the concept of scope in traditional programming languages. A coordinate space is simply an area of display space. A display whose position is unconstrained is restricted to being displayed within the coordinate space in which it is specified. Three language constructs introduce a new coordinate space: function definitions, boxes and the cond function. (Note that since boxes can be nested, so can coordinate spaces.)

Basic Primitives

There are three basic primitives: *line, arrow* and *text*. Either end of a line or arrow may be constrained with an `x` symbol. If both ends are constrained, the line or arrow is drawn exactly as it appears on the display. If either end is unconstrained, the layout rules are free to place that endpoint anywhere on the display. A completely unconstrained line or arrow may be drawn as an arc or curve. Various style attributes may be associated with a line or arrow. In the current implementation, lines may be solid, dashed, dotted or invisible. It is possible to imagine many other attributes (such as colour or thickness) that could be given to lines and arrows.

Text is displayed exactly as it is presented on the screen. If any vertex of the text is constrained, then all four vertices will be constrained. If the location of text is unconstrained, it may be drawn anywhere within the current coordinate space.

Boxes

A box primitive evaluates the contents of the box, and evaluates to a box surrounding this display. If the box's vertices are constrained, the resulting box always has the same dimensions; if the upper-right corner of the box is unconstrained, then the box is sized to fit the contents. A box has a style attribute associated with it. While many other useful styles could be envisioned, the current set includes outlined, invisible and filled boxes.

Conditions

The cond primitive takes three arguments: a condition expression, and two displays. The condition is evaluated. If it is true, then the result of the cond is the display on the left; if the condition is false then the result is the display on the right.

Functions

Figure 5 shows an example of a GVL display function definition. This example shows an abstract function, i.e. one that has not yet been bound to any particular data structure. A function definition consists of a parameter list and a body. A parameter may be an expression, a list of expressions, or another display function. GVL functions can be second order (i.e. they can take functional parameters) and polymorphic (i.e. the type of

parameters is not bound in an abstract function.) The function body contains any sequence of primitives.

Display function application is specified with the `δ` operator. In general, application is of the form:

$$\delta p : f$$

meaning that the GVL function *f* is to be applied to the parameter *p,* and the result is to be merged into the current coordinate space. The result of applying *f* is a display, which will may contain constrained and unconstrained primitives. The constrained primitives are placed within the dashed box surrounding the application. Any unconstrained primitives remain unconstrained in the current coordinate space, and can therefore be placed anywhere in the coordinate space.

When evaluating the body of a GVL function, it is guaranteed that if the same display is generated twice in a coordinate space, and the location of at least one of them is unconstrained, the two displays will be drawn in the same location. Examples following this section show how useful this property is in simplifying specifications.

Sometimes it is inconvenient to apply a GVL function directly to its arguments. At other times, it may be known in advance that a function is to be applied to some class of similar data structures. In these cases, it is helpful to be able to specialize a display function to a particular data structure or class of data structures before the display function is applied.

This specialization process consists of binding each parameter in the function to some value; each value may be a textual expression from the application program, a list of expressions, or the name of a display function. Expressions may themselves be parameterized. The binding creates a new specialized display function, with a new list of parameters. Bound functions may themselves be specialized, allowing the creation of a hierarchy of bound specifications [4]. A later section of this paper discusses the details of the binding process.

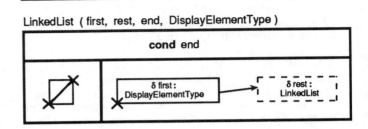

Figure 8. GVL function to draw the linked lists shown in figures 3 and 9.

An Example

An example that captures many of the features of the GVL language is the *LinkedList* function (figure 8). Figure 3 showed an example of output when the this function is applied to a list of strings.

The function takes four parameters. The *first* parameter is the value of the first item of the list; the *rest* parameter is all list elements that follow the first. The *end* parameter is a condition which specifies when there are no more elements in the list. Finally, the *DisplayElementType* parameter specifies what function is to be used to display the items themselves.

In the main part of the LinkedList function, the first element of the list is drawn in a box. An arrow is then drawn to a display of the remaining elements of the list. These remaining elements are drawn by recursively applying the LinkedList function to the *rest* parameter.

The first element of the list is displayed using the *DisplayElementType* function, which is a parameter to the LinkedList function. In this way, the same LinkedList function can be used to display a linked list of strings, a linked list of integers, or even a linked list of linked lists.

The display of the *first* element is enclosed in a box. The lower-left corner of the box is constrained with an `x` symbol, meaning that the box is to be located in the lower-left corner of the display. The upper-right corner is not constrained, meaning that the box is to be sized to fit the display of the first element. The display of the *rest* of the list is not constrained at all, meaning that the subsequent elements can be drawn anywhere in the current coordinate space.

The display is surrounded by an application of the *cond* function, which states that if the end of the list is reached (i.e., the *end* parameter evaluates to true) then a terminator box is to be drawn (the display on the left), otherwise the main display involving the recursive display of the list is to be used.

The LinkedList function can potentially be infinitely recursive. If the linked list is malformed such that it has a loop in it, then the *end* condition will never evaluate to *true*. This case is solved by the guarantee that if the same display is generated twice in the same coordinate space, and if the position of at least one them is unconstrained, the pair will be drawn in the same location. In the case of a list with a loop, at some point in the recursion, the result will consist only of elements that have already been displayed. Since the location of the recursively generated items is not constrained, the repeated items can be drawn in the same location as the items generated earlier. This means that once all the items have been drawn once, the recursion can be

terminated. (This is consistent with the traditional definition of recursion as being the fixed point of an infinite sequence of recursive applications [9,10].) The implementation of infinite recursion detection (discussed in [4]) is similar to the memoization optimization performed in many other functional language implementations [27]. Figure 9 shows the result of applying the LinkedList function to a linked list containing a cycle.

Binding

Figure 10 shows a Turing language data structure implementing a linked list. The data structure is based on an array of text lines. In order to apply the LinkedList function to this data structure, it is convenient to first bind the function to a form specialized to the data structure. This binding is expressed using the following notation:

LinkedListTextLine (pos) **is** LinkedList **where**
    first = "lines (!!pos).text :: string",
    rest = "lines (!!pos).nextLine :: lineReference",
    end = "!!pos = nilLine :: boolean",
    DisplayItemType = DisplayString
  specializing LinkedList **to** LinkedListTextLine

This says that a new function, *LinkedListTextLine*, is to be created. The new function takes one parameter (*pos*), and is defined as being *LinkedList* where the first three parameters are bound to expressions referring to the data structure, and the fourth parameter is bound to the *DisplayString* function.

The expressions used in the binding contain references to *pos*, the parameter to the new bound function. These references are introduced by a `!!` symbol that

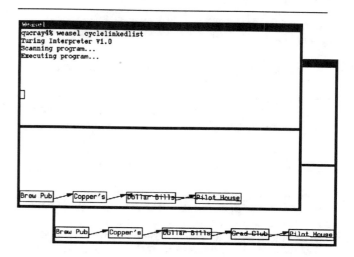

Figure 9. Result of applying the LinkedList GVL function to a broken (cyclical) linked list.

```
const nilLine := 0
const maxLines := 1000

type lineReference : nilLine .. maxLines

var lines : array lineReference of
   record
        text : string
        nextLine : lineReference
   end record
var rootLine : lineReference := nilLine
```

Figure 10. A Turing language data structure implementing a linked list as an array of records.

distinguishes between the expression source text and references to the GVL parameter. When the LinkedListTextLine function is applied, the value of the *pos* parameter is textually substituted into the expression.

Each expression also has a type specifier in the application language that indicates the type of the expression. These type specifiers are introduced by a `::` symbol. Type specifiers are required when the application programming language is statically typed (such as Turing, Pascal, C, etc.) and are optional when the language is dynamically typed. Existence of these type specifiers allows the polymorphism in GVL functions to be resolved statically.

The second part of the binding is a *specialization* clause. This clause says that in the bound version of the function, all applications of LinkedList should in fact be applications of LinkedListTextLine. Function references can only be specialized to bound versions of the same function.

The following application displays the array data structure as a linked list:

δ "currentLine :: lineReference" : LinkedListTextLine

The binding process can be modeled as a second order function over GVL functions. We define the second order function *bind* such that

$$bind : GVLfunction \times parmList \times idList \times$$
$$specializationList \rightarrow GVLfunction$$

where the first *GVLfunction* is the function to be specialized, the *parmList* is a list of values to which the parameters of the function are to be bound, the *idList* is the list of formal parameters to the new function, and the *specializationList* indicates what functions are to be replaced in the definition of the function being bound.

The definition of *bind* can then be expressed as follows:

Let f' be defined as:

$$bind\ (\ f,\ (\ b_1,...,\ b_j\ )\ ,\ (\ i_1,...,\ i_k\ )\ ,$$
$$((\ f_1,\ f'_1\ ),\ ...\ ,\ (\ f_n,\ f'_n\ ))\ )$$

then:
$$f'(\ a_1,...,\ a_k\ ) =$$
$$f\ [\ f_1\ /\ f'_1\ ;\ ...\ ;\ f_n\ /\ f'_n\ ]$$
$$(\ b_1\ [\ !!\ i_1\ /\ a_1\ ;\ ...\ ;\ !!\ i_k\ /\ a_k\ ],$$
$$...$$
$$b_j\ [\ !!\ i_1\ /\ a_1\ ;\ ...\ ;\ !!\ i_k\ /\ a_k\ ]\ )$$

That is, the bound function is defined as the original function where all applications of specialized functions are replaced, and where each formal in the bound function (the i_j) is replaced by the corresponding actual parameter to the bound function (the a_i) in the actuals to the bound function (the b_i).

For example, the binding and application of the *LinkedList* display function can be expressed as follows:

LinkedListTextLine (pos) *is defined as:*

bind (LinkedList,   *(the function being bound)*

   ("lines (!!pos).currentLine :: string",
    "lines (!!pos).nextLine :: lineReference",
    "!!pos = terminator :: boolean"),
              (the actuals to the bound function (b_i))

   ("pos"),   *(the formal of the bound function (i_i))*

   (LinkedList / LinkedListTextLine)
              (the specialization list - replace all
              uses of LinkedList with LinkedListTextLine)

)

So that the application:

LinkedListTextLine ("currentLine")

has the meaning:

LinkedList [LinkedList / LinkedListTextLine]
   ("lines (!!pos).currentLine :: string"
              ["!!pos" / "currentLine"],
    "lines (!!pos).nextLine :: lineReference"
              ["!!pos" / "currentLine"],
    "!!pos = terminator :: boolean"
              ["!!pos" / "currentLine"])

by substituting the actual parameter *"currentLine"* into the definition of *LinkedListTextLine*.

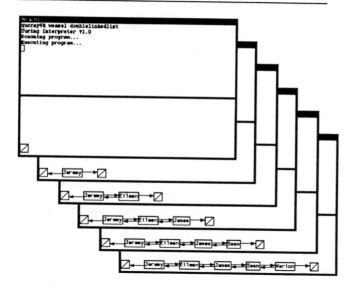

Figure 11. A series of snapshots over time of a doubly-linked list being constructed.

Other Examples

This section presents two more examples of output specifications to illustrate additional points about GVL.

Doubly Linked List

Figure 11 shows the display of a doubly linked list of strings as the list is constructed. Figure 12 shows the GVL function used to display this list. The DoubleLinkedList function is similar to that used to display a singly linked list: a *cond* function tests for the end of the list; at the end, a terminator box is drawn. The list is drawn by drawing the current element using the parameter function *DisplayElementType*. An arrow is drawn to the list on the left, and another to the list on the right. Both of these are doubly-linked lists also, and are therefore displayed recursively.

Because of the recursive description of the left and right references as doubly-linked lists, the specification is infinitely recursive. When a given element (e.g. *"Jeremy"*) is drawn, the element to its right (*"Eileen"*) is drawn as a doubly-linked list. The *"Eileen"* element redraws the element to its left (*"Jeremy"*) as a doubly-linked list, thereby starting an infinite recursion. As was seen in the singly-linked list example, the recursion is resolved by drawing repeated instances of the display in the same location as the original.

This detection and resolution of infinite recursion is a powerful specification device. The DoubleLinkedList function is actually a specification of a general binary

DoubleLinkedList (first, left, right, end, DisplayElementType)

Figure 12. GVL function to display a doubly-linked list

graph, where the display shows the current node, and edges connecting to up to two other nodes in the graph. This specification can be extended to handle *n*-ary graphs by adding additional links.

Bar Graph

A final example is an output specification to draw a bar graph. Figure 2 shows the output when a bar graph specification is applied to a list of real numbers. Figure 13 shows the GVL functions that produced this output.

To show how specifications can be built using a number of layered display functions, three functions are used to construct this example. At the highest level, a bar graph is a list of labeled bars. Each labeled bar is in turn a bar with a string label underneath it.

Applications within abstract functions pass only one parameter, which may be matched to several in the function being applied. These inconsistencies must be resolved when the abstract functions are bound. For example, in the *BarGraph* function, the first bar is displayed as a *LabeledBar,* while *LabeledBar* requires two parameters. Before *BarGraph* can be applied, either the *firstBar* parameter must be bound to a list of two expressions, or the *LabeledBar* function must be specialized to a function taking only one parameter. (To produce the given output, the first option was used.)

The *Bar* function draws a filled box of fixed width. The box surrounds an application of the *offsetY* function. This function draws an invisible line of the height specified by its parameter. The filled box is sized to surround the parameter, and is therefore made the required height. The *offsetY* function (and the corresponding *offsetX* function) can be defined recursively in terms of the primitives already given. In the current implementation these functions are built in, and are implemented in a more efficient manner.

Implementation

The *Weasel* environment is a prototype implementation of the conceptual view model. The environment consists of a front end that deals with the user, and a back end that executes the application program and displays views

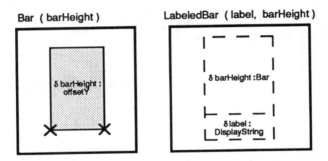

Bar (barHeight)

LabeledBar (label, barHeight)

δ barHeight : offsetY

δ barHeight : Bar

δ label : DisplayString

BarGraph (firstBar, otherBars, noMoreBars)

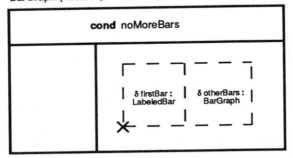

cond noMoreBars

δ firstBar : LabeledBar

δ otherBars : BarGraph

Figure 13. GVL functions to draw the bar graph shown in figure 2.

Figure 14. High-level structure of the Weasel prototype implementation of the conceptual view model.

(figure 14). The back end has been implemented, and was used to generate the output shown in this paper. (The implementation of the back end is described in detail in an earlier report [4].) The front end is currently being designed [11].

The front end (the Weasel User Interface) consists of a number of loosely integrated tools. A graphical editor allows the user to draw and edit conceptual view specifications. A binding tool allows the specifications to be specialized to a particular data structure. Specifications can be placed in a library for later reuse. A text editor is used to allow the programmer to develop the application program.

The back end (the Weasel Executor) interacts with the execution of the application program, and applies the bound form of conceptual view specifications to the running program. Currently, two versions of the Executor have been implemented; the first interprets application programs written in the Turing language [5], the second is based on compiled applications written in Turing Plus.

The interface between the front and back end consists of three components: the application program to be executed, a set of conceptual view specifications written in GVL, and control information to guide the execution.

Conceptual view specifications are presented in a textual form generated by the front end from the graphical representation. The translation is straight-forward: for each primitive in the graphical mapping language, there is a corresponding textual primitive. The semantics of this textual language and the details of the translation process are described in an earlier report [4].

Since the implementation of the Weasel Interface is incomplete, the examples of output shown in this paper were generated by entering the textual version of the GVL functions directly.

Related Work

The development of the conceptual view model and the GVL specification language was influenced by a number of different sources. Shaw has proposed a new model for input and output in programming languages [12]. This model recognizes the need for an output model to support two- dimensional display devices and the output of abstract data types. The conceptual view model extends some of these ideas by demonstrating how such a model might be realized.

Systems to aid in designing and implementing user interfaces are generally referred to as User Interface Management Systems (UIMSs); a good overview of this field can be found in [13]. The conceptual view model can be thought of as describing the output component of a UIMS.

Other language systems have used methodologies similar to the conceptual view model. Both the Smalltalk Model View Controller (MVC) methodology [14] and the use of active values in Loops [15] allow the user to encode conceptual views in the application programming language.

Work in tools to aid in program debugging [16, 17], program visualization [18, 19] and systems to support graphical output [20, 1] have contributed toward the design of the conceptual view model.

There have been a number of earlier graphical languages used in different problem domains. The ThingLab system included a graphical sublanguage used to express graphical constraints [21]. The Pict programming language is an imperative language based on flowcharts [6]. FPL is a graphical representation of the Pascal language [7]. Other such languages are described by Myers [2].

The advantages of applying a graphical notation to functional languages have been demonstrated by a number of other systems. The Prograph language and programming environment [23] is based largely on FP and provides an elegant variable-free syntax. In this syntax, data flow is represented using directed arcs, but the functional nature of the language means that these arcs are restricted and therefore more readable than Prograph's imperative counterparts. The Show-and-Tell system [24] is also based on a declarative, hierarchical box syntax. The language is relational, where parts of the program are left unspecified and are filled in as a result of 'execution'. Cardelli [25] has demonstrated a graphical syntax for a language similar to ML [26].

Other languages have been tailored to expressing output mappings. The FDL language used in the VIPS debugger [16] is a textual, Ada-like language with support for output. The GRINS language [22] is a textual language used to express program input and output. Both of these languages, while introducing the flexibility of a language tailored to output, have the disadvantage of trying to encode two-dimensional information into a one-dimensional notation.

Other systems have used graphical languages designed to express output. The Descartes system [1] allows the user to draw the desired output. It does not, however, contain any mechanisms for selection or repetition. The Garden environment [20] allows the user to draw output using a set of high-level primitives. There is no facility to build new primitives, however. The authors, for example, point out that it would be impossible to express the display of an array data structure in Garden.

The Peridot user interface management system [2] also uses a graphical language to express output. These facilities include *iterations* and *conditionals* to support repetition and selection. Because it is intended to be a convenient interface in a UIMS, Peridot's language is intentionally higher-level and hence less flexible than the language presented in this paper. For example, iterations are tied ultimately to Lisp lists, and operate at one level only. There is no way of naming a part of a specification and using it recursively.

Conclusion

This paper has described a graphical functional language designed to support the conceptual view model of output. This model of output is based on the separation of the output specification of a program from the program itself,

and the use of implicit synchronization to allow the data state of the program to be continuously mapped to a display view. The graphical, functional language GVL is used to express this mapping from the program's data state to the display.

It was argued that a notation with the full power of a programming language is necessary for this task, and it was shown that a functional language using graphical notation allows compact, convenient specification of data structure mappings. High level features such as infinite recursion detection were shown to simplify these specifications.

Earlier graphical programming languages have had problems that flow of control can become tangled in a graphical system, that variables are hard to represent graphically, and that it can be hard to combine two graphical programs with certainty that they do not interfere with each other. These problems are avoided using the functional paradigm.

Acknowledgements

The back end of the Weasel prototype was developed by the authors as part of the Programming Language Technology project at Queen's University, Kingston, Canada. Troy Spetz has designed a front end for the Weasel environment [11]. The development of the prototype was greatly aided by the helpful support of Mark Mendell and the Turing language group at the University of Toronto. This work was supported in part by the Natural Sciences and Engineering Research Council of Canada and the Information Technology Research Centre.

References

1. Mary Shaw, Ellen Borison, Michael Horowitz, Tom Lane, David Nichols, and Randy Pausch, "Descartes: A Programming-Language Approach to Interactive Display Interfaces", *SIGPLAN Notices* 18, 6, pp. 100-111 (June 1983).

2. Brad A. Myers, "Creating User Interfaces by Demonstration", Computer Systems Research Institute Technical Report CSRI-196 (May 1987).

3. T.C. Nicholas Graham and James R. Cordy, "Conceptual Views of Data Structures as a Model of Output in Programming Languages", Proc. HICSS-22, Hawaii International Conference on Systems Sciences (January 1989).

4. T.C. Nicholas Graham, Conceptual Views of Data Structures as a Programming Aid, External Technical Report 88-225, Department of Computing and Information Science, Queen's University at Kingston (August 1988).

5. Richard C. Holt and James R. Cordy, "The Turing Programming Language", *Communications of the ACM* 31, 12, pp. 1410-1423 (December 1988).

6. Ephraim P. Glinert and Steven L. Taminoto, "PICT: an interactive graphical programming environment", *IEEE Computer* 17, 11, pp. 7-25 (November 1984).

7. Nancy Cunniff, Robert P. Taylor and John B. Black, "Does Programming Language Affect the Type of Conceptual Bugs in Beginners' Programs? A Comparison of FPL and Pascal", Proc. CHI 86, Conference on Human Factors in Computing Systems, pp. 175-182 (April 1986).

8. T. Teitelbaum and T. Reps, "The Cornell Program Synthesizer: A Syntax-Directed Programming Environment", *Communications of the ACM* 24, 9, pp. 563-573 (September 1981).

9. Eric C.R. Hehner, *The Logic of Programming*, Prentice Hall International, Englewood Cliffs, New Jersey (1984).

10. Robert D. Tennent, "Denotational Semantics of Algol- like Languages", *Handbook of Logic in Computer Science*, S. Abramsky, D.M. Gabbay, and T.S. Maibaum editors, Oxford University Press (1988).

11. Troy D. Spetz, WeaselUI: A User-Interface Design for the Weasel Programming Environment, M.Sc. Thesis, Department of Computing and Information Science, Queen's University at Kingston (December 1989).

12. Mary Shaw, "An Input-Output Model for Interactive Systems", Proc. CHI 86: Conference on Human Factors in Computing Systems (April 1986).

13. Guenther E. Pfaff (ed.), *User Interface Management Systems*, Springer-Verlag, Berlin (November 1983).

14. Glenn E. Krasner and Stephen T. Pope, "A Cookbook for Using the Model-View-Controller Interface Paradigm in Smalltalk-80", *Journal of Object-Oriented Programming* 1, 3, pp. 26-49 (August 1988).

15. Mark J. Stefik, Daniel G. Brobow, and Kenneth M. Kahn, "Integrating Access-Oriented Programming into a Multiparadigm Environment", *IEEE Software* 3, 1, pp. 10-18 (January 1986).

16. Sadahiro Isoda, Takao Shimomura, and Yuji Ono, "VIPS: A Visual Debugger", *IEEE Software* 8, 3, pp. 8-19 (March 1987).

17. Brad A. Myers, "Incense: A System for Displaying Data Structures", *Computer Graphics* 17, 3, pp. 115-125 (July 1983).

18. Marc H. Brown, "Perspectives on Algorithm Animation", Proc. CHI 88, Conference on Human Factors in Computing Systems, pp. 33-38 (1988).

19. Marc H. Brown and Robert Sedgewick, "Techniques for Algorithm Animation", *IEEE Software* 2, 1, pp. 28-39 (January 1985).

20. Stephen P. Reiss and Joseph N. Pato, "Displaying Programs and Data Structures", Proc. HICSS-20, Hawaii International Conference on Systems Sciences, pp. 391-401 (1987).

21. Alan Borning, "Defining Constraints Graphically", Proc. CHI 86, Conference on Human Factors in Computing Systems, pp. 137-143 (April 1986).

22. Dan R. Olsen Jr., Elizabeth P. Dempsey, and Roy Rogge, "Input-Output Linkage in a User Interface Management System", Proc. SIGGRAPH 85, *Computer Graphics* 19, 3, pp. 225-234 (July 1985).

23. T. Pietrzykowski and S. Matwin, "Prograph: A Preliminary Report", *Computer Languages* 10, 2, pp. 91-126 (1985).

24. Takayuki Dan Kimura, Julie W. Choy and Jane M. Mack, A Visual Language for Keyboardless Programming, Washington University Technical Report 86-6 (March 1986).

25. Luca Cardelli, "Two-Dimensional Syntax for Functional Languages", Proc. Integrated Interactive Computing Systems, pp. 107-119 (1983).

26. Robin Milner, "The Standard ML Core Language", *Polymorphism* 2, 2, pp. 1-28 (October 1985).

27. Simon L. Peyton-Jones, *The Implementation of Functional Programming Languages*, Prentice-Hall, London (May 1986).

Enhancing documents with embedded programs:
How Ness extends insets in the Andrew ToolKit

Wilfred J. Hansen
Information Technology Center
Carnegie Mellon University
Pittsburgh, PA 15213-3890

Abstract: *An enhanced document responds to its reader in non-traditional ways: a button press may scroll the document, play music, ... Although such operations may be implemented as objects embedded in text, full generality requires that a programming language be available to the author of a document. This paper sketches the problems of embedding programs in documents and reviews the solutions adopted in the Ness component of the Andrew ToolKit. A key question is the connection from user actions to program functions. Other questions include the appropriate level of programming language, its string processing capabilities, and security.*

Traditionally a computer document is an emulation of a paper one; it sits there for the reader to explore at will. This present paper is no different because even though I am writing it on a computer I expect most readers will view it on paper. But suppose you were reading it at a computer; how much more could it do? Simulations, calculations, interactive examples, waving flags, music, fireworks?

The report below describes a system in which it is possible to write documents that have most of these behaviors. In order to provide the most general environment, the system incorporates a programming language, Ness, the design of which has been kept simple so as to reach a broad range of authors. The underlying system is the Andrew ToolKit (ATK).

Typical applications of such a system include

enhanced documents - with various animations and simulations to illustrate the points of the document

parameterized letter - after the user fills in a few fields in a form letter other fields are calculated and the full letter is constructed

personal data base - addresses, appointments, course records, bibliography, ...

directory editor - click on a file to see its attributes or select it for moving or deleting

system status monitor - a user builds a personal monitor for work station status by selecting from a library of system measurement tools and a library of ways to view dynamically changing values: dials, strip charts, and so on.

dungeons and dragons - the description of the world is a large text through which the reader can scroll; as the reader solves puzzles, descriptions of new rooms and objects are added to the text.

The remainder of this paper discusses the system as though it were intended for extending document: objects are inserted in the document at various places and their behavior is controlled by a *script* written in the programming language. In all cases the discussion applies equally well to programming an application; such a situation is just an image that cannot be scrolled off the screen as parts of a document can. For documents the substrate is a text; for applications the substrate is a drawing editor or some other tool for laying out the contents of a window.

Hypertext documents can be created easily within a system that supports authorship of enhanced documents. The author need only insert in the text a button extended to respond to a button press by scrolling elsewhere in the same document or another. Nor is the link constrained to always branch to the same place; the author can arrange the script so the destination is chosen among several depending on what the reader has seen so far. Because lengthy linear documents are possible, the Ness/ATK combination may reduce the disorientation readers sometimes encounter in hypertext systems with small nodes. The scroll bar in the view of the document serves as a visual indication of where the current image is within the context of the entire document. See [8] for a good discussion of the advantages of hypertext and references to the growing literature on user disorientation.

Some discussion in the multi-media mail community has focussed on using a language to describe mail documents.

With this facility, new varieties of objects can be sent if the receiving system has no more capability than the language interpreter. The work reported below is both more and less general. It is not a language suitable for describing any object, it assumes that a collection of objects will be available in the software of both sender and receiver. It does, however, provide a language tailored for the author to describe a myriad of different forms of interconnection and behavior of objects.

It is important to distinguish the notion of enhancing a document with a script from the various authoring languages for educational tutorials (good examples are cT and Best Course of Action; see [7]). With the latter, the author constructs a program which *generates* a sequence of images; this contrasts with the enhanced document approach of Ness where the program within the images. The crucial difference is in user control: with an enhanced document the reader is in control and can employ ordinary text operations to move through the text. With program generated images control lies with the system; the reader can move only to where the system allows. Experience has shown that it is not easy for authors to always imagine where readers will want to go in reviewing a tutorial, so the reader many be sometimes stymied in trying to get to a desired place.

The best known system with a programming language for enhancing what the reader sees is Hypercard [1]. However, Hypercard operates in a far more limited environment: its images are constrained to a certain small size and only two forms of object may be embedded, buttons and fields. In contrast the system described below is implemented within the far richer environment of the Andrew ToolKit, ATK. [5]

Underlying ATK is an object architecture, complete with inheritance of methods. Two principle forms of object are

> *data object* - this provides for storage and manipulation of information; every data object has at least the methods for writing the object to a data stream and reading it back.

> *view* - this provides user access to the contents of a data object by displaying it in a rectangle on the screen; it also provides user interface operations for scrolling or modifying the information.

The ATK architecture is specifically designed so that a view cannot know whether it occupies an entire window or whether it is a subrectangle in another view. If a view has embedded child views, the architecture provides for the parent view to completely control the events seen by the child, thus views can be nested arbitrarily. To describe what the user sees of the combination of view and data object, this combination is called an *inset*. It is worth noting that the architecture proved sufficiently general that little change to the underlying system was required to add Ness.

In starting Ness, it was not clear how script pieces should interface with insets and the user. The many design alternatives are outlined in the next section and the following section describes the choices made for Ness. A sketch of other facets of Ness--especially the string algebra--is in the third section, followed by a discussion of security issues in the last section.

1. How can documents be enhanced?

Define an "extension" as a sequence of code to be executed at some particular time during a user's perusal of a document. The principal semantic questions are

> 1) What sorts of events can trigger the extension?

> 2) What effect can the extension have on the containing text and surrounding objects?

It is apparent that in the usual workstation environment the set of events that can trigger an extension must include user actions with the keyboard and the mouse. In ATK, an important subset of mouse actions are selection from the popup menu. Another set of trigger events are those defined by each inset class. For instance text objects may initiate an event when some portion is selected or when the text scrolls, both of which may be caused by any of several user actions.

In principle, inset-defined events would be a sufficient set of triggers. However, user inputs are an important additional form of trigger because they enable the extension language to deal with any object, whether or not it has been constructed with the language in mind.

How is each object to be connected to the portion of the script which specifies the response to events on that object? One answer to this is given by Hypercard, which associates a script with each object. The difficulty with this approach is that scripts and their functionality get scattered all over the place. In trying to understand what happens in response to a mouse click on a button it may be necessary to look at as many as five different scripts (button, card, background, stack, and home stack); and trying to understand the interaction of several buttons requires looking at each in turn. The situation is similar to the difficulties of trying to understand a spreadsheet of even modest complexity [3].

In Ness all the scripts for a collection of objects are gathered together. Each object is named and the extensions for an object appear together in a group identified with the name of the object. Review of the script is thus reduced to looking in a single place, though it is now not as easy to see which object each name refers to, especially if many objects are extended. Ness authors can avoid this by using multiple scripts in the document, one for each section. It is the author's responsibility to clarify as far as possible the relation between script portions and objects.

A few people who have heard about Ness without seeing it have suggested that the script ought to include not only the extensions but also textual descriptions of the objects themselves. Among the claimed advantages are that the script could be editted with a plain ASCII editor and that scripts could be generated by programs. Ness has taken a very different approach. Construction of objects and their assembly into a document or application are handled with the ordinary ATK object oriented editing facilities. If a button is required in the upper left corner, the author puts a button there and it is immediately visible, just as the reader will eventually see it. Ultimately ATK data streams are indeed encoded in ASCII, so they can be editted with ASCII editors by incorrigible hackers. It is also possible for a Ness script to insert an object in the document or application. To select its size and place the script negotiates with the parent inset inset which the object is inserted.

In a fully developed system there is a point to having representations of the objects in the script so the author can click on one to request that it be highlighted in the document. At present this is handled for Ness by an "arbiter" application, part of the mechanism that handles naming of objects.

What can an extension do to its environment? A guiding principal of Ness is that the instructions in an extension ought to have at least the same capabilities as the user sitting at the workstation. Consequently, primitives are provided for simulating the user actions of mouse hits, menu selections, and key strokes. In addition, each object makes available a set of operations that Ness extensions may invoke.

One of the serious problems with allowing scripts to pretend to be the user is that ATK permits users to alter the binding from keystrokes and menu options to function calls. If the author writes a script which invoke the sequence ESC-N it may work for the author but fail for others who have ESC-N bound to a different operation. The correct approach is for the author to instead call the function which he or she has bound to the ESC-N key. Functions behave the same for all users.

How does the extension script refer to objects in the environment? For each execution of an extension there is one unique object, namely the one which triggered the extension; this object can be referred to by a special name. There is also a special name for the text in which the script is embedded; via this name the program can access any portion of the document and any of its other objects. Most commonly, however, objects are referenced by the same name which is used to associate extensions with objects.

2. The Ness 'Extend' construct

A Ness script is a sequence of attribute specifications: declarations of global variables, global functions, and *extend* blocks. An extend block associates a set of contained attributes with some named object. An extend block has the syntax:

> **extend** <name>
> <attributes>
> **end extend**

where the <name> must be a string constant giving the name of an object.

There are situations in which it might make sense that the <name> value be an expression rather than a constant and that the extend construction be executable rather than a declaration. For instance an author may wish to have different extensions for an object at different times. This design was not chosen for Ness because I felt that readers and authors would be best served by a language with relatively "static" semantics; one where the reader could tell what the program refers to without a great deal of poking around the code. There could be confusion for some authors if they were allowed an expression for <name>: they might not know when the expression would be evaluated or whether a change in the value of the expression would cause the extend construct to refer to a different object. Furthermore, the static nature of the extend construct helps suggest to the author that the behavior of documents should be constant rather than dynamic; once a reader has understood a given button, it should not change its behavior without a clear cause. Nonetheless, a button can have differing behavior if an author really so desires; the extension for the button need only test a global flag and behave differently for different values.

Suppose the author wants to dynamically create an object and insert it in the document. How can extensions be specified for it? With Ness this can be accomplished if the name of the future object is pre-known. The <name> in the extend construct can refer to an object which does not yet exist. When it is created, the extensions will be automatically applied to it. For complete generality, however, it will probably be necessary to add to Ness some form of executable **extend** operation.

In additional to declarations and function definitions, the attributes in a extend block may include *event specifications*. Each such specifies a trigger event and a list of statements to be executed when the event occurs. In a manner similar to the extend construct, an event specification is a static declaration with the form

> **on** <event-type> <specifier-string>
> >   <statements>
> **end** <event-type>

The <event-type>s are **mouse**, **menu**, **keys**, and **event**, where the first three intercept the various user events and the fourth reacts to named events initiated by objects. The interpretation of the <specifier-string>, which must be a constant, depends on the <event-type>. For **mouse** it says which button is to be intercepted and whether the interception is for the down stroke, movement while down, upstroke, or all of the above. For **menu** and **keys** it specifies which operations are to intercepted or provided for the user. In particular, the <specifier-string> for **menu** can add new options to the menu. The statements for an **on event** are executed whenever the object extended (by the surrounding **extend** construct) initates the event named by the <specifier-string>.

In writing Ness scripts one of the early discoveries is that intercepting a mouse hit means that that hit will not go to the object. In one example, the object was a slider and the final value, when the mouse is let up, is to be transferred to a computation. If the mouse is intercepted, the slider will not change its value in response to the mouse, so the script must perform an additional operation to tell the extended inset of the mouse change. A built-in function in Ness provides for passing the event along to the inset.

Passing an intercepted event along to an inset may seem similar to the "pass" operation in Hypercard, an operation that sends the current input message *up* the hierarchy to the next level (button to card to stack to ...). However, in Ness and ATK events go *down* the hierarchy so the bottommost object will not see the event at all if the surrounding script so dictates. In our estimation, this gives the script and surroundings more control with less special purpose code within the objects.

Naming of insets and interception of mouse, menu, and keystroke events is handled by the *cel* and *arbiter* insets provided by the ADEW component of ATK [4]. These mechanisms are outside the insets themselves, so their facilities can be utilized without the collaboration of the subject inset. Cels and arbiters are both examples of *wrapper* insets, ones

which have a single child to which they allocate their entire screen space. Each cel wraps around a simple inset like a button, so it can name the button and intercept events. Each arbiter wraps around a substrate inset, like text, which can have multiple embedded objects; from this vantage the arbiter collects the names from all enclosed cels and makes the names available to Ness.

Since an arbiter wraps a substrate and a substrate may contain arbitrary insets, one subinset of an arbiter may be another arbiter together with its own enclosed substrate, Ness script, and collection of insets. So how does a script refer to objects in an arbiter other than its own. It doesn't. At present, a Ness script can only refer to objects that share the same surrounding arbiter as the script itself. This restriction could be eliminated, but not without some difficulty. Consider the case where an author has defined a simulation with a collection of named insets and a Ness script that refers to them. Suppose then that the author inserts two copies of this simulation in a document. It is only because each is surrounded with its own arbiter that name conflicts are avoided: the Ness script in each simulation still refers to the local insets. As yet we have not enough experience with Ness to suggest that a capability of referring to objects within embedded arbiters is a necessary capability.

The statements within an **on** construct may refer to *currentinset* to refer to the inset whose event has triggered the current execution; they may refer to inset(<string expression>) to refer to the inset whose name is given by the <string expression>. Both constructions yield objects as their values; objects on which it is possible to invoke two classes of function that are defined in C code. First, the script may refer to methods and instance variables of the object. Since this is not well protected and can lead to incorrect behavior, it is discouraged, but there are situations in which it is crucial. More safely, the script can call functions in what is called the *proctable*. Each inset defines a set of procedures in this table, from which they are available to be called from Ness functions or to be bound to keystrokes or menu options as a user customizes his environment.

3. The String Algebra

Other than for string values, the Ness language is as simple and traditional as possible. The seven statement forms currently implemented provide for variables, functions, and flow-of-control, as sketched in Table 1 and illustrated in Appendix 1. Semicolons are optional between statements. Parentheses are used only for function call and expression nesting. Since it is implemented with ATK, programs may be typographically formatted for clarity. There are five types of data in Ness: **integer**, **real**, **boolean**, **object**, and **marker**. The first three of these are as in other common languages. An object value is a pointer to an object; it is principally of use for values that are to be passed to methods and proctable functions written in C.

variables

        declaration: *boolean* p, q   *real* x, y, z   *integer* i, j

        assignment: x := y + z   p := *not* q *or True*

function

        call: f(x, p, i)   sin(z)

        return: *return* x + y   *exit function*

flow-of-control: while-do, exit-while, if-then-elif-else

        while i < j *do*

                x := x * 2.5

                if x > y *then*

                        exit while

                end if

                i := i + 1

        end while

Table 1. The seven statement forms in Ness. Other flow-of-control statements are planned for the future.

String values in Ness had to differ from those in other languages for several reasons. Most importantly, strings in any user-level language must be able to include full typography--fonts, indentation, italic, non-ASCII characters, and so on--as well as embedded objects. In a functional language it is also important that substrings be first class objects which can be passed as arguments and returned as values. In other programming languages it is difficult to write parsing and other string processing functions because substring references are clumsy. If substrings are not an integral part of the language, each substring reference needs three components: a reference to the underlying string, an indication of the start of the substring, and an indication of the length of the substring. It is possible to retain such values by keeping three separate variables; it is even reasonable to pass them as arguments to functions. Returning such a triple of values from a function, however, is awkward at best. The situation is so bad that it is difficult to see how to write a satisfactory string package as either a set of functions or a preprocessor for C; the algebra needs to be incorporated as a fundamental part of a language.

In Ness, **marker** values serve as string values. Each such value refers to a substring of some underlying base string. In particular, for documents one base string will be the document itself and a Ness script can refer to and modify an associated text via marker values. A formal algebra underlies marker values, as detailed in [2], where it is proven that the algebra is Turing equivalent. Within this algebra, constants and

concatenation serve traditional roles: each returns a marker value for an entire, newly-created string. Five functions provide for all possible manipulations on strings: base(), start(), next(), extent(), and replace(). See table 2.

base(*s*) - returns a marker for the entire base string underlying *s*

start(*s*) - returns a marker for the empty string which starts where *s* does

next(*s*) - returns a marker for the single character which starts where *s* ends

extext(*s*, *r*) - returns a marker for the portion of the base between start(*s*) and start(next(*r*)); if the latter precedes the former, the value is an empty marker at start(next(*r*))

replace(*s*, *r*) - modifies the base string underlying *s* so the portion that *s* originally referred to will contain a copy of the value initially in *r*

Table 2. The five primitive operations in the string algebra.

The string algebra solves other problems in addition to convenience in writing string processing as function calls. The programmer need not be concerned with allocating storage for strings because that is handled by the system. Strings are not restricted to the array model found in some languages and programmers need not resort to integers, pointers, or some other non-string data type in order to refer to substrings. Strings also provide a data structuring form that may be more amenable to non-programmer computation than traditional programming constructs which are designed more for the convenience of hte machine than the human.

For data structuring, Ness markers provide not only string processing, but also all the capabilities of structures and arrays. A string is a structure when it has multiple objects embedded in it. It is an array when the embedded objects are all the same type and integer subscription functions are used to access the object. It should be noted that integer accessing does not reflect the majority of applications of arrays; in many applications an array is accessed sequentially, varying the subscript by one at each step. This corresponds to sequencing through a marker value with the *next()* function. For non-sequential access, however, it is trivial to write a function in the string algebra to access the i'th element of a marker value, see Algorithm 1. In practice, this algorithm is a primitive provided in the Ness system. (When it becomes common for users to store marker value objects within strings, garbage collection will be necessary. At the moment storage for the underlying strings is released when no markers refer to them.)

```
-- subscript(m, i)
--          Returns the i'th element of m.  If the length of m is
--          less than i, the function returns an empty marker
--          at the end of m.  If i is less than zero the function
--          returns an empty marker at start(m).
--
function subscript (m, i)
          marker s
          if i <= 0 then return start(m) end if
          s := next(start(m))  -- first element of m
          while extent(s, m) /= "" do
                    -- we are not at the end of m
                    if i = 1 then  return s  end if
                    s := next(s)   -- next element of m
                    i := i - 1
          end while
          -- we are at the end of m
          return start(next(m))
end function
```

Algorithm 1. The i'th element of a marker value. This example also illustrates typographical formatting of Ness code.

The desire for simplicity in Ness has led to a number of decisions to defer or not implement popular semantic tools. The two major such decisions are that Ness is not object oriented and functions are not first class objects. Ness does provide access to objects, but these must be written in C as augmented with the *class* preprocessor [6]. If functions were first-class, the **extend** functionality could be expressed as an assignment to an attribute of the object extended. During the design it was felt that this provision would make it possible to make more complex, less intelligible programs. For both functions and object-orientedness, only experience will suggest whether we need to augment the language.

Some observers have asked: should Ness be Lisp or be more like Lisp? One argument in favor of Lisp is that it has "less" syntax. However, this argument does not hold up when we notice that each "special form" in Lisp has its own unique syntax; and that there are many more special forms in Lisp than language constructs in Ness Another argument for Lisp is that it is a well known language. This is true, but the domain for Ness is so different that a Lisp programmer must learn a new set of functions anyway; this set of function names is a much higher hurdle to Ness than is the syntax of the language. A final argument for Lisp is that lists are a convenient data structure which is simple to learn. Ness counters this with the string algebra, which is just as powerful and may be even more intuitive for non-programmers.

4. Security

Embedding of scripts in documents does not introduce a new level of security problem, but makes more obvious a common security problem. The problem is that in small operating systems when I execute a program written by someone else it may do anything I myself may do; in particular, delete a file, modify a file, or send a copy of a file--say a forth-coming examination--to an interloper, perhaps a student about to take that examination. Since a Ness script is a program, and since it can do anything a user can, its execution is a security loophole.

Hypercard offers a security level scheme of a sort: users may choose to execute at one of five levels of privilege. However, these levels restrict the user from dangerous operations while not restricting scripts; a script may even reset the level itself. One reason this is not more of a problem in the Hypercard environment is that the equipment is less frequently connected to networks. However, stackware is shared and we can expect virus attacks via stackware in the future.

Some mainframe operating systems have implemented "capabilities", permissions that can be granted to limit the operations available to programs. These would ease the security problems, though they will still exist. Consider, for example, the user who offers a brand-new spiffy shell which gives graphical access to files. This shell will have to be given enough capabilities that it could be dangerous.

Ultimately the best and only protection is Trust; the reader must trust the person from whom he or she got a document. In a small closed community, such trust is an important factor in the free and open exchange of software. Unfortunately, the spread of networking is widening our communities and exacerbating the security problems.

The Ness implementation has features that make it more difficult--though by no means impossible--for a villain to damage an unwary user.[1] In particular, no script is ever executed--or even compiled--without permission from the reader. Users may choose among two options for this protection. The default option, automatically invoked for any user who has not chosen otherwise, is that the Ness script is surrounded with a text that describes the dangers of executing a script (see Appendix 2). The tail end of this text has buttons which allow the reader several options, including that of

---

[1] It may be no surprise that despite considerable early design work actual implementation of Ness security began November 4, 1988, two days after the infamous Morris internet virus.

Empowering the script, which compiles the script and activates any extensions it specifies. To be absolutely sure the user wants to empower the script, a click on the Empower button pops up a dialog box asking whether the user *really* intends to empower the script.

A villain should also be intimidated by the fact that Ness scripts are stored only in source form. The villain cannot know which readers will take the time to examine the script before empowering it, an examination which might ferret out any suspicious code. (Few readers will read scripts in their entirety, but enough will to provide a deterrent.) Such examination of the code is aided by **Scan**, another option among the buttons at the end of the warning text. This option compiles the script, but generates an error message for each operation which might conceivably modify any of the reader's files, whether in memory or on the disk. Without artificial intelligence, this scan is forced to be quite paranoiac; it flags many statements which are completely harmless. Nonetheless, it typically selects less than a fifth of all statements.

More experienced readers may wish a direct approach to empowering scripts. They may specify in their personal preferences that they wish to see a dialog box instead of the warning text. Then whenever a Ness appears for the first time the reader is presented a dialog box which offers the same options as the buttons at the end of the warning text.

The necessity for security adds an unfortunate complexity. It would be preferable if users did not have to know about the script and the notion of empowering it. Worse, the requirement means that an author must position the script in such a way that it will be visible on the screen, because otherwise the reader will never see it to Empower it. This can clutter the design of applications with an unwanted element. In the future Ness and ATK will have mechanisms to reveal the script at the outset and later hide it.

Evaluation

This paper has shown that document extension has considerable potential for bringing the computer revolution to information delivery. It has described the Ness language which permits an author to construct a document with a variety of behaviors.

The first problem in defining the interconnection of a language embedded in a document is to identify those user events which initiate the operations described by the language. With the **extend** construct, Ness associates event handlers with named insets. If the inset signals appropriate events, they may be handled via the **on event** construct; otherwise the script can intercept user events destined for the inset with the **on menu**, **on mouse**, and **on keys** constructs.

Next the design must specify how the language can affect the document. One general tool is to allow the script to perform all possible user operations. In addition, Ness provides a full set of functions for manipulating insets, especially the text inset for which Ness provides a string algebra.

Finally, the design must provide some control so nefarious authors are not as free to produce programs which can damage readers' files. With Ness, the reader has the option to empower a script or not and also the Scan mode which aids in reviewing the script for potentially dangerous statements.

Although apriori it may seem that enhanced documents would be excellent for mail, they turn out not to be used in mail very much. The world of electronic mail is much more a world of short immediate messages than it is a world of carefully crafted communication. Plans for multi-media mail must satisfy the requirement for transmission of a variety of kinds of bulk information--including scripts--but this will not be the majority of the traffic.

A number of other lessons have been learned from this work:

o One can go quite far with static declaration of extends, events, and functions. Simple scripts for enhancing documents do not seem to need a highly dynamic language.

o Ness shows how to do extensions in a more comprehensible manner than scattering scripts behind each individual object. By giving names to objects they can be extended in the script and can serve as the targets of operations.

o The syntax of the extension language is far less a barrier to authors than is the size of the library of functions available.

o Strings can be dealt with functionally with the string algebra. However, the algebra is not as simple for non-programmers as could be hoped. The next step will be to define a pattern matching language to see if this can make clearer the description of string processing algorithms.

Ness is currently in daily use for maintenance of a data base of bugs and a bibliography. Over time, the number of applications will grow; these will serve as the basis for a future report.

References

[1] *Hypercard User's Manual* Publication 030-3081-A, Apple Computer Inc. (Cupertino, Calif.) 1987.

[2] Wilfred J. Hansen, "The Computational Power of an Algebra for Subsequences", Information Technology Center, Carnegie-Mellon Univ., 1989.

[3] Clayton Lewis and Gary M. Olson, "Can Principles of Cognition Lower the Barriers to Programming?" Report on an informal workshop, University of Colorado, July, 1986.

[4] Thomas P. Neuendorffer, "ADEW: The Andrew Development Environment Workbench: An Overview", presented at the X Conference, Boston, MA, 1989.

[5] Andrew J. Palay, Wilfred J. Hansen, et al., "The Andrew Toolkit - An Overview", presented at the Usenix Conference, Dallas, TX, January, 1988.

[6] Paul G. Crumley, "The Andrew Class System", Information Technology Center, Carnegie Mellon University, file andrew/doc/Class.doc, 1989.

[7] Bruce A. Sherwood and Jill H. Larkin, "New tools for courseware production." *Journal of Computing in Higher Education*, vol. 1, no. 1, pp. 3-20, 1989.

[8] Ben Shneiderman and Greg Kearsley, *Hypertext Hands-On!*, Addison-Wesley, 1989.

Appendix 1: A Ness extended birthday card

After empowering the Ness in the birthday card below, the reader can click the mouse on the cake; the card plays "Happy Birthday", shows the words, and lights the candle on the cake.

Before:

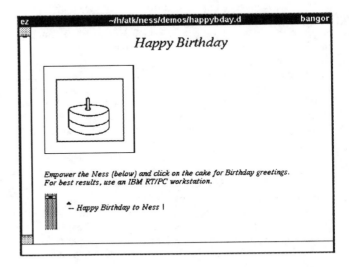

After clicking on the cake:

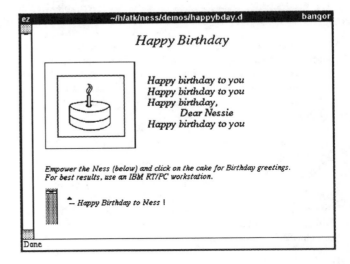

One the next page is the Ness script for the birthday card. The image area at the top of the card has two named insets: "visible cake" is the raster on the left and to its right is a text inset called "song text". The "visible cake" inset is extended so mouse clicks on it can be intercepted.

-- Happy Birthday to Ness !

```
boolean lit:= False -- "visible cake" is initially unlit
marker Cakes := "
```

```
"
```

```
extend "visible cake"   on mouse "any"
        if mouseaction = mouseleftup then
                lit := not lit
                if lit then
                        showcake(FirstObject(
                                second(Cakes)))
                        sing()
                else
                        showcake(FirstObject(Cakes))
                        replace(base(currentselection
                                (inset("song text"))), " \n")
                end if
        end if
end mouse   end extend
```

```
function showcake(object cake)
        raster_copy_subraster(cake)
        raster_select_entire(inset("visible cake"))
        raster_replace_subraster(inset("visible cake"))
        raster_center_image(inset("visible cake"))
end function
```

```
function sing()
        marker m
        m := last(base(currentselection(inset("song text"))))
        m := last(replace(m, "\nHappy birthday to you\n"))
        im_ForceUpdate()
        play_notes("L7 CC L4 DCF   E P4")
        m := last(replace(m, "\nHappy birthday to you\n"))
        play_notes("L7 CC L4 DCG   F P4")
        im_ForceUpdate()
        m := last(replace(m,
                "\nHappy birthday,\n\tDear Nessie\n"))
        play_notes("L7 CC L4 >C <A  FED P4")
        im_ForceUpdate()
        m := last(replace(m, "\nHappy birthday to you\n"))
        play_notes("L7 A#A# L4 AF G  F.")
end function
```

In function showcake, the raster_xxx() functions are proctable entires defined by the raster inset. The copy/replace sequence copies the cake to the cut buffer and then replaces the visible cake with the new image.

The text inset named "song text" initially contains a blank and a newline. The expression currentselection(inset("song text")) returns a marker value for the currently selected portion of the text in this inset; this will usually be the empty string at the beginning. It is immaterial which marker value is returned because the base() function is applied to the value to get a marker for the entire contents of "song text".

im_ForceUpdate() causes the display to update to make visible the preceding change to the text.

The function play_notes() is inserted in the proctable by a package which interprets notes strings and plays them on the keyboard speaker in the IBM RT/PC.

Appendix 2: The Warning to novices

The warning text given below is wrapped around a Ness script when it appears in a document for user perusal. (The user may set a preference option to get a dialog box instead. Such a user is presumed to know what he or she is doing.)

NESS - This inset is a Ness script. If you choose the **empower** option at the end of this inset, the script may alter the behavior of this window. It may respond in new, useful, exciting, or bizarre ways to your mouse clicks, keystrokes, and menu selections.

Warning: Empowering a Ness script is just like running a program. The author of the script or program--if malicious--can write it in such a way that it can destroy your files. If you do not trust the place or person from which you got this script, DO NOT EMPOWER IT.

To learn what this script is supposed to do, you should read the surrounding document for a description. Or, you can read the script itself if you are familiar with Ness. After reading, you have four choices: do nothing, empower the script, "scan" it for potentially dangerous statements, or change it. The last three options appear after the script.

To learn about Ness, give the command 'help ness' or see the files in /usr/andrew/doc/ness.

---- The Ness Script ----

<< the script is nested here >>

---- End of the Ness Script ----

Your Options

If you are uncertain whether to empower this script, the safest choice is to select NONE of the options below.

Also safe is the **Scan** option, which you can choose if you are familiar with the Ness language. The scan highlights each statement in the script which might conceivably change this file or other files. After choosing the Scan option, select the **Next danger** item on the **Ness** menu card to cycle through all the potentially dangerous statements.

If you know Ness and wish to modify the script, you can choose the **Author mode** option. If you do so, this help text

surrounding the script will vanish and you will be able to edit the script. You can select the **Add warning** item on the **Ness** menu card to get this help text back.

The final option is to decide to **Empower** this script. To do so means that you trust the author of the script and the person who gave you this file; it also means you are aware that the script may change how the system responds to your actions.

Scan for dangerous statements
Author mode – Let me edit the script
Empower – I trust the source of this script

ttt

PARALLEL GRAPH-REDUCTION WITH A SHARED MEMORY MULTIPROCESSOR SYSTEM

Gyorgy Revesz

IBM T.J.Watson Research Center
P.O.Box 704
Yorktown Heights, N.Y. 10598

ABSTRACT

Graph-reduction is a well-known technique for implementing lazy (i.e. non-strict) functional languages. This technique seems quite convenient for distributed computing as it involves making only local changes in the graph. However, it is very difficult implement shared subexpressions (shared subgraphs) in a distributed system and thus, the resulting communication overhead may significantly reduce the amount of possible speed-up.

As an alternative, here we study a tightly coupled multiprocessor system where each processor has direct access to a shared memory. The system we have used for our experiments has only eight processors, but it supports the concurrent "Fetch & Add" operation, which we use extensively in our graph-reducer.

The main contribution of this paper is the development of a parallel graph-reduction technique for such a system, and the measurement of its performance via some benchmark programs. As a byproduct, we have also developed a new "on-the-fly" garbage collector, which combines two different collection techniques. Also, we have developed a new read-only graph-traversal technique for any number of concurrent processes independently traversing a shared graph.

1. Problem statement

The main goal of this research was to study the possibility of using a shared memory multiprocessor system for implementing lazy functional languages. For that purpose, we have developed a parallel graph-reduction technique and measured its performance using the Advanced Computing Environment

(ACE) developed by Armando Garcia and others at the IBM T. J. Watson Research Center [6]. The ACE system is an experimental multiprocessor workstation which consists of two major sub-systems: an IBM RT workstation and a similar enclosure which houses the multiprocessor (MP) proper.

It is important to note that this shared memory multiprocessor system has been developed with a totally different set of applications in mind. This clearly distinguishes our work from reduction machines designed explicitly for the purpose of implementing functional languages, such as [9] or [2].

We use the shared memory mostly in a *Concurrent Read / Exclusive Write* manner, but we also take advantage of certain *Concurrent Write* operations whenever possible. Namely, the ACE system supports the so called concurrent "Fetch & Add" operation by automatically serializing the effect of the concurrent write accesses (additions) to the same shared memory location. If, for instance, we have N parallel processors and each

concurrently increments the same shared variable V by one, then V gets incremented by N, and each processor receives a unique answer between I and $I + N - 1$, where I represents the initial value of V. Note, however, that it is totally unpredictable which processor gets which value. Therefore, we can use these operations if and only if we do not care about the order in which they are executed. So, for example, they are perfectly reasonable for parallelizing certain matrix operations where all we care about is to make sure that each index value is assigned to one (and only one) of the available processors, but otherwise we do not care about the exact mapping of these index values to the given set of parallel processors.

There are other commutative and associative operations which are treated like "Fetch & Add" by the system. One of them, namely the concurrent "Fetch & Or" operation, turns out to be quite handy in our parallel marking algorithm, which is a key component of our on-the-fly garbage collector. But, if we need exclusive access to a shared variable, then of course we need explicit synchronization and cannot use these "Fetch & Op" instructions.

For explicit synchronization we add a lock field to every shared record that may be involved in a contention among the processors. Here a positive lock value represents exclusive write access by one of the processors, a negative value, $-K$, represents the fact that precisely K processors have concurrent read access to the given record, while zero represents the unlocked state. To test and set a lock we use the so called "Compare and Swap" instruction.

Our graph-reducer represents the first parallel implementation of the extended lambda-calculus described in [13] and [14]. Standard beta-reduction, i.e. the substitution operation is decomposed here into more elementary reduction steps whose granularity is comparable with combinator-based reduction steps using standard combinators. The arithmetic operations and some other built-in functions are implemented as curried combinators. On the other hand, we use an *infix cons operator* to represent arbitrarily nested lists. The fundamental list-manipulating functions are also implemented directly as built-in combinators. Observe the fact that our type-free calculus for list manipulation is clearly more general than polymorphic typing used in Miranda [18] and in some other functional languages, since the elements of our lists need not be of the same type.

The choice of a particular set of reduction rules is not really important for our discussion, since our graph-reduction technique works essentially with *directed cyclic graphs*, where cycles represent recursive definitions. Nevertheless, some of the reduction rules do have an impact on our reduction technique. So, for example, occasionally we do have to rename certain variables. For that purpose each processor creates unique variable names by incrementing a shared variable-counter via Fetch & Add. Also, we needed a new technique for concurrently traversing a cyclic graph by several independent processes. We have found that introducing side effects such as reversing pointers or marking off visited nodes was rather inefficient. Therefore, we have designed a concurrent graph-traversal technique for an arbitrary number of independent processes, where the graph, which is stored in the shared memory, is accessed in a strictly read-only manner.

We believe that our way of implementing speculative parallelism in a shared memory parallel processor system is quite reasonable. We do not claim that purely speculative parallelism is competitive with more analytical techniques based on strictness analysis and the like. The two approaches are, in fact, complementary to each-another. Namely, some potential for a speed-up via speculative parallelism may still remain even after the most careful analysis – short of the actual execution of the program with the given data in exactly the same environment. (Take, for example, the two arms of a conditional statement.)

We feel that our technique will give a better speed-up for larger graphs. In the near future we will run more experiments on the *IBM Research Parallel Processor Prototype* called RP3, which has become available lately. It also has a shared memory and 64 parallel processors. We expect that the new results will be available by the time of the conference.

Our results so far are non-conclusive. At the same time, we are confident that these results are not limited to a particular set of reduction rules, since our techniques can be easily generalized to other reduction rules. However, the efficiency of any graph-reduction technique depends obviously on the complexity of the pattern matching involved. As long as we have a small set of relatively simple reduction rules, for which pattern matching is easy, we can expect similar performance. Otherwise, the complexity of the pattern matching operation will have a significant impact on the results.

The next section of this paper describes the extended lambda-notation that we use as a functional language. Then we present the basic features of our graph-reduction technique and its parallel implementation. This is followed by a brief description of our new on-the-fly garbage collection technique. Finally, we include some preliminary performance figures obtained for a small benchmark. These results were measured on an experimental hardware model of the ACE system with eight parallel processors connected to a shared memory.

2. Theoretical background

Lists are usually regarded only as data structures in most programming languages. An exception is LISP where programs themselves are represented by nested lists. This has been an important step toward a uniform treatment of programs and data. Unfortunately, modern functional languages, with the exception of Backus's FP, seem to have abandoned this interesting idea.

The construction of a list of functions represents one of the basic program forming operations, called 'combining forms', in FP [1]. As a matter of fact, this combining form would be more natural in a higher-order language such as Miranda, than it is in FP, which is first-order. The standard implementation of Miranda is based on graph-reduction where both the program and its data are represented internally as graphs, which are actually combined (or merged) during the execution. So, it seems only natural that they could have similar structures. List con-

struction, however, is not used as a program forming operation in Miranda, because in that language the elements of a list must be all of the same type.

FP, on the other hand, makes a sharp distinction between programs and data. The latter are called *'objects'* and object lists are syntactically different from function lists. Function lists are formed with the aid of the *'construction'* combinator, whose defining property makes parallel processing implicitly possible without explicitly requiring it.

In [13] we showed that a minor extension of the standard lambda-calculus makes it possible to integrate 'function lists' and 'data lists' in a uniform framework. This extension is fully consistent with the standard lambda-calculus, which is, in fact, a proper part of it. Therefore, we consider arbitrarily nested lists as regular λ-expressions and define the elementary list operators as standard combinators.

Thus, our functional language is a lambda-calculus dialect with list handling capabilities where *every list has a unique applicative property*. The syntax of this extended lambda-notation can be found in the appendix. Its operational semantics is defined by a set of reduction rules as follows.

ALPHA-RULES

$(\alpha 1)$ $\{z/x\}x \to z$
$(\alpha 2)$ $\{z/x\}E \to E$ if x does not occur free in E
$(\alpha 3)$ $\{z/x\}\lambda y.E \to \lambda y.\{z/x\}E$ for every λ-expression E,
                             if $x \not\equiv y \not\equiv z$.
$(\alpha 4)$ $\{z/x\}(E_1)E_2 \to (\{z/x\}E_1)\{z/x\}E_2$
$(\alpha 5)$ $\{z/x\}[E_1, ..., E_n] \to [\{z/x\}E_1, ..., \{z/x\}E_n]$ for $n \geq 0$

Here the symbol $\{z/x\}E$ represents the operation of *renaming*, i.e. replacing all free occurrences of x in E by z. In contrast with the renaming prefix $\{z/x\}$, no substitution prefix will occur in our reduction rules, since we do not define it directly in our system. Instead, we use several β-rules which collectively implement conventional substitution:

BETA RULES

$(\beta 1)$ $(\lambda x.x)Q \to Q$
$(\beta 2)$ $(\lambda x.E)Q \to E$ if x does not occur free in E
$(\beta 3)$ $(\lambda x.\lambda y.E)Q \to \lambda z.(\lambda x.\{z/y\}E)Q$ if $x \not\equiv y$, and
                           z is neither free nor bound in (E)Q.
$(\beta 4)$ $(\lambda x.(E_1)E_2)Q \to ((\lambda x.E_1)Q)(\lambda x.E_2)Q$

Now, the question is what to do when the function body of the operator is a list. It is easy to obtain *'component-wise'* substitution via the following rule:

$(\beta 5)$ $(\lambda x.[E_1, ..., E_n])Q \to [(\lambda x.E_1)Q, ..., (\lambda x.E_n)Q]$ for $n \geq 0$

Observe, however, that this β5-rule has a strong resemblance to the defining property of *construction* in FP. The latter is formulated in our system as follows:

$$([E_1, ..., E_n])Q \to [(E_1)Q, ..., (E_n)Q]$$

So, if we distribute the abstraction prefix of a list among its elements then we can replace β5 by the above rule. That is precisely what we will do by using the following two gamma rules in place of β5:

GAMMA-RULES

$(\gamma 1)$ $([E_1, ..., E_n])Q \to [(E_1)Q, ..., (E_n)Q]$ for $n \geq 0$
$(\gamma 2)$ $\lambda x.[E_1, ..., E_n] \to [\lambda x.E_1, ..., \lambda x.E_n]$ for $n \geq 0$

The remaining rules define the operations associated with

the application of certain constants or combinators. These are usually called δ-rules and for the sake of completeness we list them below.

LIST MANIPULATING FUNCTIONS

$(\textbf{head})[] \rightarrow []$, $\qquad (\textbf{head})[E_1,E_2...,E_n] \rightarrow E_1$

$(\textbf{tail})[] \rightarrow []$, $\qquad (\textbf{tail})[E_1,E_2,...,E_n] \rightarrow [E_2,...,E_n]$

$((\textbf{cons})A)[] \rightarrow [A]$, $\qquad ((\textbf{cons})A)[E_1,...,E_n] \rightarrow [A, E_1,...,E_n]$

$(\textbf{null})[] \rightarrow \textbf{true}$, $\qquad (\textbf{null})[E_1,...,E_n] \rightarrow \textbf{false}$ for $n \geq 1$

$((\textbf{map})F)[] \rightarrow []$, $\qquad ((\textbf{map})F)[E_1,...,E_n] \rightarrow [(F)E_1,...,(F)E_n]$

$((\textbf{append})[])[E_1,...,E_n] \rightarrow [E_1,...,E_n]$

$((\textbf{append})[A_1,...,A_m])[E_1,...,E_n] \rightarrow [A_1,...,A_m, E_1,...,E_n]$

PROJECTIONS

$(1)[E_1, ..., E_n] \rightarrow E_1$ for $n \geq 1$

$(k)[E_1, ..., E_n] \rightarrow ((\textbf{pred})k)[E_2, ..., E_n]$ for $k \geq 2$, $n \geq 1$.

COMBINATORS

$((\textbf{true})A)B \rightarrow A$, $\qquad ((\textbf{false})A)B \rightarrow B$

$(Y)E \rightarrow (E)(Y)E$

OPERATORS AND PREDICATES

$((\textbf{and})\textbf{true})\textbf{true} \rightarrow \textbf{true}$ $\qquad ((\textbf{and})\textbf{true})\textbf{false} \rightarrow \textbf{false}$

$((\textbf{and})\textbf{false})\textbf{true} \rightarrow \textbf{false}$ $\qquad ((\textbf{and})\textbf{false})\textbf{false} \rightarrow \textbf{false}$

$((\textbf{or})\textbf{true})\textbf{true} \rightarrow \textbf{true}$ $\qquad ((\textbf{or})\textbf{true})\textbf{false} \rightarrow \textbf{true}$

$((\textbf{or})\textbf{false})\textbf{true} \rightarrow \textbf{true}$ $\qquad ((\textbf{or})\textbf{false})\textbf{false} \rightarrow \textbf{false}$

$(\textbf{not})\textbf{true} \rightarrow \textbf{false}$ $\qquad (\textbf{not})\textbf{false} \rightarrow \textbf{true}$

$(\textbf{zero})0 \rightarrow \textbf{true}$ $\qquad (\textbf{zero})n \rightarrow \textbf{false}$ for $n \neq 0$

$((+)m)n \rightarrow k$ if m, n are numbers and $k = m + n$

$((-)m)n \rightarrow k$ if m, n are numbers and $k = m - n$

$((*)m)n \rightarrow k$ if m, n are numbers and $k = m * n$

$((/)m)n \rightarrow k$ if m, n are numbers and $k = m / n$

$(\textbf{succ})m \rightarrow n$ if m,n are integers and $n = m + 1$

$(\textbf{pred})m \rightarrow n$ if m, n are integers, $m > 0$, and $n = m - 1$

$((<)m)n \rightarrow \textbf{true}$ if m, n are numbers and $m < n$

$((<)m)n \rightarrow \textbf{false}$ if m, n are numbers and $m \geq n$

Similar reduction rules are used for the remaining relational operators and this completes our list. Function evaluation is performed lazily, hence, we can use infinite lists without any difficulty.

A program represented by a λ-expression will be executed as a series of reduction steps, each of which consists of the application of a reduction rule to one of its subexpressions. Our parallelization of the reduction process is based on the following fundamental result:

> **Theorem:** *The extended lambda-calculus still has the Church–Rosser property.*

A formal proof of this theorem can be found in [15].

3. The highlights of a simple graph-reduction technique

Every λ-expression is translated to its graph-representation by a simple predictive parser during the input phase. This graph-representation is essentially the same as the parse tree of the input expression. It may contain the following types of nodes:

abstraction (λx) $\qquad$ *application* (:)

infix list-constructor (,) $\qquad$ *empty list* ([])

numeric value (#) $\qquad$ *variable* (x, y, z, ...)

combinator (**Y, true, false**) $\qquad$ *operator* (**head, tail,** +, −, ...)

indirection (@) $\qquad$ *renaming prefix* ({z/x})

The type of a node determines the number of its children. An application node has two children, an abstraction node has one, and a variable or constant node has none. There are no indirection or renaming nodes initially in the graph, but they are normally inserted (and eliminated) during the reduction process.

Recursive definitions are represented by *cyclic graphs* as suggested by David Turner for sequential graph-reduction using combinators [17]. Actually, we let the parser determine whether or not a function definition is immediately recursive. (We use only the **let** command but no **letrec** command.) We can assume that no mutual recursion occurs, i.e. they have been replaced by immediate ones. Hence, we do not really need the Y combinator, which also saves us the abstraction (node) corresponding to the function name being defined.

However, the use of cyclic graphs may create serious problems for the efficiency of the implementation in a parallel setting. We shall discuss these problems in more detail in Sections 5 and 6. Fortunately, we were able to solve these problems with a minimum amount of overhead. Thus, we claim that representing recursion via cyclic graphs, even for a highly parallel graph-reducer, is still much better than anything else. This seems to be an important difference between our experiments and those of others using only trees or directed acyclic graphs (see, e.g. [2]).

Renaming nodes are created only in $\beta 3$ steps and they always use a *fresh variable* generated by the system. For that purpose we use a shared variable as a counter and generate unique variable names simply by incrementing this counter via Fetch & Add.

Each of the reduction rules described in the previous section is implemented directly as an elementary local transformation of the expression graph. All the list manipulating rules are implemented lazily of course. But, once again we emphasize that our technique is applicable to a wide variety of graph-reduction rules and we do not claim that our rules are the best. Actually, the reduction rules can be treated as parameters for our reduction process whose basic features remain unchanged when we add or delete some rules.

4. Control of parallelism

The design of our parallel graph-reduction strategy is based on a multiprocessor model with the following assumptions:

(1) We assume that we have a *shared memory multiprocessor system* where each processor can read and write in the shared memory.

(2) One of the processors is designated as the *master* while the others are called *helpers*.

(3) The graph of the λ-expression being evaluated is stored in the shared memory.

(4) The master reduces the graph in normal order. But, when the master determines that a subexpression may be reduced in parallel then it places a pointer referring to it in a *task queue*. (Speculative parallelism).

(5) The helpers send requests to the task queue for subexpressions to be reduced. Each time a helper is given a subexpression it reduces it in normal order.

A similar organization was suggested by Friedman and Wise [5]. We use this model because the organization of the ACE

35

system is based on a similar hierarchy where the master and the helpers execute the same program. But, while the master is activated automatically by the system, the helpers are activated only when so requested by the master via some parallel control structure.

Our master process parses the input λ-expression and stores its graph in the shared memory before it starts any parallel computation. The helpers will take part only in the reduction process. The master never dies until the the computation is finished, i.e. normal form is reached. Then, it sends a stop signal to all the helpers and prints the result before halting itself.

The *task queue* is represented by an array and the index of the next available task is stored in a shared variable. Each helper requests a new task by asking for the current value of this shared variable while incrementing it by one via Fetch & Add. Hence, each helper receives a unique index value while the shared variable is incremented by the sum of the concurrent Fetch & Add operations. This way no explicit synchronization is needed when more than one helpers are concurrently accessing the shared task queue.

The risks and the advantages of speculative computations have been studied in various contexts throughout the literature. In connection with parallel graph-reduction, they are discussed in great detail in [12]. The author of that paper claims that a major problem is how to kill a speculative task when it becomes irrelevant. He says that irrelevant tasks should be killed; and their children, and their children, and so on. While this is usually true for the multi-tasking mechanisms of imperative languages, it is not necessarily so for a graph-reduction technique with no side effects. Indeed, a fundamental feature of our graph-reduction technique is that a partially executed task may produce useful partial results even if it is not finished. Namely, the partial execution of a subcomputation results in a partially reduced subgraph, which is readily available to subsequent computations. Therefore, both relevant and irrelevant tasks may be killed at any time between two consecutive reduction steps without significant overhead. All it takes for a processor to start working on a new task is to reset its pointer to a new node where it should continue searching for the next redex.

We take advantage of this feature in our implementation. First of all, we do not recognize parental relationships among tasks. Each task is treated as being on the same level. Secondly, each task has only a limited lifetime after which it dies automatically regardless of whether it is finished or not. The partial result is simply a semi-reduced subgraph which will be further reduced if the master gets around to work on it or places it again back in the task queue. Because of the fine grained nature of our graph-reduction technique, the master never has to wait for the completion of any subtask. Namely, each processor puts a write lock only on the top node of the redex which it is actually reducing at the moment. Thus, if the master catches up with a subtask by stumbling into a node locked by a helper it will take over by killing that helper as soon as the helper completes its reduction step and releases the node. (The helper in question is identified by the value of its write lock.) Similarly, if a helper bumps into the master or any other helper then it gets killed, i.e. sent back to get a new pointer from the task queue. Note that a task (i.e. the address of the root node of the corresponding subexpression) is removed from the task queue as soon as a helper starts working on it. Hence, nobody knows or cares about whether or not a subtask is finished except for the helper that started working on it.

The point is that the work of a helper may be interrupted between any two consecutive reduction steps. So the master has to wait only for the completion of one reduction step when it finds a helper in its way. Interrupting the current task and starting a new one is, indeed, very cheap in our system. Hence, it is reasonable to kill every task after a certain number of steps. If the task turns out to be relevant then its residual will obviously reappear in the task queue or will be picked up by the master itself. When the task queue is full, no new tasks are created, hence the overloading of the system with irrelevant tasks does not occur. Because of the speculative nature of our tasking mechanism the automatic killing of long running tasks will clearly help the system adapt itself to the actual needs of the computation at hand. The master will finish the computation when the graph is in normal form, at which point all remaining subtasks are killed.

5. An Efficient Parallel Graph Traversal

The most serious challenge to our parallel graph-reduction technique was posed by the β2-rule, which involves a search for the first free occurrence (if any) of a variable in a subexpression. As long as we have no cycles the traversal of the graph can be controlled by a local stack. But, if the graph may contain cycles then we must take some extra measures in order to avoid going in circles. One possible solution is to mark off each node that has been visited during a traversal. This, however, requires a large marker field for each node: we need as many mark bits as we have parallel processors possibly engaged in concurrently traversing the same graph. Moreover, these markers must be reset after each traversal, which makes the whole process rather cumbersome. Pointer reversal techniques are facing similar difficulties in a multiprocessor environment.

Instead of adding an extra marker field to each node, our parser inserts a special indirection node in the graph whenever it creates a back-arrow, i.e. a cycle. This is done only when a recursive definition is parsed.

Then, during the reduction process, each processor uses a private stack to control the traversal of the corresponding subgraph. Furthermore, each time a processor traverses a special indirection node, it will store this node in its private memory unless it is already there. In the latter case it will pop its stack, otherwise it will keep going. This way it can avoid traversing the same cycle twice. We claim the following:

Theorem: Our method correctly allows an arbitrary number of processors to simultaneously traverse a shared cyclic graph. Moreover, the overhead required is "small".

The proof depends on every cycle containing at least one of these special indirection nodes. These nodes are placed originally in the graph by the parser. We must, however, prove that this property is preserved throughout the reduction process. In other words, we have to make sure that every new cycle created during the reduction process contains at least one of these special indirection nodes. Fortunately, our reduction algorithm creates new cycles only when it inserts an edge representing a short cut across an existing cycle. Moreover, due to the elementary nature of our reduction rules, these short cuts are relatively easy to check: they can bypass at most three edges at a time. — It would be clearly much more difficult to maintain this property for arbitrary short cuts. This traversal technique is indeed fine tuned to our graph-reduction.

36

6. On-the-fly garbage collection

We use an improved version of the DLMSS technique designed by Dijkstra et al. [4]. The original algorithm uses three colors: white, gray, and black. At the beginning of the marking phase all nodes are white except for the root node of the active graph which is gray. During the marking phase, the gray nodes represent the boundary between the black and the white portion of the active graph. The marking algorithm proceeds by propagating the black color towards this boundary and, at the same time, shifting the gray boundary towards the unmarked (white) portion of the active graph. The marking phase terminates when no gray node is left, hence, all reachable nodes are black.

Our first improvement consists of the parallelization of both the marking phase and the collecting phase of the original algorithm by subdividing the node space into N equal subintervals, where N is the number of parallel collectors.

During the marking phase each collector scans its own subinterval, and 'shades' the children of the gray nodes while changing the color of these gray nodes to black. The shading of a node means changing its color to gray if it is white but leaving it unchanged if it is gray or black. This shading operation is performed via Fetch & Or, so that nodes having multiple parents may get marked concurrently by any number of parallel processors. This is important, since even the reducers may perform some marking activity at the same time. An explicit synchronization is needed only at the end of each sweep of the marking phase. This synchronization is implemented by a 'barrier' at the end of the basic loop. Namely, we use a shared variable and count the arrivals of the parallel processes via Fetch & Add 1. Then we wait until the value of this counter becomes equal to N.

The marking phase is finished when no more 'gray' nodes are found during the last sweep. Again we use Fetch & Add and a shared variable for counting the total number of gray nodes found independently by each of the parallel marking processes.

During the collecting phase each collector collects the white nodes from its respective subinterval. For the manipulation of the free list, which is stored as a linked list, we use standard *shared queue management techniques* ([7], [8]). Another barrier is needed for explicit synchronization at the end of the collecting phase.

Further improvement on the performance of the DLMSS technique has been achieved by combining it with a 'greedy' collector, which collects all first level garbage (orphan nodes) immediately after each marking sweep [16]. To find the orphan nodes we mark off the children of every node regardless of its color. For that purpose we need only one extra marker bit (besides the two already used by DLMSS), whose setting is combined with the operation of shading. This means that our marking algorithm performs two different markings in one Fetch & OR operation, killing two birds with one stone. According to our experiments the improvement is significant. In fact, we need the DLMSS algorithm only for collecting cyclic garbage, but most of the garbage turned out to be acyclic in our examples.

7. Sample results

The parallel version of our graph-reducer was originally written in EPEXC and tested on the RP3 simulator using the Writeable Shared Segment Operating System [10]. The EPEXC preprocessor was later ported to the ACE system which made it possible to port also the graph-reducer without any changes. Only the use of the system-clock to measure the execution time needed minor adjustments.

Here we show some performance figures for a small benchmark that we ran on the ACE system with the number of mutators varying from 1 to 4. In each case roughly half that many processors were dedicated to the task of collecting the garbage on the fly. In case of a single processor, garbage collection was done in a 'stop and go' manner and its time is shown between parentheses following the pure computing time. Execution times are given in seconds.

Mutators	1	1	2	2	3	3	4	4
Collectors	(1)	1	1	2	2	3	3	4
powerset	11(+4)	11	9	9	8	7	10	8
permute	15(+4)	15	8	11	7	7	8	8
hanoi	11(+4)	11	12	12	9	7	6	5
ack1	8(+4)	8	9	8	5	5	7	7
ack2	5(+2)	6	6	5	4	4	5	4
sieve	13(+4)	13	16	13	12	12	12	7

As can be seen from this table the pure computing time remains essentially the same when going from one processor to two, where the second processor is a dedicated on-the-fly garbage collector. This means that the latter introduces very little overhead to the mutator's work, which is very good. The amount of work done by the collector(s) was far from being negligible, because we deliberately chose a very small node space in order to make on-the-fly garbage collection nontrivial. In case of two mutators and one collector, for example, a minimum of 2997 (permute) and a maximum of 9028 (hanoi) nodes were collected while the entire node space consisted of only 1800 nodes. (No cyclic garbage was found in these examples, although the expression graphs were cyclic.)

Our benchmark contained two different versions, namely a Curried and a list oriented version of the ackermann function. Interestingly enough, the list oriented version ran much faster than the first one, which shows the advantages of our list manipulation techniques. These examples are, of course, very small for drawing significant conclusions. It seems only natural that the synchronization overhead gets relatively high when too many processors are working on a small graph. For the given examples the optimum number of mutators seems to be around three, except for 'hanoi' and 'sieve' where 4 mutators are much better.

The amount of speed-up obtained in this fashion seems relatively small, but we believe that this is due to the small size of the examples we have run so far. We have performed a deeper analysis for some cases which showed that the workload was fairly evenly distributed among the helpers and most of the delay was due to their contention in trying to get exclusive write and concurrent read access to the same nodes. In a larger graph they should be able to work together with much less interference.

Also, we should keep in mind that we are dealing with a lazy functional language with no explicit control of parallelism. All we are doing is to take advantage of the implicit parallelism of the given expression at run time in a completely automatic manner. Thus, we have not used any strictness analysis or other compile time optimization techniques, nor have we considered highly sophisticated load balancing strategies. The implicit parallelism is clearly more significant in some cases than in others, but it is treated completely automatically in our system. As we have mentioned before, we want to run further experiments on a much larger system called RP3 and hope to be able to present their results at the conference. We are convinced that simulation results are not reliable in this field, therefore we insist on running these experiments on the real thing.

Acknowledgments

The author thanks several people for their help and for their contribution to this work. Janice Stone, Alan Norton, and Whei-Ling Chang introduced the author to the RP3 simulator, the EPEXC preprocessor and the Writeable Shared Segment Operating System. Mark Gunning translated the serial version of the interpreter from Pascal to C and implemented the timing routines for performance measurements. Janice Stone designed and implemented the shared queue management technique for the free-list and a number of other parallel control routines. Tien Huynh implemented the necessary adjustments to the graph-reduction rules for supporting our concurrent graph traversal technique. Anthony Bolmarcich extended invaluable help with some of the intricacies of the EPEXC preprocessor.

References

1. Backus, J. W. Can programming be liberated from the von Neumann style? A functional style and its algebra of programs. *Communications of the ACM,* Vol. 21, No. 8, (August 1978), pp. 613-641.

2. Burkimsher, P. C. Combinator reduction in a shared-memory multiprocessor. *The Computer Journal*, Vol.30, No.3, (1987) pp. 214-222.

3. Chang, W-L. and Norton, A. *VM/EPEXC Preprocessor User's Manual Version 2.0.* RC 12246, IBM T. J. Watson Research Center, 1987.

4. Dijkstra, E. W., Lamport. L., Martin, A. J., Scholten, C. S. and Steffens, E. F. M. On-the-fly garbage collection: An exercise in cooperation. *Communications of the ACM, vol. 21, no. 11,* November 1978, pp. 966-975.

5. Friedman, D. P. and Wise, D. S. Aspects of applicative programming for parallel processing. *IEEE Trans. Comput.,* C-27, (April 1978), pp. 289-296.

6. Garcia, A., Foster, D. J., and Freitas, R. F. *The Advanced Computing Environment multiprocessor workstation* RC 14491, IBM T. J. Watson Research Center, 1989.

7. Gottlieb, A., Lubachevsky, B. D. and Rudolph, L. Coordination of very large number of processors. *ACM Transactions on Programming Languages and Systems*, 5(2), (April 1983) pp. 164-189.

8. Hwang, K. and Briggs, R. *Computer Architecture and Parallel Processing.* McGraw-Hill, 1984.

9. Magó, G. A. A network of microprocessors to execute reduction languages. *International Journal of Computer and Information Sciences* 8 (5/6) (October/December 1979) pp. 349-385/435-471.

10. Melton, E. A. and Pfister, G. F. *A Writeable Shared Segment Operating System.* RC 11371, IBM T. J. Watson Research Center, 1985.

11. Peyton-Jones, S. L. *The Implementation of Functional Languages.* Prentice-Hall, 1987.

12. Peyton-Jones, S. L. Parallel implementations of functional programming languages. *The Computer Journal*, Vol.32, No.2, (1989), pp. 175-186.

13. Revesz, G. An extension of lambda-calculus for functional programming. *The Journal of Logic Programming,* Vol.1, No.3, (1984), pp. 241-251.

14. Revesz, G. *Lambda-Calculus, Combinators and Functional Programming.* Cambridge Tracts in Theoretical Computer Science 4, Cambridge University Press, 1988.

15. Revesz, G. *A list oriented extension of the Church–Rosser Theorem.* RC 13620, IBM T. J. Watson Research Center, 1988.

16. Revesz, P. Z. *A new parallel garbage collection algorithm* Honor's Thesis, Tulane University, New Orleans, 1985.

17. Turner, D. A. A new implementation technique for Applicative languages. *Software - Practice and Experience*, 9(1), 1979, pp. 31-49.

18. Turner, D. A. An introduction to Miranda. *Appendix* in [11], pp. 431-438.

APPENDIX

THE EXTENDED SYNTAX OF λ-EXPRESSIONS

$<$λ-expression$>::=<$variable$> \mid <$constant$> \mid$

$<$abstraction$> \mid <$application$> \mid <$list$>$
$<$variable$>::=<$identifier$>$
$<$constant$>::=<$number$> \mid <$operator$> \mid <$combinator$>$
$<$abstraction$>::=$ λ$<$variable$>.<$λ-expression$>$
$<$application$>::= (<$λ-expression$>)<$λ-expression$>$
$<$list$>::= [<$λ-expression$><$list-tail$> \mid []$
$<$list-tail$>::= ,<$λ-expression$><$list-tail$> \mid]$
$<$operator$>::=<$arithmetic operator$> \mid$
$\qquad <$relational operator$> \mid <$predicate$> \mid$
$\qquad <$boolean operator$> \mid <$list operator$>$
$<$arithmetic operator$>::= + \mid - \mid * \mid / \mid$ **succ** $\mid$ **pred**
$<$relational operator$>::= < \mid \leq \mid = \mid \geq \mid > \mid \neq$
$<$predicate$>::=$ **zero** $\mid$ **null**
$<$boolean operator$>::=$ **and** $\mid$ **or** $\mid$ **not**
$<$list operator$>::=$ **head** $\mid$ **tail** $\mid$ **cons** $\mid$ **map** $\mid$ **append**
$<$combinator$>::=$ **true** $\mid$ **false** $\mid$ **Y**

Note that in an application we always put the operator, rather than the operand, between parentheses. Hence, we use *(f)x* to denote the application of a function *f* to the argument *x*.

The primitive functions **pred** and **succ** represent the predecessor and the successor functions on integers. The predicate **zero** represents the test for integer type zero while **null** represents the test for the empty list, which is denoted by []. The constant symbols **head**, **tail**, **cons**, **map**, and **append** denote the usual list operations. All functions are *Curried*, which means that they take only one argument at a time. Two or more arguments are supplied to a function by repeated applications. So, for example, we would write ((+)a)b instead of the more usual a + b.

Cache Performance of Combinator Graph Reduction

Philip J. Koopman, Jr.
Harris Semiconductor
Melbourne, Florida 32902

Peter Lee
School of Computer Science
Carnegie Mellon University
Pittsburgh, Pennsylvania 15213

Daniel P. Siewiorek
School of Computer Science
Carnegie Mellon University
Pittsburgh, Pennsylvania 15213

Abstract

The Threaded Interpretive Graph Reduction Engine (TIGRE) was developed for the efficient reduction of combinator graphs in support of functional programming languages and other applications. We present the results of cache simulations of the TIGRE graph reducer with the following parameters varied: cache size, cache organization, block size, associativity, replacement policy, write policy, and write allocation. As a check on our results, we compare the simulations to measured performance on real hardware. From the results of the simulation study, we conclude that graph reduction in TIGRE has a very heavy dependence on a write-allocate strategy for good performance, and very high spatial and temporal locality.

Keywords: functional programming, combinators, graph reduction, cache memory, architectural simulation.

Introduction

During the development of the TIGRE graph reducer [1][2], the speed of graph reduction on different hardware platforms repeatedly surprised us, in some cases failing to meet expectations, and in other cases substantially exceeding predicted performance levels. For example, the DECstation 3100 system [3] (which is based on the MIPS R2000 processor chip [4]) performed 470,000 combinator reduction applications per second (RAPS) for Turner's set of SK-combinators [5][6]. This makes TIGRE, to the best of our knowledge, the fastest SK-combinator graph reducer in existence. A VAX 8800 mainframe system [7] with a faster clock rate and a wider system bus performed only 355,000 RAPS. Finally, a Cray Y-MP [8], with a clock speed ten times that of the DECstation 3100, performed only 310,000 RAPS. Another unexpected result was that a VAX mainframe implementation of TIGRE was sped up by 20% with a slight code change to circumvent the write-no-allocate cache management strategy used by that machine.

These results have prompted us to undertake a detailed study of the architectural issues affecting the efficiency of graph reduction. The purpose of the study is twofold. First, we would like to be able to predict, on the basis of the hardware architecture, what kinds of machines will best support graph reduction (and hence functional languages). Second, we would like to obtain design-tradeoff data for both custom graph reduction hardware and new reduction techniques. This is a report of the first phase of the study — the cache behavior of SK-combinator graph reduction.

Background

The Threaded Interpretive Graph Reduction Engine (TIGRE) was developed to efficiently implement pure combinator graph reduction in support of lazy functional programming languages and other applications. The basic philosophy underlying TIGRE is the elimination of tags on data cells in order to avoid case analysis operations when accessing a graph node.

One of the most awkward aspects of graph reduction is the need to traverse the left spine of a graph, in the process "unwinding" the right-side children onto what is often referred to as the "spine" stack. Besides forcing one to implement a case analysis on graph-node tags, it seems also to require some kind of "control program" to control the traversal. This is unfortunate, since the program that we are actually interested in executing is essentially embedded in the graph; the control program really ends up being an interpreter. Hence, in this scheme we seem

Work done by Philip Koopman performed while at the Department of Electrical and Computer Engineering, Carnegie Mellon University. Research supported in part by NASA/Goddard under contract NAG-5-1046, also in part by the Office of Naval Research under contract N00014-84-K-0415 and in part by the Defense Advanced Research Projects Agency (DOD), ARPA Order No. 5404, monitored by the Office of Naval Research under the same contract. The views and conclusions contained in this document are those of the authors and should not be interpreted as representing the official policies, either expressed or implied, of DARPA or the U.S. Government.

forced to accept the efficiency penalties involved with interpretation as opposed to direct execution.

The key insight underlying TIGRE is that the graph is itself a program with two classes of instructions: pointer instructions and combinator instructions. Graph reduction then becomes a process of executing a self-modifying, threaded program which resides in the node heap. That is to say, the graph is a program that consists mainly of subroutines calls (*i.e.*, pointer instructions). One call leads to another call, which then leads to another, and so on until, finally, some other executable code (*i.e.*, a combinator instruction) is found.

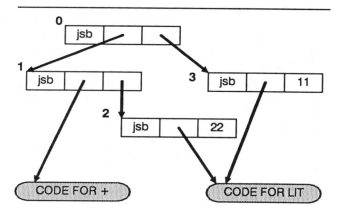

Figure 1. Example program graph for the VAX implementation of TIGRE.

Figure 1 shows a simple program graph for ((+ 22) 11) as implemented in the VAX assembly language version of TIGRE. Each node in the graph contains a VAX jsb subroutine call instruction as well as two subgraph pointers (a function pointer in the middle node cell, and an argument pointer in the rightmost node cell). Combinators and graph references are both represented by pointers. Literal values are implicitly tagged as data items by the fact that the function slot of a literal node always points to the LIT combinator code. With this representation scheme, there is only one explicit data type in the graph: the pointer. Hence there is only one type of node, and therefore no conditional branching or case analysis for tag interpretation is required at run time.

Evaluation of a program graph is initiated by performing a subroutine call to the jsb node of the root of a subgraph. The machine's program counter then traverses the left spine of the graph structure by executing the jsb instructions of the nodes following the leftmost spine. As the subroutine calls are executed, the return-address stack accumulates references to graph nodes in the manner of a spine stack. When a slot points to a combinator, the VAX simply begins executing the combinator code, with the return-address stack providing addresses of the

right-hand sides of parent nodes for the combinator's argument values.

TIGRE in no sense interprets the graph. It *directly executes* the data structure, using the hardware-provided subroutine call instruction to do the stack unwinding. When combinator bodies are reached, the arguments are popped from the return stack, the graph is rewritten, and then a jump is made to the new subgraph to continue traversing the (new) left spine. The use of the return stack for graph reduction is slightly different than for "normal" subroutines in that subroutine returns are never performed on the pointers to the combinator arguments, but rather, the addresses are consumed from the return stack by the combinators.

This technique is similar to that previously reported by Augusteijn & van der Hoeven [9]. However, to our knowledge they did not conduct an in-depth architectural study of the approach.

The execution speed of TIGRE for the Turner set of SK-combinators compares favorably with previously reported combinator graph reducers, and for supercombinators it appears to be competitive with the G-machine [10] and closure reducers such as TIM [11]. Table 1 shows a summary of TIGRE performance on a number of platforms. The numbers shown for supercombinator implementations give a RAPS rating normalized to the Turner set implementations in order to reflect speedup obtained by supercombinator compilation.

The basis for the architectural study

We conjectured that the unexpected performance variations observed among TIGRE versions were caused by hardware implementation differences among platforms, especially with regard to cache management policy. In order to better understand the operation of TIGRE, a set of cache simulations was run to measure TIGRE's use of cache memory.

The first simulation experiment was an exhaustive exploration of a number of cache design parameters to search for the optimal combination. An exhaustive search was performed to avoid the pitfalls of hill-climbing search strategies that may become trapped at local extrema. The second simulation experiment examined the sensitivity of performance to changes in individual parameters.

The MIPS R2000 was chosen as the implementation vehicle for the simulations for several reasons. Several different R2000-based machines are available to us for "reality checks" between simulator results and actual execution times. The R2000 is a simple architecture that is readily modeled, and information about the timing and operation of the R2000 is readily available. The R2000 processor lacks a subroutine-call instruction; however, the use of an interpretive loop instead of subroutine

Table 1.
TIGRE performance on a variety of platforms.

Platform	Language	Combinator Set	Program	Time (sec)	Speed (RAPS)
DECstation	ASSEMBLER	SKI Set	SKIFIB(23)	2.20	495000
3100		Turner Set	FIB(23)	1.58	470000
(16.7 MHz)			NFIB(23)	2.68	484000
			TAK	12.58	420000
			NTHPRIME(300)	2.60	364000
			QUEENS(20)	5.63	433000
		Supercombinator	FIB(23)	0.36	2046000
			NFIB(23)	0.80	1626000
VAX 8800	ASSEMBLER	SKI Set	SKIFIB(23)	2.82	387000
(22 MHz)		Turner Set	FIB(23)	2.10	355000
			NFIB(23)	3.55	366000
			TAK	16.07	329000
			NTHPRIME	3.91	242000
			QUEENS(20)	8.33	293000
		Supercombinator	FIB(23)	1.22	611000
			NFIB(23)	0.97	1339000
VAXstation 3200	ASSEMBLER	SKI Set	SKIFIB(23)	6.33	172000
		Turner Set	FIB(23)	4.80	155000
			NFIB(23)	8.23	158000
		Supercombinator	FIB(23)	2.77	269000
			NFIB(23)	2.15	605000
Cray Y-MP	C	SKI Set	SKIFIB(23)	3.09	352000
(167 MHz)		Turner Set	FIB(23)	2.40	310000
			NFIB(23)	4.25	305000
			TAK	14.69	360000
			NTHPRIME(300)	3.40	277000

threading does not affect data cache access patterns, and so is irrelevant for examining data access behavior in the second half of the study.

Phase 1: Exhaustive search of the design space

The goal of the first phase of the simulations was to use memory access traces from TIGRE and a trace-driven cache simulator to explore a wide range of values for several independent cache parameters (such as cache size, block size, and replacement policy). By simulating all possible combinations of two or three discrete values for each parameter, the performance of TIGRE over the entire cache design space was mapped. As a result, similarities and differences between the best-performing sets of parameter combinations could lend insight into what kind of cache memory organization best supports TIGRE.

The dineroIII trace-driven cache simulator program [12] was used. The simulation parameters varied were: cache size (64K and 16K bytes), cache organization (unified and split), block size (also known as line size, of 4, 8, and 16 bytes), associativity (direct-mapped and 4-way set associative), replacement policy (LRU and FIFO),

write policy (write-through and copy-back), and write allocation (allocate on write miss, and no allocation on write miss). Kabakibo et al. [13] and Smith [14] provide more information on cache management strategies and terminology.

All meaningful combinations of parameters were run. Some combinations, such as varying replacement policy on a direct-mapped cache, are meaningless. The split caches divide the available cache memory evenly between instruction and data caches, as is commonly done on real systems (e.g. a split 64K cache allocates 32K each to the instruction cache and data cache). The fib(16) benchmark using the SKI combinator set was chosen for the exhaustive design space search. A large enough heap was used to avoid the need to simulate garbage collection.

Table 2 shows the best sixteen configurations based on simulation results for the program skifib(16). The primary ranking is by miss ratio, which has a strong effect on program running time. Miss ratio is the number of memory accesses that result in cache misses normalized to the number of total accesses (e.g. 0.3000 would represent a 30% miss ratio). Traffic ratio is the number of 32-bit transfers on the data bus from the combination of

Table 2.
The sixteen best cache configurations.

CACHE SIZE	CACHE SPLITTING	BLOCK SIZE	ASSOCIA- TIVITY	REPLACE POLICY	WRITE POLICY	WRITE ALLOCATE?	MISS RATIO	TRAFFIC RATIO
64K	UNIFIED	16	4 WAY	LRU	COPY	YES	0.0096	0.0767
64K	SPLIT	16	4 WAY	LRU	COPY	YES	0.0096	0.0768
64K	UNIFIED	16	4 WAY	LRU	THRU	YES	0.0096	0.1609
64K	SPLIT	16	4 WAY	LRU	THRU	YES	0.0096	0.1610
16K	UNIFIED	16	4 WAY	LRU	COPY	YES	0.0097	0.0773
16K	UNIFIED	16	4 WAY	LRU	THRU	YES	0.0097	0.1612
64K	UNIFIED	16	4 WAY	FIFO	COPY	YES	0.0098	0.0776
16K	SPLIT	16	4 WAY	LRU	COPY	YES	0.0098	0.0777
64K	SPLIT	16	4 WAY	FIFO	COPY	YES	0.0098	0.0779
16K	SPLIT	16	4 WAY	LRU	THRU	YES	0.0098	0.1615
64K	UNIFIED	16	4 WAY	FIFO	THRU	YES	0.0098	0.1615
64K	SPLIT	16	4 WAY	FIFO	THRU	YES	0.0098	0.1617
64K	SPLIT	16	DIRECT	—	COPY	YES	0.0101	0.0795
64K	SPLIT	16	DIRECT	—	THRU	YES	0.0101	0.1627
64K	SINGLE	16	DIRECT	—	COPY	YES	0.0102	0.0799
64K	SINGLE	16	DIRECT	—	THRU	YES	0.0102	0.1632

Total data reads = 0.1585, Total Data writes = 0.1224, Total Instruction reads = 0.7191
1042523 MIPS R2000 instructions, 1449863 memory accesses, 37480 combinators.

cache misses and writes of modified cache contents to memory, normalized to the total number of accesses.

Each simulation run involved a total of 1449863 memory accesses, 1042523 of which were instruction reads. 71.9% of all memory accesses were instruction reads, 15.9% were data reads, and 12.2% were data writes. To avoid the possibility of misleading results caused by an insufficiently large simulation data set size, the simulation was rerun on several data points from various regions of the simulated design space with a data set ten times as large (created by running `skifib` with a larger input). These expanded simulations yielded essentially identical results.

Some obviously desirable characteristics can be inferred from Table 2. The write allocation policy should be set to write-allocate, and the block size should be set to 16 bytes for good performance. There is relatively little difference among the miss ratios, indicating that some of the design parameters, including the cache size, have little effect on performance. Details of the cache simulation results showed that a unified cache has a slightly better miss ratio than a split cache because the interpretive program was quite small. Thus, a unified cache gives more total cache memory for the data portion of the program. However, split caches work better in practice, since most RISC processors depend on the extra bandwidth available from a split cache scheme for high performance.

From the data in these tables, we conclude that a cache design of 64K bytes, split I/D cache (giving 32K bytes each for program and data caches), 16 byte blocks, 4-way set associative, LRU replacement, copy-back, and write-allocate is the optimal strategy.

Phase 2: Parametric analysis

The initial exhaustive search of the design space gave a good starting point for determining the optimal cache design parameters. But, there was no precise indication of the sensitivity of the performance to variation in the parameters. For this reason, a second set of cache simulations was conducted to measure the performance effects of changing the parameters.

For this second set of simulations, the cache design obtained from the first phase of the simulation study was used as a baseline. Individual parameters were then altered, one at a time, across a wide range to observe performance trends. The first set of simulations confirmed that the instructions needed to run the combinator reducer were almost immediately loaded into cache and stayed in cache throughout the program execution. Therefore, the parametric analysis simulations modeled only the data accesses of the programs and collected statistics for just the data cache (assuming a split I/D cache scheme). The baseline configuration, against which sensitivity to change was measured, was: 32K byte data-cache size, 16 byte block size, 4-way set associative, LRU replacement, copy-back, and write-allocate. The benchmark program run was `fib(18)`, with data collected for three implementations of the program: the SKI combinator set, the Turner set, and supercombinator compilation with strictness analysis.

The importance of a write-allocate strategy

Table 3 shows the results of varying the write allocation policy. We have found that this design parameter is more important by far than any of the other parameters, with very poor cache hit ratios of 76% to 85% awaiting the user of a machine which incorporates a write-no-allocate policy. A 95% or higher cache hit ratio is generally considered desirable for systems running conventional software.

Table 3.
TIGRE performance with varying cache write allocation strategy.

MISS RATIOS

Allocation Strategy	SKI set	Turner set	Super.
write allocate	0.0341	0.0300	0.0528
write no allocate	0.1914	0.1522	0.2433

The reason for the extreme sensitivity to write-allocation lies with the allocation of heap nodes. As heap nodes are allocated, the addresses of the new cells are generated without accessing heap memory (using a stop-and-copy garbage collection algorithm). The first time the node is written, a cache miss is generated. A write-allocate strategy will load the node into the cache, while a write-no-allocate strategy will simply write the node value into main memory. The problem comes on the subsequent read of this node, which typically happens within several hundred clock cycles. A write-no-allocate policy will experience a second cache miss, while a write-allocate policy will get a cache hit on the previously written element. This second cache miss with a write-no-allocate policy significantly degrades performance. The effect becomes even more pronounced when a long sequence of writes (each generating a cache miss) is performed in succession before the first read, as can happen when performing a sequence of graph rewrites on a small portion of the program graph.

The Turner set data showed the least degradation from using write-no-allocate because it does not create a large number of superfluous nodes as the SKI set does (by using the B and C combinators instead of less efficient sequences of the S and K combinators). But, the Turner set does have a large number of redundant accesses to elements for intermediate graph rewriting that are eliminated by the supercombinator approach, so the supercombinator version shows marked degradation in performance from using a write-no-allocate strategy.

Strong spatial locality means large block size

Figure 2 shows the results of varying block size over a range of 4 bytes to 8K bytes. The cache miss ratio decreases up to a cache size of 2K bytes for the SKI and Turner Set methods, and up to 8K bytes (the limit to block size given 4-way set associativity) for the supercombinator method. This suggests very strong spatial locality. This spatial locality is probably due to the fact that short-lived cells are allocated from the heap space in sequential memory locations. (This sequentiality is an inherent property of compacting garbage collection and heap allocation schemes, such as the stop-and-copy garbage collector used by TIGRE.)

One could, at first glance, decide to build a machine with a 2K byte cache-block size based on the miss ratios alone. For conventional programs, this decision would be

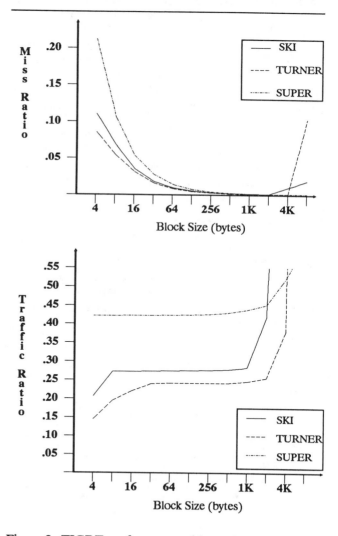

Figure 2. TIGRE performance with varying cache block size.

unwise, because the traffic ratio (the number of words of data moved by the system bus) usually increases dramatically with an increased block size. This heavy traffic can slow a system down by greatly increasing the time required to refill a cache block after a miss. With combinator graph reduction, this effect is much less pronounced. The traffic ratio does not increase appreciably until the block size is between 1K and 4K bytes in size. So, a machine with a 256 byte or 512 byte cache-block size is entirely reasonable for this application.

The fact that the miss ratio stays very low until the cache-block size increases to within a factor of between four and sixteen of the total cache size gives further insight into the behavior of graph reduction. The code in this experiment tends to access approximately four to sixteen regions of memory at a time, since the miss ratio begins to climb when the 32K byte cache can hold fewer than sixteen cache blocks. This suggests excellent temporal locality.

The observed temporal locality bodes well for virtual memory access behavior. Since most translation lookaside buffers are limited in size (for example, 64 entries addressing 4K bytes each on a MIPS R2000), good spatial locality is important to limit the number of TLB misses. At a second level, good spatial locality also limits thrashing of virtual memory pages between main memory and secondary storage devices. The result is that combinator graph reduction seems to provide excellent virtual memory behavior even without the use of compacting techniques (since no garbage collections were done for these simulation runs).

High temporal locality means small cache size
Figure 3 shows the results of varying cache size over a range of 128 bytes to 128K bytes. Since most newer designs tend to use large cache memories to improve performance (with 64K bytes in a data cache often the minimum acceptable amount for a RISC implementation), it is surprising to see that performance for all three

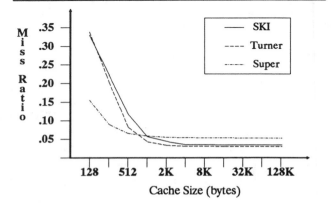

Figure 3. TIGRE performance with varying cache size.

implementations stays at approximately 95% to 98% hit ratio with a cache as small as 2K bytes, which corresponds to only 256 graph nodes. This suggests that combinator graph reduction may have better temporal locality than conventional programs. This temporal locality may be due in part to a high infant mortality rate among allocated heap nodes.

High temporal locality suggests that generational garbage collection techniques [15] may be useful with combinator graph reduction, but this issue has not been explored in detail.

A word of caution on the interpretation of the cache-size data collected here is in order. The benchmarks used are rather small a certain sense. They access a large amount of heap space, so it cannot be said that the programs are too small to exercise a large cache. However, only a few thousand heap nodes are actually active (i.e., not garbage) at any given time during a computation, so it might be argued that the good performance observed for small caches is due to running small test programs. Final resolution of this question will have to wait until a diverse body of large programs is available for measurement. This is particularly important for the measurements involving supercombinator compilation.

Write-through policy
Table 4 shows the results on miss ratio and traffic ratio for a write-through versus copy-back memory update policy. The cache miss ratios are the same, as expected, since this policy does not affect whether misses occur. However, the bus traffic generated for the write-through method is significantly higher than for copy-back. This can cause severe problems with system performance, even on a uniprocessor.

With a write-through policy with a block size of 16 bytes (4 words), 14.3% of data cache accesses for the SKI implementation generate a bus transaction. This is manageable on most systems. Unfortunately, it is more common for processors to have narrower buses to memory, with most microprocessors supporting only a 4-byte bus. In this case, a memory bus access would be generated on average on 57.2% of data accesses, which

Table 4.
TIGRE performance with varying
memory update strategy.

Memory Update	MISS RATIO / TRAFFIC RATIO		
	SKI set	Turner set	Super.
copy-back	0.0341	0.0300	0.0528
	0.2721	0.2209	0.4223
write-through	0.0341	0.0300	0.0528
	0.5721	0.5431	0.6849

can swamp a bus, causing memory-bandwidth performance limitations. This bus overloading takes place because a microprocessor bus can only sustain a data transfer every 4 to 8 clock cycles, whereas a 57.2% bus-access rate demands bandwidth corresponding to a transfer for every 1.7 data memory accesses, which could correspond to 1.7 clock cycles. Clearly, a copy-back policy is desired to limit the effects of bus saturation.

The supercombinator implementation has even worse bus-write characteristics. This is caused by a higher percentage of bus-write operations, since supercombinator code does less graph traversing (and hence fewer reads) per combinator. This effect is exacerbated by the fact that supercombinator compilation reduces the redundancy of computations, resulting in fewer instances of repeated overwriting of nodes. This, in turn, limits the effectiveness of the copy-back strategy (which attenuates bus-write traffic only to the extent that nodes are written more than once while the node is resident in the cache memory). Thus, with supercombinators it is even more important to use a copy-back strategy, but even this strategy is likely to generate significant demands on bus bandwidth.

Associativity & Replacement Policy

Simulation results of varying the associativity of the cache from direct-mapped (1-way associative) to 8-way associative showed a variation in miss ratios of less than 0.2%. 2-way set associative seems to bring a slight performance improvement over direct-mapped, but beyond that there is no discernible advantage to adding cache sets.

Simulation results of varying the replacement policy for the cache similarly showed variations of less than 0.1% in miss ratios. Least Recently Used (LRU) replacement was found to be the best by a small margin. In the original simulation with both program and memory sharing a unified cache, LRU replacement was more important, since it prevented the program words from being flushed from the cache when using more than 1-way associativity.

Neither associativity nor replacement policy seem to matter much for combinator graph reduction.

The optimal cache strategy

Based on the analysis of the findings of these simulations, a cache design which minimizes complexity and cost while achieving reasonable performance would have the following characteristics: cache size of 16K bytes each for split instruction and data caches, 16-byte block size, direct-mapped, write-allocate, and copy-back. This cache configuration was simulated to have a 98.94% hit ratio overall for the SKI method (96.24% data hit ratio, and 99.99 + % instruction hit ratio), and a traffic ratio of 0.0827 words transferred on average per memory access.

Unfortunately, even though data prefetching or sub-block filling could efficiently support a block size of 16

bytes, most microprocessors in workstations support block sizes of 4 bytes. The same cache configuration with a 4-byte block size was simulated to have a 96.80% hit ratio overall (92.13% data hit ratio, and a 99.99 + % instruction hit ratio) with bus traffic of 0.0599 words transferred on average per memory access. This difference of 2.14% in cache hit ratio between 16-byte and 4-byte block sizes represents approximately a 44000 RAPS (nearly 10%) speed penalty for a DECstation 3100 class machine.

Comparison with actual measurements

Cache simulation results are an important architectural design tool. However, there is always the question of whether the results of such simulations correspond to the "real world". In order to establish some confidence in the simulation results, a comparison was made between the results of a simulation of the DECstation 3100 and the results of actual program execution. The DECstation 3100 has a split cache with 64K bytes in each cache, a block size of 4 bytes, direct-mapped organization, and uses write-through memory updating with write-allocate cache management. [3]

Simulation indicates that for skifib, the R2000 processor executes 27.82 instructions per combinator reduction application (on average). The R2000 also performs 33.95 memory reads (including both instruction reads and data reads) per combinator reduction application, which when multiplied by a simulated miss ratio of 0.0097, gives 0.33 cache read misses per combinator reduction. The DECstation 3100 has a cache read miss latency of 5 clock cycles, resulting in a cost of 1.65 clock cycles per combinator because of cache misses. This, when added to the 27.82 cycle instruction execution cost (27.82 instructions at one instruction per clock cycle), yields an execution time of 29.47 clock cycles per combinator.

The DECstation 3100 has a cost of zero clock cycles for a cache write miss, so long as the write buffer does not overflow. With an average of 4.74 writes (at 6 clock cycles per write) plus 0.33 cache miss reads (at 5 clock cycles per read) per combinator, a total of at least 30.09 clock cycles is needed per combinator to provide adequate memory bandwidth for the write-through strategy. This is somewhat longer than the 29.47 clock cycle instruction execution speed, leading to the conclusion that the DECstation 3100 implementation of TIGRE is constrained by memory bandwidth.

As a result of this analysis, we calculate the simulated execution speed of the DECstation 3100 to be 30.09 clock cycles per combinator. At 16.67 MHz, this translates into a speed of 554000 RAPS between garbage collections.

When actually executing the skifib benchmark, the DECstation 3100 performed approximately 475000 reduction applications per second (RAPS) including garbage collection time. Garbage collection overhead was measured at approximately 1%. This rather low cost is attributed to the fact that a small number of nodes are actually in use at any given time, so a copying garbage collector must typically copy just a few hundred nodes for each collection cycle on the benchmark used. Virtual memory overhead can be computed based on a 0.0091 miss ratio for a block size of 4K bytes, with 6.67 data access per combinator, giving a computed virtual memory miss ratio of 0.00136 per combinator. Assuming 13 clock cycles overhead per TLB miss (based on an 800 ns TLB miss overhead for a MIPS R2000 with a 16 MHz clock as reported by Siewiorek & Koopman [16]), and noting that an average combinator takes 30.09 clocks, this gives a penalty of:

$$0.00136 * 13 / 30.09 \text{ (clocks per combinator)}$$
$$= 0.06\%$$

Together with the 1% garbage collection overhead, this 1.06% overhead predicts a raw reduction rate of:

$$475000 * 1.0106 = 480000 \text{ RAPS}$$

This rate is 15% slower than the 554000 RAPS predicted raw reduction rate. Some of this 15% discrepancy is due to the overhead of cache cold starts on a multiprogrammed operating system. The rest of the discrepancy is probably caused by bursts of traffic to the write buffer, which stalls the processor when full.

The potential of special-purpose hardware

DECstation 3100 as a baseline

We have described various implementation methods and performance data for TIGRE. This section uses those data points to propose architecture and implementation features which could be used to speed up the execution of TIGRE. The reason for examining such features is to determine the feasibility of constructing special-purpose hardware, or, if construction of special-purpose hardware is not attractive, the features that should be selected when choosing standard hardware to execute TIGRE.

Since the best measured performance for TIGRE was for the MIPS R2000 assembly language implementation, the approach used for examining processor features to support TIGRE will be made in terms of incremental modifications to the MIPS R2000 processor. This approach will give a rough estimate for the potential performance improvement, while maintaining some basis in reality. For the purposes of the following performance analysis, the characteristics of the SKI implementation of the fib benchmark executing on the DECstation 3100 shall be used.

Since TIGRE has been shown to have some unusual cache access behavior, the first area for improvement that will be considered is changing the arrangement of cache

memory. Then, improvements in the architecture of the R2000 will be considered.

Improvements in cache management

Copy-back cache

The most obvious limitation of the DECstation 3100 cache is that it uses a write-through cache. This caused the limiting performance factor to be bus bandwidth for memory write accesses, instead of instruction read or data read miss ratios. A simple improvement, then, is to employ a copy-back cache. A cache simulation of fib for the DECstation 3100 shows that this reduces the data cache traffic ratio from 0.5461 to 0.2078, removing the bus bandwidth as the limiting factor to performance. This reduces the execution time of an average combinator from 30.09 clock cycles (the bus bandwidth-limited performance) to 29.47 clock cycles (the cache hit ratio-limited performance).

Increased block size

A second parameter of the cache that could be improved is the block size. TIGRE executes well with a large block size, so increasing the cache-block size from 4 bytes to, say, 256 bytes, should dramatically decrease the cache miss ratio, but would suffer from the limited width of the memory bus. Using a wide bus-write buffer with a 4 byte cache-block size can capture many of the benefits of a large block size, and reduce bus traffic. A write buffer width of 8 bytes (one full graph node) can be utilized efficiently by a supercombinator compiler to get a very high percentage of paired 4-byte writes to the left-and right-hand sides of cells when updating the graph.

However, even if a very sophisticated cache mechanism were used to reduce cache misses to the absolute minimum possible (ideally, 0.0000 miss ratio), the speedup possibilities are somewhat small. This is because only 1.65 clock cycles of the 29.47 clock cycles per combinator are spent on cache misses to begin with.

Improvements in CPU architecture

The opportunities for improvement by changing the architecture of the R2000 are somewhat more promising than those possible by modifying the cache management strategy. In particular, it is possible to significantly increase the speed of stack unwinding and performing indirections through the stack elements.

Stack unwinding support

The one serious drawback of the R2000 architecture for executing TIGRE is the lack of a subroutine call instruction. The current TIGRE implementation on the R2000 uses a five-instruction interpretive loop for performing threading (i.e. stack unwinding). Since 1.37 stack unwind operations are performed per combinator, this represents

6.85 instructions which, assuming no cache misses, execute in 6.85 clock cycles.

But, there is a further penalty for performing the threading operation through graphs with the R2000. A seven-instruction overhead is used for each combinator to perform a preliminary test for threading, and to access a jump table to jump to the combinator code when threading is completed. (One of these instructions increments a counter used for performance measurement. It can be removed for production code, as long as measuring the number of combinators executed is not important.) This imposes an additional 7.00 clock cycle penalty on each combinator.

So, the total time spent on threading is 13.85 clock cycles per combinator. It takes three clock cycles to simulate a subroutine call on the R2000:

```
# store current return address
    sw      $31, 0($sp)
# subroutine call
    jal     subr_address
# branch delay slot instruction follows
# decrement stack pointer
    addu    $sp, $sp, -4
```

so it is reasonable to assume that a hardware-implemented subroutine call instruction could be made to operate in three clock cycles. Thus, if the instruction cache were made to track writes to memory (permitting the use of self-modifying code), a savings of 10.85 clock cycles is possible. One important change to the instruction set would be necessary to allow the use of subroutine call instructions — the subroutine call instruction would have to be defined to have all zero bits in the opcode field (so that the instruction could be used as a pointer to memory as well). An alternate way to implement a subroutine call with a modifiable address field is to define an indirect subroutine call that reads its target address through the data cache, eliminating the need to keep the instruction cache in synch with bus writes.

Stack access support
An important aspect of TIGRE's operation is that it makes frequent reference to the top elements on the spine stack. In fact, 4.61 accesses to the spine stack are performed per average combinator. Most of the load and store instructions that perform these stack accesses can be eliminated by the use of on-CPU stack buffers that are pushed and popped as a side effect of other instructions.

For spine-stack unwinding, two of the three instructions used to perform a subroutine call could be eliminated with the use of hardware stack support, leaving just a single jal instruction to perform the threading operation at each node. Of course, the R2000 has a built-in branch delay slot, so it probably not the case that the actual time for the threading operation could be reduced to less than two clock cycles. But, the second clock cycle could be used to allow writing a potential stack buffer overflow element to memory.

Of the 4.61 instructions that access the spine stack, the threading technique just described may be used to eliminate the effect of 1.37 of the instructions per combinator. The remaining 3.24 instructions can also be eliminated by introducing an indirect-through-spine-stack addressing mode to the R2000. All that would be required is to access the top, second, and third element of a spine-stack buffer as the source of an address instead of a register. A simple implementation method could map the top of stack buffer registers into the 32 registers already available on the R2000. This gives a potential savings of 3.24 clock cycles, since explicit load instructions from the spine stack need not be executed when performing indirection operations.

Double word stores
TIGRE is usually able to write cells in pairs, with both the left-and right-hand cells of a single node written at approximately the same point in the code for a particular combinator. Thus, it becomes attractive to define a "double store" instruction format. Such an instruction would take two source register operands (for example, an even/odd register pair), and store them into a 64-bit memory doubleword. If the processor were designed with a 64-bit memory bus, such a "double store" could take place in a single clock cycle instead of as a two-clock sequence. The savings of using 64-bit stores is 0.895 clock cycles per combinator for the SKI implementations of fib, and 1.192 clock cycles per combinator for the Turner set implementation of fib (measured by instrumenting TIGRE code to count the opportunities for these stores as the benchmark program is executed). Support of 64-bit memory stores would speed up supercombinator definitions even more, since the body of supercombinators often contains long sequences of node creations. For example,

Table 5.
Summary of possible performance improvements.

cumulative optimizations	clocks per combinator
current implementation	30.09
copy-back cache	29.47
100% cache hit ratio	27.82
subroutine call + self-modifying code	16.97
hardware stack for jal	15.60
hardware stack indirect addressing	12.36
8-byte store instructions	11.47

the supercombinator implementation of `fib` can make use of 1.33 64-bit stores per combinator.

Table 5 summarizes the efficiency improvements that may be gained through the cache and processor architecture changes just discussed. Nearly a three-fold speed improvement is possible over the R2000 processor with just a few architectural changes.

Further work

We recognize the fact that our benchmarks are not very realistic. Larger benchmarks are required, as well as more benchmarks based on supercombinators rather than the simple SK-combinators. Unfortunately, we have been hindered by the unavailability of good benchmark suites. We are working to develop a good range of benchmark programs.

Results

We have found that an efficient cache for combinator graph reduction has several unusual characteristics, including: a very strong dependence on the write-allocate strategy, very modest cache size requirements, and the ability to effectively use very large block sizes.

The results of this research should help users of combinator graph reduction select commercial machines which will perform efficiently. They may also influence the course of design of special-purpose graph reduction hardware in the future.

References

[1] Koopman, P. (1989) *An Architecture for Combinator Graph Reduction*, Ph.D. Dissertation, Carnegie Mellon University.

[2] Koopman, P. & Lee, P. (1989) A Fresh Look at Combinator Graph Reduction. In *Proceedings of SIGPLAN '89 Conference on Programming Language Design and Implementation, Portland OR, June 21-23, SIGPLAN Notices*, 24(7), July 1989, 110-119.

[3] Digital Equipment Corporation (1989) *DECstation 3100 Technical Overview (EZ-J4052-28)*, Digital Equipment Corporation, Maynard MA.

[4] Kane, G. (1987) *MIPS R2000 RISC Architecture*, Prentice Hall, Englewood Cliffs, NJ.

[5] Turner, D. A. (1979) A new implementation technique for applicative languages. *Software - Practice and Experience*, 9(1):31-49, January.

[6] Turner, D. A. (1979) Another algorithm for bracket abstraction. *Journal of Symbolic Logic*, 44(2):67-270.

[7] Burley, R. (1987) An overview of the four systems in the VAX 8800 family. *Digital Technical Journal*, 4:10-19, February.

[8] Pittsburgh Supercomputer Center (1989) *Facilities and Services Guide*, Pittsburgh PA.

[9] Augusteijn, A. & van der Hoeven, G. (1984) Combinatorgraphs as self-reducing programs. University of Twente, the Netherlands.

[10] Peyton Jones, S. L. (1987) *The Implementation of Functional Programming Languages*, Prentice-Hall, London.

[11] Fairbairn, J. & Wray, S. (1987) TIM: A simple, lazy abstract machine to execute supercombinators. In Kahn, G. (ed.), *Proceedings of the Conference on Functional Programming and Computer Architecture, Portland*, pages 34-45, Springer Verlag, 1987.

[12] Hill, M. D. (1984) Experimental evaluation of on-chip microprocessor cache memories, *Proc. Eleventh Int. Symp. on Computer Architecture*, Ann Arbor, June.

[13] Kabakibo, A., Milutinovic, V., Silbey, A. & Furht, B. (1987) A survey of cache memory in modern microcomputer and minicomputer systems. In: Gajski, D., Milutinovic, V., Siegel, H. & Furht, B. (eds.) *Tutorial: Computer Architecture*, IEEE Computer Society Press, pp. 210-227.

[14] Smith, A. J. (1982) Cache memories, *ACM Computing Surveys*, 14(3):473-530, September.

[15] Appel, A., Ellis, J. & Li, K. (1988) Fast garbage collection on stock multiprocessors. In *Proceedings of the Conference on Programming Language Design and Implementation, Atlanta*, June.

[16] Siewiorek, D. & Koopman, P. (1989) *A Case Study of a Parallel, Vector Workstation: the Titan Architecture*, Academic Press, Boston. In Press.

A Self-applicable Partial Evaluator for the Lambda Calculus

(extended abstract)

Neil D. Jones, Carsten K. Gomard, Anders Bondorf, Olivier Danvy, Torben Æ. Mogensen

DIKU – Computer Science Department, University of Copenhagen

Universitetsparken 1, 2100 Copenhagen Ø, Denmark

e-mail: neil@diku.dk, gomard@diku.dk, anders@diku.dk, danvy@diku.dk, torbenm@diku.dk

Abstract

We describe theoretical and a few practical aspects of an implemented self-applicable partial evaluator for the call by value untyped lambda calculus with constants, conditionals, and a fixed point operator.

This paper's main points are first: to announce the existence of and to describe a partial evaluator that is both higher-order and self-applicable; second: to describe a surprisingly simple solution to the central problem of binding time analysis; and third: to state that the partial evaluator has been proven correct when it terminates.

While λ-mix (the name of our system) seems to have been the first higher-order self-applicable partial evaluator to run on the computer, it was developed mainly for academic reasons. Two recently developed systems are much more powerful for practical use but also much more complex: Similix (Bondorf and Danvy) and Schism (Consel).

Our partial evaluator is surprisingly simple, completely automatic, and is implemented in a side-effect free subset of Scheme. It has been used to compile, to generate compilers, and to generate a compiler generator.

1 Introduction

1.1 Overview

This paper describes a self-applicable partial evaluator (to our knowledge the first) for the call-by-value untyped lambda calculus with constants, conditionals, and a fixed point operator. Abstractly it may be viewed as an optimizing Curry combinator or, in other words: a nontrivial implementation of Kleene's S_n^m theorem. Practically viewed it takes a program in the form of a lambda expression and some but not all of its arguments and it yields a *specialized* or *residual* program which, if applied to the values of the remaining arguments, evaluates to the same result that the original program would have evaluated to when applied to all its arguments.

The purpose of partial evaluation is to produce a residual program from a source program and some of its data.

Our partial evaluator produces a residual λ-expression given a source λ-expression and the values of some of its arguments. When given the rest of the values, the residual program yields the same result as the source program would when applied to all its arguments.

The partial evaluator is surprisingly simple and is implemented in a side effect free subset of Scheme. Since it is self-applicable it can be used both to compile and to generate a compiler when given a programming language definition written in the lambda calculus, as for example, a denotational semantics. Both target programs and the generated compiler are in the form of lambda expressions. A simple example is given of the partial evaluator's application to semantics-directed compiler generation; some engineering work would need to be done, however, to apply it to really large language definitions.

As an example of compilation by partial evaluation: given the denotational semantics for *Tiny*-programs (in section 4) and the *Tiny*-version of the factorial program (figure 1), our system produces automatically the target program of figure 2 where @ denotes function application. Note that since the residual program is *single-threaded* in the store variables [Schmidt 85] these can all be replaced by a single global variable. With the store arguments removed and the access to the store sequentialized, the residual program looks like assembly code. Figure 2 displays a target program obtained by partially evaluating the Tiny interpreter with respect to the Tiny Factorial program of figure 1; the corresponding generated compiler is given in section 4.1.

```
variables:  result x;
result := 1;
x    := 6;
while x
        { result := result * x;
          x    := x - 1 }
```

Figure 1: Source *Tiny* Factorial program

Earlier semantics-directed compiler generators

```
(@ (fix (lam fac
            (lam store-1
                (if (@ (@ =? 0) (@ (@ access 1) store-1))
                    store-1
                    (@ fac (@ (lam store-3
                                 (@ (@ (@ update 1)
                                       (@ (@ - (@ (@ access 1) store-3)) 1))
                                     store-3))
                             (@ (lam store-2
                                   (@ (@ (@ update 0)
                                         (@ (@ * (@ (@ access 0) store-2))
                                            (@ (@ access 1) store-2)))
                                       store-2))
                                store-1)))))))
    (@ (@ (@ update 1) 6) (@ (@ (@ update 0) 1) i-store)))
```

Figure 2: Factorial Residual Program – the *Tiny* interpreter has been specialized with respect to Factorial

[Mosses 79, Paulson 82, Appel 85, Weis 87] involved numerous program components and intermediate languages. These are obviated in a self-applicable partial evaluator since self-application allows us to generate compilers from language definitions automatically and even to generate a compiler generator. Target programs, compilers and the compiler generator are efficient and have natural structures. In contrast with much other work in the field, our partial evaluator is completely automatic.

What is new in this paper This article has three points. First: to report that the open problem of specializing higher-order programs is solved; second: to describe a surprisingly simple solution to the central problem of binding time analysis using types and third: to state that the partial evaluator has been proven correct when it terminates.

There have been three breakthroughs in Spring '89, with significantly distinct methods. This paper describes the simplest and easiest to understand of the three systems, a self-applicable partial evaluator for the lambda calculus. The two other systems treat Scheme programs, and extend existing self-applicable partial evaluators. One is based on collecting closures at their site of application [Bondorf 90], and the other represents closures as partially static structures [Consel 89].

Primary goals of this article Our first main goal is the complete removal of the computational overhead of implementating denotational semantics directly. (Denotational semantics defines the meanings of programs in a programming language by translating them into the lambda calculus. Our point is to produce target programs that contain only those lambda calculus operations needed to execute the source program and to handle control flow.) Our second main goal is to have a *self-applicable* partial

evaluator. This makes it possible not only to compile from an interpretive language specification, but also to generate stand-alone compilers from language definitions and even a stand-alone compiler generator.

What is not done in this article Our system does not yield production quality compilers, or target code near machine level. As in SIS [Mosses 79], the target code consists of lambda expressions (these could, however, be translated further into machine code as in [Paulson 82, PeytonJones 87]). Also, we have not yet tried to implement a large programming language from a formal definition.

Binding Time Analysis and Program Annotation As in all previous self-applicable partial evaluators, an essential component is the use of a *binding time analysis* of the program to be specialized. Its effect is to *annotate* the program by marking as "eliminable" those parts which may be computed during partial evaluation and by marking the remaining parts as "residual". Partial evaluation then proceeds by nonstandard execution. The nonresidual part of the program is interpreted as usual (by beta-reducing applications, unfolding fixed point operators, *etc.*), whereas the corresponding residual applications, abstractions, *etc.* are regarded as base functions whose effect is to generate code (lambda expressions) to appear in the residual program.

The source code of a non-residual application has the form operator @ operand, and is to be performed. The source code specifying a residual application of form operator @-r operand, where @-r is regarded as a base function with type *Code × Code → Code*. During partial evaluation, once the code operator has been generated for the operator and the code operand for the operand, @-r assembles them together to build the residual application operator @ operand.

The program must be *well-annotated* for this scheme to succeed, otherwise type errors can occur during partial evaluation, *i.e.*, at "compile time". In section 3 we set up a simple type system to define well-annotatedness. To paraphrase Milner, well-annotated programs cannot cause the partial evaluator to go wrong. The effect of the type system is to clarify the boundary between compile-time and run-time types in partial evaluation, and the role and nature of binding time analysis is to determine this boundary before partial evaluation begins.

Only Static Computations Must be Well-typed
Using the partial evaluator to compile from an interpreter requires the interpreter's static computations to be well-typed, but its dynamic computations need not be. This makes it possible to partially evaluate interpreters for both strongly typed and untyped languages, and still to guarantee absence of type errors during compilation without need for "type tags". Since the target program is a lambda expression, run-time type security for strongly typed languages can be obtained by type checking as usual.

Our two-level lambda calculus differs in several important respects from that of [Nielson 88c]. First, we use the second level (our "residual", their "run-time") is used for code generation, not execution. Second, we do not require programs to be strongly typed and so definitions of untyped languages can easily be handled. Third, our version has naturally led to building a self-applicable partial evaluator.

The task of binding time analysis (abbreviated BTA) is this: given program p and information as to which arguments will be available during partial evaluation, we must annotate enough parts of p as residual so the result is well-annotated. Binding time analysis is thus a sort of type inference, in which type conflicts are resolved not by reporting type errors but by *changing the conflicting parts*, by relabelling them as residual, *i.e.* to be evaluated at run time.

For efficiency as few parts of p as possible should be marked as residual, consistent with well-typedness of its annotated version. The annotations also have other uses which are important but not discussed in this paper: to avoid generating infinitely large residual programs or duplicating code, *i.e.*, generating multiple copies of the same target operations.

1.2 Lambda Calculus

A very simple language, the classical lambda calculus, is used here in order to achieve simplicity and allow a more complete description than would be possible for a larger and more practical language. One intention is to give useful background for reports on the more advanced, complex and practically oriented higher order partial evaluators recently developed by Bondorf, Danvy, and Consel.

A lambda calculus program is an *expression* together

with an initial *environment*. The program takes its input through its free variables whose values are supplied by the environment. The environment is also expected to map base function names, such as cons, to the corresponding functions. The expression abstract syntax is

$$\text{exp} \quad ::= \quad \text{var} \mid \text{exp @ exp} \mid \lambda\, \text{var.exp} \mid$$
$$\text{if exp exp exp} \mid \text{fix exp} \mid \text{const constant}$$

Since we use lambda calculus both as a programming language and as a meta-language, we need to distinguish notationally lambdas that appear in source programs from lambdas that denote functions. Syntactic lambda expressions are written in sans serif style: exp @ exp, λ var.exp, fix exp ..., and the meta-language is in *slanted* style: *exp @ exp*, λ *var.exp*, *fix exp* .... When a lambda expression is presented as generated by machine, it is written in `type-writer` style: `(@ exp exp)`, `(lam var exp)` etc.

For an example, consider the power function computing x to the nth where x and n are free (input) variables. (In the concrete syntax we omit some of the explicit application nodes, *e.g.*, for testing whether n' equals zero.)

(fix λ p.λ n'.λ x'.if (= n' 0) 1   (* x' (p @ (− n' 1) @ x')))
@ n @ x

1.3 Partial Evaluation and the Futamura Projections

Following earlier papers on partial evaluation (*e.g.*, [Jones 89]), we take **L** *power* [*2*, *3*] to denote the result of running the **L**-program *power* on its two input data, *2* and *3*. The idea is to consider a language as mapping a program text into the function it computes, which has proven valuable in this framework where programs are data objects. Here **L** is the lambda calculus. It thus holds that **L** *power* [*2*, *3*] = 9. Given an **L**-program *p* a *residual* program for *p* with respect to partial data *d1* is a program p_{d1} such that

$$\textbf{L}\, p\, [d1,\, d2] = \textbf{L}\, p_{d1}\, d2$$

Suppose *p* is the power program shown above and *d1* is n = 2, then a residual program p_2 is

$$(* \text{x} (* \text{x} 1))$$

with free variable x. The knowledge that n = 2 is incorporated in the residual program.

A *partial evaluator* is a program *mix* which has the property that when given *p* and the partial data *d1* produces the residual program p_{d1}. This is captured by the *mix equation*:

$$\textbf{L}\, p\, [d1,\, d2] = \textbf{L}\, (\textbf{L}\, mix\, [p,\, d1])\, d2$$

Let **S** and **T** be programming languages, perhaps (but not necessarily) different from **L**. An **S**-interpreter *int* written in **L** is a program that fulfills **S** *pgm data* = **L**

int [*pgm, data*] and an S-to-T-compiler *comp* written in
L is a program that fulfills **S** *pgm data* = **T** (**L** *comp pgm*)
data.

The *Futamura projections* [Futamura 71, Ershov 78]
state that given a partial evaluator *mix* and an interpreter
int it is possible to compile programs, and even to generate stand-alone compilers and compiler generators by
self-applying *mix*. The three Futamura projections are:

$$
\begin{array}{rcl}
\mathbf{L}\ mix\ [int, pgm] &=& target \\
\mathbf{L}\ mix\ [mix, int] &=& compiler \\
\mathbf{L}\ mix\ [mix, mix] &=& compiler\ generator \\
&& \text{or shorter: } cogen
\end{array}
$$

The equations are easily verified using the definitions of
interpreters, compilers and the mix equation. These proofs
and a more detailed discussion can be found in [Jones 89].
Their first non-trivial computer realization was reported in
[Jones 85], where **L** was a first order language of recursive
equations. The system we are describing here realizes all
three Futamura projections with unlimited use of higher
order functions.

1.4 Related Work

The present work overlaps with two areas: *partial evaluation* which has emphasized automatic program optimization and transformation; and *semantics-directed compiler
generation* whose main goal has been to take as input a
denotational semantics definition of a programming language, and to obtain automatically a compiler that is both
correct and efficiently implements the defined language.

1.4.1 Partial Evaluation

Early work in partial evaluation viewed partial evaluation
as an optimizing phase in a compiler (constant folding),
as a device for incremental computations [Lombardi 67],
or as a method to transform imperative Lisp programs
[Beckman 76]. The latter system was able to handle FU-
NARGs, but it was not self-applicable (although the Red-
compile program amounts to a hand-written version of
cogen). Later work aimed to partially evaluate higher-
order and imperative Scheme programs [Schooler 84,
Guzowski 88], but still it was not in a self-applicable way.

The potential of self-application was realized independently in Japan and The Soviet Union [Futamura 71,
Turchin 80, Ershov 78] in the early 1970's and experiments
were made without conclusive results. The first actual
self-application was realized in 1984 [Jones 85, Jones 89]
for first order recursive equations. Since then several other self-applicable systems have been developed
([Bondorf 89a] for programs in the form of term rewriting systems, [Gomard 89] for a simple imperative language, [Fuller 88] for Prolog, [Romanenko 88] for a subset of Turchin's Refal language, [?] and [Bondorf 89b] for
stronger systems handling first order Scheme programs).

These systems are reasonably efficient for first order languages, the generated compilers were typically between 3

and 10 faster than compiling by partial evaluation of an
interpreter. In all cases a binding time analysis was seen
to be essential for efficient self-application (the reasons for
this are detailed in [Bondorf 88]). To our knowledge no
nontrivial and fully automatic self-applicable higher order
solutions have been developed prior to the one presented
here.

Although it can give dramatic speedups and has much
promise, partial evaluation is no panacea. A characteristic so far is that obtaining good results requires careful attention to programming style (a workman must know the
strengths and limitations of his tools, even when they are
very powerful); an alternative is to use or source to source,
binding-time oriented program transformations (staging)
to change program style in deeper ways [Jørring 86].

1.4.2 Semantics-directed compiler generation

The pathbreaking work in this field was SIS: the Semantics Implementation System of [Mosses 79]. SIS implements a pure version of the untyped lambda calculus using the call by need reduction strategy. Compiling from
a denotational semantics is done by translating the definition into a lambda expression, applying the result to
the source program, and simplifying the result by reducing wherever possible. This is clearly a form of partial
evaluation. SIS has a powerful notation for writing definitions, but it is unfortunately extremely slow, and is prone
to infinite loops when using, for example, recursively defined environments. In our opinion this is due to the fact
that the reduction strategy is "on-line", and the problem
could be eliminated by annotations such as we have used.
(Choosing the annotations so as to avoid nontermination
is admittedly a challenging problem, but we feel it is one
that should be solved *before* doing partial evaluation rather
than during it.)

Systems based on the pure (typed) lambda calculus include [Paulson 82, Weis 87, Nielson 88b]. The first uses
partial evaluation at compile time. It is considerably faster
at compile time than SIS, but still very slow at run time.
Weis's system [Weis 87] is probably the fastest in this category that has been used on large language definitions. In
the Nielsons's work the greatest emphasis is put on correctness, rather than efficiency.

Systems by Pleban and Appel [Pleban 84, Appel 85]
achieve greater run-time efficiency at the expense of less
pure semantic languages – one for each language definition
in the former case, and the lambda calculus with dedicated
treatment of environments and stores in the latter. Finally
Wand's system and methodology [Wand 84, Wand 82] require so much cleverness from the user that it is not clear
how it may be automatized.

To our knowledge none of these systems is so powerful
that one could consider using the system to construct its
own components; and all are quite complex, with many
stages of processing and intermediate languages. In contrast, the partial evaluator to be presented here involves

only one language (with annotations), and all components are derived from a single program: mix. Regarding automation, partial evaluation of an interpreter gives the compiling algorithm of [Wand 82] for free.

2 Partial Evaluation Using a 2-level Lambda Calculus

The result of applying the BTA (binding time analysis) to an expression is an *annotated* expression where the parts that are *not* to be evaluated at partial evaluation time are marked. We achieve this with a 2-level lambda calculus, similar in syntax but different in semantics from [Nielson 88a]. In the second phase we blindly obey the annotations: we reduce all redexes not marked as residual and generate residual target code (also a lambda expression) for the marked operations. The focus of this section is the syntax and semantics of our 2-level lambda calculus.

The 2-level lambda calculus contains two versions of each operator in the ordinary lambda calculus: for each of the "normal" operators: λ, @, ... there is also a residual version: λ-r, @-r, ...in the 2-level calculus. The abstract syntax of 2-level expressions is thus

$$2exp \quad ::= \quad 2exp \text{ @ } 2exp \mid \lambda \text{ var}.2exp \mid \text{if } 2exp \text{ } 2exp \text{ } 2exp \mid$$
$$\text{fix } 2exp \mid \text{const } constant \mid$$
$$2exp \text{ @-r } 2exp \mid$$
$$\lambda\text{-r } var.2exp \mid \text{if-r } 2exp \text{ } 2exp \text{ } 2exp \mid$$
$$\text{fix-r } 2exp \mid \text{const-r } constant \mid \text{var} \mid \text{lift } 2exp$$

Intuitively, for all operators λ, @, ... the denotations given by the semantic function $2\mathcal{E}$ in figure 3 are the same as they would be for 1-level semantic function, and the operators: λ-r, @-r, ... are suspended yielding as result a piece of *code* for execution at run-time. The lift operator builds a constant expression with the same value as lift's argument. lift is used when a residual expression has a subexpression with a constant value.

The valuation functions for 2-level lambda calculus programs are given in figure 3. We expect the result of partially evaluating a program to be a new program, so function $2\mathcal{P}$ checks that its result is in the *Code* summand which is equal to the syntactic category of 1-level expressions. The rules contain explicit type checks; section 3 will discuss suffcient criteria for omitting these.

If f is a value from *2Funval* we take $f{\uparrow}\textit{2Funval}$ to be the value f injected into summand *2Funval*. Informally: $f{\uparrow}\textit{2Funval}$ puts a type tag on f. If *val* is a value from *Val*, $val{\downarrow}\textit{2Funval}$ removes the type tag, provided *val* is from the *2Funval* summand. If not, $val{\downarrow}\textit{2Funval}$ produces an error (It is assumed that *Val* has an error element and that applications *etc.*, are strict in errors; details are omitted for notational simplicity.)

The function *build-@* has type $Code \times Code \to Code$ and is purely syntactic: it builds a residual 1-level expression which is the application of its two arguments. The other *build*-functions have analogous meanings.

3 Program Annotation

An *annotated* lambda expression exp[ann] is a 2-level expression obtained by replacing some occurrences of @, λ, ... in exp by the corresponding marked operator: @-r, λ-r, ... Clearly the annotations have to be placed consistently so that a summand error is not produced in the rules in figure 3. We say that an expression exp[ann] is *well-annotated* for initial environment ρ if $2\mathcal{E}[\![\text{exp}^{\text{ann}}]\!] \rho$ does not produce a summand error. Hence, if exp[ann] is well-annotated the type checks are superfluous and can be omitted from the partial evaluation algorithm. Our algorithm proceeds like this:

1. Given an expression exp apply BTA yielding a well-annotated exp[ann].

2. Apply the mix program to exp[ann]. The mix program is the $2\mathcal{E}$-rules written as a lambda expression *without* the type checks.

To develop a sufficient criterion for well-annotatedness, we introduce a type system for 2-level expressions. The abstract syntax for a 2-level type T is

$$type \quad ::= \quad const \mid type \to type \mid code$$

We take the assertion form $\tau \vdash 2exp: type$ to mean that when given type assumptions τ on the free variables of 2exp the 2-level expression 2exp is well-annotated and of type *type*. ρ and τ are related by: $\tau \vdash var: const$ iff $\rho(var)$ is in *Const* (and similarly for *code*). The type rules of figure 4 express the type checking part of the 2-level semantics. It is easy to verify that if for some type t, $\tau \vdash 2exp: t$ then $2\mathcal{E}[\![2exp]\!] \rho$ is in the corresponding summand T, and no type error is produced.

The task of BTA Given a type assumption τ for the free variables of exp, the task of BTA is to annotate it such that $\tau \vdash 2exp: code$. This is done by marking some parts as residual and inserting lift-operators where necessary. (The lift-operator converts an expression of type *const* into an expression of type *code*, so that the expression appears in the residual program.) This is in fact always possible by making *all* operators residual and inserting lift-operators around all free variables of type *const*. Such an annotation is of course not desirable since partial evaluation would just return the original exp with no computation done at all.

$2\mathcal{E}$ can "go wrong" in other ways than by committing type errors. If $2\mathcal{E}$ reduces too many redexes reduction might proceed infinitely, or residual code might be duplicated. To avoid this, some redexes should be left in the the residual program, and it is the job of the BTA to decide which. A BTA algorithm would proceed like this

Semantic Domains

$$
\begin{aligned}
2Val &= Const + 2Funval + Code \\
2Funval &= 2Val \rightarrow 2Val \\
Code &= Expression \\
2Env &= Var \rightarrow 2Val
\end{aligned}
$$

$2\mathcal{P}:\ 2Expression \rightarrow 2Env \rightarrow 2Val$
$2\mathcal{P}[\![exp]\!]\ \rho \qquad\qquad = \quad 2\mathcal{E}[\![exp]\!]\ \rho{\downarrow}Code$

$2\mathcal{E}:\ 2Expression \rightarrow 2Env \rightarrow 2Val$
$2\mathcal{E}[\![var]\!]\ \rho \qquad\qquad = \quad \rho(var)$

$$
\begin{aligned}
2\mathcal{E}[\![\lambda\,var.exp]\!]\ \rho &= \lambda\,value.(2\mathcal{E}[\![exp]\!]\ \rho[var \mapsto value]){\uparrow}2Funval \\
2\mathcal{E}[\![exp_1\ @\ exp_2]\!]\ \rho &= 2\mathcal{E}[\![exp_1]\!]\ \rho{\downarrow}2Funval\ (2\mathcal{E}[\![exp_2]\!]\ \rho) \\
2\mathcal{E}[\![fix\ exp]\!]\ \rho &= fix\ 2\mathcal{E}[\![exp]\!]\ \rho \\
2\mathcal{E}[\![if\ exp_1\ exp_2\ exp_3]\!]\ \rho &= 2\mathcal{E}[\![exp_1]\!]\ \rho{\downarrow}Const \rightarrow 2\mathcal{E}[\![exp_2]\!]\ \rho,\ 2\mathcal{E}[\![exp_3]\!]\ \rho \\
2\mathcal{E}[\![const\ c]\!]\ \rho &= c{\uparrow}Const \\
2\mathcal{E}[\![lift\ exp]\!]\ \rho &= build\text{-}const(2\mathcal{E}[\![exp]\!]\ \rho{\downarrow}Const){\uparrow}Code
\end{aligned}
$$

$$
\begin{aligned}
2\mathcal{E}[\![\lambda\text{-}r\,var.exp]\!]\ \rho &= let\ nvar = newname(var) \\
&\quad\ \ in\ \ build\text{-}\lambda(nvar, 2\mathcal{E}[\![exp]\!]\ \rho[var \mapsto nvar]{\downarrow}Code){\uparrow}Code \\
2\mathcal{E}[\![exp_1\ @\text{-}r\ exp_2]\!]\ \rho &= build\text{-}@(2\mathcal{E}[\![exp_1]\!]\ \rho{\downarrow}Code,\ 2\mathcal{E}[\![exp_2]\!]\ \rho{\downarrow}Code){\uparrow}Code \\
2\mathcal{E}[\![fix\text{-}r\ exp]\!]\ \rho &= build\text{-}fix(2\mathcal{E}[\![exp]\!]\ \rho{\downarrow}Code){\uparrow}Code \\
2\mathcal{E}[\![if\text{-}r\ exp_1\ exp_2\ exp_3]\!]\ \rho &= build\text{-}if(2\mathcal{E}[\![exp_1]\!]\ \rho{\downarrow}Code, \\
&\qquad\qquad\ \ 2\mathcal{E}[\![exp_2]\!]\ \rho{\downarrow}Code, \\
&\qquad\qquad\ \ 2\mathcal{E}[\![exp_3]\!]\ \rho{\downarrow}Code){\uparrow}Code \\
2\mathcal{E}[\![const\text{-}r\ c]\!]\ \rho &= build\text{-}const(c){\uparrow}Code
\end{aligned}
$$

Figure 3: 2-level Lambda Calculus Semantics

1. Given exp with initial type assumptions τ, annotate exp yielding exp^{ann} such that $\tau \vdash$ exp^{ann}: $code$.

2. Apply finiteness and code duplication analysis. If this step adds any annotations, go back to step 1.

4 Compilation and Compiler Generation

In this section we give an interpreter for an imperative language, *Tiny* with while-loops and assignments. We give a denotational semantics in lambda calculus form and use it to compile and to generate a stand-alone compiler. The syntax of *Tiny*-programs is

program	::=	var-declaration command
var-declaration	::=	variables: variable*
command	::=	while expression command |
		command; command |
		variable := expression

The semantic functions are given in figure 5. The semantic functions may easily be written in lambda calculus form to be partially evaluated. The resulting lambda calculus program, a *Tiny*-interpreter, has two free variables: the initial store istore and the program to be interpreted. Suppose that a *Tiny*-program is given but that istore is unknown. In other words, suppose that we have the type assumptions $\tau \vdash$ istore: $code$ and $\tau \vdash$ program: $const$. When we apply the $2\mathcal{E}$ rules to a well-annotated version of the *Tiny*-interpreter and the factorial program of figure 1, we get the lambda expression of figure 2. (Both programs are shown in the introduction.)

4.1 An Example of Compiler Generation

Self-applying the partial evaluator with respect to the *Tiny*-interpreter yields a *Tiny* to lambda calculus compiler $\mathcal{C}_c$. The compiling function $\mathcal{C}_c$ is essentially a syntactically curried version of the semantic function $\mathcal{C}$. The operators annotated as residual in the *Tiny*-interpreter have been replaced by the corresponding code generating actions.

To emphasize these striking structural similarities we have renamed the machine generated variables into names close to those of $\mathcal{C}$. Figure 6 displays the generated compiling function $\mathcal{C}_c$, syntactically sugared. On the right hand

$$\frac{\tau[x \mapsto T_2] \vdash \mathsf{exp}: T_1}{\tau \vdash \lambda x.\mathsf{exp}: T_2 \to T_1}$$

$$\frac{\tau \vdash \mathsf{exp}_1: T_2 \to T_1, \quad \tau \vdash \mathsf{exp}_2: T_2}{\tau \vdash \mathsf{exp}_1 \ @ \ \mathsf{exp}_2: T_1}$$

$$\frac{\tau \vdash \mathsf{exp}: T \to T}{\tau \vdash \mathsf{fix} \ \mathsf{exp}: T}$$

$$\frac{\tau \vdash \mathsf{exp}_1: const, \quad \tau \vdash \mathsf{exp}_2: T, \quad \tau \vdash \mathsf{exp}_3: T}{\tau \vdash \mathsf{if} \ \mathsf{exp}_1 \ \mathsf{exp}_2 \ \mathsf{exp}_3: T}$$

$$\tau \vdash \mathsf{const} \ c: const$$

$$\frac{\tau(x) = T}{\tau \vdash x: T}$$

$$\frac{\tau[x \mapsto code] \vdash \mathsf{2exp}: code}{\tau \vdash \lambda\text{-}r \ x.\mathsf{2exp}: code}$$

$$\frac{\tau \vdash \mathsf{exp}_1: code, \quad \tau \vdash \mathsf{exp}_2: code}{\tau \vdash \mathsf{exp}_1 \ @\text{-}r \ \mathsf{exp}_2: code}$$

$$\frac{\tau \vdash \mathsf{exp}: code}{\tau \vdash \mathsf{fix}\text{-}r \ \mathsf{exp}: code}$$

$$\frac{\tau \vdash \mathsf{exp}_1: code, \quad \tau \vdash \mathsf{exp}_2: code, \quad \tau \vdash \mathsf{exp}_3: code}{\tau \vdash \mathsf{if}\text{-}r \ \mathsf{exp}_1 \ \mathsf{exp}_2 \ \mathsf{exp}_3: code}$$

$$\tau \vdash \mathsf{const}\text{-}r \ c: code$$

$$\frac{\tau \vdash \mathsf{exp}: const}{\tau \vdash \mathsf{lift} \ \mathsf{exp}: code}$$

Figure 4: Type rules checking well-annotatedness

Semantic Domains

$$Store = Location \to Nat$$
$$Environment = Variable \to Location$$

$\mathcal{P}: program \to Store \to Store$
$\mathcal{P}[\![\underline{\text{variables:}} \ v_1, \ldots, v_n; \ \mathsf{cmd}]\!] \ \sigma_{init} = \mathcal{C}[\![\mathsf{cmd}]\!] \ (\mathcal{D}[\![v_1, \ldots, v_n]\!] \ \textit{first-location}) \ \sigma_{init}$

$\mathcal{D}: variable^* \to Location \to Environment$
$\mathcal{D}[\![v_1, \ldots, v_n]\!] \ loc = \lambda \ id.id = v_1 \to loc, \ (\mathcal{D}[\![v_2, \ldots, v_n]\!] \ \textit{next-loc(loc)})(id)$
$\mathcal{D}[\![\,]\!] \ loc = \lambda \ x.error_{loc}$

$\mathcal{C}: command \to Environment \to Store \to Store$
$\mathcal{C}[\![c_1; \ c_2]\!] \ \rho \ \sigma = \mathcal{C}[\![c_2]\!] \ \rho \ (\mathcal{C}[\![c_1]\!] \ \rho \ \sigma)$
$\mathcal{C}[\![\mathsf{var} := \mathsf{exp}]\!] \ \rho \ \sigma = \sigma[\rho(\mathsf{var}) \mapsto \mathcal{E}[\![\mathsf{exp}]\!] \ \rho \ \sigma]$
$\mathcal{C}[\![\underline{\text{while}} \ \mathsf{exp} \ c]\!] \ \rho \ \sigma = (\mathsf{fix} \ \lambda \ f.\lambda \ \sigma_1.\mathcal{E}[\![\mathsf{exp}]\!] = 0 \to \sigma_1, \ f(\mathcal{C}[\![c]\!] \ \rho \ \sigma_1)) \ \sigma$

$\mathcal{E}: expression \to Environment \to Store \to Nat$
... as usual ...

Figure 5: *Tiny* Semantics

$$\mathcal{C}_c[\![\mathsf{c_1};\ \mathsf{c_2}]\!]\ \rho \qquad\ = \mathrm{let}\ \sigma_1 = \textit{new-name}(\textit{const}\ \sigma)\ \mathrm{in}$$
$$\mathcal{C}_c[\![\mathsf{c_2}]\!]\ \rho\ \text{``}@\text{''}\ (\mathcal{C}_c[\![\mathsf{c_1}]\!]\ \rho\ \text{``}@\text{''}\ \sigma_1)$$
$$\mathcal{C}_c[\![\mathsf{var} := \mathsf{exp}]\!]\ \rho = \mathrm{let}\ \sigma_1 = \textit{new-name}(\textit{const}\ \sigma)\ \mathrm{in}$$
$$\mathbf{update}\ \text{``}@\text{''}\ \rho(\mathsf{var})\ \text{``}@\text{''}\ (\mathcal{E}_c[\![\mathsf{exp}]\!]\ \rho\ \sigma_1)\ \text{``}@\text{''}\ \sigma_1$$
$$\mathcal{C}_c[\![\underline{\mathsf{while}}\ \mathsf{exp}\ \mathsf{c}]\!]\ \rho = \mathrm{let}\ \sigma_1 = \textit{new-name}(\textit{const}\ \sigma)$$
$$\sigma_2 = \textit{new-name}(\textit{const}\ \sigma)$$
$$f1 = \textit{new-name}(\textit{const}\ f)\ \mathrm{in}$$
$$(\text{``fix''}\ \text{``}\boldsymbol{\lambda}\text{''}\ f1.\text{``}\boldsymbol{\lambda}\text{''}\ \sigma_2.\ \text{``if''} = \text{``}@\text{''}\ 0\ \text{``}@\text{''}\ (\mathcal{E}_c[\![\mathsf{exp}]\!]\ \rho\ \sigma_2)$$
$$\sigma_2$$
$$f1\ \text{``}@\text{''}\ (\mathcal{C}_c[\![\mathsf{c}]\!]\ \rho\ \text{``}@\text{''}\ \sigma_2))\ \text{``}@\text{''}\ \sigma_1$$

Figure 6: Generated compiling function – $\mathcal{C}_c$ is a syntactically curried version of $\mathcal{C}$

side of the equations there, we use for brevity the syntax-font: "$@$", "$\boldsymbol{\lambda}$", ... where the compilation algorithm builds syntactic expressions, instead of writing *build-@*, *build-λ* ... . Comparing of figures 5 and 6 shows that in the generated compiler the run-time (residual) actions of the interpreter have been replaced by code building operations.

5   Assessment

The table below shows the run-times of our example programs. In the following, *fac* denotes the factorial program written in *Tiny* (figure 1), *target* denotes the factorial residual program (figure 2), *tiny* denotes the *Tiny*-interpreter, *comp* denotes the generated *Tiny*-compiler. All the timings are measured in Sun 3/50 cpu milliseconds using Chez Scheme. The sizes are measured as the number of cons cells plus the number of atoms in the S-expressions representing the programs.

run		run-time	ratio
L tiny [fac,6]	=	70	
L target 6	= 720	10	7.0
L mix [tiny,fac]	=	700	
L comp fac	= target	20	35.0
L mix [mix, tiny]	=	17600	
L cogen tiny	= comp	380	46.3
L mix [mix, mix]	=	64600	
L cogen mix	= cogen	1330	48.6

program	size	ratio
fac	71	
target	221	3.1
tiny	743	
comp	927	1.3
mix	3206	
cogen	3811	1.2

The interpretative overhead in the mix program is rather large since all free variables (input variables and function names) are looked up in the initial environment which is linearly organized in our implementation. Since mix is

able to remove interpretational overhead the speed-ups gained when mix is partially evaluated are accordingly large (perhaps artificially so; in earlier work consistent speedups of 5 to 15 have been reported). The size ratio between *comp* and *tiny* is quite small since the two programs are very similar in structure. Some operations in *tiny* have been replaced by the corresponding code generating operations. The same relation holds between *mix* and *cogen*. That the absolute sizes of *mix* and *cogen* are large is because the initial environments are inlined pieces of code.

6   Conclusion and Future Work

We have developed and successfully self-applied a higher-order partial evaluator. The partial evaluator is based on very simple principles but is powerful enough to remove completely interpretative overhead from a denotational language definition of *Tiny*; and to generate a stand-alone compiler with a very natural structure. Future papers will concentrate on more powerful systems; BTA-algorithms; correctness proofs; and how to combine the ideas presented here with the ideas of function specialization used in most previous papers on partial evaluation.

References

[Appel 85] Appel, A. Semantics-Directed Code Generation. In *12th ACM Symposium on Principles of Programming Languages*, pages 315–324. 1985.

[Beckman 76] Beckman, L. et al. A Partial Evaluator, and Its Use as a Programming Tool. *Artificial Intelligence* 7(4):319–357, 1976.

[Bondorf 88] Bondorf, A., Jones, N.D., Mogensen, T., and Sestoft, P. *Binding Time Analysis and the Taming of Self-Application*. Draft, 18 pages, DIKU, University of Copenhagen, Denmark, August 1988.

[Bondorf 89a] Bondorf, A. A Self-Applicable Partial Evaluator for Term Rewriting Systems. In Diaz, J. and Orejas, F. (editors), *TAPSOFT '89. Proc. Int. Conf. Theory and Practice of Software Development, Barcelona, Spain, March 1989. (Lecture Notes in Computer Science, Vol. 352)*, pages 81–95. Springer-Verlag, 1989.

[Bondorf 89b] Bondorf, A. and Danvy, O. Automatic Autoprojection for Recursive Equations with Global Variables and Abstract Data Types. 1989. (submitted for publication).

[Bondorf 90] Bondorf, A. Automatic Autoprojection of Higher Order Recursive Equations. 1990. (to appear in the proceedings of ESOP 90).

[Consel 89] Consel, C. *Analyse de Programme, Evaluation Partielle, et Génération de Compilateurs.* PhD thesis, Université Paris VI, 1989. (in French).

[Ershov 78] Ershov, A.P. On the Essence of Compilation. In Neuhold, E.J. (editor), *Formal Description of Programming Concepts*, pages 391–420. North-Holland, 1978.

[Fuller 88] Fuller, D.A. and Abramsky, S. Mixed Computation of Prolog Programs. *New Generation Computing* 6(2,3):119–141, 1988.

[Futamura 71] Futamura, Y. Partial Evaluation of Computation Process – An Approach to a Compiler-Compiler. *Systems, Computers, Controls* 2(5):45–50, 1971.

[Gomard 89] Gomard, C. K. and Jones, N. D. Compiler Generation by Partial Evaluation: a Case Study. In Gallaire, H. (editor), *Information Processing 89*, IFIP. 1989.

[Guzowski 88] Guzowski, M.A. Towards Developing a Reflexive Partial Evaluator for an Interesting Subset of LISP. Master's thesis, Dept. of Computer Engineering and Science, Case Western Reserve University, Cleveland, Ohio, January 1988.

[Jones 85] Jones, N.D., Sestoft, P., and Søndergaard, H. An Experiment in Partial Evaluation: The Generation of a Compiler Generator. In Jouannaud, J.-P. (editor), *Rewriting Techniques and Applications, Dijon, France. (Lecture Notes in Computer Science, Vol. 202)*, pages 124–140. Springer-Verlag, 1985.

[Jones 89] Jones, N.D., Sestoft, P., and Søndergaard, H. Mix: A Self-Applicable Partial Evaluator for Experiments in Compiler Generation. *Lisp and Symbolic Computation* 2(1):9–50, 1989.

[Jørring 86] Jørring, U. and Scherlis, W.L. Compilers and Staging Transformations. In *Thirteenth ACM Symposium on Principles of Programming Languages, St. Petersburg, Florida*, pages 86–96. 1986.

[Lombardi 67] Lombardi, L.A. Incremental Computation. In Alt, F.L. and Rubinoff, M. (editors), *Advances in Computers, Vol. 8*, pages 247–333. Academic Press, 1967.

[Mosses 79] Mosses, P. *SIS — Semantics Implementation System, Reference Manual and User Guide.* DAIMI Report MD-30, DAIMI, University of Århus, Denmark, 1979.

[Nielson 88a] Nielson, F. A Formal Type System for Comparing Partial Evaluators. In Bjørner, D., Ershov, A.P., and Jones, N.D. (editors), *Partial Evaluation and Mixed Computation*, pages 349–384. North-Holland, 1988.

[Nielson 88b] Nielson, F. and Nielson, H. R. *The TML-Approach to Compiler-Compilers.* Technical Report 1988-47, Department of Computer Science, Technical University of Denmark, 1988.

[Nielson 88c] Nielson, H. R. and Nielson, F. Automatic Binding Time Analysis for a Typed λ-calculus. In *15th ACM Symposium on Principles of Programming Languages*, pages 98–106. 1988.

[Paulson 82] Paulson, L. A Semantics-Directed Compiler Generator. In *9th ACM Symposium on Principles of Programming Languages*, pages 224–233. 1982.

[PeytonJones 87] Peyton Jones, S. L. *The Implementation of Functional Programming Languages.* Prentice-Hall, 1987.

[Pleban 84] Pleban, U. Compiler Prototyping Using Formal Semantics. *SIGPLAN Notices* 19(6):94–105, 1984.

[Romanenko 88] Romanenko, S.A. A Compiler Generator Produced by a Self-Applicable Specializer Can Have a Surprisingly Natural and Understandable Structure. In Bjørner, D., Ershov, A.P., and Jones, N.D. (editors), *Partial Evaluation and Mixed Computation*, pages 445–463. North-Holland, 1988.

[Schmidt 85] Schmidt, D. A. Detecting Global Variables in Denotatinal Specifications. *ACM Transactions on Programming Languages and Systems* 7(2):299–310, 1985.

[Schooler 84] Schooler, R. Partial Evaluation as a Means of Language Extensibility. Master's thesis, 84 pages, MIT/LCS/TR-324, Laboratory for Computer Science, MIT, Cambridge, Massachusetts, August 1984.

[Turchin 80] Turchin, V.F. The Use of Metasystem Transition in Theorem Proving and Program Optimization. In Bakker, J. De and van Leeuven, J. (editors), *Automata, Languages and Programming. Seventh ICALP, Noordwijkerhout, The Netherlands.*

(Lecture Notes in Computer Science, Vol. 85), pages 645–657. Springer-Verlag, 1980.

[Wand 82] Wand, M. Semantics-Directed Machine Architecture. In *9th ACM Symposium on Principles of Programming Languages*, pages 234–241. 1982.

[Wand 84] Wand, M. A Semantic Prototyping System. In *SIGPLAN '84 Symposion on Compiler Construction*, pages 213–221. 1984.

[Weis 87] Weis, P. *Le Systeme SAM: Métacompilation très efficace à l'aide d'opérateurs sémantiques.* PhD thesis, Université Paris VII, 1987. (in French).

A Language for Distributed Applications

Mario R. Barbacci and Jeannette M. Wing

Software Engineering Institute and School of Computer Science
Carnegie Mellon University

Abstract

Durra is a language designed to support the development of distributed applications consisting of multiple, concurrent, large-grained tasks executing in a heterogeneous network.

An application-level program is written in Durra as a set of *task descriptions* that prescribes a way to manage the resources of a heterogeneous machine network. The application describes the tasks to be instantiated and executed as concurrent processes, the intermediate queues required to store the messages as they move from producer to consumer processes, and the possible dynamic reconfigurations of the application.

The application-level programming paradigm fits very naturally a top-down, incremental method of software development. Although we don't claim to have solved all problems or identified all the necessary tools, we would like to suggest that a language like Durra would be of great value in the development of large, distributed systems.

1. Programming Heterogeneous Machines

A computing environment consisting of loosely-connected networks of multiple special- and general-purpose processors constitutes a *heterogeneous machine*. Users of heterogeneous machines are concerned with allocating specialized resources to tasks of medium to large size. They need to create processes, which are instances of tasks, allocate these processes to processors, and specify the communication patterns between processes. These activities constitute *application-level programming*, to distinguish them from the activities leading to the development of the individual component tasks.

This work is sponsored by the U.S. Department of Defense. The views and conclusions contained in this document are solely those of the author(s) and should not be interpreted as representing official policies, either expressed or implied, of Carnegie Mellon University, the U.S. Air Force, the Department of Defense, or the U.S. Government.

Currently, users of a heterogeneous machine follow the same pattern of program development as users of conventional processors: Users write individual tasks as separate programs, in the different programming languages (e.g., C, Lisp, Ada) supported by the processors, and then hand code the allocation of resources to their application by explicitly loading specific programs to run on specific processors at specific times. Often, these programs are written with built-in knowledge about the cooperating programs, thus making them difficult to reuse in alternative applications, or with knowledge about the network structure, making them difficult to reuse in a different environment. Tailoring the programs to the application or the environment further complicates the development of applications whose structure might change as a result of requirements of the application (e.g., mode changes in signal processing) or to support fault-tolerance (e.g., restarting a program in a different processor after the original processor fails).

We believe that a better approach is to separate the concerns of the developers of the individual component programs from those of the developers of the applications using these programs. We claim that developing software in this style is qualitatively different from developing software at the level of the component programs. It requires different kinds of languages, tools, and methodologies; and in this paper we address some of these issues by presenting a language, Durra, and showing how it can support a top-down, incremental software development methodology. In this paper we only address language and methodology issues. For a description of the Durra runtime environment and tools see [4].

2. The Durra Language

Durra [2, 5] is a language designed to support the development of distributed applications. An application is written in Durra as a set of *task descriptions* that prescribes a way to manage the resources of a heterogeneous machine network. The result of compiling a Durra application description is a set of resource allocation and scheduling directives, as suggested in Figure 1.

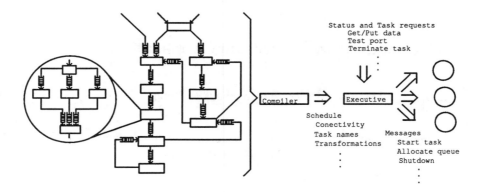

Figure 1: Compilation of an Application Description

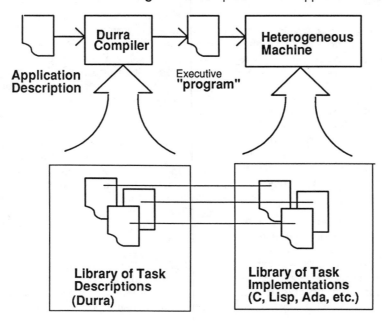

Figure 2: Scenario for Developing a Distributed Application

2.1. Scenario for Developing an Application

We see three distinct phases in the process of developing an application using Durra: the creation of a library of tasks, the creation of an application using library tasks, and the execution of the application. These three phases are illustrated in Figure 2.

During the first phase, the developer writes (in the appropriate programming languages) the various tasks that will be executed as concurrent programs in the heterogeneous machine. For each of these task implementations, the developer writes (in Durra) a corresponding task description.

Task descriptions are used to specify the properties of a task implementation (a program). For a given task, there may be many implementations, differing in programming language (e.g., C or Ada), processor type (e.g., Motorola 68020 or DEC VAX), performance characteristics, or other properties. For each implementation of a task, a task description must be written in Durra, compiled, and entered in the library. A task description includes specifications of a task implementation's performance and functionality, the types of data it produces or consumes, the ports it uses to communicate with other tasks, and other miscellaneous attributes of the implementation.

```
task task-name                        -- Name of the task or task family
  ports
    port-declarations         -- Used for communication between a process and a queue

  attributes
    attribute-value-pairs         -- Used to specify miscellaneous properties of the task

  behavior                    -- Used to specify functional and timing behavior of the task
    requires predicate
    ensures predicate
    timing timing expression

  structure                   -- A graph describing the internal structure of the task
    process-declarations        -- Declaration of instances of internal subtasks
    bind-declarations           -- Mapping of internal ports to this task's ports
    queue-declarations        -- Means of communication between internal processes
    reconfiguration-statements    -- Dynamic modifications to the structure
end task-name
```

Figure 3: A Template for Task Descriptions

During the second phase, the user writes an *application description*. Syntactically, an application description is a single task description and could be stored in the library as a new task. This allows writing of hierarchical application descriptions. When the application description is compiled, the compiler generates a set of resource allocation commands to be interpreted by the executive.

During the last phase, the executive loads the task implementations (i.e., programs corresponding to the component task descriptions) into the processors and issues the appropriate commands to execute the programs.

2.2. Task Descriptions

Task descriptions are the building blocks for applications. Task descriptions include the following information (Figure 3): (1) its interface to other tasks (**ports**); (2) its **attributes**; (3) its functional and timing **behavior**; and (4) its internal **structure**, thereby allowing for hierarchical task descriptions.

Interface information.- This portion defines the ports of the processes instantiated from the task.

```
ports
    in1: in heads;
    out1, out2: out tails;
```

A port declaration specifies the direction and type of data moving through the port. An **in** port takes input data from a queue; an **out** port deposits data into a queue.

Attribute Information.- This portion specifies miscellaneous properties of a task. In a task description, the developer of the task lists the actual value of a property; in a task selection, the user of a task lists the desired value of the property. Example attributes include author, version number, programming language, file name, and processor type:

```
attributes
    author = "jmw";
    implementation = "program_name";
    Queue_Size = 25;
```

Behavioral Information.- This portion specifies functional and timing properties about the task. The functional information part of a task description consists of a pre-condition on what is required to be true of the data coming through the input ports, and a post-condition on what is guaranteed to be true of the data going out through the output ports. The timing expression describes the behavior of the task in terms of the operations it performs on its input and output ports. For additional information about the syntax and semantics of the functional and timing behavior description, see [1].

Structural Information.- This portion defines a process-queue graph (e.g., Figure 1) and possible dynamic reconfiguration of the graph.

A process declaration of the form

  process_name : **task** *task_selection*

creates a process as an instance of the specified task.

Task selections are templates used to identify and retrieve task descriptions from the task library. A given task, e.g., convolution, might have a number of different implementations that differ along dimensions such as algorithm used, code version, performance, or processor type. In order to select among a number of alternative implementations, the user provides a task selection as part of a process declaration. This task selection lists the desirable features of a suitable implementation. Syntactically, a task selection looks somewhat like a task description without the structure part. Figure 4 shows a template for a task selection.

A queue declaration of the form

  queue_name [*queue_size*]:
    src_port > *data_transformation* > *dst_port*

```
task  task-name                      -- REQUIRED. Name of a task or task family.
   ports                             -- OPTIONAL. Interface of the desired task
      port-declarations

   attributes                 -- OPTIONAL. Miscellaneous properties of the desired task
      attribute-expression

   behavior          -- OPTIONAL. Functional and timing behavior of the desired task
      requires  predicate
      ensures  predicate
      timing  timing expression                              -- OPTIONAL.
   end  task-name
```

Figure 4: A Template for Task Selections

creates a queue through which data flow from an output port of a process (src_port) into the input port of another process (dst_port). Data transformations are operations applied to data coming from a source port before they are delivered to a destination port.

A reconfiguration statement of the form

```
if  condition  then
      remove  process-and-queue-names
      process  process-declarations
      queues  queue-declarations
      reconnect  queue-reconnections
      exit  condition
end if;
```

is used to specify changes in the current structure of the application (i.e., process-queue graph) and the conditions under which these changes take effect, and the conditions under which the changes are undone, thus reverting to a previous configuration. Typically, a number of existing processes and queues are replaced by new processes and queues, which are then connected to the remainder of the original graph. The reconfiguration and exit conditions are Boolean expressions involving time values, queue sizes, signals raised by the processes, and other information available to the executive at runtime.

3. A Task Emulator as a Prototyping Tool

To support the prototyping of distributed, large-grained applications, we have developed a program that acts as a "universal" task emulator. This program, MasterTask [3], can emulate any task in an application by interpreting the timing expression describing the behavior of the task, performing input and output in the proper sequence and at the proper time (within the precission of Durra time values and the executive clock.)

MasterTask is useful to both application developers and task developers. Application developers can build early prototypes of an application by using MasterTask as a substitute for task implementations that have yet to be written. Task developers can experiment with and evaluate proposed changes in task behavior or performance by rewriting and reinterpreting the corresponding timing expression.

3.1. Timing Expressions

Timing expressions are the critical piece of information used by MasterTask. Tasks send and receive messages following a task-specific pattern provided by a timing expression. This expression describes the behavior of the task in terms of the operations it performs on its input and output ports; this is the behavior of the task seen from the outside.

Queue operations constitute the basic events of a timing expression. An event represents a queue operation (i.e., "Enqueue" and "Dequeue") on the queue attached to a specific port. In addition, a pseudo-operation, "delay", is used to represent the time consumed between (real) queue operations.

A timing expression (Figure 5) is a regular expression describing the patterns of execution of operations on the input and output ports of a task. The optional keyword **loop** can be used to indicate that the pattern of operations is repeated indefinitely.

A timing expression is a sequence of parallel event expressions. Each parallel event expression consists of one or more event expressions separated by the symbol || to indicate that their executions overlap. Since the expressions might take different amounts of time to complete, nothing can be said about their completion, other than a parallel event expression terminates when the last event terminates.

A basic event expression is either a queue operation (including "delay") or a timing expression enclosed in parentheses. The latter form also allows for the specification of a guard, an expression specifying the conditions under which a sequence of operations is allowed to start or repeat its execution.

When MasterTask starts, it reads the timing expression for the task it wants to emulate and assigns a number of concurrent, light-weight processes (Ada task objects in the current implementation) to interpret the timing expression. These processes are responsible for evaluating the guards and for invoking the queue operations.

Syntax:

```
TimingExpression  ::= {``LOOP''} SequentialEvent
SequentialEvent   ::= ParallelEvent_List_spaces
ParallelEvent     ::= BasicEvent_List_double_vertical_bar
BasicEvent        ::= Event |
                      {Guard ``=>''} ``('' SequentialEvent ``)'')
Event             ::= PortName |
                      ``DELAY'' TimeWindow
TimeWindow        ::= ``['' TimeValue ``,'' TimeValue ``]''
TimeValue         ::= Number_Of_Seconds {TimeBase} |
                      ``*''                            -- Indeterminate amount of time
TimeBase          ::= ``DTIME'' |                      -- Time since start of day
                      ``ATIME'' |                      -- Time since start of application
                      ``PTIME'' |                      -- Time since start of process
Guard             ::= ``REPEAT'' IntegerValue |
                      ``BEFORE'' TimeValue |            -- Absolute time
                      ``AFTER'' TimeValue |             -- Absolute time
                      ``DURING'' TimeWindow |           -- Time interval
                      ``WHEN'' Expression               -- A Boolean expression
```

Examples:

```
3615.5 atime                -- An application relative time: 1 hour and 15.5 seconds
                            -- after the start of the application.

delay[10, 15]               -- A delay interval lasting between 10 and 15 seconds.

delay[*, 10]                -- A delay interval taking at most 10 seconds.

delay[10, *]                -- A delay interval taking at least 10 seconds.

in1 || in2                  -- Two parallel input operations, starting simultaneously.

in1 delay[10,15] out1       -- Three sequential operations.

repeat 5 => (in1 delay[10,15] out1)
                            -- Same as above but as a cycle repeated five times.
before 64800 DTIME => ( .  .  . )
                            -- A sequence constrained to start before 6 pm.
                            -- (64,800 seconds after the start of the day)
after 64800 DTIME => ( .  .  . )
                            -- A sequence constrained to start after 6 pm.
during [40.5 PTIME, 100] => ( .  .  . )
                            -- A sequence constrained to start between 40.5 and 140.5 seconds
                            -- from the start of the process.
when (Current_Size(in1) > 0) and (Current_Size(in2) > 0) => ((in1 || in2) out1);
                            -- A sequence that starts after both input queues have data.
loop when (Current_Size(in1) > 0) and (Current_Size(in2) > 0) => ((in1 || in2) out1);
                            -- The same sequence as above but repeated indefinitely.
```

Figure 5: Timing Expressions

3.2. Using the Task Emulator

The task emulator described above provides natural support for system development methodologies based on successive refinements, such as the Spiral method [8]. Users of the spiral model selectively identify high-risk components of the product, establish their requirements, and then carry out the design, coding, and testing phases. It is not necessary that this process be carried out through the testing phase -- higher-risk components might be identified in the process and these components must be given higher priority, suspending the development process of the formerly riskier component.

Durra allows the designer to build mock-ups of an application, starting with a gross decomposition into tasks specified by their interface and behavioral properties. Once this is completed, the application can be emulated using MasterTask as a stand-in for the yet-to-be written task implementations.

The result of the emulation would identify areas of risk in the form of tasks whose timing expressions suggest are more critical or demanding. In other words, the purpose of this initial emulation is to identify the component task more likely to affect the performance of the entire system.

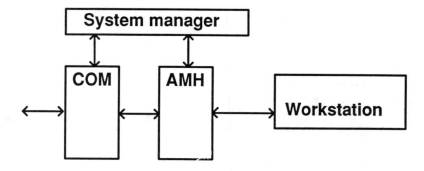

Figure 6: Initial Structure of the C^3I Node

The designers can then experiment by writing alternative behavioral specifications for the offending task until a satisfactory specification (i.e., template) is obtained. Once this is achieved, the designers can proceed by replacing the original task descriptions with more detailed templates, consisting of internal tasks and queues, using the structure description features of Durra. These, more refined, application descriptions can again be emulated, experimenting with alternative behavioral specifications of the internal tasks, until a satisfactory internal structure (i.e., decomposition) has been achieved. This process can be repeated as often as necessary, varying the degree of refinement of the tasks, and even backtracking if a dead-end is reached. It is not necessary to start coding a task until later, when its specifications are acceptable, and when it is decided that it should not be further decomposed.

Of course, it is quite possible that a satisfactory specification might be impossible to meet and a task implementation might have to rejected. The designers would then have to backtrack to an earlier, less detailed design and try alternative specifications, or even alternative decompositions of a parent subsystem. This is possible because we are following a strictly top-down approach. The effect of a change in an inner task would be reflected in its impact on the behavioral specifications of a "parent" task. The damage is, in sense, contained and can not spread to other parts of the design.

4. An Example of Incremental Development

To illustrate an incremental development process using Durra, in this section we show an application, a C^3I node [6]. The top level structure of the node is shown in Figure 6. The node consists of four subsystems: System Manager, Communications (COM), Application Message Handler (AMH), and Workstation. These subsystems correspond to the first four process declarations in Figure 7. In addition to these task, there are two auxiliary tasks which are used for communications between the system manager and the communication and application message handler subsystems.

One of these auxiliary tasks broadcasts commands from the system manager to the other two subsystems, and the other merges their responses to the system manager. **Broadcast** and **merge** are predefined in Durra and implemented directly by the Durra runtime executive. A broadcast task takes data from a single input port and copies it to multiple output ports (the number of output ports is specified in the task selection.) A merge task takes data from multiple input ports and copies them into a single output port (the number of input ports is specified in the task selection.)

Figure 8 shows the tasks descriptions for the subsystems of the initial configuration. At the start of the development process we might not be ready to commit to any particular structure for the subsystems and simply opt to describe them as simple, unstructured tasks. This information is sufficient to do static checks, including port (i.e., type) compatibility and graph connectivity. However, if we want to carry out some preliminary dynamic checks, we need to provide a pseudo-implementation for each subsystem. That is, we need to write ad hoc programs that emulate the input/output behavior of each of the subsystems and then specify these programs as the "implementation" attributes in the subsystem task descriptions.

Alternatively, if a subsystem's behavior is relatively simple and repetitive, we could use MasterTask as a subsystem emulator by specifying "master" as its "implementation" attribute. In fact, we can mix the two approaches and have some subsystems emulated by ad hoc programs, while other subsystems are emulated via MasterTask, as illustrated in Figure 8.

After some experimentation with the gross decomposition outlined above, we can proceed to expand the subsystems. For example, the Message Handler subsystem (Figure 9) consists of five internal tasks. Three of these tasks, AMHS_control, AMHS_inbound, AMHS_outbound, are user-implemented. The other two tasks are instances of the predefined broadcast and merge tasks described before.

```
task configuration
structure
    process
        --      real system processes
          sm      : task system_manager;
          com     : task comm;
          amh     : task amhs;
          wp      : task wkstn;
        --      auxiliary system processes
          bc  : task broadcast                -- command broadcast
                ports
                        in1         : in  system_command;
                        out1, out2  : out system_command;
                end broadcast;
          mg  : task merge                    -- response multiplexor
                ports
                        in1, in2    : in  subsystem_response;
                        out1        : out subsystem_response;
                attribute
                        mode = fifo;
                end merge;
    queues
        -- system command propagation
        q_c1    : sm.SM_Out          >> bc.in1;
        q_c2    : bc.out1            >> com.SM_Commands;
        q_c3    : bc.out2            >> amh.SM_Commands;
        -- subsystem response propagation
        q_r1    : com.SM_Responses   >> mg.in1;
        q_r2    : amh.SM_Responses   >> mg.in2;
        q_r3    : mg.out1           >> sm.SM_In;
        -- inbound message propagation
        q_i1    : com.Inbound       >> amh.COMM_Inbound;
        q_i2    : amh.WS_Inbound     >> wp.Inbound;
        -- outbound message propagation
        q_o1    : wp.Outbound       >> amh.WS_Outbound;
        q_o4    : amh.COMM_Outbound >> com.Outbound;
end configuration;
```

Figure 7: Initial Application Description

The subsystem is an abstraction and does not correspond to an executable program. Its ports (SM_Commands, SM_Response, COMM_Inbound, COMM_Outbound, WS_Inbound, and WS_Outbound) must be implemented by internal-process ports. This is the purpose of the **bind** declarations, which declare which internal-process ports implement the subsystem ports.

The development of the Message Handler does not necessarily stop here. Each of the three user-implemented tasks (AMHS_Control, AMHS_inbound, and AMHS_outbound) could in turn consist of multiple, concurrent internal programs. The task description for AMHS_Control, for example, would declare internal processes and queues, and would bind internal ports to implement the interface of the task (i.e., the SM_In, SM_Out, Cmd_Out, and Resp_In ports.) This level of detail is not visible in the description of Figure 9.

We can continue the design in this fashion, successively refining the subsystem descriptions until, at the end, the application is fully described as a hierarchical graph in which the innermost nodes are implemented as separate programs, specified by the "implementation" attribute of the corresponding task descriptions.

An application description does not use language features beyond those used in a compound task description. An application description is simply a compound task description which is compiled and stored in a Durra library and, conceivably, could be used as a building block for a larger application. From the point of view of the users of Durra, the main difference between a task description and an application description is that application descriptions are translated into directives to the runtime executive by executing an optional *code generation phase* of the Durra compiler.

For brevity, we will not describe the complete design process of the C^{3}I node. See [7] for details about the Durra task descriptions and the task implementations.

5. Related Work
CONIC [12] address the problem of dynamic reconfiguration of real-time systems in the design of the CONIC language. Originally, CONIC restricted tasks to be programmed in a fixed language (an extension to Pascal with message passing primitives) running on homogeneous workstations. This restriction was later relaxed to support multiple programming languages.

System Manager Subsystem

```
task system_manager
    ports       SM_In   : in  subsystem_response;
                SM_Out  : out system_command;
    attributes  implementation = "system_manager_emulator";
                processor = "Vax";
end system_manager;
```

Communications Subsystem

```
task comm
    ports       SM_Commands   : in  system_command;
                SM_Responses  : out subsystem_response;
                Inbound       : out comm_if_message;
                Outbound      : in  comm_if_message;
    attributes  implementation = "comm_emulator";
                processor = "Vax";
end comm;
```

Application Message Handler Subsystem

```
task AMHS
    ports       SM_Commands   : in  system_command;
                SM_Responses  : out subsystem_response;
                COMM_Inbound  : in  comm_if_message;
                COMM_Outbound : out comm_if_message;
                WS_Inbound    : out workstation_if_message;
                WS_Outbound   : in  comm_if_message;
    attributes  implementation = "amhs_emulator";
                processor = "Vax";
end AMHS;
```

Workstation Subsystem

```
task wkstn
    ports       Inbound   : in  workstation_if_message;
                Outbound  : out comm_if_message;
    behavior
        timing loop ( (Inbound delay[5, 60]) || (delay[*, 180] Outbound) );
    attributes  implementation = "master";
                processor = "Vax";
end wkstn;
```

Figure 8: Top Level Subsystem Descriptions

MINION [MINION89] consists of a language for describing distributed applications and a graphics editor for interactive modification of the application structure. MINION allows a user to expand, contract, or reconfigure an application in arbitrary ways during execution time. Hermes [1] hides from the programmers all knowledge about storage layout, persistency of objects or even operating system primitives. Processes communicate through ports, connected via message queues although the semantic of queue operations are similar to an Ada entry call/accept mechanisms, albeit the binding of processes to ports is dynamic, as in Durra, CONIC, and MINION.

RNET [8] is language for building distributed real-time programs. An RNET program consists of a configuration specification and the procedural code, which is compiled, linked with a run-time kernel, and loaded onto the target system for execution. The language provides facilities for specifying real-time properties, such as deadlines and delays that are used for monitoring and scheduling the processes. These features place RNET at a lower level of abstraction, and thus RNET cannot be compared directly to Durra. Rather, it can be considered as a suitable language for developing the runtime executived required by Durra and other languages in which the concurrent tasks are treated as black boxes.

Specifying a data transformation in a queue declaration is a way to support the transmission of structured data types between heterogeneous processors or languages. For example, two tasks written in different languages are likely to use different layouts for record data types. The Durra runtime executive will not alter the presentation of the data to hide the layout differences and will transmit a record type as a block of bytes, without attempting to modify the data. It is up to the source and destination tasks to implement the appropriate packing and unpacking of the data.

Interfacing heterogeneous machines or language environments is not a new problem. Several techniques have been proposed to generate type declarations and routines which perform the appropriate packing and unpacking of the data [10, 11, 13, 14]. These and other similar facilities could be adopted by the application developers without difficulty in the data transformation tasks or in the application tasks proper.

```
task AMHS
    ports       SM_Commands       : in  system_command;
                SM_Responses      : out subsystem_response;
                COMM_Inbound      : in  comm_if_message;
                COMM_Outbound     : out comm_if_message;
                WS_Inbound        : out workstation_if_message;
                WS_Outbound       : in  comm_if_message;
        structure
        process ac: task AMHS_control;
                ai: task AMHS_inbound;
                ao: task AMHS_outbound;
                pb: task broadcast
                        port   in1          : in  system_command;
                               out1, out2 : out system_command;
                    end broadcast;
                pm: task merge
                        port   in1, in2 : in  subsystem_response;
                               out1     : out subsystem_response;
                        attribute mode = fifo;
                    end merge;
        bind    SM_Commands       = ac.SM_In;
                SM_Responses      = ac.SM_Out;
                COMM_Inbound      = ai.COMM_Inbound;
                COMM_Outbound     = ao.COMM_Outbound;
                WS_Inbound        = ai.WS_Inbound;
                WS_Outbound       = ao.WS_Outbound;
        queue   q1: ac.Cmd_Out   >> pb.in1;
                q2: pb.out1      >> ai.Cmd_In;
                q3: pb.out2      >> ao.Cmd_In;
                q4: ai.Resp_Out  >> pm.in1;
                q5: ao.Resp_Out  >> pm.in2;
                q6: pm.out1      >> ac.Resp_In;
    end AMHS;
```

Figure 9: Message Handler Subsystem Description

6. Conclusions

Application-level programming, as implemented by Durra, lifts the level of programming at the code level (task implementations) to programming at the specification level (task descriptions), separating the structure of an application from its behavior. This separation provides users with control over the evolution of an application during application development as well as during application execution. During development, an application evolves as the requirements of the application are better understood or change. This evolution takes the form of changes in the application description, selecting alternative task implementations from the library, and connecting these implementations in different ways to reflect alternative designs.

During execution, an application evolves through application mode changes or in response to faults in the system. This evolution takes the form of conditional, dynamic reconfigurations, removing processes and queues, instantiating new processes and queues, and building a new process-queue graph without affecting the remaining processes and queues.

The application-level programming paradigm fits very naturally a top-down, incremental method of software development. Although we don't claim to have solved all problems or identified all the necessary tools, we would like to suggest that a language like Durra would be of great value in the development of large, distributed systems. It would allow the designer to build mock-ups of an application, starting with a gross decomposition into tasks described by templates specified by their interface and behavioral properties. In the process of developing the application, component tasks can be decomposed into simpler process-queue graphs and at each stage of the process, the application can be emulated using MasterTask as a stand-in for the yet-to-be written task implementations.

In our prototype implementation, we have intentionally sacrificed semantic complexity in favor of simpler task selection based only on interface and attribute information, and have limited the performance and reliability by implementing a centralized executive. As a result, we gained the advantage of being able immediately to test our general idea about application-level programming with a real environment (Durra compiler, runtime system, and debugger/monitor) that runs on a heterogeneous machine (various kinds of workstations connected via an Ethernet). Expanding task selection features and distributing the runtime executive are in our plans for the future.

References

[1]   D.F. Bacon, R.E. Strom, and S.A. Yemini.
        Hermes User Manual.
        Technical Report, IBM Thomas J. Watson
             Research Center, 1988.

[2]   M.R. Barbacci and J.M. Wing.
        Specifying Functional and Timing Behavior for
             Real-time Applications.
        Lecture Notes in Computer Science. Volume
             259, Part 2.*Proceedings of the Conference on
             Parallel Architectures and Languages Europe
             (PARLE).*
        Springer-Verlag, 1987, pages 124-140.

[3]   M.R. Barbacci, C.B. Weinstock, and J.M. Wing.
        Programming at the Processor-Memory-Switch
             Level.
        In *Proceedings of the 10th International
             Conference on Software Engineering.*
             Singapore, April, 1988.

[4]   M.R. Barbacci.
        MasterTask: The Durra Task Emulator.
        Technical Report CMU/SEI-88-TR-20 (DTIC AD-
             A199 429), Software Engineering Institute,
             Carnegie Mellon University, July, 1988.

[5]   M.R. Barbacci, D.L. Doubleday, C.B. Weinstock,
        and J.M. Wing.
        Developing Applications for Heterogeneous
             Machine Networks: The Durra Environment.
        Computing Systems 2(1), March, 1989.

[6]   M.R. Barbacci and J.M. Wing.
        *Durra: A Task-Level Description Language
             Reference Manual (Version 2).*
        Technical Report CMU/SEI-89-TR-34, Software
             Engineering Institute, Carnegie Mellon
             University, September, 1989.

[7]   M.R. Barbacci, D.L. Doubleday, C.B. Weinstock,
        S.L. Baur, D.C. Bixler, M.T. Heins.
        *Command, Control, Communications, and
             Intelligence Node: A Durra Application
             Example.*
        Technical Report CMU/SEI-89-TR-9 (DTIC AD-
             A206575), Software Engineering Institute,
             Carnegie Mellon University, February, 1989.

[8]   C. Belzile, M. Coulas, G.H. MacEwen, and
        G. Marquis.
        RNET: A Hard Real Time Distributed
             Programming System.
        In *Proceedings of the 1986 Real-Time Systems
             Symposium*, pages 2-13. IEEE Computer
             Society Press, December, 1986.

[9]   Barry W. Boehm.
        A Spiral Model of Software Development and
             Enhancement.
        Computer 21(5), May, 1988.

[10]   P.H. Gibbons.
        A Stub Generator for Multilanguage RPC in
             Heterogeneous Environments.
        IEEE Transactions on Software Engineering
             13(1):77-87, January, 1987.

[11]   M.B. Jones, R.F. Rashid, and M.R. Thompson.
        Matchmaker: An Interface Specification Language
             for Distributed Processing.
        In *Conference Record of the Twelfth Annual ACM
             Symposium on Principles of Programming
             Languages*, pages 225-235. ACM, January,
             1984.

[12]   J. Kramer and J. Magee.
        A Model for Change Management.
        In *Proceedings of the IEEE Workshop on Trends
             for Distributed Computing Systems in the
             1990's*, pages 286-295. IEEE Computer
             Society, September, 1988.

[13]   S.A. Mamrak, H. Kuo, and D. Soni.
        Supporting Existing Tools in Distributed
             Processing Systems: The Conversion
             Problem.
        In *Proceedings of the 3rd International
             Conference on Distributed Computing
             Systems*, pages 847-853. IEEE Computer
             Society Press, October, 1982.

[14]   Sun Microsystems, Inc.
        XDR: External Data Representation Standard.
        RFC 1014, SRI Network Information Center,
             June, 1987.

FLAME: a language for distributed programming

Flavio De Paoli*   Mehdi Jazayeri

Hewlett-Packard Laboratories
Palo Alto, CA 94304

Abstract

FLAME is an experimental language for distributed programming. It is intended for applications that run on a collection of computers connected by a network. It is part of a project that deals with the building of open software systems. Open systems place stringent requirements on both the type of language one uses and the style of programming. FLAME tries to address the difficulties of writing such open, distributed applications with current technology. FLAME is based on C++ and its main contribution is to integrate the notions of objects and process groups at the programming language level. The result is a powerful language which nevertheless raises several new questions. We present the current state of FLAME and potential areas for future development.

1   Introduction

FLAME is an experimental language for distributed programming. It supports the writing of applications that consist of several processes that may execute on different machines connected by a network. The FLAME project is part of a larger project[Wilkes88] that deals with the building of "open" software systems. An open system may be modified dynamically, i.e. features may be added or modified without having to bring the system down. Open systems place stringent requirements on both the type of language one uses and the style of programming.

FLAME tries to address the difficulties in writing such open, distributed applications with current technology, which consists of embedding calls to operating system and network services in a traditional program. Remote procedure call packages help, but they lack the security and convenience that a programming language can offer. Such a language must provide the programmer with abstractions for distributed programming that make the important features of traditional operating system and network services available in a safe and secure setting. This paper presents the key ideas of FLAME and its constructs for dealing with processes and process groups. FLAME is itself an "open" language in the sense that it evolves as we encounter new problems.

Underlying the design of FLAME are two ideas which we believe are important for distributed programming: object orientation and process groups. Object-oriented notation provides a clean and powerful schema in which each process is an object. Objects can only communicate by exchanging messages rather than sharing data structures. The group concept allows the programmer to consider a collection of processes as a unique entity. The group interface hides its implementation, that is, the constituent processes, from the group clients.

*Present address: Dipartimento di Elettronica, Politecnico di Milano, Milan, ITALY

In the object-oriented approach, an object is defined as data and some code to handle that data. Objects are independent units from which the system is built. This decomposition of a system into disjoint entities is appropriate for a distributed environment because it allows objects to be spread over the network naturally. Each object contains all the information it needs, so it can potentially be a process, with its own thread of control. Such a process can be moved to run on any node: objects, by definition, hide their execution from the outside world.

An object-oriented approach simplifies even the exchange of messages. The system is composed of homogeneous elements: each object sends messages to other objects and receives messages from objects. There are no designated servers—any object can respond to remote invocations. The object-oriented relationship is inherently symmetrical. Furthermore, the only information needed to access an object is its identifier. This simplifies the parameter passing mechanism: each object can be represented by a unique, location-independent, identifier. Requirements for objects in a distributed environment are discussed in [Jazayeri89].

Once we have the ability to design systems using such active objects, we are able to design "classic" systems, that is, conventional systems as implemented in any sequential style, to be able to run in a distributed environment. But process groups enable us to tap the potential of a distributed architecture even more. The basic idea is to group processes of the same kind and give them a unique name. We call this entity a process group.

A first feature of process groups is the ability to send broadcast messages to group members. That is, in order to send a message to each member of a group, the client can send a single message to the group, relying on the runtime system to deliver the message to the individual members. This level of indirection provided by the group concept also allows us to send messages to processes whose identities we don't know explicitly. This allows the programmer to design an interface that hides the real implementation of a part of the system. This is the first requirement for being able to to design dynamic, open, systems. Imagine a group of processes providing some service. The client sends a request for a service and gets the answer but it doesn't know who really answered its request. The group can be composed of an arbitrary number of processes at any given time. This flexibility allows the system manager, for example, to run as many processes as needed at any time, depending on the number of requests, without affecting any of the (running) clients. Or, if a process crashes, the remaining group members can collaborate to start a new one without notifying anyone outside the group.

Other uses of the group concept can be found in failure recovery or system maintenance. During system maintenance, we can add or remove processes without pausing or stopping the system. Let us suppose that we have designed a new component that should replace the old one in the system. By using groups, the new component can be run before the old one is killed. The result is that for a while two components are running, but the group can respond to incoming requests at all times.

An important issue in a distributed architecture is the ability to handle site failures or just single process failures. By using a replicated data technique and groups, a failure can be handled easily. Different process members of a group can run on different machines. When a crash is detected, the remaining processes can jointly restore the previous state of the system. Another important feature provided by groups is the ability to deal with any number of processes. This allows us to modify the dimension of the system dynamically, for instance we can increase or decrease the number of running processes in order to maintain a certain level of performance.

In the next section we review some related languages. In section 3, we present FLAME's constructs for processes and groups in an object oriented environment. To demonstrate the power of FLAME, a complete example of a replicated, fault-tolerant directory service will be given in section 4. Section 5 will conclude the paper and discuss some open issues.

2 Related work

A popular model adopted in many programming languages is that a program contains several independent threads of control. That is, a program consists of several classical sequential processes which may execute concurrently. A first example is CSP [Hoare78], where processes are used to implement in a different way traditional "main" programs. Processes are highly coupled: their lifetimes are interconnected because everything is defined statically and traditional (static) scope rules apply. The communication model requires that the sender knows the identity of the receiver and vice versa. If the two partners agree, the communication, i.e. data transfer, is performed.

Languages like Ada [Ada80], or SR [Andrews82], try to define different threads as more independent units of a single process. In SR a program is defined as a collection of resources, which interact by means of operations. Each resource is composed of two parts, an interface and a body. The interface is a collection of declarations of components, like types, variables and operations. Operations declared in the interface are callable by external processes, i.e. resources. When a process wants to use an operation provided by another resource, it explicitly imports that resource into its declarative part. This means that a communication is asymmetrical: the caller names explicitly the callee that does not know the caller. The communication model is defined as message exchanges, but shared memory is also allowed inside a single resource. When a process is created, an access to that object is returned and assigned to a variable. This gives the creator the capability to access the process. It is used, for example, to send messages. The receiver can accept communication in Ada style, i.e. accept any among a set of incoming messages, or can specify by using guards and scheduling expressions an order of preferences. Such a model considers each resource as independent and potentially executable on a different machine. The latest version of the language[Andrews88] allows the programmer to specify the machine on which a newly-created process can execute and also implements different operations of a resource as different threads.

Models like those provided by SR are sometimes called "object-based", because each component, i.e. resource, can be viewed as an object, but they do not have all the characteristics of an object-oriented language. That is, components do not define types, instead they can define types in the interface, and full inheritance, another fundamental aspect of object orientation, is not supported. The latest version of SR defines a form of inheritance: a resource can inherit the interface of another one. This allows the definition of classes of objects.

Languages like SR are useful for implementing concurrent activities, but they do not pay attention to the environment in which the system will be executed. By providing a language with particular features for distributed architectures, the different problems that arise from a distributed architecture can be handled. For example, a process can run on any machine or it can move to another machine; a machine can crash and part of a system crashes with it. Languages Argus [Liskov88], NIL [Strom85] and Emerald [Black87] have been designed to pay attention to these problems.

Argus is designed for programs that maintain online data for long periods of time. These systems require data consistency in spite of failures, they may need to be reconfigured dynamically and programmers may need to put information and processes at a particular node. The basic entity of an Argus program is a guardian. A guardian encapsulates one or more resources accessible by calling special guardian procedures called handlers. Each guardian reside at a single node of the network, although it can change its node of residence. Several guardians can reside at the same node. A guardian is resilient to the crash of its host node. It is composed of stable and volatile objects: stable objects are written periodically to a stable storage device; when a crash occurs, the current consistent state can be restored from those objects. In Argus, any action is an atomic transaction: if a failure occurs in the middle of an action, it is possible to restore the state and rerun the last action.

A NIL system is defined as a dynamically evolving network of loosely coupled processes, communicating by asynchronous message passing. Processes are the single modular building block, supporting both concurrency and data abstraction. There is no form of shared data, communication is performed by ownership transfer. To send an object means to send a pointer; the receiving process becomes the new owner of that object. The sender loses the capability to access the object sent. An interesting feature provided by NIL is the concept of typestate. Each operation available for a type has associated pre- and post conditions. This ensures security: it is possible to detect and raise exceptions. The system cannot reach an unknown state.

Emerald is the closest language to FLAME. It defines objects as basic building blocks. Any object has an identity, data, a set of private and public operations and an optional thread which operates in parallel with invocations of the object's operations. The interface of an object is defined by an abstract data type that defines the set of operations supported, their signatures and their semantics. Each object belongs to a node, but it is a unit of mobility, that is, any object can be moved to another node in the network. Emerald exploits this possibility to perform parameter passing: when a remote invocation is done, the referenced object is moved to the node of the invokee. Such a "call by move" is intended to mirror the traditional call by reference in a distributed environment.

An object-oriented approach is very important in a distributed environment. An object hides its data, implementation and execution. This makes any object a perfect unit of distribution by definition. Actually, there are many attempts to support object-oriented distributed programming, but they can be characterized as multithreaded rather than distributed. Furthermore, there are many attempts to use object-based languages for object-oriented programming, e.g. [Booch87] which uses Ada. Examples of new object-oriented concurrent languages or systems are concurrent C++ [Gehani88] and PRESTO [Bershad88]. Concurrent C++ is Concurrent C with interfaces built in C++, this allows to hide the real processes from the user. PRESTO provides a C++ library and a runtime system that allows to write parallel programs in a multiprocessor environment. PRESTO defines a thread class that allows to execute any regular class, or, better, any operation of a regular class as a separate thread.

More recent projects that share our goal of supporting the writing
of distributed fault-tolerant programs are Arjuna[Shrivastava88], Avalon/C++[Detlefs88], and Aeolus[LeBlanc85]. These are all based on the notions of atomic actions and transactions, which are not part of FLAME.

All languages discussed above are concerned with systems built of independent processes. So far, concepts like groups of processes and broadcast facility have been considered in operating systems[Cheriton85], or in a limited way at the language level[Gehani84]. Gehani defines BSP, Broadcasting Sequential Processes, as a set of primitives to send and to reply to broadcast messages, but BSP does not emphasize the concept of a group. Systems like ISIS[Isis89], provide low level commands to define and handle process groups. We believe that the next step to build a new generation of languages is to provide group facilities in an object-oriented environment. This is crucial to provide programmers a new methodology and a new environment for developing more dependable and less error prone open, distributed, software.

3 Constructs for managing processes and groups

FLAME is based on C++[Stroustrup87]. Instead of designing a completely new language, we have decided to add our distributed programming constructs to complement the sequential C++. We are not aiming to maintain compatibility with C++ but simply use it as a starting point. Our current implementation uses ISIS[Isis89] as a runtime system. In this section, we present the process management constructs of FLAME.

3.1 Process definition

Processes are the basic building blocks for writing a distributed FLAME program. A FLAME process is a class with its own thread of control. Syntactically, we use the keyword "process" instead of "class". A process defined this way can just respond to incoming function calls. In this case there are no logical differences between a passive object, i.e. C++ style, and an active object: the object provides some features and external objects use them. What makes the FLAME process different from a C++ object, however, is that a function of the FLAME process executes in its own address space, which is distinct from the caller's. Each call also executes as a new thread. A function call thread is not pre-empted by the system but may be suspended as a result of some explicit action by the programmer. This makes it possible for different threads to be logically active simultaneously. Any inter-thread concurrency control is the responsibility of the programmer.

In addition to a thread devoted to each incoming call, a process can also have its own thread, independent of the outside world. A special function, called Body, can be defined in the private part of the process declaration, to define those activities. The form of a process declaration is the following:

```
process TypeName {
  // private part: object and function declarations
  [ Body( FormalParameterDeclaration ); ]
public:

  // The constructor:
  TypeName( FormalParameterDeclaration );
  // public part: object and function declarations
};
```

When an object of type process is created, the constructor initializes the new process and then the function Body, if any, is called. The Body function is like all the other functions except that it is implicitly called after process initialization. Another difference is that it never returns: it can stay alive along with the process, or it terminates when the execution of its code terminates. But the process stays alive also if the body terminates. A process will stay alive until it explicitly asks to terminate calling exit(), or the creator kills it.

Let's see an example. Throughout this section, we will present a first version of a phone directory service system. We want to design a process that maintains a list of phone numbers. Each entry is defined as follow:

```
struct PhoneEntry {
  char Name[20];
  char Number[12];
};
```

The system provides facilities to insert and delete an entry and, retrieve a number. A declaration for this process can be:

```
process SinglePhoneServer {
  // an array to store entries:
  PhoneEntry PhoneList[MAX_NUMBERS];
  int NumberOfEntries;
public:
  PhoneServer() { NumberOfEntries=0; };
  void AddNumber(char* name, char* number);
  char* FindNumber(char* name);
  int DelNumber(char* name);
};
```

The implementation of each function can be written in regular C++ and is not shown here. A complete implementation of a more sophisticated phone server system is given in Section 4.

3.2 Processes and groups

As discussed before, a group provides an interface between processes that are members of the group and the outside world. It should also provide some added facilities to take advantage of this new situation, i.e. it is possible to control the system by monitoring the group. A process group provides its members with some standard features; the members may extend this set by supplying group-specific features. The private part of a FLAME process declaration may contain a section to describe the group features. This section is introduced by the keyword "group:" and contains object and function declarations. The syntax is shown below:

```
process TypeName {
  // private part: object and function declarations
  [ Body( FormalParameterDeclaration ); ]
[ group:
  // group part: object and function declarations ]
public:
  // The constructor:
  TypeName( FormalParameterDeclaration );
  // public part: object and function declarations
};
```

Any declarations included in the group part can be accessed by the group members only. The objects declared in this section form the "group state" and are known by all group members. All members of a group execute the same code and update their own copy of the group state.

The FLAME runtime system maintains a group manager for each group. The group manager is a special, replicated, process object that holds the group description and provides the group with general features. For example, when a new member joins the group, the group manager contacts one of the existing members for a copy of the group state and sends it to the new member.

The only function allowed in this group section is a special function that the programmer can customize in order to describe what should be done to handle special situations affecting the group. This function, called GroupChange, is called by the group manager any time a member joins or leaves the group. With this function the programmer can, for instance, define what has to be done when a member process crashes.

The procedure GroupChange can be viewed as a sort of exception handler. Some languages (i.e. Ada) allow the user to provide special code to be executed automatically by the runtime system when a special situation occurs, for example, when the program attempts to execute illegal operations such as division by zero. In our case, the runtime system is able to detect changes to the group; what is defined in the group section is used to handle this special situation. For example, when the exception "member leaves the group" is detected, procedure GroupChange is executed before the processes are allowed to continue their normal activities. Or when an exception of type "member joins the group" occurs, the automatic exception handler provided by the runtime system sends a copy of the group state to the new member, then GroupChange is executed. Our decision to keep the group-related code in a separate section is explained by the above remarks: it should be executed only by the group manager, that is, the runtime system, and only when something special happens external to the process.

Group managers are objects of built-in process type Group. The interface of this class is:

```
process Group {
  // private declarations
public:
  int NClient();        // number of clients
  int NMember();        // number of members
  void* NewMember();    // new member address if any
  void* Clients(int);   // id of specified client
  void* Members(int);   // id of specified member
  void Deliver(...);    // collected replies
};
```

Let's go back to the PhoneServer process. We can build a replicated phone directory by designing a group of processes to manage the phone directory. We can write a new version of PhoneServer with a new interface. New public functions should be designed to take advantage of the group. The declaration of this new process can be:

```
process PhoneServer {
  PhoneEntry PhoneList[MAX_NUMBERS];
  int NumberOfEntries;
  void AddNumber(char* name, char* number);
  char* FindNumber(char* name);
  int DelNumber(char* name);
  Group PhoneDirectory;
group: // visible by group members only
  struct State {
    PhoneServer* his_addr;
    int his_index;
  };
  State Server[MAX_SERVER];
  void GroupChange(int WhatChange);
public:
  PhoneServer();
  void Add (char* name, char* number);
  char* Lookup (char* name);
  void Del (char* name);
};
```

Inside the group section, a list of all servers available is defined; when a new process joins the group, Server is updated by the process group PhoneDirectory. The function GroupChange is provided to handle any changes inside the group. The parameter WhatChange tells the process which kind of change occurred: a failure or a new member joined the group. In this version of PhoneServer, we have duplicated all the declarations we had in the previous version. In the next section, we discuss the inheritance mechanism which allows us to derive PhoneServer from SinglePhoneServer.

3.3 Inheritance

We can combine the C++ inheritance mechanism with FLAME processes. Below, process B is derived from a previously-defined process A:

```
process B : public A { ... };
```

The resulting process A will have two bodies, those of A and B, and as public functions the union of the public functions of A and the functions defined in B. A public function declared in A may be redeclared in B, in which case the first declaration will be hidden by the second one. When an object of type B is created, the constructors of the two processes are executed, first A then B. After initialization, the body of A is called and then the body of B. If the process A is not declared public, all the public functions declared in A become private in B. That is, they become regular passive functions that any thread inside B can call. In this case, only the body and GroupChange are threads.

Let's go back to the phone service example. The PhoneServer process defined in the previous section can be rewritten in the following way:

```
process PhoneServer : SinglePhoneServer {
  Group PhoneDirectory;
group:
```

```
struct State {
  PhoneServer* his_addr;
  int his_index;
};
State Server[MAX_SERVER];
void GroupChange(int WhatChange);
public:
  PhoneServer();
  void Add (char* name, char* number);
  char* Lookup (char* name);
  void Del (char* name);
};
```

By using inheritance, it is possible to let a process join different groups. If processes A and B of the previous example have a group declaration, the resulting object will belong to two different groups. The function GroupChange and the objects defining the group state are overloaded, that is, each group is able to call the proper GroupChange function and transfer the proper state. The only limitation to the inheritance mechanism is that a regular class cannot be derived from a process class: we cannot create a passive object from an active one. But a process can inherit a class as private.

3.4 Process objects

We have now seen the basic object types in FLAME. In this section, we show how a process object is declared, created, and used. Later, we will show how processes are used to build a *system*. First, an object has to be declared. The declaration has the usual form:

```
ProcessTypeName ObjectId;
```

A declaration creates an access to a process of a particular type; before using it we must initialize it as described below. An object can be initialized, or assigned if already initialized, with the operators *create* and *lookup*. Here are the possible forms:

```
ObjectId = create "ObjectName";
ObjectId = create;
ObjectId = lookup "ObjectName";
```

The create operator creates a new process of the type specified in the declaration and returns an access to that object. Process identifiers have a global scope and can be passed from one process to another. If ObjectName is specified, this becomes the name of the process, otherwise the process is anonymous. The only way to access an anonymous process is through a group. That is, the new process must join a group before it can receive messages from other processes. The lookup operator does not create a new process, it just looks up an existing process and returns the address of that process or a NULL address. The lookup operator is the only way to grant access to a process. After initialization, ObjectId can be used as any other object, in particular it can be passed as parameter and it is possible to send messages to it. For processes of type Group, the special operator join is provided. The possible forms are the following:

```
ObjectId = join "GroupName";
ObjectId = join;
```

The first form looks up a process group with the given name. If that group does not exist, a new one is created. The second case, *join* without argument, means to look up any group with members of the same type as the process executing the statement. After the execution of a *join*, the process becomes a member of the joined group. The operators *create* and *lookup* are also valid for processes of type Group in the following forms:

```
ObjectId = create "GroupName";
ObjectId = lookup "GroupName";
```

That is, GroupName must be provided.

An example of *join* can be in our PhoneServer process. The constructor can be written this way:

```
process PhoneServer {
  ...
  Group PhoneDirectory;
  ...
public:
  PhoneServer()
  { NumberOfEntries=0;
    PhoneDirectory=join "PhoneService"; };
  ...
};
```

When a process of type PhoneServer is created, it joins a group called PhoneService. The object PhoneDirectory holds the address of this group.

3.5 Process communication

Once access to a process is obtained using the operators *create*, *lookup*, or *join*, a message can be sent to that object by using the usual notation:

```
ObjectId.Procedure(Arguments);
```

There are no syntactic differences between a local call and a remote procedure call. The compiler will trap a remote call and translate it into a proper format. Going back to the PhoneServer example, a client can execute the following code:

```
PhoneServer P;
char* number;
...
P = lookup;
...
number = P.Lookup("john");
```

If the client wants to send a broadcast message to the group PhoneService, the code will be modified in this way:

```
Group G;
char* number;
...
G = lookup "PhoneService";
...
G.Deliver("Lookup",1,number,"john");
```

The first argument of a Deliver call is the name of the function to which the message should be delivered; the second one is the number of replies wanted; the third is a pointer to an area where the returned results will be stored. The rest of the arguments will be passed on to the function to the function being called. The programmer is responsible for providing an area large enough to collect the incoming replies. For example, if n replies are wanted, an array of n elements should be provided. All arguments are passed by value. The number of replies can be replaced by the keywords ALL or MAJORITY.

Parameter passing is effectively by value. If the parameter is a pointer, the value pointed by it is copied across. If a pointer result is expected, the value is copied to a temporary area and a pointer to it is returned. Pointers themselves may not be passed across processes because processes have distinct address spaces.

The function Lookup of all the members in group G is called. The last argument is the number replies requested by the caller; 1 is the default value. All other arguments are passed as parameters to the function being called. The number of replies can be replaced by the keywords ALL or MAJORITY. The programmer must provide an object to collect the incoming replies. For example, if n replies are wanted, an array of n elements should be provided. All arguments are passed by value.

3.6 System structure

A typical system is composed of class declarations, process declarations and a driver. The driver is a "main" process in C++ style, designed to be the supervisor of the system. It can be viewed as the interface between the system and the user. Logically, it is a process like any other except that it does not define a type.

Each process class will be compiled in a different file. This allows the user to create objects by running the associated files. In this case, the driver can be omitted: the control of the system is done directly by the user. He can run processes on different machines or kill them as any other program, and so on.

System definitions can be contained in a single file or can be split into different files, each one containing a declaration of a process. The links will occur at run time; only the type definitions need to be provided at compile time.

4   An example: phone directory service

In this section, we will present a complete, sophisticated phone directory service to maintain a list of phone numbers in FLAME. We will define a group of servers, called PhoneService. The list is partitioned among the members, each of which maintains a portion of the list. The number of servers is not known and may vary at runtime. Therefore, the details of partitioning can only be determined at runtime. We also want the service to be fault-tolerant in the sense that the failure of any single member of the group should not cause any data or service to be lost. Therefore, in addition to partitioning the list, we also replicate each partition so that each partition is maintained by two members of the group.[1] The service must be capable of repartitioning the data among the members in the case that a member dies or a new member joins the group.

Each entry of the list is defined as a name-number pair:

```
struct PhoneEntry {
    char Name[20];
    char Number[12];
```

---

[1] A discussion of data replication, partitioning and their relationship may be found in [Jazayeri88].

```
};
```

Let's define process PhoneServer as a member of the group PhoneService:

```
process PhoneServer {
    PhoneEntry PhoneList[MAX_NUMBERS];
    int NumberOfEntries;
    int MyIndex;
    int NServers;
    void AddNumber(char* name, char* number) {
        strcpy (PhoneList[NumberOfEntries].Name,
                name);
        strcpy (PhoneList[NumberOfEntries].Number,
                number);
        NumberOfEntries++;
    };
    char* FindNumber(char* name) {
        for (i=0; i<NumberOfEntries; i++){
            if (strcmp(name, PhoneList[i].Name) == 0)
                //found it
                return PhoneList[i].Number;
        }
        return 0;
    };
    int DelNumber(char* name) {
        for (i=0; i<NumberOfEntries; i++) {
            if (strcmp(name, PhoneList[i].Name) == 0) {
                //found it
                // shift all entries up by one
                // starting with entry i+1 to end
                for (j=i; j<NumberOfEntries; j++){
                    strcpy(PhoneList[j].Name,
                            PhoneList[j+1].Name);
                    strcpy(PhoneList[j].Number,
                            PhoneList[j+1].Number);
                }
                --NumberOfEntries;
                return TRUE;
            }
        }
        return FALSE;
    };
    int HashNumber(char* name) {
        int i = 0;
        int h = 0;
        while (name[i] != NULL) {
            h+= (int)name[i];
            i++;
        }
        return h;
    };
    Group PhoneDirectory;
group:
    struct State {
        PhoneServer* his_addr;
        int his_index;
    };
    State Server[MAX_SERVER];
    void GroupChange(int WhatChange);
public:
    PhoneServer() {
```

```
  MyIndex=0; NumberOfEntries=0;
  PhoneDirectory=join "PhoneService";
};
void Add (char* name, char* number);
char* Lookup (char* name);
void Del (char* name);
PhoneEntry GetAll() { reply PhoneList; };
};
```

The array Server defines the state of the group, it will be passed to any new member who joins the group. Function GroupChange will be discussed later. Inside the constructor, the process joins the group called PhoneService. A definition for function Add can be the following:

```
void PhoneServer::Add (char* name, char* number) {
  int master;
//store the number only if you are
//the master or the backup copy
  master= HashNumber(name) % NServers + 1;
  if (master == MyIndex || (master+1) == MyIndex)
    AddNumber(name, number);
  if (master == NServers && MyIndex == 1)
    AddNumber(name, number);
  reply;
}
```

Each member of the group has a unique index from 1 to number of members. To decide who has to store an entry, we compute a hash value of the name modulo the number of members. The resulting number is the index of the member that takes care of that entry. We call this process Master. The member with the next index holds the backup copy for that entry. To understand the code, remember that each process executes the same code. The function Lookup can be implemented in this way:

```
char* PhoneServer::Lookup (char* name) {
  int i=0;
  char* number;
  int master;
  master= HashNumber(name) % NServers + 1;
  if (master == MyIndex) number=FindNumber(name);
  if (number)
    reply number;
  else
    reply;
}
```

Each member of the group checks whether or not it is the master for the name requested. If not, a null reply is sent. For better performance, we could have the backup process also reply with its entry: the callee can accept the faster reply and ignore the second one.

The code for the last public function is:

```
void PhoneServer::Del (char* name) {
  int master;
  master= HashNumber(name) % NServers + 1;
  if (master == MyIndex || (master+1) == MyIndex)
    DelNumber(name);
  if (master == NServers && MyIndex == 1)
    DelNumber(name);
  reply;
}
```

We still use the notion of master to know if the information being deleted belongs to the process.

The most interesting function is GroupChange. It is called, by the group, any time there is a member that joins or leaves the group. Here is the code:

```
void PhoneServer::GroupChange(int WhatChange) {
  int OldIndex= MyIndex;;
  int OldNServers=NServers;
  int OldMaster, Master;
  int CrashIndex;

  // update the group state and compute a
  // new MyIndex if necessary
  NServers = PhoneDirectory.NMember();
  if (WhatChange == 1) {
    // a new process joined the group
    Server[NServers-1].his_addr=(PhoneServer*)
        PhoneDirectory.Members(NServers-1);
    Server[NServers-1].his_index=NServers;
    if (MyIndex==0) {
      // I'm the new process with the last index
      MyIndex=NServers;
      cout << form("\nNew Server: MyIndex= %d,
              NServers= %d", MyIndex, NServers);
    }
  }
  else  // a process left the group
    i=0;
  while (Server[i].his_addr ==
          PhoneDirectory.Members(i)) i++;
  CrashIndex=Server[i].his_index;
  while (i<NServers) {
    Server[i].his_addr=Server[i+1].his_addr;
    // note: his_index doesn't change
    if(Server[i].his_addr == this) {
      MyIndex=i+1;
      cout << form("\nGroupChange: old_index= %d,
                my_index= %d, NServers= %d",
                OldIndex, MyIndex, NServers);
    }
    i++;
  }
}

// redistribute information among members
if (NServers != 1) {
  for (i=0; i<NumberOfEntries; i++){
    OldMaster= HashNumber(PhoneList[i].Name)
            % OldNServers + 1;
    Master= HashNumber(PhoneaList[i].Name)
            % NServers + 1;
    if (OldMaster == OldIndex){
      // send number and delete
      PhoneDirectory.Deliver("Add",0,,
        PhoneList[i].Name, PhoneList[i].Number);
    }
    if (OldMaster == CrashIndex){
      // send number and delete
      PhoneDirectory.Deliver("Add",0,,
        PhoneList[i].Name, PhoneList[i].Number);
    }
  }
}
```

```
      NumberOfEntries=0;
    }
  }
```

The function is divided into two parts. The first one updates the state, i.e. Server. We need information stored in Server because if a crash happens, we need to compute the index of the crashed process. This allows any process to decide what information it has to send to other members. This is what happens in the second part of the function: each process sends the entries of which it was the master or, if the process was the backup for the failed process, all entries. In any case, all the entries have to be distributed again because their master number has changed.

The phone directory system is completed by a client process that uses the features provided by group PhoneService. Process PhoneClient does not have any public functions, it just has a body that provides an interface between the user and PhoneService. Here is the code:

```
process PhoneClient {
 char* ReplyNumber;
 int ReplyNEntries[MAX_SERVERS];
 PhoneEntry ReplyPhoneList[MAX_SERVERS][MAX_NUMBERS];

 printlist() {
   for (server_no=0; server_no<MAX_SERVERS;
        server_no++)
     for (i=0; i<MAX_NUMBERS; i++)
       if (ReplyPhoneList[server_no][i].Name)
         cout << form("%2d: %20s : %10s\n",
              server_no+1,
              ReplyPhoneList[server_no][i].Name,
              ReplyPhoneList[server_no][i].Number);
 }

 Body () {
   int MyIndex;
   char Name[20],
        Number[10],
        Action;
   Group PhoneDirectory;

   PhoneDirectory = Lookup "PhoneService";
   if (PhoneDirectory == NULL) {
     cout << form(
     "\nSorry! Phone service is not available\n");
     exit(0); // ABORT;
   }

   // Loop asking queries
   cout << form(
   "Yes? {a,l,d,p} [Name [Number]] (^D to quit)\n");
   while (scanf(" %c", &Action) != EOF) {
     switch (Action) {
       case 'a': //add entry
         cin >> Name >> Number;
         PhoneDirectory.Deliver
              ("Add", 0,, Name, Number);
         break;
       case 'l': //lookup entry
         cin >> Name;
         PhoneDirectory.Deliver
              ("Lookup", 1, ReplyNumber, Name);
         if (length(ReplyNumber)>0)
           cout << form(" %20s : %10s\n",
                Name, ReplyNumber);
         else
           cout << form(
           " %20s : ***NOT FOUND***\n", Name);
         break;
       case 'd': //delete entry
         cin >> Name;
         PhoneDirectory.Deliver ("Del", 0, ,Name);
         break;
       case 'p': //print the list
         PhoneDirectory.Deliver
              ("GetAll",ALL,ReplyPhoneList);
         printlist();
         break;
       default:
         cout<<form("Invalid command, try again\n");
         break;
     }
     cout << form(
     "Yes?{a,l,d,p}[Name [Number]](^d to quit)\n");
   }
   cout << form("Bye.\n");
   exit(0); // ABORT;
 }

 public:
   PhoneClient() {};
};
```

With the current implementation of FLAME, we can compile these two processes and obtain two executable files that we can run. It is possible to run and kill processes to change the configuration of the system, and so on. Better would be to be able to support a special process main that helps the user to handle the system. Here is an example:

```
main () {
  PhoneServer ProcessPointer[5];
  char Action;
  int Index=0;
  for (int i=1; ;i++) {
    cout << form("%d => ", i); cin >> Action;
    switch (Action) {
    case 'a': // add process server
      if(index < 5) {
        // create an anonymous process
        ProcessPointer[index] = create;
        Index++;
      } else cout << form(
           "Sorry. Too many processes. ");
      break;
    case 'd': //delete process
      Index--;
      delete ProcessPointer[Index];
      break;
    case 'q':
      exit(0);
      break;
    default:
```

```
      cout<<form("%c:Invalid command, try again\n",
                 Action);
      break;
    }
  }
}
```

We are currently investigating the desirability of such a facility. Some comments on this issue are given in the next section.

5 Conclusions and future work

While FLAME has made some applications easier to write, its use has also shown some of its limitations. Currently, FLAME requires group members to know that they belong to a group. But it is also important to deal with groups of processes that do not know that they belong to a group and are gathered into a group dynamically. A good example is the operators *lookup* and *join* introduced above. They can really be viewed as group operators. That is, the statement:

```
PhoneDirectory = lookup "PhoneService";
```

really means: lookup inside the group of groups if there is a group called PhoneService.

The possibility of collecting processes can be useful for building new systems from existing processes, or reconfiguring old systems. For example, the system presented in the previous section can be used to create a PhoneServer group for each letter of the alphabet. It requires the ability to create a new process group that at runtime starts the proper number of processes and delivers incoming messages to them.

Using these concepts we can define a new main for the phone service system:

```
main () {
  Group Service;
  PhoneServer ProcessPointer;
  char Action;
  char Machine[20];
  int index;
  for (int i=1; ;i++) {
    cout << form("%d => ", i); cin >> Action;
    switch (Action) {
    case 'a': // add process server
        cout << form("On what machine? ");
        cin >> Machine;
        if (Machine[0] == '*')
          ProcessPointer = create;
        else
          ProcessPointer = create on Machine;
        Service.ADD(ProcessPointer);
        break;
      case 'd': //delete process
        // first show all processes in the group
        Service.PRINTLIST();
        cout << form("What process? ");
        cin >> index;
        Service.DEL(index);
        break;
      case 'q':
        exit(0);
```

```
        break;
      default:
        cout<<form(
          "%c:Invalid command,try again\n",Action);
        break;
    }
  }
}
```

where all processes are collected into a new group that helps the user to control the system. We can imagine a process group that provides feature like ADD, DEL and PRINTLIST to handle the new situation. Of course, the usual functions provided by groups are still available. We are currently working on defining possible constructs to handle groups of processes with no embedded knowledge of group membership.

In conclusion, we believe that the group construct is a fundamental one for programming with processes. We have presented our current ideas on how this feature is combined with object orientation in the FLAME language. An interesting extension worth pursuing is that of heterogeneous process groups. In this paper, we have only considered process groups with identical members. It is possible to generalize the notion to heterogeneous member processes. Of course, members must all share a common property—that of being able to be group members. This question is related to the classic object-oriented typing issues, e.g. the ability to have a stack of geometric objects such as lines, points, triangles, etc.

References

[Ada80] *Reference manual for the Ada programming language* (July 1980). United States Department of Defense.

[Andrews82] G. R. Andrews. The distributed programming language SR—mechanisms, design and implementation. *Software—Practice and Experience*, **12**:719–53 (1982).

[Andrews88] G. R. Andrews, R. A. Olsson, M. Coffin, I. Elshoff, K. Nilsen, T. Purdin, and G. Townsend. An overview of the SR language and its implementation. *ACM Transactions on Programming Languages and Systems*, **10**(1):51–86 (January 1988).

[Bershad88] B. N. Bershad, E. D. Lazowska, and H. M. Levy. PRESTO: a system for object-oriented parallel programming. *Software—Practice and Experience*, **18**(8):713–32 (August 1988).

[Black87] A. Black, N. Hutchinson, E. Jul, H. Levy, and L. Carter. Distribution and abstract types in Emerald. *IEEE Transactions on Software Engineering*, **SE–13**(1):65–76 (January 1987).

[Booch87] G. Booch. *Software Components with Ada—Structures, Tools, and Subsystems*, The Benjamin/Cummings Series in Ada and Software Engineering (1987). The Benjamin/Cummings Publishing Company, Incorporated.

[Cheriton85] D. R. Cheriton and W. Zwaenepoel. Distributed process groups in the V kernel. *ACM Transactions on Computer Systems*, **3**(2):77–107 (May 1985).

[Detlefs88]   D. L. Detlefs, M. Herlihy, and J. Wing. Inheritance of synchronization and recovery properties in Avalon/C++. *IEEE Computer*, **21**(12):57–69 (December 1988).

[Gehani84]   N. H. Gehani. Broadcasting sequential processes (BSP). *IEEE Transactions on Software Engineering*, **10**(4):343–51 (July 1984).

[Gehani88]   N. Gehani and W. D. Roome. *The Concurrent C Programming Language* (1988). Silicon Press, 25 Beverly Rd, Summit, NJ 07901.

[Hoare78]   C. A. R. Hoare. Communicating sequential processes. *Communications of the ACM*, **21**(8):666–77 (August 1978).

[Isis89]   K. Birman, R. Cooper, T. Joseph, K. Kane, and F. Schmuck. *The ISIS System Manual, Version 1.1* (8 June 1989). Cornell University.

[Jazayeri88]   M. Jazayeri. Distributed software design techniques. Technical report HPL–DSD–88–40 (14 December 1988). Distributed Systems Department, Hewlett-Packard Laboratories.

[Jazayeri89]   M. Jazayeri. Objects for distributed systems. *ACM SIGPLAN Workshop on Object-based Concurrent Programming* (San Diego, September 26-27, 1989). Published as G. Agha, P. Wegner, and A. Yonezawa, editors, *SIGPLAN Notices*, **24**(4):117–19 (April 1989).

[LeBlanc85]   R. J. LeBlanc and C. T. Wilkes. Systems programming with objects and actions. *5th International Conference on Distributed Computing Systems* (Denver), pages 132–9 (May 1985).

[Liskov88]   B. Liskov. Distributed programming in Argus. *Communications of the ACM*, **31**(3):300–12 (March 1988).

[Shrivastava88]   S.K. Shrivastava, G. N. Dixon, F. Hedayati, G. D. Parrington, and S. M. Wheater. A technical overview of Arjuna: a system for reliable distributed computing. *IT–88 Conference Pub.* (Swansea (U.K.)), pages 601–5 (July 1988).

[Strom85]   R. Strom and S. Yemini. The NIL distributed systems programming language: a status report. *SIGPLAN Notices*, **20**(5):36–44 (May 1985).

[Stroustrup87]   B. Stroustrup. *The C++ Programming Language* (1987). Addison-Wesley, Reading, Mass. & London.

[Wilkes88]   J. Wilkes. Maxwell—an overview. Technical report HPL–DSD–88–37rev1 (22 December 1988). Distributed Systems Department, Hewlett-Packard Laboratories.

EXPERIENCE WITH DISTRIBUTED PROGRAMMING IN ORCA

Henri E. Bal *   *M. Frans Kaashoek*   *Andrew S. Tanenbaum*

Dept. of Mathematics and Computer Science
Vrije Universiteit
Amsterdam, The Netherlands

ABSTRACT

Orca is a language for programming parallel applications on distributed computing systems. Although processors in such systems communicate only through message passing and not through shared memory, Orca provides a communication model based on logically shared data. Programmers can define abstract data types and create instances (objects) of these types, which may be shared among processes. All operations on shared objects are executed atomically. Orca's shared objects are implemented by replicating them in the local memories of the processors. Read operations use the local copies of the object, without doing any interprocess communication. Write operations update all copies using an efficient reliable broadcast protocol.

In this paper, we briefly describe the language and its implementation and then report on our experiences in using Orca for three parallel applications: the Traveling Salesman Problem, the All-pairs Shortest Paths problem, and Successive Overrelaxation. These applications have different needs for shared data: TSP greatly benefits from the support for shared data; ASP benefits from the use of broadcast communication, even though it is hidden in the implementation; SOR merely requires point-to-point communication, but still can be implemented in the language by simulating message passing. We discuss how these applications are programmed in Orca and we give the most interesting portions of the Orca code. Also, we include performance measurements for these programs on a distributed system consisting of 10 MC68020s connected by an Ethernet. These measurements show that significant speedups are obtained for all three programs.

1. INTRODUCTION

Orca is a new programming language intended for implementing parallel applications on loosely-coupled distributed systems. Unlike the majority of other languages in this category [7], Orca supports a communication model based on shared data. We have taken this decision because we feel that, for many applications, it simplifies programming. Since distributed systems lack shared memory, however, this sharing of data is logical rather than physical.

Two important issues arise out of this decision: how to *implement* logically shared data efficiently and how to *use* it. The first issue has been addressed in several other publications [8, 5, 4]. The key ideas in an efficient distributed implementation of Orca are *replication* of shared data and the use of a highly efficient *broadcast protocol* for updating copies of shared data.

In this paper, we will focus on our experiences in using Orca. Thus far, Orca has been used for a number of small to medium size applications. Small applications include: matrix multiplication, prime number generation, sorting, the All-pairs Shortest Paths problem, the Traveling Salesman Problem, alpha-beta search, Fast Fourier Transformation, and Successive Overrelaxation. As a somewhat larger application, we have implemented a distributed chess problem solver. Some of these applications could just as easily have been written in a language providing only message passing and no shared data. Others, however, greatly benefit from the support of logically shared data. The chess problem solver, for example, uses several shared data structures, such as a transposition table and a killer table [12].

Below, we will look at three parallel applications with different needs for shared data. The first application, the Traveling Salesman Problem, is a good example demonstrating the usefulness of logically shared data. Although the algorithm we use can be (and has been) implemented with message passing, such an implementation is much more complicated and has an inferior performance.

The second application, the All-pairs Shortest Paths (ASP) problem, basically requires broadcast messages for efficiency. ASP could be implemented efficiently in a message-passing language that supports broadcasting. The Orca implementation of ASP is rather elegant, since the physical broadcasting is hidden in the implementation of the language; it is not visible to the programmer. In addition to this higher-level of abstraction, the performance is at least as good as with explicit one-to-many message passing.

The third and last application we discuss is Successive Overrelaxation (SOR). This application merely needs point-to-point message passing. We include this application to show how message-passing can be implemented in Orca.

The outline of the rest of the paper is as follows. In Section 2, we will present a short description of Orca, together with its underlying model. We will also briefly describe the current implementations of the language. In Sections 3 to 5 we will discuss the three applications mentioned above. For each application, we will give the most interesting portions of the Orca program. In addition, we will show the speedup of each program, to give an idea of the performance of parallel Orca programs. The implementation used for these measurements runs on an Ethernet-based distributed system. Finally, in Section 6, we will present some conclusions.

2. THE ORCA PROGRAMMING LANGUAGE

In this section we will give a concise introduction to Orca. A much more thorough description can be found in [4]. We will first describe Orca's underlying model, called the *shared data-object model*. Next, we will look at the most important aspects of the language design. We will conclude with a brief description of the language implementation.

* This research was supported in part by the Netherlands organization for scientific research (N.W.O.) under grant 125-30-10.

2.1. The shared data-object model

The shared data-object model provides the programmer with logically shared data. The entities shared in our model are determined by the programmer. (This is in contrast with Kai Li's Shared Virtual Memory [22], which only allows fixed-size pages to be shared.) In our model, shared data are encapsulated in *data-objects**, which are variables of user-defined abstract data types. An abstract data type has two parts:

- A specification of the operations that can be applied to objects of this type.
- The implementation, consisting of declarations for the local variables of the object and code implementing the operations.

Instances (objects) of an abstract data type can be created dynamically. Each object contains the variables defined in the implementation part. These objects can be shared among multiple processes, typically running on different machines. Each process can apply operations to the object, which are listed in the specification part of the abstract type. In this way, the object becomes a communication channel between the processes that share it.

The shared data-object model uses two important principles related to operations on objects:

1. All operations on a given object are executed *atomically* (i.e., *indivisibly*). To be precise, the model guarantees *serializability* [13] of operation invocations: if two operations are applied simultaneously to the same data-object, then the result is as if one of them is executed before the other; the order of invocation, however, is nondeterministic.

2. All operations apply to *single* objects, so an operation invocation can modify at most one object. Making *sequences* of operations on different objects indivisible is the responsibility of the programmer.

These two principles make the model easy to understand and efficient. Moreover, in our experience, they provide sufficient support for many medium to large grained parallel applications. Distributed applications like banking and airline reservation systems can profit from more support (e.g., atomic multi-object operations), but such applications are not our major concern here. Other languages address this application domain, for example Argus [23] and Aeolus [28]. Also, parallel applications on *closely-coupled* (shared-memory) systems can use a finer grain of parallelism (e.g., parallelism within objects), but again these are not the type of applications we are interested in here.

The shared data-object model is related to several other models for parallel or distributed programming, such as the distributed object-based model of Emerald [18] and the monitor model of Concurrent Pascal and Mesa [9, 14]. The primary distinguishing property of our model is the total lack of centralized control of shared data. Operations on monitors, for example, are usually implemented using semaphores and are executed one at a time. Our model, on the other hand, only guarantees serializability, but does not actually serialize all operations. As we will see, our model can be implemented efficiently by replicating objects and performing read operations on shared objects in parallel on local copies.

---

* We will sometimes use the term "object" as a shorthand notation for data-objects. Note, however, that unlike in most parallel object-based systems, objects in our model are purely passive.

The model is also related to Linda's Tuple Space [2]. It differs from Tuple Space by allowing programmers to define operations of arbitrary complexity on shared data structures. Linda supports a fixed number of low-level primitives for manipulating single tuples, which we feel is a disadvantage [19].

Other differences between the two models are the way shared data are addressed and modified. Data in Tuple Space are addressed associatively and are modified by first taking them out of Tuple Space, then modifying them, and then putting them back. In our model, shared objects are addressed and modified directly, much like normal variables, so the implementation of our model is somewhat simpler and using it more closely resembles ordinary programming.

2.2. Linguistic support for the shared data-object model

We have designed a new programming language called *Orca*, which gives linguistic support for the shared data-object model. Orca is a simple, procedural, type-secure language. It supports abstract data types, processes, a variety of data structures, modules, and generics. Below, we will look at the expression of parallelism and synchronization in Orca and we will discuss Orca's data structuring mechanism, which was especially designed for distributed programming.

Parallelism in Orca

Parallelism in Orca is based on explicit creation of sequential processes. Processes are similar to procedures, except that procedure invocations are serial but newly created processes run in parallel with their creator. Initially, an Orca program consists of a single process, but new processes can be created explicitly through the **fork** statement:

    fork name(actual-parameters) [**on**(cpu-number)] ;

This statement creates a single new process, which can optionally be assigned to a specific processor by specifying the processor's identifying number. Processors are numbered sequentially; the total number of processors available to the program can be obtained through the standard function NCPUS. If the **on** part is omitted, the new process will be run on the same processor as its parent.

A process can take parameters, as specified in its definition. Two kinds are allowed: input and shared. A process may take any kind of data structure as value (input) parameter. In this case, the process gets a copy of the actual parameter, which is passed by its parent (creator) in the **fork** statement. The data structures in the parent and child are thereafter independent of each other—changing one copy does not affect the other—so they cannot be used for communication between parent and child thereafter.

The parent can also pass any of its *data-objects* as a shared parameter to the child. In this case, the data-object will be shared between the parent and the child. The parent and child can communicate through this shared object, by executing the operations defined by the object's type. This mechanism can be used for sharing objects among any number of processes. The parent can spawn several child processes and pass objects to each of them. The children can pass the objects to *their* children, and so on. In this way, the objects get distributed among some of the descendants of the process that created them. If any of these processes performs an operation on the object, they all observe the same effect, as if the object were in shared memory, protected by a lock variable. Note that there are no "global" objects. The only way to share objects is by passing them as parameters.

Synchronization

Processes in a parallel program sometimes have to synchronize their actions. This is expressed in Orca by allowing operations to *block* until a specified predicate evaluates to *true*. A process that invokes a blocking operation is suspended for as long as the operation blocks.

An important issue in the design of the synchronization mechanism is how to provide blocking operations while still guaranteeing the indivisibility of operation invocations. If an operation may block at any point during its execution, operations can no longer be serialized. Our solution is to allow operations only to block *initially*, before modifying the object. An operation may wait until a certain condition becomes true, but once it has started executing, it cannot block again.

The implementation of an operation has the following general form:

```
operation op(formal-parameters): ResultType;
    local declarations
begin
        guard condition₁ do statements₁ od;
        guard condition₂ do statements₂ od;
        ...
        guard conditionₙ do statementsₙ od;
end;
```

The *conditions* (guards) are side-effect free Boolean expressions that depend only on the internal data of the object and the parameters of the operation. The *statements* may read or modify the object's data.

If the operation is applied to a certain object, it blocks until at least one of the guards is true. If a guard initially fails, it can succeed at a later stage after another process has modified the internal data of the object. As soon as one or more guards succeed, one true guard is selected nondeterministically and its corresponding statements are executed.

The testing of the guards and the execution of the statements of the selected guard together are an indivisible action. As long as all guards fail, the operation has no effect at all, as the object's data can only be modified by the statements. This means that serializability is still easy to achieve, so all operation invocations are executed as atomic actions.

Data structures

We will now turn our attention to the data structuring facilities of Orca. Data structures are important to the design of any language, whether sequential or distributed. Below, we will look at *distribution* of data structures and at *type-security*.

First, we want data structures to be treated similar to scalar variables. In particular, any data structure can be passed as a parameter to processes and operations. This is especially important if data structures are encapsulated within abstract data types, because we want to be able to pass any object as an input or shared parameter to a remote process, no matter what its internal data look like. In contrast, most other distributed languages only allow scalar data or arrays to be sent to a remote process or require the programmer to write code that converts data structures into a transmittable form [15].

Second, we want the data structuring mechanism to be type-secure. Erroneous usage of data structures should be detected either during compile-time or run-time, but should never wreak havoc. This is critical, as it makes debugging distributed programs easier.

The basic idea behind the data structuring mechanism of Orca is to have a few built-in primitives that are secure and suitable for distribution. More complicated data structures can be defined using the standard types of the language (integer, real, boolean, char) and the built-in data structuring capabilities. Frequently, new data structures will be designed as abstract data types. To increase the usefulness of such types, Orca supports *generic* abstract data types.

Orca has the following type constructors built-in: arrays, records, unions, sets, bags, and graphs. Arrays in Orca are similar to flexible arrays in Algol 68 [27]. They have dynamic bounds that can be changed during run-time by assigning a new value to the array. The graph type-constructor can be used for building arbitrary complex data structures, such as lists, trees, and graphs. Most of the other type constructors are similar to their Modula-2 counterparts, except that each data type in Orca can have components of any type.

At run time, data structures are represented by *descriptors*. These descriptors are used for two different purposes. First, descriptors allow any data structure to be passed as a (value) parameter to a remote process. The run time system (RTS) is capable of transmitting variables of any type, even graphs.

In Orca, nodes can be added to, and deleted from, a graph through the following constructs:

```
n := addnode(G);      # add a new node to G
deletenode(G, n);     # delete node n from G
```

The first statement allocates a new node for graph G and stores its name in the variable n. The second statement deallocates this node. The RTS keeps track of which nodes constitute a given graph; this information is stored in the graph's descriptor. Whenever the graph is sent to a remote machine, the RTS uses this information for marshalling the nodes of the graph into transmittable form.

The second purpose of descriptors is to allow extensive run-time type checking to be done. The RTS, for example, checks all array and graph references. If a node is deleted from a graph and subsequently referenced, a run-time error will be given. This is in sharp contrast to languages such as C and Modula-2, in which references to deallocated memory may cause severe damage.

2.3. Implementation

An implementation of Orca consists of two parts: a compiler and a run time system. A prototype Orca compiler has been built using the *Amsterdam Compiler Kit* [26], which is a toolkit for building portable compilers. The compiler generates the EM intermediate code, extended with calls to library routines implemented by the run time systems. The library routines are used for the management of processes, data-objects, and complex data structures.

The compiler performs several important optimizations. Foremost, it analyses the implementation code of operations and determines which ones are read-only. As explained before, this allows the RTSs to apply read operations to local copies of objects.

At present, we have three prototype implementations of the run time system, on two different machines. One RTS runs on a shared-memory multiprocessor, consisting of 10 MC68020 CPUs and 8 MB shared memory, connected through a VME bus. Each CPU board contains 2 MB of local memory, used for storing programs and local data. This RTS was written mainly for comparison purposes, since Orca is intended for distributed systems.

The second RTS runs on a distributed system containing 10 nodes that are connected by a 10Mbit/sec Ethernet. Each node consists of a CPU board, identical to the ones used in the multiprocessor, and an Ethernet controller board using the Lance chip. This RTS runs on top of the Amoeba distributed operating system [24]. It uses Amoeba's Remote Procedure Call for interprocess communication.

The third RTS, which is used for this paper, also runs on the distributed system. Unlike the Amoeba RTS, it runs on top of the bare hardware. It uses the reliable broadcast protocol described in [20] for communication. It replicates all shared data-objects on all processors. Operations that only read (but do not modify) their object's data are applied to the local copy of the object. Write operations are applied to all copies, by broadcasting the operation and its parameters. Since our broadcast protocol is very fast, this scheme is efficient for many applications, as we will see. The implementation of this RTS is described in more detail in [5]. Below, we will study three parallel applications that have been implemented in Orca. Also, we will give measurements of the performances of these programs on the broadcast RTS.

3. THE TRAVELING SALESMAN PROBLEM

In the Traveling Salesman Problem (TSP), the goal is to find the shortest route for a salesman to visit (exactly once) each of the n cities in his territory. The problem can be solved using a parallel *branch-and-bound* algorithm. Abstractly, the branch-and-bound method uses a *tree* to structure the space of possible solutions. A *branching rule* tells how the tree is built. For the TSP, a node of the tree represents a partial tour. Each node has a branch for every city that is not on this partial tour. Figure 1 shows a tree for a 4-city problem. Note that a leaf represents a full tour (a solution). For example, the leftmost branch represents the tour New York - Chicago - St. Louis - Miami.

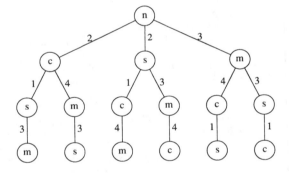

Fig. 1. Search tree for 4-city TSP (New York, Chicago, St. Louis, Miami).

A *bounding rule* avoids searching the whole tree. For TSP, the bounding rule is simple. If the length of a partial tour exceeds the length of any already known solution, the partial tour will never lead to a solution better than what is already known. In Figure 1 for example, the leftmost full route has length 6, so the partial route starting with New York - Miami - Chicago (of length 7) cannot lead to an optimal solution.

3.1. Parallel TSP in Orca

Parallelism in a branch-and-bound algorithm is obtained by searching parts of the tree in parallel. A *manager process* traverses the top part of the tree, up to a certain depth D. For each node at depth D, the manager generates a job to be executed by *worker* processes. A job consists of the evaluation of the subtree below a given node. Effectively, the search tree is distributed among several processes. The manager process searches the top D levels; one or more worker processes traverse the nodes at the lower N − D levels.

To implement the bounding rule, the workers need to keep track of the shortest full route found so far. On a distributed system, one might be tempted to let each worker keep a local minimum (i.e., the length of the shortest path found by the worker itself). After the entire tree has been searched, the lowest value of these local minima can be determined. This scheme is easy to implement and has little communication overhead. Unfortunately, it also makes the bounding rule far less effective than in a sequential program. In the example of Figure 1, only the worker that has evaluated the leftmost route will know there exists a path of length 6. Other workers will be ignorant of this fact, and may start working on partial routes longer than 6, which cannot lead to an optimal path.

In our implementation, the length of the best route so far is kept in a data-object `minimum`, which is shared among all the workers (see Figure 2). This object is of type `IntObject`, which is a predefined object type encapsulating a single integer variable. Each process can directly read the value through an operation invocation. The Orca RTS will automatically replicate the object on all processors, so reading the object does not involve any interprocess communication. Whenever the object changes (i.e., whenever a new better full route is found), all copies are updated immediately.

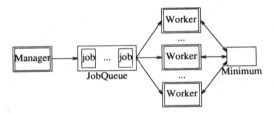

Fig. 2. Structure of the Orca implementation of TSP. The Manager and Workers are processes. The JobQueue is a data-object shared among all these processes. Minimum is a data-object of type IntObject; it is read and written by all workers.

The manager and worker processes communicate through a shared `JobQueue` data-object. The manager adds jobs to this queue, which are subsequently retrieved and executed by the workers. The JobQueue is an instantiation of a *generic* object type (see Figure 3).

Three operations are defined for JobQueue objects. `AddJob` adds a new job to the tail of the queue. In the TSP program, this operation will only be invoked by the manager process. The operation `NoMoreJobs` is to be called when all jobs have been added to the queue. Finally, the operation `GetJob` tries to fetch a job from the head of the queue. If the queue is not empty, `GetJob` removes the first job from the queue and returns it through the **out** parameter `job`. If the queue is empty and `NoMoreJobs` has been invoked, the operation returns "false". In this way, it is easy to determine when

```
generic (type T)
object specification GenericJobQueue;
    # add a job to the tail of the queue:
    operation AddJob(job: T);
    # invoked when no new jobs will be added:
    operation NoMoreJobs();
    # Fetch a job from the head of the queue.
    # This operation fails if the queue is
    # empty and NoMoreJobs has been invoked.
    operation GetJob(job: out T): boolean;
end generic;
```

Fig. 3. Specification of generic object type GenericJobQueue.

the workers can be terminated. If none of these two conditions—queue not empty or NoMoreJobs invoked—holds, the operation blocks until one of them becomes true.

The type definitions and constants used by the TSP program are shown in Figure 4. The distances between the cities are stored in a two-dimensional array of type DistTab. The entries in a given row C of this array are *presorted* by the distances to city C. Entry [C, i] of the array contains the *i*th closest city to C and the distance from C to that city. With this representation, it is easy to implement the nearest-city-first heuristic.

```
# distances, sorted by nearest-city-first heuristic.
type pair =
    record
        ToCity: integer;  # to which city
        dist: integer;    # distance to that city
    end;
type DistArray = array[integer] of pair;
type DistTab = array[integer] of DistArray;
# job type:
type PathType = array[integer] of integer;
type JobType =
    record
        len: integer;   # length of partial route
        path: PathType; # the partial route itself
    end;
const NrTowns = 12;  # number of towns
const MaxHops = 3;   # search depth of manager
```

Fig. 4. Declarations for types and constants used by the TSP program.

Figure 4 also declares a type JobType, which defines the jobs to be executed by the workers. A job consists of an initial (partial) route for the salesman and the length of this partial route. The latter number is included for efficiency reasons only; it could also be derived from the path itself.

An outline of the Orca code for the manager process is shown in Figure 5. The manager creates and initializes the shared object minimum, initializes the distance table, and forks one worker process on each processor except its own. Subsequently, the manager generates the jobs and stores them in a shared object of type TspQueue, which is an instantiation of the generic type GenericJobQueue of Figure 3. When all jobs have been generated, the manager forks a worker process on its own processor and waits until all work has been done. In this way, job generation overlaps with

most of the worker processes. The final worker process is not created until all jobs have been generated, so job generation will not be slowed down by a competing process on the same processor. The manager uses a shared counter (WorkersActive) to keep track of the number of active worker processes. When the counter drops to zero, all workers have terminated. The manager then prints the final value of minimum (i.e., the length of the optimal solution).

```
process manager(distance: DistTab);
    # length of current best path (shared object):
    minimum: IntObject;
    # the job queue (shared object):
    q: TspQueue;
    i: integer;
    # number of active workers (shared object):
    WorkersActive: IntObject;
begin
    # initialize minimum to infinity:
    minimum$assign(MAX(integer));
    # initialize number of workers:
    WorkersActive$assign(NCPUS());
    for i in 1.. NCPUS() - 1 do
      # fork one worker per cpu, except current cpu
      fork worker(minimum,q,distance,WorkersActive) on(i);
    od;
    Generate the jobs for the workers and store them in q.
    Each job is an initial path of MaxHops hops.
    q$NoMoreJobs(); # all jobs have been generated now
    fork worker(minimum,q,distance,WorkersActive) on(0);
    # jobs have been generated; fork a worker on this
    # cpu too and wait until workers have finished:
    WorkersActive$AwaitValue(0);
    # length of shortest path:
    WriteLine("minimum = ", minimum$value());
end;
```

Fig. 5. Outline of Orca code for the manager process of the TSP program

In the implementation of Figure 5, a job contains an initial path with a fixed number of cities (MaxHops). Basically, the manager process traverses the top MaxHops − 1 levels of the search tree, while the workers traverse the remaining levels. The manager process generates the jobs in "nearest-city-first" order. It is important that the worker processes execute the jobs in the same order they were generated. This is the reason why we use an ordered queue rather than an unordered bag for storing the jobs.

The code for the worker processes is shown in Figure 6. Each worker process repeatedly fetches a job from the job queue and executes it by calling the function tsp. The tsp function generates all routes that start with a given initial route. If the initial route passed as parameter is longer than the current best route, tsp returns immediately, because such a partial route cannot lead to an optimal solution. A worker process obtains the length of the current best route by applying the value operation to the shared object minimum. This operation returns the current value of the integer stored in the object. Since the operation does not modify the object's data, it uses a local copy of the object, without doing any interprocess communication.

If the route passed as parameter is a full route (visiting all cities), a new best route has been found, so the value of minimum should be updated. It is possible, however, that two or more worker processes simultaneously detect a route that is better than the current

83

```
process worker(minimum: shared IntObject;
         q: shared TspQueue;
         distance: DistTable;
         WorkersActive: shared IntObject);
      job: JobType;
begin
   while q$GetJob(job) do  # while there are jobs to do:
         # search subtree:
         tsp(MaxHops,job.len,job.path,minimum,distance);
   od;
   WorkersActive$dec();  # this worker becomes inactive
end;

function tsp(hops: integer; len: integer;
         path: shared PathType; minimum: shared IntObject;
         distance: DistTable);
      city, dist, me, i: integer;
begin
   # Search subtree starting with initial route "path"
   if len >= minimum$value() then return; fi;  # cut-off
   if hops = NrTowns then
      # We found a full route better than current.
      # best route. Update minimum, using
      # indivisible "min" operation:
      minimum$min(len);
   else
      # "path" really is a partial route.
      # Call tsp recursively for each
      # subtree, in "nearest-city-first" order.
      me := path[hops];  # me := last city on path
      for i in 1.. NrTowns do
         city := distance[me][i].ToCity;
         # is city on path?
         if not present(city, hops, path) then
            # no, append city to path:
            path[hops+1] := city;
            # distance me->city:
            dist := distance[me][i].dist;
            tsp(hops+1, len+dist, path, minimum,
                  distance);
         fi;
      od;
   fi;
end;
```

Fig. 6. Orca code for the worker processes of the TSP program

best route. Therefore, the value of minimum is updated through the indivisible operation min, which checks if the new value presented is actually less than the current value of the object. If the value is really changed, the run time system automatically updates all copies of the object.

3.2. Performance of parallel TSP

We have determined the performance of the TSP program on the broadcast RTS by measuring its execution time for solving three randomly generated input graphs with 12 cities each. The manager process searches 2 levels of the tree, so it generates $11 \times 10 = 110$ jobs, each of which solves a 10 city TSP problem. Figure 7 shows the average speedups obtained for these three problems. (The speedup on P processors is defined as the ratio of the execution times on 1 and P processors. Thus, by definition, the speedup with

1 processor is always 1.0.) With 10 processors, the Orca program is 9.96 times faster as with one processor.

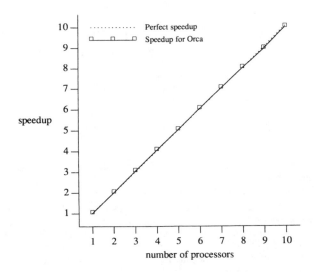

Fig. 7. Measured speedup for the Traveling Salesman Problem, averaged over three randomly generated graphs with 12 cities each.

Since the compiler and run time system used for our measurements are prototypes, it is not very meaningful to compare the performance of Orca programs with languages such as C and FORTRAN, which have highly optimized implementations. Many of the sequential parts of the language have been implemented in a preliminary, inefficient way. Furthermore, Orca does heavy run-time checking. Although this slows down execution, we feel the overhead is justified by the type security thus obtained. Orca programs typically are 3 to 5 times slower than similar programs written in C.

It is interesting to compare the performance of the Orca TSP program with an earlier implementation of TSP in C, on top of Amoeba [6]. The C/Amoeba version uses Remote Procedure Call for interprocess communication. It is similar to the Orca version, except that replication of the shared variable minimum is dealt with by the programmer rather than the RTS. If a worker in the C/Amoeba version finds a better full route, it does not update the shared variable immediately, because the RPC model makes it difficult for servers to return intermediate results. Instead, the worker completes the analysis of the subtree assigned to it and then returns the best path. Moreover, the other worker processes do not update their local copies of the shared variable until they have finished their current jobs.

As a result, worker processes in the C/Amoeba version often will have an out-of-date value of the shared variable. Therefore, they will frequently search more nodes than is necessary. This search overhead may become quite significant. For one of the input graphs we obtained the following statistics:

Total number of nodes in the tree:	108,505,112
Nodes searched by sequential program:	1,272,076
Nodes searched by 10-CPU C/Amoeba program:	1,763,552
Nodes searched by 10-CPU Orca program:	1,149,270

In this example, the C/Amoeba version of TSP searches 39% more nodes than a sequential algorithm. The Orca version running on the broadcast RTS, on the other hand, searches 10% *fewer* nodes. It achieves superlinear speedup in this case (a speedup of 10.75 with 10 processors). Such anomalous behavior of parallel branch-and-bound programs has also been reported by other authors [21]. It is due to the different search order of the parallel algorithm. One processor quickly finds a near-optimal solution, which other processors use for pruning parts of their trees. However, if we were to make a large number of runs with different input data, we would not see a superlinear effect on the average, of course.

THE ALL-PAIRS SHORTEST PATHS PROBLEM

In the All-pairs Shortest Paths (ASP) problem it is desired to find the length of the shortest path from any node i to any other node j in a given graph. Sequential solutions to the ASP problem are given in several text books on algorithms and data structures [1, 16]. We will first review the standard sequential algorithm, due to Floyd, for solving the ASP problem and then discuss how it can be parallelized. The algorithm assumes that the nodes of the graph are numbered sequentially from 1 to N (the total number of nodes) and that each edge in the graph is assigned a positive length (or weight).

The standard sequential solution to the ASP problem uses an iterative algorithm. During iteration k it finds the shortest path from every node i in the graph to every node j that only visits intermediate nodes in the set {1..k}. During iteration k, the algorithm checks if the current best path from i to k concatenated with the current best path from k to j is shorter than the best path from i to j found so far (i.e., during the first k-1 iterations).

Before the first iteration, such a path only exists if the graph contains a direct edge from node i to node j. After the last iteration, the resulting path may visit any other node, as the set {1..k} includes all nodes if k = N. Therefore, after the last iteration, the resulting path is the shortest path from node i to node j.

The standard algorithm uses a sequence of matrices for storing the lengths of all these paths. After iteration k, element $C^k[i,j]$ contains the length of the shortest path from i to j found so far (i.e., the best path visiting only nodes between 1 and k). During iteration k, the matrix C^{k-1} is transformed into a matrix C^k as follows:

$$C^k[i,j] = MINIMUM(C^{k-1}[i,j], C^{k-1}[i,k] + C^{k-1}[k,j]) \quad (1 \le i,j \le N)$$

Note that the value of row k of matrix C^k is equal to row k of matrix C^{k-1}, because

$$C^k[k,j] =$$
$$MINIMUM(C^{k-1}[k,j], C^{k-1}[k,k] + C^{k-1}[k,j]) =$$
$$MINIMUM(C^{k-1}[k,j], C^{k-1}[k,j]) =$$
$$C^{k-1}[k,j]$$

Parallel ASP in Orca

This sequential algorithm can be transformed into a parallel algorithm by computing the rows of the matrices $C^k[i,j]$ in parallel. There are two ways for structuring such a parallel ASP algorithm. First, we can have a single master process that executes N iterations. During iteration k, the master forks one or more slave processes and passes part of the matrix C^{k-1} to each slave. A slave computes one or more rows of C^k, sends these values back to the master, and then terminates.

An alternative way for structuring the parallel algorithm is to let each slave execute an iterative algorithm. In this case, the master process forks a number of slave processes and then terminates. Each slave process performs N iterations and then outputs its results. The latter approach is more efficient, because it requires fewer **fork**

statements. Also, it has more parallelism, because different slave processes may be working on different iterations.

We therefore use the second approach and structure the algorithm as a number of iterative slave processes. Each slave process computes a fixed number of rows of the C matrices. The different rows of C^k cannot be computed completely independently from each other, however. Suppose a slave process wants to compute row i of matrix C^k. That is, it has to compute the values

$$C^k[i,j], \text{ for all } j \text{ between 1 and N.}$$

To compute the value $C^k[i,j]$, the values of $C^{k-1}[i,j]$, $C^{k-1}[i,k]$, and $C^{k-1}[k,j]$ are needed. The first two values have been computed by this process during the previous iteration. The value of $C^{k-1}[k,j]$, however, has been computed (during iteration k-1) by the process that takes care of row k. The above argument applies to any value of i and j between 1 and N. Therefore, during iteration k, each process needs to know the value of the entire row k of matrix C^{k-1}. So, after each iteration k, the process that computed the value of row k+1 of matrix C^k has to send this value to all other processes. Furthermore, a process should not continue computing its part of C^k until it has received row k of the previous iteration. Clearly, the processes must be *synchronized* to achieve this.

In conclusion, the ASP problem can be solved in parallel by letting each slave process taking care of some of the rows of the C matrices. Each process performs an iterative algorithm. During iteration k, a processor that is assigned rows lb up to ub computes the values

$$C^k[i,j], \text{ for all } i \text{ between lb and ub, and all } j \text{ between 1 and N.}$$

A processor should not start working on iteration k until the value of row k of matrix C^{k-1} is available. Apart from this restriction, the processors do not depend on each other. In particular, they need not all be working on the same iteration.

The synchronization constraint described above is implemented through an object of type RowCollection, whose specification is shown in Figure 8. This object type defines two operations, AddRow and AwaitRow. Whenever a process has computed row k of matrix C^{k-1}, it executes the operation AddRow, passing the iteration number (k) and the value of the row (an array of integers) as parameters. Before a process starts working on iteration k, it first waits until the value of row k for this iteration is available. It does so by invoking AwaitRow(k).

```
module specification AspTypes;
    const N = 200;  # number of nodes in the graph
    type RowType = array[integer] of integer;
end;


object specification RowCollection;
    from AspTypes import RowType;

    # Object used to exchange row k before an iteration
    operation AddRow(iter: integer; R: RowType);
        # Add the row for the given iteration number
    operation AwaitRow(iter: integer): RowType;
        # Wait until the row for the given iteration is
        # available, then return it.
end;
```

Fig. 8. Specification of module AspTypes and object type RowCollection

The implementation of object type RowCollection is shown in Figure 9. The internal data of an object of this type consist of an array of rows (i.e., the variable `tab`). There is one row for each iteration of the algorithm. As different processes may be working on different iterations, all these rows are retained during the entire execution of the program.

The variable `tab` is of type `collection`, which is an array of N elements of type `RowType`. The declaration for `RowType` (see Figure 8) does not specify actual bounds for the rows. This means that the rows of `tab` will initially be empty. Since Orca allows entire arrays to be reassigned, however, the rows can be initialized with a single assignment statement. The `AddRow` operation assigns a non-empty array to a certain entry of the table. The `AwaitRow` operation blocks until the specified entry of the table is non-empty. (An empty array has a lower bound that is higher than its upper bound.)

```
object implementation RowCollection;
    from AspTypes import N, RowType;

    # The local data of objects of type RowCollection
    # consists of an array of rows, one row per
    # iteration. Initially, each row is an empty array.

    type collection = array[integer 1..N] of RowType;
    # the local data of RowCollection objects:
    tab: collection;

    operation AddRow(iter: integer; R: RowType);
    begin
        # fill in the row for given iteration
        tab[iter] := R;
    end;


    operation AwaitRow(iter: integer): RowType;
    begin
        # wait until row "iter" is defined,
        # i.e. tab[iter] is non-empty.
        guard lb(tab[iter]) < ub(tab[iter]) do
            # return the requested row:
            return tab[iter];
        od;
    end;
end;
```

Fig. 9. Orca code for the implementation of object type RowCollection.

An outline of the code for the ASP program itself is shown in Figure 10. It is structured using one master process and a number of slave processes. The master process forks one slave process per processor. Each slave is assigned part of the initial C matrix. A slave initializes its part of the C matrix. Each slave takes a shared object of type `RowCollection` as a parameter. This object, called `RowkColl`, is used for synchronizing the slaves, as described above.

Conceptually, the slave processes compute a sequence of matrices C^0, C^1, ... , C^N. In the implementation, however, each slave simply uses a single array variable, which gets modified in place. There is basically only a single C matrix, which is partitioned among all the slaves.

Each slave process executes N iterations. At the beginning of iteration k, it first obtains the value of row k. This value may either have been computed by itself (if `lb` ≤ k ≤ `ub`) or by some other

```
module implementation asp;
    import RowCollection;
    from AspTypes import N, RowType;
    # table with distances:
    type DistTable = array[integer] of RowType;

    process manager();
        # shared object for sending row k:
        RowkColl: RowCollection;
        i, lb, ub: integer;
    begin
        for i in 0 .. NCPUS()-1 do
            determine interval [lb, ub] for next slave
            fork slave(RowkColl, lb, ub) on(i);
        od;
    end;


    process slave(RowkColl : shared RowCollection; lb,
                  ub: integer);
        # table with distances between nodes:
        C: DistTable;
        i,j,k: integer;
        RowK: RowType;
    begin
        initialize rows lb to ub of C matrix
        for k in 1 .. N do  # do N iterations
            if (k >= lb) and (k <= ub) then
                RowK := C[k]; # I have row k
                # add it to shared object RowkColl:
                RowkColl$AddRow(k, RowK);
            else
                # Someone else is computing row k;
                # wait for it.
                RowK := RowkColl$AwaitRow(k);
            fi;
            for all elements C[i,j] of rows C[lb] .. C[ub] do:
                C[i,j] := MINIMUM(C[i,j], C[i,k] + RowK[j])
        od;
        print final results
    end;
end;
```

Fig. 10. Outline of Orca implementation of ASP.

slave. In the first case, it sends the value to all other slaves, using the `AddRow` operation on `RowkColl`. In the second case, it obtains the value by invoking the `AwaitRow` operation, which blocks until the value is available. In either case, the slave process proceeds by updating the values of its rows. As soon as a slave process has finished all N iterations, it is ready to print its results.

3.3. Performance of parallel ASP

The performance of the ASP program for a graph with 200 nodes is shown in Figure 11. The speedup is only slightly less than perfect. The main reason why the speedup for ASP is not perfect is the communication overhead. Before each iteration, the current value of row k must be transmitted across the Ethernet from one processor to all the others.

Despite this overhead, the Orca program obtains a good speedup. With 10 processors, the speedup is 9.17. One of the most important reasons for this good performance is the use of broadcast messages for transferring the row to all processors. Each time the operation `AddRow` is applied to `RowkColl`, this operation and its

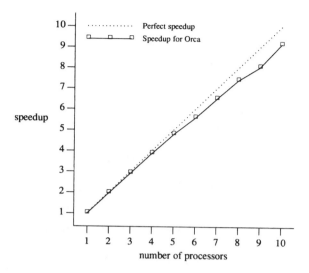

Fig. 11. Measured speedup for the All-pairs Shortest Paths problem, using an input graph with 200 nodes.

called *relaxation parameter* [25]. The entire process terminates if, during the current iteration, no single point has been changed by more than a certain quantity.

Parallel implementations of SOR have been described in several research papers [10, 11]. The SOR program described below is based on the parallel Red/Black SOR algorithm used for the Amber system [11]. This algorithm treats the grid as a checkerboard and alternately updates all black points and all red points. As each point only has neighbors of the opposite color, each update phase can easily be parallelized. The grid can be partitioned among the available processors, which can all update different points of the same color in parallel.

3.4. Parallel SOR in Orca

As explained in the Amber paper, the distribution of the grid among the processors is of vital importance to the performance of parallel SOR. We have used a similar distribution scheme as in the Amber implementation. The grid is partitioned into regions, each containing several rows of the grid. Each region is assigned to a separate processor. Alternative distribution schemes of the grid would be less efficient. Putting the entire grid in a single shared object would create a severe bottleneck, since the grid is read and written very frequently. The other extreme, putting each point of the grid in a separate shared object, is also inefficient, since it would introduce a very high communication overhead.

With the above distribution scheme, all processors repeatedly compute new values for the points in their region, based on the current value of the point and its four neighbors. For a point on the upper or lower boundary of a region, however, one of the neighbors is stored on a remote processor. The processors, therefore, have to exchange the values of their boundary points before each iteration. This is illustrated in Figure 12.

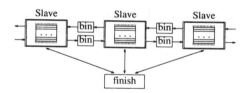

Fig. 12. Structure of the Orca implementation of Successive Overrelaxation. Each slave process maintains some portion of the rows of the grid. The dotted boxes are copies of the last row of the left neighbor and the first row of the right neighbor. These rows are transferred through shared "bin" objects. The processes also communicate through a shared barrier object "finish," to decide when the convergence criterion has been reached.

parameters are broadcast to all processors. In our broadcast protocol [20], this causes one point-to-point packet and one multicast packet to be sent over the Ethernet.

The performance of the program also compares favorably with the parallel ASP program described in [17]. Jenq and Sahni have implemented ASP on an NCUBE/7 hypercube, using a work distribution similar to ours. For a graph with 112 nodes they report speedups of approximately 6.5 with 8 processors and 10.5 with 16 processors. As the NCUBE/7 does not support broadcast in hardware, they have used a binary tree transmission scheme for simulating broadcast. The elapsed time for a simulated broadcast message is proportional to the logarithm of the number of processors. In contrast, the protocol used in our broadcast RTS typically only uses two messages per reliable broadcast. The time needed for broadcasting a message is almost independent of the number of receivers [20].

The bends in the graph of Figure 11 are caused by the slightly unbalanced work distribution. With 8 CPUs, for example, each processor manages exactly 25 rows of the distance matrix; with 9 CPUs, however, some processors will have 22 rows, but others will have 23 rows. As the elapsed computation time is determined by the processor that terminates last, the speedup with 9 processors cannot exceed $200/23 \approx 8.7$.

SUCCESSIVE OVERRELAXATION

Successive overrelaxation (SOR) is an iterative method for solving discretized Laplace equations on a grid [25]. The sequential SOR algorithm works as follows. During each iteration, the algorithm considers all non-boundary points of the grid. For each point, SOR first computes the average value of its four neighbors. Next, it determines the new value of the point through the following correction:

$$Gnew\,[r,c\,] \,=\, G\,[r,c\,] + \omega \times (av - G\,[r,c\,])$$

where *av* is the average value of the four neighbors and ω is the so-

In Orca, the SOR program uses one *slave* process per processor. The slaves execute a number of iterations. Each iteration consists of two phases, one for the black points and one for the red points of the grid. Before each phase, a slave sends its first row to its left neighbor and its last row to its right neighbor. Next, it waits for the last row of its left neighbor and the first row of its right neighbor. Subsequently, it updates those points in its regions that have the right color.

The exchange of the rows is implemented through shared objects of type RowBin, which is an instantiation of the generic type GenericBin (see Figure 13). Basically, a bin object is a message buffer capable of holding a single message, in this case a row of the grid. The put operation on a bin blocks while the bin is full; the get operation blocks while the bin is empty.

```
generic (type T) object specification GenericBin;
    # put item in the bin; block while bin is full:
    operation put (e: T);
    # fetch item from bin; block while bin is empty:
    operation get (e: out T);
end generic;


generic object implementation GenericBin;
    bin: T;          # the buffer containing the item
    # indicates if there's an item in the buffer now:
    empty: boolean;

    operation put (e: T);
    begin
        # wait until bin is empty
        guard empty do
            bin := e;        # put item in bin
            empty := false; # bin is no longer empty
        od;
    end;

    operation get (e: out T);
    begin
        # wait until there's an item in the bin
        guard not empty do
            e := bin;        # fetch the item
            empty := true;  # bin is now empty
        od;
    end;
begin
    empty := true;  # bin is initially empty
end generic;
```

Fig. 13. Specification and implementation of generic object type GenericBin

As mentioned above, the SOR program should continue updating points until each point has reached a stable value, approximately the average value of its four neighbors. Each slave process therefore keeps track of the maximum change of all points in its region. If, at the end of an iteration, the slaves agree that no point has changed by more than a certain value, the program terminates. This is implemented through an object finish, which basically implements barrier synchronization [3]. After each iteration, each slave determines if it wants to continue the SOR process or not. If all slaves want to stop, the entire SOR program terminates; otherwise, the slaves continue with the next iteration.

3.5. Performance

The SOR program described above is a difficult one for our broadcast RTS, since SOR mainly uses point-to-point communication. Apart from the termination protocol, each processor only communicates with its left and right neighbor.

The broadcast RTS replicates all shared objects on all processors. If, for example, one processor wants to send a row to its left neighbor, all processors will receive the put operation and apply it to their local copies of the bin. Despite this inefficiency, the broadcast RTS still achieves a remarkably good performance (see Figure 14), due to the highly efficient broadcast protocol being used. (To

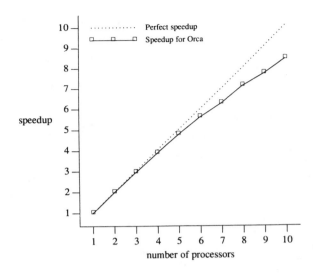

Fig. 14. Measured speedups for Successive Overrelaxation, using a grid with 80 columns and 242 rows.

be fair, the hardware we use does not have hardware floating point processors; with hardware floating point, the relative communication overhead would be higher, so the speedup would be lower.) The speedup on 10 processors is approximately 8.5. The speedup is comparable to that of the Amber implementation, which runs on a collection of Firefly multiprocessor workstations [11].

4. CONCLUSIONS

We have discussed a new programming language, Orca, designed for implementing parallel applications on distributed computing systems. Orca's most distinctive feature is its support for logically shared data. Processes on different machines can share data that are encapsulated in instances (objects) of abstract data types. The implementation (i.e., the compiler and run time system) takes care of the physical distribution of the data among the local memories of the processors. The Orca implementation used for this paper replicates all shared objects. Read operations on shared objects are applied to local copies. After a write operation, all copies are updated, using a reliable broadcast protocol.

We have discussed the usefulness of logically shared data in the context of three applications. The first application, the Traveling Salesman Problem, is a good example of when our approach is most effective. The TSP program uses a shared object with a high read/write ratio. As this object is replicated and the copies are updated immediately after each change, the application is very efficient.

The second program, which solves the All-pairs Shortest Paths problem, uses a shared object for transmitting rows of the distance matrix from one processor to all the others. Since updating objects is implemented through broadcasting, this again is highly efficient. An interesting aspect of this program is the fact that the programmer need not be aware of the broadcasting, as it is handled entirely by the run time system.

The third application, Successive Overrelaxation, does not need shared data or efficient broadcasting. Instead, it uses simple point-to-point message passing. This application is easy to implement in Orca, but the broadcast RTS is somewhat inefficient here. For this application, a selective (heuristic) replication strategy would be better. (This has been demonstrated by another RTS for Orca, described in [4]). Still, even under these unfavorable circumstances the broadcast RTS achieves a speedup of 85% of the theoretical maximum.

The reliable broadcast protocol we use scales well to a large number of processors. Therefore, we expect the RTS to scale well too, especially when heuristic replication is used.

In conclusion, our approach to distributed programming looks promising, at least for the applications discussed in this paper. In the near future, we intend to study more applications and compare our work with that of others. It will be interesting to compare our model with message-passing models as well as with other models supporting logically shared data.

ACKNOWLEDGEMENTS

We would like to thank Wim van Leersum for implementing the Orca compiler and Erik Baalbergen and Susan Flynn Hummel for giving useful comments on the paper.

REFERENCES

[1] Aho, A.V., Hopcroft, J.E., and Ullman, J.D., "The Design and Analysis of Computer Algorithms," Addison-Wesley, Reading, MA (1974).

[2] Ahuja, S., Carriero, N., and Gelernter, D., "Linda and Friends," *IEEE Computer*, vol. 19, no. 8, pp. 26-34 (Aug. 1986).

[3] Almasi, G.S. and Gottlieb, A., "Highly Parallel Computing," The Benjamin/Cummings Publishing Company, Redwood City, CA (1989).

[4] Bal, H.E., "Programming Distributed Systems," Silicon Press, Summit, NY (1990). "revision of Ph.D. thesis"

[5] Bal, H.E., Kaashoek, M.F., and Tanenbaum, A.S., "A Distributed Implementation of the Shared Data-object Model," *USENIX Workshop on Experiences with Building Distributed and Multiprocessor Systems*, pp. 1-19, Ft. Lauderdale, FL. (Oct. 1989).

[6] Bal, H.E., Renesse, R. van, and Tanenbaum, A.S., "Implementing Distributed Algorithms Using Remote Procedure Calls," *Proc. AFIPS Nat. Computer Conf.*, vol. 56, pp. 499-506, AFIPS Press, Chicago, IL (June 1987).

[7] Bal, H.E., Steiner, J.G., and Tanenbaum, A.S., "Programming Languages for Distributed Computing Systems," *ACM Computing Surveys*, vol. 21, no. 3, pp. 261-322 (Sept. 1989).

[8] Bal, H.E. and Tanenbaum, A.S., "Distributed Programming with Shared Data," *Proc. IEEE CS 1988 Int. Conf. on Computer Languages*, pp. 82-91, Miami, FL (Oct. 1988).

[9] Brinch Hansen, P., "The Programming Language Concurrent Pascal," *IEEE Trans. Softw. Eng.*, vol. SE-1, no. 2, pp. 199-207 (June 1975).

[10] Butler, R., Lusk, E., McCune, W., and Overbeek, R., "Parallel Logic Programming for Numeric Applications," *Proc. 3rd Int. Conf. on Logic Programming*, pp. 375-388, London (July 1986).

[11] Chase, J.S., Amador, F.G., Lazowska, E.D., Levy, H.M., and Littlefield, R.J., "The Amber System: Parallel Programming on a Network of Multiprocessors," *Proc. 12th Symp. Operating Systems Principles*, ACM SIGOPS, Litchfield Park, AZ (Dec. 1989).

[12] Elias, R-J., "Oracol, A Chess Problem Solver in Orca," Master thesis, Vrije Universiteit, Amsterdam, The Netherlands (July 1989).

[13] Eswaran, K.P., Gray, J.N., Lorie, R.A., and Traiger, I.L., "The Notions of Consistency and Predicate Locks in a Database System," *Commun. ACM*, vol. 19, no. 11, pp. 624-633 (Nov. 1976).

[14] Geschke, C.M., Jr., J. H. Morris, and Satterthwaite, E.H., "Early Experience with Mesa," *Commun. ACM*, vol. 20, no. 8, pp. 540-553 (Aug. 1977).

[15] Herlihy, M. and Liskov, B., "A Value Transmission Method for Abstract Data Types," *ACM Trans. Program. Lang. Syst.*, vol. 4, no. 4, pp. 527-551 (Oct. 1982).

[16] Horowitz, E. and Sahni, S., "Fundamentals of Data Structures," Pitman Publishing, London (1976).

[17] Jenq, J.-F. and Sahni, S., "All Pairs Shortest Paths on a Hypercube Multiprocessor," *Proc. 1987 Int. Conf. Parallel Processing*, pp. 713-716, St. Charles, IL (Aug. 1987).

[18] Jul, E., Levy, H., Hutchinson, N., and Black, A., "Fine-Grained Mobility in the Emerald System," *ACM Trans. Comp. Syst.*, vol. 6, no. 1, pp. 109-133 (Feb. 1988).

[19] Kaashoek, M.F., Bal, H.E., and Tanenbaum, A.S., "Experience with the Distributed Data Structure Paradigm in Linda," *USENIX Workshop on Experiences with Building Distributed and Multiprocessor Systems*, pp. 175-191, Ft. Lauderdale, FL. (Oct. 1989).

[20] Kaashoek, M.F., Tanenbaum, A.S., Flynn Hummel, S., and Bal, H.E., "An Efficient Reliable Broadcast Protocol," *Oper. Syst. Rev.*, vol. 23, no. 4, pp. 5-20 (Oct. 1989).

[21] Lai, T.H. and Sahni, S., "Anomalies in Parallel Branch-and-Bound Algorithms," *Proc. 1983 Int. Conf. Parallel Processing*, pp. 183-190 (Aug. 1983).

[22] Li, K., "IVY: A Shared Virtual Memory System for Parallel Computing," *Proc. 1988 Int. Conf. Parallel Processing (Vol. II)*, pp. 94-101, St. Charles, IL (Aug. 1988).

[23] Liskov, B., "Distributed Programming in Argus," *Commun. ACM*, vol. 31, no. 3, pp. 300-312 (March 1988).

[24] Mullender, S.J. and Tanenbaum, A.S., "Design of a Capability-Based Distributed Operating System," *Computer J.*, vol. 29, no. 4, pp. 289-299 (Aug. 1986).

[25] Stoer, J. and Bulirsch, R., "Introduction to Numerical Analysis," Springer-Verlag, New York, NY (1983).

[26] Tanenbaum, A.S., Staveren, H. van, Keizer, E.G., and Stevenson, J.W., "A Practical Toolkit for Making Portable Compilers," *Commun. ACM*, vol. 26, no. 9, pp. 654-660 (Sept. 1983).

[27] Wijngaarden, A. van, Mailloux, B.J., Peck, J.E.L., Koster, C.H.A., Sintzoff, M., Lindsey, C.H., Meertens, L.G.L.T., and Fisker, R.G., "Revised Report on the Algorithmic Language Algol 68," *Acta Informatica*, vol. 5, pp. 1-236 (1975).

[28] Wilkes, C.T. and LeBlanc, R.J., "Rationale for the Design of Aeolus: A Systems Programming Language for an Action/Object System," *Proc. IEEE CS 1986 Int. Conf. on Computer Languages*, pp. 107-122, Miami, FL (Oct. 1986).

David R. Hanson   Makoto Kobayashi†

Department of Computer Science
Princeton University
Princeton, NJ 08544 USA

ABSTRACT

EZ is a system that integrates the facilities provided separately by traditional programming languages and operating systems. This integration is accomplished by casting services provided by traditional operating services as *EZ* language features. *EZ* is a high-level string processing language with a persistent memory. Traditional file and directory services are provided by *EZ*'s strings and associative tables, and tables are also used for procedure activations. This paper describes processes in *EZ*, which are procedure activations that execute concurrently and share the same, persistent virtual address space. They are semantically similar to 'threads' or 'lightweight processes' in some operating systems. Processes are values. They are just associative tables and have all of the characteristics of other EZ values, including persistence. Examples of their use and a brief overview of their implementation are included.

1. Introduction

EZ[1, 2] is a system that integrates the facilities provided separately by traditional programming languages and operating systems. This integration is accomplished by casting services provided by traditional operating systems as *EZ* language features. The result is a system that is intended to be a complete computing environment that—ultimately—can replace both conventional languages and operating systems.

EZ is a high-level string processing language with a persistent memory in which values exist indefinitely or until changed. Traditional file and directory services are provided by *EZ*'s strings and associative tables [1]. Associative tables are also used for procedure activations, providing low-level services such as activation record creation, references to local variables, and access to state information. This approach permits traditionally separate editing and debugging services both to be provided by an editor written in *EZ* that edits *EZ* values [2].

The design challenge in *EZ* is finding the natural 'linguistic encapsulation' of operating system facilities. Earlier work focussed first on encapsulating file system facilities as strings and tables, then on accessing the details of sequential execution by casting procedure activations as tables. This paper describes the encapsulation of processes in *EZ*, which permits *EZ* to provide

some of the functions of conventional operating systems at the programming-language level. Sections 2 and 3 briefly describe the *EZ* language and procedures. Processes and I/O are described in §4, the implementation is sketched in §5, and §6 summarizes experience to date and current and future work.

2. The Language

EZ is a high-level string processing language that has its roots in Icon [3] and its predecessors. It has late binding times and considerable run-time flexibility. For example, variables can be assigned values of any type, automatic conversions are performed for most operations, and structures are heterogeneous.

EZ has four basic types of values: numerics, strings, procedures, and tables. Numerics (integers and reals) and strings (of arbitrary length) are scalars, and tables are heterogeneous, one-dimensional associative arrays that can be indexed by and can contain arbitrary values. Procedures are described below.

Since values persist until changed, assigning strings to variables is like creating 'files' in conventional systems. Substring access and assignment provide random access facilities; $s[i:j]$ specifies the substring of s between character positions i and j. Tables are like directories in conventional operating systems. For example, the fragment

```
paper["title"] = "EZ Processes"
paper["authors"] = drh || "\n" || mk
```

creates a table for a paper and assigns it to **paper**, and assigns two entries to the new table (double vertical bars, ||, denote string concatenation). The notation $e.id$ is equivalent to $e["id"]$ so tables can be used as records, too. Tables can contain tables; for example, if **references** is a table containing entries for a reference list,

```
paper.references = references
```

adds the reference list to **paper**. Tables can be used to construct hierarchical directories, as in UNIX, as well as arbitrary cyclical structures. Except as noted below, tables expand automatically to accommodate their contents. Entries are removed by the built-in procedure **remove**, so **remove(paper,"title")** removes the entry for **title** in the example above.

Expressions usually compute values, but, as in Icon, some expressions may fail to yield values. For

---

† Present address: IBM Tokyo Research Laboratory, IBM Japan, 5-19 Sanban-cho, Chiyoda-ku, Tokyo 102, Japan

90

example, the relational operators return their right operand only if the relation is satisfied. The absence of values drives control structures such as if statements and for and while loops. For example,

```
sum = 0
for (i = 1; i <= 10; i += 1)
    sum += x[i]
```

computes the sum of x[1] through x[10]. As long as i is less than or equal to 10, i <= 10 yields 10 and the loop body is executed. When i becomes 11, i <= 10 fails to yield a value, which terminates the loop. For some operators, such as assignment, the absence of a value inhibits the execution of the operation. Thus, max = max < a updates max only if a is greater than max.

File system operations are usually provided by 'utilities' in conventional operating systems. Such programs often reduce to simple code fragments in *EZ*. For example, the 'list directory' utility in UNIX, ls, lists the names in a directory, and the *EZ* equivalent can be done by

```
for (i in paper)
    s = s || " " || i
```

which assigns " title authors references" to s. The for-in loop sequences through the table paper assigning the value of each 'index' (which can be of any type) to i and executing the loop body.

Automatic conversions between data types obviate the need for 'conversion' functions and utilities found in conventional languages and operating systems. Numeric operators convert their operands to integers or reals as necessary. Similarly, operands of string operators are converted to strings as necessary. For some operators, the operation performed depends on the type of the operands. For example, the relational operators perform lexical comparison if both operands are strings and numeric comparison (with the appropriate conversions) if either operand is numeric.

Conversions between tables and strings are also provided. Tables are converted to strings by concatenating their elements, and strings are converted to tables by constructing a table with the string associated with the index 1. Thus, for example, simply typing the name of a table displays its contents.

3. Procedures

Procedures are values that contain executable code; a procedure 'declaration' amounts to an assignment of the procedure 'constant' to the identifier. The fragment

```
procedure ls(t) local i, s = ""
    for (i in t)
        s = s || " " || i
    return s
end
```

assigns to ls a procedure that returns a list of the indices in the table passed as the argument. Conversions between procedures and strings are performed automatically. Procedures are converted to strings by returning their source code. Thus, entering "ls" displays its code. Strings are converted to procedures by compiling them; in a sense, compilation is an optimization in *EZ*. Scope rules depend on tables interrogated by the compiler. Unlike other systems, these 'symbol tables' are *EZ* tables, which can be manipulated at the source-language level. This facility is described in more detail below and in Reference 2.

Procedures can be invoked as usual, for instance,

```
list = ls(paper)
```

assigns " title authors references" to list.

In addition, conversion from a procedure to a table, provided by the built-in function table, yields a table that is an activation record for the procedure. This table contains entries for each of the arguments and locals declared in the procedure and entries describing the current state of the activation.

Arguments and locals in an activation can be accessed by indexing the table. For example, after executing

```
d = table(ls)
```

d.i and d.s access the local variables i and s in that activation of ls. Such activations may be invoked like procedures, so both

```
d(paper)
```

and

```
d.t = paper
d()
```

begin execution of ls with paper as its argument.

In addition to the arguments and locals, activations also have the index Procedure, which contains the procedure itself, and the index Resumption, which is the resumption point or 'location counter' for the activation. Resumption points can also be used to access and alter the execution and the source code for the procedure; details are given in Reference 2.

Since activations are just tables, entries can be added, removed, or changed as desired. For example, the Procedure entry need not correspond to the procedure from which the activation was created; it can be changed to any procedure. Missing local variables and parameters are created as necessary. It is typical, for example, for tables to contain *both* data and activation information. For example, a procedure to format a paper can be included as the **Procedure** entry in the table **paper**, described above. Indeed, activations can be constructed from scratch by constructing the table from the appropriate pieces as follows:

```
paper = [
   "title": "EZ Processes",
   "authors": drh || "\n" || mk,
   "body": ...,
   "references": references,
   "Procedure": formatter
]
```

The table constructor $[i_1\!:\!e_1,\ldots,i_n\!:\!e_n]$ constructs a table with n index-value pairs $(i_1,e_1),\ldots,(i_n,e_n)$. Assuming **formatter** is a procedure that formats a document defined by

```
procedure formatter(title, authors,
      body, references)
   ...
end
```

paper() produces the formatted document.

4. Processes

Processes in *EZ* are activations that execute concurrently. All processes share the same, persistent virtual address space. Thus, they are semantically similar to 'threads' or 'lightweight processes' in some operating systems [4]. Processes are just tables; they have all of the normal characteristics of other *EZ* values, including persistence, and all table operations apply to processes. There is no analog of 'heavyweight processes' with separate address spaces as in most operating systems. As described below, the protection benefits of such processes can be obtained by appropriate exploitation of *EZ*'s scope rules.

Processes are manipulated explicitly as *EZ* values and by a set of built-in procedures.

```
create(p, args...)
```

instantiates a new process. It creates a new process, passes *args* to the new process, begins its execution, and returns the process. If **p** is a table (i.e., a procedure activation) a copy is made and instantiated; if **p** is a procedure, **table(p)** is instantiated. If the process cannot be instantiated, **create** does not return a value. Other values are converted to procedures and instantiated as just described. For example, at startup, the *EZ* server (see below) executes

```
create(procedure ()
   while (1) pause()
end)
```

to instantiate an idle process. The argument is compiled into an anonymous procedure, an activation is created, and the activation is instantiated. **pause()** is a built-in procedure that causes the calling process to relinquish its processor. *EZ* uses preemptive scheduling, so **pause** is strictly unnecessary, but **pause** is useful in applications that involve waiting, such as interactive user interfaces [5, 6].

In the current implementation, *EZ* is a server. Local and remote clients connect to the server much like the remote login mechanism on UNIX. Once connected, clients initiate a 'command interpreter,' which is a single process written in *EZ*. The default is a simple line-by-line command interpreter process created by the following code.

```
create(procedure main()
   while (1) read()()
end)
```

read() returns a line, which is converted to a procedure (i.e., compiled) and invoked. Alternatives, which mirror the structure of the UNIX shell, execute each command as a process:

```
create(procedure main() local p
   while (1)
      if (p = create(read()))
         join(p)
end)
```

The built-in procedure **join(p)** causes the calling process to waiting until process **p** terminates.

As shown, the command interpreter process runs forever. Terminating and disconnecting a client need not terminate running processes; they continue running and the command interpreter continues running when the client reconnects. Clients can also terminate and kill all running processes. This is accomplished by explicit manipulation of the table of processes described below.

More elaborate user interfaces, such as the editor that edits *EZ* values [2], permit users to identify code fragments, perhaps by selecting them on the screen, and executing the fragments directly or as processes as suggested above. Thus, when these interfaces run as processes, they work like the simple one above differing only in their presentation to the user.

Processes terminate execution by returning or calling the built-in procedure **die()**. Note that the table remains and may be used again if it is accessible. In *EZ*, accessibility determines the lifetime of data, but not the lifetime of process execution (a garbage collector reclaims inaccessible data). For example,

```
d = create(
   procedure nextmove(x, y)
      local t = f(x, y)
      y = g(x, y)
      x = t
   end,
   0, 0)
```

creates a process for **nextmove** that, given a current position **x,y** computes a new position (perhaps a time-consuming computation) and terminates. The next move is computed by

```
d = create(d)
```

because **d** contains the values of **x** and **y** from the first instantiation.

The built-in procedure **kill(p)** terminates the execution of the process indicated by **p**, but has no affect on the accessibility of **p**.

4.1 The Process Table

Whenever a process is instantiated by **create**, a record describing the new process is entered into the table **Processes**. **Processes** is indexed by each process (i.e., each table); an entry for a process **p** is inserted by executing the equivalent of the assignment

```
Processes[p] = record [
    priority: 0,
    process: p,
    join: ,
    queue:
]
```

The **record** constructor builds a table with the indicated fields, which must be identifiers. Fields with omitted values are uninitialized. Such tables are equivalent to other tables except new entries cannot be added and existing entries cannot be removed.

The value of the **priority** field gives the execution priority of the process in the usual manner (except that all processes are guaranteed some execution time to prevent starvation). The priority of process **p** can be changed by simply changing **Processes[p].priority**. By default, all processes are given the same priority. 'System' processes are assigned other priorities; the idle process is given a low priority while command interpreters are given a high priority. The **process** field is the process itself. The **join** field is a list of processes (threaded through the **queue** fields of the records described above) waiting for this process to terminate.

The process table can be manipulated like any other table. For example,

```
create(procedure()
    local old = 0, new
    while (1) {
        new = size(Processes)
        if (new ~= old)
            write("process count = ",
                old = new)
        pause()
    }
end)
```

instantiates a process that reports changes in the number of processes; **size** is a built-in procedure that re-

turns the size of its operand, e.g., the number of entries in a table, the length of a string, etc.

Most operating systems have a 'process status' utility that gives information on the currently running processes; **ps** in UNIX is an example. The following procedure provides a similar facility in *EZ*.

```
procedure ps() local p
    for (p in Processes)
        write(p.Procedure, "\n")
end
```

ps() prints the source code for the initial procedure in each process.

4.2 Synchronization

Semaphores are used for low-level process synchronization. Higher-level synchronization mechanisms, such as events and message passing, can be implemented in *EZ* with semaphores.

P(s) and **V(s)** are the usual atomic P and V operations on a general semaphore **s**. A semaphore is a table with an appropriately initialized **count** entry. Processes waiting on **s** are linked together via the **queue** fields mentioned above; this list emanates from the **queue** field of **s**, which is created if necessary.

Mutual exclusion can be implemented as usual:

```
mutex = record [ count: 1, queue: ]

procedure update()
    P(mutex); { access resource }; V(mutex)
end
```

Any table can be used as a semaphore; a **count** field with a value of 0 is added if necessary. For example,

```
printer = create(procedure server()
    local head = 0, tail = 0,
        mutex = [ "count": 1 ]
    while (1) {
        P(printer)
        print(printer[head += 1])
        remove(printer, head)
    }
end)
```

creates a simple print server process and assigns it to **printer**. **printer** is a table that serves three purposes. First, it's the activation record for procedure **server**. Second, it's a semaphore that controls the producer-consumer relationship between the single process **printer** and its multiple clients. Since there's no **count** field in **printer**, one is added at the first **P(printer)** (or **V(printer)**) with the value 0, which causes **printer** to wait for something to print. (This implicit creation of a **count** field can be avoided by declaring a local variable `count`.) Third, `printer` is also the print queue; `printer[head+1]` through `printer[tail]` contain the values to be printed. `head` and `tail` are simply incremented; aside from integer overflow, there is no need to keep them within specific bounds.

`mutex` is a semaphore that synchronizes access to the tail of the queue, i.e., `printer[tail]`. Such synchronization is necessary because, while `printer` is the single consumer, there are many producers. As shown above, `printer` blocks on `printer` until a client executes a `V(printer)`. Clients call `lpr`, which appends a value to the queue, using `mutex` gain exclusive access, and then issues a `V` on `printer`:

```
procedure lpr(s)
    P(printer.mutex)
    printer[printer.tail += 1] = s
    V(printer.mutex)
    V(printer)
end
```

Although not recommended, semaphore `count` values and queues can be changed explicitly; they are just table entries.

4.3 Encapsulating I/O

EZ has no I/O primitives; procedures, like `read` and `write` used the examples above, do I/O by communicating with built-in processes connected to devices. These built-in processes use semaphores to synchronize producer-consumer interactions in the usual manner. Other fields are included depending on the specific device. (Of course, there are no 'disk files' as in conventional systems, *per se*, since *EZ* strings and tables provide equivalent facilities.)

For example, the value of `Input` is a built-in process that continually reads lines from the client's terminal. `Input` is initialized by the internal equivalent of

```
Input = create(
    procedure(filename)
        local line, empty, full
        empty = record [ count: 1, queue: ]
        full  = record [ count: 0, queue: ]
        while (1) {
            P(empty)
            doio
            V(full)
        }
    end,
    "terminal"
)
```

where *doio* represents the internal code that performs the actual input operations. When this process runs, *doio* reads the next line from the terminal and assigns it to `line`, and the process signals using `V` that the line is available. It then waits for a consumer to retrieve the

line. Actual implementations for other devices might read more than a single line with a single I/O operation and buffer the excess.

`read` gets the next line by synchronizing appropriately and accessing `Input.line`:

```
procedure read()
    local line
    P(Input.full)
    line = Input.line
    V(Input.empty)
    return line
end
```

Terminal output is similar; the value of `Output` is a built-in process that writes the value of `Output.line` to the terminal.

Other I/O devices are accommodated by changing the details and fields of the process to suit the device. A mouse, for example, can be represented by a process with fields that encode the possible mouse events.

Uses of *EZ* 'I/O processes' thus far have been relatively simple. More ambitious applications, such as building a window system (based on NeWS or X windows) for *EZ*, are underway.

4.4 Protection

EZ provides memory protection for its processes with its scope rules, which can be used to create a 'protected' environment for a process.

Scope rules, which dictate the interpretation of free identifiers, depend on the contents of tables interrogated by the compiler. Unlike most other systems, these 'symbol tables' are *EZ* tables and can thus be manipulated by *EZ* code. As suggested above, use of identifiers declared `local` is restricted to the associated procedure in the usual manner. An interpretation of free identifiers is made by searching the table that is the current value of the variable `root` for an index value lexically equal to the identifier. Each process has its own `root`. Thus, the assignment

```
message = "I'll return soon"
```

is equivalent to

```
root.message = "I'll return soon"
```

If the identifier is not found in `root`, the compiler searches the chain of tables given by

```
root[".."]
root[".."][".."]
root[".."][".."][".."]
...
```

until the identifier is found or a table without a `".."` entry or whose `".."` entry is not a table is encountered.

If this search fails to locate the identifier, it is entered in `root`.

By changing the value of `root` and altering the path given by the `".."` entries, rules such as the inheritance rules in Smalltalk [7], the 'search lists' in UNIX, and the protection benefits of separate address spaces can be obtained. When a new client connects to the *EZ* server, it executes the following initialization code.

```
for (i in root[".."])
    root[i] = root[".."][i]
root.System = root[".."]
remove(root, "..", "i")
```

This code makes a copy of the system root table, which contains the builtin values and values maintained by the server (e.g., `Processes`), arranges for `System` to refer to the system root table, and then removes the `".."` and `i` entries. Doing so prevents subsequent processes from changing system-wide values or unintentionally inferring with other clients. `System` provides an alternative path to the root table, however, for those applications with a legitimate need to manipulate system tables. Clients wishing total isolation from the server and other clients can execute

```
remove(root, "System")
```

5. Implementation

The current version of *EZ* is derived from the earlier implementation and is written in ANSI C [8] and runs under UNIX. The implementation consist of about 7,000 lines of C and a several hundred lines of *EZ*. The *EZ* code consists of the procedures described above as well as other utility and start-up procedures.

EZ source code is compiled into code for a virtual machine that mirrors the primitive operations in the language. The implementation details are similar to those in other very high-level languages, like Icon [9]; additional details are given in Reference 2.

The persistent virtual address space resides on secondary storage and is allocated in units of logical pages. To accommodate small values efficiently, logical pages are 512 bytes regardless of the physical page size of the host. All values, including tables representing activations and processes, are allocated in the virtual address space. The few necessary 'internal' structures, such as an internal pointer to the process table, are also allocated in the virtual address space.

Software caching provides access to the virtual address space. Value representations are designed to increase reference locality, which helps a large cache (≈ 1000 logical pages) minimize paging. Simply flushing the cache saves the system state.

The server multiplexes a single interpreter among the running *EZ* processes initiated by the clients. This implementation is similar to implementations of 'lightweight' processes in UNIX [10, 11] and in other operating systems [4]. Execution of virtual machine instructions and of most built-in procedures is atomic. Context switching is limited to a few built-in procedures that deal with processes (e.g., `join`, `pause`, `die`) and I/O. Preemption is implemented by context switching every n (≈ 1000) virtual machine instructions. I/O interrupts can also cause a context switch.

Multiple representations for values, particularly tables, are used to provide a representation that is best suited for the inferred use. For example, tables that are indexed only by integers have a different representation (sparse arrays) than those indexed by other values (hash tables). The conversion from the simpler to the more complex representation is automatic and performed only when necessary.

Most activations, including processes, are never accessed as tables, and the 'default' activation representation anticipates this pattern of 'transient' activations. While the space for all activations is logically allocated in the virtual address space, activations that are never used as tables are not written to secondary storage. Furthermore, the space for these activations is reused without incurring any paging overhead. Thus, for procedures invoked in the 'normal' functional manner, activations are allocated in a stack-like fashion as in most languages, and the allocation is nearly as efficient as stack allocation, once a pool of available activation pages accumulates.

When an activation is accessed as a table, its representation is converted to a representation that caters to both indexed access and access from the generated virtual machine code. This is accomplished by building a hash table for the indexed access and what amounts to a transfer vector that points into the hash table for access from the generated code.

To terminate the *EZ* server, all accessible activations are converted to the representation just described. This is necessary because the representation of transient activations cannot be written to secondary storage.

As described in References 2 and 12, an off-line garbage collector reclaims inaccessible pages in secondary storage representation of the virtual address space. Reclaimed pages are added to a pool of free pages for subsequent allocation. Pages from this pool are also used for transient activations.

6. Discussion

Initial use of the *EZ* process facility, though limited, has been revealing. While the persistent nature of processes is useful, it can be confusing if processes are used in the traditional, throw-away fashion. It's easy to forget that processes are just persistent values; uninitiated users are often surprised when `ps` (see above) reports days-old processes that are either blocked or computing away. More experience is necessary to understand fully the ramifications of persistent processes and to develop an methodology for their effective use.

Work is currently underway in several areas: Language issues, multi-process applications, a multiprocessor implementation, and multiple representations.

Introducing processes into *EZ* at the language level has been accompanied with some semantic problems whose 'correct' resolution remains open. One of the most interesting issues is the interaction between the process table and *EZ*'s scope rules. As described above, the compiler binds identifiers by consulting a list of symbol tables, which are just *EZ* tables. `Processes` is simply another identifier and, in each client environment, `Processes` points to the single, system-wide process table, which is also an *EZ* table. An alternative is to have many process tables and have `Processes` point to a separate table in each client. The linguistic implications of this alternative and its implementation consequences are yet to be completely investigated.

Another open question concerns 'runaway' inaccessible processes. For instance,

```
p = create(procedure ()
    while (1) pause()
end)
remove(Processes, p)
p = 0
```

creates a non-terminating process, removes it from the process table, and changes `p` so that it no longer refers to the process. The running process is inaccessible and, unless special measures are taken, will be ultimately reclaimed by the garbage collector. Currently, this situation is handled by keeping a 'hidden' pointer to all executable processes so that they *are* accessible, but not from the source-language level. An alternative under investigation would have the garbage collector terminate such processes. More experience may suggest the 'right' choice or other alternatives.

Applications of *EZ* processes thus far have been relatively simple; more ambitious applications will contribute understanding and help identify problems in the current implementation. An example is a current project to use the X window system in the *EZ* clients. Not only will this application provide a more usable system, but will help refine the mechanisms used to have *EZ* processes respond to interrupts. It will also require I/O processes that deal with bitmapped displays.

The current implementation runs on a uniprocessor UNIX system. An implementation for a recently acquired 4-processor DEC 'Firefly' is also planned. The Firefly's shared memory architecture is matched perfectly to *EZ*'s abstract view of a single large, flat address space. A multi-processor implementation will also test the suitability of the process mechanism and its implementation. For example, the decision to make virtual machine instructions atomic helped evolve the implementation of 'sequential' *EZ* to include processes, but is inappropriate on a multiprocessor. Significant redesign of the virtual machine will be required to deal with 'big' operations, such as compilation and concatenation of long strings, that simply cannot be atomic in a multiprocessor system.

Implementing *EZ* tends to require specialized techniques because the semantics are so different from traditional languages and operating systems. While all implementations to date have used multiple representations, processes stress the current implementation to its limit. New representations for processes are being investigated; the approach taken for transient activations, mentioned in the previous section, is an example. Measurements to confirm the efficacy of alternative representations are also contemplated.

Implementing and using *EZ*'s processes has also suggested numerous areas for future work. Examples include a concurrent garbage collector as an *EZ* process [13], performance monitoring for persistent processes, and long-term reliability mechanisms. A particularly interesting area is in building a 'distributed' *EZ*, perhaps by adapting the recent implementations of shared virtual memory [14, 15] to, in effect, distribute the *EZ* virtual address space across a network of workstations.

Acknowledgements

Chris Fraser's comments helped clarify several sections of this paper.

References

1. C. W. Fraser and D. R. Hanson, A High-Level Programming and Command Language, *Proc. of the SIGPLAN '83 Symp. on Programming Language Issues in Software Systems*, San Francisco, CA, June 1983, 212–219.

2. C. W. Fraser and D. R. Hanson, High-Level Language Facilities for Low-Level Services, *Conf. Rec. 12th ACM Symp. on Prin. of Programming Languages*, New Orleans, LA, Jan. 1985, 217–224.

3. R. E. Griswold and M. T. Griswold, *The Icon Programming Language*, Prentice-Hall, Englewood Cliffs, NJ, 1983.

4. M. J. Accetta, R. V. Baron, W. Bolosky, D. B. Golub, R. F. Rashid, A. Tevanian, Jr., and M. W. Young, Mach: A New Kernel Foundation for UNIX Development, *Proc. of the Summer USENIX Conf.*, Atlanta, GA, July 1986, 93–112.

5. *NeWS 1.1 Manual*, Sun Microsystems Inc., Mountain View, CA, Jan. 1988.

6. *NeWS Technical Overview*, Sun Microsystems Inc., Mountain View, CA, Jan. 1988.

7. A. Goldberg, D. Robson, and D. H. H. Ingalls, *Smalltalk-80: The Language and Its Implementation*, Addison Wesley, Reading, MA, 1983.

8. B. W. Kernighan and D. M. Ritchie, *The C Programming Language, Second Edition*, Prentice-Hall, Englewood Cliffs, NJ, Second Edition, 1988.

9. R. E. Griswold and M. T. Griswold, *The Implementation of the Icon Programming Language*, Princeton Univ. Press, Princeton, NJ, 1986.

10. E. C. Cooper and R. P. Draves, C Threads, Tech. Rep. CMU-CS-88-154, Computer Science Dept., Carnegie Mellon Univ., Pittsburgh, PA, June 1988.

11. G. V. Cormack, A Micro-Kernel for Concurrency in C, *Software—Practice & Experience* **18**, 5 (May 1988) 485–492.

12. C. W. Fraser and D. R. Hanson, The *EZ* Reference Manual, Tech. Rep. 84–1, Dept. of Computer Science, The Univ. of Arizona, Tucson, AZ, Jan. 1984.

13. A. W. Appel, J. R. Ellis, and K. Li, Real-time Concurrent Collection on Stock Multiprocessors, *Proc. SIGPLAN '88 Conf. on Programming Language Design and Implementation*, Atlanta, GA, June 1988, 11–20.

14. K. Li, *Shared Virtual Memory on Loosely-Coupled Multiprocessors*, Ph.D. Diss., Yale Univ., New Haven, CT, Oct. 1986.

15. K. Li and P. Hudak, Memory Coherence in Shared Virtual Memory Systems, *Proc. 5th Annual Symp. on Principles of Distributed Computing*, Calgary, Alberta, Aug. 1986, 229–239.

Data–Oriented Exception Handling in Ada[†]

Qian Cui
McCabe & Associates
Twin Knolls Professional Center
5501 Twin Knolls Road, Suite 111
Columbia, Maryland 21045

John Gannon
Department of Computer Science
University of Maryland
College Park, Maryland 20742

Abstract

Exception handling mechanisms were added to programming languages to segregate normal algorithmic processing from error processing. However, attaching handlers to control statements clutters source text in much the same way that testing operations' parameters and results does. In this paper, we present a set of language features that can be added to Ada that associate exceptions with the operations of a data type and exception handlers with data objects. We call our notation *data-oriented exception handling* to distinguish it from more conventional, control–oriented mechanisms. The implementation of a preprocessor from our notation to Ada is described. Empirical studies indicate that control–oriented exception handling mechanisms are more complex than necessary for the tasks they perform, and that data–oriented exception handling can be used to produce programs that are smaller, better structured, and easier to understand and modify.

Introduction

Exceptions are defined as "errors or other exceptional situations that arise during program execution" [5]. Although generally signalled in response to software failures (e.g., domain failures when operations are invoked with parameters that do not satisfy the operations' input assertions or range failures when operations cannot produce results satisfying their output assertions), exception conditions can also be used in normal processing situations to supply extra information about results or monitor the progress of a computation [3].

Exception handling mechanisms permit users to define exceptional conditions and handlers, and to indicate the occurrence of an exception. When an exception is detected, normal processing is suspended and control is passed to a handler associated with the exception. When the handler finishes processing the exception, control is either returned to the point following the signalling statement (resumption), returned to the invoker of the signalling operation (termination), or passed to another exception handler by raising another exception (propagation). Generally, handlers are associated with exceptions via control components in a program, either dynamically by executing a statement making a handler available for a particular exception (as in PL/I) or statically by attaching a handler to a statement or procedure [7] or to an expression [10]. Exceptions that are not handled are propagated at least one–level along the calling chain and until a handler (if any) is found. This presumes that an operation's invoker knows why the operation was called and how best to respond to any exceptional conditions [9].

Proponents of exception handling mechanisms claim these features improve programs in several ways.

Algorithms are not punctuated with conditional statements which divert readers from the main control path and increase nesting depth.

The same checks are not performed by both an operation's caller and its implementation.

Less efficient checks done by the caller are replaced by more efficient checks in the operation's implementation.

Some exceptions (e.g., those caused by resource depletion) cannot be checked before a call is made.

Despite gains in programming simplicity, the use of exceptions, particularly those that are automatically propagated, remains fault–prone because they are the least well documented and tested parts of an interface [4].

Ada is the first widely–used language since PL/I to include exception handling features, and its design reflects many improvements suggested by research on exception handling [2,6]. Handlers are attached to the end of blocks of statements statically rather than being enabled dynamically by executing a statement containing the handler body sometime before an exception is signalled.

However, Ada's exception handling mechanism might still be altered to improve our ability to understand and

† This work was supported by the Air Force Office of Scientific Research under grant AFOSR–87–00130.

validate programs. Handlers are still associated with exceptions via the control components of a program. Although handlers appear at the end of any block after the block's algorithmic code, introducing blocks in the middle of statement lists for the sole purpose of attaching handlers actually inserts error handling code in the middle of algorithmic code. Handlers and packages are not well integrated since such handlers apply only to the initialization sequences of the packages and not the operations in the package bodies. If a subprogram is terminated by an exception, then the values of out and in out parameters present problems. While scalar parameters will not have been updated, aggregate parameters may or may not be changed since a compiler may adopt either reference or copy–in, copy–out implementation strategies. Automatic propagation of unhandled exceptions (rather than explicit propagation of re–named exceptions) makes it impossible to determine statically the set of handlers that can catch an exception. Thus, axiomatizations of Ada's exception handling features limit automatic exception propagation [8].

We have designed and implemented an alternative exception handling mechanism for Ada in which exceptions are associated with data objects rather than with control features. While it does not address all the problems with exceptions in Ada, our mechanism does remove handler code from algorithmic code, improving program structure and aiding user understanding.

Language Features

We raise exceptions only in response to implementation insufficiencies [1] when the storage reserved for an object is inadequate to represent its value or when performance constraints cannot be met. Although defining resource requirements in an operation's specification might permit programmers to test for such conditions explicitly before invoking an operation, such requirements complicate specifications. Our view of exceptional conditions as implementation insufficiencies results in an exception handling mechanism that is tightly coupled with Ada's package construct implementing abstract data types. Exceptions are defined and raised only in packages because such conditions are defined in terms of an object's representation, which can be manipulated only in a package body. Each data object declared has its own set of (exception, handler) binding pairs specified in its declaration.

Three new syntactic structures are defined to implement this design: #exception, #when, and #raise. Exceptions are declared by attaching an #exception clause to the type exported from the specification part of a package. Handlers are associated with exceptions in an object's declaration by attaching a #when clause to the declaration

that specifies handler procedures for the exceptions defined on the object's type. Exceptions are signalled by #raise statements that transmit parameters indicating the object suffering from an implementation insufficiency.

The following package specification defines an abstract data type for stacks whose size can be expanded incrementally.

```
generic
    type e_type is private;
    tentative_size_limit : positive;

package stack_pkg is

    type stack is limited private
        #exception overflow(S: in out stack),
          no_space(S: in out stack; place: string);

    procedure create(S: out stack);
    procedure push(S: in out stack; E: e_type);
    procedure pop(S: in out stack; E: out e_type);
    procedure copy(S: stack; T: out stack);
    function  size(S: stack) return natural;
    function  max_size(S: stack) return natural;
    procedure expand(S: in out stack; amt: positive);

private

    type stack_object;
    type stack is access stack_object;

end stack_pkg;
```

The #exception clause attached to the type definition specifies two exceptions: overflow and no_space. An object of type stack raises the exception overflow when it grows beyond its predefined initial maximum size. This is resolved by increasing the initial maximum size and allocating more storage for the object. Once the overflow problem is corrected, the original computation can be resumed. In the event where all system memory resources have been exhausted, the more severe exception no_space is raised.

All exceptional conditions have parameters to facilitate communication between their signalers and handlers. The two exceptions declared in the previous example both take a parameter of type stack to indicate which object needs more storage. In addition, no_space takes a string parameter that it uses to produce an error message.

Handlers are associated with exceptions when an object is declared by attaching a #when clause to the declaration.

```
with stack_pkg;
procedure main is

    package integer_stack is
        new stack_pkg(integer, 20);
    use integer_stack;

    S1, S2: stack
        #when overflow(S: in out stack ) =>
            expand(S, 40);

begin
    ...
end main;
```

When `overflow` is raised by an operation trying to
update `S1` or `S2`, `expand` is executed to increase the
object's storage capacity by 40%. The names of the
formal parameters of the exception (e.g., `S`) can be used
in the handler body, which is restricted to a single
statement (generally a procedure call). The actual
parameters supplied by a `#raise` statement are passed
along to the corresponding handler procedure as actual
parameters.

Default handlers for exceptions can be specified in a type
declaration and inherited by variables declared with that
type.

```
type stack is limited private
    #exception overflow(S: in out stack) =>
        expand(S, 10),
    no_space(S: in out stack; place: string) =>
        put_line( place );
    ...
```

Thus, the declaration of `S1` and `S2` above would cause
both data objects to override the default handler for
`overflow` (i.e., `expand(S,10)`) and inherit the one for
`no_space`.

In the body of a package that implements an abstract data type,
exceptions can be signalled by executing a `#raise` statement,
e.g., `#raise overflow(S)`. The numbers, types, and
positions of the actual parameters supplied in a `#raise`
statement should agree with those of the formal
parameters declared in the corresponding `#exception`
clause. When an exception is raised, if there is a handler
associated with the object for that condition, the handler
is executed and control returns to the point following the
`#raise` statement. However, if there is no handler,
program execution is terminated.

In many cases, the exception handler is an exported
operation declared in the visible part of a package. Since
the exception is defined on a type whose implementation
is hidden, operations in the package body can deal with
implementation insufficiencies more efficiently than users
can. However, users can supply a procedures of their
own to implement unplanned responses to insufficiencies
(e.g., removing the older elements in the stack to make
room for newer entries).

Handlers that are visible operations of a package can
raise other exceptions. For example, `expand` can raise the
exception `no_space` if no more storage is available to
create new stack objects. To avoid endless recursion, a
handler is not permitted to raise the same exception with
which it is associated. Thus, `expand` is not allowed to
raise the exception `overflow`. Also, care must be taken
to prevent indirect recursion involving two or more
handlers.

We have implemented a preprocessor for translating
pseudo–Ada programs with data–oriented exception
handling into logically equivalent Ada programs. Since
Ada does not permit procedures to be passed as
parameters, the implementation of the preprocessor is not
as straightforward as might be imagined. The details of
the implementation are presented in the Appendix.

Case Study

We analyzed about two dozen programs in the Simtel20
Ada Repository and categorized their use of exceptions
into the following seven categories:

(1) sending error messages (including error logging, etc.);

(2) propagating exceptions upward by re–raising the
    same exceptions or by converting them to other
    exception names;

(3) initializing and/or finalizing operations on objects
    (e.g., open/close a file, set/flush a buffer, etc.);

(4) terminating a block/sub–program or aborting a task;

(5) changing the values of global variables to record the
    significance of raised exceptions for later treatment;

(6) ignoring the exception being raised (null handlers);

(7) performing significant repair or diagnostic actions
    (e.g., determining the site where a
    CONSTRAINT_ERROR is raised).

The results of the analysis in Table 1 show that most of
the handler actions apply only the simplest form of
exception handling, such as propagating the raised
exception upward until termination, or printing out error
messages without doing anything else.

Of the 26 programs analyzed, 15 have trivial exception
handling (2 have no exception handling and another 13
just print messages and propagate errors). Only 2
programs have more than 15% of their exception
handling statements belonging to the last category (i.e.,
non–trivial algorithms). Few programs have deeply
nested exception handlers, and not surprisingly, these
programs are very hard to understand.

Table 1

File Name	Stmt Number	Handler Number	Stmt in Handlers	Error Message	Propa- gation	Init & Final	Term & Abort	Change Globals	Ignore (null)	Control & Others
expert.ada	400	0								
mins.src	856	20	45	6	7	22	3	2	2	3
ed2.src	771	11	42	20	4	13	2	2		1
wpcommon.src	1552	9	9				5	2	2	
wpcrt.src	2197	0								
wpformat.src	4902	31	51	19	2	7	17	6		
wpeditor.src	2035	39	59	18	3	20		9	3	6
ftp.src	2993	179	334	152	153	14	4	7	4	
iface.src	573	9	10	5	5					
smtp.src	1001	71	118	66	46	5				1
smtpwicat.src	1139	70	118	68	47	3				
tcpstand.src	217	1	1	1						
tcpsub.src	3981	141	224	218	6					
tcptest.src	667	5	17	17						
tcpwicat.src	2706	168	252	233	6		12		1	
telnet.src	2476	94	198	104	94					
telwicat.src	2242	95	188	97	91					
wicatmisc.src	297	3	3	2				1		
form2.src	2869	160	320	66	90	12	7	21	32	92
formtest.src	163	2	2	2						
compord.src	1052	44	140	52	2	1	5	2	12	66
mman.src	784	27	31	8		7	4	8	4	
mmgr.src	2633	209	398	158	181	33	1	9	3	13
manpower.src	350	13	17	11		6				
pplanner.src	5112	161	480	266	89	35	45	3	7	35
tracker.src	4343	97	325	294	10	6		14	1	

To determine the effects of transforming a procedure with control–oriented exception handling into one with data–oriented exception handing, we examined compord.src, one of the two programs with non–trivial handlers. This program calculates the correct compilation order of Ada source program units. One of its procedures, put_info_in_dag, uses the data type direct acyclic graph, to represent objects containing compilation dependencies of Ada program units. If a new edge added to the withs_dag results in a cycle, the newly added nodes and edge will then be entered into cycle_dag for later processing. Three exceptions are declared in dag_pkg: illegal_node is raised when a node is not in a dag, or when it is and should not be; duplicate_edge is raised by attempts to add an edge already in the graph; and makes_cycle is raised if a newly added edge would cause a cycle. A slightly edited version of the body of this procedure appears below. Two procedures, add_node_to_dag and add_to_cycle_dag, have replaced inline code to make comparisons between methods more fair.

This program has 4 blocks containing exception handlers, and nests 3 of these blocks within one another. Handler responses to exceptions vary for different data objects. For example, when makes_cycle is raised by add_edge on line 17, the signaler is working on withs_dag. The handler (at line 33) puts the related information into cycle_dag. A similar situation exists when makes_cycle is raised on line 21 and handled on line 23. However, when makes_cycle is raised inside add_to_cycle_dag on lines 25 and 35, the signalers are processing cycle_dag. In such cases, the handlers (on lines 29 and 39) ignore the exception.

Examining the code more carefully, we found the exception handling code on lines 33–40 to be unreachable. In order for control to arrive at line 33, the procedure add_edge (line 17) must raise the exception make_cycle. This implies that procedure add_node (line 16) completed without raising any exceptions that would have terminated the block on lines 14–41. Thus, add_node's argument, with_node, is a fresh node just added into withs_dag. In addition, with_node must be a node different from parent_node or illegal_node would have been raised. Since there is no edge connected to with_node when it is added to withs_dag and with_node is different from parent_node, adding an edge from parent_node to with_node will never generate a cycle.

```
 1 begin
 2    label := ... ;
 3    value := wdag.get_value(withs_dag, parent_node);
 4    ...
 5    if not gen_inst then ...
 6        wdag.set_value(withs_dag, parent_node );
 7    end if;
 8 exception
 9    when wdag.illegal_node => ... ; add_node_to_dag(withs_dag, ... );
10 end;
11 ... ;
12 while id_list_pkg.more(i) loop
13    id_list_pkg.next(i, with_name);
14    begin
15        ...
16        wdag.add_node(withs_dag, with_node );
17        wdag.add_edge(withs_dag, parent_node, with_node );
18    exception
19        when wdag.illegal_node =>
20            begin
21                wdag.add_edge(withs_dag, parent_node, with_node );
22            exception
23                when wdag.makes_cycle =>
24                    begin
25                        add_to_cycle_dag(cycle_dag, parent_node, with_node );
28                    exception
29                        when idag.illegal_node | idag.makes_cycle => null;
30                    end;
31                when wdag.duplicate_edge => null;
32            end;
33        when wdag.makes_cycle =>
34            begin
35                add_to_cycle_dag(cycle_dag, parent_node, with_node );
38            exception
39                when idag.illegal_node | idag.makes_cycle => null;
40            end;
41    end;
42 end loop;
```

To demonstrate the impact our view of exceptions might have on programs, we rewrote put_info_in_dag. The transformed program declares exceptions on the dag data type. Since all objects ignore duplicate edges and nodes, null handlers are associated with these exceptions as defaults.

```
package dag_pkg is
    type dag is private #exception
        duplicate_node(g: dag; l: label)=>null,
        node_not_in_dag(g: dag; l: label),
        duplicate_edge(g: dag; l1,l2: label)=>null,
        makes_cycle(g: dag; l1, l2: label);
    ...
end dag_pkg;
```

All handler actions associated with exceptions raised concerning cycle_dag are null actions. Therefore, in the transformed version, we attach a handler for makes_cycle to cycle_dag in the latter's declaration.

```
cycle_dag: idag.dag
    #when makes_cycle(g: dag; l1, l2: label) => null;
```

The situation is not as simple for withs_dag since it is an in-out parameter with different exception bindings in other scopes. However, introducing a new local variable, temp_dag, and attaching handlers to it is straightforward.

```
temp_dag: wdag.dag
    #when node_not_in_dag(g: dag; l: label) =>
                add_node_to_dag(g, l),
        makes_cycle(g: dag; l1, l2: label) =>
                add_to_cycle_dag(cycle_dag, l1, l2);
```

The revised version of the procedure is shown below.

```
temp_dag := withs_dag;
label := ... ;
value := wdag.get_value(temp_dag, parent_node);
    ...
if not gen_inst then ...
    wdag.set_value(temp_dag, parent_node );
end if;
    ... ;
while id_list_pkg.more(i) loop
    id_list_pkg.next(i, with_name);
        ...
    wdag.add_node(temp_dag, with_node );
    wdag.add_edge(temp_dag,parent_node,with_node);
end loop;
withs_dag := temp_dag;
```

The original procedure and the revised version (including the extra procedures) have about the same number of statements. Since the two versions of the procedure accomplish the same task with the same algorithm, we should not expect this number to change greatly. However, the new version breaks the original code into three smaller procedures, resulting in better modularity and functionality. As for the complexity, the original version has up to three levels of nested handlers, one of which was unreachable. In contrast, the revised version has no handler code mixed with the main code of computation, thus emphasizing the main algorithm and enhancing readability. Sample executions on worst–case data show no difference in execution time between the two versions and approximately a 5% space penalty in the compiled code of the data–oriented version.

Empirical Studies

We conducted two studies to investigate the effects of different exception handling mechanisms on program construction, comprehension, and modification. The subjects were senior undergraduate students taking an advanced Ada course in the University of Maryland, University College for adult continuing education. All of the students were experienced programmers working for commercial software companies. These studies were performed on relatively small programs written by students to help substantiate claims about benefits provided by data–oriented exception handling. Although the results cannot be generalized to large systems, the data encourages us to apply our methods to these systems.

Program Construction

In our first study, subjects solved the same problem twice, first with Ada and then with our version of Ada with data–oriented exception handling. Our preprocessor translated pseudo–Ada programs so they could be compiled by the Ada compiler.

We tested four pairs of null and alternative hypotheses that compare the sizes of programs, numbers of statements per subprogram, and maximum and average nesting depths of statements. We conjectured that programs with data–oriented exception handling would have smaller measures of each of these metrics than similar programs with control–oriented exception handling. Although we evaluate the results of this study as if it were a controlled experiment, substantial learning effects may bias the results.

Subjects designed and implemented a test driver and a generic package supporting a hash table represented as a variable–size, one–dimensional array. Two hashing functions need to be supplied when instantiating the package: an efficient hashing function that resolves key

conflicts with simple linear probing and a more complicated algorithm that produces better key distribution. When it becomes too full, the hash table can be expanded and if too many key collision occur, the hashing function can be switched. Several exceptions (e.g., `too_many_nonhit`, `table_half_full`, `no_more_storage`) are defined to facilitate function switching and table expansion. The driver routine reads a list of keys and uses the exceptions to take specified actions when performance constraints are violated.

Subjects completed two programs, the first using Ada with its control–oriented exception handling mechanism and the second with our data–oriented mechanism. Of the eleven subjects who remained in the class to the end of the semester, nine turned in both programs. Study of these programs shows that using data–oriented exception handling resulted in simpler and smaller code. On average, the driver routines in the first project have 152.67 Ada statements, about 25% more statements than their counterparts in the second project (122.11 statements). There were also improvements in program structure in the second project. On average, the subjects divided the driver routines into more sub–modules (procedures and functions) in the data–oriented versions — 9.33 sub–modules, compared to 7.11 sub–modules used in the control–oriented version. Since data–oriented exception handling resulted in both fewer statements and more modules, the average size of the modules decreased greatly from the first project to the second (22.22 statements/sub–module to 13.58). Other improvements in program structure in the data–oriented versions can be demonstrated by examining the main program of the drivers. On average, there are more than twice as many executable statements in the main programs in the first project than in the second (36.89 to 16.56 statements) and the statements were more deeply nested (average maximum nesting depth 5.89 to 3.22). While some improvement must be attributed to learning effects, the differences are all highly statistically significant (using a Wilcoxon rank–sum test).

Program Comprehension and Modification

Our second study was designed to test how the choice of the different exception handling mechanisms would affect program comprehension and modification. Since this study was conducted after concluding the previous study, the subjects were already familiar with both exception handling mechanisms.

This experiment took the form of in–class quiz. Each subject studied two problems. For each problem, the subjects were asked to read a program of four to five pages and then answer several questions, some of which involved comprehension and others modification. In order to investigate the effect of different exception handling mechanisms on program comprehension and modification, we designed two equivalent versions of programs for each of the problems: a control–oriented exception handling version (C) and a data–oriented exception handling version (D), respectively. A subject assigned to work on version C of one problem studied version D of the other problem, and vice versa. We tested two pairs of null and alternative hypotheses that compared test scores and solution times. We conjectured that test scores would rise and solution times fall for subjects using data–oriented exception handling.

The questions for the problems were designed so that it was possible to grade them objectively according to certain uniform grading rules that apply to both versions. The final score assigned to a student on a problem was calculated by counting the number of correct solutions divided by the number of questions.

The analysis shows that the average score for the problems in version C (0.591) is somewhat lower than the average score for the corresponding problems in version D (0.697). Dividing the questions into two groups (comprehension and modification), we determined that the differences of total scores mainly come from the latter group. Thus, our data–oriented exception handling mechanism may have greater impact on modification activities (a more realistic programming task) than on a programmer's ability to understand and answer questions about a program.

In addition to giving solutions, subjects were also asked to record the time spent on each question. The total time given for the quiz is 150 minutes. The average time spent on a problem for version C was 57.227 minutes, while that for version D was 53.455 minutes. Thus subjects spent less time on problems for data–oriented exception handling versions, but still got better results.

The difference in test scores between the two groups is mildly significant (at the 20% level) while that for solution time is not significant. The relatively small differences between the respective averages for time consumed and small number of subjects both contribute to the lack of significant differences.

Summary

Exception handling mechanisms were introduced into programming languages to segregate normal algorithmic processing from error handling. Attaching handlers to control statements clutters source text in much the same way that testing suitability of inputs for an operation and the significance of its results does. In contrast, declaring exceptions with a type's operations and associating handlers with objects in declarations centralize information about exceptional processing and separate it from algorithmic processing. Experimental results indicate that data–oriented exception handling can be used to produce programs that are smaller, better structured, and easier to understand and modify. With the exception of pre–processing time, no significant time or space penalty results from this change. We are currently working on proof rules and test coverage metrics that will permit us to compare these alternative exception handling mechanisms in other ways.

References

(1) A.P. Black. Exception Handling: the Case Against. Ph.D. Thesis, TR 82–01–02, Dept. of Computer Science, Univ. of Washington, (May 1983).

(2) C.M. Geschke, J.H. Morris, and E.H. Satterthwaite. Early experience with Mesa. *Comm. ACM*, 20, 8, 540–553, (Aug. 1977).

(3) J.B. Goodenough. Exception Handling: Issues and a Proposed Notation. *Comm. ACM*, 18, 12, 683–696, (Dec. 1975).

(4) J.J. Horning. Effects of Programming Languages on Reliability. in *Computing Systems Reliability*, (T. Anderson and B. Randell, eds.), Cambridge University Press (1979).

(5) J.D. Ichbiah, et al. Rationale for the Design of the Ada Programming Language. *SIGPLAN Notices* 14, 6, Part B (June 1979).

(6) R. Levin. Program Structures for Exceptional Condition Handling. Ph.D. Thesis, Carnegie–Mellon University, (June 1977).

(7) B.H. Liskov and A. Snyder. Exception handling in CLU. *IEEE Trans. Software Eng.*, SE–5, 6, 546–558, (Nov. 1979).

(8) D.C. Luckham and W. Polak. Ada exception handling: an axiomatic approach. *ACM TOPLAS* 2, 2, 225–223, (April 1980).

(9) D.L Parnas and H Wurges. Response to Undesired Events in Software Systems. Proceedings of the Second International Conference on Software Engineering, (1976), 437–446.

(10) S. Yemini and D.M. Berry. A Modular Verifiable Exception–Handling Mechanism. *ACM TOPLAS, 7,2*, (1985), 214–243.

Appendix: Implementation

We have implemented a preprocessor to translate a pseudo–Ada program with data–oriented exceptions to a logically equivalent Ada program. The preprocessor uses Ada's generic facility to pass automatically–generated dispatch procedures (one per defined exception) to an objects' defining package. A dispatch procedure accepts parameters that permit it to identify objects in order to execute the appropriate handler statement for the object. `raise` statements in the bodies of operations are translated into calls on dispatch procedures.

In the specification part of the generic package, the preprocessor translates each exception into a generic formal procedure.

```
with system; use system;
generic
     type e_type is private;
     tentative_size_limit : positive;

     with procedure overflow_handler
        (zzz_obj1: integer; zzz_addr1: address);
     with procedure no_space_handler
        (zzz_obj1: integer; zzz_addr1: address;
         place: string);

package stack_pkg is

     type stack is limited private;
--     #exception overflow( S : in out stack ),
--        no_space(S: in out stack; place: string);
     ...
     procedure push(S: in out stack;
                    zzz_obj1: integer;
                    zzz_addr1: address; E: e_type);
     ...
```

Each formal parameter of type stack in the package specification is augmented by two additional formal parameters: an integer identifying the object which is used by a dispatch procedure to select the object's handler, and the address of the object which is used by a dispatch procedure to access objects that might not be visible. Of course, any calls to these procedures are similarly translated, e.g.

```
push( S, 4, S'address, X );
```

When a package is instantiated with appropriate parameters (e.g., defining the type of the stack elements and the initial size of the stack):

```
package int_stack is new stack_pkg(integer, 20);
```

the preprocessor introduces two dispatch procedures for the exceptions defined in the package specification and uses them in the instantiation:

```
procedure zzz_int_stack_overflow
     (zzz_obj1: integer; zzz_addr1: address);
procedure zzz_int_stack_no_space
     (zzz_obj1: integer; zzz_addr1: address;
      place: string);
package int_stack is new stack_pkg
     (integer, 20 , zzz_int_stack_overflow,
      zzz_int_stack_no_space );
```

For each type in a user's program, the preprocessor assigns sequential integers to all objects of the type. These numbers are used as selectors in the case statement in the appropriate dispatch procedure. In the following sample user program, S1, S2, and S3 are assigned the numbers 1, 2 and 3 respectively.

```
with text_io, stack_pkg; use text_io;
procedure try is
     zzz_abort : exception;
     procedure my_handler
        (S: in out int_stack.stack;
         zzz_obj1: integer;
         zzz_addr1: address; amt: positive );
     S1, S2 : int_stack.stack;
--     #when overflow(S: in out stack)=>expand(S, 40);
--          no_space(S: in out stack; place: string)
--                    => put_line( place );
begin
     ...
     declare
        S3: int_stack.stack;
--          #when overflow(S: in out stack) =>
                  my_handler(S, 30);
        begin  ...  end;
     ...
end try;
```

The preprocessor generates the exception zzz_abort to halt the main program if an exception is raised on an object without a corresponding handler.

Implementation considerations led us to limit an exception handler's actual parameters to formal parameters from the exception specification (i.e., identifiers appearing before =>), literals, or global variables in the user program. The preprocessor inserts dispatch procedures in the outermost unit of scope in a user's program. Thus, variables declared in inner units of scope and actual subprogram parameters are not visible to the dispatch procedures.

One dispatch procedure is constructed for each exception defined on a type. Each dispatch procedure contains a case statement whose body is the collection of #when clauses for each of the objects in the user's program. The dispatch procedure for int_stack.stack's overflow exception is shown below.

```
with unchecked_conversion;
separate( try )
procedure zzz_int_stack_overflow
     ( zzz_obj1: integer; zzz_addr1: address) is

     type zzz_ptr is access int_stack.stack;
     function zzz_addr_to_ptr is
        new unchecked_conversion(address,zzz_ptr);
     zzz_p1: zzz_ptr := zzz_addr_to_ptr(zzz_addr1);
begin
     case zzz_obj1 is
          when  1 => int_stack.expand
                     (zzz_p1.all,1,zzz_addr1,40);
          when  2 => int_stack.expand
                     (zzz_p1.all,2,zzz_addr1,40);
          when  3 => my_handler
                     (zzz_p1.all,3,zzz_addr1,30);
          when others => raise zzz_abort;
     end case;
end zzz_int_stack_overflow;
```

When constructing a handler in a dispatch procedure from the corresponding #when clause in a declaration, the actual parameters that are global variables or literals are

simply copied textually. However, those actual
parameters that are formal parameters of an exception
need special treatment since some of the identifiers (e.g.,
S3) would not be visible in a dispatch procedure declared
on the outer level of a user's program. The preprocessor
converts the addresses of objects passed to dispatch
procedures to the objects themselves. To convert an
address to an object, the preprocessor uses
unchecked_conversion to initialize an access variable
(pointer) so that it points to an object with proper
structure. The access variable can then be de–referenced
to produce an object as expected. In our example,
zzz_addr1 is converted to an access value pointing to an
object of type int_stack.stack and is then used to
initialize zzz_p1. When invoking my_handler, a stack
object is obtained by de–referencing zzz_p1 (i.e.,
zzz_p1.all). The object number and address of each
stack object are passed as actual parameters so that any
other exceptions raised for the object can be properly
handled.

A #raise statement is translated to an invocation of the
corresponding generic formal procedure with the object's
number, e.g.,

```
procedure push(S: in out stack; zzz_obj1: integer;
               zzz_addr1: address; E : e_type ) is
begin
    if S.top = S.storage'last then
--      #raise overflow( S );
        overflow_handler( zzz_obj1, zzz_addr1 );
    ...
end push;
```

GARTL: A Real-time Programming Language Based on Multi-version Computation

Chris Marlin   Wei Zhao   Graeme Doherty   Andrew Bohonis

Department of Computer Science, The University of Adelaide,
G.P.O. Box 498, Adelaide, South Australia 5001, Australia.

Abstract

The increasing importance of real-time computing systems is widely known and such systems are presently the subject of much research. A particularly attractive approach to the programming of hard real-time systems is the identification of multiple versions of the task to be carried out. If this is done, then the system scheduler used by a real-time system can select the version which gives the most precise results in the time available – the more time available, the more precise the results. This approach to programming hard real-time systems is called *multi-version computation*. This paper explores the question of suitable language support for multi-version computation through the description of GARTL, a real-time programming language. Some aspects of the implementation of GARTL are also discussed.

1. Introduction

In the last few years, there has been increased interest in the design and analysis of real-time computer systems [11,14,16]. New, complex real-time applications are being envisioned, such as the space station, teams of mobile robots performing undersea exploration, and the integration of expert systems into embedded real-time applications such as avionics and process control. In all these systems, real-time software plays a critical role.

The principal problem in writing software to execute in a hard real-time environment is well-known: the software must be written so that the various hard real-time deadlines are met without fail. Since the real-time system will, in general, consist of various components or *tasks*, the above problem becomes in practice the more difficult problem of setting and achieving a number of subsidiary deadlines, one for each task which has to be carried out. Some of the tasks to be carried out will be periodic, such as those concerned with sensors on the external world. Other tasks will be aperiodic; examples of these include tasks which are activated by other tasks.

For all tasks, it may be possible to identify multiple versions of the task, which may have quite different resource requirements. In particular, the different versions may require different lengths of time for their execution. Typically, the version which takes the longest time to execute will also produce the most accurate result, yield the most information, or be superior to the others in some significant manner. The other versions will take smaller and smaller amounts of time to execute, but will produce results of lower and lower quality.

For example, consider a missile detection and identification system on, say, a ship. One would expect that, provided some minimum amount of time is available, this system would be capable of at least detecting the presence of a missile near the ship and indicating that it appears to be getting closer to the ship. If more time is available,

the system may be able to provide more detailed information on the missile, such as its speed and altitude. If still more time is available, it might be possible for the system to also identify the missile type. These levels of information correspond to different versions of the missile detection and identification task.

The question of how long a particular version will take to execute is clearly a complex one and this execution time will frequently depend critically on parameter values and other conditions prevailing in its environment at the time of invocation. It will also be necessary to have some estimate of the time available for the task to execute; we will assume in the remainder of this paper that this latter estimate is available when required.

The focus of this paper is the design of a programming language called GARTL to support the above approach to programming hard real-time systems, and is part of a larger project concerned with multi-version computation as an approach to meeting hard real-time deadlines [3,6,7,8,9,10,12,15]. In terms of language support, it is necessary to provide the ability to declare the multiple versions of a task; among other things, this declarative mechanism will need to indicate the attributes of task upon which the execution is thought to depend. The other major aspect of language support is, of course, the invocation of the tasks; this language mechanism must have the ability to specify the task to be activated, the lowest acceptable version of the task and the deadline for completion of the task, among other things. An important innovation in the GARTL language is the way it permits interaction between the tasks and the system scheduler; this kind of interaction is extremely useful in programming hard real-time systems.

In the remainder of this paper, the GARTL language features to support the multi-version computation approach to real-time programming are first described. Then, some aspects of the implementation of the language are discussed. Finally, some conclusions are presented and planned future work is outlined.

2. The GARTL Language

The GARTL language has been designed as an extension of the C language[5]. In this section, the more important of the extensions are described and some of the design issues discussed.

2.1 Task specification

As shown in Figure 1, a GARTL task is specified in the form of a section of code similar to a C function of type void. This code executes in parallel with other tasks. A task may not access any variables which are not either declared locally, or declared as parameters to the task – the reason for this restriction is to make the dependencies of the task as clear as possible, and to simplify

```
[preemptable] task ⟨task name⟩
    [#⟨version variable⟩:⟨maximum version⟩]
    (⟨parameter list⟩)
    [⟨parameter type list⟩]
    [monitor ⟨monitor list⟩]
    [using ⟨resource use list⟩]
{
    ⟨statement list⟩
}
```

Figure 1. The form of a task specification in GARTL.

the process of predicting the execution times of its various versions. As described later, tasks may be scheduled to start at some specified time in the future, a deadline for their execution may be specified, and they may be started periodically, possibly up to some specified stopping time. The various components of the syntactic form shown in Figure 1 will now be explained.

Resources

The resources specified in the "⟨resource use list⟩" may be files, I/O ports, or other system resources. The specific operations allowed on a resource will depend on the nature of the system resource concerned. Thus, for example

- a file resource might be readable and writeable via the relevant system functions,

- an input port resource might be read-only, again via system functions, and

- a global RAM resource might be readable and writeable via the relevant system functions.

The resources that a task requires must be specified in the task declaration as one of *readable*, *writeable* or *readable and writeable*; to acheive this, the syntax of each element in "⟨resource use list⟩" above has the following syntax (in its simplest form):

[read | write | readwrite] on ⟨name list⟩;

The scheduler will allow a number of tasks to be scheduled for possibly simultaneous execution if they only require read access on a particular resource; if a task is scheduled that requests write (or readwrite) access on a resource, then no other task can be scheduled for possibly simultaneous execution which also requests that resource either for reading or for writing. For example, the task "T1" in Figure 2 requires read access on resources "r1", "r2", "m1" and "r3", and write access on "m1" and "f1".

```
task T1(r1)
    resource r1;
    using
        read on r1, r2;
        readwrite on m1;
        read on r3;
        write on f1;
{
    /* body */
}
```

Figure 2. A GARTL task using various resources.

Figure 2 also shows that a resource may be passed as a parameter; in such situations, the resource ("r1" in Figure 2) must be declared in the "⟨parameter type list⟩" part of the task. In this way,

it is possible for the required resource to remain unspecified until the time that the task is scheduled for execution.

Global resources

Each resource which is not a parameter of the task can only be a resource which is *globally declared*. This allows the specification of an association between a name to be used within the program and an operating system resource (such as a file or an I/O port). Such a declaration has the form:

resource ⟨name⟩ is "⟨system name⟩" [raises ⟨exception name⟩];

where "⟨name⟩" is the name by which the resource will be known throughout the program, "⟨system name⟩" is some identification of the system resource, and "⟨exception name⟩" is the name of an exception (see Section 2.4 below). For example, the declaration

resource DB is "./database" raises missing_DB;

declares a file resource with the local name "DB", and which is actually the file called "database" in the current directory; if it is not found, the exception "missing_DB" is raised, which might perhaps result in the creation of the file.

When a program begins execution, an exception is raised for each declared resource that is not present. The order in which the exceptions occur is not specified, but all are guaranteed to occur before the body of the main task begins execution. If the user specifies an exception name in the resource declaration, then this exception is raised for the main task. If the user does not specify an exception, however, then the exception "resource_missing" is raised. The default action for dealing with any exception which has no handler specified for it (including the "resource_missing" exception) is to terminate program execution. The exception handling facility described in Section 2.4 can be used to create the resource and then continue execution.

Preemptable tasks

As shown in Figure 1, the task specification may be prefixed by the keyword "**preemptable**" to indicate that it can be interrupted. When a task is scheduled, it has guaranteed access to all of its requested resources, and no other task should be scheduled that will violate this access. In designing a task, the programmer can assume that any changes that occur to a resource during the task's execution will not be the result of the action of some other task. That is, any changes that occur will only be caused either by the task itself or by some external stimuli, such as the arrival of data on an I/O port.

However, this can lead to the inefficient application of available resources to meet deadlines. For example, imagine that a task "T1" which will take 20 seconds has a deadline in 25 seconds and has just been scheduled on a system with one processor. Now imagine that another task "T2" requests scheduling; this task has a deadline in 5 seconds and will take 5 seconds. If "T1" could be interrupted, or *preempted*, then both deadlines can be met; on the other hand, if "T1" is not interrupted, "T2" will certainly not meet its deadline. Rather than have the GARTL language implementation attempt to discern whether it is possible to interrupt a task's execution without unfortunate effects, the present version of the language requires the programmer to indicate whether a task can be safely interrupted by prefixing the task specification with the keyword "**preemptable**".

Version numbers

Another aspect of the task specification is the provision of version numbers. As indicated in Section 1, the GARTL language supports an approach to the programming of hard real-time systems which involves the provision of multiple versions of a task. The scheduling of tasks is always based on the assumption a higher numbered version of a task is more desirable (say, in terms of the accuracy of the result) than a lower numbered version. It is up to the programmer to use version numbers consistent with this assumption. Consequently, the task specification includes the ability to specify a range of version numbers and to provide access to the version number of the current instance of the task through a *version variable*, in the following manner:

$$\#\langle \text{version variable}\rangle:\langle \text{maximum version}\rangle$$

The version variable is implicitly an unsigned integer. Within the declarations and body of the task, the version variable can only have its value read. To facilitate the construction of the database of performance measurements and resource requirements used by the implementation (see Section 3), an upper limit on the version number must be specified by the user. For example, the task specification for "Refine" in Figure 3 indicates that the task has 30 versions, numbered from 1 to 30. In this case, the version number is held in the version variable "Ver" and is used to control the execution of a refinement loop in a simple manner. Declaring a task without any specification of multiple versions is equivalent to declaring the same task with a maximum version number of 1.

```
task Refine#Ver:30(x)
    int x;
{
    int i;
    for (i=0; i<=Ver; i++) { /* refine "x" */ }
}
```

Figure 3. A simple GARTL task which has multiple versions.

When a task has multiple versions, the different versions may not all have the same resource requirements. For example, a low numbered version may use a global RAM resource to hold a previously calculated approximate result, while a higher numbered version might look up a file and calculate a more accurate result. This is illustrated in Figure 4, where the task "GetName" has two versions: the first version requires only access to "last", whereas the second version also requires access to "the_file". The example in Figure 4 also shows how the memory requirements of a task can depend on the version number, in that version 1 has an array with 100 elements and version 2 has an array of size 200.

```
task GetName#V:2(id,name)
    int id;
    char *name;
    using
        readwrite on last : 1, 2;
            /* Both versions use "last" */
        read on the_file : 2;
            /* Only the second version uses "the_file" */
{ int my_array[V*100];
    ...
}
```

Figure 4. A GARTL task where the multiple versions have different resource requirements.

Monitored variables

As will be explained in more detail later, when a request for a task to be scheduled is submitted to the scheduler, the scheduler looks at the values of a subset of the parameters passed to the task, and uses its knowledge of past executions to determine if it is possible to successfully schedule a suitable version of the task. The parameters to be regarded as significant in predicting execution time from past executions of the task are specified by the programmer.

These are known as *monitored variables*. Using knowledge of the computation carried out by the task, the programmer must choose the parameters which are important in deciding how long a task will execute. Assignments can be made to monitored variables within a task, but it is only their values at the time of the scheduling request that is important in deciding how long it will take. If a task has no monitored variables, it is assumed that the time of execution of the task will be independent of the inputs, and always the same for a particular version of the task.

For example, Figure 5 depicts a task with monitored variables. The declaration of a monitored variable, such as that for "len", contains a list of collections of possible values for the monitored variable. Each collection is enclosed in square brackets and defines an equivalence class of values of the corresponding variable from the point of view of predicting the execution time of the task. Thus, the declaration in Figure 5 defines three equivalence classes of values and indicates to the language implementation that maintaining three sets of execution time records for this task will be sufficient to predict future execution times. The three equivalence classes for monitoring "len" defined by the declaration in Figure 5 are:

(1) the values between 0 and 25 inclusive, along with the values between 27 and 49 inclusive,

(2) the value 26, and

(3) the values from 50 up to the maximum representable integer.

It is the programmer's responsibility to ensure that actual parameter values fall within one of the equivalence classes declared; if this assumption is violated, a "monitor_range" exception will be raised for the calling task. Only parameters with scalar types (such as "int" and "char"), or with floating point number types may be used as monitored variables. Because of the difficulty of specifying ranges of values for floating point number types, whenever a value occurs in a number of equivalence classes, the value is regarded as belonging to the last of the classes specified.

```
task T1#V:2(int len, struct list_array list)
    /* "len" is the number of elements of "list"
        actually used */
    monitor
        len: [0..25,27..49],[26],[50..maxint];
{
    /* body */
}
```

Figure 5. A task with monitored variables.

2.2 Mailboxes and messages

The message facility of GARTL provides a means for tasks to communicate among themselves, and for communication between tasks and the system scheduler. (In the remainder of this section on mailboxes and messages, the term "tasks" may be assumed to include the scheduler.) As far as the programmer is concerned, *messages* may be regarded as blocks of memory copied between tasks, via the system scheduler, using library routines of system calls. On the other hand, *mailboxes* are areas of memory local to task instantiations, and messages are sent to these areas.

Mailboxes may only be declared as variables local to tasks; in particular, they may not be declared within functions. When a message is sent, it must be sent to a particular mailbox. If the task that owns the mailbox is active, then the message will be copied via the system scheduler into the mailbox, where it can be read by the receiving task at some later point. Messages sent to mailboxes whose owning task is not active are simply lost. The last place in a mailbox is special in that if a mailbox is full, any new arriving messages will overwrite the last message in the mailbox.

Figure 6 depicts a task which declares two mailboxes: "MBint" and "MBpers". The mailbox "MBint" is intended to receive up to four messages containing integers, and "MBpers" is a mailbox which can hold only receive one message at a time, each such message containing a structure of the type shown.

```
task R() {
    mailbox int MBint[4];
    mailbox
        struct {
            char name[8];
            int age;
        } MBpers[1];

            /* body */

}
```

Figure 6. A task containing two mailboxes.

In order to describe the location of a mailbox, there is a prede-fined type called "**mail_address**". The mail address of a mailbox can be found using the "**mailaddr**" operator on a mailbox. For example, the code in Figure 7 sets the variable "MA" to the mail address of the mailbox "MB", where the contents of the latter are structures of the type shown in the figure.

```
/* declarations */
mailbox struct {
    char name[8];
    int ID;
} MB[20];

mail_address MA;

/* code */
MA = mailaddr MB;
```

Figure 7. Declaring and using mail addresses.

A message can be sent to a mailbox using the "send" library function. This takes as arguments the address of a message, and a mail address. It sends a copy of the message to the mailbox ad-dressed. The number of bytes sent is just enough to fill one of the mailbox's messages and is not related to the type of the local copy of the message. Thus, it is the programmer's responsibility to make sure the messages are of the correct size. In a similar manner, messages can be recieved from a mailbox using the "recv" library function, but only if the mailbox has been declared local to the current task. When a message is received, a copy is placed into the memory starting at the address given by the second parameter to "recv". When this is done, the mailbox is allowed to reuse the space for another message; thus, if the mailbox is full, it will be able to receive one more mes-sage before it has to start overwriting messages again. The "recv" function returns the number of messages that the mailbox contained prior to the message being read out. If an attempt is made to read a message from a mailbox not declared locally, or if an attempt is made to read a message from a mailbox that does not currently hold a message, the returned message is undefined. The number of messages that have arrived in a locally declared mailbox can be tested with the "arrived" library function.

2.3 Task invocation

At any one time, there are likely to be a number of tasks exe-cuting, and a number that are ready to be executed. Except for the main task, the execution of every task is initiated by another task. In order to start a new (or *child*) task, the existing (or *parent*) task makes a scheduling request to the system scheduler. The parent task informs the scheduler of

- the parameters to pass to the child task,
- which versions of a multiple-versioned task are acceptable, and
- how the child is to be executed.

There are essentially two ways in which a child can be executed: *synchronously* and *asynchronously*. In addition, there are two ways that the scheduler can be called; again, these are known as calling the scheduler *synchronously* and *asynchronously*. All four combinations of these possibilities are allowed and are discussed below.

When the scheduler receives a scheduling request, it estimates what the resource requirements of the new task will be, including processor time, and decides on the highest numbered version of the task that can be executed. If the highest version number the sched-uler expects to be able to complete is nevertheless smaller than the minimum specified by the programmer, then the child task is not scheduled and is hence not executed.

A scheduling request will specify the task to be scheduled, the minimum allowable version number and the parameters to be trans-mitted to the task if it is successfully invoked. For example, the scheduling request

call T1#3(x,y,z)

will schedule task "T1" with parameters "x", "y" and "z" only if version three or higher can execute successfully, and the request

call T2#(a+b)*c (d,e)

schedules "T2" with parameters "d" and "e" only if the best version which can be scheduled is greater than or equal to the result of the expression "(a+b)*c". If no minimum version is specified, then any version is regarded as acceptable. Note, however, that it is still possible that no child will be scheduled (in the case that even the lowest version cannot be scheduled in the time allowed).

Scheduler results

It is often desirable to know if a task has been successfully scheduled or not. In order to obtain this information back from the scheduler, it is possible to pass to the scheduler the address of a mailbox where the scheduler can write an integer representing the results of its efforts; this is done by giving its name before the task name in the invocation command. As soon as the scheduler has decided whether the child task can be scheduled or not, it sends an integer message to the given mailbox. This integer is the maximum version of the child task which can be executed. As mentioned above, if the integer is less than the minimum specified by the programmer for the task, then the child task is not actually scheduled for execution.

For scheduling requests that request multiple instances of a task (see "Periodically scheduled tasks" below), the scheduler may be provided with a mailbox that can hold multiple integer messages. Each element in the mailbox will hold the scheduler's result for that instance of the child. That is, the first element will hold the maximum version for the first instance, the second element will relate to the the second instance, and so on. If the mailbox fills up, the results will keep overwriting the last message in the mailbox.

As an example, consider the code in Figure 8. In this fragment of code, the integer variable "SR" is used to hold the result from the scheduler via the message in the mailbox "SMB". The parent task then uses the contents of this variable to decide what action to take.

```
{
    mailbox int SMB[1];
    mail_address MA = mailaddr SMB;
    int SR;
    int give_up=0;

    call (MA) recognise#4( ); /* the first attempt at "recognise" */
    recv(MA, &SR); /* now know scheduler has sent message */
    upto 100 while ((SR<4) && (! give_up)) {
        if (SR=0)
            give_up = 1; /* we are never going to succeed */
        else {
            slow_down( ); /* take recovery action */
            call (MA) recognise#4( ); /* and try again */
            recv(MA, &SR);
        }
    }
}
```

Figure 8. Using results returned by the scheduler.

Synchronous task scheduling

When a child task is scheduled synchronously, the parent task suspends execution until the child finishes. As mentioned earlier, the scheduler may be invoked either synchronously or asynchronously in the case that the task is to be scheduled synchronously. If the scheduler is to be invoked synchronously, which is illustrated in Figure 9(a), the call syntax seen earlier is used and the parent suspends itself as soon as the scheduling request is made. In Figure 10, for example, the parent requests that the task "T1" be executed syn-

```
    mailbox int SR;
    call (mailaddr SR) T1#3( );
```

Figure 10. An example of synchronous task scheduling.

chronously. At the point immediately after the scheduling request on the second line of Figure 10, the programmer can assume that the scheduler has decided whether or not "T1" will be scheduled. To find out the nature of this decision, the "SR" mailbox will need to be checked.

If, on the other hand, the scheduler is to be invoked asynchronously, one uses the keyword **asyn_call** in place of **call**; in this case, shown in Figure 9(b), the parent continues execution until the scheduler is finished the process of deciding if the child can execute. If the child can execute, the parent will then suspend and wait until the child has terminated; this would normally be used where the child needs access to some resource being used by the parent. The parent will not terminate until all synchronously scheduled children have terminated. Note that the child does not neccessarily start executing immediately (see "Timing constraints" below) and so the parent may have a long wait.

For scheduling requests which potentially invoke multiple instances of a task (see "Periodically scheduled tasks" below), the parent does not continue execution until the scheduler has decided on the success or failure of the scheduling of all the child tasks, and until the last child task which was successfully scheduled has terminated. If the scheduler was called asynchronously, the parent continues execution until the scheduler has decided if the first child can be scheduled successfully before suspending its own execution.

Asynchronous task scheduling

When a parent task makes a successful request for a child to be executed asynchronously, the child may be executed at any time within its timing constraints. This means that the parent task may terminate before the child task. Again, the scheduler may be called synchronously or asynchronously:

- if the keyword **sched** is used, then the scheduler is called synchronously, and
- if **asyn_sched** is used, the scheduler is called asynchronously.

The synchronous scheduler call is illustrated in Figure 11(a) and would be used if the parent was interested in knowing what the scheduler results were; Figure 11(b) shows the asynchronous version, which would be used if the parent was not interested in these results. In a similar fashion to synchronous task scheduling, a synchronous call to the scheduler will cause the parent task to wait until the

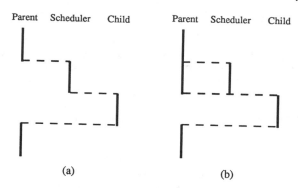

Figure 9. Synchronous task scheduling.

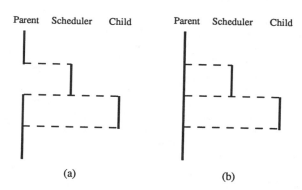

Figure 11. Asynchronous task scheduling.

scheduler has decided on the success of the scheduling of all instances of the child task, but it will not wait for the actual execution of the children. An asynchronous call to the scheduler will allow the parent to continue regardless of whether the scheduler or the child tasks have finished.

Consider the code in Figure 12, in which "T1" is scheduled asynchronously and the parent will be forced to wait until the scheduler has decided on the success of the request before continuing. This means that the parent can be guaranteed access to a non-empty mailbox at the point shown, since the scheduler will have finished its work by that point. If the version chosen is then found to be less than the minimum, some recovery action is taken.

```
sched (mailaddr MBX) T1#7();
recv(mailaddr MBX, &SchedRes);
                /* MBX holds result messages */
if (SchedRes<7) recovery_action();
```

Figure 12. An example of asynchronous task scheduling.

<u>Timing constraints</u>

Various timing constraints can be specified in GARTL on a scheduling request:

- the *starting time* of the task,
- the *deadline*, which is the time by which the task must finish, and
- the *periodicity* of the task, which is the way in which an instance of a task may be requested to be started at given time intervals.

Child tasks are not neccessarily started as soon as the request for them is accepted by the scheduler, in that the programmer may wish to start a task at some time in the future. This is achieved by specifying an earliest start time in the scheduling request, as in

sched Radar_Scanner() at 10*ticks_per_sec;

where "ticks_per_sec" is intended to be a number which is the number of system ticks that occur in one second. In fact, the task may not be started at exactly the time specified, as the scheduler may decide that the task should start later so that other tasks may also execute that require the same resources or are more urgent and require the processing time. Hence, it is only guaranteed that the child task will not execute before the start time specified. The expression that the user gives following the keyword "**at**" is and used as the time when the child task will start. If a number of instances are requested (via periodicity), then the start time given is the start time requested for the first instance. The time given is an interval in system ticks from the current time. If no start time is specified, then it is assumed that the task start time should be the current time.

If it is vital that a task be completed by a certain time, then the programmer should specify a deadline. The scheduler then uses its past knowledge of the execution time and resource requirements of this task in a manner which is outlined in Section 3 to try to decide which is the highest numbered version that can be executed between the start time and the deadline. A deadline is specified in the manner illustrated by the following example:

call (mailaddr CanDoMBX) ReadSign() **in** 3000;

which specifies that the "ReadSign" task must execute before 3000 system ticks are up. The expression following the keyword "**in**"

represents the time allowed for the execution of that task. Note that it is, like the start time, an interval in system ticks, but it is measured from the start time of the task (or from the current time if no start time is specified). In the case of a periodically scheduled task, the deadline is taken to be relative to the start time for each instance, rather than from the start time specified for the first instance.

As another example, consider

call (mailaddr TurnedMBX) TurnMissile#2(HORIZ,15)
at 3000 **in** 1000;

which indicates that the "TurnMissile" task is to be executed at least 3000 ticks from now, and before 4000 ticks from now.

<u>Periodically scheduled tasks</u>

Some tasks are of a nature that they perform some processing repeatedly, such as monitoring a gauge. This is most effectively achieved by starting some task to do this processing once every so often. Periodically scheduling a task is indicated as shown in the example

asyn_sched GaugeReader(THERMOMETER) **every** 1000;

in which the parent task schedules a "GaugeReader" task every 1000 system ticks. The parent does not suspend waiting to find out if the scheduling was successful. The expression following "**every**" specifies the interval in system ticks in between the start times of consecutive instantiations of the task.

It is also possible to include a stopping constraint, to indicate that only a fixed number of periodic instantiations are to be invoked; this is achieved with an "**until**" expression. For example, the scheduling request

sched T1() **at** 100 **every** 10 **until** 133;

tries to schedule instances of "T1" at times 100, 110, 120 and 130 ticks. The expression given represents the an interval measured from the time of the scheduling call in system ticks. During this interval from the start time to this stopping time, the scheduler will continue to try to schedule new instances of the task. Note that an **until** expression is only syntactically correct if it is preceeded by an **every** expression.

The task version for a periodically scheduled task can change at each instantiation. Hence if the system is heavily loaded, the the task instance may be a low version if that is all that can be achieved, but a higher version may be used if the system is less heavily loaded.

<u>Missed deadlines</u>

If a task has not finished execution by the time its deadline arrives, then it is said to have missed its deadline. This is something of a disaster, because it means that the scheduler has not accurately estimated the execution time for the scheduled version of the task. Reflecting its serious nature, this situation is considered a run-time error and a "missed_deadline" exception is raised for that task. This exception can be handled using the facilities described in Section 2.4 below.

<u>Non-terminating tasks</u>

The notion of being able to predict task execution times from past behaviour is based on the assumption that tasks will always have finite execution times. Thus, non-terminating tasks are to be avoided.

In order to assist the programmer to avoid non-terminating tasks, there is no **goto** statement in GARTL and all loop statements must have a specified upper limit on the number of iterations. The GARTL loop statements, of which there are three kinds, are thus all preceded by "**upto** ⟨limit⟩". A "limit_exceeded" exception will be raised if the specified limit, which must be a statically-evaluable constant, is exceeded at run-time.

Function definitions in GARTL require the specification of the maximum number of possible instantiations of that function by a single task. Once again, this maximum number must be statically-evaluable, and the "limit_exceeded" exception is raised if its value is exceeded during execution.

2.4 Exceptions and exception handlers

Exceptions occur at unpredictable times. They may occur because deadlines are missed, resources are discovered to be missing, or due to the occurrence of other user-specified situations. Exceptions are always raised on behalf of some task, meaning that the task is somehow responsible for the exception. Every task can choose the exceptions that it will catch; however, if an exception is raised for a task that is not handled in the exception handler section of the task (see below), the default handler for that exception is invoked. If there is no user-specified default handler, then the default action is to terminate execution of the entire program.

User-specified exceptions can be declared in the simple manner illustrated by the following example:

exception my_exception;

In this case, no default exception handler is given (and so the exception must either be handled in the task in which it is raised or program execution will be terminated). Specifying a default exception handler for a user-defined or predefined exception is a matter of giving a statement after the declaration of the exception name, as illustrated in Figure 13. Figure 13(a) defines a default exception handler for the user-defined exception "fatal_exception" which is being introduced, and Figure 13(b) defines a default exception handler for the predefined exception "missed_deadline".

```
exception fatal_exception
    exit(FATAL_EXCEPTION_ERROR);
    /* Cause termination of the program. */
```

(a)

```
exception missed_deadline {
    cleanup(); /* Perform some cleanup actions. */
    return; /* Cause the task responsible to exit. */
}
```

(b)

Figure 13. Specifying a default exception handler.

The way in which a programmer can specify that a task is to handle a particular exception is to include an exception handler section in the main body of the task. The form of this section is illustrated by the example in Figure 14. In this case, if a "missed_deadline" exception is raised for an instance of "T1", then "T1" will stop whatever it was doing, execute the "clean_up" routine, then exit the entire program. If a "my_exception" exception is raised for "T1", it stops what it was doing, schedules the "my_handler_task" task with parameters 1, 2, and 3, and then exits. If a "fatal_exception" exception is raised for "T1", then "T1" exits, but the execution of the rest of the program continues.

```
task T1() {
    ...
exceptions :

    missed_deadline {
        cleanup();
        exit(MISSED_DEADLINE_ERROR);
    }

    my_exception
        asyn_sched my_handler_task(1,2,3);

    fatal_exception
        /* Do nothing. */
}
```

Figure 14. Specifying an exception handler in a task.

3. Implementation

There are two major components in the implementation of the GARTL language described in the previous section:

- a compiler for translating GARTL to C, and

- an operating system, called GARTOS, to support real-time applications.

These are both components of GARTEN, an environment for the development of real-time software, which will also include facilities for testing and debugging hard real-time systems. At this stage, GARTEN is reasonably primitive, but we plan to improve the integration of the various components along the lines of multiple window, multiple view programming environments such as MultiView[1], also being developed at the University of Adelaide.

As mentioned above, the current GARTL implementation compiles GARTL source programs to C, which is then compiled in the standard way. The GARTL-to-C compiler has been generated using the GNU BISON[4] compiler generation system. The generated C code assumes a high level of operating system support for mailboxes, message-passing, scheduler interaction, and so on.

These facilities are provided by the GARTOS operating system in the form of a number of C-callable routines. Since the GARTOS operating system is not the focus of this paper, it will not be described fully here; nevertheless, some of its more important aspects for the implementation of GARTL will be highlighted.

A particularly important aspect of the GARTOS operating system is the ability of the scheduler to predict the computation time for a task. For each task, GARTOS sets up a database of m dimensions, where m is equal to the number of monitored variables of the task plus one. The structure of this database is illustrated in Figure 15, which shows that there are two monitored variables for the task "task4". Thus, the database for this task is three-dimensional, being addressed by various equivalence classes for the two variables and by version number.

The database for a task is used to store information about computation times for the task. A cell in the database corresponds to a given version of the task and a given set of input value ranges classified by the monitored variables. In each cell, statistical data on computation time for the task, such as the mean, variance, the maximum, and minimum, are recorded. Such data is collected whenever the task is executed. In the case that the variance and/or the difference between the average and maximum/minimum is too large, the GARTOS operating system gives a suitable warning message to the

Table of databases

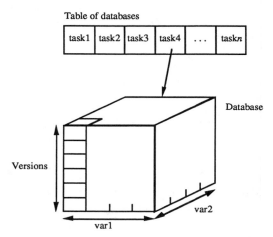

| task1 | task2 | task3 | task4 | ... | task*n* |

Figure 15. The structure of the GARTOS database for a task having two monitored variables.

programmer, indicating the possible misidentification of the monitored variables and/or the misclassification of their ranks.

At run time, when a scheduling request for a task is received, its database is searched and the maximum likely computation time for the indicated values of the monitored variables is computed. The database has been designed in such a way that this run-time search and computation can be carried out efficiently. The details of the structure and operations of the database will be reported elsewhere.

It is clear that the scheduler plays a critical role in any real-time system. It is the scheduler which makes the decision as to which task to run at what time, on what processors, and so on. The scheduler must be very fast and reliable. In implementing GARTEN, we have adopted the idea used in the Spring project[13] that the scheduler and many other important operating systems functions should be implemented in a separate, dedicated system processor. In our present implementation, we employ only two processors: one for system functions and one for the real-time application. However, we hope to be able to further improve the performance of real-time systems by using more extensive multiprocessors, such as the Leopard multiprocessor workstation[2], which is also under development at the University of Adelaide.

The main advantage of removing the scheduler's load from the processor used by the application is to improve the predictability of the execution time of application tasks. We believe that this approach is justified in view of the current low cost of microprocessors.

4. Conclusions and Future Work

The GARTL language described in this paper has been designed to support the multi-version computation approach to programming hard real-time systems described in Section 1. Support for this paradigm has many consequences in terms of language features, both with regard to the specification of the tasks to be executed, for interaction with those tasks and the scheduler, and for the form of scheduling requests. These consequences have been outlined through the description of the appropriate GARTL features. The GARTL language has been specifically designed to provide direct support for the multi-version computation approach to programming hard real-time systems.

The FLEX programming language[6,7,10] supports a similar approach to programming real-time software, which is known as *imprecise computation*. In FLEX, there is a mechanism which keeps the partial (imprecise) computation results of a task. In the case a task which has to be preempted (due to the expiration of its deadline), these partial resutls are avaiable to the caller of the task. In GARTL, a different approach is taken so that the partial result mechanism is not necessary. In the case of GARTL, the system scheduler is called when a task is to be invoked. The scheduler decides if this task can be finished by its deadline and if so which of its versions will be executed. Once such a decision has been made, the task is *guaranteed* to complete by its deadline. No preemption is needed due to the expiration of its deadline. As we mention below, this allows a missed deadline to be detected earlier; hence, the necessary recovery action can be taken earlier by the task's invoker.

An important aspect of GARTL is the way it permits interaction between the application program and the system scheduler. Many other programming languages do allow an application task to invoke another application task at run-time. However, in those languages, there is no feedback from the system to the invoking task about the timing of invoked task. That is, the invoker only knows that the execution of the invoked task will be logically correct, but has no information on when the execution will be made and if the deadline of that invoked task can be met. As a result, a missed deadline cannot be detected by the invoking block, making it difficult to take necessary recovery actions. This is important for many real-time applications and amounts to a special kind of fault tolerance: a missed deadline fault is being detected at the earliest possible time – the time at which the task is being submitted. Part of our planned future work is to extend GARTL to allow the scheduling of multiple instances of a task on different processors; in this way, some hardware faults may be tolerated.

The operating system support required for a language supporting the multi-version computation approach to real-time systems has been indicated by outlining some aspects of GARTOS, the operating system which supports the GARTL implementation. One aspect of GARTOS which is of particular importance is the way in which it makes use of information about the past execution of the multiple versions of tasks to select the appropriate one to execute within the specified deadline (if this is possible). This approach is necessary because the execution of the multiple versions does lend itself to an *a priori* analysis which enables us to choose the appropriate version. The information about past execution of a task is stored in a database which tabulates each version's execution time and other resource needs against attributes of the task on which the resource requirements are thought (by the programmer) to depend.

The present means of predicting the execution time of a task from past execution times under similar circumstances is presently reasonably crude and we are currently investigating other, more sophisticated techniques. These include techniques based on various heuristics.

As mentioned in the previous section, we expect to incorporate the GARTL language into an integrated environment for the development of real-time software. This environment will include various debugging, testing, and editing tools for supporting development of real-time systems. A salient feature of these tools is that they must necessarily be oriented towards the timing characteristics of real-time software. The environment will also contain facilities for browsing the database of information about task execution histories.

References

[1] R. A. Altmann, A. N. Hawke and C. D. Marlin, "An Integrated Programming Environment Based on Multiple Concurrent Views", *Australian Computer J.*, Vol. 20, No. 2 (May 1988), pp. 65–72.

[2] P. J. Ashenden, C. J. Barter and C. D. Marlin, "The Leopard Workstation Project", *A.C.M. SIGARCH Computer Architecture News*, Vol. 15, No. 4 (September 1987), pp. 40–51.

[3] E. K. P. Chong and W. Zhao, "Task Scheduling for Imprecise Computer Systems with User Controlled Optimization", in *Computing and Information*, R. Janicki and W. W. Koczkodaj (Ed.), pp. 441–446 (North-Holland, Amsterdam, 1989).

[4] C. Donnelly and R. Stallman, "BISON: The YACC-compatible Parser Generator", Free Software Foundation (1988).

[5] B. W. Kernighan and D. M. Ritchie, *The C Programming Language* (Prentice-Hall Inc., Englewood Cliffs, New Jersey, 1978).

[6] K. Lin, S. Natarajan and J. Liu, "Imprecise Results: Utilizing Partial Computations in Real-Time Systems", *Proc. I.E.E.E. Real-Time Systems Symposium 1987*, pp. 210–217.

[7] K. Lin, S. Natarajan and J. Liu, "Expressing and Maintaining Timing Constraints in FLEX", *Proc. I.E.E.E. Real-Time Systems Symposium 1988*, pp. 96–105.

[8] J. Liu, K. Lin and C. Liu, "Concord Prototype System and Real-Time Scheduling", *Proc. I.E.E.E. Fourth Workshop on Real-Time Operating Systems* (July 1987), pp. 27–30.

[9] J. Liu, K. Lin and S. Natarajan, "Scheduling Real-Time, Periodic Jobs Using Imprecise Results", *Proc. I.E.E.E. Real-Time Systems Symposium 1987*, pp. 252–260.

[10] S. Natarajan and K. J. Lin, "FLEX: Towards Flexible Real-Time Programs", *Proc. I.E.E.E. Int. Conf. on Computer Languages 1988*, pp. 272–279.

[11] K. G. Shin (Ed.), Special Issue on Real-Time Systems, *I.E.E.E. Transactions on Computers*, Vol. 36, No. 8 (1987).

[12] J. Stankovic, "Misconceptions about Real-Time Computing: A Serious Problem for Next-Generation Systems", *I.E.E.E. Computer*, Vol. 21, No. 10 (October 1988), pp. 10–19.

[13] J. Stankovic and K. Ramamritham, "The Design of the Spring Kernel", *Proc. I.E.E.E. Real-Time Systems Symposium 1987*, pp. 146–157.

[14] J. Stankovic and K. Ramamritham, *Hard Real-Time Systems* (I.E.E.E. Press, 1988).

[15] W. Zhao and E. K. P. Chong, "Performance Evaluation of Scheduling Algorithms for Dynamic Imprecise Soft Real-Time Computer Systems", *Australian Computer Science Communications*, Vol. 11, No. 1 (February 1989), pp. 329–340.

[16] W. Zhao (Ed.), Special Issue on Real-Time Operating Systems, *A.C.M. Operating Systems Review*, Vol. 23, No. 3 (1989).

Coercion as a Metaphor for Computation

Suresh Jagannathan*
Department of Computer Science
Yale University

Abstract

The idea of *coercion* – taking objects of one type and transforming them into objects of another – is not a new one, and has been an important feature of language design since the advent of Fortran. This paper considers a generalization of coercion that permits structured transformations between *program* and *data structures*. The nature of these coercions goes significantly beyond what is found in most modern programming languages.

Our intention is to develop a programming model that permits the expression of a wide-range of superficially-diverse modularity constructs within a simple and unified framework. We base the design of this model on the observation that a variety of program structures found in modern programming languages are represented fundamentally in terms of an environment. Given suitable transformations that map the environment representation of a program structure into a data object, we can enable the programmer to gain explicit control over his naming environment.

We investigate the semantics of program/data coercion in the presence of a non-strict parallel evaluation semantics for environments. Parallelism and program/data coercion form an interesting symbiosis and it is the investigation of their interaction that forms the primary focus of this paper.

Key Words and Phrases: Namespace management, modularity, first-class environments, reflection, object-oriented programming, actors, non-strictness, interpreters.

1   Introduction

The idea of *coercion* – taking objects of one type and transforming them into objects of another – is not a new one, and has been an important feature of language design since the advent of Fortran. Most languages provide a limited form of coercion, *e.g.,* integers are usually allowed to be coerced into reals (and *vise versa*); some languages come equipped with more wide-ranging coercion mechanisms: APL and Algol 68 allow coercion between array and scalar types; PL/1 permits coercion between numeric and string types. This paper considers a generalization of coercion that permits structured transformations between *program* and *data structures*. The nature of these coercions goes significantly beyond what is found in most modern programming languages.

Our intention is to develop a programming model that permits the expression of a wide-range of superficially-diverse modularity constructs within a simple and unified framework. We base the design of this model on the following observation: a variety of program structures (*e.g.,* closures, packages [8], classes [12, 17], etc.) are represented fundamentally in terms of an environment structure[1]. Given suitable transformations that map the environment representation of a program structure into a data object, we can enable the programmer to gain explicit control over his naming environment. Inverse transformations that permit a data object to be transformed or "lifted" into an environment image allow the programmer to build his own customized environments. A data object so-transformed can be used in any context where an environment is expected; similarly, an environment so-transformed can be used wherever a data value can.

Making the representation of environments explicit within the language leads to a number of important expressivity gains. We describe some of these briefly below and expand on these points in the remainder of the paper.

1. We can customize the naming environment of any expression by evaluating the expression within the context of a coercion operation that transforms a user-specified data structure into an environment. New binding protocols can be introduced dynamically and the binding-environment of any expression can be customized appropriately.

2. Given the ability to compose data structures together, we can now compose environments in arbitrary ways. Data structure/environment composition allows us to capture the essence of object-oriented programming

---

*Funding for this work provided in part by NSF grants CCR-8601920, CCR-8657615 and ONR N00014-86-K-0310.

[1] Two examples: (a) A closure is a binding-environment coupled with an expression that is constrained to evaluate within that environment. (b) The definitions found along a given chain in a class-based inheritance hierarchy may be used to implicitly affect the evaluation of expressions that refer to a class instance found at the lowest level of the hierarchy.

models that support inheritance. With an appropriate parallel evaluation semantics, transformations between program and data structure can be used to realize an actor-based programming model.

3. An expression can examine the environment within which it is evaluated. The ability of an expression to examine its own evaluation environment forms the basis of reflective programming models. A reflective procedure applied in the context of a parallel programming model can be used to implement process daemons, processes that can examine an evaluation environment in parallel with other expressions that access and manipulate this environment.

4. We can characterize program structures in terms of the coercion operators provided by the model. We can specify an interpreter, for example, without having to implement data structures and operations that explicitly manipulate an environment representation. A coercion-based interpreter of the sort discussed below is *self-describing* in the sense that the structures it manipulates can be given a well-defined representation within the language itself.

The paper is organized as follows: in the next section, we give a brief description of the programming model. The essence of the model is captured by two coercion operators that effect transformations between environment structures and data structures. The model also defines a specific data representation for environments; this representation takes the form of a non-strict record object. The presence of non-strictness makes parallelism an integral part of the model. Section 2.3 provides a formal semantics of a kernel language containing these operators. Section 4 examines a set of paradigms and applications that result from the interaction of non-strict data structures with program/data coercion. We begin by arguing that binding protocols typically "hard-wired" as part of the semantics of a language can in fact be customized as suits the convenience of the programmer. We then go on to consider the relationship between the environment structure produced by a meta-circular evaluator and the structure manipulated by an object-based program. Reflection is considered to be a consequence of first-class environments and non-strict data structures. Actor systems are examined in the context of a reflective programming environment; we show how the actor model can be simplified without loss of expressive power through the use of the coercion mechanisms developed here. Section 5 presents conclusions.

2 The Nature of the Model

We present a model that permits structured transformations between data objects and environments. An environment is a collection of bindings of names to values that is maintained by a programming language's interpreter. The names defined by a program structure are represented as elements of some environment. Environments can be coerced into data objects that broadly resemble conventional record structures. Users can manipulate such a record using the operations allowed upon it. In addition, a record object may in turn be coerced into an environment which can then be used (implicitly) to affect the evaluation of other expressions.

The semantics of the model is first given in terms of the simply typed λ-calculus augmented with record types and the transformation operations. We then examine the implication of injecting these operators into Scheme, a richer language that supports assignment.

2.1 Records

Records define a collection of mutually-recursive bindings of possibly heterogeneous type. An expression of the form

[id_1 = e_1, id_2 = e_2, ..., id_n = e_n]

denotes an n-field record with field names id_1, id_2,..., id_n; each of the e_i evaluate in an environment containing bindings for the id_i. Since our intention is to understand how to apply this model in a variety of different contexts, including some involving the use of parallelism, we ascribe a parallel-evaluation semantics to our record objects: each of the e_i evaluate in parallel subject only to the standard data flow dependency constraints. Record objects are also non-strict. Thus, a record object can be made available for inspection even if some of its elements are still under evaluation *provided* that the names it defines have been noted. In particular, a record has a well-defined meaning even if its component elements diverge. Non-strictness of this kind also implies parallelism since expressions can access a record structure even as other expressions proceed to compute the value of the record's fields.

The value of a record field can be retrieved using the "." operator: if r is a record, then evaluating $r.id$ returns the binding-value of id as defined in r; if r does not contain a field named id, an error results. The non-strict semantics of records means that we can evaluate a "." expression even if not all fields in its record argument yield values; thus,

[m = $\perp$, n = 1] . n

yields 1 (where $\perp$ denotes a diverging computation). The expression M.x is *blocked* until a value has been computed for the field named x in record M.

We provide one other operation over records. Let r_1 and r_2 be two records and let $Dom(r)$ be the set of names defined within record r. Then the "join" or composition of r_1 and r_2 (written ($r_1 \bullet r_2$) can be expressed as follows:

$$(r_1 \bullet r_2).x = \begin{cases} r_2.x \text{ if } x \in Dom(r2) \\ r_1.x \text{ otherwise} \end{cases}$$

Like ".", $\bullet$ is also non-strict: it does not require its arguments to be values before it returns its result. Thus, the join of r_1 and r_2 can be computed even if both record expressions are still under evaluation.

2.2 The Coercion Operators: ↑ and ↓

In addition to providing record types, the model supports two operations (denoted ↑ and ↓) that implement our coercion semantics. The ↓ operator is used to coerce the environment representation of an expression into a record. If e_1 is an expression, then ($\downarrow e_1$) yields a record with two fields, val and env bound to the value denoted by e_1 and to the record-image of e_1's environment representation, resp. (Informally, every expression has a representation in terms of an environment; the environment structure associated with an expression, in general, contains the set of bindings accessible to and introduced by the expression during the course of its evaluation; we give a more precise definition below.) Suppose that e_1's environment image contains a binding for x to v. The env field in the record-object yielded by evaluating ($\downarrow e_1$) will contain a field named x bound to v.

The inverse of the ↓ operator is ↑. Given an expression e_1 that yields a record, we can evaluate an expression e_2 in the context of e_1's environment image by evaluating ($e_1 \uparrow e_2$). The (non-strict) record-object yielded by evaluation of e_1 is coerced into an environment that contains a binding for each field-name found in the record. The binding-value of a free identifier found in the body of e_2 *not* defined within the environment image of e_1's record-object is resolved within e_2's lexical environment.

2.3 Formal Semantics

We give a formal semantics to a functional base language that supports the operators defined in the previous section. The term set Λ of our base language is defined inductively over a set of constants and variables:

$$
\begin{aligned}
E ::= &\ 0 \mid 1 \mid 2 \ldots \\
&\ \text{true} \mid \text{false} \mid \\
&\ [\text{id}_1 = E, \text{id}_2 = E, \ldots, \text{id}_n = E] \mid \\
&\ \lambda\text{id}.E \mid (E\ E) \mid E \to E; E \mid \\
&\ E.\text{id} \mid (E \bullet E) \mid (E \uparrow E)\ (\downarrow E)
\end{aligned}
$$

where id ranges over variables. λ abstractions stand for call-by-name (non-strict) procedures.

We give meaning to expressions in our base language by associating each expression with an element of a sum domain **V** that satisfies the following isomorphism:

$$\mathbf{V} \cong \mathbf{N} + \mathbf{B} + \mathbf{R} + (\mathbf{V} \to \mathbf{V})$$
$$\mathbf{R} = \mathbf{Env} \cong \mathbf{Id} \to \mathbf{V}$$

where **N** is the flat domain of natural numbers and **B** is the flat domain of Booleans. The continuous function space operator is denoted by →. **R** and **Env** denote the domain of functions that map identifiers to values. Details regarding the construction of **V** can be found in [7].

We use the following conventions throughout:

- d in **V**, where d belongs to a summand **S** of **V** denotes the injection of d into **V**.

- If $v = (d$ in **V**$)$ for some $d \in$ **S**, then $v \mid_S = d$. Otherwise $v \mid_S = \bot$.

- $\bullet$ = yields $\bot$ whenever either of argument does.

2.3.1 Operations over Environments

If A is a domain, then $\tilde{A}$, the domain extension of A, is defined by:

$$\tilde{A} = A + \{none\} + \{formal\}$$

The special values *none* and *formal* are used to distinguish unbound identifiers and the formals of an abstraction from ordinary binding-values: if x is mapped to *none* in some environment $\tilde{A}$, it implies that x is unbound in $\tilde{A}$; if x is mapped to *formal* by $\tilde{A}$, it indicates x is defined as a formal parameter within $\tilde{A}$.

We define a projection operation that maps elements from $\tilde{A}$ back to A with the function *proper*:

$$
\begin{aligned}
proper :&\quad \tilde{A} \to A \\
proper &\quad \tilde{a} \quad = a \mid_A \\
proper &\quad none \quad = \bot \\
proper &\quad formal = \bot
\end{aligned}
$$

If A is a set of identifiers and B is a domain of values, then the domain of environments binding elements of A into B is given by $A \to \tilde{B}$. We define singleton environments using the $\mapsto$ constructor:

$$[i \mapsto v]\rho = \lambda x. x = i \ \to \ v; \rho(x)$$

Let ρ_1 and ρ_2 be environments. Then, the *composition* of ρ_1 and ρ_2 (denoted ∘) is defined thus:

$$\rho_1 \circ \rho_2 = \lambda x.\ \rho_1(x) \ = \ none \ \to \rho_2(x); \rho_1(x)$$

2.3.2 The Meaning Function

The denotation function for Λ is given in figure 1. We use c to range over numerical and Boolean constants, x and *id* to range over identifiers, ρ to range over environments, and E to range over general Λ terms.

The meaning of our coercion operators is given in terms of an auxiliary function, $\mathcal{D}$, that captures our notion of *evaluation environment*. Every expression is associated with an environment image that can be captured and manipulated via the coercion operators. If $e \in \Lambda$, then $\mathcal{D}[\![e]\!]_\rho$ yields the environment image of e when evaluated in environment ρ. We give the definition of $\mathcal{D}$ in figure 2.

The environment image of a constant is simply its lexical environment; the environment image of an identifier is the environment image of its binding-value. A record has as its environment image the join of its lexical environment with the bindings it defines locally. The environment image of a λ-abstraction is the function's lexical environment augmented with a binding for its formal parameter to the distinguished value *formal*. The lexical environment of a function joined with the environment that associates a binding of the function's formal to the value of the actual defines the environment image of an application expression.

$$[\ ] : \Lambda \rightarrow \mathbf{Env} \rightarrow \mathbf{V}$$

$$
\begin{aligned}
[c]_\rho &= c \\
[x]_\rho &= proper(\rho(x)) \\
[[id_1 = E_1, id_2 = E_2, \ldots, id_n = E_n]]_\rho &= fix(\lambda f.[id_i \mapsto [E_i]_{f \circ \rho}](\lambda x.none)), 1 \leq i \leq n \\
[\lambda x.E]_\rho &= \lambda v.[E]_{\rho \circ \lambda id.id = x \rightarrow v; none} \\
[(E_1\ E_2)]_\rho &= [E_1]_\rho \mid_{\mathbf{V} \rightarrow \mathbf{V}} ([E_2]_\rho) \\
[E_1 \rightarrow E_2; E_3]_\rho &= [E_1]_\rho \mid_{\mathbf{B}} \rightarrow [E_2]_\rho; [E_3]_\rho \\
[E_1 \bullet E_2]_\rho &= [E_1]_\rho \mid_{\mathbf{Env}} \circ [E_2]_\rho \mid_{\mathbf{Env}} \\
[E.id]_\rho &= [E]_\rho \mid_{\mathbf{Env}} (id) \\
[E_1 \uparrow E_2]_\rho &= [E_2]_{\mathcal{D}[E_1]_\rho} \mid_{\mathbf{R}} \\
[\downarrow E]_\rho &= (\lambda v_1.\lambda v_2.[[\mathbf{val} = v_1, \mathbf{env} = v_2]]_\rho)[E]_\rho\ \mathcal{D}[E]_\rho
\end{aligned}
$$

Figure 1: The meaning function for Λ.

$$\mathcal{D}[\ ] : \Lambda \rightarrow Env \rightarrow Env$$

$$
\begin{aligned}
\mathcal{D}[c]_\rho &= \rho \\
\mathcal{D}[x]_\rho &= \mathcal{D}[[x]_\rho]_\rho \\
\mathcal{D}[[id_1 = E_1, id_2 = E_2, \ldots, id_n = E_n]]_\rho &= \rho \circ [[id_1 = E_1, id_2 = E_2, \ldots, id_n = E_n]]_\rho \\
\mathcal{D}[\lambda x.E]_\rho &= \rho \circ \lambda id.id = x \rightarrow formal; none \\
\mathcal{D}[(E_1\ E_2)]_\rho &= \lambda id.\mathcal{D}[E_1]_\rho(id) = formal \rightarrow [E_2]_\rho; \mathcal{D}[E_1]_\rho(v) \\
\mathcal{D}[E_1 \rightarrow E_2; E_3]_\rho &= [E_1]_\rho \mid_{\mathbf{B}} \rightarrow \mathcal{D}[E_2]_\rho; \mathcal{D}[E_3]_\rho \\
\mathcal{D}[E_1 \bullet E_2]_\rho &= \mathcal{D}[[E_1 \bullet E_2]_\rho]_\rho \\
\mathcal{D}[E.id]_\rho &= \mathcal{D}[[E.id]_\rho]_\rho \\
\mathcal{D}[E_1 \uparrow E_2]_\rho &= \mathcal{D}[[E_1 \uparrow E_2]_\rho]_\rho \\
\mathcal{D}[\downarrow E]_\rho &= \mathcal{D}[[\downarrow E]_\rho]_\rho
\end{aligned}
$$

Figure 2: Environment Representation of Λ terms

3 Manifestation of the Model

To make our discussion concrete, we define a language COE that supports the operators and structures described in the previous section. The syntax and semantics of COE most closely resembles that of Scheme [13]. In essence, COE is Scheme augmented with a record data type and the two coercion operators described above.

The semantics of the coercion operators in COE differs from their semantics in Λ because of Scheme's support for assignment. Consider the COE expression (↓ e). The **env** field in the record-object yielded by evaluating this expression will contain a *reference* to the binding-values of all identifiers found in e's evaluation environment. Thus any changes made to **env** will be reflected in e's environment. Similarly, in an ↑ operation of the form (↑ e_1 e_2) evaluated in COE, the binding-value of an identifier in the coerced environment image of e_1 will be a reference to the corresponding value in the record object that e_1 denotes. Here again, changes made to an environment binding by e_2 are reflected in the record structure denoted by e_1.

3.1 Some Simple Examples

The value yielded by the expression

```
(let ((f (↓ (let ((x 2
                   (y 5))
              nil))))
  ((lambda (z) (+ z.x z.y)) f.env))
```

is 7. The evaluation-environment of the ↓-operator's argument contains (among possibly other things) a binding for **x** to 2 and a binding for **y** to 5; this environment is coerced into a record object which is then applied as the argument to the function, (lambda (z) (+ z.x z.y)).

As we mentioned above, side-effects on a coerced record are reflected in the corresponding environment. Thus, the value yielded by evaluating

```
(let ((x 1)
      (y (lambda (z) (+ z 1)))
      (z (↓ y)))
  (begin
    ((lambda (f) (set! f.x 10)) z.env)
    x))
```

is 10; the assignment to **f.x** is reflected in the corresponding evaluation environment, *i.e.*, in the evaluation environment of the closure bound to **y**. It is precisely the ability to side-effect an environment via its data structure representation that justifies the use of the term *coercion* in describing our transformation operators. The component elements of the record object yielded by ↓ is shared with the binding-value of the corresponding element in its environment image. The ↓ operator simply manifests the environment image within the value domain of the language.

Since COE is based on a programming model that permits records to be explicitly denoted, we can define a record and use it as the evaluation environment of an expression via ↑. For example, the evaluation of

```
(↑ [ x = 2, y = 3 ]  (+ x y))
```

yields 5. The coerced environment image of the record object yielded by evaluation of the expression [x = 2, y = 3] is used as the binding environment in the evaluation of the expression (+ x y). As we mentioned above, free names referenced during the evaluation of ↑'s second argument not defined in the environment-image of its first argument are resolved in the expression's lexical environment. Thus, evaluating

```
[ b = 3,
  f = (lambda (x) (↑ x (+ a b)))
  (f [a = 2])]
```

yields

```
[ b = 3,
  f = closure of (lambda (x) (↑ x (+ a b))),
  5 ]
```

A lambda expression that is the second argument to ↑ has its free variables evaluated first in the environment-image of the ↑ operator's first argument and then in the context of its lexical environment. The environment captured by a lambda closure is superseded by a user-specified environment whenever a lambda expression is evaluated in context of an ↑ operation.

Thus, the value of the expression

```
(let ((x 1)
      (z 2))
  (let ((y (↑ [z = 20] (lambda () (+ x z)))))
    (let ((x 3)
          (z 4))
      (y))))
```

is 21. The free variable **x** in the lambda expression is bound to its value in the function's lexical environment whereas the reference to free variable **z** is resolved relative to its binding-value in the environment image of the record expression.

4 Paradigms and Applications

Building and manipulating environments is a fundamental part of any computation; most languages, however, come equipped with only a small number of (fairly-limited) namespace devices to help the user manipulate his naming environment. The manner in which these devices are constructed rarely allow a computation direct access to the naming environments it builds. In the remainder of this section, we investigate the ramifications of allowing computations direct control over the naming environments they access.

4.1 Binding Protocols

Most languages that come equipped with a default binding protocol rarely provide facilities by which this protocol can be overridden in a semantically-clean way. Scheme is a good case in point. Scheme's primary environment-building structure, the *closure*, is built and maintained by the underlying interpreter: users can't write down an expression that defines the representation of a closure, nor can they examine a closure-object from within Scheme. Thus, it becomes problematic to implement variations on the lexical-binding protocol; since users don't have access to the binding environment within which expressions are evaluated, they can't alter the environment in any way not originally prescribed by the language design. This is an important limitation in the expressivity of the language; it often necessitates Scheme dialects to provide either *ad hoc* constructs to realize other binding disciplines (*e.g.*, the fluid-let [1] construct to achieve dynamic-binding) or significant extensions to the base language (*e.g.*, extensions for supporting late-binding and object-based programming [3, 9, 18]).

COE, like Scheme, also represents functions in terms of closures. The fact that the language provides operations to explicitly capture an environment, however, makes the lexical-binding rule logically unnecessary. We could, in other words, have ascribed a purely dynamic binding semantics to lambda expressions and used this binding protocol to define a fully lexically-binding variant. Consider an alternative semantics for lambdas, one in which lambda expressions are viewed as simple constants. Under such a semantics, the evaluation of a lambda expression simply yields the text representation of that expression. In the absence of any environment-capturing operations, the resulting language would be capable of only supporting dynamic binding. In COE, however, we can implement higher-order lexically-scoped functions on top of a dynamic binding protocol *without* having to extend or alter the underlying interpreter.

To see why, consider an extension to the base language that includes a dynamically-binding version of lambda, call it lambda$_d$. We wish to show that given lambda$_d$ we can specify the meaning of lambda. The basic idea is simple: an expression of the form:

(lambda (x1 x2 ... xn) Exp)

is rewritten as a record:

[τ_1 = ($\downarrow$ nil),
  τ_2 = (lambda$_d$ (x1 x2 ... xn) Exp)]

(τ_1 and τ_2 are assumed to be fresh identifiers.)

This record is, in effect, a closure – it consists of two parts, a representation of an environment and the text of the function: it can be passed freely, embedded within data structures, or returned as the result of an application. The expression ($\downarrow$ nil) evaluates to the lexical environment of the lambda expression. In the absence of any coercion operations τ_2, when applied to arguments, will retrieve the binding-values of free names in its body based on the apply-time environment.

We can write an application expression that essentially behaves as though its first argument were statically scoped by using the $\uparrow$ operator. An application of the form, (e1 e2 ...en) is equivalent to the following expression:

(let ((τ_3 e1)
      (arg1 e2)
      ⋮
      (argn en))
  ($\uparrow$ τ_3.τ_1.env (τ_3.τ_2 arg1 arg2 ... argn)))

Arg1, ... argn are fresh names introduced to avoid the unwanted capture of free names occurring in the actuals by $\uparrow$. The above expression evaluates the application relative to the function's lexical environment.

The particular transformation of functions and applications shown above is basically the same as one which would have been performed by a Scheme interpreter [27] with one important difference: in Scheme, there is no primitive representation of a naming environment nor are there any primitive operations that correspond to either the $\uparrow$ or $\downarrow$ operators. The Scheme meta-circular evaluator must maintain and update its environment image explicitly. In COE, environments have a well-defined representation and can be manipulated directly. Thus, the specification of lexical-binding and closure application can be given via simple rewrite rules; there is no need to define a complete evaluator in order to specify their semantics.

The same technique used to build a closure can be used to specify an arbitrary evaluation environment; for example, if we wish to evaluate a function in the context of a user-specified library we can do so by building a record of the same sort as above:

[τ_1 = L, τ_2 = (lambda$_d$ ...)]

L is an expression that yields a record containing the bindings defined by the library. Applying this closure as we did above causes the lambda$_d$ expression to evaluate in the context of the bindings defined by this library object. In general, the object bound to τ_1 may be the result of a complex expression that builds and composes records; the result of evaluating this expression is used as the evaluation environment for the function bound to τ_2. The ability to evaluate an expression in the context of a user-specified environment is also a key requirement in an object-based programming methodology; we discuss this issue in detail in the sections following.

Note that a slightly different translation scheme would allow us to get the effect of dynamic binding via a lexical binding protocol. An expression of the form:

(lambda$_d$ (x1 x2 ... xn) Exp)

can be rewritten thus:

(lambda (Env)
    ($\uparrow$ Env (lambda (x1 x2 ... xn) Exp)))

We rewrite a dynamically-binding function into a higher-order lexically-scoped one that takes as its argument the record image of the dynamic environment and returns a function that evaluates in the context of this environment. Thus, an application expression that is to be evaluated under a dynamic binding protocol:

(e1 e2 ... en)$_d$

is equivalent to:

(let ((τ_1 ($\downarrow$ nil))
      (τ_2 e1))
  ((τ_2 τ_1.env) e1 ... en))

This translation differs from a purely dynamic binding protocol in one respect: free names referenced in the body of the function not present in the dynamic environment are resolved relative to their binding-value in the lexical environment. It's easy to augment the translation scheme to handle this case, but we omit the translation here.

4.2 Modularity

The front-end (FE) of most interpreted languages is implemented by a `read-eval-print` loop – the FE acts as a virtual machine that repeatedly reads a new input expression, evaluates it on the basis of the internal environment structure maintained by the `eval` procedure, and prints the result. Users usually do not have access to the internal state of `eval` – programs to access and manipulate the environment image of an interpreter session must usually be provided as part of the evaluator package.

The COE front-end, on the other hand, implements a parallel *transparent* evaluator – expressions input by the user are added as a new element on top of the current environment; old bindings are superseded by new ones by layering the new binding expression on top of the old one; the non-strict evaluation semantics of records allows input expressions to be evaluated in parallel upto the ordinary serialization rules imposed by the name evaluation rule.

The outline FE (ignoring issues of printing and formatting) can be written as follows:

```
[FE =
  (lambda (user-env io-stream)
    (let ((next (↑ user-env
                    (read (first io-stream)))))
      (FE (• user-env next)
          (rest io-stream))))]
```

Expressions input by the user are represented as strings in a stream called `io-stream`. (A `stream` is a (potentially) infinite queue. It is represented in COE as an abstraction whose representation allows elements to be appended to the end in constant-time. We provide four operations on streams: `make-stream` (which returns a new empty stream), `first` (which returns the head element, blocking if the stream is empty), `rest` (which returns the rest of the stream, blocking if the stream contains zero or one element), and `attach` (which adds a new element to the end.).)

Read coerces its input (which is assumed to be a string representation of a single element record) into a COE record object. This object is then evaluated in `read`'s dynamic environment. In the above example, the record yielded by `read` is evaluated relative to the bindings found in `user-env`. Because records have a non-strict evaluation semantics, each expression input may be evaluated concurrently with every other. Thus, if `io-stream` is structured as follows:

```
( "[y = 3]"
  "[f = (lambda (x) (+ x y)]"
  "[a1 = (f 2)]"
  "[y = 4]"
  "[a2 = (f 2)]" )
```

the corresponding structure of `user-env` after these expressions have been read (and evaluated) would be:

```
[ y  = 4,
  f  = closure of (lambda (x) (+ x y)),
  a1 = 5,
  a2 = 5 ]
```

Because `lambda`s are lexically-scoped functions, rebinding `y` to 4 does not change the apply-time behaviour of `f`; changing the behaviour of `f` requires side-effecting `y`. If, instead of the binding declaration `y = 4`, the user input, `(set! y 4)`, the second application of `f` would have used the new value of `y`. This property of the COE top-level front-end is in contrast to the behaviour of most Lisps but is consistent with other lexically-scoped interpreted languages such as ML [23].

Languages that use program objects such as packages or classes would be hard-pressed to support this kind of structure because they provide no operations to compose new environments dynamically. For example, given a Simula or Smalltalk class C, one cannot dynamically construct a new class C' that differs from C based on conditions known only at runtime. This is a fundamental requirement in the above example – each new expression input results in the construction of a new environment. Note that simply modeling environments as records would also not suffice. A record is a simple data object and its standard semantics does not permit its bindings *implicitly* to affect the evaluation of other expressions.

Language interpreters are arguably esoteric, but the modularity requirements they impose are found in a number of other paradigms as well. An object-oriented, inheritance-based programming style is a good example. There are several competing paradigms for general object-based programming: in Simula-67[12] instances are similar to records with function-valued components and message-passing is realized as field selection and application over these records; Smalltalk[17] (followed by CommonLoops[9] and Flavors[18]) treats message-passing as function call. Amber[10, 11] also models objects as records, but expresses inheritance as subtype relations among these records.

We pose an alternative view: in COE an object is considered a record, but inheritance is captured by simple record composition. The ↑ operator is used to coerce a record object into an evaluation environment. Message-send is realized by evaluating an expression in the context of the environment-image of a record object. In a coercion-based model, then, inheritance is viewed as essentially a namespace management problem; the inheritance hierarchy specifies a namespace that is composed from a collection of records that may define different bindings for the same name.

Thus, in thinking of objects as records, we see that an instance of a subclass in an inheritance hierarchy is simply a record that is the "fusion" of the environments defined by the associated instances of all its super-classes. The inheritance hierarchy determines how the record is to be constructed: nameclashes between a subclass instance and a superclass instance are always resolved in favour of the subclass. The coercion operation allow us to transform simple record objects into environments.

Let O_1 and O_2 be two classes such that O_1 is a subclass of O_2. Let O_1 define methods and instance variables m_1, m_2, ..., m_j and let O_2 define methods and instance variables $n_1, n_2, ..., n_k$ and assume that there exists a non-empty intersection of method/instance variable names defined by these two objects. We represent O_1 as a record:

```
O₁ = [ create =
          (lambda ()
             (• O₂.(create)
                (• O₁.(instance-vars)
                   O₁.methods)))

       instance-vars =
          (lambda ()
             [ O₁'s instance variables ]

       methods = [ O₁'s methods ] ]
```

O_2 is structured similarly. Evaluating $(O_1.\text{create})$ yields a record that contains a fresh copy of O_1's instance variables, O_1's methods and the instance variables and methods of O_2 (and all its superclasses). Note that because of the semantics of "•", instance variables and methods defined in O_2 (and its superclasses) also defined by O_1 are superseded with O_1's definition in all of O_1's instances. Thus, if O_1 and O_2 both define a method named M, bound to definitions D_1 and D_2 resp., the record returned as a result of evaluating $(O_1.\text{create})$ will contain a binding for M to D_1, not D_2.

Message-passing in this model is simply expression evaluation within the environment-image of the record object. If I_1 is an instance of O_1, then $(\uparrow I_1\ exp)$ evaluates exp using the instance variables and methods defined in I_1; if M occurs free in exp, and I_1 contains a binding for M, then the value of M in exp will be the binding value of M in I_1. Changes made to environment variables within exp that correspond to field-names in I_1 become visible to other expressions that subsequently access I_1.

The Smalltalk-style expression

```
(send object method args)
```

is, therefore, represented in COE as

```
((↑ object method) args)
```

Because of the non-strict semantics of records, the system we have described here is essentially a *parallel* object-based system: many objects may send (and receive) messages to (and from) one another concurrently. We expand on this point below. Note also that modeling objects in terms of records also allows us to support multiple-inheritance; the order in which the multiple superclasses of an object are layered determines how method and instance variable name clashes between superclasses are to be resolved. This is essentially the same view taken in [10].

As a final point, note that the object returned as a result of interpreter-session is structurally the same as the objects built in an inheritance system. Both define a complex naming environment. In the inheritance example, the record/environment structure was created at the time of object instantiation and object creation allowed superclass methods to be superseded by subclass ones; in the front-end example, the environment structure is built recursively allowing new definitions to supersede old ones.

4.3 Reflection and Non-Strictness

Reflection [29, 26] refers to an activity in which an executing process can examine its evaluation environment, store and continuation. COE supports a restrictive form of reflection that allows an expression to examine its evaluation environment. Unlike standard reflective systems, however, the language's non-strict evaluation semantics allows an expression to examine its evaluation environment *concurrently* with the manipulation of the same environment by other executing expressions. We discuss the implications below.

A process daemon is a passive process that watches a program or data structure for interesting developments. It's difficult to support the construction of such processes in conventional languages because of the enforced separation between program and data structures. On the other hand, it's easy to implement processes of this kind in the framework of a model that permits computations access to their evaluation environment. Consider, as a simple example, the implementation of a daemon process that is to print a message whenever a user redefines the keyword "lambda" at the top-level (see figure 3).

When applied, the function waits for a new element to be added onto the environment; this information is conveyed through a data stream named `signal`. When a new input element has been added, the daemon checks whether the environment now contains a definition for "`lambda`" by evaluating the expression `my-env.lambda` where `my-env` is defined to be the join of a record containing a dummy definition of `lambda` with `user-env`. It prints an appropriate message whenever the result yields a definition for `lambda` that is not identical to the dummy one. We can install this daemon within an interpreter session that is managed by a front-end similar to the one described earlier. However, we need to change the definition of the front-end slightly so that (a) it builds the environment object via side-effect rather than recursion and (b) it builds a data stream indicating whenever a new element has been added to the current environment object:

```
[FE =
  (lambda (user-env io-stream signal)
     (let ((next (↑ user-env
                    (read (first io-stream)))))
       (begin
         (attach signal t)
         (set-record user-env
                     (• user-env next))
         (FE user-env
             (rest io-stream)
             signal))))]
```

(`Set-record` mutates the object referenced by its first argument with the value yielded by its second.)

Suppose, given this implementation, the user inputs

```
"[check-lambda = (redefine user-env
                           signal)]"
```

to the interpreter built by the application of `FE`. `Check-lambda` can monitor the environment-object and io-stream of the evaluator responsible for its evaluation. New data values that augment `user-env` are visible to

```
[ redefine =
    (lambda (user-env signal)
        (letrec ((id (gensym))
                    (loop
                        (lambda (signal)
                            (let ((my-env (• [lambda = id] user-env)))
                                (begin
                                    (first signal)
                                    (if (not (equal? my-env.lambda id))
                                        (write "Redefining lambda"))
                                    (loop (rest signal)))))))))
            (loop signal)))]
```

Figure 3: Parallel Process Daemons

this application despite the fact that check-lambda exists within user-env. Many different monitors can be written that all examine user-env notified via signal whenever a new element is added. Note that even though check-lambda runs forever, the FE doesn't hand – because FE creates a non-strict record object, it is ready to accept new input even as previously input expressions continue to evaluate.

The ability to build a reflective daemon process comes fundamentally from the ability to treat program structures as data objects via coercion. Because the environment defined by a program structure can be treated as a simple non-strict data object, one can examine the internal structure of a program even if it is still in mid-evaluation. Viewing programs as *transparent* data objects encourages an interesting program methodology not supported by other programming models. For example, one can write a program essentially unencumbered by calls to i/o routines. Programmers are free to drape this program with routines that monitor its evaluation, format and display results as they see fit. Many different display routines can be written for the same program; the original core is left untouched. This style of programming, in essence, is no different from the reflective daemon described above: an i/o routine is a daemon that monitors the evaluation of a program structure.

4.4 Parallelism and Coercion

As a final example, we consider the realization of an actor-based programming model [4, 19] within our base language. In an actor-based paradigm, the fundamental computational entities are long-lived *concurrent objects* that communicate through message-passing. We can express the essence of the actor model in COE by organizing an actor program as a collection of concurrent processes that communicate with one another via specified data streams. The coercion operators allow us to examine the current evaluation environment of any given actor from the outside by treating the actor's environment as a data object, and by using the bindings defined within a given actor to affect the evaluation of other actors. This latter property is especially useful, as we will see, if we wish to dynamically compose different actor subsystems together.

The context of our example will be a translation of a static dataflow program (implemented in terms of a dataflow

graph) into COE[2]. The nodes in such a graph are actors; they have long-lived local state and communicate with one another via a simple form of message-passing. The COE version of the dataflow graphs is to be faithful to the semantics of the dataflow actors with respect to the synchronization and firing rules obeyed by these actors.

The translation treats nodes in the dataflow graph as perpetually running process monitors and edges as streams. Each process watches the stream corresponding to the input edges for the node it represents and computes a result based on input values found in these map streams. These results are then written to the stream corresponding to the node's output edge. Monitors execute asynchronously (in the same way that actors in a real dataflow system do). In the particular translation given here, acknowledgment arcs between nodes are not used: data written onto streams are queued; the translation guarantees that the order in which output values are emitted by a node is preserved when writing onto the appropriate edge by explicitly serializing the writing of an output value with the reading of new inputs[3].

Consider the following program fragment written in Val[2] to compute the factorial of a number:

Function *Factorial* (n : integer returns integer)
    for i : integer := 0;
        p : integer := 1;
    do if $i = n$ then p
        else
            iter i := $i + 1$;
              p := $p * i$
           enditer
        endif
    endfor
  endfun

The iter construct creates a new "local" environment for i and p and evaluates the expressions to which they are bound in the context of this new environment.

---

[2] For our purposes, a static data flow language is one in which the structure of the base language graphs is fixed at compile time; there are no function application operators that can instantiate new copies of function graphs at runtime. Iteration is supported by allowing cyclic graphs to be constructed. Readers unfamiliar with the dataflow model of computation should consult [5] which gives a comprehensive introduction to the subject.

[3] In other words, this simulation assumes unlimited queuing on edges.

A possible translation of this function into a static dataflow graph representation is shown in Figure 4.4. Edges entering into the sides of actors are signals – they generate boolean tokens. True and False gates pass their input only if the current value on their signal line is either true or false, resp.; they consume their input otherwise.

The corresponding representation in COE is given below:

```
[ fact =
    (lambda (n)
        (let ((graph REP))
            (begin
                (attach graph.i 0)
                (attach graph.p 0)
                graph.answer))) ]
```

where REP is a record:

```
[ i = (make-stream),
  p = (make-stream),
  answer = *,
  edge1 = (make-stream),
  edge2 = (make-stream),
  edge3 = (make-stream),

  false-gate =
    (lambda (input signal result)
        (begin
            (if (= (first signal) "false")
                (attach result
                    (first input)))
            (false-gate (rest input)
                    (rest signal)))),

  =actor =
    (lambda (i n)
        (begin
            (if (= (first i) n)
                (attach edge1 "true")
                (attach edge1 "false"))
            (=-actor (rest i) n))),

  true-gate =
    ((lambda (p edge1)
        (begin
            (if (= (first edge1) "true")
                (set! answer (first p)))
            (true-gate
                (rest p)
                (rest edge1))))
        p edge1)

  false-gate-1 = (false-gate i edge1
                            edge2),
  false-gate-2 = (false-gate p edge1
                            edge3),

  +-actor =
    ((lambda (edge2)
        (begin
            (attach i (1+ (first edge3)))
            (+-actor (rest edge2))))
        edge3)

  *-actor =
    ((lambda (edge3 i)
        (begin
            (attach p (* (first edge3)
                        (first i)))
```

```
            (*-actor (rest edge3)
                    (rest i))))
        edge4 i)) ]
```

It is often convenient to allow the binding-value of names defined within a record to be supplied by expressions found outside the record. To support this facility, we provide an explicit synchronization mechanism (denoted *) that acts as an unbound value; an expression that accesses a record field bound to * blocks until some other expression replaces the * with a non-unbound value. Insofar as it provides an explicit synchronization mechanism, unbound values in COE correspond roughly to I-structures [6] found in Id [24] or logical variables [22, 30] found in logic languages.

Each actor executes the same high-level process repeatedly: (1) wait for new input, (2) attach result to the output stream and (3) recurse. For example, the +-actor waits for a new value for i to be attached to edge2 by false-gate-1. Once a value is written, the actor increments it and attaches the result to its output stream and waits again for new input. Despite the fact that all actors and gates can run asynchronously, the serialization introduced by the begin form guarantees that an output will not be produced until the corresponding inputs are received. Moreover, because every edge has only one producer, it is easy to see that merging of output values from different nodes cannot occur. The final result is given by the true gate which evaluates the set! expression that stores the result into answer. The true gate is activated only when all iterations have completed, i.e., only when i = p.

We can probe the state of any given actor using the ↑ and ↓ operators. Suppose we wish to monitor the construction of various edges during the evaluation of (fact 10). To do this, we simply evaluate:

```
(let ((fact-env (↓ (fact 10))))
    (↑ fact-env.env inspect edges))
```

The translation given here is limited in one respect relative to a more general actor model: the static dataflow graph has a fixed number of actors; it is not possible to dynamically change or compose the set of actors in a simple static dataflow program. COE however is not bound by this limitation and it is straightforward to extend the base dataflow model to permit dynamic composition and generation of actors.

For example, suppose we require the stream of integers produced by the +-actor to be channeled as an input to another dataflow graph; we'd like to do this dynamically and *non-invasively* without altering the fact program. Dynamic composition of actor systems is possible using coercion. The record object that contains the individual actors in our program is coerced into an environment; once the coercion is performed, we can evaluate another program in the context of the bindings found in this environment. Thus, a function that siphons the elements produced by the +-actor (in the activation (fact 10)) to another (unrelated) dataflow program that multiplies these elements by 10 can be written as follows:

```
(let* ((fact-env (↓ (fact 10)))
       (input-stream
            fact-env.env.graph.edge3))
```

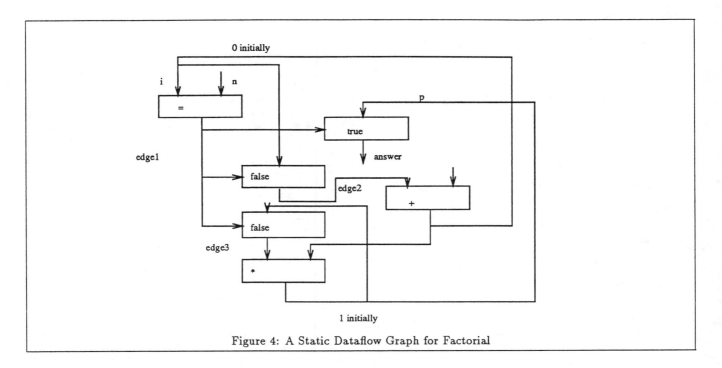

Figure 4: A Static Dataflow Graph for Factorial

```
(mult-10 input-stream))
```

The actor-based model described here is a simpler realization of the standard model formalized in [4]. Actors traditionally have been represented in terms of a set of components that represent both the computational as well as the communication behaviour of the object they manifest. The communication of an actor consists of the set of all other actors to which this actor responds. An actor's computational behaviour may include the monitoring of other actors, the creation of new "replacement" actors or the evaluation of a simple expression in response to input becoming available on the mail queue. In the COE framework, the specification of an actor is separated from the specification of its communication: an actor is an element of a record structure. Its state and environment may be examined by other actors via the coercion operators. The communication medium is represented via streams which are themselves represented as a recursive (potentially infinite) list of records (*i.e.*, actors). Abstracting the essence of actor behaviour (*i.e.*, the ability to model objects as computational entities with *visible* state) from communication (*i.e.*, stream generation) results in a simpler but no less expressive programming model.

5 Conclusions

In its support for non-strict evaluation of record objects COE's operational semantics most closely resembles various dataflow and graph reduction languages [21, 25, 28]. The coercion operators in COE distinguish it from these languages in obvious ways however; in terms of COE's support for direct manipulation of naming environments, it bears a strong resemblance to Symmetric Lisp [15, 16, 14], a non-strict language that provides support for first-class naming

environments. Symmetric Lisp is based on a programming model that unifies program and data structures via a single environment generating mechanism. There is a strong similarity between COE's ↑ operator and Symmetric Lisp's with expression; both constructs in essence use the bindings defined within a user-specified record structure to influence the evaluation environment of other expressions. One can view COE as an extension of the Symmetric Lisp effort insofar as it permits arbitrary record/environment transformations.

The goal of providing a uniform basis for reasoning about a number of superficially-different modularity constructs motivated our investigation into the semantics of a model that supports explicit representation of naming environments. The symbiotic interaction of parallelism with first-class environments leads to a number of interesting paradigms; the structure of a process daemon or the organization of a parallel object-based system are two cases in point. In [20], we present other examples illustrating the utility of the model, *e.g.,*the construction of a guarded horn clause logic system, the implementation of a parallel blackboard structure, and the design of a monolingual parallel programming environment. We plan to continue investigation of the semantics and implementation of languages that are based on the model described here; an extensive implementation effort is currently under way.

References

[1] Harold Abelson and Gerald Sussman. *Structure and Interpretation of Computer Programs.* MIT Press, 1985.

[2] William Ackerman and Jack Dennis. VAL – A Value-Oriented Algorithmic Language: Preliminary Reference Manual. Technical Report 218, MIT, 1979.

[3] Norman Adams and Jonathan Rees. Object-Oriented Programming in Scheme. In *Proceedings of the 1988 Conference on Lisp and Functional Programming*, pages 277–288, 1988.

[4] Gul Agha. *Actors: A Model of Concurrent Computation in Distributed Systems*. PhD thesis, MIT Artificial Intelligence Laboratory, 1985. Published as AI-TR-844.

[5] Arvind and David Culler. *Dataflow Architectures*, volume 1, pages 225–253. Annual Reviews Inc., 1986.

[6] Arvind, Rishiyur Nikhil, and Keshav Pingali. I-Structures: Data Structures for Parallel Computing. In *Proceedings of the Workshop on Graph Reduction*. Springer-Verlag, 1986. Lecture Notes in Computer Science, Number 279.

[7] H. Barendregt. *The Lambda Calculus*. North-Holland, 1981.

[8] J.G.P. Barnes. An Overview of Ada. *Software Practice and Experience*, 10:851 – 887, 1980.

[9] Daniel Bobrow, Kenneth Kahn, Gregor Kiczales, Larry Masinter, Mark Stefik, and Frank Zdybel. Common-Loops:Merging Lisp and Object-Oriented Programming. In *Object Oriented Programming Systems, Languages and Applications*, pages 17–30, September 1986.

[10] Luca Cardelli. A Semantics of Multiple Inheritance. In *International Symposium on Semantics of Data Types*. Springer-Verlag, 1984. Lecture Notes in Computer Science, Number 173.

[11] Luca Cardelli. Amber. Technical Report 11271-840924-10TM, AT&T Bell Laboratories, 1984.

[12] O.J. Dahl, B. Myhruhaug, and K. Nygaard. The Simula67 Base Common Base Language. Technical report, Norwegien Computing Center, 1970.

[13] William Clinger *et. al.* The Revised Revised Revised Report on Scheme or An UnCommon Lisp. Technical Report AI-TM 848, MIT Artificial Intelligence Laboratory, 1985.

[14] David Gelernter and Suresh Jagannathan. A Symmetric Language. Technical Report YALEU/DCS/RR-568, Yale University, May 1989.

[15] David Gelernter, Suresh Jagannathan, and Thomas London. Environments as First-Class Objects. In *14th ACM Symposium on Principle of Programming Languages Conf.*, 1987.

[16] David Gelernter, Suresh Jagannathan, and Thomas London. Parallelism, Persistence and Meta-Cleanliness in the Symmetric Lisp Interpreter. In *SIGPLAN '87 Conf. on Interpreters and Interpretive Techniques*, 1987.

[17] Adele Goldberg and David Robson. *Smalltalk-80: The Language and its Implementation*. Addison-Wesley Press, 1983.

[18] R. Greenblatt, T. Knight, J. Holloway, D. Moon, and D. Weinreb. The LISP Machine. In *Interactive Programming Environments*, pages 326–352. McGraw-Hill, 1984.

[19] Carl Hewitt. Viewing Control Structures as Patterns of Passing Messages. *Journal of Artifical Intelligence*, 8(3):323–364, 1977.

[20] Suresh Jagannathan. *A Programming Language Supporting First-Class, Parallel Environments*. PhD thesis, Massachusetts Institute of Technology, December 1988. Published as LCS-Technical Report 434.

[21] Thomas Johnsson. *Compiling Lazy Functional Languages*. PhD thesis, Department of Computer Sciences, Chalmers University of Technology, Goteborg, Sweden, 1987.

[22] R. Kowalski. Algorithms = Logic + Control. *Communicatiosn of the ACM*, 22(7):424–436, July 1979.

[23] Robin Milner. The Standard ML Core Language. Technical Report CSR-157-84, Edinburgh University, 1984.

[24] Rishiyur Nikhil. ID Reference Manual (Version 88.0). Technical report, MIT, 1988. Computation Structures Group Technical Report.

[25] Simon L. Peyton Jones, Chris Clack, Jon Salkild, and Mark Hardie. GRIP – A High Performance Architecture for Parallel Graph Reduction. In *Proceedings of the 3rd. International Conference on Functional Programming and Computer Architecture, Portland, Oregon*, September 1987.

[26] Brian Smith and J. des Rivières. The Implementation of Procedurally Reflective Languages. In *Proceedings of the 1984 Conf. on Lisp and Functional Programming*, pages 331–347, August 1984.

[27] Guy Steele Jr. and Gerry Sussman. The Art of the Interpreter, or the Modularity Complex. Technical Report AI-TM 453, MIT Artificial Intelligence Laboratory, 1978.

[28] D. A. Turner. A New Implementation Technique for Applicative Languages. *Software - Practice and Experience*, 9:31–49, 1979.

[29] Mitchell Wand and Daniel Friedman. The Mystery of the Tower Revealed: A Non-Reflective Description of the Reflective Tower. In *Proceedings of the 1986 Conf. on Lisp and Functional Programming*, pages 298–307, August 1986.

[30] David H. Warren. Logic Programming and Compiler Writing. *Software Practice and Experience*, 10(2):97–127, February 1980.

Multi-Dimensional Organization and Browsing of Object-Oriented Systems

Harold Ossher

IBM Thomas J. Watson Research Center
P. O. Box 704, Yorktown Heights, N.Y. 10598

This paper describes a two-dimensional organization for object-oriented systems, and a browser supporting that organization. The organization provides sites for documenting both generic functions and object types, allows convenient browsing and information hiding according to both function and type, and supports the notion of *abstract types*. The paper then describes extension of the organization and browser to multiple dimensions to allow for *multi-methods* that are split into separate implementations based on criteria in addition to receiver type. Inheritance and information hiding in the multi-dimensional case are discussed briefly. The multi-dimensional browser has been implemented on top of the RPDE³ environment framework.

1 Introduction

Class- or type-based object-oriented programs have a natural two-dimensional structure: each method is an implementation of a particular generic function for a particular object type. It therefore makes sense to group methods according to either generic function or type.

Grouping of methods according to type is common and important, and dates back to the data abstraction languages, such as CLU [9]. A type encapsulates a data structure. Representation details (instance variables) are hidden, and all access is via the methods. If you want to see what operations can be performed on a type, you look at the interfaces of the methods associated with that type, including inherited methods. If you want to find all the code that directly uses the representation of a type, you look at the collection of methods associated with that type (and, in most systems, with its subtypes).

Since types are usually arranged in an inheritance hierarchy, grouping of methods according to type is particularly attractive: all methods can be found by navigating the hierarchy. Hierarchy browsers are, in fact, the standard tool for browsing and manipulating object-oriented systems.

Grouping of methods according to generic function is less common, but is also important. Object-oriented programming, properly done, relies heavily on the fact that a generic function can be called with no foreknowledge of the exact type of the object to which the call is directed, yet with confidence that the appropriate thing will be done. This means that the generic function itself must have some meaning, and that all methods implementing it must conform to that meaning. Collecting these methods together helps to emphasize that fact, and also provides a site for documenting, or formally specifying, the meaning.

Grouping of methods by generic function can also be useful for browsing. A programmer wishing to write a new method that implements a generic function for some type might wish to examine other implementations of the same generic function. A programmer wishing to change the meaning of a generic function will need to find and perhaps change all methods implementing that function. Not all generic functions are implemented, either directly or via inheritance, for all types. A programmer wishing to use a generic function might need to find out all the types that support it, and perhaps to write additional implementations for some types that do not currently support it.

Environments for object-oriented systems typically support grouping by type effectively, by means of some form of hierarchy browser, but grouping by generic function much less effectively. This paper proposes a two-dimensional matrix organization that gives generic function and type equal status. It provides suitable sites for documenting or specifying both generic functions and types, and makes browsing according to either equally convenient. A browser that supports this organization has been built under RPDE³ [5], a framework for building structured environments. This browser is for the object-oriented Pascal extension supported by RPDE³ and in which RPDE³ is implemented, but all the ideas and even many of the details are directly applicable to other languages and systems. Section 2 describes the two-dimensional matrix organization and browser.

Some object-oriented languages allow multiple implementations of a single generic function for a single type, discriminated on some other criteria such as types or values of parameters. Examples are *multi-methods* in Common-Loops [3] and CLOS [2], and *subdivided methods* in RPDE³ [5]. Organizational problems are now more acute, because grouping according to these other criteria can be impor-

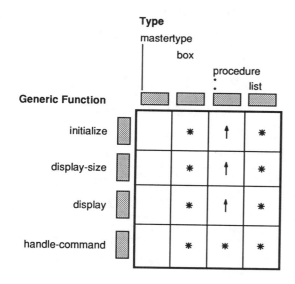

Figure 1: A Simple Function/Type Matrix

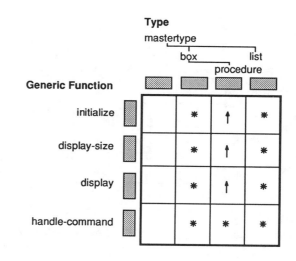

Figure 2: Function/Type Matrix showing Inheritance

tant also. Section 3 discusses these organizational issues, shows how the matrix organization can be extended to multiple dimensions to handle them, and presents a browser for multi-dimensional matrices.

2 Two-Dimensional Organization

The crux of the proposed organization is a two-dimensional matrix, called a *function/type matrix*, in which each row corresponds to a generic function and each column to a type. A simple function/type matrix is shown in fig. 1.

Each row has a *header*, shown as a small shaded box in the figure, that is a site for information about the associated generic function, such as its name, its parameters and its semantics. Just how the semantics are specified is beside the point here; the key fact is that the row header provides a suitable site for a (formal or informal) semantic specification, documentation and any other information about a generic function.

Similarly, each column has a header that is a site for information about the associated type, such as its name, its representation (instance variables), documentation, and perhaps a semantic specification also.

Each entry in the matrix is a *method*: the code that implements a particular generic function for a particular type. Methods are indicated by asterisks in the figure: they can be thought of as hypertext-like links to the method code. Upward arrows in the figure indicate inherited methods.

Details of inheritance are determined by an *inheritance hierarchy*. This hierarchy is a directed graph whose nodes are object types (matrix columns) and whose edges represent inheritance links; an edge (t_1, t_2) in the hierarchy means that t_2 inherits from t_1. In the common case of sin-

gle inheritance, the hierarchy is a tree. The inheritance hierarchy can be drawn adjacent to the matrix, as shown in fig. 2. All nodes, whether internal nodes or leaves, correspond to columns. Note that the matrix organization in no way constrains the nature of the inheritance hierarchy, nor its semantics.

By virtue of the separate generic function dimension, the two-dimensional organization conveniently supports the *abstract type* model of Emerald [1], a particularly elegant approach to type specification that provides the advantages of static type checking without reducing the flexibility of object-oriented programming. An abstract type in Emerald is an interface that specifies collections of operations, their parameters, and, at least in principle, their semantics. In other words, an abstract type is a set of generic functions. There is no forced relationship between abstract types and a code inheritance hierarchy. Instead, an object conforms to an abstract type if and only if it implements, either directly or via inheritance, all the generic functions that make up the type. Thus, any number of object types can conform to a given abstract type, and one object type can conform to any number of abstract types. All type specification is done in terms of abstract types, and static type checking is performed using the carefully defined notion of type conformity [1]. A similar model is employed by RPDE[3]; abstract types are called *roles* [5,6], and any object type that implements all the generic functions in a role is able to fulfil that role.

In the two-dimensional organization an abstract type, being a set of generic functions, is represented by a set of rows. Abstract types can thus be shown as a directed acyclic graph whose leaves are rows; following RPDE[3] terminology this graph is referred to as the *role hierarchy*. An object type satisfies an abstract type if and only if the column representing the type has non-empty entries for all rows included in the abstract type. It does not matter

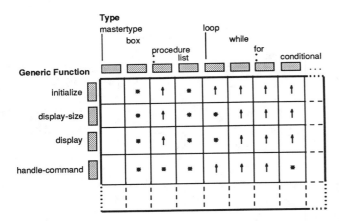

Figure 3: Function/Type Matrix Presented with Elision

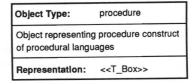

Figure 4: Type Header

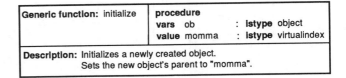

Figure 5: Generic Function Header

where the object type is in the inheritance hierarchy.

One of the key aspects of data abstraction and object-oriented programming is *information hiding*: the fact that instance variables of a type are visible only to methods associated with that type. It is this fact primarily that leads to the customary organization of systems according to type. This restriction can be expressed simply in terms of the matrix organization: the method located at position (f, t) in the matrix can access only the instance variables of type t (depending on the details of the language involved, this might include inherited instance variables). The restriction is thus easily specified, and it can be easily enforced by an environment.

In fact, the matrix organization permits information hiding in the generic function dimension also. Variables that are intended for use only by methods implementing specific generic functions, but across multiple types, traditionally have to be made global. Use restriction is then by convention only. The matrix organization allows such variables to be associated with generic functions or roles. The method located at position (f, t) in the matrix can then use those variables associated with generic function f or with some role containing it.

For example, several RPDE[3] environments are structured environments for different programming languages. These environments support a "code-generation" operation that produces a standard textual program from the object representation used by the environments themselves. This operation is implemented by means of "code-generate" methods associated with the objects representing programming language constructs. These methods make use of some variables, containing information such as the target language currently being generated and the comment delimiters to be used for that language. These variables are properly associated with the "code-generate" generic function, for use only by implementations of that generic function.

In summary, the primary advantages of the two-dimen-

sional organization are as follows:

- Identification and documentation, and the possibility of specification, of generic functions as well as types.

- Information hiding based on generic function as well as type.

- Convenient support for the abstract type model. The organization is appropriate, however, even in systems where type specification is not of interest.

2.1 The Two-Dimensional Browser

The previous section described an organization. This section describes a structured environment built under RPDE[3] that supports that organization, presents it to the user and allows the user to work within it. Some features that have been planned but not yet implemented are included in the description.

The starting point when using the environment is the function/type matrix, which is presented to the user as shown in fig. 1. In a large system, the whole matrix will obviously not fit on the screen. The RPDE[3] display manager presents a display based on user-specified points of focus. In other words, the user can indicate types and/or generic functions of interest, and will be presented with a display that includes them and as much surrounding context as will fit in the window. An example is shown in fig. 3

The boxes at the heads of rows and columns stand for headers with detailed information. By positioning the cursor on any one and issuing the *header* command, the user can see the details. Type headers contain the name, description and representation of the type, as illustrated in fig. 4. Generic function headers contain the name, parameters and description of the generic function, as illustrated in fig. 5. Descriptions are informal. Semantic specifications

```
initialize_list  procedure
                 vars   ob          :  istype  object
                 value  suboptionx  :  istype  suboption
                 value  obx         :  istype  virtualindex
                 value  momma       :  istype  virtualindex
                 var    u           :  istype  t_obj_cursor

Initializes a newly-created list object.

variable  instype :  istype    obtype
variable  zero    :  istype    virtualindex
variable  restval :  boolean

Set instance variables
↳ob.rep.parent    := momma.v
  ob.rep.showing   := 0
  ob.rep.children  := 0
Set the cursor to point to the new list
↳u.obtab_index.r   := obx.v + basemap[obx.f]
  u.obtab_index.f   := obx.f
  u.subobtab_index  := 0
  u.subobject_index := 0
Insert an initial entry if required
↳instype := obtype_type_parameter( ob.typeofob, suboptionx, 11 )

  instype <> empty  zero.v := 0
                    zero.f := obx.f
                    retval := insert_object( ob, suboptionx, obx,
                                             zero, zero, instype, u )
```

Figure 6: A Method as Displayed by RPDE[3]

could be accommodated by the browser simply by adding an extra component to each header; determining the nature of such specifications, however, remains a research issue. The precise nature and content of headers will vary from language to language, but the general approach to browsing described here is applicable to any object-oriented language or system.

The function/type matrix is intended to be presented in a very compact manner, to give the user an overview of as many types and generic functions as possible in a single display. Accordingly, no attempt is made to present either the inheritance hierarchy or the role hierarchy in the same display as the matrix. Instead, the user can click on any type header to see a display of the inheritance hierarchy in another window, focused on the selected type. The user can navigate the inheritance hierarchy and click on any node to get back to the corresponding type in the matrix. Similarly, the user can gain access to the role hierarchy by clicking on a generic function header.

In the environment, the asterisks in the matrix really are hypertext links to methods. The user can click on an asterisk to see the code, presented in another window. In the case of this particular environment, the code is written in an object-oriented extension of Pascal using a structured RPDE[3] environment for Pascal programming [8]. Accordingly, the method is an RPDE[3] object representing a procedure or function, and containing within it objects representing declarations, statements, and the other constructs making up Pascal procedures. An example is shown in fig. 6. When a method displayed, the appropriate RPDE[3] coding environment is automatically available for manipulating it; no mode change or environment transition is even apparent to the user. The user can click on the procedure to get back to the corresponding asterisk in matrix.

The arrows represent inherited method implementations. The user can click on an arrow to see the matrix slot from which the inheritance takes place, and can go from there to the code, if desired. This feature of the environment allows the user to see at a glance what generic functions are implemented for a type and to find the code for any of the implementations, without having to search the type hierarchy manually.

The manner in which the RPDE[3] display manager operates opens up a number of interesting possibilities when it comes to the issue of which generic functions and types to display, and in what order. In brief, the display manager starts with the focal points specified explicitly by the user, and then adds "surrounding context" until the window is full. Each displayable object must implement a generic function called "increase-presence" that the display manager can call to find out what surrounding context is appropriate for the object in question. Great freedom is available when writing "increase-presence" methods, and this can be exploited to good effect. For example, if the user focuses on a type, its supertype chain can be displayed to its left and its immediate subtypes to its right. Types can be omitted from the display if they do not implement any of the generic functions currently of interest. Full exploitation of this mechanism to present interesting and useful portions of the function/type matrix remains an area for further investigation.

In summary, the primary advantages of the two-dimensional browser are:

- Compact, visual presentation of what generic functions are implemented by object types, directly or via inheritance.

- Support for browsing by generic function as well as type.

- Inheritance tracking: the use of arrows to show which methods are inherited, and the ability to find the code without manually searching the class hierarchy.

- Structured editing environments for code: the method code is not treated as text, but rather as object structures presented visually to the user and manipulated directly.

3 Beyond Two Dimensions

The organization and browser described in the previous section support the standard object-oriented approach of providing a separate implementation of a generic function for each object type that needs one. There are many cases, however, where the implementation must choose what to do based on some criteria in addition to object type. For example, the same object can often be displayed in different ways, perhaps showing different levels of detail. The user might set an environment variable called "perspective" that indicates which perspective he/she wants. The "display" method for each type would then have to behave differently for different values of this variable.

Just as there are advantages to providing separate implementations for separate types, rather than a combined implementation for all types, so there are advantages, described below, to splitting such separate cases into separate implementations. We refer to this process as *method subdivision*. Multi-methods in CommonLoops [3] and CLOS [2] are examples of mechanisms for subdividing methods. Subdivision is usually on the basis of the types of selected generic function parameters, but CLOS also permits subdivision based on the values of parameters.

RPDE³ supports and makes extensive use of a mechanism called subdivisions [5]. A generic function can be declared to be subdivided on the basis of one *subdivision criterion*, either the value of a parameter or of a global environment variable. For any object type, separate implementations of such a generic function can be provided for all subdivision values of interest. A default implementation can also be provided for use in all other cases. For example, we subdivide methods in the display management role on perspective, as described above. We subdivide "handle-command" on the kind of command, so that separate handlers can be written for different commands. We subdivide "code-generate" on target language. For most structured constructs, like conditionals and loops, we can generate textual PC Pascal, VS Pascal and C from the same RPDE³ object via three subdivisions of the "code-generate" method. More than one of these have been worked on at the same time by different people.

Experience has demonstrated the desirability of extending the subdivision model to more than one subdivision criterion. For example, command handlers might be subdivided not only on the kind of command but also on the language currently in use, or on the current display perspective. A companion paper in these proceedings describes an extended subdivision model in detail [7].

Some of the advantages of method subdivision are:

- Each subdivided implementation is very specific, and its context is clear: it implements a specific function for a specific type under specific, clearly identified circumstances (such as for a particular display perspective). One does not have to wade through complex conditional statements to understand this context.

- Different programmers can work on different subdivisions simultaneously without interference and without worrying about affecting one another.

- By far the most important advantage of subdivisions is that new situations can be handled by adding implementations rather than by modifying existing ones:

  - If one wishes to introduce a new perspective, for example, one can simply add it and provide implementations for it. Types that are not affected can be ignored: the default will be used automatically.

  - If one wishes to subdivide a generic function that is not currently subdivided, one can simply specify that it be subdivided on the appropriate criterion and provide special implementations for types that need them. Types that are not affected can be ignored: the default will be used automatically.

The rest of this section shows how subdivided methods can be accommodated in the matrix organization by extending it to multiple dimensions. The RPDE³ subdivision model is used for detailed description, but the ideas are directly applicable to other languages and mechanisms.

Within a generic function header is a place to specify that the function is to be subdivided, and on what criterion. Separate implementations can now be provided not just for different object types, but within each type for different values of the subdivision criterion. Each slot in the function/type matrix row corresponding to the generic function can thus contain multiple methods. They can be organized by introducing a third dimension representing the subdivision criterion.

For example, Fig. 7 shows subdivisions of the "display" generic function, based on perspective. Three perspectives are shown:

- The default, which shows all detail.

- The "structure" perspective, which shows just the top-level structure of a system. In this perspective, lists display as hierarchies, and procedures just as names.

- The "interface" perspective, which shows procedure parameters and descriptions, but not their code.

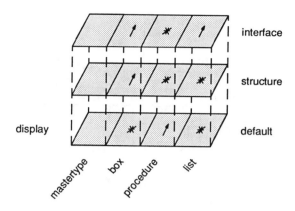

Figure 7: Subdivisions of "display"

Once again, asterisks indicate explicit implementations, and arrows indicate inheritance. Details of inheritance are discussed shortly.

If a generic function is not subdivided, its function/type matrix row is a one-dimensional matrix, with one slot for each type. If it is subdivided on the basis of one criterion, the row is a two-dimensional matrix: one dimension is type, the other is the subdivision criterion, such as perspective. If it is subdivided on the basis of more than one criterion, the row is a matrix with one dimension for type, and one for each subdivision criterion. Putting all generic functions together, one therefore gets a collection of matrices of different dimensionalities. This can also be thought of as a single multi-dimensional matrix, with one dimension for generic function, one for object type, and one more for each different subdivision criterion. This unified approach is superior, because some generic functions might share some subdivision criteria, and this sharing is explicit in the multi-dimensional matrix organization.

A sparse, multi-dimensional matrix is conceptually elegant, but might seem cumbersome to work with in practice. Fortunately, only a few dimensions need be considered at any time, determined by the generic function(s) under consideration. The next section describes the environment for browsing and manipulating the matrix, and shows how just relevant portions of the matrix can be presented to the user. First, however, we briefly consider two interesting areas for future research opened up by this organization: multi-dimensional inheritance and information hiding.

In the two-dimensional case discussed in section section 2, inheritance was determined by the inheritance hierarchy in the object type dimension. In the multi-dimensional case, the various subdivision dimensions can have their own inheritance hierarchies also, and inheritance is determined by a combination of these. One way to do this, in the case of single inheritance, is as follows. Suppose generic function f is subdivided on criteria $s_0, s_1, ..., s_n$, in that order, where s_0 is object type. Suppose that for each value, x, of some subdivision criterion, $i(x)$ denotes another value

of that subdivision criterion from which x inherits. Then if the matrix slot $(f, x_0, x_1, ..., x_n)$ contains an arrow, the inherited implementation is

$$inherit((f, x_0, x_1, ..., x_n), (x_0, x_1, ..., x_n))$$

where

$$inherit((f, x_0, x_1, ..., x_n), (y_0, y_1, ..., y_n))$$

is the method in slot $(f, y_0, y_1, ..., y_n)$ if one is specified explicitly, and is equal to

$$inherit((f, x_0, x_1, ..., x_n), (y_0, y_1, ..., y_{j-1}, i(y_j), x_{j+1}, ..., x_n))$$

otherwise, where j is the largest number between 0 and n such that $i(y_j)$ is not null. This expresses formally the simple rule that inheritance is according to the latest possible subdivision criterion in the list associated with the generic function. Other ways of handling multi-dimensional inheritance, including handling of multiple inheritance, remain topics for future research.

The two-dimensional organization described in section 2 supported two-dimensional information hiding, in which a method could have access to information associated with both its object type and its generic function. This extends to the multi-dimensional case, where private information can be associated with subdivision criteria also. A particularly interesting case of this is where a generic function is subdivided on the basis of the type of a parameter other than the receiver. For example, if separate implementations of the generic function "add(a, b)" are provided for different types of a and b, multi-dimensional information hiding could allow each implementation to access the representations of both a and b. The word "could" was used advisedly. Rather than decreeing that both representations can always be used, the matrix organization makes it possible to specify in simple terms what is to be accessible and what is not. Just how this should be done and how to exploit it remain topics for further research.

3.1 The Multi-Dimensional Browser

Even if excellent 3D graphics were used, presenting the entire multi-dimensional function/type matrix in a single presentation would not be viable. Instead, the multi-dimensional browser allows the user to view two-dimensional slices of his/her choice.

The crux of the environment is still the two-dimensional matrix with generic functions as rows and object types as columns. Non-empty entries in the matrix for subdivided generic functions show up not as asterisks, however, but as icons indicating sub-matrices. A simple example is shown in fig. 8.

First consider the case of single subdivision criteria. The user can click on a sub-matrix icon, or issue the *subdivision* command on the generic function header, in which case a

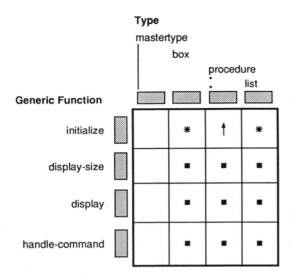

Figure 8: Home View of Multi-Dimensional Matrix

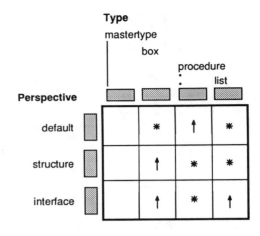

Figure 9: Subdivision View of Multi-Dimensional Matrix

different view of the matrix is presented, such as that shown in fig. 9. The columns are still object types, but the rows now correspond to subdivision values. The generic function is "frozen" at the one selected, so that all the information presented pertains just to that generic function. In other words, this is the slice through the function/type matrix that corresponds to the particular generic function of interest.

If the generic function is subdivided on multiple criteria, non-empty slots in the subdivision view will again contain sub-matrix icons, and the user can repeat the process of clicking on the icons or issuing *subdivision* commands. Each time this is done, one more subdivision criterion is frozen at a particular value, and the next one is displayed. The user can return to the original function/type view at any time via the *home* command.

The user can also select two-dimensional presentations explicitly. He/she can request presentation of the list of all dimensions in the function/type matrix, and can select from this list the dimensions to be displayed as rows and columns. He/she can also specify values at which to "freeze" the dimensions not currently displayed.

4 Summary and Conclusions

This paper presented a multi-dimensional matrix organization for object-oriented systems, and an environment supporting that organization. The organization is appropriate for any object-oriented language or system, though some details will differ from language to language. The environment presents two-dimensional slices of the matrix under user control. Implementation of the first version of the environment under the RPDE[3] framework is currently almost complete. Once it has been completed, the RPDE[3] system

itself will be manipulated using the environment, providing feedback as to its effectiveness and indicating additional function that would help the user.

The primary advantages of the multi-dimensional matrix organization and environment over the traditional class hierarchy organization and browser are:

- Identification and documentation, and the possibility of specification, of generic functions, types and subdivision criteria.

- Compact, visual presentation of what generic functions are implemented, directly or via inheritance, for types and subdivisions.

- Convenient browsing by generic function, type, or subdivision criteria.

- Convenient support for the abstract type model, if desired.

- Support for information hiding based on generic function, type, or subdivision criteria.

- Support for inheritance based on type and subdivision criteria.

Some additional advantages of the environment, not directly dependent on the matrix organization, are:

- Inheritance tracking.

- Structured, direct manipulation editing environments for method code.

Much interesting work remains to be done on the browser and the underlying multi-dimensional organization, including the following:

- The browser currently supports fairly primitive user

commands. It should be enhanced to support directly and conveniently more complex operations commonly performed by users. Examples include creating new object types or generic functions, introducing new subdivision criteria, changing generic function interfaces, and finding and reworking an existing method as the fastest means of writing a new one. Taking this further, the browser should provide *task-oriented* support for common user activities. Since the browser is built upon the RPDE³ framework, which supports extension of environments, adding such support should not be difficult.

- There is potential for the browser to perform a variety of checks to give the user immediate notification of inconsistencies introduced by his/her editing. We have designed a scheme for performing type-checking based on roles that ensures both type-correctness of code and consistency between code and persistent objects in a repository [6]. We plan to implement this checking within the browser.

- The paper discussed information hiding with respect to instance variables, but not with respect to methods. Generic functions and methods are commonly considered to be universally accessible. Explicitly controlling their visibility, however, can significantly aid system understanding and maintenance, and some languages do allow for methods that are private or otherwise restricted. The multi-dimensional organization allows visibility to be specified in each dimension, or across dimensions. For example, one can specify which roles can use which other roles, which types can use which other types, which types can use which roles, and so on. The author has done some work in this area in the context of the *grid mechanism* [10] and an extension of objects to support multiple *views* with access control [4]; this work can and should be integrated with the organization and browser described here.

- Semantic specification was mentioned briefly, but not explored in this paper. The primary challenge is to develop a means of specifying the semantics of generic functions independently of specific types, and of types independently of generic functions.

- The browser would be considerably enhanced by the use of more sophisticated visual techniques, such as three-dimensional graphics and animation.

References

[1] Andrew Black, Norman Hutchinson, Eric Jul, Henry Levy, and Larry Carter. Distribution and abstract types in Emerald. *IEEE Transactions on Software Engineering*, SE-13(1):65–76, January 1987.

[2] D. G. Bobrow, L. G. DeMichiel, R. P. Gabriel, S. E. Keene, G. Kiczales, and D. A. Moon. Common Lisp object system specification X3J13. *SIGPLAN Notices*, 23, September 1988.

[3] Daniel Bobrow, Kenneth Kahn, Gregor Kiczales, Larry Masinter, Mark Stefik, and Frank Zdybel. Common-Loops: Merging Lisp and object-oriented programming. In *Conference on Object-Oriented Programming Systems, Languages, and Applications*, pages 17–29, ACM, Portland, September 1986.

[4] Brent Hailpern and Harold Ossher. *Extending Objects to Provide Multiple Interfaces*. Research Report RC 14016, IBM Thomas J. Watson Research Center, Yorktown Heights, NY, September 1988.

[5] William Harrison. RPDE³: A framework for integrating tool fragments. *IEEE Software*, 4(6):46–56, November 1987.

[6] William Harrison and Harold Ossher. Checking evolving interfaces in the presence of persistent objects. Submitted for publication.

[7] William Harrison and Harold Ossher. Subdivided procedures: A language extension supporting extensible programming. In *Proceedings of the IEEE 1990 International Conference on Computer Languages*, March 1990.

[8] William H. Harrison, Jack L. Rosenfeld, Ching C. Wang, and Brian A. Weston. Structured editing with RPDE. *Computer Language*, 3(9):93–101, September 1986.

[9] B. H. Liskov, A. Snyder, R. Atkinson, and J. C. Schaffert. Abstraction mechanisms in CLU. *Communications of the ACM*, 20(8):564–576, August 1977.

[10] H. L. Ossher. A mechanism for specifying the structure of large, layered systems. In Bruce Shriver and Peter Wegner, editors, *Research Directions in Object-Oriented Programming*, pages 219–252, MIT Press, 1987.

An Object Model for Shared Data

Gail E. Kaiser
Columbia University
Department of Computer Science
New York, NY 10027

Brent Hailpern
IBM Research Division
T.J. Watson Research Center
Yorktown Heights, NY 10598

Abstract

The classical object model supports private data within objects and clean interfaces among objects, and by definition does not permit sharing of data among arbitrary objects. This is a problem for certain real-world applications, where the same data logically belongs to multiple objects and may be distributed over multiple nodes on the network. Rather than give up the advantages of encapsulated objects in modeling real-world entities, we propose a new object model that supports shared data in a distributed environment. The key is separating distribution of computation units from information hiding concerns. We introduce our new object model, describe a motivating example from the financial services domain, and then present a new language, PROFIT, based on the model.

Introduction

The classical object model [27] supports private data within objects and clean interfaces among objects. The standard mode of communication between objects is for a client object to send a message to a server object to request some service defined in the server's interface; the client is not aware of the private data hidden within the server and cannot manipulate this data except through side-effects of the server's responses to its messages. This encapsulation makes it impossible for two or more arbitrary objects to transparently and symmetrically *share* data in a tightly-coupled manner. This is reflected in both the compile-time view of objects as information hiding units and their execution-time view as processes. Our goal is to extend the classical object model to support transparent, symmetric, tightly-coupled sharing.

The classical object model permits code and data definitions to be shared via inheritance, but not data values. Data values can be shared symmetrically but non-transparently, by encapsulating the shared data in a third object accessed through message passing [1]. Data can be shared asymmetrically by encapsulating it within one of the objects, which may access it transparently, but the only access available to other objects is through message passing; any sharing is by convention and outside the programming model. It is possible to share data symmetrically and transparently, but only among all instances of a certain class (class variables) or a certain set of classes (pool variables), or all objects (global variables) [11]. We know of one previously proposed object model that does support shared data among arbitrary objects: Self [25] treats all data as potentially shared, transparently and symmetrically, but the data is loosely-coupled. There is no mechanism for compile-time consistency checking of access to any data; instead, all access is through message passing. We drew upon many ideas pioneered in Self during the development of our object model.

We are concerned with operation in a distributed environment, where the client and server may reside in different processes, and processes may themselves be multi-threaded. (By process, we mean the standard operating system process with its own address space; by thread, we mean a context consisting of registers and a control stack.) Distribution complicates sharing because two objects that share a common subpart may not reside in the same address space, and in these cases apparently direct access must be implemented via message passing. A few distributed object systems (e.g., [26], [22]) support some form of partitioning of subobjects among different nodes, but subobjects cannot be shared.

We propose a new object model that supports data sharing among arbitrary objects in a distributed environment by separating compile-time and execution-time concerns. There are three important components: *facets*, *objects* and *processes*. Facets are subobjects, the minimal unit of data and control; facets may be shared among multiple objects and may be replicated in multiple processes. Our objects reflect the compile-time aspect of classical objects: each object encapsulates one or more facets and provides an external interface. Our processes reflect the execution-time aspect: each process colocates one or more facets within a single address space and manages a number of *threads*. Objects and processes are orthogonal: objects are not contained in processes nor vice versa.

Our new model is motivated by an important application domain, financial services. Advanced financial services, e.g., "programmed trading", involve: (1) enormous amounts of data; (2) sharing of data among large numbers of users; (3) logical representation of this data as local variables as opposed to entities in an external database; (4) rapidly changing data (e.g., prices); (5) changes to data outside the control of the system (e.g., from the stock exchange wire); and (6) severe economic penalties for making decisions based on obsolete data. These problems have been articulated by other researchers, but not solved (e.g., [20]). In this paper, we are concerned primarily with points 1-3; we have considered points 4-6, but due to space limitations, we mention timing concerns only as needed to explain our decisions regarding other aspects of the design.

Objects are naturally suited for modeling such real-world phenomena, except there is no provision for sharing data among objects. This is the motivation for our extension of the classical object model to support transparent, symmetric, tightly-coupled sharing of data. Transparency is needed since the shared data is logically part of each sharing object. Symmetry is needed to treat multiple users uniformly. Tight coupling is required to guarantee static semantic consistency at compile-time. Tight-coupling is also important at run-time, since our rapidly changing data is similar to the real-time data of manufacturing and telecommunications: the data changes when it changes, and cannot be blocked until convenient. However, financial applications are more like telecommunications than manufacturing, since operation can degrade gracefully (to a point) as changes are sometimes missed and changes arise on the order of seconds rather than microseconds.

Financial services is also one of the primary motivating applications for database management systems, which support shared data (the database) and separate compile-time (data definition) from execution-time (data access). But conventional databases do not support encapsulation within objects, or even a clear notion of "object", while object-oriented databases [9] do not support sharing among objects. Neither makes execution-time issues such as threads of control and data placement among nodes explicit in the programming model, but buries concurrency and distribution in the underlying database manager. Our object model addresses these problems, although it does not treat persistence or queries. Our object model is not specific to financial services, but is suitable for other applications, such as intelligent network management [18], weather modeling and animation [12], with similar requirements.

We start by discussing an extended financial services example in general terms to motivate our new object model. Then we give an overview of a new programming language, PROFIT (PROgrammed FInancial Trading), based on our model. PROFIT is an extension of C, and most statements and declarations will be written in C. We then present PROFIT's facets, objects and processes. Discussion of timing constraints is outside the scope of this paper. We briefly compare to related work, and summarize our contributions. A subset of PROFIT has been implemented in a pilot study.

Example Portfolio Management System

Consider a financial market, with both stocks and options, collectively called instruments. Our example system manages portfolios made up of combinations of such instruments. For the sake of the example, we assume there are only three companies, *Institutional Books and Materials*, *Domestic Educational Corporation* and *Supplies, Umbrellas and Novelties*, abbreviated INS, DOM and SUP. Options on their stocks are available with various expiration dates. The system, called *Stock Environment Calculator* (SEC), monitors the current prices of the stocks and options and executes the appropriate purchases and sales (according to certain constraints associated with the particular portfolio by a financial analyst) as market conditions change. We describe three aspects of SEC: consistent access to the current prices of a stock and its options (the 9am stock price along with the 9:10am option price could result in disastrous financial strategies); easy programming of the objects that track the changing prices to determine when action must be taken; and transparent sharing of the prices by all the users of the system.

An individual portfolio consists of a set of instruments, their current prices and a set of strategies for when to buy and sell. Each portfolio is organized into subparts, where each part represents the instruments for a particular company, together with any aspect of the strategy specific to that company (see Figure 1). For example, if the price of a stock increased 10% since purchase, buy more. Additional subparts support strategies that cut across companies and maintain any other data needed. A subpart representing the instruments of a particular company contains the current prices of the stock and options. Multiple portfolios will refer to the same company with independent criteria for when price changes are significant to the financial analysts's strategies.

The difficult problem is how to notify the computations reflecting the strategies of these portfolios when the prices of the stocks and options change. There are three ways to structure the solution. The *active value* approach propagates each change to every interested portfolio. *Polling* requires every interested portfolio to poll the current value. The third approach uses *daemons*. We compare these three approaches at an abstract level, and describe PROFIT's implementation of the daemon approach in the remainder of the paper.

In the active value approach (e.g., [23]), any change to any value can be propagated to other parts of the program. The propagation invokes code associated in advance with the data and the kind of change. An exemplary application is changing the speed of a simulated car, resulting in an updated display of the speedometer reading and the consumption rate of fuel. In Figure 2, the active value approach combines the shared data (D) and whatever computation is necessary to monitor (M) the changes to the data in the same object. The monitoring is not a separate thread of control, but instead a side-effect of the procedures that update the data. The monitor code has the responsibility to notify all other interested computations (C) of changes.

The active value approach has a significant flaw with respect to this application: since price changes are frequent and typically small (1/4 point), some changes may be insignificant from the point of view of some portfolios. Thus the system can be flooded by many notification messages to which few portfolios are paying attention. One solution is for the monitor code to know the separate criteria for each interested portfolio regarding what changes are considered important. This would add a significant computational component to the active value and greatly complicate the programming of the monitor code.

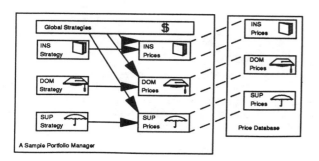

Figure 1: Example Portfolio

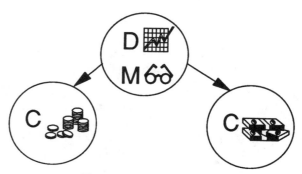

Figure 2: Active Value Approach

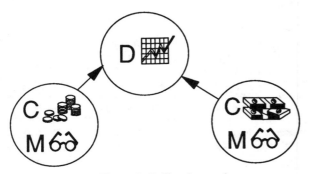

Figure 3: Polling Approach

Polling is the traditional means for implementing device drivers, and can be implemented in any imperative programming language. The idea is to check over and over again whether a data item has changed. Figure 3 illustrates this approach: the shared data (D) is passive, and the interested computation objects (C) directly incorporate the monitoring (M) of changes to the data. The computation code must include explicit statements to check whether the shared data has been changed in a manner considered significant by the particular computation.

Polling overcomes the problems with the active value approach, since each portfolio can decide how often to check each price and under what criteria to take action. Unfortunately, a naive implementation — consisting of tedious busy-wait loops — obscures the logic of the main portfolio program. This is not a serious impediment when polling only a single price, but is complicated when the latest prices of multiple instruments must be considered both individually and in combination (Figure 4).

```
INS_up_10%:                 int old_INS, old_DOM;
    {sell_INS();}               while (1) {
                                   if (INS_price>(1.1*old_INS))
INS_down_15%:                          {sell_INS();old_INS=INS_price;}
    {buy_INS();}               if (INS_price<(0.85*old_INS))
                                       {buy_INS();old_INS=INS_price;}
INS_exceeds_DOM:              if (INS_price>DOM_price && old_INS<old_DOM)
    {buy_DOM(); sell_INS();}           {buy_DOM(); sell_INS();
                                   old_INS=INS_price;
                                   old_DOM=DOM_price;}


   without explicit               with explicit polling
       polling
```

Figure 4: Complexity of Polling

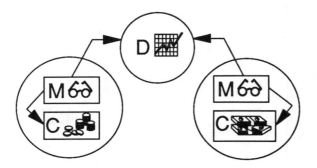

Figure 5: Daemon Approach

We prefer a more sophisticated solution in which the shared prices are monitored by simple daemons [2]. Each daemon contains a trigger that informs the main-line strategy when something "interesting" happens. Active values and polling both employ two objects, one representing the prices and the other the portfolio manager. The daemon approach uses three objects, adding an intermediate object that polls the prices and behaves as an active value with respect to the portfolio manager. The advantages include a simpler programming model and the capability for each portfolio to decide how best to use its computational resources. Figure 5 shows the three objects: passive shared data (D) as in polling, the strategic computation (C) as in the active value solution, and a separate daemon (M).

Overview of PROFIT

We have designed our programming model to provide the appropriate building blocks to easily represent the daemon solution as well as active values and polling. Our contribution is an explicit programming model for *shared data* in a concurrent object system. This is reflected in our design of the PROFIT programming language. There are three main concepts:

- *Facet*, the minimal unit of data and control, in particular, the unit of shared data. A facet consists of a number of named slots, each of which may contain either a data value or procedure code. A facet may execute a single thread of control at any one time.

- *Object*, a statically defined collection of facets representing an information hiding unit. An object defines a context for binding references between facets in the same object and an external interface for passing messages to and from other objects.

- *Process*, a statically defined collection of facets — orthogonal to objects — that must execute at the same physical location. That is, a process represents a single virtual address space. Creation and scheduling of threads, employing single or multiple processors, is handled by processes.

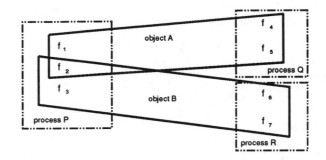

Figure 6: Facets, Objects and Processes

Every facet is a member of one or more objects and one or more processes. In the simplest case, there is exactly one process in the program, and all objects execute on the same machine within the same virtual address space. When there are multiple processes, different facets of the same object may reside in different processes.

Processes are units of separate compilation, while objects may be treated as declarations included during compilation as needed or as source code also compiled separately. Objects and facets can be written independently of processes, and later configured into a system by defining processes; any configuration will provide a logically correct program, although one may be more efficient than another on a given concurrent architecture.

We posit one SEC process containing all the prices, and one additional process for each individual user of the SEC. Each user would define one object corresponding to each of his portfolios, consisting of computation and daemon facets and the relevant previously defined prices facets. The computation and daemon facets would live in the user's process, while the prices facets would be updated only in the SEC process but replicated and thus read in the user processes. The analogy to traditional database servers is not accidental. This relationship between facets, objects and processes is illustrated in Figure 6.

A program specifies the objects and processes that together make up a single application, the physical locations of the processes at execution-time and the initialization code to start the application running. For the purposes of this paper, we assume that facets, objects, processes and programs are all defined statically, so it is not possible to add new components while a program is executing. In the more general case, however, it would be necessary to be able to add user-defined objects (portfolios) and processes to an already-executing system.

PROFIT's facets and objects provide abstractions for programming each of the three approaches to our example above:

- In the active values approach (Figure 2), a prices facet is shared among several objects. This facet must provide the data, change monitoring and notification of interested objects. Each of these objects also contains a non-shared facet that receives the notification and carries out the appropriate financial strategy.

- In the polling approach (Figure 3), the prices facet contains only shared data. Each interested object includes a non-shared facet that carries out both computation and change monitoring. Although this permits the programmer to set the priority of monitoring change, that is, the time interval between polls, it unnecessarily complicates the overall computation by mixing polling activities and the control associated with the main-line strategy.

- In the daemon-based approach (Figure 5), the prices facet contains only shared data. Each interested object includes two non-shared facets, one that carries out the computation and the other that monitors changes. The latter is devoted to polling the shared facet, performing only that computation necessary to determine which changes are interesting to its object, and notifying the strategy facet accordingly.

Processes support the run-time behavior of our example: the execution of a thread within a particular facet makes it possible for the programmer to easily control the rapidity with which change is monitored and acted upon. That is, all relevant timing constraints are expressed directly by the procedures provided within a facet, so each daemon facet can poll/notify at the time intervals appropriate for the portfolio management object(s) containing it. It is the responsibility of the enclosing process to schedule execution of facet threads. Only one replica of a facet can be executing a thread at a time in the general case, requiring significant synchronization overhead, which we ignore in this paper. However, we expect most shared facets will contain only data slots (e.g., shared prices) and no procedure slots, so

replication could be optimized to allow multiple reading threads with no contention and no synchronization. Alternatively, prices facets might not be replicated, in which case the daemon facet would have to poll via interprocess communication, perhaps across a network.

PROFIT is more a language extension than an entirely new language, in that it does not define the details of the base language, in this case the data and procedures that may appear in slots. We intend these to be written in conventional programming language(s); for now we assume C. Thus data slots contain C data values and procedure slots contain C functions. Macros and subroutines will be provided for evaluating slots within the same facet, handling indirection to other facets and objects, referring to any facets and objects returned by these evaluations, interacting with threads, and so on. One issue is whether multiple data slots, of the same or different facets, can point to the same data structure. This is a problem since different facets might reside in different processes, so direct sharing is not always possible. One solution might be distributed virtual memory [15]. We follow a simpler approach: no sharing of data structures, only entire facets (i.e., there is no pointer aliasing). Data structures are copied when transmitted as arguments, whether within the same process or across process boundaries.

Facets

The facet is the minimal unit of data and control. A facet has a unique name and a set of named slots, each of which may contain either a data value or procedure code. Slots are typed, either the type of the data (a C datatype) or the return value of the procedure (a C datatype or void). Procedure slots must be equated to specific C functions at compile-time. Evaluating a data slot returns the value, while evaluating a procedure slot executes the procedure (with the parameters provided) and returns the result of the execution, if any. (Facets correspond closely to Self objects.)

For example, the set of prices for the instruments of the INS company would be represented as a facet, called INS-instruments (Figure 7). The only operations are (implicit) get and put. In this example, there is one possible writer — some agent external to SEC representing the stock exchange wire — and multiple readers from different portfolios. Another example would be the daemon that monitors the changing prices of DOM's instruments (Figure 8). The daemon would keep certain local data such as high and low trigger values, used when deciding whether to notify the corresponding portfolio manager.

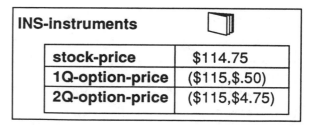

Figure 7: INS-instruments Facet

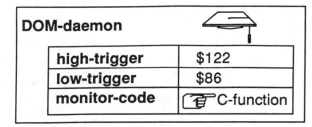

Figure 8: DOM-daemon Monitor

There is a distinguished slot within each facet, called `active`, that represents the currently executing thread of control. There can be at most one thread executing within a facet. Among other things, the thread indicates its originating object (see next section). If the `active` slot is null, then the facet is not doing anything. A prices facet, for example INS-instruments, would normally be passive except while `get` or `put` is running. The `get` operation must be able to return multiple prices from the INS-instruments facet to ensure consistent access, while the `put` operation could be restricted to a single value since price changes are independent. A portfolio management strategy, say involving statistics specific to the INS instruments, would also normally be passive, until the daemon wakes it up after a significant change.

A facet represents a closed scope, meaning every use of an identifier matches an identifier defined within the facet. There are no free variables. Of course, each procedure in a procedure slot of a facet is also a scope, with its own local variables. The facet's other procedure and data slots are global to the procedure, that is, the facet is treated as the procedure's enclosing scope and the procedure can call the other procedure slots and access the data slots. In order to support references between facets, a slot may be declared *indirect*, as in Figure 9. The containing object is then obliged to provide a *binding*, to a slot in some other facet within the same object or to an entry in the interface of another object; see next section. Every object has a *binding table* for this purpose. When code references an indirect slot, then the semantics are to refer to the current object's binding table to resolve the reference. Thus, a procedure in one facet can call procedures or access data in other facets via the corresponding indirect slot in its own facet.

This approach is based on delegation [16], where when one object cannot handle a message, it defers it to another. We modify traditional delegation by binding at the enclosing object level rather than separately for each individual facet.* This means a facet can be written without knowledge of which specific other facets it will delegate to (see Figure 10).

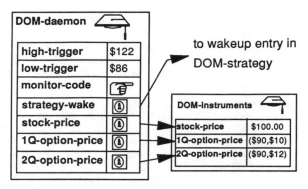

to wakeup entry in DOM-strategy

Figure 10: Binding

Objects

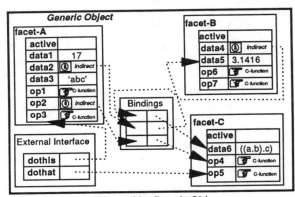

Figure 11: Generic Object

Binding Table	
(facet-A,data2)	(facet-B,data5)
(facet-A,op2)	(facet-C,op4)
(facet-B,data4)	(facet-C,data6)

Figure 12: Generic Binding Table

As in the classical object model, a PROFIT object is the compile-time unit of information hiding. It defines an external interface and encapsulates its internal data and procedures. The interface defines the object's unique name and the set of entries (procedures) visible to other objects. PROFIT objects are different in that the internal data and procedures are supplied by a set of facets with bindings between the facets. A generic object is shown in Figure 11. The binding table maps each indirect slot of every facet within the object, either to a slot of a facet in the same object or to an entry in the interface of another object. Figure 12 shows how several facets may be bound together within an object, and Figure 13 the bindings for the SUP portfolio manager object.

---

*Further, we fully delegate to the receiving facet's own context (its own slots) rather than evaluating a slot from the receiving facet as if it were a slot in the delegating facet, i.e., there is no "self pointer". This is relevant if the evaluated slot is a procedure that references other slots.

DOM-daemon	
high-trigger	$122
low-trigger	$86
monitor-code	☞ C-function
strategy-wake	ⓐ *indirect*
stock-price	ⓐ *indirect*
1Q-option-price	ⓐ *indirect*
2Q-option-price	ⓐ *indirect*

Figure 9: Indirect Slots

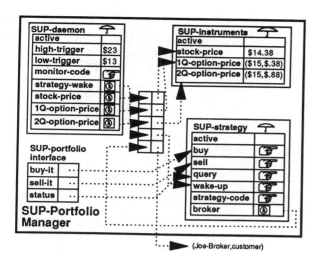

Figure 13: SUP Portfolio Manager Object

When a procedure is executing within a facet, it may directly access only those slots defined in the same facet. Accesses to indirect slots are resolved through the binding table. First we describe calls within a facet, and then calls from one facet to another. A call within a facet is treated like a conventional procedure call. The actual parameters and caller's return point are pushed on the stack maintained by the current thread (i.e., each thread has a separate stack), and control is transferred to the called procedure. Calling a procedure slot means calling a C function. The local variables of the C functions are stored on the stack. All external references made by the C function must appear as slots in the facet. When the procedure returns, any result is left on the stack, and control is transferred back to the calling procedure.

For calls between facets, we consider first the callee and then the caller. If a call arrives while the callee facet is already active, the call is queued. When a call reaches the front of its queue, the facet accepts the call and sets its `active` slot and binding table according to the calling object. Subsequent indirection is with respect to this binding table. When the call completes, the response is sent to the caller and the facet goes on to the next queued call. The caller initiates a call by pushing the actual parameters and return point on its stack. The caller facet is then released, and can accept a new call. When the call returns, it simply adds itself to the end of the original caller's queue. Note that the caller is not suspended, but may continue by accepting the next call in its queue. When the call returns and reaches the front of the queue, the caller continues execution of that thread at the point where it left off.

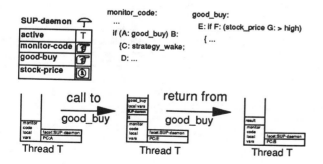

Figure 14: SUP-daemon Call Within Facet

These discussions of both caller and callee viewpoints are equally valid for indirection to another facet in the same object or to an entry in the interface of another object (and ultimately a facet in this other object). However, when a call is made across processes, the calling thread must be suspended at the process level (i.e., the calling facet is not suspended) and a new stand-in thread created in the called process.[**] On return, the suspended thread is resumed by the process. In the next section we discuss the details of implementing these synchronous calls, and also describe mechanisms that permit asynchronous calls.

Consider the following example: The SUP-daemon periodically polls the SUP-instruments prices, to compare to its own trigger values. If the criteria are met, the daemon notifies the SUP-strategy computation. The SUP-daemon's call to evaluate a data slot within its own facet is shown in Figure 14, while the SUP-daemon call to get data from the SUP-instruments facet is depicted in Figure 15. The asynchronous call needed for the SUP-daemon to notify SUP-strategy is discussed later.

When a facet is shared among multiple objects, each of these objects provides a different binding table that must resolve all the shared facet's indirect slots (Figure 16). When a facet is active, only one binding is actually used, the one belonging to the object from which the facet was invoked. Since a shared facet may be invoked from another shared facet, it is necessary for the appropriate binding table (i.e., its pointer or index) to be passed as an implicit parameter.

Communication between objects is a simple extension of the communication between facets. When a call is received at the interface of an object, the object maps the call to a procedure slot of one of its member facets. When the call returns, the object sends the result back to the calling object. Because objects can communicate with many other objects, we associate a queue with each object's external interface. As soon as a call in this queue has been mapped to a particular facet, it is moved from the object's queue to the facet's queue, and the object goes on to resolve the next external call.

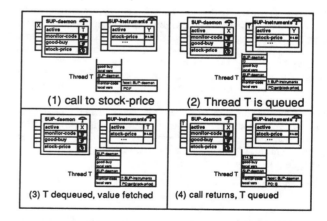

Figure 15: SUP-daemon Call to SUP-instruments

[**]The thread is not copied, so up-level addressing of non-local variables cannot be supported, since the semantics would be different depending on how the object was distributed. Fortunately this is not a problem when C is the base language.

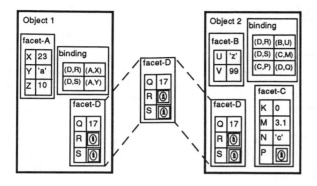

Figure 16: Shared Facet

Processes

The classical object model does not specify a particular role for processes. There is a spectrum of relationships between objects and processes reflected in existing concurrent object-based systems ([7, 24, 8, 4]). A PROFIT process represents a single address space and contains one or more threads of control. Each facet may be replicated in multiple processes, and any threads executing in a replica are managed by its containing process. The system support for processes is also responsible for maintaining consistency among all the replicas of the same facet [10]; we do not address how replication is implemented in this paper, but note only that symmetric read/write replication is required. Processes thus represent the execution-time organization of facets. In contrast, objects represent the compile-time organization of facets: Objects do not "live" anywhere, and facets of the same object may reside in different processes. The external interface and binding table of every object are replicated in every process, with no run-time overhead since this information is determined at compile-time and is not modifiable.

There are also many notions of thread, running a spectrum from light-weight as in Mach's raw threads [21] to medium-weight as in Mach's C-thread package [6] to heavy-weight as in a full Unix process [2]. The common concept is that a thread has a single locus of control. What distinguishes the variety of threads is the ownership of data (address space) and context (registers, control stack). We have in mind medium-weight threads. Along with a simple locus of control, a PROFIT thread maintains context between nested calls (evaluations of procedure slots), thereby permitting recursion. Alternatively, light-weight threads without their own control stacks would preclude recursion or dynamic variables; heavy-weight threads on a per-facet basis, resulting in one facet per process, would likely lead to terrible performance.

In the previous section, we discussed the notion of queuing calls for facets and for objects. Each call in a facet queue is represented by a thread, which provides the context of the call. Since objects have no physical representation, object queues are implemented as separate queues in each process, and processes take over the objects's run-time role in mapping external calls. First we discuss the manipulation of threads in facet queues, and then the creation of threads in response to calls (messages) queued for processes. If a call arrives while the facet is already active, the thread associated with the call is queued. When a thread reaches the front, the facet sets its `active` slot to reference the dequeued thread; when the call

completes, the thread is queued for the caller. This works only among facets within the same process, where enqueuing and dequeuing of threads is managed by pointer operations. When calls are made across process boundaries, the calling thread must be suspended and a stand-in thread created in the remote process.

There are two situations in which processes create new threads: when a call is made across process boundaries and when an asynchronous call is made. When a facet calls another facet that resides in another process, the calling thread is suspended at the process level. The calling facet accepts the next thread in its queue. Meanwhile, the process sends a message to the other process, indicating (facet, slot), parameters, return point and some identification of the calling object, needed to select the appropriate binding table. The message is appended to the receiving process's queue. The receiving process removes the first message in its queue, creates a corresponding thread and queues the thread for the indicated facet. When the call is completed, the process sends a message back to the sending process's queue. The sending process matches the message with the suspended calling thread, and queues it for the calling facet.

Asynchronous calls work the same as synchronous calls as explained above — with two differences. The first is that the calling facet does not release its thread, but instead continues execution. The second is that there is no return point; when an asynchronous call completes, its thread is deleted.[***] Note that this does not permit the calling facet to wait for the completion of the asynchronous call (or, more generally, wait for a particular asynchronous call from another facet).

This lack of blocking uncovers an apparent flaw in the PROFIT design: there is no way to make an *atomic* call, except for the trivial cases of `gets`, `puts` and procedures whose only calls (direct and transitive) happen to be synchronous calls to other procedures within the same facet. When a facet makes a synchronous call to another facet, it relinquishes its thread and serves the next thread in its queue. This context switching may result in arbitrary changes to its data slots. In those cases where it is necessary for certain data items to maintain their current values during a synchronous call to another facet, this data must be stored in the local variables of the calling procedure (C function) — and thus in the thread's stack, where there is no danger of being overwritten by unrelated threads queued for the same facet. This lack of atomicity is intentional, since atomicity directly conflicts with the need for rapid reaction to change: an "atomic" call that can be interrupted (and not rolled back), say to meet timing constraints, is of course not really atomic.

Related Work

Among existing languages, PROFIT is probably closest to Argus [17]. PROFIT facets are similar to Argus objects. If PROFIT objects and processes were not distinct, but instead every object was also a process, the result would closely match Argus guardians. Argus's lightweight processes are analogous to PROFIT's threads. Hermes [3] is another similar language that provides both objects and processes. In Hermes, the process defines the external interface, in terms of typed ports; objects are encapsulated inside processes. Hermes objects are thus like PROFIT facets except they cannot be shared or replicated, although they can be passed by value as arguments across ports.

[***]An important optimization is to return the thread to a pool for later reuse, rather than deallocating it.

It is also interesting to compare PROFIT to Linda [5], which defines a paradigm for parallel programming quite different from Argus or Hermes. Communication among processes in Linda is via tuples in a global tuple space. Facets can be viewed as the static analog of tuples. On the other hand, facets may be treated as the dynamic analog of Flavors's mixins [19]. Mixins provide data and procedure slots that may be inherited by arbitrary objects. Such inheritance is concerned with structure, however, not contents. In particular, each inheriting object may have different values in the data slots inherited from the same mixin. Facets, in contrast, provide direct sharing of data slot values as well as definitions, in the style of Self. The most significant difference between PROFIT and Self is that PROFIT supports concurrency, both multiple threads and multiple processes, while Self is a purely sequential language. Another important difference is that PROFIT data and procedure slots are provided in C, allowing access to existing application code — which is obligatory for the financial applications envisioned, while Self is a uniform language.

Conclusions

The primary contribution of this paper is our new object model for shared data (facets) based on the separation of compile-time information hiding (objects) and execution-time computation concerns (processes). We have demonstrated by our portfolio manager example a methodology for using our new object model in a practical application domain with specialized requirements.

Acknowledgments

Isai Shenker has completed an implementation of a subset of PROFIT, in C, that supports most facilities except multiple processes and provides timing-related constructs not presented here. Ari Gross is working on a separate subset implementation in C++. We would like to thank Steve Popovich for developing, jointly with Kaiser, an earlier notion of facets as a proposed extension to the Meld language [13]. We would also like to thank Tien Huynh and Catherine Lassez for motivating the financial services example [14], and Dan Schutzer for discussions of pragmatic financial industry concerns. Nasser Barghouti and Travis Winfrey made extensive comments on a previous draft.

Kaiser is supported by NSF grants CCR-8858029 and CCR-8802741, by grants from AT&T, Citicorp, DEC, IBM, Siemens, Sun and Xerox, by the Center for Advanced Technology and by the Center for Telecommunications Research.

References

[1]   Gul Agha.
        Actors A Model of Concurrent Computation in Distributed Systems.
        The MIT Press, Cambridge MA, 1986.

[2]   Maurice J. Bach.
        The Design of the UNIX Operating System.
        Prentice-Hall, Englewood Cliffs NJ, 1986.

[3]   David F. Bacon and Robert E. Strom.
        Implementing the Hermes Process Model.
        Technical Report RC 14518, IBM T.J. Watson Research Center, March, 1989.

[4]   Andrew Black, Norman Hutchinson, Eril Jul and Henry Levy.
        Object Structure in the Emerald System.
        In *OOPSLA '86*, pages 78-86. September, 1986.

[5]   Nicholas Carriero and David Gelernter.
        Linda in Context.
        Communications of the ACM 32(4):444-458, April, 1989.

[6]   Eric C. Cooper and Richard P. Draves.
        C Threads.
        Technical Report CMU-CS-88-154, CMU Department of Computer Science, June, 1988.

[7]   Partha Dasgupta, Richard J. Leblanc Jr. and William F. Appelbe.
        The Clouds Distributed Operating System: Functional Description, Implementation Details and Related Work.
        In *8th ICDCS*, pages 2-9. June, 1988.

[8]   David Detlefs, Maurice Herlihy and Jeannette Wing.
        Inheritance of Synchronization and Recovery Properties in Avalon/C++.
        Computer 21(12):57-69, December, 1988.

[9]   Klaus Dittrich and Umeshwar Dayal (eds).
        1986 International Workshop on Object-Oriented Database Systems.
        September, 1986

[10]   David K. Gifford.
        Weighted Voting for Replicated Data.
        In *7th SOSP*, pages 150-162. December, 1979.

[11]   Adele Goldberg and David Robson.
        Smalltalk-80 The Language and its Implementation.
        Addison-Wesley, Reading MA, 1983.

[12]   Paul E. Haeberli.
        ConMan: A Visual Programming Language for Interactive Graphics.
        In *SIGGRAPH '88*, pages 103-111. August, 1988.

[13]   Gail E. Kaiser, Steven S. Popovich, Wenwey Hseush and Shyhtsun Felix Wu.
        Melding Multiple Granularities of Parallelism.
        In *3rd ECOOP*, pages 147-166. July, 1989.

[14]   Catherine Lassez and Tien Huynh.
        An Expert Decision-Support System for Option-Based Investments Strategies.
        Journal of Computers and Mathematics with Applications , 1990.
        In press.

[15]   Kai Li and Paul Hudak.
        Memory Coherence in Shared Virtual Memory Systems.
        In *5th PODC*, pages 229-239. August, 1986.

[16]   Henry Lieberman.
        Using Prototypical Objects to Implement Shared Behavior in Object Oriented Systems.
        In *OOPSLA '86*, pages 214-223. September, 1986.

[17]   Barbara Liskov.
        Distributed Programming in Argus.
        Communications of the ACM 31(3):300-312, March, 1988.

[18]   Subrata Mazumdar and Aurel A. Lazar.
        Knowledge-Based Monitoring of Integrated Networks.
        In *IFIP TC 6/WG 6.6 Symposium on Integrated Network Management*, pages 235-243. May, 1989.

[19]   David A. Moon.
        Object-Oriented Programming with Flavors.
        In *OOPSLA '86*, pages 1-8. September, 1986.

[20]   Peter Peinl, Andrea Reuter and Harald Sammer.
        High Contention in a Stock Trading Database: A Case Study.
        In *SIGMOD*, pages 260-268. June, 1988.

[21]   Richard Rashid, Avadis Tevanian, Michael Young, David Golub, Robert Baron, David Black, William Bolosky and Jonathan Chew.
        Machine-Independent Virtual Memory Management for Paged Uniprocessor and Multiprocessor Architectures.
        In *ASPLOS II*, pages 31-39. October, 1987.

[22]   Marc Shapiro, Philippe Gautron and Laurence Mosseri.
        Persistence and Migration for C++ Objects.
        In *3rd ECOOP*, pages 191-204. July, 1989.

[23]   Mark J. Stefik, Daniel G. Bobrow and Kenneth M. Kahn.
        Integrating Access-Oriented Programming into a Multiparadigm
            Environment.
        IEEE Software 3(1):11-18, January, 1986.

[24]   Robert Strom and Nagui Halim.
        A New Programming Methodology for Long-Lived Software
            Systems.
        IBM Journal of Research and Development 28(1), January, 1984.

[25]   David Ungar and Randall B. Smith.
        Self: The Power of Simplicity.
        In *OOPSLA '87*, pages 227-242. October, 1987.

[26]   Horst F. Wedde, Bogden Korel, Willie G. Brown and Shengdong
            Chen.
        *Transparent Distributed Object Management Under Completely
            Decentralized Control.*
        Technical Report, Wayne State University, 1989.

[27]   Peter Wegner.
        Dimensions of Object-Based Language Design.
        In *OOPSLA '87*, pages 168-182. October, 1987.

Specification and Automatic Prototype Implementation of Polymorphic Objects in TURING Using the TXL Dialect Processor*

James R. Cordy

Eric Promislow

Department of Computing and Information Science
Queen's University at Kingston
Kingston, Canada K7L 3N6

Abstract

Object-oriented dialects of existing programming languages are often implemented using a preprocessor that translates from the dialect to an equivalent program in the original programming language. Unfortunately, the nature of the preprocessing done by these implementations is hidden in the ad-hoc algorithms of the preprocessors themselves except as demonstrated by examples. This paper describes an attempt to catalogue and generalize these syntactic transformations using a simple set of applicative transformation rules expressed in the TXL dialect description language. Example transformation rules for implementing object types and parametric polymorphism in an object-oriented dialect of the Turing programming language are given in the paper. These rules easily generalize to other languages of the Pascal family and have been used to automatically implement Objective Turing.

Introduction

Object-oriented dialects of existing programming languages such as C are commonly prototyped using a preprocessor that translates from the object-oriented dialect to the base language. This was the case, for example, for C++ [1] and Objective C [2]. However, the nature of the preprocessing done by these implementations is often hidden in the ad-hoc algorithms of the preprocessors themselves, and is at best exposed by a few simple examples of the results of the preprocessing.

The Objective Turing project is an attempt to rectify this situation by explicitly specifying each key feature of object-oriented programming as a context-sensitive syntactic transform to the (non-objective) Turing programming language [3] using the TXL dialect specification language [4]. By specifying each feature

using an independent TXL transformation rule which clearly and compactly encodes the necessary syntactic transforms, we can compile a reference catalog for preprocessor implementation of object-oriented features that can be used to guide future preprocessor implementations for other languages.

This paper introduces the TXL dialect specification language and gives a complete set of applicative transformation rules to implement polymorphic object types as a dialect of Turing. These rules have been used to automatically implement Objective TURING using the TXL dialect processor.

The TXL Dialect Processor

TXL, the Turing eXtender Language [4] is a system designed to allow easy description and automatic prototype implementation of new programming language features as dialects of an existing programming language such as Turing. The goal of TXL is to provide some measure of the power and flexibility of interpretive extensible languages for traditional Pascal-like compiled languages. TXL uses a context-sensitive syntactic transformation algorithm that is not limited by the constraints typical of other preprocessors and extensible languages, and is driven by a concise, readable dialect specification language that conveniently expresses the syntax and semantics of new language features.

Using Turing (or any other language) as a base, TXL provides the ability to describe new language dialects at a very high level, and automatically provides prototype implementations. Each dialect is described in two parts, the context-free syntactic forms (described in terms of the syntactic forms of the base language using a BNF-like notation), and the run time model of the dialect (expressed as a set of applicative syntactic transformations to the base language). The TXL Processor uses these descriptions to automatically transform dialect programs to programs in the base language.

---
* This work was supported by the Natural Sciences and Engineering Research Council of Canada.

145

The syntactic forms of the base language are described using the same BNF-like notation used to describe syntactic forms of the dialect. These base language syntactic forms serve as a data base of syntactic forms used to describe the syntax of the dialect. For example, the syntactic forms of the Turing language base include the forms *declarationsAndStatements, variableReference, assignment,* and so on. The semantics of the dialect are described as a set of recursive context-sensitive transformations from the syntactic structures of the dialect to base language structures.

As a simple example dialect, consider the addition of coalesced assignment short forms (i.e., the "+=", "−=" etc. of C) to the Turing language. The desired syntactic forms can be described in terms of the Turing base forms as a replacement of the *statement* syntactic form to include the original Turing statements plus a new form we call *coalescedAssignment* (Figure 1).

The new definition of the *statement* syntactic form replaces the original Turing form in the grammar of the dialect, so that the dialect includes all of original Turing plus the new coalesced assignment statement. The form of the coalesced assignments themselves is described using the new syntactic form *coalescedAssignment* and its sub-form *coalescedOperator*.

The meaning of the new syntactic form is described using a transformation to equivalent Turing base language code. In this case, for example, the transformation rule would change the coalesced assignment $a += b$ to the semantically equivalent Turing statement $a := a + (b)$.

Transformation is achieved by applying the transformation rules to the abstract syntax tree of each dialect language program. For example, the main transformation rule of the coalesced assignment dialect (figure 1) specifies that in each subtree below a *statement* node, any subtree matching the pattern *variableReference coalescedOperator = expression* should be replaced by another *statement* subtree containing the assignment statement $V := V \ Op \ (E)$ where V, Op and E are the original subtrees for the *variableReference, coalescedOperator* and *expression* matched by the pattern.

Objective TURING

Turing [3] is a new general purpose programming language in the tradition of Pascal. In addition to the features provided by Pascal, Turing provides other modern programming features such as encapsulation using modules, varying-length character strings, type-safe variant records, safe dynamic storage and pointers, parametric procedures, and run-time constants. Turing does not however provide any object-oriented features such as object types, polymorphism, inheritance or dynamic binding.

```
% Trivial coalesced assignment dialect;
% allows  a += b etc.

% Part 1:  Syntactic forms

define statement      % replaces Turing base
                      % syntactic form of same name
   choose
      [coalescedAssignment] % new dialect
                      %      statement form
      [assignment]        % original Turing
      [assert]            %      statement forms
      . . .
      [get]
end define

define coalescedAssignment
   order
      [variableReference]
            [coalescedOperator] = [expression]
end define

define coalescedOperator
   choose + - * /
end define


% Part 2:  Semantic transformations

rule replaceCoalescedOperators
   replace [statement]
      V [variableReference]
         Op [coalescedOperator] = E [expression]
   by [statement]
      V := V Op ( E )
end rule
```

Figure 1. TXL Description of a Simple Coalesced Assignment Dialect.

*In Part 1, the syntactic forms of the dialect are described using a BNF-like notation in which the keyword **order** indicates sequence and the keyword **choose** indicates alternation. The dialect syntactic forms are integrated into the base language grammar by replacing an existing base language syntactic form with a new form. In the above example, the new form of* statement *replaces the original Turing syntactic form of the same name in the dialect grammar.*

In Part 2, the semantics of the dialect are described using a set of rules that transform the syntactic forms of the dialect to semantically equivalent base language structures. In this case, every occurrence of a statement containing the dialect syntactic form coalescedOperator *is transformed to an assignment statement using the corresponding Turing operator.*

Modules and Information Hiding

One feature of object-oriented systems that the Turing language already provides is information hiding in the form of *modules*. Turing modules collect a set of data structures and the procedures that manipulate them into a single opaque package. Only the *exported* attributes of the module can be accessed from outside it. From an object-oriented point of view, a Turing module is a single instance object, and its exported procedures are the methods of the object. Figure 2 shows an example of a Turing *stack* module.

Although we will use them as a vehicle to implement object types in this paper, modules are not a prerequisite for the transformations presented. Because the information hiding provided by modules can itself be expressed as a syntactic transform to procedures and records [5], our transformations are easily extended to apply to languages without modules such as Pascal.

```
module stack
    import (error)
    export (push, pop)

    const maxdepth := 100
    var storage : array 1 .. maxdepth of int
    var depth : 0 .. maxdepth

    procedure push (e : int)
        if depth <= maxdepth then
            depth := depth + 1
            storage (depth) := e
        else
            error ("stack overflow")
        end if
    end push

    procedure pop (var e : int)
        if depth > 0 then
            e := storage (depth)
            depth := depth - 1
        else
            error ("stack underflow")
        end if
    end pop

    depth := 0
end stack
```

Figure 2. A Stack Module in Turing.

Object Types

The distinction between Turing modules and true objects is that modules are not first-class types and can not be used as the type of variables, parameters and so on. The obvious way to add objects to Turing, then, is to allow modules to be types. Using such an extension, the *stack* module could be used as the body of a type declaration and the resulting type used to declare instances (figure 3).

Since we intend to extend rather than modify Turing, our syntax will explicitly use the keyword *object* in place of *module* for module types. This additional syntactic form can be expressed in TXL by replacing the Turing base syntactic form *typeSpec* with an extension that adds object types :

```
define typeSpec
    choose
        [objectType]      % added new syntactic form
        [standardType]    % original Turing
        [arrayType]       %      type spec syntactic forms
        . . .
        [namedType]
end define

define objectType
    order
        object
            [importList]
            [exportList]
            [moduleBody]
        'end [id]
end define
```

The syntactic forms *importList, exportList* and *moduleBody* used to specify the *objectType* syntactic form are inherited from the Turing base grammar.

This syntactic specification is deceptively simple. However, its semantics have no direct reflection in Turing, and the problem of transforming *objectTypes* into equivalent Turing programs will involve several steps, each specified using a TXL transformation rule. Overall, the transformation we will be specifying works as follows:

Every declaration of an *objectType* in the dialect program will be transformed into a Turing module with the same body. The internal variables of the object type will be gathered together into a data record type that will be exported from the module. Global (initializing) statements of the object type will be gathered into an initializing procedure for object data records that will also be exported. Each exported procedure (method) of the object type will be transformed to take an extra parameter of the data record type, representing the private data of the calling object instance.

```
type stack :
    object
        import (error)
        export (push, pop)

        . . . same body as the Stack
                module of figure 2 . . .

    end stack

var stack1 : stack
var stack2 : stack

stack1.push (5)
stack1.push (7)

stack2 := stack1        % assign entire stack1 object
                        %          to stack2
var x : int
stack2.pop (x)
assert  x = 7
```

Figure 3. A Stack Object Type in the Objective Turing Dialect and Example Instances.

In the scope of the object type's declaration, each variable declaration of the object type will be replaced by a variable declaration of the exported data record type followed by a call to the initializing procedure. Finally, all calls to procedures (methods) of the variable instance will be transformed into calls to the corresponding procedures of the module, passing the instance's data record as an extra argument.

The transformation is governed by a *mainRule* that simply serves to get things started, since for efficiency reasons TXL limits the extent of a rule's pattern search to a specified scope of the abstract syntax tree. This main rule simply says that the rule *fixObjects* should be applied to every scope of the program.

```
rule mainRule
    replace [declarationsAndStatements]
        P [declarationsAndStatements]
    by [declarationsAndStatements]
        P [fixObjects]
end rule
```

Step 1. Convert Object Types to Modules.

The rule *fixObejcts* syntactically converts each object type declaration to a Turing module and specifies the scopes in which several sub-rules are to be applied.

```
rule fixObjects
    replace [declarationsAndStatements]

        type ObName [id] :
            object
                ObImport [importList]
                ObExport [exportList]
                ObBody [declarationsAndStatements]
            'end ObName
        RestOfScope [declarationsAndStatements]

    by [declarationsAndStatements]

        module ObName
            ObImport
            ObExport  [addObjectAndInitializerExport]
            ObBody
                [sortDeclarationsAndStatements]
                [makeObjectRecordTypeAndEnterFields]
                [makeObjectInitializerProcedureAndEn-
                    terStatements]
                [addObjectParameterToProcedures]
        'end ObName
        RestOfScope
                [transformObjectReferences ObName]
end rule
```

The rule states that in each scope containing a type declaration of an *objectType*, the declaration should be replaced by a module with the same import list, export list and body as modified by several other rules, and that the rule *transformObjectReferences* should be applied to the scope of the type declaration itself.

Step 2. Add Exported Names for the Object Data Record Type and the Object Initializer Procedure.

The rule *addObjectAndInitializerExport* adds two new names to the list of identifiers exported from the module: the name of the object data record type, *DataRecordType,* and the name of the object data record initializer procedure, *InitializeDataRecord.* These names need not be unique since they are hidden inside a Turing module. If unique names were needed, the *gensym* TXL primitive would be used to generate them.

```
rule addObjectAndInitializerExport
    replace [exportList]
        export ( First [id]  Rest [repCommaId] )
    by [exportList]
        export ( DataRecordType,
                InitializeDataRecord, First Rest )
end rule
```

The missing comma between *First* and *Rest* in the export list is not an error. The Turing base grammar uses the recursive production *repCommaId* to specify any number of repetitions (including zero) of a comma followed by an identifier. Because application of this rule is bound (by the *fixObjects* rule) to the export list of the object module, it will match only that one export list.

Step 3. Sort the Declarations and Statements in the Object Module.

The Turing programming language allows interspersing of declarations and statements in a scope. In particular, variable declarations, procedures and initializing statements in a module body may be arbitrarily intermixed. In order to create a record type containing all the private variables of the object, and the initializing procedure for object data records, the module body must be re-ordered to gather all variable declarations and all initializing statements together. (This does not change the semantics of the module.) The following rules specify the re-ordering.

```
rule sortDeclarationsAndStatements
    replace [declarationsAndStatements]
        ObBody [declarationsAndStatements]
    by [declarationsAndStatements]
        ObBody
            [sortDS]    % declarations before statements
            [sortTV]    % constants and types before
                        %     variables and procedures
            [sortVP]    % then variables, then procs
end rule
```

```
rule sortDS
    replace [declarationsAndStatements]
        S [statement]
        D [declaration]
        R [declarationsAndStatements]
    by [declarationsAndStatements]
        D
        S
        R
end rule
```

```
rule sortTV
    replace [declarationsAndStatements]
        V [variableOrSubprogramDeclaration]
        T [constantOrTypeDeclaration]
        R [declarationsAndStatements]
    by [declarationsAndStatements]
        T
        V
        R
end rule
```

```
rule sortVP
    replace [declarationsAndStatements]
        P [subprogramDeclaration]
        V [variableDeclaration]
        R [declarationsAndStatements]
    by [declarationsAndStatements]
        V
        P
        R
end rule
```

Each of these sub-rules specifies a bubble sort that bubbles up instances of one kind of declaration or statement before another. For example, the *sortDS* rule specifies that every occurrence of the pair (*statement, declaration*) should be replaced by the same pair in reverse order. This rule is repeatedly applied until there are no more occurrences of the misordered pair it is looking for in its scope of application (the body of the object module). Although it is tempting to think of TXL rules as algorithmic, they are in fact applicative and can be applied any time their pattern matches any subtree in their scope of application.

Step 4. Gather the Object Module's Private Variables into the Object Data Record Type.

As the object module's variable declarations are grouped together by the sorting rules, they can be gathered into a new record type. This type will be used as the type of an additional parameter to each procedure of the module giving the data fields of the object instance associated with each call. The transform has two parts: first a new empty record type declaration is inserted before the first variable in the scope, then each variable declaration is moved in as a field of the record type. These two steps will necessarily happen in sequence since the pattern of the second rule will never match until the first rule has been successfully applied.

```
rule makeObjectRecordTypeAndEnterFields
    replace [declarationsAndStatements]
        ObBody [declarationsAndStatements]
    by [declarationsAndStatements]
        ObBody
            [makeObjectRecordType]
            [enterObjectRecordTypeFields]
end rule
```

```
rule makeObjectRecordType
    replace [declarationsAndStatements]
        V [variableDeclaration]
        Rest [declarationsAndStatements]
    by [declarationsAndStatements]
```

```
            type DataRecordType :
              record
              'end record
            V
            Rest
      end rule

      rule enterObjectRecordTypeFields
        replace [declarationsAndStatements]
            type DataRecordType :
              record
                    R [repRecordField]
              'end record
            var V [id] : T [typeSpec]
            RestOfScope [declarationsAndStatements]

        by [declarationsAndStatements]
            type DataRecordType :
              record
                    V : T
                    R
              'end record
            RestOfScope [fixObjectVariableReferences V]
      end rule
```

Step 5. Change References to the Object's Private Variables to Reference the Data Record Parameter of the Object Procedures.

As each private variable is moved into the object's data record type by the *enterObjectRecordTypeFields* rule, all internal references to it are changed to refer to the corresponding field of the data record parameter of the procedure containing the reference. This rule is parameterized by the identifier of the variable whose references are being transformed.

```
      rule fixObjectVariableReferences Var [id]
        replace [id]
            Var
        by [reference]
            DataRecord . Var
      end rule
```

Step 6. Gather the Object Module's Initializing Statements into the Object Data Record Initializer Procedure.

Since the sorting rules gather the initializing statements together at the end of the module's scope, creating the initializer procedure is relatively straightforward. The rule *makeObjectInitializerProcedureAndEnterStatements* simply grabs everything from the first statement to the end of the sorted body and puts it in a new procedure named *InitializeDataRecord*.

```
   rule makeObjectInitializerProcedureAndEnterStatements
     replace [declarationsAndStatements]
        P [subprogramDeclaration]
        S [statement]
        Rest [declarationsAndStatements]
     by [declarationsAndStatements]
        P
        procedure InitializeDataRecord
                (var DataRecord : DataRecordType)
           S
           Rest
        'end InitializeDataRecord
   end rule
```

Step 7. Add an Object Data Record Parameter to Each Procedure of the Module.

This rule adds an additional object data record type parameter called *DataRecord* as the first parameter to each procedure of the object module. Nullary procedures, which for brevity are not handled here, would require a slightly different rule to be applied in addition to this one.

```
   rule addObjectParameterToProcedures
     replace [declarationsAndStatements]

        procedure PName [id]
           ( Arg1 [parameterDeclaration]
             RestOfArgs [repCommaParameterDecl] )
        PBody [subprogramBody]
        procedure InitializeDataRecord
           InitPList [optParameterList]
           IBody [subprogramBody]
        RestOfScope [declarationsAndStatements]

     by [declarationsAndStatements]

        procedure InitializeDataRecord  InitPList
           IBody
        procedure PName
           ( var DataRecord : DataRecordType,
             Arg1  RestOfArgs )
        PBody
        RestOfScope
   end rule
```

In order to avoid an infinite sequence of matches, the *addObjectParameterToProcedures* rule keeps track of which procedures it has already transformed by moving each one below the *InitializeDataRecord* procedure after it has been done, and matching only the procedure immediately above it.

Step 8. Transform Declarations of Instances of the Object Type into Declarations of Object Data Records.

The rule *transformObjectReferences* handles the final two steps of the transform. The first of these is the change of declarations of instance variables of the object type into declarations of variables of the *DataRecordType* exported by the object module followed by a call to the *InitializeDataRecord* procedure of the module.

```
rule transformObjectReferences ObName [id]
    replace [declarationsAndStatements]
        var ObVar [id] : ObName
        RestOfScope [declarationsAndStatements]
    by [declarationsAndStatements]
        var ObVar : ObName . DataRecordType
        ObName . InitializeDataRecord (ObVar)
        RestOfScope [changeObjectProcedureCalls
                        ObVar ObName]
    end rule
```

Step 9. Change Calls to the Object Instance's Procedures into Calls to the Object Module.

The second step is the *changeObjectProcedureCalls* rule, applied by the *transformObjectReferences* rule to the scope of each object instance variable. This rule takes two TXL parameters, the name of the instance variable and the name of the object type. The *repCommaExpn* production is similar to the *repCommaId* production explained earlier, and includes the leading comma in the rest of the argument list to the procedure (if any).

```
rule changeObjectProcedureCalls ObVar [id]
ObName [id]
    replace [procedureCall]
        ObVar . PName [id] ( FirstArg [expn]
                    RestOfArgs [repCommaExpn] )
    by [procedureCall]
        ObName . PName (ObVar, FirstArg
                    RestOfArgs)
    end rule
```

Figure 4 shows the result of applying the entire transform to the example stack object type of figure 3.

Parametric Polymorphism

Most proponents of the object-oriented paradigm consider some kind of polymorphic capability to be essential. While true dynamic polymorphism might be desirable in some contexts, many systems bow to the requirements of efficient compilability and settle for some lesser form, such as static parametric polymorphism in the sense of [6] instead. C++, for example, limits its class

```
module stack
    import (error)
    export (DataRecordType, InitializeDataRecord,
            push, pop)

    const maxdepth := 100

    type DataRecordType:
        record
            storage : array 1 .. maxdepth of int
            depth : 0 .. maxdepth
        end record

    procedure InitializeDataRecord (var DataRecord :
                        DataRecordType)
        DataRecord.depth := 0
    end InitializeDataRecord

    procedure push (var DataRecord : DataRecordType,
                    e : int)
        if DataRecord.depth <= maxdepth then
            DataRecord.depth := DataRecord.depth + 1
            DataRecord.storage (DataRecord.depth) := e
        else
            error ("stack overflow")
        end if
    end push

    procedure pop (var DataRecord : DataRecordType,
                    var e : int)
        if DataRecord.depth > 0 then
            e := DataRecord.storage (DataRecord.depth)
            DataRecord.depth := DataRecord.depth - 1
        else
            error ("stack underflow")
        end if
    end pop
end stack

var stack1 : stack.DataRecordType
stack.InitializeDataRecord (stack1)
var stack2 : stack.DataRecordType
stack.InitializeDataRecord (stack2)

stack.push (stack1, 5)
stack.push (stack1, 7)

stack2 := stack1        % assign entire stack1 object
                        %        to stack2
var x : int
stack.pop (stack2, x)
assert x = 7
```

Figure 4. The Result of Transforming the Stack Object Type of Figure 3 to a Turing Module Using the Rules of the Object Type Dialect.

```
type class  stack (maxdepth, elementType) :
   object
      import (error)
      export (push, pop)

      var storage :
         array 1 .. maxdepth of elementType
      var depth : 0 .. maxdepth

      procedure push (e : elementType)
         ... same body as before ...
      end push

      procedure pop (var e : elementType)
         ... same body as before ...
      end pop

      depth := 0
   end stack

type smallStackOfString : instance stack (10, string)
type bigStackOfInt : instance stack (100, int)

var stringStack :  smallStackOfString
var intStack :  bigStackOfInt

stringStack.push ("Hi there")
stringStack.push ("Hello yourself")
```

Figure 5. A Polymorphic Stack Object Type in the Objective Turing Dialect and Example Instances.

polymorphism to either static parametric polymorphism (using C preprocessor macros), or opaque polymorphism using pointers [1].

Objective Turing follows this same static parametric model and uses type parameters to provide polymorphic objects. Syntactically, we introduce a new declaration for a *type class,* which is simply a type-parameterized type declaration. The dialect allows type classes of any type, in particular object type classes.

Figure 5 shows the *stack* object type extended to be an object type class for stack object types with any depth limit and any type of elements. Instances of the object type class yield an object type, as shown in the declaration of the *smallStackOfString* type and its subsequent uses.

We can specify the syntax of type classes in TXL by adding the *typeClassDeclaration* as an alternative declaration form, *instanceType* as an alternative type specification form, and using the new productions:

```
define typeClassDeclaration
   order
      type class [id]  ( [list id] ) : [typeSpec]
end define

define instanceType
   order
      instance [id]  ( [list expnOrTypeSpec] )
end define

define expnOrTypeSpec
   choose
      [expn]
      [typeSpec]
end define
```

This grammar allows type classes to be parameterized by either a type or an expression. We will assume that expression parameters to type classes are to be passed by name, although pass by value could easily be implemented by the transform if required.

The basic strategy for transforming type classes is to delete the type class declaration itself and transform instances of the it into copies of the class' type specification with the actual argument types and expressions of the instance substituted for the formal parameters of the class. The main rule starts things off, applying the *fixTypeClasses* rule to every scope in the program before applying the *fixObjectTypes* rule.

```
rule mainRule
   replace [declarationsAndStatements]
      P [declarationsAndStatements]
   by [declarationsAndStatements]
      P [fixTypeClasses]
        [fixObjectTypes]
end rule
```

FixTypeClasses deletes the type class declaration and applies the *fixInstantiations* rule to search its scope of declaration of instances to transform.

```
rule fixTypeClasses
   replace [declarationsAndStatements]
      type class TCname [id] ( Formals [list id] ) :
         TCbody [typeSpec]
      RestOfScope [declarationsAndStatements]
   by [declarationsAndStatements]
      RestOfScope
         [fixInstantiations TCname Formals TCbody]
end rule
```

FixInstantiations searches the scope for instances of the type class and replaces the instance clause with a copy of the type class' type specification body in which the actual arguments of the instance have been substituted for the formal parameters of the type class.

```
rule fixInstantiations TCname [id] Formals [list id]
                        TCbody [typeSpec]
    replace [declaration]
        type ITname [id] :
            Instance TCname
                ( Actuals [list expnOrTypeSpec] )
    by [declaration]
        type ITname :
            TCbody [substitute Formals Actuals]
end rule

rule substitute Old [id] New [expnOrTypeSpec]
    replace [id]
        Old
    by [expnOrTypeSpec]
        New
end rule
```

The application of the *substitute* rule takes advantage of another feature of TXL - its ability to automatically apply rules to corresponding elements of two lists of items. In this case, *Formals* and *Actuals* are lists of *ids* and *expnOrTypeSpecs* respectively. TXL automatically applies the rule successively to each corresponding (*id, expnOrTypeSpec*) pair in the lists.

Figure 6 shows the result of using these transforms on the example polymorphic stack object type of figure 5, to yield monomorphic object types that can then be transformed by the *fixObjectTypes* rule to yield a true Turing language program.

Conclusion

We have shown that it is possible to clearly specify both object types and parametric polymorphism using independent syntactic transformation rules. These transformations have been expressed in the TXL dialect specification language and fed to the TXL processor to yield a viable prototype implementation of Objective Turing. With little significant change, these same transformation rules can be used for any compiled language of the Pascal family and so form a convenient and compact specification of the general features.

Two other features commonly associated with object-oriented programming are *inheritance* and *dynamic binding*. These have also been specified as independent TXL transformation rules and are features of the full Objective Turing dialect [10].

```
type smallStackOfString :
    object
        import (error)
        export (push, pop)

        var storage : array 1 .. maxdepth of string
        var depth : 0 .. 10

        procedure push (e : string)
            ... same body as before ...

        end push

        procedure pop (var e : string)
            ... same body as before ...

        end pop

        depth := 0
    end smallStackOfString

type bigStackOfInt :
    object
        import (error)
        export (push, pop)

        var storage : array 1 .. maxdepth of int
        var depth : 0 .. 100

        procedure push (e : int)
            ... same body as before ...

        end push

        procedure pop (var e : int)
            ... same body as before ...

        end pop

        depth := 0
    end smallStackOfString

var stringStack : smallStackOfString
var intStack : bigStackOfInt

stringStack.push ("Hi there")
stringStack.push ("Hello yourself")
```

Figure 6. Result of Applying the *fixTypeClasses* Rules to the Example of Figure 5.

Scope and Limitations of TXL

The TXL transformations given in this paper, while quite viable, are deceptively simple and transparent, in part because of the necessity of simplifying the syntax of the dialect for concise presentation in this paper. In practice, rule sets can be much larger than the set given here, and it is often very difficult to see how to achieve the desired result using TXL transformation rules.

The scope of possible transformations implementable in TXL is however much greater than the simple syntactic transforms shown in this paper. TXL rule sets are capable of implementing all of the traditional programming language implementation tasks, including parsing, name and scope analysis, type checking, operator precedence analysis, interface matching, anti-aliasing, and even (in theory) code generation. In fact, it has been shown that the computational power of TXL rule sets is equivalent to that of Turing machines [11], so there is no theoretical limit to the translation that can be done short of the bounds of computability.

From a practical standpoint, however, TXL is severely limited by the complexity of the rule sets and by the performance of the TXL processor, which necessarily uses a variant of Prolog unification to apply rules. The performance of the rule set given in this paper is quite reasonable, taking about 8 seconds to translate a 200 line Objective Turing program into Turing on a Sun 3/50, but it is very easy to write rule sets that can take much longer. A detailed discussion of the scope and limitations of TXL appears in [11].

Acknowledgements

TXL was designed by J.R. Cordy and C.D. Halpern at the University of Toronto, and was implemented by the authors at Queen's University. The Turing programming language was designed by R.C. Holt and J.R. Cordy at the University of Toronto. The ideas for the run-time models used in the transformations described in this paper come from various sources, including the implementations of C++ [1], Euclid [7] [8] and Force One [9]. This work was supported by the Natural Sciences and Engineering Research Council of Canada.

References

1. B. Stroustrup, *The C++ Reference Manual,* Addison-Wesley, 1986.

2. B.J. Cox, *Object Oriented Programming : An Evolutionary Approach,* Addison-Wesley, 1986.

3. R.C. Holt and J.R. Cordy, "The TURING Programming Language", Comm. of the ACM 31,12 (December 1988), pp. 1410-1423.

4. J.R. Cordy, C.D. Halpern and E. Promislow, "TXL: A Rapid Prototyping System for Programming Language Dialects", Proc. IEEE 1988 International Conference On Computer Languages, October 1988, pp. 280-285.

5. R.D.Tennent, *Principles of Programming Languages,* Prentice-Hall, 1981.

6. L. Cardelli and P. Wegner, "On Understanding Types, Data Abstraction, and Polymorphism", ACM Computing Surveys 17,4 (December 1985), pp. 471-522.

7. B.W. Lampson, J.J. Horning, R.L. London, J.G. Mitchell and G.J. Popek, "Report on the Programming Language EUCLID", ACM SIGPLAN Notices 12,2 (February 1977).

8. R.C. Holt and D.B. Wortman, "A Model for Implementing Euclid Modules and Prototypes", ACM Trans. on Programming Languages and Systems 4,4 (October 1982), pp. 552-562.

9. G.V. Cormack and A.K. Wright, "Polymorphism in the Compiled Language Force One", Proc. HICSS-22 1987 Hawaii International Conference on System Sciences, Volume II (Software), January 1987, pp. 284-292.

10. J.R. Cordy and E. Promislow, "Specification and Automatic Prototype Implementation of Object-Oriented Concepts Using the TXL Dialect Processor", External Technical Report 89-251, Department of Computing and Information Science, Queen's University at Kingston, March 1989.

11. Eric Promislow, A Run-Time Model for Generating Semantic Transformations from Syntactic Specifications, M.Sc. thesis, Department of Computing and Information Science, Queen's University at Kingston, September 1989.

Conflict Propagation

Nissim Francez*
Ira R. Forman
Microelectronics and Computer Technology Corp.
Austin, Texas

December 26, 1989

Abstract. The multiparty interaction is a synchronous communication primitive for concurrent systems. When all processes are ready for an interaction, it is enabled and may be executed. Processes may ready many interactions, but can execute only one at a time. This gives rise to a conflict situation when two enabled interactions have a common process. This paper studies the requirements for abstraction constructs encapsulating multiparty interactions. Several alternatives are explored for the meaning of an abstraction invocation when used in the position of a guard. The conclusion is that in order to support a stepwise-refinement design methodology conflicts must be propagated across invocations to achieve a proper coordination at the abstraction level. The presentation is in terms of a language *Interacting Processes (IP)* for high-level expression of distributed programs.

1   Introduction

The purpose of this paper is to introduce the notion of *conflict propagation* as a major aid in the design of distributed programs, supporting *refinement* in a context of *multiparty interactions*.

The refinement of an action is long recognized as an important program design tool. However, most often refinement is studied in such a way that a refined action is in a "stand alone" context. Theoretically, it is known [Bac88b][Bac88a] that in order to support *stepwise* refinement as a design method, refinement should be *monotonic* when viewed as partial-order inducing among programs. In other words, if S' refines S, then $P[S']$ should refine $P[S]$, for any context $P[\ ]$.

In this paper, we consider an aspect of refinement that involves refinement of actions in a *guard position*. Guarding actions (in contrast to pure boolean expressions) were first introduced in CSP [Hoa78], with its *input/output* guards. Here we consider more elaborate guarding actions, referred to as *multiparty interactions*, that serve as the interprocess synchronization and communication mechanism, involving an arbitrary number of participants. The synchronous *send - receive* of CSP is a special case of such interactions. In particular, we are interested in the issue of *encapsulation* of the refining section as an *abstraction*, replacing the refined action by an invocation of the abstraction. This is explained in greater detail below.

In order to make the presentation more self contained, we embody conflict-propagation in a language called *IP (Interacting Processes)*, and review its main features. The core language of IP was first introduced in [Fra89]. The kind of abstractions dealt with appeared first in [FHT86] and [For87]. The language, its accompanying theory (*verification, fairness,* etc.) and the design methodology based on it are the contents of a forthcoming book [FF90].

Section 2 presents the IP language and examples of its usage. Section 3 introduces *conflict propagation* and classifies its variants. Section 4 considers the bearings of conflict propagation on design by refinements.

2   The IP language

In this section we review the mini-language, called *IP (Interacting Processes)*. Its main features are:

- The usage of *multiparty interactions* as *guards*, thereby generalizing both Dijkstra's original guarded commands language [Dij75], which has only boolean guards, and CSP [Hoa78], using synchronous binary communication as guards.

- The usage of *team abstractions* and *enrolements* as guards, supporting a methodology for program refinement.

We present here an informal description of the language constructs. The formal definition of the core

---

*On sabbatical from Computer Science Dept., Technion, Haifa, Israel

language can be found in [Fra89] or [AFG90]. Some recent approaches to *fairness* in the context of multiparty interactions in *IP* can be found in [AFG90].

The language is parametrized by some *underlying expression language*. In examples, we use arithmetic expressions, list or queue expressions, etc. The *interpretation* of such expression in some structure over which computations take place is also assumed known, and not further elaborated here. Thus, we are not defining standard data structure operation like *push* (for *stacks*) or *enqueue* (for *queues*).

2.1 The IP core-language

A program $P :: [P_1 \parallel \cdots \parallel P_n]$ (alternatively[1] denoted also as $[\parallel_{i=1,n} P_i]$), consists of a *concurrent composition* of $n \geq 1$ (fixed n) *processes*, having *disjoint* local states (i.e., no shared variables). A *process* $P_i, 1 \leq i \leq n$, consists of a statement S, called its *body*, where S may take one of the following forms:

- Dummy statement - *skip*: A statement with no effect on the state.

- Assignment statement - $x := e$: The variable x is local to P_i and e is an expression over P_i's local state. Assignments have their usual meaning of state transformation.

- Interaction statement - $a[\bar{v} := \bar{e}]$: Here a is[2] the *interaction name* and $a[\bar{v} := \bar{e}]$ is an *interaction part*, containing an optional parallel assignment. The process P_i is a *participant* of the interaction a. All variables in $\bar{v}$ are local to P_i and different from each other. The expressions $\bar{e}$ may involve variables *not local* to P_i (belonging to other participants of that interaction). An interaction a is *readied* by a process P_i, if control of P_i has arrived to a point where executing a is one of the possible continuations. The *readiness set* $\mathcal{R}_i$ of P_i consists of all actions (either local or interaction parts) readied by P_i (at some given stage in a computation). An interaction a is *enabled* only when all its participants have readied it. Thus, an interaction synchronizes all its participants, with all the parts executed in parallel. The assignments in an interaction body are the means for *interprocess communication*, in addition to synchronization. When an interaction starts, a temporary *combined state* is formed, allowing participating processes to access variables in the local states of other participants, by means of the computed expressions. Thus, this

is a *symmetric* interprocess communication construct, involving an arbitrary number of participating processes. The usual synchronous *send - receive* constructs (*handshaking, rendezvous*) are special cases of interactions.

Upon termination of a local interaction part a participating process resumes its local thread of control (i.e., no synchronization at the end of an interaction). Note that if the body $\bar{v} := \bar{e}$ is empty for some participating process, the effect of the interaction on that process is pure synchronization. Note also that a process may have several local interaction parts with the same interaction name, allowing it to execute different assignments in different executions of the interaction. Local interaction parts with the *same* interaction name, residing in different processes, are said to be *syntactically matching*. They are *semantically matching* once they constitute parts of an enabled interaction.

In view of the above, an assignment statement $x := e$ can be seen as an abbreviation to an *anonymous* one-party interaction $[x := e]$, containing the assignment within its (only) part. By having nameless interactions, one enforces purely local actions.

- *Sequential composition -*

$$S_1; S_2$$

First S_1 is executed; if and when it terminates, S_2 is executed. We freely use $S_1; \ldots S_k$ for any $k \geq 2$.

- *Nondeterministic selection -*

$$[\![\parallel_{k=1}^m B_k \& a_k[\bar{v}_k := \bar{e}_k] \to S_k]\!]$$

Here $B_k \& a_k[\bar{v}_k := \bar{e}_k]$ is a *guard*, having two components. The component B_k is a boolean expression over the local state of P_i, while the component $a_k[\bar{v}_k := \bar{e}_k]$ is an interaction (part) guard. S_k is any statement. When a nondeterministic selection statement is evaluated in some state, the k'th guard is *open* if B_k is true in that state. We say that the interaction a_k is *readied* by P_i at that state; the guard is *enabled* [3] if it is open and the interaction a_k is enabled. Executing the statement involves the following steps. First, an evaluation of all boolean parts to determine the collection of open guards. If this collection is empty the statement *fails*.

---

[1] When convenient, mnemonic process names are used, e.g., [*Producer* $\parallel$ *Consumer* $\parallel$ *Buffer*].

[2] See below the meaning of an *absent* interaction name.

[3] Note that both interactions and guards may be enabled.

Otherwise an enabled guard is passed (simultaneously with the execution of all the other matching bodies in the other participating parties) and then S_k is executed. In case no open guard is enabled, execution is *blocked* until some open guard is enabled (possibly forever).

- *Nondeterministic iteration -*

$$*[\![_{k=1}^m B_k \& a_k[\bar{v}_k := \bar{e}_k] \to S_k]$$

Similar to the nondeterministic selection, but the whole procedure is repeated after each execution of a guarded command, and execution terminates once none of the guards are open. At this point, no restrictions are imposed on consecutive choices during the execution of a nondeterministic iteration, and they are assumed to be *arbitrary*. Thus, *fairness* assumptions (see [Fra86]) are not considered here.

The *participants* of an interaction a, are *all* the processes having a reference to the interaction name a anywhere in their program. The collection of participants of interaction a is denoted by $\mathcal{P}_a$. Because interaction names are not storable, $\mathcal{P}_a$ is *syntactically determinable*.

Conflict: Two enabled interactions a_1 and a_2 are in *conflict* iff both interactions are enabled and they have some common participants, i.e., $\mathcal{P}_{a_1} \cap \mathcal{P}_{a_2} \neq \emptyset$.

Conflicts are resolved nondeterministicly. A survey of algorithms for conflict resolution appears in [Lev88]; several of the algorithms appear in [Bag89] where their performance is analyzed.

Indexing

Many programs have a *replicated* process structure, where all processes have similar programs but operate on different, but similarly structured, states. For such programs, the index of a process (or any static [4] expression over such indices) can be used in the text of the process. For clarity, variable names of indexed processes are always indexed. Thus s_i is the s-variable of P_i.

Another frequently used form of replicated structures is that of an indexed family of interactions, e.g., $a_i[\ldots], 1 \leq i \leq m$, for some m. Participation of P_i in interactions can also be determined by indexing, e.g., P_i may refer to $a_{i+1}[\ldots]$, or to $a_{2i}[\ldots]$, provided all indices are in range.

Note that *computed indexing*, depending on values of program variables, as in $a_{x+y}[\ldots]$, is forbidden.

---

[4] Known also as *compile-time*.

$$PHIL :: [P_1 \| \ldots \| P_n \| F_1 \| \ldots \| F_n], \text{ where}$$
$$P_i :: s_i :=' t';$$
$$*[\quad s_i =' t' \to s_i :=' h'$$
$$\qquad]\!]$$
$$\qquad s_i =' h' \& get\text{-}forks_i [s_i :=' e']$$
$$\qquad\qquad \to give\text{-}forks_i [s_i :=' t']$$
$$\qquad],$$
$$F_i :: *[\ get\text{-}forks_i [\,] \to give\text{-}forks_i [\,]$$
$$\qquad]\!]$$
$$\qquad get\text{-}forks_{i+1} [\,] \to give\text{-}forks_{i+1} [\,]$$
$$\qquad].$$

Table 1: A solution of the dining philosophers problem in *IP*

The typical index ranges used are $[0..m-1]$ and $[1..m]$. Unless otherwise stated, index operations are always *cyclic*.

Example: dining philosophers

A typical problem the solution of which can be conveniently expressed in the core-language of *IP* is the famous *dining philosophers* problem [Dij68].

There are n processes $P_i, 1 \leq i \leq n$ ("philosophers"), each capable in being in one of three states: *thinking*, *hungry* and *eating*, respectively abbreviated to $'t'$, $'h'$ and $'e'$. The only transitions of P_i are from $'t'$ to $'h'$, from $'h'$ to $'e'$ and from $'e'$ back to $'t'$. In addition, there are n *resources* $f_i, 1 \leq i \leq n$ ("forks"). In order for the transition of P_i from $'h'$ to $'e'$ to take place, P_i needs exclusive access to both f_i and f_{i-1}.

A solution formulated in the *IP* core-language is presented in Table 1. The forks are represented by additional processes $F_i, 1 \leq i \leq n$. The state of P_i is represented by the variable s_i. When the i'th philosopher P_i is *hungry* ($s_i = 'h'$) it can *eat* ($s_i = 'e'$) by interacting in the three-party interaction $get\text{-}forks_i$ (together with fork F_i and fork F_{i-1}). Thus, acquiring the resources is represented as synchronizing with the corresponding processes in an interaction. A free resource is represented by the corresponding process readying the respective interaction. After P_i finishes eating, it becomes *thinking* ($s_i = 't'$) by interacting with the same forks once again in the $give\text{-}forks_i$ interaction, thereby releasing the resources.

2.2 Abstractions: Teams, Roles and Processes

In this subsection we describe one of our main modularization constructs, the *team*. It serves as an encapsulation mechanism that both hides the details of *interaction patterns*, and allows multiple use of each definition of such patterns.

The role of *interprocess communication abstraction* was stressed by the *script* construct [FHT86] and by the *team* construct in *Raddle*[For87]. We consider it to be a cornerstone in high-level distributed programming and design.

An additional, though more marginal, function of a team is to facilitate structured *dynamic process creation*, not discussed in this paper.

A team is comprised of *roles* and *processes*. Processes are actual executing agents, while roles are *formal processes*, to which actual processes may *enrole* [5] in order to activate their computations. By organizing a distributed program as a collection of teams, it is possible to structure it hierarchically, limiting the interactions in which a role can participate to the ones within the team containing the role. Thus, teams form also a natural unit of scope. The team structure is not intended to impose any additional synchronization means among collections of interacting processes. Synchronization remains solely an effect achievable via multiparty interactions.

A program now comprises a set of *team declarations*, together with a *designated initial team*. The execution of the program starts by an instantiation of the initial team followed by an execution of the instantiated team. We defer for the moment the discussion of interteam relationships. A *team declaration* specifies the following items.

- A unique team-name, used as the means of team identification.

- Team (formal) parameters and their respective types. The team parameters are accessible to all the roles and processes declared in that team. The parameter-passing modes are *value*, *value-result*, and *result*.

- A *prologue*, which is a loopless statement, used as the initialization section of the team. Typically, within this section local team variables may be initialized to values depending on the teams value-parameters, while the team result parameters may be bound to their returned value. Also, team-instantiations may take place in the prologue. This has the effect of instantiating all the teams in the program before processes start to execute. Relaxation of this restriction is not considered here.

- A *body*, consisting of a concurrent composition of *roles* and *processes*. The body specifies the pattern of interaction among the team's roles and processes.

When a team is *instantiated*, its formal parameters are bound to the actual parameters provided by the team instantiation statement (described below), and its processes begin execution immediately after termination of the team's prologue. The instantiation of a team terminates in a unique *team-instance identifier*, which is returned as the value of the instantiation. This value maybe assigned to a *team designator* and used later for uniquely identifying specific team instances. A process is local to the team and its body obeys the same rules as processes of the core language. A role, which may itself be parametrized, is a certain formal process, having as its body a statement of the core language. Both a process and a role have, in addition, the ability to enrole into other roles (possibly of the same team) if the designator of the team containing the target role is known. The *team-enrolement* statement (described below) provides the actual parameters, to which the formal role parameters are bound during enrolement.

If there is no enrolement for a role, any attempt to interact with that role is *blocked*. Of course, an attempt to interact with a process which does not ready its part of the interactions also delays, as in the core language.

Example: bounded buffer

Consider the bounded buffer as an abstraction, allowing for multiple instances of bounded buffers used by different pairs of interacting processes. Here the expression language is assumed to have the standard queue operations:

enqueue(q, x): Add x to the end of queue q and return the new queue

dequeue(q): remove first element from q (undefined if $q = nil$)

first(q): Return the first element of the queue (undefined if $q = nil$).

The program appears in Table 2. Both the consumer and the producer interact with the buffer in binary interactions. The buffer readies the *consume* interaction only if the queue is not empty ($size > 0$) and the *produce* interaction only if the queue is not full ($size < n$). If the queue is neither empty nor full, the buffer readies both *produce* and *consume* interactions, which in this case are in conflict. The *consume* interaction illustrates all the rules for dealing with expressions. Note that the variable q is referenced by

---

[5] This is not a misspelled word. After an arduous search, we have concluded that a new word is appropriate for our model. Although *enroll* has a related origin to *role*, we feel that it is inappropriate to stretch any of its contemporary meanings to our desire, which is *to enter a role*.

```
team BB (value bound : integer) ::
[
role sender(value x) :: produce[]
‖
role receiver(result y) :: consume[y := first(q)]
‖
process buffer
    size : integer := 0; q : queue := nil;
   *[size < bound & produce[q := enqueue(x, q)]
        → size := size + 1
     ‖
     size > 0 & consume[q := dequeue(q)]
        → size := size − 1]
].
```

Table 2: An abstraction of the bounded buffer in *IP*

both parties of the interaction and is assigned to only
by the part of *buffer*, to which it is local. Because
the assignments are parallel, the value of y upon the
completion of the *consume* interaction is the first element of q at the start of *consume*.

The bound of the buffer is a team parameter, so
that buffers of different bounds can be obtained as
instances of this team. The parameter is used by the
buffer process to control the interactions. The item
produced and consumed, x and y, respectively, are
role parameters, supplied by the processes that enrole
as the sender and receiver, respectively. Note that
the buffer process does not terminate, while both the
sender and receiver roles terminate after one interaction. A sequence of deposits and retrievals of values
would involve multiple enrolements to the respective
role, one per each communicated value.

2.2.1 Team instantiation

The *team instantiation* statement creates *instances*
of team declarations to which enrolements can take
place. We are considering here only static process
configurations. Therefore, teams can be instantiated
only in the prologue of other teams. A team instantiation is the following form.

$<varname> := $ **new** $<teamname> (<parameters>)$

The effect of this statement is to create a new
team instance of the type referred to by the team
name, bind the actual parameters to the team formal
parameters (which match in number and types), and
execute the prologue of the created team. Upon termination of the prologue, a unique identifier of the
newly created team instance is stored in the named

```
team BUFFER–USERS ···

small–buffer := new BB(1);
large–buffer := new BB(1000);
  :
```

"Roles specification"

Table 3: Example: Team instantiations

variable, whose type is **team designator**. The designator can subsequently be used for team enrolements,
as described in the next subsection.

Note that if the prologue of the newly created
team instance itself contains further team instantiations, there is a chain-effect. The original instantiation statement does not terminate until all the team
instantiations in the prologue terminate.

Example: Instantiating bounded buffers

Suppose that it is required to create two instances
of the bounded buffer, of sizes 1 and 1000, serving
different interacting pairs of roles within some team.
We might have the following (Table 3).

This example shows the typical use of team parameter passing, which is mostly done by value. However, occasionally there is also a need for a retrieval of
data from a team, in addition to its returned unique
designator. This is achieved via **result** parameters,
examples can be found in [FF90].

Below we relate to some additional features of
team instantiation.

Conditional instantiation: Because teams have parameters, predicates over these parameters
   could be used at instantiation time to control
   further team instantiations. Both **value** parameters of the team itself and **result** parameters of teams created in some prior stage of the
   prologue can be referred to within such predicates. Such a statement would have the form
   $[B → t := $ **new** $T ‖ ¬B → t := nil]$.

Recursive instantiation: If within a prologue of team
   T a **new** T instantiation appears (possibly with
   different actual parameters), we obtain a chain
   of instantiations of teams of type T. To make
   beneficial use of this feature, the creation should
   be guarded by a condition that should eventually hold and stop the chain of instantiations.
   Otherwise, if the chain does not terminate, the
   program can never start ... .

---

team $ETERNAL\text{-}CREATIONS$
$t := $ **new** $ETERNAL\text{-}CREATIONS$;

$process\ R :: \cdots$

Table 4: Example: Nonterminating team instantiations

For example, the team in Table 4 does not terminate, creating an ever growing collection of processes unable to start execution.

2.2.2 Enrolement

In this subsection, we consider the *enrolement* statement, activating a role in some team. At a first stage, we consider only "stand alone" enrolements, sequentially composed. Later we extend the treatment and consider enrolements in guard position, being in conflict with other actions of the role.

The form of an enrolement statement is the following.

$<rolename> @ <teamdesignator> (<parameters>)$

Again, matching in number and type between formal and actual role parameters is assumed. The designator of the team must be known at the enrolement point. It can be either a designator of a team instantiated in the prologue of the enclosing team, or a designator received as a team or role parameter, or a designator received in a previous interaction with other roles. The role name has to be a name of a role within the designated team.

Upon enrolement, the enroler is *suspended*, control is passed to the role in the body of the designated team. The enrolement *terminates* as soon as the execution of the body of role itself terminates (if ever). When an enrolement statement terminates, the enroler resumes its activity within the original team. Note that enrolement is not a coordinated activity, and does not synchronize the enrolers. Only interactions within the target team may cause the enrolers to synchronize, either with other enrolers or with processes within the designated team.

For example, within a role of the team $BUFFER\text{-}USERS$, an enrolement of the form $sender@small\text{-}buffer(xx+1)$ may take place, where xx is a local variable of the enroler. After binding xx to x, the formal parameter representing the transmitted value, the enroler is synchronized with the buffer in *produce* interaction, once the latter has

been readied by the buffer. No synchronization of the *sender* with an enroler as *receiver* is caused, as expected in buffered communication. Upon termination of that interaction the *sender* role body has terminated, and the enroler resumes activity in the $BUFFER\text{-}USERS$ team.

Note well that we do allow recursive enrolement, whereby a chain of enrolements lead from a role back to itself. Because the presence of recursive enrolement plays a crucial role in conflict propagation (as described in the next section), the next example demonstrates the need for recursive enrolement.

Example: Distributed towers of Hanoi

As an example of recursive team instantiation, we present a distributed solution of the famous problem known as *Towers of Hanoi*. This solution is a variant of the one first presented in [FHT86]. The game consists of three poles, named *source, destination,* and *spare*, respectively. Initially, n discs of different diameters are placed on the source pole in such a way that no disc is placed above a smaller disc. The goal of the game is to move all n discs from the source pole to the destination pole, using the spare pole as temporary storage, subject to the following two constraints.

1. Only the top disc on a pole can be moved.

2. No disc can be placed on top of a smaller disc.

We can define three "interactions" between the poles, called *step1, step2,* and *step3,* which execute sequentially.

step1: $n-1$ discs are moved, using a recursive invocation of the procedure, from the source pole to the spare pole, using the destination pole as intermediate storage.

step2: The (only) remaining disc on the source pole (which is the largest of the discs participating in the current enrolements) is moved to the destination pole.

step3: $n-1$ discs are moved from, using another recursive invocation of the procedure, from the spare pole to the destination pole, using the source pole as intermediate storage.

step1 and *step3* are not primitive operations allowed by the problem statement, but they are instances of the problem for $n-1$ discs. This property can be used to create a recursive solution.

In the recursive team *Hanoi* (in Table 5), each one of the poles is represented by a role of the same name. The variable *self* denotes the team designator of the

160

```
team Hanoi() ::
[
  role source( value n : integer,
                value-result s : stack ) ::
    [ n > 1 → source@self(n − 1, s)
    ⫿ n = 1 → skip ]
    ; step2 [ s := pop(s) ]
    ; [ n > 1 → spare@self(n − 1, s)
    ⫿ n = 1 → skip ]
  ‖
  role spare( value n : integer,
                value-result p : stack ) ::
    [ n > 1 → destination@self(n − 1, p)
    ⫿ n = 1 → skip ]
    ; step2 [ ]
    ; [ n > 1 → source@self(n − 1, p)
    ⫿ n = 1 → skip ]
  ‖
  role destination( value n : integer,
                value-result d : stack ) ::
    [ n > 1 → spare@self(n − 1, d)
    ⫿ n = 1 → skip ]
    ; step2 [ d := push(d, top(s)) ]
    ; [ n > 1 → destination@self(n − 1, d)
    ⫿ n = 1 → skip ]
].
```

Table 5: The Towers of Hanoi solved with recursive enrolement.

current team instance. Each role has a **value - result** parameter of type **stack of discs**. Due to these stacks, the first constraint is trivially met. The parameter n represents the number of discs to be moved. The second step, that of an actual disc movement, is realized by an interaction between the three roles. Note that no further synchronization among roles is needed; the three-party interaction is sufficient to prevent the *spare* enroler from moving ahead into the *source* role and stealing an interaction.

3 Enrolement within guards

In this section we consider another feature of the *IP* language, which turns to be of utmost importance for program development via refinements and other correctness-preserving transformations and which raises the issue being the subject of this paper. So far, we considered enrolement as a "stand alone" local action, sequentially composed with other actions. We now want to consider the semantics of an enrolement action when in a guard position, either in a nondeterministic selection or nondeterministic iteration. We refer to this as a *guarding enrolement*. This feature allows for *conditional enrolement*, when accompanied by a boolean part of a guard, having other alternative actions (local actions, interactions or other enrolements).

However, due to the conflict resolution mechanism controlling choices, part of the definition of this feature is the contribution of such an action to the readiness-set and the influence of conflict resolution on the intended meaning of such enrolements. We shall explore several possibilities for the semantics of guarding enrolement and discuss their respective bearings on design methodology.

One principle which we will preserve is that synchronization in *IP* is accomplished *solely* with multiparty interactions. Adherence to this principle rules out some of the possible semantics one might consider. For example, guarding enrolement may not *delay* directly an enroler (as was the case for enrolements in [FHT86]). Any delaying effect should be obtained by interactions which the enroler encounters when executing a role.

First, the syntactic form of a guarding enrolement is as follows.

$$B \& <rolename> @ <designator> (<parameters>) \rightarrow S$$

where such an enrolement appears as an alternative in nondeterministic selection or iteration; the team designator, as before, has to be known at the point of enrolement, and the role name is a name of a role in the designated team instance. Once again, S is an arbitrary *IP* statement.

A necessary condition for readying a guarding enrolement is the satisfaction of B, the boolean component of the guard. Our main concern is what to take as a sufficient condition. We start by distinguishing between two approaches, *uncoordinated enrolement* and *coordinated enrolement*.

Uncoordinated enrolement

According to this approach, the (guarding) enrolement is considered as a *local action* of the enroler; the enrolement is directly included in the readiness set and is taken to be in conflict with any other enabled action. In other words, the necessary condition for readying mentioned above is also taken as sufficient. Consequently, enrolers can not coordinate joint enrolements into the same team instance whenever this approach is adopted.

The main advantage of this approach is its simplicity and locality, rendering it efficient and easy to implement. The obvious disadvantage is the inability of enrolers to coordinate enrolements into some team instance. In particular, if an interaction is encapsulated in a team, the enrolements into the team cannot be substituted for the parts of the interactions which might have been in guard positions. This is because (under the uncoordinated enrolement approach) one partner could get stuck in the enrolement while the other partners make alternate choice (that is, never enrole in the team).

In order to see that clearly, consider the program fragment in Figure 1, which is termed the *basic conflict situation*. According to *IP* semantics if P_2 engages in one of its alternative interactions (a or b), it is always in conjunction with its respective partner engaging in the *same* interaction, each in its respective part.

Now suppose interactions a and b are refined to teams Ta and Tb, respectively, with roles R_1 and R_2 in Ta and R_2 and R_3 in Tb. We assume that ta and tb are team designators for instances of Ta and Tb. After the enrolements are substituted for the interaction parts, the program fragment would look as follows:

$$
\begin{array}{l}
[\\
\quad P_1 :: \ ...; \ [\ R_1@ta(\ ... \ ) \ \rightarrow \ S_1 \\
\qquad\qquad\quad [\!] \\
\qquad\qquad x[\,...\,] \ \rightarrow \ T_1 \ ]; \ ... \\
\| \\
\quad P_2 :: \ ...; \ [\ R_2@ta(\ ... \ ) \ \rightarrow \ S_2 \\
\qquad\qquad\quad [\!] \\
\qquad\qquad R_2@tb(\ ... \ ) \ \rightarrow \ T_2 \ ]; \ ... \\
\| \\
\quad P_3 :: \ ...; \ [\ R_3@tb(\ ... \ ) \ \rightarrow \ S_3 \\
\qquad\qquad\quad [\!] \\
\qquad\qquad y[\,...\,] \ \rightarrow \ T_3 \ ]; \ ...
\end{array}
$$

The conflicts among a, b, x, and y are lost! Instead, the uncoordinated enrolement forces P_2 to commit to executing either a or b without knowing whether the partner will ever ready its part of the interaction (which implies that P_2 could get "struck" in the enrolement").

This approach is a major obstacle to a large family of refinements, where interactions are refined into teams and an interaction part in a guard position becomes a guarding enrolement.

If uncoordinated enrolement is chosen, then the ability to substitute a team instance for an interaction would be lost, and subsequently detract from the usefulness of multiparty interactions. In order to maintain this property, we next explore alternate meanings for enrolement, which are clearly distinct from our usual notions of procedure invocation.

$$
\begin{array}{l}
P_1 :: \ ...; \ [\ a[\,...\,] \ \rightarrow S_1 \\
\qquad\qquad\quad [\!] \\
\qquad\qquad x[\,...\,] \ \rightarrow T_1 \ ]; \ ... \\
\| \\
P_2 :: \ ...; \ [\ a[\,...\,] \ \rightarrow S_2 \\
\qquad\qquad\quad [\!] \\
\qquad\qquad b[\,...\,] \ \rightarrow T_2 \ ]; \ ... \\
\| \\
P_3 :: \ ...; \ [\ b[\,...\,] \ \rightarrow S_3 \\
\qquad\qquad\quad [\!] \\
\qquad\qquad y[\,...\,] \ \rightarrow T_3 \ ]; \ ...
\end{array}
$$

Figure 1: The basic conflict situation.

Coordinated enrolement

Here the guarding enrolement is not an action capable of being in a direct conflict with other actions. Rather, its conflicts is *propagated*, that is, interactions in the body of the target role are in conflict with interactions in the context of the enrolement.

Coordinated enrolement has several variants; the common theme to all of them is the reliance on a *lookahead* (into the body of the enrolement) in order to determine the contribution to the readiness set. By means of conflict propagation the ability to reach agreement for coordinated joint enrolement is restored in many cases.

The basic idea in conflict propagation is to determine a collection of *first actions* within the role targeted by a guarded enrolement. This is a collection of interaction parts that would be readied if enrolement had indeed taken place. Once such a collection has been determined, it is added to the readiness set of the enroler. If and when one of these first actions is chosen (via conflict resolution) as the next action to be executed, only then is the guarding enrolement *committed* and takes place with the actual parameter binding and the respective transfer of control.

To see the implication of this provision on coordinated enrolement, consider the following example. Suppose that coordinated enrolement is required for roles R_1, R_2 and R_3 of a team instance of team definition T, which has designator t. Then, the definition of team T may look like the one in Table 6.

```
team T ::
[
        role R_1 :: a[ ]; ···
    ‖
        role R_2 :: a[ ]; ···
    ‖
        role R_3 :: a[ ]; ···
].
```

Table 6: Example of a coordinated enrolement

Suppose that three processes, P_{i_1}, P_{i_2} and P_{i_3} wish to coordinate joint enrolement into $R_1@t$, $R_2@t$ and $R_3@t$, respectively but also have alternative interaction parts $b[\,]$, $c[\,]$ and $d[\,]$. Thus, P_{i_1} has the form

$$\cdots; [R_1@t \to \cdots \| b[\,] \to \cdots]; \cdots$$

and the P_{i_2}, P_{i_3}, respectively, have similar choices

$$\cdots; [R_2@t \to \cdots \| c[\,] \to \cdots]; \cdots$$

$$\cdots; [R_3@t \to \cdots \| d[\,] \to \cdots]; \cdots.$$

As a result of the conflict propagation, each of the three processes readies interaction $a[\,]$. So, if $a[\,]$ is the next chosen interaction, all three of them commit to the enrolements. Otherwise, none of them will commit to its enrolement, choosing other alternatives instead. In other words, interaction $a[\,]$ conflicts (indirectly) with $b[\,]$, $c[\,]$ and $d[\,]$.

Returning to the basic conflict situation of Figure 1, the coordinated enrolement again restores the joint enrolements of P_1 and P_2 to a or of P_2 and P_3 to b, ensuring that no process gets stuck in any role.

The determination of the contribution of each guarding enrolement to the readiness set was easy in the situation depicted in Table 6, because the readiness set is independent of any runtime computation. As a first indication of the complexity involved in this lookahead, consider the following variant of a coordinated enrolement, shown in Table 7, where the determination of the readiness set depends on the evaluation of boolean conditions. In this example, each of the roles R_i may ready either interaction $a[]$ or interaction $e[]$ or both, depending on the evaluation of the various boolean conditions B_i and C_i, which in turn may depend on the role parameters n_i.

However, the source of the most serious complications is the fact that guarding enrolements may be *nested*, propagating the conflict across further teams. To see that, suppose interaction e (of Table 7) is encapsulated into a team as shown in Table 8, where one of the first actions within R_1 is yet another guarding

```
team T ::
[
    role R_1(value n_1 : integer) ::
        [ B_1 & a[ ] → ···
        ‖
          C_1 & e[ ] → ···]
  ‖
    role R_2(value n_2 : integer) ::
        [ B_2 & a[ ] → ···
        ‖
          C_2 & e[ ] → ···]
  ‖
    role R_3(value n_3 : integer) ::
        [ B_3 & a[ ] → ···
        ‖
          C_3 & e[ ] → ···]
].
```

Table 7: Example of a dynamic coordinated enrolement

enrolement! In this example, the contribution of R_1 to the conflict set, in addition to the readied interaction $a[\,]$, depends on deepening the lookahead into the first actions contributed by role R' in team instance t'! Clearly, by means of such nesting the conflict can be propagated deeper and deeper, causing longer and longer local computations before commitment, most of which have to be undone.

Note that commitments are made to interactions. That is, if an interaction part (in a readiness set) is selected for execution, then the process is committed to the entire chain of enrolements that leads to the selected interaction.

The main advantage of this approach, in all its variants, is this restoration of coordinated enrolement, which allows an interaction in any context to be encapsulated in a team. The main disadvantages are its complexity and the presence of some pathological programs that arise from unguarded recursion (as is described below). In view of this extra complication, three variants of this approach of coordinated guarding enrolement can be distinguished.

Direct Propagation: To realize this variant, the structure of roles needs to be constrained in such a way that there always exist an *immediate* first actions within the role, and only proper actions, either local or interactions, serve as such. In other words, a role can not enrole into some other role before executing at least one proper action. Basically, this variant disallows guarding enrolements in a "top-level" selection or iteration.

The advantage of this approach is by immediately bounding the conflict propagation and the amount of computation that is irrelevant to the selected enrolement (e.g., guarding conditions inside enrolements that must be computed). The disadvantage is that in the refinement process, [6] there are actions that cannot be further refined, because of their function of conflict carriers.

Bounded Propagation: In this variant, guarding enrolements *can* serve as alternatives in top-level selections and iterations, provided these are *not recursive*. The propagation of conflict has a non-trivial depth, but is still bounded. This seems to be more helpful in supporting refinements and still avoiding some pathological cases.

Full Propagation: A full *lookahead* is computed to determine the readiness set. That is, all enrolements are followed including recursive enrolements.

There are three aspects of full propagation that must be discussed: the potential for unbounded lookahead, the void readiness set, and the infinite readiness.

Unbounded Lookahead: In general, an improperly guarded sequence of recursive enrolements can lead to an unbounded lookahead. This would have a very detrimental effect on the most direct way of determining the readiness set, that is, computing the readiness set by expanding the enrolements.

Void Readiness Set: In case *all* the first actions in a role consist of merely another recursive guarding enrolement to the same role, the readiness set is empty. In any effective implementation, the search for a readiness set will last forever. This should have the same meaning as any other situation where the readiness set is empty, that is, the role or process fails. An example appears in Table 9. The lookahead caused by a guarding enrolement to $R_1@t(\cdots)$ will evaluate B_1, B_2. Suppose both are false. At that point, there is no action to inherit the original conflict of the guarding enrolement. If there are other actions in the readiness set, this means

```
team T ::
[
    role R₁(value n₁ : integer) ::
        [ B₁ & a[ ] → ···
        ‖
          C₁ & R₁′@t′(n₁) → ···]
    ‖
    role R₂(value n₂ : integer) ::
        [ B₂ & a[ ] → ···
        ‖
          C₂ & R₂′@t′(n₂) → ···]
    ‖
    role R₃(value n₃ : integer) ::
        [ B₃ & a[ ] → ···
        ‖
          C₃ & R₃′@t′(n₃) → ···]
].
    team T′ ::
[
    role R₁′ (value n₁ : integer) ::
        e [ ] → ···
    ‖
    role R₂′ (value n₂ : integer) ::
        e [ ] → ···
    ‖
    role R₃′ (value n₃ : integer) ::
        e [ ] → ···
].
```

Table 8: Example of a deeper propagated conflict in a coordinated enrolement

---

[6] This approach is similar to the one found in [BK88], though no abstractions are present there. However, their *joint actions* have always an initialization section. When a joint action is refined into an action system, the initialization section of the refining system inherits the conflict of the refined action.

```
team T ::
[
    role R₁(value n₁ : integer) ::
        [ B₁&a[ ] → ···
        ‖
          B₂&b[ ] → ···]
    ‖
    ⋮
].
```

Table 9: Example of an empty readiness set in a co-ordinated enrolement

that this enrolement can not be selected, but some other action can proceed. However, if the original guarding enrolement was the only action at hand, the *whole* readiness set is empty, amounting to a global failure of the whole program. This is a natural generalization of failing due to all guards being closed within an IP selection statement.

Infinite Readiness Set: In case the body of the role has in the top level two choices, one a recursive enrolement to the same role and the other some proper action, the ultimate readiness set is infinite. If the semantics dictates that eventually one member of this infinite set must always be chosen, this renders the semantics to be noneffective, similar to *fairness* or *random assignments*[7], both transcending bounded nondeterminism.

Now that we have explored the possible meanings of enrolement within a guard, for IP we choose coordinated enrolement with **full propagation** of conflicts. At first the decision to use such a complex mechanism will seem odd, but this decision supports the most powerful design methodology. Further the decision to use full propagation does not create problems that are not already created by either the use of fairness or unguarded recursion.

To appreciate the subtleties of conflict propagation, consider the following example. Let a team T have roles R_i, $i = i, n$ and let t designate an instance of T. Suppose an enroler P encounters the following nondeterministic selection

$$[\underset{i=1,n}{\|} R_i@t(...) \to S_i]$$

which is intuitively interpreted as the willingness to

coordinate enrolement in any role in t, provided there are other enrolers for all the other roles in t.

In addition, suppose that interaction a is first in each of the roles R_i, $i = i, n$. Then, by the conflict propagation, all those parts of a are members in $\mathcal{R}_P$; yet this does not render interaction a enabled. Consequently, we see that the IP semantics also induces *identity propagation*, that is, a role assumes the indentity of its enroler while the enrolement lasts. If, on the hand, we had n pairwise distinct processes P_i, $i = 1, n$ each of which is about to execute the above selection, then the interaction a is enabled (actually, in $n!$ ways) and conflict resolution will select one of the enableness patterns and assign processes to roles consistently if a is selected for execution.

4   A Larger Example

It is time to present an example large enough to illustrate the merit of our proposal. Let us consider the problem of designing a debit card system. Debit cards are by now familiar artifacts of the EFT world. When a customer presents it to a merchant for a purchase, the debit card is used to initiate a three party interaction, a *request*, in which funds are transferred from the customer's bank to the merchant's bank. The debit card system has three components: the point-of-sales terminals, the computers that hold the customer accounts, and the computers that hold the merchant accounts. A debit card system has three basic requirements:

- All requests must transfer funds correctly.

- A customer account must never have a negative balance.

- All requests must eventually be processed.

More detailed presentations of this problem can be found in [FE87],[Sta88]. We would like a design process that allows the capture of the requirements in an operational form.

Table 10 contains a design for a debit card system. The design contains three kinds of processes: *pos* is a point-of-sales terminal, *cbank* is a customer's bank, and *mbank* is a merchant's bank. Variables of type *sale* are records that contain the sale amount, the merchant identification number and the customer identification number. A variable of type *database* is a set of record that contain account information. For the sake of simplicity we have assumed that the account databases are already initialized and that the sale request is set non-null by some outside mechanism. The essence of the design is captured in the set of three-party interactions *xaction*, which checks

---

[7]These are of the form $v := ?$, which assigns to v an arbitrary natural number within a finite time.

```
[
  ‖     pos_i ::
 i=1,I
        s : sale := null,
        okay : boolean ;
      *[    ‖      s ≠ null ∧ bank(s.customer) = j
        j=1,J, k=1,K
                              ∧ bank(s.merchant) = k
               &xaction_{i,j,k}[okay := approved(cbalances, s),
                                s := null ]
              → skip
      ]
  ‖
 j=1,J  cbank_j ::
        cbalances : database ;
      *[    ‖       xaction_{i,j,k}[ cbalances :=
        i=1,I, k=1,K
                         if approved(cbalances, s)
                         then debit(cbalances, s)
                         else cbalances ]
              → skip
      ]
  ‖
 k=1,K  mbank_k ::
        mbalances : database ;
      *[    ‖       xaction_{i,j,k}[ mbalances :=
        i=1,I, j=1,J
                         if approved(cbalances, s)
                         then credit(mbalances, s)
                         else mbalances ]
              → skip
      ]
]
```

Table 10: Debit Card System.

the balance of the customer and if sufficient, transfers the funds. In Table 10 there are I point-of-sale processes, J customer banks, and K merchants banks. There are $I * J * K$ interactions $xaction_{i,j,k}$ defined in Table 10; each pos process contains $J * K$ interactions; the pos initiates an interaction based on the identification numbers of the merchant and the customer. The function $bank$ is used to map customer and merchant identification numbers into indices. For the sake of simplicity, we do not allow merchants to be customers. The functions $debit$ and $credit$ are used to update the appropriate accounts in the databases by either debiting or crediting the sale amount.

Now that a high level solution to the design of a debit card system has been presented, let us return to our main point – the encapsulating of interactions in teams and the vital part that conflict propagation

plays in its facilitation. In Table 11 the parts of the $xaction$ interaction are replaced with enrolement to $Xaction$, a team, in which the interaction is encapsulated. It must be emphasized that there is no difference in the meaning of the designs described in Table 10 and Table 11. Note that in the two different types of banks the enrolements appear in the context of a choice; without conflict propagation there is no way to encapsulate $xaction$ without a large restructuring of the solution (the reader might try this for himself).

It should also be noted that in neither table is the context of $xaction$ as general as possible; two of the parties to $xaction$ are persistent (i.e., will always come back to the interaction if some other choice is made) and the third party is insistent (i.e., readies only one interaction and will do nothing else until that interaction is executed). In some other design, $xaction$ might be persistent in all three roles, yet one could still encapsulate $xaction$ in a team.

Interactions are encapsulated because many refinements are possible. Table 12 expresses one such refinement. Here the $cbank$ is given the responsibility of transferring the funds to the $mbank$ after the pos has been informed (this gets the customer through the check-out line faster).

The refinement in Table 12 is effected with an initial synchronization of all parties (the interaction $sync$); this is an essential if the refinement is to be correct in all contexts. Table 13 gives a refinement that does not have the initial synchronization. This refinement is correct only because the set of processes that enrole as $cbanks$ does not intersect with the set of processes that enrole as $mbanks$. If the same processes enroled as both $cbanks$ and $mbanks$, a deadlock could arise by having a set of banks in which each insists on transferring funds ($xfer$) to another bank in the set. The characterization of contexts in which refinements are correct is still an open problem in our methodology and is currently under investigation. A more detailed account and more examples of the whole approach will appear in [FF90].

5   Conclusions

This paper is part of a larger body of work in the area of the definition and application of multiparty interactions that has been on-going for a number of years. Here just the requirements for abstraction constructs encapsulating multiparty interactions were studied. This problem is different from that of abstractions in sequential models in that processes can ready multiple interactions but execute only one at a time, which leads to conflict situations. To have a viable abstraction for encapsulating interactions, the

```
team Xaction ::
[
role pos( s : sale, okay : boolean ) ::
  xaction[ okay := approved(cbalances, s),
        s := null ]
‖
role cbank( cbalances : database ) ::
  xaction[ cbalances :=
              if approved(cbalances, s)
              then debit(cbalances, s)
              else cbalances ]
‖
role mbank( mbalances : database ) ::
  xaction[ mbalances :=
              if approved(cbalances, s)
              then credit(mbalances, s)
              else mbalances ]
].


team DCS( I, J, K : integer ) ::
        for all
   i=1,I, j=1,J, k=1,K   x_{i,j,k} = new Xaction()
[
  ‖    process pos_i ::
 i=1,I
    s : sale := null,
    okay : boolean;
  *[      ‖
      j=1,J, k=1,K
        s ≠null ∧ bank(s.customer) = j
              ∧ bank(s.merchant) = k
          & pos@x_{i,j,k}(s, okay) → skip
  ]
‖
  ‖    process cbank_j ::
 j=1,J
    cbalances : database;
  *[      ‖         cbank@x_{i,j,k}(cbalances) → skip ]
      i=1,I, k=1,K
‖
  ‖    process mbank_k ::
 k=1,K
    mbalances : database;
  *[      ‖         mbank@x_{i,j,k}(mbalances) → skip ]
      i=1,I, j=1,J
].
```

Table 11: Encapsulating the transaction in a team.

```
team Xaction ::
[
role pos( s : sale, okay : boolean ) ::
  sync[];
  approve[ okay := approved(cbalances, s), s := null ]
‖
role cbank( cbalances : database ) ::
    okay : boolean, sokay : sale;
  sync[];
  approve[ okay := approved(cbalances, s), sokay := s ];
  [ okay → xfer[ cbalances := debit(cbalances, sokay) ]
  ‖¬ okay → continue[] ]
‖
role mbank( mbalances : database ) ::
  sync[];
  [ xfer[ mbalances := credit(mbalances, sokay) ]
          → skip
  ‖ continue[] → skip ]
].
```

Table 12: Refinement of the transaction.

```
team Xaction ::
[
role pos( s : sale, okay : boolean ) ::
  request[];
  approve[ okay := cbank.okay ]
‖
role cbank( cbalances : database ) ::
    okay : boolean, sokay : sale;
  request[ sokay := s ];
  okay := approved(cbalances, s);
  approve[];
  [ okay → xfer[ cbalances := debit(cbalances, sokay) ]
  ‖¬ okay → skip
  ]
‖
role mbank( mbalances : database ) ::
  xfer[ mbalances := credit(mbalances, sokay) ]
].
```

Table 13: Refinement of the transaction without initial synchronization.

abstraction must be applicable in all contexts, including interactions appearing as guards. Several alternatives were explored for the meaning of enrolement when used in the position of a guard. The conclusion is that in order to support a stepwise-refinement design methodology conflicts must be propagated across enrolements to achieve proper coordination at the abstraction level.

References

[AFG90] Paul Attie, Nissim Francez, and Orna Grumberg. Fairness and hyperfairness in multi-party interactions. In *17th ACM-POPL*, January 17-19 1990.

[Bac88a] R. J. R. Back. A calculus of refinements for program derivations. *Acta Informatica*, 25:593–624, 1988.

[Bac88b] R. J. R. Back. *Refining Atomicity in Parallel Programs*. Technical Report Ser. A, No 57, Abo Academi, 1988.

[Bag89] R. Bagrodia. Synchronization of asynchronous processes in csp. *ACM Trans. on Programming Languages and Systems*, 11(4):585–597, October 1989.

[BK88] R.-J. J. Back and R. Kurki-Suonio. Distributed cooperation with action systems. *ACM Transactions on Programming Languages and Systems*, 10(4):513–554, October 1988.

[Dij68] E. W. Dijkstra. Cooperating sequential processes. In F. Genuys, editor, *Programming Languages*, pages 43–112, Academic Press, New York, 1968.

[Dij75] E. W. Dijkstra. Guarded commands, nondterminacy and, formal derivation of programs. *Communications of the ACM*, 18(8):453–457, August 1975.

[FE87] I. R. Forman and M. Evangelist. *EFT: A Case Study in Design using Raddle*. Technical Report STP-121-87, Microelectronics and Computer Technology Corp., April 1987.

[FF90] Nissim Francez and Ira R. Forman. *Interacting Processes: A Multiparty Approach to Coordinated Distributed Programming*. Forthcoming, 1990.

[FHT86] Nissim Francez, Brent T. Hailpern, and Gadi Taubenfeld. Script- a communication abstraction mechanism and its verification. *Science of Computer Programming*, 6(1):35–88, January 1986.

[For87] Ira R. Forman. On the design of large distributed systems. In *First international conference on computer languages*, pages 84–95, October 1987.

[Fra86] N. Francez. *Fairness*. Springer-Verlag, New York, 1986.

[Fra89] Nissim Francez. Cooperative proofs for distributed programs with multi-party interactions. *IPL*, 32:235 –242, September 22 1989.

[Hoa78] C. A. R. Hoare. Communicating sequential processes. *Communications of the ACM*, 21(8):666–677, August 1978.

[Lev88] E. Levy. *A Survey of Distributed Coordination Algorithms*. Technical Report STP-271-88, Microelectronics and Computer Technology Corp., September 1988.

[Sta88] M. Staskauskas. The formal specification and design of a distributed electronic funds-transfer system. *IEEE Trans. on Computers*, 37(12):1515–1528, December 1988.

Reliable Distributed Computing with Avalon/Common Lisp

Stewart M. Clamen, Linda D. Leibengood, Scott M. Nettles, and Jeannette M. Wing

School of Computer Science
Carnegie Mellon University
Pittsburgh, PA 15213

Abstract

Avalon is a set of linguistic constructs designed to give programmers explicit control over transaction-based processing of atomic objects for fault-tolerant applications. These constructs, designed as extensions to familiar programming languages such as C++ and Common Lisp, are tailored for each base language so the syntax and spirit of each language are maintained. We present here an overview of these novel aspects of Avalon/Common Lisp: (1) support for *remote evaluation* through a new **evaluator** data type; (2) a generalization of the traditional client/server model of computation, allowing clients to extend server interfaces and server writers to hide aspects of distribution, such as caching, from clients; (3) support for *failure atomicity* through automatic commit and abort processing of transactions; and (4) support for *persistence* through automatic crash recovery of atomic data. These capabilities provide programmers with the flexibility to exploit the semantics of an application to enhance its reliability and efficiency. Avalon/Common Lisp runs on IBM RT's on the Mach operating system. Though the design of Avalon/Common Lisp exploits some of the features of Common Lisp, e.g., its packaging mechanism, all of the constructs are applicable to any Lisp-like language.

1. Introduction

Large networks of computers supporting both local and distributed processing are now commonplace. Application programs running in these environments concurrently access shared, distributed, and possibly replicated data. Examples of such applications include electronic banking, library search and retrieval systems, nation-wide electronic mail systems, and overnight-package delivery systems. Such applications must be designed to cope with failures and concurrency, ensuring that the data they manage remain *consistent*, that is, are neither lost nor corrupted, and *available*, that is, accessible even in the presence of failures such as site crashes and network partitions.

A widely-accepted technique for preserving consistency in the presence of failures and concurrency is to organize computations as sequential processes called *transactions*. Transactions must satisfy three properties: serializability, failure atomicity, and persistence. *Serializability* means that transactions appear to execute in some serial order. *Failure atomicity* ("all-or-nothing") means that a transaction either succeeds completely and *commits*, or *aborts* and has no effect.

Persistence means that the effects of a committed transaction survive failures. We use the term *atomic* to stand for all three properties.

Although transactions are widely used in the database community, demonstrating that they can be a foundation for general purpose distributed systems remains a challenge and is currently of active interest. Appropriate programming language support for application programmers would greatly enhance the usability and thus, generality, of such systems.

Avalon is a set of linguistic constructs designed as extensions to familiar high-level programming languages such as C++ [25] and Common Lisp [16]. The extensions are tailored for each base language, so the syntax and spirit of each language are maintained. The constructs include new encapsulation and abstraction mechanisms, as well as support for concurrency and recovery. The decision to extend existing languages rather than to invent a new language was based on pragmatic considerations. We felt we could focus more effectively on the new and interesting issues such as reliability if we did not have to redesign or reimplement basic language features, and we felt that building on top of widely-used and widely-available languages would facilitate the use of Avalon outside our own research group.

This paper presents an overview of some of the more novel aspects of Avalon/Common Lisp. The distinguishing characteristic of Avalon/Common Lisp, in contrast to Avalon/C++ [6] and other transaction-based distributed programming languages (see Section 6), is its support for *remote evaluation* [23]. Lisp's treatment of code as data provides a natural and easy way to implement remote evaluation since we simply transmit code, as well as data, between clients and servers. Moreover, we exploit remote evaluation to extend and generalize the traditional client/server model of distributed computing. Thus, the programmer gains more flexibility in structuring an application, while often simultaneously improving its performance.

We have implemented the Avalon/Common Lisp constructs presented herein on top of Camelot [21], a distributed transaction management system (written in C) built at Carnegie Mellon. Camelot provides low-level facilities like lock management, two-phase commit protocols, and logging to stable storage.

The particular extensions we designed for Common Lisp are applicable to any Lisp-like language, though for concreteness, all our examples will be expressed in Avalon/Common Lisp. We assume the reader has a reading knowledge of Common Lisp.

In Section 2 we give an overview of Avalon/Common Lisp's model of computation and program structure as they relate to distribution, persistence, and concurrency. Sections 3 and 4 explain the novel features of Avalon/Common Lisp related to distribution, in particular remote evaluation and our generalization of the traditional client/server model. Section 5 illustrates features of Avalon/Common Lisp related to persistence. Section 6 compares Avalon/Common Lisp with other transaction-based, distributed programming languages and closes with a summary of our current status.

2. Overview

Distribution

An Avalon/Common Lisp computation executes over a distributed set of *evaluators* (Figure 1), each of which is a distinct Lisp process. An evaluator resides at a single physical site, but each site may be home to multiple evaluators. A user starts a computation at an *initiating* evaluator, which may communicate with other *remote* evaluators. To a first approximation, evaluators communicate through remote procedure calls with call-by-value semantics. The dotted lines in the figure indicate possible call paths between evaluators.

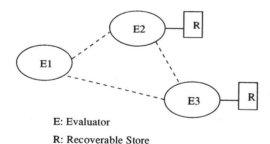

E: Evaluator

R: Recoverable Store

Figure 1: Model of Distributed Evaluators and Recoverable Storage

As in Common Lisp, an Avalon/Common Lisp program consists of a set of *packages*. Each evaluator is host to one or more packages. We map the standard client/server model of distributed computing onto our more general architecture as follows: We put a client's code in one package and execute it on the initiating evaluator, and for each server, we put its code in a separate package and execute it on a remote evaluator.

Section 3 will explain how we extend this standard client/server model by using remote evaluation in combination with the feature that an evaluator can be host to multiple packages. The combination frees us from the above one-to-one correspondences between client

code (or server code) and a package, and between a client process (or server process) and an evaluator. In short, in our full extended client/server model, client code can cross evaluator boundaries, can be split into more than one package, or can coexist with server code at the same evaluator. Similar remarks hold for server code.

Persistence

Since Avalon/Common Lisp provides *transactions*, we need to provide a way to support failure atomicity and persistence. When a crash occurs, we need to recover the state of the system to some previously saved consistent state, one that reflects all changes performed by all committed transactions.

Each evaluator has access to at most one private *recoverable store* (see Figure 1), which itself is managed by a separate process.[1] Normally, there would be no recoverable store associated with the evaluator where the client code resides, but there would be one per evaluator that is host to a server.

At the programming language level, each server package encapsulates a set of *object bindings* and exports a set of *functions*. Each object binding is a mapping between a symbol and an object. A binding can be declared to be *persistent*; otherwise it is considered to be *volatile*. Persistent bindings (and the objects to which they map) are allocated from recoverable store; hence, persistent bindings survive crashes, while volatile ones do not. By convention, a server's functions should provide the only means for a client and other servers to gain access to the server's object bindings, and thus its recoverable objects.

It makes sense to access recoverable objects only when executing a transaction so Avalon/Common Lisp provides control primitives to begin, commit and abort transactions. Section 5 shows a use of these primitives.

Concurrency

Avalon/Common Lisp supports concurrent transactions ("heavyweight" processes), but no concurrency within a transaction. Serializability of transactions is guaranteed by using standard two-phase read/write locks on objects [8]. A transaction holds its locks until it commits or aborts.

Since Common Lisp does not support multiple threads of control, in particular "light-weight" processes as in C Threads [5], we have a simpler model of computation with respect to concurrency than that for other languages such as Avalon/C++. Specifically, only one thread of control executes within an evaluator at once. For example, suppose two clients each make a request at a single server. The (server's)

---

[1]Each recoverable storage manager is a C process since we currently use Camelot's implementation of recoverable storage; hence, each of our Lisp processes communicates with a C process whenever recoverable storage is accessed.

evaluator processes these two requests serially. On behalf of the first request, it accesses the recoverable store, acquires appropriate read or write locks, and returns appropriate result values. The evaluator then services the second request. If the second request creates a lock conflict, the (server's) evaluator blocks until the lock is freed. Lock conflicts can arise because locks are released as transactions complete, not when function calls return.

Avalon/Common Lisp supports nested transactions, but, again because of the limited kind of concurrency we can support in Common Lisp, each transaction can have at most one active child transaction. A transaction commits only if its child has committed or aborted; a transaction that aborts aborts its child. A transaction's effects become persistent only when it commits at the top level.

The most interesting and novel aspects of Avalon/Common Lisp relate to its way of handling distributed computing, and not persistent storage or concurrency. Thus, the next two sections will focus on the issues related to distribution: remote evaluation and the extended client/server model.

3. Remote Evaluation

3.1. Example Uses of Extensions

Suppose, for simplicity, there are two evaluators, one *local* and one *remote*, where the local evaluator might be the initiating evaluator for some computation. The following expressions:

```
(let ((a 123) (b 45)) (+ a b))
(let ((a 123) (b 45)) (remote (+ a b)))
(let ((a 123) (b 45))
     (remote (+ (local a) (local b))))
```

all return the same value to the user, namely the number 168. Given that the function + refers to the built-in generic addition function, all three expressions have the same semantic meaning. How they differ is where the various subexpressions are evaluated.

In the first expression, all computation (new binding creation, variable lookup, function application) occurs on the local evaluator.

In the second expression, the creation of bindings for a and b occurs on the local evaluator, while the remote special form directs the evaluation of the (+ a b) to be performed on the remote evaluator. The lexical environment, containing the local bindings for a and b, is transmitted along with the expression (+ a b) to the remote evaluator.

The evaluation of the third expression occurs similarly to the second, except that the evaluations of the expressions a and b (within the

(+ (local a) (local b)) expression) are performed back on the local host. Since + is already defined on the remote evaluator, this process is equivalent to a traditional remote procedure call (RPC), where the arguments (and not the actual function) are evaluated locally and then transmitted to a remote server for application.

3.2. New Functions, Special Variables, and Macros

As an extension, Avalon/Common Lisp provides one new data type, the **evaluator**, two new special variables, *remote-evaluator* and *local-evaluator*, and a small number of new special forms, the most important of which are remote and local. Intuitively, the two forms are used to translate the thread of computation from one evaluator to another, e.g., from the designated local evaluator to some remote evaluator. Below we give the meaning of each in the style of the Common Lisp manual [16].

make-evaluator *string*   [*Function*]

This function finds and returns the evaluator whose name is specified by the string argument. If none exists, it builds and returns a new evaluator object. Evaluators are *first-class* objects: one can store an evaluator away in other data structures, perform remote evaluations on it at some future time, and transmit them.

remote-evaluator   [*Variable*]

This special variable names the evaluator used to evaluate expressions of the form (remote *expr*). On an initiating evaluator, it is bound by default to the initiating evaluator itself until the user changes it to point to some other (remote) evaluator. On a remote evaluator, it is bound by default to the remote evaluator itself. If desired, the programmer can explicitly reset this binding dynamically.

local-evaluator   [*Variable*]

This special variable names the evaluator used to evaluate expressions of the form (local *expr*). In the case of an initiating evaluator, it is normally unbound. In the case of a remote evaluator, it is bound by default to the evaluator from which the remote was called. If desired, the programmer can explicitly reset this binding dynamically.

remote *expr* &optional *evaluator*   [*Macro*]

This special form's semantics is identical to identity except that: (1) The actual computation is performed by the evaluator bound to *remote-evaluator* (or to the evaluator specified as the optional argument) with the same lexical environment as the current evaluator, but a different current package and dynamic state; and (2) the object returned is a *copy* of the result, as opposed to the result object itself. Even in the case where the evaluator bound to `*remote-evaluator*` is specified to be or defaults to the current evaluator, a copy of the resulting object is returned.

Since the process for transmitting data from one evaluator to another necessitates creating copies of objects, mutable objects[2] are not eq to their remotely referenced analogues. This is the primary incompatibility introduced by the use of `remote` expressions in a program. Despite the loss of identity, we still preserve sharing of common substructures among transmitted objects, so that values that are comparable on one evaluator are still comparable on another. Hence, we have:

```
(let* ((a (the (not (or number symbol character))
               <arbitrary lisp object>))
       (b a))

  (eq a (remote a))                  ⟹ nil
  (remote (eq a (remote a)))         ⟹ nil

  (equalp a (remote a))              ⟹ t
  (remote (equalp a (remote a)))     ⟹ t

  (remote (eq a b))                  ⟹ t
  (eq (remote a) (remote b))         ⟹ unspecified
```

Here an object that is neither a number, symbol, nor character is locally bound to a and b. The first two comparisons return `nil` since the object bound to a and its copy are different objects, regardless of where the comparison is evaluated. The next two comparisons return t because the values of a's object and its copy are the same. The next comparison shows that remotely comparing the identities of a and b is identical to comparing them locally. Finally, the last comparison shows that while remote and local copies are not identical, the results of different `remote` calls to the same evaluator may return the same object.

local *expr*   [*Macro*]

This special form has meaning only when evaluated dynamically within a `remote` expression. Its semantics is identical to `identity` except that: (1) Computation occurs at the evaluator specified in `*local-evaluator*`; normally, this is the evaluator where the most dynamically immediate `remote` expression was evaluated; and (2) the object returned is a copy of the object, instead of the object itself.

---

[2]In Common Lisp, all objects, except for numbers, characters and symbols, are mutable.

Avalon/Common Lisp gives the programmer the flexibility to redirect the thread of computation, if desired, by using the optional parameter to `remote`, or by explicitly setting `*remote-evaluator*` to an evaluator different from the default. Hence, the user can make *third-party calls*, i.e., calls by one remote evaluator to another evaluator. Third-party calls would be common when one server calls another server on behalf of the original computation performed for the client. The calling evaluator is then defined to be the local evaluator and the third evaluator to be the remote evaluator. For example, in Figure 1, if E1 remotely calls E2 which then remotely calls E3, then E3's `*local evaluator*` is automatically set to E2 and its `*remote-evaluator*`, to E3.

Note that since special variables can be set dynamically, they need not reflect the call chain, though normally they would. In the previous scenario, for example, if E3's `*local-evaluator*` is explicitly reset to E1, then `local(...)` expressions would be evaluated at E1, not E2, even though E2 made the remote call to E3. Results are still returned to the evaluator that initiated the `remote` call; hence they would be returned to E2, not E1.

3.3. Abstract Interpreter

Figure 2 shows a simplified abstract interpreter, giving a more formal semantics to the evaluation of the special forms, `remote` and `local`. It does not handle the case of preserving (remote) side effects on shared, mutable objects.

We first define a `dynamic-state` to include the (current) lexical environment, control-related tags and labels, and names of the local and remote evaluators. The lexical environment includes both local variable and local function bindings. We define an `evaluator` to be a name and a set of packages.

To see what `eval` does, we first explain what the helping function `handle-remote` does. It takes four arguments: the expression being evaluated; a dynamic state that includes some lexical environment; and two evaluators, one to indicate where `local` expressions are to be evaluated and one to indicate where `remote` expressions are to be evaluated. A new dynamic state is created and used as the state in which the argument expression is evaluated. The `deep-copy` function preserves internal sharing of objects. It is similar to the `read` of a `print` on printable Common Lisp objects. The recursive calls to `eval` and `deep-copy` ensure that expressions with nested `remote`'s and `local`'s are handled properly.

The `eval` function itself takes three arguments, the expression being evaluated, a dynamic state that includes some lexical environment, and an evaluator. If the expression to be evaluated is a `remote` then first a check is made to see if a specific evaluator is bound to the optional argument in the `remote` call; if not, then the

```
(defstruct dynamic-state
  lexical-env
  catch-tags
  labels
  local-evalr
  remote-evalr
  )

(defstruct evaluator
  name
  packages
  )

(defun eval (expr state evalr)
  (case expr
         ;; other cases ...

         (remote
           (handle-remote (remote-body expr)
                          state evalr
                          (or (remote-evalr expr)
                              (dynamic-state-remote-evalr evalr))))
         (local
           (handle-remote (remote-body expr)
                          state evalr
                          (dynamic-state-local-evalr evalr)))))

(defun handle-remote (expr state oevalr nevalr)
  (deep-copy
    (eval
      expr
      (make-dynamic-state
        :lexical-env  (deep-copy (dynamic-state-lexical-env state))
        :catch-tags   (dynamic-state-catch-tags state)
        :labels       (dynamic-state-labels state)
        :local-evalr  oevalr
        :remote-evalr nevalr
        )
      nevalr)))
```

Figure 2: Abstract Interpreter for Handling Remote Evaluation

remote evaluator bound in the dynamic state is passed as the new remote evaluator to `handle-remote`. Handling a `local` is simpler; the local evaluator bound in the dynamic state is passed as the new remote evaluator to `handle-remote`.

3.4. More Examples

The environment passed as part of a `remote` call does not include the Common Lisp "special" (global) bindings. In the following example:

```
(defvar a 123)
(let ((b 45))
    (remote (+ (local a) b)))
```

an explicit call *back* to the initiating evaluator (using `local`) is required in order to ensure that the special value of a is retrieved; otherwise, the global binding of a on the remote evaluator would be used. Note that the default binding of `*local-evaluator*` will cause `local` to direct a computation back to its originating evaluator.

Since one of Avalon's design goals is to minimize interference with the target language's semantics, nearly all Common Lisp expressions can be "wrapped in" a `remote` to give the desired and expected effects. The lambda expression below is transmitted to the remote evaluator along with its argument for evaluation, illustrating that even procedural objects are permissible within `remote` expressions:

```
(remote ((lambda (x) (* x x)) 4))
```

We also support the remote application of recursively defined functions such as:

```
(labels ((fact (n) (if (< n 2)
                       1 (* n (fact (- n 1)))))))
  (remote (fact 20)))
```

since the current lexical environment is transmitted along with the expression. During the evaluation of the above code, the recursive function `fact`, bound in the lexical environment, is applied to 20 on the remote evaluator, and the result is transmitted back to the local evaluator.

The effects of mutating operations in the lexical environment are preserved across evaluator boundaries. For example, the following returns 10:

```
(let ((a 5))
  (remote (setq a 10))
  a)
```

We also handle exits, both local and dynamic, transparently. The result below will be 12, just as if the `remote` call had never existed:

```
(block tag
  (remote (+ 9 (return-from tag 12))))
```

Likewise with the following, the result is also 12:

```
(progn
  (remote (defun add9 (x)
              (+ x (throw 'foo 12))))
  (catch 'foo (remote (add9 1))))
```

3.5. Transmission of Objects

Avalon/Common Lisp supports transmission of all Common Lisp readable types. A type is *readable* if all its instances can be created through the Common Lisp reader using the type's default print representation. Some examples of readable types include `simple-arrays`, `lists`, and `structs`. Most readable types are trivially transmissible since from one evaluator we simply pass an object's print representation and at the other evaluator we reconstitute a copy of the object using the built-in `read` function. We also support transmission of some non-readable Common Lisp types like `functions` and `hash tables`. For a more complex type, like object classes, users would need to define their own *marshall* function, which traverses an object's abstract representation and creates a transmissible version, and *unmarshall* function, which reverses that mapping.

As an optimization, we plan to add to our current implementation support for both partial transmission of large objects and transmission of partially evaluated objects. For large readable objects, such as a complex network of `structs`, we would not copy and transmit the entire object but just its root and its descendants up to *n*-levels deep, where *n* is user-definable. Hence transmitted objects might include *remote references*, i.e., names of objects that reside remotely. Currently our support for partial transmission of large objects is limited to only immutable `structs`. Finally, for conceptually infinite objects akin to *streams* in Scheme [1], we need transmit only a partial evaluation of their values.

4. Extended Client/Server Model

The client/server model is a common paradigm for distributed computing, especially in systems based on remote procedure call. By introducing remote evaluation into Avalon/Common Lisp we can extend this model in useful and powerful ways. In this section, we explore these extensions, by presenting several models of how distributed programs may be structured in Avalon/Common Lisp .

In the traditional client/server model, the RPC interface serves two purposes. It defines both the calling interface between a client and server and the boundary along which a computation is distributed. The caller (client) is also the initiator process of some computation; the callee (server) is also some initiated process executing on behalf of the caller.

Avalon/Common Lisp separates these two functions. We use the terms *client* and *server* to distinguish between the caller and callee. This client/server distinction defines the interface between the facilities provided by the server programmer, and those provided by the client programmer, just as is true for interfaces in non-distributed programs. We use the terms *local* and *remote* to distinguish between the initiator and initiated processes, i.e., evaluators, of a distributed computation. The local/remote distinction serves to define the boundary along which a computation is distributed. A computation is local if it is performed at the evaluator initiating the computation, while it is remote if it occurs at some evaluator different from the initiator. Remote evaluation is the mechanism by which Avalon/Common Lisp expresses this change in computational locus.

In what follows, we suggest alternative ways to organize the remote and local aspects of client and server interfaces, ranging from traditional RPC to a scheme where both the client and the server do computation both remotely and locally.

As a motivating example, we consider a simple distributed database of bibliography entries such as that used for Scribe or LaTex .bib files. We assume that the user of the database is computing on some local site, e.g., a personal workstation, while the database itself resides on some remote site. The database interface consists of set operations like `intersection` and `union`; a `matches` function that takes as input a query and returns a set of matching bibliography entries; and a `print-bib-entrys` function that takes as input a set of bibliography entries and returns its print representation. Thus, a typical bibliography database user might write:

```
(print-bib-entrys
  (union
    (matches author-named-Edsger)
    (matches author-named-Butler)))
```

to print all the database entries authored by people named Edsger or Butler.

The Traditional Client/Server Model

To get the effects of RPC as used in the traditional client/server model in Avalon/Common Lisp, we simply put a `remote` around the outermost function call. If the database, the set operations, and the printing and matching functions all reside remotely, then the following code fragment shows how our original single-site query would be expressed:

```
(remote
  (print-bib-entrys
    (union
      (matches author-named-Edsger)
      (matches author-named-Butler))))
```

The Extensible Server Model

In Avalon/Common Lisp, a client can extend a server's interface by transmitting function definitions to the server and can then execute them remotely. In our example, the client first uses a remote `defun` to define a more complicated match function:

```
(remote
  (defun match-Edsgers-or-Butlers ()
    (union
      (matches author-named-Edsger)
      (matches author-named-Butler))))
```

The client executes the following code locally, which evaluates the newly defined function remotely:

```
(remote
  (print-bib-entrys (match-Edsgers-or-Butlers)))
```

A client would normally make multiple remote definitions at one time, perhaps as part of its initialization code. There are several advantages to providing extensible servers. The client programmer gains flexibility by tailoring the server interface to the needs of his or her application. Concrete examples of software with extensible interfaces are Emacs and Postscript [26]. The programmer also can greatly enhance the application's performance by allowing a complex computation to take place near the resource it is manipulating. For example, NeWS [13], an extensible windowing system, can support the smooth rubber-banding of spline curves, while X [20], which essentially uses the standard RPC paradigm, has difficulty smoothly rubber-banding even straight lines.

The Hidden Distribution Model

By permitting some or all server code to run locally, that is, at the local evaluator, Avalon/Common Lisp allows clients to be completely unaware of the distributed nature of a computation. Server writers are free to hide some or all of the distributed aspects of the program from a client. In the most extreme case, the client may never even know that it is using a distributed service.

In the hidden distribution model, our example looks as follows. On the local side, the server writer makes the following definitions (we define macros instead of functions to suppress one level of evaluation):

```
(defmacro matches (query)
  `(remote (matches ,query)))
(defmacro union (setA setB)
  `(remote (union ,setA ,setB)))

(defmacro print-bib-entrys (db)
  `(remote (print-bib-entrys ,db)))
```

The client code is the same as for the non-distributed case:

```
(print-bib-entrys
  (union
    (matches author-named-Edsger)
    (matches author-named-Butler)))
```

Here, when the client calls the three functions provided in the local side of the server code, the server makes the explicit remote calls to the remote side of the server code.

The Full Model

The full model allows both the client and the server to compute both at the local and the remote evaluators. Figure 3 depicts this situation where again, the dotted lines indicate possible call paths. Support for this generality is useful if we want both the ability to perform complex client computations at the remote site, and to allow the server to hide key aspects of the distributed computation, such as caching.

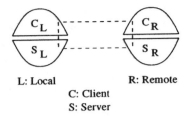

L: Local   R: Remote
C: Client
S: Server

Figure 3: The Full Extended Client/Server Model of Distributed Evaluators

To illustrate both of these capabilities, suppose the server writer implements the `matches` and `union` functions to manipulate the database entries using some compact, but incomplete representation of each entry, while `print-bib-entrys` must have the entire entry before printing it. Caching the complete entries at the local site prevents them from being repeatedly shipped from evaluator to evaluator (i.e., remote to local) while hiding this caching in the server interface allows the client to ignore the complications introduced by the cache.

For our example, on the local side, the server writer makes the following definitions:

```
(defun print-bib-entrys (s)
  (set-map #'print-db-entry s))
(defun print-db-entry (set-entry)
  (unless (value-cached-p set-entry)
    (add-to-cache (get-remote-object set-entry)))
  (print-entry (cached-value set-entry)))
```

The client makes the following remote definition (as before in the Extensible Server Model):

```
(remote
  (defun match-Edsgers-or-Butlers ()
    (union
      (matches author-named-Edsger)
      (matches author-named-Butler))))
```

The client executes it:

```
(print-bib-entrys (remote
                   (match-Edsgers-or-Butlers)))
```

The reader should compare the above call to that used in the Extensible Server Model.

The above example illustrates what would commonly be done for querying a large database. In general, application programmers need the ability to write *split queries*, where part of the query is performed remotely through a server interface, and part performed locally through client code. A typical query might be split into a *search predicate* executed remotely and a *filter predicate* executed locally. For example, the search predicate might return a stream of bibliography entries to the client who might then further filter out every fifth entry.

5. Persistence

In this section we show how Avalon/Common Lisp supports failure atomicity through the `with-transaction` construct and persistence through declarations of persistent bindings. We first illustrate these features by showing the relevant pieces of the package for the bibliography database server.

5.1. Example Uses of Extensions

Here we make the database's binding persistent and initialize it:

```
(defpersistent $bib-database$
               (make-persistent (empty-set)))
```

By convention, we use the "$" characters to distinguish those symbols used for persistent bindings from those used for volatile ones. `Make-persistent` creates a recoverable object; `defpersistent` defines $bib-database$ as a special symbol whose binding is recoverable, and creates a binding between $bib-database$ and the recoverable empty set.

We use transactions for standard database operations such as adding, modifying, and deleting entries. Consider the function for adding a bibliography entry:

```
(defun add-bib-entry (entry)
  (with-transaction
    (if (valid-bib-entry-p entry)
        (adjoin $bib-database$
                (make-persistent entry))
        (abort-transaction 'invalid-bib-entry))))
```

If the entry is valid, i.e., well-formed and not already in the database, then we make the volatile value of the `entry` argument persistent and add it to the database. Otherwise, we abort the transaction signalling the abort condition `invalid-bib-entry`. Since the update is done within a transaction, if a crash occurs during the update, the state of the bibliography database will be as if the update never occurred; Camelot's recovery algorithm will guarantee the database is restored to a previously saved consistent state.

The counterpart to `make-persistent` is `make-volatile`. Since an evaluator communicates with a recoverable store, retrieving a persistent binding from it gives us a handle on a recoverable object. Upon retrieval, we are free to continue to use the object as a recoverable object until we need to either call a standard Common Lisp function or transmit the object back to the local evaluator. Thus as a server writer, we have some latitude as to when to make the `make-volatile` call. For example, both `print-bib-entrys` below have the same eventual effect:

```
(defun print-bib-entrys ()
  (set-mapc #'(lambda (set-entry)
                 (print-bib-entry
                    (make-volatile set-entry)))
             $bib-database$))

(defun print-bib-entrys ()
  (set-mapc #'print-bib-entry
               (make-volatile $bib-database$)))
```

In the first version, `set-mapc` operates on a persistent set (and uses `rec-car`, `rec-cdr`, etc. to traverse the $bib-database$[3]). In the second, `set-mapc` operates on a volatile object. `Make-persistent` and `make-volatile` are each idempotent and are inverses of each other.

Avalon/Common Lisp currently supports recoverable versions of a large subset of Common Lisp's built-in types, e.g., `fixnum`, `list`, `simple-string`, `simple-vector`, as well as any type constructed using `struct`'s.

5.2. New Macros and Functions

Here is the programmer's interface to the new macros and functions:

`defpersistent` *variable* [*initial-value*]   [*Macro*]

This form is similar to the `defvar` form, except that any binding to *variable* is recoverable, i.e., survives crashes and supports failure atomicity. If given, *initial-value* is assigned to *variable*, as long as

variable has not previously been bound. *Initial-value* must evaluate to a recoverable object and is only evaluated if it is used to initialize the binding.

All subsequent `setq` operations to *variable* will change the binding atomically; `setq` operations to persistent variables can be aborted if evaluated within a transaction.

`make-persistent` *object*   [*Function*]
`make-volatile` *object*   [*Function*]

These functions create a persistent (volatile) representation of *object*. If *object* is already persistent (volatile), it is returned as the result.

`with-transaction` *body*   [*Macro*]
`with-top-level-transaction` *body*   [*Macro*]

Both forms initiate a new transaction and evaluate *body*. `With-transaction`, if evaluated dynamically within another transaction, will begin a nested transaction; otherwise it starts a top-level transaction. `With-top-level-transaction` always initiates a new top-level transaction. Both forms return a mutiple value consisting of a status signifying whether or not the transaction committed, and the result of the last expression in *body*.

Normal evaluation of either form results in a committed transaction. Exceptional exits from the *body* (via `catch`/`throw` and local exits) result in the transaction aborting. Transactions can also be explicitly aborted via use of `abort-transaction`.

`abort-transaction` *retval* &optional `top-level`[*Macro*]

This form aborts the currently executing transaction. If the optional argument is nil (the default), the innermost dynamically nested transaction is aborted and the value of *retval* is returned as the status in the multiple-value result of `with-transaction`. Otherwise, the current (dynamically scoped) top-level transaction is aborted.

6. Related Work and Discussion

Our work on remote evaluation is closest in spirit to Stamos's Ph.D. work [23] for which he designed extensions to the programming language CLU to support remote evaluation in the context of atomic transactions. Since the target languages differ, so do our concrete designs. We designed and packaged our language extensions in a way that avoids modifying the compiler and instead exploits the interpretative programming style of Common Lisp. Since CLU is a compile-time (strongly) typed language, Stamos defines static checks

---

[3]Avalon/Common Lisp supports "recoverable" versions of some standard Lisp functions like `car`, `cdr`, `eq`, `eql`, etc. They operate on objects retrieved from recoverable store, rather than normal non-recoverable Lisp objects.

that must be performed to ensure a remote evaluation request is valid. Client extensions to servers and code arguments further complicate both these checks and the compiler's subsequent encoding of a remote evaluation request. We avoid some of these difficulties since our new **evaluator** data type gives us not only a run-time boundary (each is a process), but a compile-time boundary (each defines a global namespace for a set of packages).

Our extensions to the client/server model are similar to that supported by Falcone's Heterogeneous Distributed System architecture, prototyped at DEC [10]. Falcone focuses on support at the operating-system level, rather than at the programming-language level, though he does provide a small Lisp-like language interface to the system facilities. By our extending Common Lisp rather than defining a new language, we have the advantage of completely integrating our extensions with an existing, familiar, and widely-available programming language. Also, Falcone handles only primitive data types such as lists and byte vectors, and does not address persistent and recoverable storage of data.

Avalon/Common Lisp is distinct from other distributed programming languages such as CSP [15], SR [2], Linda [12], Nil [24], and Ada [19], since we have direct support not only for remote evaluation, but for transactions, and in particular the following features: commit and abort processing, crash recovery, atomic objects, and management of persistent data.

Even though Avalon/Common Lisp lacks light-weight processes, there are some similarities between it and other "concurrent Lisp" efforts such as Qlisp [11] and Multilisp [11], both of which support concurrent computation using light-weight, shared-memory processes. Qlisp's *qlambda* construct creates a closure and a process that will be used to evaluate any future application of the closure. Like qlambda instances, Avalon/Common Lisp's evaluators are each identified with a separate process. The lexical environment inherited in a `remote` call could be passed to a Qlisp process as an argument, and the evaluator-specific global environment could be simulated using the environment of the qlambda's closure. Avalon/Common Lisp's `remote` construct is also similar to Multilisp's *future* construct. Both allow the programmer to dispatch arbitrary forms to another process for evaluation. A key difference is that Multilisp's processes, being light-weight, are created on-demand, while the evaluators in Avalon/Common Lisp are heavy-weight, and, therefore, long-lived.

Transactions themselves have been a primary focus in both distributed and centralized data bases ([3], [8], [14], [9]). Several research projects have chosen transactions as the foundation for constructing reliable general-purpose distributed programs, including Argus [17], Arjuna [7], Clouds [18], TABS [22], and Camelot [21]. Of these projects, however, only Argus and Arjuna have addressed the linguistic aspects of the problem. Argus extends CLU and Arjuna

extends C++. None of these projects have direct support for remote evaluation or our extended client/server model.

Avalon/C++ and Avalon/Common Lisp differ in significant ways even though they address the same application domain, reliable distributed computing, and are motivated by the need to provide programming level support for transactions. Avalon/C++'s primary design focus was on user-defined atomic data types, in particular, support for *hybrid atomicity*. Programmers can define (hybrid atomic) objects that provide higher degrees of concurrency than that provided by using standard two-phase read/write locks, such as that used for Avalon/Common Lisp. In contrast, Avalon/Common Lisp's primary design focus is on remote evaluation and support for a client/server model more general and flexible than the traditional one such as that used for Avalon/C++. Thus, Avalon/Common Lisp relies on well-known techniques for dealing with serializability (read/write locks) and persistence (write-ahead logging, recoverable virtual memory), but introduces a new model for distributed computing.

Currently, all Avalon software runs on IBM RT's in the Mach and Camelot environments. Avalon/C++ runs on Sun's and Vaxes as well. Avalon/C++ has been operational for a year and we are not doing any further design or implementation work with it.

Avalon/Common Lisp is nearly complete as of this writing. All Avalon/Common Lisp code presented in this paper runs. Besides the bibliography database, other Avalon/Common Lisp examples include a simple array server and a factory-parts database. Further details on the Avalon/Common Lisp programmer's interface are in [4].

In summary, Avalon is a set of linguistic constructs that extend the capability of existing programming languages by directly supporting transactions. For each of our target languages, C++ and Common Lisp, we designed our extensions to be unintrusive and modular. For example, a Common Lisp programmer can load one set of packages if support for only remote evaluation is desired, a different set if support for only recoverable store is desired, or both sets if both features are desired. These language extensions relieve users from the burden of doing low-level system activities such as locking and managing stable storage, and instead allow them to concentrate on the logic required of their application. At the same time, however, they are given enough flexibility to exploit the semantics of their applications to increase their programs' reliability and efficiency.

Acknowledgments

We thank Gene Rollins who has helped motivate some of the design of Avalon/Common Lisp through his willingness to be our first user. He and Karen Kietzke also gave useful comments on earlier drafts of this paper.

We also thank Dave McDonald for providing us with a barebones Common Lisp interface to Camelot's recoverable storage manager, and Alfred Spector and the rest of the former Camelot crew for providing us with basic run-time support.

This research was sponsored by the Defense Advanced Research Projects Agency (DOD), ARPA Order No. 4976, monitored by the Air Force Avionics Laboratory Under Contract No. F33615-87-C-1499. Additional support was provided in part for J.M. Wing by the National Science Foundation under grant CCR-8620027 and for S.M. Clamen by the Office for Naval Research under grant ONR-N00014-88-12-0641.

The views and conclusions contained in this document are those of the authors and should not be interpreted as representing the official policies, either expressed or implied, of the Defense Advanced Research Projects Agency, the National Science Foundation, the Office for Naval Research or the U.S. Government.

References

[1] H. Abelson and G.J. Sussman with J. Sussman. *Structure and Interpretation of Computer Programs*. MIT Press, Cambridge, MA, 1985.

[2] G.R. Andrews. Synchronizing resources. *ACM Transactions on Programming Languages and Systems*, 3(4):405–430, October 1981.

[3] P.A. Bernstein and N. Goodman. A survey of techniques for synchronization and recovery in decentralized computer systems. *ACM Computing Surveys*, 13(2):185–222, June 1981.

[4] S.M. Clamen, L.D. Leibengood, S.M. Nettles, and J.M. Wing. The avalon/common lisp programmer's guide. 1989. Avalon Design Note 14.

[5] Eric C. Cooper and Richard P. Draves. *C Threads*. Technical Report CMU-CS-88-154, Computer Science Department, Carnegie Mellon University, June 1988.

[6] D.L. Detlefs, M.P. Herlihy, and J.M. Wing. Inheritance of synchronization and recovery properties in avalonc++. *IEEE Computer*, 57–69, December 1988.

[7] G. Dixon and S.K. Shrivastava. Exploiting type inheritance facilities to implement recoverability in object based systems. In *Proceedings of the Sixth IEEE Symposium on Reliability in Distributed Software and Database Systems*, 1987.

[8] K.P. Eswaran, J.N. Gray, R.A. Lorie, and I.L. Traiger. The notion of consistency and predicate locks in a database system. *Communications ACM*, 19(11):624–633, November 1976.

[9] B.G. Lindsay et al. *Notes on Distributed Databases*. Technical Report RJ2571, IBM San Jose Research Laboratory, July 1979.

[10] J.R. Falcone. A programmable interface language for heterogeneous distributed systems. *ACM Transactions on Computer Systems*, 5(4), November 1987.

[11] R. P. Gabriel and J. McCarthy. Queue-based multi-processing lisp. In *ACM Symposium on Lisp and Functional Programming*, pages 25–44, August 1984.

[12] D. Gelernter. Generative communication in linda. *ACM Transactions on Programming Languages and Systems*, 7(1):80–112, January 1985.

[13] J. Gosling, D.S.H. Rosenthal, and M. J. Arden. *The NeWS Book: An Introduction to the Networked Extensible Window System*. Springer-Verlag, 1989.

[14] J.N. Gray. *Notes on Database Operating Systems*, pages 393–481. Springer-Verlag, Berlin, 1978.

[15] C.A.R. Hoare. Communicating sequential processes. *Communications of the ACM*, 21(8):666–677, August 1978.

[16] G. Steele Jr. *Common LISP*. Digital Press, 1984.

[17] B. Liskov and R. Scheifler. Guardians and actions: linguistic support for robust, distributed programs. *Transactions on Programming Languages and Systems*, 5(3):381–404, July 1983.

[18] M.S. McKendry. Clouds: a fault-tolerant distributed operating system. *IEEE Tech. Com. Distributed Processing Newsletter*, 2(6), June 1984.

[19] Dept. of Defense. Reference manual for the ada programming language. 1983. ANSI/MIL-STD-1815A-1983.

[20] R.W. Scheifler and J. Gettys. The x window system. *ACM Transactions on Graphics*, 5(2), April 1986.

[21] A.Z. Spector, J.J. Bloch, D.S. Daniels, R.P. Draves, D. Duchamp, J.L. Eppinger, S.G. Menees, and D.S. Thompson. The camelot project. *Database Engineering*, 9(4), December 1986. Also available as Technical Report CMU-CS-86-166, Carnegie Mellon University, November 1986.

[22] A.Z. Spector, J. Butcher, D.S. Daniels, J.L. Eppinger D.J. Duchamp, C.E. Fineman, A. Heddaya, and P.M. Schwarz. Support for distributed transactions in the tabs prototype. *IEEE Transactions on Software Engineering*, 11(6):520–530, June 1985.

[23] J.W. Stamos. *Remote Evaluation*. Technical Report 354, MIT Labxooratory for Computer Science, January 1986.

[24] R.E. Strom and S. Yemini. Nil: an integrated language and system for distributed programming. In *SIGPLAN '83 Symposium on Programming Language Issues in Software Systems*, June 1983. Also an IBM research report (RC 9499 (44100)) from April 1983.

[25] B. Stroustrup. *The C++ Programming Language*. Addison Wesley, 1986.

[26] Adobe Systems. *Postscript Language Reference Manual*. Addison-Wesley, 1985.

Using Languages for Capture, Analysis and Display of Performance Information for Parallel and Distributed Applications

Carol Kilpatrick   Karsten Schwan

School of Information and Computer Science
Georgia Institute of Technology
Atlanta, GA

David Ogle

IBM
B673/F93
Research Triangle Park, NC

Abstract

A graphical performance display tool can offer insights into the nature of a program's performance that would be difficult, and sometimes impossible, to achieve with a traditional textual view of performance activity. We offer two languages with which programmers can specify the collection and the display of performance information about parallel and distributed application programs.

Introduction

The programming of parallel machines remains ill-understood, in part because the attainment of high performance is the 'raison d'etre' for parallelism. Namely, a parallel program is not 'complete' until its performance has been optimized. Therefore, any system for parallel programming must offer support for program performance improvement[10]. Part of such support is the collection, analysis, and presentation of information about program performance[11,8].

This paper describes a system for the graphical presentation of program performance information. Our approach differs from previous work in several ways:

- *Hierarchical views of performance information* – the system allows the graphical and textual presentation of multiple views[9] of the target application, ranging from low-level views directly mapped to the executing program to higher level abstract views based on user-defined program performance models. Multiple, hierarchical views are supported because programmers typically need to consider many different attributes of their parallel applications when improving their performance. The use of graphics is motivated by the large amounts of program

information collected for large-scale parallel application programs. It is difficult and sometimes impossible to view such information textually.

- *Real-time viewing* – the information required for graphical views is collected, analyzed, and filtered[11] in real-time, during program execution. View presentation can be dynamic and in real-time or static, after program execution. Dynamic view presentation is useful for the on-line improvement of program performance, which requires that timing constraints attached to monitoring activities guarantee bounds on the 'age' of the presented information.

- *Uniform information model* – the specification, collection, analysis, and presentation of monitoring information is based on a uniform and high-level information model[10,11], which is an extension of the entity-relationship model. In addition to providing a uniform base, the model also offers powerful operations for the manipulation of large amounts of monitoring information[12].

- *Tool integration* – the information model is also the basis for the integration of monitoring into a system for parallel programming[10], containing program construction tools, hardware information, and runtime system support.

Problem Description and Solution

The generation of graphical displays of performance information requires the monitoring of the program's execution and the display of such information. This requires that a user must (1) specify what to monitor and (2) describe how to display the monitored information. These are two separate concerns and so we offer two languages:

1. the *view language* is used to specify what to monitor, i.e., what information the monitor is to collect, analyze, and store as the program executes, and

2. the *display language* is used to specify how to display monitored (*view*) information.

While the view and display languages clearly address separate concerns, it is not reasonable to expect programmers to master several languages in order to solve a single problem (i.e., to specify and display monitoring information). Our solution to this issue is to define both languages using a single base model, an entity-relationship model that is extended to include sets, called an E-R-S model. The model is used to capture all program and monitoring information of interest to the user. Since both the view and display languages manipulate information in terms of this model, they differ only in the specific manipulations offered by each.

In contrast to other research in program monitoring[6], we are primarily concerned with the evaluation of program performance. This implies that the base model must capture attributes of both the program to be evaluated and the program's execution environment (e.g., target hardware configuration). Therefore, the base model is not simply a mirror image of the target program. Instead, it is an E-R-S abstraction of the program and of all other information of interest to the user. We use an active E-R-S database to store and manipulate information described with the model[10]. Such information includes program views to be monitored, views of the target hardware, display mappings (generated by the display language), display object definitions, and display frames. The database is shared by all tool components of the parallel programming system and thus, acts as the integrating agent. The two tools discussed in this paper are the real-time monitor and the display tool. Both interact via the database, as well.

Before discussing the languages used for display and monitoring specification, we present a brief overview of their use, their relationships to each other, and their roles in a parallel programming system (see Figure 1).

As stated above, we specify monitoring in terms of an abstraction of the target program using the E-R-S model. This abstraction captures what *can be* monitored; it is created by the program construction system and the programmer through specification of the *entities* of the program (typically generated by the program construction system) and the *attributes* of those entities of interest to the programmer (typically mapped to specific program variables). Attribute specification is performed with an *attribute language* developed by Ogle in his Ph.D. thesis[8] and derived from the work of Snodgrass[11]. A *basic entity* in our previous and current work on parallel pro-

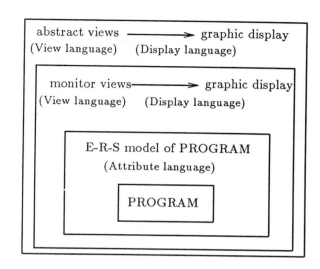

Figure 1: program and program execution information

gramming environments is the E-R-S abstraction for an *object* within the target program. In a distributed Unix system, such an entity might be mapped to a *process*[8,7].

In addition to basic entities and attributes, certain *relationships* between basic entities and *sets* of basic entities (or relationships) are of interest. A sample relationship is the 'communicates with' relationship in a Unix system that describes all processes that are able to communicate with each other (using standard Unix communication primitives). A sample set of interest might be all processes located on the same workstation.

The specification of what to monitor (i.e., the program views to monitor) is performed with *monitor views* stated with the *view language*, using the entities, relationships, and sets defined earlier. Thus, monitor views are based on program abstractions rather than language or implementation dependent program variables and need not be mapped directly to the program. The advantage of this approach is that anything represented in the database can be monitored, including the database's representation of the various tools of the programming system.

Once monitor views have been stated, *abstract views* specified with the view language are used to: (1) filter monitor view information; (2) combine several views, possibly with the intent to express similarities between different low-level views; and (3) create new views based on timing relationships between underlying monitor views.

The graphical representation of views defined with

the view language is specified with the *display language*. This language allows the user to map the view to a variety of displays including histograms, pie charts, dials, and graphs as well as displays tailored for particular performance models, such as a queueing model. Graphics are defined on a per view basis, resulting in a hierarchy of displays that show views of performance activity at various levels of abstraction.

The last step before program execution is to compile both view and display definitions. As part of the compilation process, all view and display definitions are stored in the database. In addition, collection code is generated during view compilation and is used to instrument the target application. Such code is inserted into the program by the user.

Finally, as the program executes, the *display tool* is used to turn views on and off (i.e., to control monitoring), to turn displays on and off, and to control the displays (e.g., speed, direction and for a particular abstract view, visibility of its various underlying component views).

The three languages, the *attribute language*, the *view language*, and the *display language* allow a user to build a hierarchy of abstractions concerning the target program. Our current focus is on graphical abstractions related to the **performance** of parallel application programs.

System description

The prototype system, consists of a central monitor and display tool, and of local monitors that reside on each node of the distributed and parallel target architecture. The current version of the monitoring system is derived from work performed at Ohio State[8] and executes on the network of SUN workstations; it is now being extended to operate efficiently on two parallel machines, a Sequent Symmetry and a BBN Butterfly.

A first prototype of the programming environment depicted in Figure 2 was completed Spring 1988 at Ohio State. A new system targeting multiple parallel architectures is now being constructed for object and threads-based parallel programs. This system has the following components: a program construction system (PCS); a monitoring system; a display tool; and loader/operating system components on each target machine (e.g., threads packages on the BBN Butterfly and the Sequent Symmetry). These components will be integrated through the database as shown in Figure 2:

- Program construction system (PCS) – it is used for program entry, editing, compiling, linking and loading.

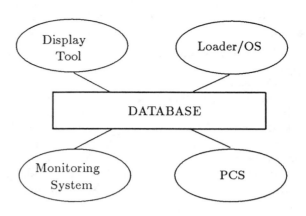

Figure 2: components of the programming environment

- Monitoring system – the monitoring system is responsible for collecting, analyzing, conveying, and storing dynamic program execution information.

- Display tool – it consists of a library of graphics routines and reusable display objects. It provides the user-interface through which the user (1) chooses what information the monitor collects during a particular execution and (2) controls the display of monitored information.

- "Database" – the database is an active E-R-S database that is used as a vehicle for tool integration. It also offers the view, display, and low-level access languages for manipulation of information based on the E-R-S model.

Related work

Our work on the graphical display of parallel program performance is primarily related to two research areas: (1) program visualization and (2) the monitoring of parallel and distributed programs.

Program visualization. Several program visualization/algorithm animation systems have been developed with the goal of showing dynamic properties of computer programs for sequential systems. These include Balsa[4], TANGO[13] and PV[3].

While none of these systems address issues in parallel program display, such work has made clear that any system for program display must offer capabilities such as the concurrent display of multiple program views, zooming, speed control, dynamic display editing, and default representations of typical views.

Monitoring. Two previous efforts in program monitoring are directly related to this research:

- Snodgrass' monitoring system for a target parallel architecture[11]; and

- Ogle's real-time monitoring system for distributed and parallel programs [8], which is based on Snodgrass' work.

Snodgrass provides a language for sensor specification, and a temporal query language, TQUEL[12] to specify what information is desired and therefore, what sensors to enable. Information collected by sensors is analyzed centrally, then entered into a temporal database, from which it is retrieved with TQUEL statements. In this fashion, TQUEL statements can ask about current, past, or future program events in a uniform fashion. Program display is performed after program execution. Ogle's work concerns the distribution of the information analysis performed for TQUEL-like statements across the multiple nodes of target distributed and parallel architectures[8]. In addition, Ogle is concerned with real-time monitoring, which requires the extension of TQUEL with specifications of (1) timing constraints and (2) target processes to be notified of the existence of new monitoring information.

We extend Ogle's work by adding: (1) abstract views; (2) the specification of display information; and (3) the implicit temporal attributes available in TQUEL.

The work by Bates and Wileden[1] in distributed debugging is also of interest. Somewhat similar in spirit to our view language, they provide an Event Description Language (EDL) to describe a hierarchy of event-based abstractions.

Sample Application

The application. The parallel quicksort algorithm[5] described below motivates our ideas concerning the graphical display of performance information. We choose parallel quicksort in part because of the algorithm's well-known interesting dynamic performance properties which include: (1) tradeoffs regarding the use of parallel vs. sequential sorting due to communication delays or contention effects[5]; (2) load balancing among multiple quicksort servers; and (3) contention on centralized algorithm components, such as queues, etc.

Our implementation is object-based, consisting of multiple instantiations of both a quicksort server object and a queue object and an array object. Each server object receives two indices defining a sub-array of the array to be sorted from the queue object, then acquires the corresponding sub-array from the array object (in a multiprocessor implementation, this would simply require accesses to the array stored in memory). Given the sub-array and depending on its size, the server either sorts it using some sequential sort algorithm or partitions it into smaller sub-arrays to be sorted in parallel. Therefore, this application consists of: (1) one or more array objects maintaining the array to be sorted; (2) one or more queue objects managing the index pairs that define unsorted sub-arrays; (3) multiple quicksort server objects performing the partitioning and the sequential sort. We assume that each quicksort server sequentially sorts its sub-array whenever the sub-array's size is less than the value of partitionTOsort, which is a local variable in the server. When the sub-array's size exceeds partitionTOsort, it is partitioned, the resulting two index pairs are returned to the queue object, and the corresponding sub-arrays are returned to the array object.

Performance measurements. Considering this implementation, programmers might be interested in the following seven performance measurements:

- for each object: (1) the number of accesses and (2) the total computation time;

- for the array object: (3) the number of elements in the array being sorted;

- for the queue object: (4) the current length of the queue of index pairs; and

- for the quicksort object: (5) the computation time per invocation; (6) the value of partitionTosort; and (7) the number of elements of the sub-array currently being processed.

To motivate the usefulness of these measures, consider a configuration of the parallel quicksort program consisting of a single array object, a single queue object, and multiple quicksort servers. Such a configuration might exhibit contention for the services of the single array and queue objects, leading to performance degradation. Such contention may be evaluated using the 'number of accesses' and 'total computation time' measurements of each object. Computation time will increase due to excessive waiting. Similarly, load imbalances may be detected with the 'queuelength' attribute of the queue object: an excessively long queue implies an insufficient number of servers or a value of partitionTosort that is too small.

Note that measurements like those listed above will be of use in most parallel applications, as is apparent from their use in queueing models that may evaluate 'service time' (i.e., the execution time per object invocation), 'wait time' (i.e., the time from an object's invocation to the completion of the operation), etc.

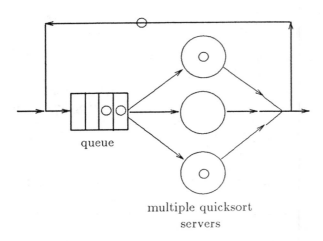

queue

multiple quicksort
servers

Figure 3: display of queueing model

Graphical display of performance. In our system, displays that depict performance measurements like those listed above may be fashioned using a 1-to-1 mapping of program attributes to well-known graphical objects like dials, dot charts, time graphs, or histograms, all of which are icons that may represent either finite or infinite numbers of states and are present in most modern program visualization systems. For example, we might graphically depict a histogram for the number of invocations of each quicksort object, or alternatively use a dial displaying the same information for each quicksort object, where each dial is positioned according to the object-processor map.

Our system provides not only the ability to display such 1-to-1 mappings, but also to display higher level descriptions of the same or of derived information. One example of such a description is a performance model. Such a model would first be described as a derived abstract view, then displayed by attachment of graphical views. An example performance model is a queueing model with attached display as shown in Figure 3. It is interesting to note that programmers routinely make use of performance models, which might range from naive models capturing desired relationships between objects (e.g., object A shouldn't issue more invocations to object B than are actually received by it) to complex models for performance analysis or performance prediction.

Next, we will show how such models and associated graphical displays are constructed with the three languages explained in the previous section.

The E-R-S Model and the Attribute Language

The E-R-S model is the basis for the user's concep-

tual model of the parallel application program and of the underlying system. Specifically, all program components and their interesting states are represented as basic entities (E-entities), relationships (R-entities), and sets of both (S-entities).

As mentioned previously, the *attribute language* is used for E-, R- and S-entity specification. For example, an E-entity that describes the interesting attributes of a single object of type queue in the sample parallel program would describe `invocationTime` and `size` (in the examples below, reserved words are capitalized and user-specified words are in mixed upper and lower case):

```
ATTRIBUTE DEF
FOR OBJECT  queue
    invocationTime: (exitInvocationTime -
                    beginInvocationTime);
    size:          q_size;
END ATTRIBUTE DEF
```

The application expressions, `q_size` and (`exitInvocationTime-beginInvocationTime`) are program variables that are mapped to the object attributes `invocationTime` and `size` respectively. These attributes (and any others defined for object queue) are compiled into an E-entity structure and provide the basis for the user's model of the target application object, queue. Similar definitions are made for all target application objects of interest.

Next, relationships between E-entities may be defined using R-entities. Relationship specific attributes may be defined, though we require these attributes be mapped to expressions involving attributes of the underlying relationship members. Consider the 'invocation' relationship named `quicksortINVOKESarray` between the objects quicksort and array with relationship specific attribute `frequency`:

```
RELATIONSHIP DEF  quicksortINVOKESarray
    RELATES quicksort TO array
END DEF

ATTRIBUTE DEF
FOR RELATIONSHIP quicksortINVOKESarray
    frequency:  quicksort.InvFreq_array;
END ATTRIBUTE DEF
```

Note that this implementation of the attribute frequency relies on the instrumentation of the invoker, the quicksort object, with the frequency count variable, `InvFreq_array`.

E- and R-entities can also be placed into sets, S-entities, for which set-specific attributes may again be defined. As with relationships, set specific attributes must be mapped to expressions involving attributes of the set members. For example, all binary relationships of invokers to invokees regarding the quicksort objects may be collected in the set named `setOFquicksortINVOKESarray`:

```
SET DEF setOFquicksortINVOKESarray
   CONTAINS quicksortINVOKESarray
END SET DEF
```

Monitoring and the View Language

The user-specified E-R-S model of the program is a static model – it is an abstraction built on top of the target code. For program monitoring, a temporal dimension has to be added[12]. Temporal statements are used to give instructions concerning what should be monitored when. Also, timing constraints are specified and associated with the ensuing data collection and analysis. The *view language* described in this section is provided for the specification of what to monitor and includes these temporal statements and timing constraints. However, prior to that description, we provide a brief description of the monitoring collection mechanisms our system uses.

Two collection mechanisms are used, called probes and sensors (see [8,11] for a detailed description of probes and sensors). Probes *sample* attribute values and do not execute synchronously with program execution. The monitor can probe the executing program at any time for an attribute value, which results in the return of the most recent value of that attribute. Sensors are used for *tracing*, since they are executed synchronously with the application program (sensors are physically located in the application code). Sensors transmit information to the monitor when executed.

Sensor code can be automatically inserted into a program for predefined program events, like procedure calls. Insertion is not easily automated for arbitrary program events[11]; it is performed by programmers.

Monitor views. We discuss two kinds of views, termed *monitor views* and *abstract views*.

Monitor views specify what can be monitored. They are compiled to collection code, to E-, R-, or S-entities and to code associated with those entities (action routines), such that the entities stored in the database are properly updated in response to the receipt of monitoring information. Each view specification includes: (1) the condition that makes the view active; (2) real-time timing constraints that may be used to determine the collection mechanisms (probes or sensors) to be used for collection and analysis

of the view's contents; (3) the action to take when the view becomes active, either **update** the database with the current view information or **notify** specified processes that the view is active; (4) references to the components of the target application stored in the database that are to be accessed when the view is active, i.e., the attributes (and therefore basic entities, relationships and sets) that capture the **state** associated with the view; and (5) temporal attributes that specify when the state information associated with the view is considered **valid**.

Views are defined in terms of the attributes of the entities, relationships, and sets that model the program. The following is an example of a monitor view specification for the sample sort application discussed previously:

```
VIEW DEF QueueLimitsExceeded
   ACTIVE CONDITION
      (queue[1].size > 24) and
         (queue[2].size > 24);
   CORRECT TO WITHIN (25 UNITS);
   NOTIFY (display_tool)
      WITHIN (876 UNITS);
   STATE
      queSize1: queue[1].size;
   VALID (INTERVAL)
END VIEW DEF
```

The ACTIVE CONDITION statement contains a boolean expression that specifies when to collect monitored information. A value of 'true' implies that the view is 'active' and state information is collected. The 'analysis' associated with monitoring is the determination of view 'activity' along with the computations required (if any) to compute STATE.

Errors are introduced in the results returned by the monitor because of the distribution of the target application and the monitor, due to the lack of a centralized clock and due to latencies associated with data transmissions between nodes. The CORRECT TO WITHIN statement provides a mechanism to allow the user to specify how correct results must be (see [8] for examples and a detailed description) – it is used to specify timing constraints for real-time monitoring and guides the monitor in making decisions about which collection mechanisms to use (sensors or probes) and how to route collected information to the database.

When a view changes state, possible actions are (1) UPDATE the database with the new monitored information and (2) NOTIFY specified processes that a view is active and pass each specified process the new view information. Again, because of the distributed nature of the program and the monitor, delays exist between the event occurrence and its reporting to a notified process. The NOTIFY command has a WITHIN clause that specifies how quickly a notified process needs information. The monitor uses this timing constraint to optimize monitoring[8].

The STATE statement includes named attributes that specify what target application information to collect and to associate with the view. When the view is active, the values of these expressions are returned through sensors and/or monitor probes and are stored as a new view instance in the database.

The VALID statement is used to associate temporal information with a view. We use ideas developed by Snodgrass in his work on historical databases and include in our views, the notion of temporal view types POINT in time and INTERVAL. During program execution, a timestamp is associated with each new view instance and is generated by the sensor (or monitor if view attributes are probed). POINT in time views consist of information that represents a state that is meaningful at a particular point in time, i.e., at time, t1, the timestamp associated with the view. An INTERVAL view consists of information that represents a state that is considered meaningful over an interval of time. For example, an interval view might become active at time t1. State information is collected and associated with the view instance. This state information is considered valid until time t2, when either (1) the view is no longer active or (2) the view is still active, but the state associated with the view changes and a new view instance is created. We use Snodgrass' notation and include the temporal attribute AT with a POINT in time view and the temporal attributes FROM and TO with an INTERVAL view. These temporal attributes specify when a view is to be considered active, i.e., when the state information is valid.

Temporal attributes provide a vehicle to build abstract views based on timing relationships between views. Also, like any of the other view attributes, temporal attribute values can drive some aspect(s) of a display.

In summary, given a view specification, the monitor (1) generates a database entity associated with the view and (2) determines the collection methods, tracing and/or sampling, to be used and then (3) automatically generates collection and analysis mechanisms. During execution, when a view becomes active, instances of these views are stored in a historical database.

Abstract views. View abstractions provide the mechanism for filtering and synthesizing monitor view information. Before giving an abstract view example, we note that our database is an active

database. An operation that modifies the information in the database can trigger procedures (action routines) that themselves either modify the database and/or send database information to particular processes. When new monitor view information is added to the database, action routines are triggered to update all associated abstract views.

Abstract views are built by relating underlying views through STATE attributes, temporal attributes, and the ACTIVE CONDITION associated with these views. For example, suppose we are interested in the sublist sizes that are processed by the various quicksort objects. We choose to look at a count of the number of "small", "medium" and "large" sublists that are processed for the set of all quicksort objects. We choose "small" as sublist length < partitionTOsort, i.e., when the quicksort object is doing the sequential sort on the sublist. Below, we give an abstract view specification named, Global_SmallPartition, that captures the information just described. First, however, we give the view specification for the underlying view, PartitionSize, (a monitor view). Each of the quicksort objects will be associated with a view of this type during program construction:

```
VIEW DEF PartitionSize
   CORRECT TO WITHIN (10) UNITS
   STATE
     Size: (quicksort.last_index -
            quicksort.start_index)+1
   VALID (POINT)
END DEF
```

When this view is compiled sensor code is generated and associated with the view. The user then instruments the quicksort object with this sensor code. Note that as no ACTIVE CONDITION statement is included, when the sensor code is executed, the ACTIVE CONDITION is implicitly met and the view becomes active.

The abstract view Global_SmallPartition is active when any monitor view of the type specified above is active. In order to reason about this set of views we define the following set of PartitionSize views:

```
SET DEF setOFPartitionSize
   CONTAINS PartitionSize
END DEF
```

The abstract view specification appears next. Note that the COMPUTE statement is a new construct not included with our discussion on monitor views.

```
VIEW DEF Global_SmallPartition
```

```
ACTIVE CONDITION
  <there exists i:
    PartitionSize[i].ACTIVE_CONDITION &
    (PartitionSize[i].Size <
        quicksort[i].partitionTOsort)>
NOTIFY (display_tool)
COMPUTE
    static int    small_cnt = 0;
    small_cnt = small_cnt + 1
STATE
    Small_Count : small_cnt
VALID AT PartitionSize[i].AT
END VIEW DEF
```

There is a `PartitionSize` view for each Quicksort object. The derived view, `Global_SmallPartition` is active when one of the `PartitionSize` views is active, say i, and when its (`Size < partitionTOsort`). The ACTIVE CONDITION is described in pseudocode, because the data manipulation language to be used with views is now being defined. Eventually, the ACTIVE CONDITION statement will be followed by a data manipulation program evaluating to a boolean value.

The CORRECT TO WITHIN statement is, in general, meaningless in an abstract view. Recall that with monitor views, this statement determines what collection mechanisms to generate. With abstract views, (in most cases) we automatically associate a correctness value – the maximum correctness value of the underlying views. The exception to this is when the ACTIVE CONDITION statement includes entity attributes that require monitor collection of the attribute value. In this case, a CORRECT TO WITHIN specification is appropriate.

The NOTIFY and STATE statements play the same role for abstract views as for the previously discussed monitor views.

Abstract views can have state associated with them for counting, averaging, etc. The COMPUTE statement includes variable declaration and code. Note that the scope of the COMPUTE variables includes the STATE statement.

Recall that for monitor views the time the view is to be considered valid is specified using either a VALID (POINT) or VALID (INTERVAL) statement. Abstract views are also either POINT in time or INTERVAL views. However, for abstract views, the time during which the view is considered valid must be explicitly stated. The user decides what temporal attributes make sense for the new view. S/he bases this decision on both the abstraction and the temporal attributes of the underlying views. Consider the following three VALID statement examples for abstract views:

1. VALID AT underlyingView1.AT;
2. VALID FROM underlyingView1.FROM
       TO underlyingView2.TO;
3. VALID FROM underlyingview2.FROM
       TO NEXT INSTANCE

The first is an example for a POINT in time view specification. The second is an example for an INTERVAL view specification. View instances are VALID over the interval specified with the FROM and TO attributes. The third is an example for an INTERVAL view specification. It is relevant when abstract views are generated in real-time through action routines and the TO endpoint is not yet known. It is VALID over the interval starting with the specified FROM attribute and ends at the same time as the FROM attribute of the next view instance (recall that we use a historical database to store view history and when a view changes state, a new view instance is created.)

If an abstract view is defined before program execution, action routines are generated and associated with the underlying views in the database. When new underlying view instances are added to the database, action routines are triggered that add new abstract view instances to the database. This means abstract views contain "traced" information from the underlying views.

If an abstract view is defined as the program executes, the view is compiled to a query on the database. In this case, underlying view values are "probed", i.e., the user must tell the monitor when and how often to build new abstract view instances. The display tool discussed in a later section is used to tell the monitor when to query the database, for example, periodically or for some time period.

Abstract views allow the user to ask questions on the fly, like "if this view is active, how about this?," i.e., the user can experiment and display the state of the objects from various perspectives when a particular view is

Views and the Display Language

View instances contain information about the state of the execution at particular points in time and/or over time intervals. In order to display this information, we associate each view of interest with a display object and then use the display language to map view information (attributes) to display object attributes.

Each display object consists of two parts: (1) graphics attributes and (2) a display-drawing routine. The attributes of a particular display object are modified according to a display map that establishes a relationship between a specified view and a display object. The display-drawing component is an active component, implemented as a database action routine[2] that includes code that draws on the screen. The code gets attribute values, performs computations and makes calls to the appropriate graphics routines in order to draw the desired display.

The structure of a display object is given next:

```
ATTRIBUTES
    graphic attributes
ACTION
    display drawing code
```

The structure and some of the semantics of the display language are similar to the view language:

```
DISPLAY MAP 3_bins
    RELATES VIEW        Small_Medium_Large
    TO GRAPHICAL OBJECT barChart1;
    DISPLAY LAG WITHIN  (25 UNITS);
    MAP
        background_color: red
        Nbars:            3
        bar[1].height:    small_cnt
        bar[2].height:    medium_cnt
        bar[3].height:    large_cnt
END DISPLAY DEF
```

This display is named 3_bins and specifies a relationship between the view Small_Medium_Large and the display object barChart1. Though not included in this example, an ACTIVE CONDITION statement can be included in a display map and provides a filter mechanism.

The DISPLAY LAG statement is the timing specification of interest for display that is analogous to the CORRECT TO WITHIN statement that is the timing specification of interest for views. For real-time display, the display lag statement specifies an acceptable amount of time the display may lag behind the program's execution. The correctness constraint values of the associated view along with upper bound timing estimates for rendering are used to predict whether or not the desired lag can be met. During execution, the number of views displayed concurrently will contribute to the actual display lag. The user can be notified that display lag constraints are not being met and s/he can adjust the number of visible views if desired.

The MAP statement is used to bind view attributes to display object attributes such as position, color, etc and is analogous to the STATE statement for views. In the example given above, the attributes on the left are a partial list of the display attributes for the

display object barChart1. Any bindings not specified are bound to default values in the object.

If the display map specification is made prior to program execution, action routines are generated to update the display object attributes when corresponding view attributes are updated. If specification is made during or after execution, the display tool must query the database to get needed view information.

Display Tool

The display tool is an interactive tool that provides the user interface between (1) the user and the monitor and (2) the user and the database.

The pre-compile-time, user-specified views and display maps define what information and displays can be generated during program execution. When a view is turned on, view information about that view is collected. With an abstract view, underlying view information is collected and database action routines are triggered that build the abstract views.

We propose three "viewing" modes that give the user control over what monitoring information to store and when to display monitored information:

1. Real-time display mode – real-time display mode is synchronous with the generation of low-level monitor views;

2. Collect view mode – in collect view mode, view information is collected and stored in the database. Display of these views at a later point during program execution or after program execution is then possible.

3. Historical display mode – in historical display mode, displays are turned on after information has been collected for the associated view (or its component lower level views).

The user also needs to control the rate at which a display changes, i.e., in continuous mode, from fast to slow or in single-step mode where the steps can be a frame at a time or at a larger granularity, with continuous update between steps.

In our current design, layout is done by the user. S/he positions a display on the screen and opens a window that determines size. For example, to display a dial showing *total compute time per invocation* for each of the queue objects, the user opens the appropriate display window for each object and may position all windows in a row. The user can also set display attributes (other than the position attributes which are set when the window is positioned), for example, background color or dial color.

In summary, the display tool is the interface between (1) the user and the monitor and (2) the user and the database of monitored information. It is an interactive tool that allows the user to view program execution information either in real-time or through historical queries to the database.

Conclusions and Future Work

This paper demonstrates the feasibility of a system for the graphical presentation of program performance information. More generally, we have demonstrated that visual environments for program information display may be developed within a uniform conceptual framework. The specific innovative attributes of our work are: (1) the ease of specification and presentation of multiple, graphical views concerning a single parallel program, ranging from low-level views directly mapped to the executing program to abstract views based on user-defined program performance models; (2) the efficient collection, analysis, and filtering of the information required for such graphical views during program execution, which permits the presentation of view information in real-time, as well; (3) the specification and presentation of monitoring information based on a uniform and high-level information model that offers powerful operations for the manipulation of large amounts of monitoring information; (4) the use of that information model for the integration of monitoring and display into a system for parallel programming[10]; and (5) the use of an information model to define three closely related languages for view specification and presentation, the *attribute language*, the *view language*, and the *display language*.

The current display language allows the user to create displays tailored for viewing the performance of various monitored application components. The next step is to use this monitored information as input to a variety of user-specified performance models. We see these performance models as abstract views. We plan to use and modify the current view language in order to offer a declarative framework for performance model specification. The performance model can then be mapped to a variety of displays. The user can turn the performance model on and off and watch the associated display along with any of the underlying input information (in the form of monitor or abstract views) used by the model.

Acknowledgements. Abhijit Chaudhari and Joubert Berger are responsible for the current monitor implementation at Georgia Tech. David Ogle is responsible for the work in real-time monitoring of parallel applications, which is one of the foundations of this work. Carol Kilpatrick is responsible for extending David Ogle's work to include abstract views, temporal specifications and the specification of display information. Nancy Griffeth was involved in the early stages of this work.

References

[1] Peter Bates and Jack C. Wileden. An approach to high-level debugging of distributed systems. *SIGPLAN Notices*, 18(8):107–111, August 1983.

[2] Win Bo. *Topologies – Distributed Abstract Objects in Multicomputers*. PhD thesis, Department of Computer and Information Sciences, The Ohio State University, Sept. 1989.

[3] Gretchen P. Brown, Richard T. Carling, Christopher F. Herot, David A. Kramlich, and Paul Souza. Program visualization: graphical support for software development. *IEEE Computer*, 18(8):27–35, August 1985.

[4] Marc H. Brown. Exploring algorithms using Balsa-II. *IEEE Computer*, 21(5):14–36, May 1988.

[5] J. Deminet. Experience with multiprocessor algorithms. *IEEE Transactions on Computers*, C-31(4), April 1982.

[6] Mellor-Crummey J. Leblanc, T. Debugging parallel programs with instant replay. *IEEE Transactions on Computers*, (36), 1988.

[7] Dave Ogle, Karsten Schwan, and Richard Snodgrass. *The Real-Time Collection and Analysis of Dynamic Information in a Distributed System*. Technical Report, Computer and Information Science, The Ohio State University, OSU-CISRC-TR-85-12, Sept. 1985.

[8] David Ogle. *The Real-Time Monitoring of Distributed and Parallel Systems*. PhD thesis, Department of Computer and Information Sciences, The Ohio State University, Aug. 1988.

[9] Karsten Schwan and Jim Matthews. Graphical views of parallel programs. *ACM SIGSOFT Notices*, 1986.

[10] Karsten Schwan, Rajiv Ramnath, Sridhar Vasudevan, and Dave Ogle. A language and system for parallel programming. *IEEE Transactions on Software Engineering*, April 1988.

[11] Richard Snodgrass. A relational approach to monitoring complex systems. *ACM Transactions on Computer Systems*, 6(2):157–196, May 1988.

[12] Richard Snodgrass. The temporal query language tquel. *ACM Transactions on Database Systems*, 12(2):247–298, 1987.

[13] John Stasko. *The TANGO Algorithm Animation System*. Technical Report CS-88-20, Brown University, December 1988.

Subdivided Procedures: A Language Extension Supporting Extensible Programming

William Harrison and Harold Ossher

IBM Thomas J. Watson Research Center
P. O. Box 704, Yorktown Heights, N.Y. 10598

This paper describes an extension of conventional procedures in which procedure bodies handling multiple cases can be *subdivided* into separate bodies handling a single case each. Subdivision is based on criteria specified by the programmer. Underlying call support selects the body to execute in response to each call.

Subdivided procedures support a programming style in which great attention is paid to facilitating subsequent extensions. Normally, extensions have to be made by changing source code; subdivided procedures allow them to be made instead by adding new bodies.

Subdivided procedures can be implemented on top of procedural languages with a preprocessor that examines just a file of definitions; it does not need to examine procedure code. A restricted version of the mechanism implemented within the RPDE³ environment framework has been in constant use for more than two years. Experience has shown that it does facilitate extensible programming, and at little or no cost in call-time overhead.

1 Introduction

This paper describes an extension of conventional procedure call that is specifically intended to support *extensible programming*. It can been implemented on top of standard procedural languages by means of a preprocessor that processes a separate file of definitions but does not process procedure code at all. We begin by discussing what we mean by extensible programming and why it is important, and then describe the extension.

Programs, especially large ones, are almost always modified significantly after they are written. Some of the modifications are to fix bugs, but many are to extend scope or functionality, often in major and unanticipated ways. The ease with which such extensions can be made depends greatly on how the original program was written and structured. We use the term *extensible programming* to denote a style of programming that explicitly supports subsequent extension.

There are two primary reasons why extensible programming is important. The first is that a great deal of extension is done in practice. This includes both continual enhancement of programs by authors or support teams, and user customization and enhancement of purchased packages or applications. Effective extensible programming could reduce the costs of these activities significantly. The second reason is related and even more compelling: a great deal of extension and customization are *not* done because they would be too difficult and expensive, or even too dangerous, to attempt. As a result, many users put up with obsolete systems or with systems that are not quite suited to their needs. Effective extensible programming could make such extension and customization possible.

The art of extensible programming is one that is still largely unexplored, and unpracticed. Certainly the good programming and software engineering practices that have been developed over the past decades, such as structured programming [6], information hiding [17] and data abstraction [14] play an important part. Yet designing and programming specifically for extensibility imposes special demands and requires special techniques. Full analysis of these remains a research issue and is beyond the scope of this paper. We concentrate here on one aspect of extensible programming: the ability to add extensions without disturbing existing code and without fear of damaging existing functionality. We term this approach *extension by addition*.

We discuss extension by addition in detail in section 2, motivating and illustrating it by means of an example. We then describe the subdivided procedure mechanism in section 3, and show, in section 4, how it supports extension by addition and hence extensible programming. Section 5 describes a somewhat restricted version of subdivided procedures supported by the RPDE³ environment framework and our experience with its use. Section 6 discusses implementation and performance issues. Finally, section 7 discusses the relationship between subdivided procedures and methods, multi-methods and other related work.

2 Extension by Addition

Consider a simple example: a procedure *draw* that draws a geometric figure on a display. The code used to do this

```
procedure draw(f: figure)
    initial code common to all cases
    case f.kind of
        line:
            initial code common to lines
            case current-display of
                EGA:     code to draw line on EGA display
                VGA:     code to draw line on VGA display
                Megapel: code to draw line on Megapel
            end case
            final code common to lines
        circle:
            case current-display of
                EGA:     code to draw circle on EGA display
                VGA:     code to draw circle on VGA display
                Megapel: code to draw circle on Megapel
            end case
        square:
            case current-display of
                EGA:     code to draw square on EGA display
                VGA:     code to draw square on VGA display
                Megapel: code to draw square on Megapel
            end case
    end case
end case
```

Figure 1: A Sample Procedure

depends on the kind of figure to be drawn and the kind of display involved. The code written in conventional procedural style might have the form shown in fig. 1, assuming that details of the figure are given in a single record parameter and that the kind of display is stored in an environment variable *current-display*. In the interests of brevity, "common code" has been shown in a few representative locations rather than in all possible locations.

The most obvious extensions to procedure *draw* are to add new kinds of figures to be drawn and new kinds of displays. What do these extensions require? Firstly, access to the source code and the ability to change it and then rebuild the system. Given that, one of the extensions (adding a new kind of figure) requires adding a new top-level case, whereas the other (adding a new kind of display) requires adding a second-level case to each of the top-level cases. Let us now discuss the implications of these requirements.

Requiring access to source code usually precludes user extension and customization, since source code is seldom shipped. A user who has purchased an application containing this draw procedure and who has just obtained a new kind of display will have to wait for the vendor to support the new display. It is interesting to note that object-oriented environments, such as Smalltalk [8], that emphasize extensibility are usually shipped with a substantial amount of source code. Applications must also be shipped with source code if they are to be extensible.

Extensibility can be achieved without access to source code, however. Operating systems provide means for users to write their own commands or macros, without providing access either to kernel source code or even source code of supplied commands. Similarly, many editors provide means for users to write their own commands or functions as free-standing entities without a need to modify source code. These are widespread examples of effective extensibility using the technique of extension by addition. It works primarily for two reasons: an invocation mechanism that allows user-defined commands to be executed in the same way, from the user's point of view, as built-in commands, and the provision of a suitable notation and set of primitives for the user to use when building his extensions. Variations in the power of the notation and the completeness of the set of primitives primarily account for variations in extensibility across operating systems or editors.

Extension by addition is an important technique even when source code is available. The wide availability of source code for systems like Unix[1] has encouraged improvements in various tools to be made by many independent contributors, for example the multiplicity of "shells." Unfortunately, the tool users are then confronted by the availability of a multiplicity of tools, each containing some desired features, but not all. Extension by addition allows for the simple integration of independently made tool extensions. For example, suppose that one programmer extends *draw* to handle a new kind of figure, while another programmer extends it to handle a new kind of display. If these extensions are performed by modifying source code, two separate versions of the procedure will result, and detailed reconciliation will have to be performed if both are to made available in the same version of the entire system. If the extensions are performed by adding independent fragments of code, however, all these can simply be included in a single system which will then support both the new figure and the new display. Only the single case of drawing the new figure on the new display will not be handled, and will have to be coded as an extra fragment if it is needed.

Another advantage of extension by addition is that it cannot corrupt existing functionality. The new function either works or does not, but it cannot cause other functions to stop working (except by corrupting shared data structures). This is in marked contrast to extensions made by changing source code, where deliberate or inadvertent changes can have devastating effects. In the *draw* example it is quite likely that, in the course of adding a new figure, the programmer will want to change some of the common code. If he does so, he assumes the risk of inadvertently affecting other cases he might not understand adequately.

For the reasons outlined in the course of discussing the example above, we hold that extension by addition is an important aspect of extensible programming, and that it requires a special invocation mechanism. Such a mechanism is not usually provided by programming languages. We describe an extension to conventional procedures, called *subdivided procedures*, that does provide it.

---

[1] Unix is a trademark of AT&T Bell Laboratories.

191

As discussed in section 7, subdivided procedures are generalizations of *methods* in object-oriented systems [8] and are quite similar to multi-methods in CommonLoops [3] and CLOS [2]. They are defined and implemented, however, in the domain of conventional procedural languages. The implementation requires processing of a collection of special subdivision specifications, but requires no extension of language syntax and no preprocessing of procedure bodies. From the programmer's point of view, therefore, it provides a significant new capability without the need to adopt a new language.

3 Subdivided Procedures

This section describes the details of the subdivided procedure mechanism. The concepts defined here are illustrated using the *draw* example from section 1

A *subdivided procedure* consists of an interface, a subdivision specification, and one or more bodies. An interface to a subdivided procedure is no different from a standard procedure interface. It is an entity with the following attributes:

- *Procedure name.* A name by which the procedure is identified, usually chosen to denote the function performed.

- *Formal parameters.* Declarations of parameters to be passed when the procedure is called.

- Optional declarations of *return values.* Though the term "procedure" is used throughout this paper, subdivision applies equally to functions.

The interface to the *draw* procedure is thus simply *draw(f: figure)*.

A *subdivision specification* is an entity with the following attributes:

- *Subdivision criteria.* A tuple of expressions, $(e_1, e_2, \ldots, e_n)$, whose values at call time will determine which body to execute. The expressions must be valid in the environment of the procedure itself, *not* the environment of the call. They can refer to the formal parameters of the procedure, and to any other identifiers visible at the site of the procedure definition.

It makes sense to subdivide the *draw* procedure on two criteria: the kind of figure to be drawn and the current display type. The subdivision criteria are thus the pair (*f.kind, current-display*), referring to a field within a formal parameter and to a global environment variable. This choice of subdivision criteria will permit a separate body to be written for each of the separate cases in fig. 1, as shown below.

A *subdivided procedure body* is an entity with the following attributes:

> **procedure** draw **body for** (line, EGA)
> *initial code common to all cases*
> *initial code common to lines*
> *code to draw line on EGA display*
> *final code common to lines*

> **procedure** draw **body for** (circle, Megapel)
> *initial code common to all cases*
> *code to draw circle on Megapel display*

> ...

Figure 2: The Sample Procedure Subdivided

- One or more *body names.* Each body name is a tuple of constants, $(b_1, b_2, \ldots, b_n)$, called *selectors.* The selectors are values of the subdivision criteria that distinguish this particular body. Multiple body names permit the same body to be used in multiple contexts without duplication.

- The code to be executed in response to a call.

The single, composite body of the *draw* procedure of fig. 1 would be replaced by nine separate bodies, two of which are shown in fig. 2. Each body deals with a particular figure kind and display type, and has a body name that identifies them explicitly. If the blocks of common code are substantial, they can be placed in auxiliary procedures that are called from the subdivided bodies.

A call to a subdivided procedure does not differ in any way from standard procedure call, which is an executable statement with the following attributes:

- *Procedure name*, denoting the function to be performed and hence the procedure to be called.

- *Actual parameters* to be bound to the formal parameters.

No explicit mention of subdivision criteria or body names are made in calls.

There are some restrictions on subdivision criteria and body names:

- The value of each subdivision criterion, e_i, must be of a type that supports testing for equality. This includes integers, strings, symbols in languages that support symbols as values, or even arrays, records, or abstract data types. The actual types available will depend on the particular programming language or program involved.

- Each selector b_i in a body name must be either a compile-time constant of the same type as the corresponding subdivision criterion, e_i, or the special symbol **default**. The requirement that selectors be manifest at compile time might seem at first a gratuitous restriction, but in fact it has important implications for extensibility, discussed in section 4.

- All body names associated with a single procedure must be distinct.

- If a body name has fewer selectors than there are subdivision criteria specified for the procedure, it is considered to be padded with **default** symbols. This permits addition of subdivision criteria without explicitly changing existing body names. A body name cannot, however, have more selectors than there are subdivision criteria.

A partial order relation, **matches**, is defined on selectors, as follows: If s and t are selectors, then s **matches** t if and only if $s = t$ or t is the special symbol **default**. Two partial order relations are defined on tuples of selectors. Let $x = (x_1, x_2, \ldots, x_n)$ and $y = (y_1, y_2, \ldots, y_n)$ be tuples of selectors. Then x **matches** y if and only if x_i **matches** y_i for each $1 \leq i \leq n$. Also, x **is more specific than** y if and only if x **matches** y and

$$\exists i.(1 \leq i \leq n \wedge \forall j.(1 \leq j < i \supset x_j = y_j) \wedge$$
$$x_i \neq \textbf{default} \wedge y_i = \textbf{default})$$

Loosely stated, the latter condition requires that the leftmost unequal occurrence of **default** must be later in x than in y. Note that for a particular selector type, this relation is independent of any ordering relation defined for that type, but does depend on equality as defined for that type. It follows from these definitions that, if x, y, and z are tuples of selectors for which x **matches** y and x **matches** z, then either $y = z$ or y **is more specific than** z or z **is more specific than** y.

Consider some simple examples based on the *draw* example:

(line, EGA) **is more specific than** (line, default)
(line, default) **is more specific than** (default, EGA)
(default, EGA) **is more specific than** (default, default)

Procedure resolution is the process of finding the procedure body that is to be executed in response to a call. In the case of subdivided procedures, there are two aspects to this: finding the appropriate *procedure* first, and then choosing the appropriate *body* from the collection of bodies implementing that procedure. Subdivision affects only the choice of the appropriate body; any desired scheme can be used to find the procedure itself, including any of the scoping and naming schemes currently used in procedural languages.

Given a call and the procedure P it refers to, the body to be executed is determined as follows:

1. Evaluate the subdivision criteria, $(e_1, e_2, \ldots, e_n)$, specified in P's subdivision specification. The result is a tuple of values, $v = (v_1, v_2, \ldots, v_n)$.

2. Execute the body with the most specific body name that v matches. Formally: Let B be the set of all body names b associated with bodies of P such that

$$\forall b \in B.(v \textbf{ matches } b)$$

If B is empty, the call is in error. Otherwise, there is a unique body name $b = (b_1, b_2, \ldots, b_n) \in B$ such that

$$\forall b' \in B.(b = b' \vee b \textbf{ is more specific than } b')$$

The existence and uniqueness of b follow from the definitions of "**matches**" and "**is more specific than**".

For example, consider the call *draw(myline)*, where *myline.kind = line* and *current-display = EGA*. This call would resolve to the body named (line, EGA) in fig. 2. If this body did not exist, it would resolve to the first one in the following sequence that did: (line, **default**), (**default**, EGA), (**default**, **default**). If none of these bodies existed, a runtime error would result.

The description above deliberately did not specify whether evaluation of subdivision criteria and matching of the results against body names takes place at compile time or at run time. If, for any call, the values of the subdivision criteria are manifest at compile time, the call can be fully resolved at compile time. Compile-time resolution implies, however, that addition of new bodies or body names requires recompilation of callers. Since the primary motivation behind subdivided procedures is extension by addition, the ability to add bodies to handle new cases is important, so runtime resolution is preferable.

As a further illustration of subdivided procedures, consider message passing in Smalltalk [8]. A Smalltalk message type (generic function) can be characterized as a subdivided procedure with one subdivision criterion: the class of the *receiver* (the object to which the message is sent). Bodies are methods, and body names are classes. Each method has at least one body name: the class that contains the method code. An inherited method also has an additional body name for each class that inherits it. The Smalltalk system determines the value of the subdivision criterion at message send time, and then selects the appropriate method to execute. It is interesting to note that code-sharing inheritance schemes can be defined simply yet precisely in terms of association of body names with bodies, in the manner suggested by this example. This is a matter of definition only, and places no restrictions on implementation.

4 Extensible Programming using Subdivided Procedures

This section discusses just how subdivided procedures support extensible programming.

To start with, let us revisit the extensions of the *draw*

procedure mentioned in section 1: adding a new kind of figure or a new type of display. Either of these extensions can be accomplished simply by writing additional bodies with body names specifying the new cases being covered, compiling these bodies and linking them together with the appropriate system facilities. These new bodies cannot interfere with existing ones, and so cannot corrupt existing functionality.

It is easy to add a new subdivision criterion to a subdivided procedure. For example, the *draw* procedure migh be subdivided on another environment variable, *filled*, that specifies whether or not the drawn figure must be filled with the current fill pattern or not. This can be accomplished initially by changing the subdivision criteria of *draw* from (*f.kind*, *current-display*) to (*f.kind*, *current-display*, *filled*). Because short body names are automatically padded with **default**, all existing bodies will still work, and will be invoked irrespective of the value of *filled*. One can now write new bodies just for those specific cases where this behavior is incorrect. For example, drawing of lines is unlikely to be affected by issues of fill, so no extra bodies need be written for cases involving lines. This example illustrates both the addition of a new subdivision criterion and the fact that separate bodies are seldom needed for all cases, since default behavior is often correct.

Subdividing an ordinary procedure for the first time is similar to the case of adding a new criterion. The original body becomes the **default** one, and new bodies can be written for cases that require different treatment. It is even possible for the default body to contain explicit discrimination among cases, like the *draw* procedure in fig. 1. This is not recommended, but allows the graceful introduction of subdivided procedures to handle new cases being added to a program written in conventional style.

Subdivided procedures support customization and modification as well as extension. For example, if one is unhappy with an existing body for some particular case, one could go and change it. If the source code is not available, however, or if one does not wish to modify it, one could write a new body for that case and have it replace the existing one.

The restriction that body names be composed of compile-time constants rather than arbitrary expressions is motivated by considerations of extensibility. A programmer adding a new body to handle a particular case will not necessarily know about all other cases, yet will need to be sure that calls resolve to his new body whenever appropriate. The use of constants in body names ensures that the conditions under which a body will be executed are simple and clear, and in no way dependent on dynamic properties of the system. More complex resolution schemes involving call-time evaluation of body names leave open the possibility of unexpected clashes or selection of a body other than the one the programmer intended. The programmer will have to understand a lot more about cases other than his

own to be sure that such problems do not arise.

Another advantage of constant body names, and the reason for using simple equality matching with defaulting rather than more complex pattern matching, is that it establishes a simple and useful static structure for systems. The *n* subdivision criteria associated with a subdivided procedure establish an *n*-dimensional matrix whose axes are labeled with the values of the subdivision criteria and whose entries are the bodies. These matrices are often sparse, because defaulting is used in many cases. Their regularity helps with locating code and with determining the cases for which bodies need to be written.

5 Experience

RPDE³ [10] is a framework for building structured, object-oriented environments. It supports *subdivided methods*, a somewhat restricted version of subdivided procedures described by Harrison [10]. This section introduces RPDE³ briefly, and discusses subdivided methods and our experience with their use. A browser based on the *n*-dimensional matrix structure described above has been implemented as an RPDE³ environment, and is described elsewhere [16].

An example of an environment built under RPDE³ is a structured editor for system development using refinement [11]. A system is represented as a collection of objects, like modules, procedures, declarations and statements. The editor presents portions of the system to the user in a graphical form that clearly displays the underlying structure. Interacting directly with the graphical presentation, the user issues editing commands that cause the underlying system representation to be modified. Each type of object supports its own particular set of commands. For example, a pseudo-code statement supports refinement, whereas a statement list supports insertion and deletion of its statements.

We build environments such as this upon the RPDE³ framework, which provides a number of standard services. These include an object repository, display manager, keystroke and command handler, object-based mark/move/-copy, and a facility for routing messages around networks of objects. All environments use the framework. In addition to the advantage of reuse, this allows different environments to be integrated easily and ensures that different environments have a uniform feel to the user.

An environment is built upon the framework by defining types of objects that are appropriate to the domain of the environment, such as those mentioned in the example above. The object type definitions are split into small code fragments, such as representation definitions and method implementations.

A simple method[2] in RPDE³ is a subdivided procedure with one, standard subdivision criterion: the type of ob-

---

[2] In RPDE³ terminology, "method" means method interface or generic function, whereas "method implementation" means the code or body.

ject passed as the first parameter. A subdivided method has one additional subdivision criterion. It can be chosen by the programmer to be either the value of an integer parameter to the method, or the value of an integer global variable. For example, the methods responsible for displaying objects on the screen are subdivided on a global variable that the user can set by command to indicate the display perspective he desires. Multiple perspectives allow, for example, displaying of lists in linear indented form or as trees.

The RPDE³ system is written in Pascal [12], extended by an implementation of simple and subdivided methods. Each method implementation (body) is a Pascal procedure with a unique Pascal identifier as its name. *Method interface definitions* identify subdivision criteria, and *method implementation definitions* map body names to the Pascal names. Inheritance of method implementations is also supported, but is not discussed further here. A processor converts these definitions to run-time support, described briefly in section 6.

For example, suppose the following declarations are global:

var perspective: integer; **const** tree = 3

The display method interface can then be defined as follows:

method display(...) **subdivided on** perspective

Implementations of this method for object type "list" can be defined as follows:

type list
    display **for** perspective **default**: display_list_default
    display **for** perspective tree: display_list_as_tree

Method calls are standard Pascal procedure calls, such as

display(...)

The caller does not need to know whether a simple Pascal procedure, a simple method or a subdivided method is being called. Calls to methods will be fielded by the generated run-time support and resolved correctly.

Subdivided methods were introduced into RPDE³ more than two years ago, and have been used extensively since then. The current RPDE³ system contains 58 methods, of which 11 are subdivided based on a total of 8 criteria. There are 238 cases in which non-default method implementations are used. Few of these bodies had to be written from scratch: most are inherited or shared. More detailed statistics regarding the nature and number of code fragments making up RPDE³ and the environments built upon it are given in a recent paper by Harrison [9].

The fine-grained splitting made possible by subdivided methods has proved to be a major benefit. For example, the main application of RPDE³ to date has been the construction of the environment for development by refinement mentioned earlier. This environment supports programming in multiple languages, including C [13] and two different dialects of Pascal. Programs are represented as networks of appropriate objects, such as procedures, statements and expressions, and users view and manipulate these objects directly. The standard textual form of programs can be generated from the object representation, for presentation to compilers.

Though different languages are involved, most of the object types used to represent programs are the same, emphasizing the semantic similarities between the languages whenever possible. Differences that do occur, such as differences in the generated textual form, are specified using subdivisions based on one or other of three environment variables: *source-language*, which specifies the language the user is currently working in, *target-language*, which specifies the specific textual dialect to be generated, and *perspective*, which specifies how objects should be displayed to the user (e.g. variable declarations in Pascal or C style). Many of the objects involved exhibit some different behavior based on the current values of these variables, though much of their behavior remains unchanged.

The use of subdivided methods has made it possible to build support for a new language upon existing support for a similar language by adding bodies. Different people have developed support for different languages concurrently by adding separate collections of bodies. Simply linking all these together has resulted in a combined system supporting all the languages.

We are constantly finding new uses of subdivided methods, some of which require more than one subdivision criterion per method. This need was one of the factors motivating the development of the more general subdivided procedure mechanism described in this paper.

6 Implementation and Performance

This section outlines the nature and performance of the implementation of simple and subdivided methods in RPDE³, and discusses the issue of extending it to the more general subdivided procedure mechanism described in this paper.

The run-time support for RPDE³ method call, written about five years ago, is a variant of the tag-key approaches described by Rose for doing fast message dispatch on stock hardware [18]. A processor generates transfer vectors and associated code from method interface and implementation definitions. There is an entry point corresponding to every method interface. The code at each entry point examines the the first parameter of the method call to determine its type, and picks up the appropriate entry in a transfer vector. If the method is not subdivided, the transfer vector entry is the address of the method body; the code branches to it. If the method is subdivided, the transfer vector entry is the address of a secondary transfer vector; the code examines the appropriate subdivision criterion and branches to the appropriate entry.

Transfer vectors can be compacted to save space using a simple scheme that depends on known method call patterns and the semantics of inheritance in RPDE³. Compaction splits each transfer vector into a fast part, for frequently called methods, and a slower but more compact part, and shares secondary vectors among subdivisions when they are inherited without modification. Call-time overhead for calls resolved through fast parts is about 24 Intel 8086 machine instructions for non-subdivided methods, and about 48 for subdivided methods. Overheads on the IBM RT/PC are about 22 and 44 machine instructions. Calls resolved through slow parts involve searching, and have an additional overhead dependent on just how much searching is required.

This implementation can readily be extended to the more general subdivided procedure mechanism by adding additional levels of transfer vectors, allowing for evaluation of more complex subdivision criteria, and hashing subdivision values if necessary. The additional levels of transfer vectors add no overhead to calls that do not actually use them. They do require space, of course, and since the compaction scheme that works well in RPDE³ is unlikely to work as well in general, more sophisticated approaches to transfer vector compaction will probably be required. This is an area for future research.

Stating the overhead of subdivided procedures relative to simple procedures, as was done above, can be misleading. Resolving a call to a subdivided procedure involves determining what code is to be executed on the basis of a set of criteria. In the absence of subdivided procedures, this determination would usually still have to be made, by means of explicit code within the procedure bodies. If the subdivision support can make this determination as efficiently as such explicit code, then there is in fact no overhead associated with subdivision at all. Even if it cannot, the difference is much smaller than the overheads given above.

Detailed analysis and optimization of performance are topics for future research. Advances in message dispatching techniques in object-oriented languages (see, for example, [19,7,4]) suggest that substantial efficiency improvement will be possible. For the present, our experience with RPDE³ has shown that even a carefully crafted but simple implementation is viable in a real, interactive system.

7 Related Work

The notion of resolving a procedure call to a procedure body based on criteria in addition to the procedure identifier is not new. A great deal of the work in this area has been done to support *polymorphism* by allowing different implementations of the same procedure for different argument types. Overloading in Ada [1], message passing in object-oriented languages such as Smalltalk [8] and SELF

[20], and multi-methods in CommonLoops [3] and CLOS [2] are all examples of this. Except for multi-methods, these approaches perform resolution based on fixed criteria: Ada overloading on the type signature of the call, and object-oriented message passing on the class of the receiver (e.g. Smalltalk) or the receiver itself (e.g. SELF). Subdivided procedures permit greater flexibility by supporting subdivision on the values of user-defined expressions rather than just on such fixed criteria.

Multi-methods are usually described as permitting resolution to be based on the *types* of multiple arguments. However, they are implemented within Lisp systems, and Lisp is flexible enough to allow values to be treated as types. It is therefore possible to achieve as much flexibility with multi-methods as with subdivided procedures, and our experience with subdivided methods in RPDE³ suggests that this flexibility is valuable. The primary distinction of subdivided procedures relative to multi-methods is that they are defined and implemented as extensions of conventional procedural languages rather than being integrated features within extremely rich object-oriented languages. They can thus bring extensible programming to the ordinary programmer without the need for introducing a new and substantially different language.

There are also languages and systems in which code to be executed is determined using pattern matching, unification, or evaluation of predicates associated with code. Some examples are production systems [15], rules in Prolog [5], and *constraint-based invocation* being developed by Van Biema [21]. Described in terms of the subdivided procedure model, such schemes have body names that are not compile-time constants. This permits even greater flexibility, but at the cost of complicating the static structure of programs and the runtime tests for matching and specificity. This additional complexity reduces the opportunities for performance optimization, makes it harder for a programmer examining code to determine just which body applies in a particular circumstance, and increases the likelihood that a new body added for one purpose will end up being called in unanticipated and inappropriate circumstances.

The subdivided procedure mechanism thus represents a particular tradeoff between simplicity and flexibility. It can be characterized as the most flexible mechanism for splitting procedures that provides the advantages of body names that are constants.

8 Conclusions

This paper presented a mechanism that allows procedures to be subdivided into separate bodies based on criteria specified by the programmer. Such subdivision allows code that is applicable in different situations to be written and examined separately, and support for new situations to be provided by addition rather than modification of code. The mechanism can be implemented on top of a standard procedural language with no change to the language or its compiler. Experience within the RPDE³ system has shown that use of subdivided procedures can ease the important tasks of system modification and extension.

We believe that, with systems continually growing in size and complexity, programming for extensibility is a critical issue. There is much interesting work to be done in developing programming styles and language mechanisms to support it. Subdivided procedures are one such mechanism, and hence a step in that direction.

Acknowledgements

We wish to thank Brent Hailpern, Gail Kaiser, John Shilling and Peter Sweeney for helpful comments on drafts of this paper.

References

[1] American National Standards Institute. *The Programming Language Ada Reference Manual.* Springer-Verlag, 1983.

[2] D. G. Bobrow, L. G. DeMichiel, R. P. Gabriel, S. E. Keene, G. Kiczales, and D. A. Moon. Common Lisp object system specification X3J13. *SIGPLAN Notices*, 23, September 1988.

[3] Daniel Bobrow, Kenneth Kahn, Gregor Kiczales, Larry Masinter, Mark Stefik, and Frank Zdybel. Common-Loops: Merging Lisp and object-oriented programming. In *Conference on Object-Oriented Programming Systems, Languages, and Applications*, pages 17–29, ACM, Portland, September 1986.

[4] Craig Chambers, David Ungar, and Elgin Lee. An efficient implementation of SELF, a dynamically-typed object-oriented language based on prototypes. In *Conference on Object-Oriented Programming Systems, Languages, and Applications*, pages 49–70, ACM, New Orleans, October 1989.

[5] W. F. Clocksin and C. S. Mellish. *Programming in Prolog.* Springer-Verlag, second edition, 1984.

[6] O.-J. Dahl, E. W. Dijkstra, and C. A. R. Hoare. *Structured Programming.* Academic Press, 1972.

[7] L. P. Deutsch. Efficient implementation of the Smalltalk-80 system. In *Conference Record of the Eleventh Annual Symposium on Principles of Programming Languages*, pages 297–302, ACM, January 1984.

[8] Adele Goldberg and David Robson. *Smalltalk-80: The Language and its Implementation.* Addison-Wesley, 1983.

[9] William Harrison. *Building Extensible Tools and Applications from Small Fragments.* Research Report RC 14533, IBM Thomas J. Watson Research Center, Yorktown Heights, NY, March 1989.

[10] William Harrison. RPDE³: A framework for integrating tool fragments. *IEEE Software*, 4(6):46–56, November 1987.

[11] William H. Harrison, Jack L. Rosenfeld, Ching C. Wang, and Brian A. Weston. Structured editing with RPDE. *Computer Language*, 3(9):93–101, September 1986.

[12] K. Jensen and N. Wirth. *Pascal User Manual and Report.* Springer-Verlag, second edition, 1978.

[13] Brian W. Kernighan and Dennis M. Ritchie. *The C Programming Language.* Prentice-Hall, 1978.

[14] B. H. Liskov, A. Snyder, R. Atkinson, and J. C. Schaffert. Abstraction mechanisms in CLU. *Communications of the ACM*, 20(8):564–576, August 1977.

[15] Nils J. Nilsson. *Principles of Artifical Intelligence.* Tioga Publishing Company, 1980.

[16] Harold Ossher. Multi-dimensional organization and browsing of object-oriented systems. In *Proceedings of the IEEE 1990 International Conference on Computer Languages*, March 1990.

[17] D. L. Parnas. Information distribution aspects of design methodology. In C. R. Freeman, editor, *Information Processing 71: Proceedings of IFIP Congress 71. Volume 1: Foundations and Systems*, pages 339–344, IFIP, August 1971.

[18] John R. Rose. Fast dispatch mechanisms for stock hardware. In *Conference on Object-Oriented Programming Systems, Languages, and Applications*, pages 27–35, ACM, San Diego, September 1988.

[19] N. Suzuki and M. Terada. Creating efficient systems for object-oriented languages. In *Conference Record of the Eleventh Annual Symposium on Principles of Programming Languages*, pages 290–296, ACM, January 1984.

[20] David Ungar and Randall B. Smith. Self: The power of simplicity. In *Conference on Object-Oriented Programming Systems, Languages, and Applications*, pages 227–242, ACM, Orlando, October 1987.

[21] Michael van Biema. The integration of rule-based and object-oriented programming paradigms. April 1988. Dissertation proposal, Columbia University.

LEGEND : A LANGUAGE FOR
GENERIC COMPONENT LIBRARY DESCRIPTION

Nikil D. Dutt
Information and Computer Science
University of California at Irvine
Irvine, CA 92717

ABSTRACT

LEGEND is a novel generator-generator language for the definition, generation and maintenance of generic component libraries used in high level hardware synthesis. Each LEGEND description generates a library generator GENUS, which is organized as a hierarchy of generic component generators, templates and instances. High level synthesis systems typically transform the abstract behavior of a design into an interconnection of generic component instances derived from a library such as GENUS. Although existing hardware description languages (such as VHDL) can effectively describe particular component libraries, they lack the capability of *generating* these component libraries from a higher-level description. LEGEND complements a language such as VHDL by providing a component library generator-generator with behavioral models for simulation and subsequent synthesis. LEGEND generated components have realistic register transfer semantics, including clocking, asynchrony and data bi-directionality. LEGEND's simple and extensible syntax allows users to add and modify component types easily. LEGEND is currently implemented on SUN3's under C/UNIX and is used by a suite of behavioral synthesis tools at U. C. Irvine.

1. Introduction

The task of high level hardware synthesis involves the mapping of abstract behavioral design descriptions into structural designs at the register transfer level, composed of components drawn from a generic component library. The synthesized structural design must functionally implement the abstract behavior under the set of high-level constraints given by the user. Once a feasible structural design of generic components is synthesized, it is passed on to a set of logic and layout synthesizers to implement the design in a particular target technology, such as 3-micron CMOS. With rapid advances in fabrication and layout technologies, it becomes increasingly important to insulate lower-level technological changes from higher-level design decisions, since these technology-specific designs become obsolete with even small changes in the technology. This creates a huge bottleneck in the design cycle, since the entire design process has to be restarted for every small change in the technology. A key to solving this design crisis in VLSI systems is *technology independence*: the concept of keeping higher level design descriptions and decisions independent of the target technology. High-level hardware synthesis systems use components drawn from a *generic component library* to effect this technology independence; structural designs composed of components drawn from a generic library can be re-targeted to different technologies at the backend, without having to redo the task of high-level synthesis for every new technology.

There are several advantages in maintaining a library of generic components:

- it permits efficient synthesis by generating the structure for *only* the functionality desired, instead of using predefined components.
- since the components are "generic", the task of behavior-to-structure synthesis is insulated from technological details.
- details of control encoding for components can be hidden from behavioral synthesis by requiring one control line per function; a technology mapper and logic optimizer can perform the encoding later.
- we can associate cost functions for components which return estimates for area, power and delay based on the parameters used to invoke a component; this permits feedback of low-level information.
- it simplifies retargetting of a design to new libraries.
- it is extensible; new component types can be characterized and added to the library.
- it is general; allows modeling of buses, storage elements, functional units and finite state controllers.

This paper describes a novel generator-generator language, LEGEND, for the definition, generation and maintenance of generic component libraries used in high level synthesis. LEGEND's simple syntax and strong register-transfer semantics, coupled with its extensibility, makes it a powerful language for facilitating efficient high-level synthesis.

Each generic component from a generated library is instantiated by specifying its parameters which define its structural, operational and performance attributes. Typical parameters include the component's *style* (eg. slow or fast), *functionality* (eg. add and increment for an arithmetic unit), *input-output characteristics* (ports on the component), *size* (eg. number of words for a memory), *bit-width* and *representation* (eg. two's complement). Hence each LEGEND generator is a template for a generic microarchitectural component; depending on the design requirements, components may be built from these templates by supplying the necessary parameters.

The rest of this paper is organized as follows. Section 2 describes previous work on hardware description languages, component generators and libraries. Section 3 briefly introduces the LEGEND language, and the semantics of the generated generic component library. Section 4 illustrates how generic components and their instances are created and used. Section 5 uses a simple example to show how components derived from LEGEND are simulated in VHDL. Section 6 concludes with the status of this research.

2. Previous Work

2.1. Hardware Description Languages

Although a number of good hardware description languages have been described in the literature (DDL [4], AHPL [8], ISPS [2], etc.), these have been used primarily for behavioral specification and synthesis; none of them have addressed the issue of how to describe, generate and maintain generic component libraries.

More recently, VHDL [12] was proposed as a "standard" hardware description language for the specification and maintenance of design descriptions transcending several design levels including behavior, data-flow and micro-architectural structure. Although VHDL has good constructs for describing *specific* libraries and component instances, it does not have the capability of *generating* customized component libraries. This is particularly important in a high-level synthesis environment, since a higher-level description could customize VHDL component libraries for different application domains. VHDL is also closely tied to a simulation model of computation, hence and lacks several hardware semantics at the register transfer level.

2.2. Generic Component Characterization

Abstract component characterization is an important task in high level synthesis, since these component models determine the "goodness" of a synthesized design. Currently, most behavioral synthesis systems use a two level representation for the component data base. The parent level describes the components with their attributes and characteristics, while the lower level describes instances duplicated from these components, possibly with some limited amount of parameterization for the size or bit-width [10]. For instance, an ALU component can be instantiated with a specified bit-width, but the functions performed by the ALU are fixed. This two-level representation is not powerful enough to handle more general types of components which have almost all of their attributes (including functionality and structural ports) parameterized. A hierarchical representation, using the notion of of "types", "generators", "components" and "instances" introduced in this paper, overcomes this problem.

Quite often, the component data base is embedded within the synthesis system as part of the synthesis code. This makes the task of generic library management cumbersome. Since there is no clean separation between the synthesis code and the underlying component database, modification of an existing component or the addition of a new component necessitates rewriting parts of the synthesis code. Furthermore, since the underlying models of these components are often tied to a particular technology library, a lot of effort is required to retarget the components to a new technology library. What is desired is a clean separation between the synthesis tasks and the components used for synthesis.

Another problem with existing representations is that they treat "components", "wires", "ports", "buses", etc. differently. This limits the kinds of optimizations that can be performed by the synthesis tools. For instance, the concept of "unit merging" is similar to that of "bus merging", but these tasks are treated differently since "units" and "buses" have different representations.

Although components can perform several operations simultaneously, it is a difficult task to characterize operational simultaneity in a component for the task of synthesis. Since most behavioral languages have the notion of a single assignment operation, mapping an operation to a component that performs several operations simultaneously can be unwieldy. This requires a many-to-one mapping from the language operators to a structural component which performs the operations. In fact, the component may generate outputs for which there are no corresponding behavioral variables (the carry-out on an adder, for example). The other problem is with the representation of costs for simultaneous operations performed by a component. As an example, the carry-out on an adder component is obtained for no cost when the adder is explicitly performing an "add" operation in the language. However, if only the carry-out is required (without the sum), the cost of this operation is now that of the addition. Hence we need the notion of "operation classes" introduced in this paper, which permit the representation of simultaneous operations and combined costs for synthesis.

Finally, many high level synthesis systems do not have explicit behavioral models for components in the data base. These models are essential for the verification of the behavior of the synthesized structural design using simulation.

2.3. Related Work

Similar work on hierarchical library generator-generators has been described at lower levels of the design process. At the layout level, DPL [1] describes an object-oriented hierarchical representation of layout (cell) objects. Palladio [15] describes another object-oriented representation to model designs across a number of design levels; however, it was never used in any synthesis environment. More recently, Fred [14] describes an interesting object-oriented approach for representing designs and constraints at the module and layout level. Fred uses the ETHEL language to describe a module's physical and layout characteristics. None of this work has examined the representation of generic component libraries for high level synthesis and generators for such libraries.

3. LEGEND: The Generator-Generator

LEGEND is a language used to generate a particular instance of a generic component library, **GENUS** [6], for use in a high-level synthesis system. In order to understand the syntax and semantics of LEGEND, it is necessary to examine the organization of a typical GENUS component library. This section will briefly outline the GENUS organization and its semantics, before describing the LEGEND language.

3.1. GENUS System Overview

Every high-level synthesis system uses an implicit or explicit generic component library. The abstract behavior of the design is implemented as a structural realization of interconnected component instances drawn from this generic library. GENUS is hierarchical generic component library used by several high-level synthesis tools at U.C. Irvine (EXEL [5], VSS [9], MILO [11], ICDB [16], etc.). This section describes the hierarchy in GENUS, the functions used to create and access elements in GENUS. It also describes how a particular technology library may be used to restrict the generators to produce only those generic components that can be feasibly realized using that library.

3.1.1. GENUS Hierarchy

GENUS is organized into 4 levels of hierarchy, where each level inherits attributes from its parent level. This representation closely models a hierarchical object oriented database.

Figure 1 shows a sample GENUS snapshot, where instances I1 through I5 are children of the class of 4-bit register components. The register components are generated from the class of register generators by specifying some or all of the register parameters (in this particular example, only the number of bits was specified). Finally, the register generator class belongs to the sequential type class, where all elements are activated by a clock.

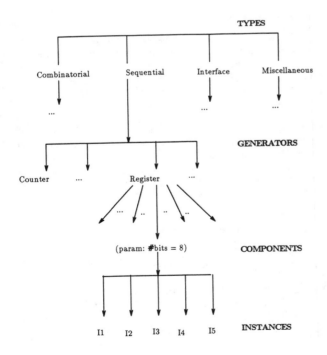

Figure 1. Hierarchy in GENUS

The *type* class describes the abstract functionality of elements in GENUS. Sample type attributes include *combinatorial*, *sequential*, *interface* and *miscellaneous*.

A *generator* class is used to generate a family of similar components and instances. LEGEND descriptions (described later in this section) are used to maintain lists of all possible parameters and definitions for every possible operation performed by a generated component.

A *component* is generated by passing a list of parameters to the parent LEGEND generator descriptor. For instance, in Figure 1, a 4-bit register component is generated by specifying the bit-width attribute to the register generator. All possible parameters for a particular generator need not be specified; missing parameters are assigned default values.

Instances are "carbon-copies" of a generated component, with unique names. These GENUS elements are the ones actually used for connectivity in the structural design. Since an instance inherits all of its attributes from the parent component, only the connectivity of the instance is stored in its representation.

3.1.2. Using GENUS

The most common operations performed on the generic component library are the creation of components and instances, and the querying of a GENUS library for various attributes.

Since the library is organized hierarchically, any attempt to create a new component or instance must begin at the parent generator class. Functions for creating new components are passed a parameter list; the parent generator class is searched to see if a component is already generated by matching the parameter values. Similarly, the request to create a new instance of a component is passed as a parameter list to the root generator class. If a component for this parameter list does not already exist, a new one is created. Finally, the instance itself is created.

A variety of query functions access the GENUS database at each level. Queries may be initiated at the root (generator), or at a particular level of the hierarchy. For instance, a query to find the number of 4-bit registers instantiated in the database starts at the register generator (the root of the register hierarchy) with the appropriately configured parameter list. On the other hand, a query to check if instance I4 in Figure 1 has a RESET port begins at the instance level and necessitates a look-up of its parent's attribute list (the 4-bit register component) for the existence of a RESET port.

When the completed structural (generic) design is to be mapped to a particular technology library, certain generic components may not exhibit a clean mapping to the corresponding technology library components. The task of performing this technology mapping can become very cumbersome unless the user provides technology specific hints to GENUS so that a only "feasible" set of components are generated for the particular technology library.

This task can be accomplished through a *technology library restrictor*, which prunes the parameter list for a generator so that only "well-behaved" generic components are generated for that technology library.

3.2. LEGEND Overview

A LEGEND description uses a special notation for describing individual generic component generators. Each generic component generator is characterized by a unique name and a list of attributes describing the type class, implementation styles, parameters, port information and functionality. The LEGEND description can be tailored to a particular generic component library by specifying the necessary component generator types. In addition, each component generator can produce simulatable VHDL behavioral models for the generated components; these models can be used to verify the behavior of a synthesized design. The LEGEND library description is parsed into the internal data structures used to represent the GENUS library. [7] contains the complete description of the LEGEND language; we will use the LEGEND definition for a counter generator, shown in Figure 2, as a running example in this section. The ports for a component are categorized into data inputs (INPUTS) and outputs (OUTPUTS), while control-specific ports are listed under the entries CLOCK, ENABLE, CONTROL and ASYNC.

3.2.1. Name

This specifies a unique name for a generator.

```
NAME:              COUNTER
CLASS:             Clocked
MAX_PARAMS:        7
PARAMETERS:  GC_COMPILER_NAME, GC_INPUT_WIDTH (%w),
             GC_NUM_FUNCTIONS, GC_FUNCTION_LIST,
             GC_SET_VALUE, GC_STYLE, GC_ENABLE_FLAG
NUM_STYLES:        2
STYLES:            SYNCHRONOUS, RIPPLE
NUM_INPUTS:        1
INPUTS:            I0[%w]
NUM_OUTPUTS:       1
OUTPUTS:           O0[%w]
CLOCK:             CLK
NUM_ENABLE:        1
ENABLE:            CEN
NUM_CONTROL:       3
CONTROL:           CLOAD, CUP, CDOWN
NUM_ASYNC:         2
ASYNC:             ASET, ARESET
NUM_OPERATIONS:    3
OPERATIONS:
      (      (LOAD)
             (INPUTS:    I0)
             (OUTPUTS:   O0)
             (CONTROL:   CLOAD)
             (OPS:  (LOAD: O0 = I0)))
      (      (COUNT_UP)
             (OUTPUTS:   O0)
             (CONTROL:   CUP)
             (OPS:  (COUNT_UP: O0 = O0 + 1)))
      (      (COUNT_DOWN)
             (OUTPUTS:   O0)
             (CONTROL:   CDOWN)
             (OPS:  (COUNT_DOWN: O0 = O0 - 1)))
VHDL_MODEL:        counter_vhdl.c
OP_CLASSES:        default
```

Figure 2. LEGEND Description For a Counter Generator

3.2.2. Class

This specifies if the generator is of type class *clocked* or *combinational*. When a component is *clocked*, certain semantics are associated with the ports on the component.

The CLOCK entry specifies the name of the clock line(s) for the component (currently only one clock line is assumed). For edge-triggered components, the attribute "RISING_EDGE" or "FALLING_EDGE" indicates when the clock is active.

The ENABLE attribute, when assigned a port name, activates the component for clocked behavior. For instance, in Figure 2, the counter exhibits synchronous operation only when CEN is high. If no port is specified for the ENABLE entry, a clocked component is assumed to be enabled at all times.

The CONTROL attributes specify the clocked control with one line per function. For instance, the counter in Figure 2 has separate lines for the synchronous operations LOAD, COUNT_UP and COUNT_DOWN.

The ASYNC ports specify control lines that invoke asynchronous behavior: they override any clocked control that may be simultaneously active. For example, the ASET port in Figure 2 is an asynchronous set line for the counter.

The semantics of the CLOCK, ENABLE, CONTROL and ASYNC lines are implicit in the definition of a component.

For *combinational* generators, there are no entries under CLOCK and ASYNC in the LEGEND description. The ENABLE entry is optional; if it is specified, a component is generated with an enable line. For combinational generators exhibiting multi-function behavior, each function is assigned a unique CONTROL line.

3.2.3. Parameters

The MAX_PARAMS and PARAMETERS entries indicate the number and global symbols used to describe the generic generator. For the counter in Figure 2, the parameterized input width is represented by the variable "%w"; this is treated as a parameterized variable in the rest of the component description.

3.2.4. Styles

The STYLES entry indicates the list of possible implementation styles for generating instances of the component. For the counter in Figure 2, the implementation styles are SYNCHRONOUS and RIPPLE.

3.2.5. Ports

Ports are specified under the INPUTS, OUTPUTS, INPUT_OUTPUTS, CONTROL, CLOCK, ASYNC and ENABLE entries. Ports specified under CONTROL, CLOCK, ASYNC and ENABLE are assumed to be one bit wide by default. For the INPUTS and OUTPUTS, each port has a bit-width specified within the pair "[" and "]". A parameterized variable (which starts with the character "%") may be used when necessary.

3.2.6. Operations

Each operation that can be performed by a generated component is described by its name, input, output and control port information.

3.2.7. VHDL_MODEL

The behavioral operation of a generated component is modeled in VHDL. This VHDL model is generated by the C routine indicated in this entry. The VHDL models are described further in section 5.

3.2.8. Op_classes

Each entry here describes the list of possible operations that may be performed in parallel for the generated component. We can associate cost functions for implementing any combination of these operations in each OP_CLASS. This permits realistic modeling of structural components. A "default" op_class indicates that each operation is mutually exclusive and cannot be performed simultaneously with any other operation.

3.2.9. Macro Expansion and Port Naming

For generated components that have a parameterizable number of ports (or operations), the list of port names are generated by calling special functions that return a name or a list of names. These function names start with the special symbol "&" to distinguish them from other names in the LEGEND description. Similarly, the operations performed by a component may depend on some arguments in the parameter list. Hence the "macro-expand" feature is used to describe this functionality. Figure 3 shows a sample LEGEND definition for a MUX component. The index of the macro-expand loop is a variable whose name begins with a "$". Note that in the parameter list, the input width and the number of inputs are parameterized (and represented by %w and %n respectively). Since the input port names depend on the number of inputs, we use the function "&get_component_pin_name_list" to generate the list of pin-names for the MUX inputs.

Further, in Figure 3, the operation of the MUX component is dependent on the number of inputs, the input and control port names, all of which are parameterized. Hence we use the macro-expand feature to describe the functionality by looping through every pair of inputs and control signals.

3.2.10. Estimation Functions

The initial version of each generated GENUS generic component library used estimators derived from Chippe's model of function units [3]. Functions for area, speed and power returned estimates based on the size, functionality and bit-width of a generated component. However, these estimates were derived from a technology-specific library (LSI CMOS macrocells). Work is under way to incorporate generic

```
NAME:          MUX
CLASS:         Combinatorial
MAX_PARAMS: 5
PARAMETERS: GC_COMPILER_NAME, GC_INPUT_WIDTH (%w),
               GC_NUM_INPUTS (%n), GC_ENABLE_FLAG,
               GC_INVERT_FLAG
NUM_INPUTS:    %n
INPUTS:                    &get_component_pin_name_list
                                   (MUX, INPUT, %n, %w)
NUM_OUTPUTS:              1
OUTPUTS:       O0[%w]
NUM_CONTROL:             %n
CONTROL:       &get_component_pin_name_list
                                   (MUX, CONTROL, %n, 1)
NUM_ENABLE: 1
ENABLE:         CEN
NUM_OPERATIONS:         %n
OPERATIONS:
macro_expand ($i = 0 to %n-1)
   {
    ( (&get_component_function(MUX, $i))
       (INPUTS:   &get_component_pin_name
                              (MUX, INPUT, $i))
        (OUTPUTS:  O0)
        (CONTROL:  &get_component_pin_name
                              (MUX, CONTROL, $i))
        (OPS:   (  O0 = &get_component_pin_name
                              (MUX, INPUT, $i))))
   }
VHDL_MODEL: mux_vhdl.c
OP_CLASSES:   default
```

Figure 3. Macro-Expand Feature

cost functions from the IIF descriptions for GENUS components as described in [16]. These estimates are based on generic gate counts assuming a custom layout synthesis environment.

4. LEGEND: Semantics and Usage

As mentioned earlier, LEGEND-generated components in the GENUS library belong one of several type classes, based on their properties and/or functions. This section describes the semantics, assumptions and naming conventions associated with these components. It then describes how components and instances can be accessed.

4.1. Port Naming Convention

Ports on each component are categorized into *data input*, *data output*, *data input-output*, *control*, *asynchronous*, *enable* and *clock* types. Input ports names begin with an "I", output port names begin with an "O", input-output port names begin with a "B" (for Bidirectional), control and enable port names begin with a "C", the clock is labeled "CLK", while async ports begin with an "A".

4.2. Port Semantics

Sequential components are assumed to have a clock input; synchronous operations are performed when the clock is high and the enable line (if any) is high. Asynchronous operations override the clocked operations. For combinatorial components, there is no port of type "CLOCK"; operations are inhibited only if the associated "ENABLE" line for the component is low. Non-sequential components do not have asynchronous ports.

4.3. Component Control

In our model of a generic component, a multi-operation component has a *separate control line* for each operation. This feature makes each component in a generated library truly generic, since the task of control encoding is left to a technology mapper at the time of circuit realization. Because of this assumption, a component which is controlled by a line wider than a single bit has this control line labeled as an input. An example is the *select* input for a SELECTOR component which is wider than a single bit for more than 2 data inputs; this line is labeled "ISEL" and is treated as an input port for consistency. Similarly, the address lines for memories and register files are treated as inputs.

4.4. Combinatorial Components

Figure 4 shows a table of combinatorial components available in the generic component library. Both primitive logic gates and bit-wise logic gates are described in the table. Except for the primitive and bit-wise logic gates, each component has an optional enable input. The logic unit (LU) performs all 16 possible logical functions of two inputs. The MUX component selects input $I<i>$ when control line $C<i>$ is high, and permits the generation of an inverted output. The selector component chooses the input whose guard value matches the value on the single input line ISEL. The DECODER takes an n-bit input and outputs 2^n single bit lines, where line i is 1 when the input equals the value of i.

LIST OF COMBINATORIAL COMPONENTS					
Type	Functions	Data I/O	Control	Async	Attributes
Logic Gates (Single)	GAND, GOR, GNAND, GNOR GXOR, GXNOR GNOT	I0: input O0: output			#input bits
Bitwise Logic Gates	AND, OR, NAND, NOR XOR, XNOR	$I0..I<n-1>$:input O0: output			#inputs (n) #bits
Logic Unit	ZERO, ONE AND, NAND RINHI(xy') LNOT, LID LINHI(x'y) RID(y) XOR, OR NOR, XNOR RNOT(y') LIMPL(x+y') RIMPL(x'+y)	I0,I1: input O0: output	CZERO, CONE CAND, CNAND CRINHI CLNOT, CLID CLINHI CRID CXOR, COR CNOR, CXNOR CRNOT CLIMPL CRIMPL		#input bits, #functions, func. list
Mux	Mux input i	$I0..I<n-1>$: input O0: output	$CI0..CI<n-1>$		#bits, #inputs inv?
Selector	Select (on guard val)	$ISEL,I0..I<n-1>$: input O0: output			#bits, #inputs, guards, c-width, else_flag
Decoder		I0: input $O0..O2^n$-1			input_width(n), type, else-option
Encoder		$I0..I2^n$-1 $O0..O<n-1>$			#outputs(n), type
Comparator	EQ, NEQ GT, LT GEQ, LEQ	I0, I1: inputs OEQ, ONEQ, OGT, OLT,OGEQ,OLEQ: outputs	CEQ, CNEQ, CGT, CLT, CGEQ, CLEQ		#bits #functions func-list
Shifter	SHR0, SHR1, SHL0, SHL1, ROTR, ROTL, ASHL, ASHR	I0, ILIN, IRIN, ISHNUM: input O0: output	CSHR0, CSHR1, CSHL0, CSHL1, CROTR, CROTL CASHL, CASHR		#bits, #functions, func-list, mode, fill, maxshift
Barrel Shifter	SHR, SHR, ASHL, ASHL, ROTR, ROTL,	I0, ISHNUM, ILR, IROT,IFILL,IMODE: input O0: output	CSHR, CSHR, CASHL, CASHL, CROTR, CROTL		#bits, maxshift, #functions, func-list
Adder/ Subtractor	+, -	I0, I1, ICIN: input O0, OCOUT: output	CADD CSUB		#bits, #fns, fn-list, style, #pipe-st
ALU	{+,-,INC,DEC} {>,<,=,!=,ZRO} {16 logic fns}	I0, I1: input O0, 5-cond, OCOUT: output	1-per fn		#bits, style, #fns func-list, #pipe-st
Multiplier	*	I0, I1: input O0: output			#bits, style, #pipe-st
Divider	/	I0, I1: input O0: output			#bits, style, #pipe-st

Figure 4. Combinatorial Components

Conversely, an ENCODER component takes 2^n boolean inputs and produces n encoded outputs (where the encoding is determined by the encoder type). The COMPARATOR, SHIFTER, ADD_SUB, MULT and DIV components are self-explanatory. The ALU can perform four arithmetic, five comparison and all sixteen logical operations. At the time of instantiation, an appropriate subset of these functions may be chosen for implementation.

4.5. Sequential Components

Figure 5 shows the list of available sequential components. As mentioned earlier, each sequential component is assumed to have a port named "CLK". If asynchronous ports exist for the component, they override the clocked, synchronous behavior of the component. A register component may have the positive output "OQ", the negated output "OQN" or

both outputs generated. Both registers and counters must have a set-value specified at instantiation time. The counter component can count up and down, besides doing a synchronous load and an asynchronous set and reset. For the register-file component, each port pair (I<i>,O<i>) has associated with it an address line A<i>, and a port-attribute which indicates if that port is of type *input*, *output* or *bidirectional*.

4.6. Interface and Miscellaneous Components

Figure 6 shows the list of interface, bus, switchbox, clock and delay components. An interface component has several attributes that describes its function (buffer/clock_driver/...), mode (input/output/...), level (CMOS/TTL/...), output_type(inverting/non-inverting) and drive (L/M/H). The port component models ports on a design, with the

LIST OF SEQUENTIAL COMPONENTS					
Type	Functions	Data-i/o	control	async	attributes
Register	load, shl, shr,	I0, LIN, RIN: input, OQ, OQN: output	CLOAD, CSHL, CSHR, CEN	ACLEAR, ASET	#bits, #fns, type, set-val, en OQ?, OQN?
Counter	load, up, down, clear, set	I0: input O0: output	CLOAD, CUP, CDOWN, CEN	ACLEAR ASET	#bits, #fns, set-val, style, type, enable
Register File		I0,..,I<n-1> IA0,..,IA<n-1>	CR0,CW0,.. CR<n-1>,CW<n-1>		#bits, #words #ports, port_attr, en
Stack/ FIFO	push, pop	I0: input, O0: output	CPUSH, CPOP, CEN		#bits, #words, type, enable
Memory	read, write	I0, IADDR, IA_VALID: input OD_READY, O0: output	CWRITE,CREAD, CEN		#bits, #words, enable

Figure 5. Sequential Components

LIST OF INTERFACE, BUS, SWITCHBOX AND MISC. COMPONENTS					
Type	Functions	Data I/O	Control	Async	Attributes
Interface Units	Buffer Clock Driver Schmidt Trigger Tristate	I0: input O0: output	CEN		#bits, function mode:(i, o, i/o), level:(CMOS,TTL, ..) output:(inv/non-inv) drive:(l, m, h)
Port		I0: input O0: output			#bits, mode:(i, o, i/o)
BUS		I0..I<n-1>: input O0: output	C0..C<n-1>		#bits, n-in, fan-out
WIRED-OR		n-inputs 1-output			#bits, n-in, fan-out
Switchbox Concat	O0 = I0Q..QI<n-1>	I0,..,I<n-1>: input O0: output			#inputs, width0,..,width<n-1>
Switchbox Extract	O1 = I0{i:j}	I0: input O1: output			inp-width, l,r index
Clock Generator		O0: output	CEN		clock-period, duration-high
Delay	Delay δ	I0:in, O0:out			delay-value (δ)

Figure 6. Interface and Miscellaneous Components

attributes number_of_bits and port_mode. The port component is useful in constructing a hierarchy of designs. The BUS and WIRED-OR components are similar to each other, except that the BUS component has tristate drivers at each input to the bus. CONCAT and EXTRACT components simply model switchbox operations for merging streams of data and extracting substreams of data. At present, the clock generator component is used for modeling a very simple system clock, using the attributes clock-period and duration-high. The DELAY component is used to model a delay element on a logic path.

4.7. Accessing Components

Library generators, components and instances are accessed using the appropriate access function with the generator name and a variable number of arguments. Figure 7 shows the general form of an access function. This call specifies the name of the library component and a list of attributes, with the list being terminated by a "0". The call to a *generic_component_routine* returns an object of the appropriate type (generator, component or instance). A set of standard query routines can be applied to the object to extract any attribute or characteristic for it. Figure 8 shows a sample call used to generate an instance of an ALU. The arguments in the call consist of pairs of reserved global symbols (which begin with the letters "GC_") and the appropriate value or list. The size of a list must **always** precede the list itself. For instance, in Figure 8, GC_NUM_FUNCTIONS is assigned the value "8" before specifying the GC_FUNCTION_LIST which consists of 8 operations that the ALU instance will perform. Figure 9 and Figure 10 show the list of global symbols reserved for indicating the type of argument specified in a

```
<generic_component_routine>
    (GC_COMPILER_NAME, <name>,
    <attribute_list>, 0)
```

Figure 7. Generic Component Access: General Form

```
get_gc_instance(  GC_COMPILER_NAME, ALU,
                  GC_BIT_WIDTH, 16,
                  GC_NUM_FUNCTIONS, 8,
                  GC_FUNCTION_LIST, +, -,
                      INC, DEC, >, <, =, AND,
                  GC_ENABLE_FLAG, FALSE,
                  GC_STYLE, CLA,
             0)
```

Figure 8. Sample ALU Instance Call

call, together with their possible values. Appendix A in [6] has a complete list of generator calls for all the generic components.

5. VHDL Models for LEGEND Descriptions

LEGEND generates VHDL models for specifying the behavior of generated components. LEGEND thus complements and overcomes a deficiency in VHDL by providing a generator-generator language for VHDL component libraries. These VHDL models can be used for functional simulation of synthesized register-transfer designs, and can also be used for lower-level synthesis of individual components at the logic and gate levels.

A typical VHDL model generated for a 4-bit up/down counter is shown in Figure 11. These VHDL models are currently simulated on the Vantage VHDL simulator [13].

```
use work.defs.all;
entity counter is
port (In1 : in bit_vector(3 downto 0);
      CLK, Cen : in bit;
      CLOAD, CUP, CDOWN : in bit;
      Out1 : out bit_vector(3 downto 0);
      Aset, Areset : in bit
      );
end counter;

architecture counter_behavior of counter is
begin
      process
variable temp : bit_vector(3 downto 0);
      begin
          if (Aset or Areset) = '0' then
              if (CLK and Cen) = '1' then
                  if Cload = '1' then
                      temp := In1;
                  else
                  if Cup = '1' then
                      temp := inc(temp);
                  else
                  if Cdown = '1' then
                      temp := decr(temp);
                  end if;
                  end if;
                  end if;
              end if;
          else
              if Aset = '1' then
                  temp := "1111";
              else
                  if Areset = '1' then
                      temp := "0000";
                  end if;
              end if;
          end if;
          Out1 <= temp;
          wait on CLK, Aset, Areset;
      end process;
end counter_behavior;

configuration counter_config of counter is
    for counter_behavior
    end for;
end counter_config;
```

Figure 11. Generated VHDL Model for 4-Bit Up/Down Counter

GENERIC COMPONENT GLOBALS		
Name	Possible Values	Default Value
GC_COMPILER_NAME	*< component-name >*	
GC_NUM_FUNCTIONS	*< integer >*	
GC_FUNCTION_LIST	*< list-of-character-strings >*	
GC_NUM_PORTS	*< integer >*	
GC_PORT_ATTRIBUTE_LIST	*< list-of-character-strings >*	
GC_NUM_GUARDS	*< integer >*	
GC_GUARD_LIST	*< list-of-guard-values >*	
GC_INPUT_WIDTH_LIST	*< list-of-integers >*	
GC_NUM_WORDS	*< integer >*	
GC_NUM_INPUTS	*< integer >*	
GC_NUM_OUTPUTS	*< integer >*	
GC_INPUT_WIDTH	*< integer >*	
GC_CONTROL_WIDTH	*< integer >*	
GC_ADDER_STYLE	GC_RIPPLE_CARRY, GC_CARRY_LOOKAHEAD	GC_RIPPLE_CARRY
GC_ALU_STYLE	GC_RIPPLE_CARRY, GC_CARRY_LOOKAHEAD	GC_RIPPLE_CARRY
GC_MULT_STYLE	GC_ARRAY, GC_WALLACE_DADDA, GC_ITERATIVE	GC_ARRAY
GC_DIV_STYLE	GC_RESTORING, GC_NON_RESTORING, GC_MULTIPLICATIVE	GC_RESTORING
GC_COUNTER_STYLE	GC_RIPPLE_CARRY, GC_CARRY_LOOKAHEAD	GC_RIPPLE_CARRY
GC_ENABLE_FLAG	TRUE, FALSE	FALSE
GC_INVERT_FLAG	TRUE, FALSE	FALSE
GC_ELSE_FLAG	TRUE, FALSE	FALSE
GC_SET_FLAG	TRUE, FALSE	FALSE
GC_RESET_FLAG	TRUE, FALSE	FALSE
GC_PIPELINE_FLAG	TRUE, FALSE	FALSE
GC_PIPELINE_STAGES	*< integer >*	
GC_PIPELINE_DELAY	*< integer >*	

Figure 9. List of Compiler Global Symbols

GENERIC COMPONENT GLOBALS		
Name	Possible Values	Default Value
GC_DECODER_TYPE	GC_BINARY, GC_BCD	GC_BINARY
GC_ENCODER_TYPE	GC_BINARY, GC_BCD	GC_BINARY
GC_REGISTER_TYPE	GC_LATCH, GC_D_FF	GC_D_FF
GC_COUNTER_TYPE	GC_BINARY, GC_BCD, GC_JOHNSON, GC_GRAY	GC_BINARY
GC_STACK_TYPE	GC_STACK, GC_FIFO	
GC_SHIFT_MODE	GC_FILL, GC_EXTEND	GC_FILL
GC_FILL_INPUT	0, 1	0
GC_SHIFT_DISTANCE	*< integer >*	
GC_CLOCK_PERIOD	*< integer >*	
GC_CLOCK_HIGH	*< integer >*	
GC_DELAY_VALUE	*< integer >*	
GC_LEFT_INDEX	*< integer >*	
GC_RIGHT_INDEX	*< integer >*	
GC_INTERFACE_FUNCTION	GC_BUFFER, GC_CLOCK_DRIVER, GC_SCHMIDT, GC_TRISTATE	
GC_INTERFACE_MODE	GC_INPUT, GC_OUTPUT, GC_BIDIRECTIONAL	
GC_INTERFACE_LEVEL	GC_CMOS, GC_TTL, GC_ECL	
GC_INTERFACE_DRIVE	GC_LOW, GC_MEDIUM, GC_HIGH	
GC_FAN_OUT	*< integer >*	
GC_SET_VALUE	*< integer >*	
GC_COUNTER_MODE	GC_SYNCHRONOUS, GC_RIPPLE	GC_SYNCHRONOUS
GC_REG_POS_OUT	TRUE, FALSE	TRUE
GC_REG_INVERT_OUT	TRUE, FALSE	FALSE

Figure 10. List of Compiler Global Symbols (Cont'd)

6. Summary

This paper described the features of LEGEND, a novel language used to define, generate, maintain, and upgrade generic component libraries used in high level synthesis. LEGEND provides a powerful generator-generator environment with a consistent hierarchical organization of generic components and instances. LEGEND complements VHDL, a standard hardware description language, by providing a library generator facility. Each generated component has a simulatable VHDL model generated for it. The semantics of LEGEND model register-transfer behavior such as asynchrony and clocking realistically. The LEGEND generator-generator is implemented on SUN3's under C/UNIX, and is used by a suite of behavioral synthesis tools at U.C. Irvine. Future work will address the modeling of better estimators for generic components in the generated libraries.

7. Acknowledgements

The author would like to thank Dan Gajski for initial discussions on the GENUS representation, and Forrest Brewer and Barry Pangrle for discussions on the characterization of costs for multi-output, multi-operation components.

8. References

[1] J. Batali and A. Hartheimer, "The Design Procedure Language Manual," A.I. Memo No. 598, MIT A.I. Laboratory, Sept. 1980.

[2] M.R. Barbacci, "Instruction Set Processor Specification (ISPS)," *IEEE Transactions on Computers*, vol. c-30, no. 1, January 1981.

[3] F.D. Brewer, D.D. Gajski, "Knowledge Based Control in Micro-Architecture Design" *24th IEEE Design Automation Conference* Miami, Fl (July, 1987).

[4] J.R. Duley and D.L. Dietmeyer, "A Digital System Design Language (DDL)," *IEEE Trans. Computers*, Vol C-17, Sept. 1968.

[5] N.D. Dutt and D.D. Gajski, "EXEL: A Language for Interactive Behavioral Synthesis," *Proc. Ninth International Symposium on Computer Hardware Description Languages*, Washington D.C., June 1989.

[6] N.D. Dutt, "GENUS: A Generic Component Library for High Level Synthesis," *Tech Rep* 88-22, U.C. Irvine, Sept. 1988.

[7] N.D. Dutt, "LEGEND: A Language for Generic Component Definition," *Tech Rep* 89-30, U.C. Irvine, Sept. 1989.

[8] F.J. Hill and Z. Navabi, "Extending Second Generation AHPL," *Fourth International Symposium on Hardware Description Languages*, Palo Alto, Oct. 1979.

[9] J.S. Lis and D.D. Gajski, "Synthesis from VHDL," 1988 *International Conference on Computer Design*, Rye Brook, NY, Sept. 1988.

[10] M.C. McFarland, A.C. Parker and R. Camposano, "Tutorial on High Level Synthesis," *25th Design Automation Conference*, July 1988.

[11] N. Vander Zanden and D.D. Gajski, "MILO: A Microarchitecture and Logic Optimizer," *Proc. 25th Design Automation Conference*, Anaheim, CA, June 1988.

[12] *VHDL Tutorial for IEEE Standard* 1076 *VHDL*, CAD Language Systems Inc., June 1987.

[13] *Vantage VHDL Simulator*, Vantage Analysis Systems Inc., 1989.

[14] W. Wolf, "How to Build a Hardware Description and Measurement System on an Object-Oriented Programming Language," *IEEE Trans. Computer Aided-Design*, Vol. 8, No. 3, March 1989.

[15] H. Brown, C. Tong and G. Foyster, "Palladio: An Exploratory Environment for Circuit Design," *IEEE Computer*, Vol. 16, No. 12, Dec. 1983.

[16] G.D. Chen and D.D. Gajski, "An Intelligent Component Database for Behavioral Synthesis," *Technical Report* 89-39, University of California at Irvine, November 1989.

IMPROVING MODULE REUSE BY INTERFACE ADAPTATION

James M. Purtilo   Joanne M. Atlee

Computer Science Department
University of Maryland
College Park, MD 20742

*This research was supported by the Office of Naval Research under contract N00014-87-K-0307,
and by the University of Maryland Institute for Advanced Computer Studies.*

ABSTRACT: Most reuse techniques that involve adaptation of software components focus on transformations at either the design level or the source code level (i.e., individual modules). We propose a third fundamental type of transformation: interface adaptation. By introducing transformations at the point where module interfaces are bound, programmers can reduce coupling between modules in a design, and simultaneously increase cohesion within modules. We have created a language called Nimble for programmers to implement interface adaptations. This paper motivates and describes Nimble in detail.

The emerging technologies for reusing software components make it increasingly likely that designers will be presented with valid program units whose interfaces slightly differ from the specification: parameters may appear in a different order, data types may not exactly match, and some data may need to be either initialized or masked out when the reusable module is integrated within a new application. This situation arises because process models supporting reuse make it more difficult for programmers to anticipate a particular context of use when implementing a module.

Rather than force developers to alter the reusable module's source, we have investigated techniques for *externally* adapting the module for use in a new application: we have created a declarative language called NIMBLE that allows designers to describe how the actual parameters in a procedure call are to be transformed at run time. Application source code need not contain complex, manually-introduced coercion code, and it is therefore simpler. As we will show, it is also easy to automatically implement the transformations themselves. NIMBLE has been implemented on a variety of Unix hosts, and is part of a broader reuse project at the University of Maryland. Our current system is suitable for use either in conjunction with existing module interconnection languages, or stand-alone with C, Pascal and Ada source programs.

NIMBLE is a notation for describing how to transform the actual parameters of a procedure invocation. Such parameter manipulation is required in strongly-typed systems when the parameters being passed do not conform to the arguments accepted by the procedure. The central idea is to provide this parameter-coercion capability without changing the source code of the modules involved. Programmers and designers can use this notation to specify a mapping from the actual parameter list to a new parametric structure that matches the needs of the procedure being invoked. Our system provides a *translator* which takes the NIMBLE specification map and creates an execution-time module to actually perform the coercion during each invocation. This constructed module contains code for extracting the necessary arguments from the actual parameter list, creating a new parameter list (meeting the NIMBLE specifications), and completing the invocation with the new parameter list.

The *type*, *order*, and *structure* of variables in the actual parameter list (at the point of the call) and the formal parameter list (in the procedure definition) are referred to as *interface patterns*. Hence, NIMBLE is a system for *direct manipulation of interface patterns*. Examples of transformations which can be requested through NIMBLE include reordering of arguments, restructuring of argument types, and coercion of a primitive datum's representation (often needed when the procedure call is actually an RPC). By using NIMBLE to interconnect module interfaces, the procedures themselves need not be altered to conform to a given context of use. This characteristic is important in modern software development environments, where the alteration of source code for a particular use is discouraged due to the potential for error (in the application) and additional complexity (in managing all the versions).

Our implementation of NIMBLE is oriented for use in the POLYLITH [9,11] software interconnection system, a so-called "toolbus-based system." The combination of these two systems affords us a powerful resource for developing application structures, and then reusing previously implemented modules to execute those designs. Our research results are applicable to any software development environment that supports separate packaging of reusable modules.

1. MOTIVATION

Reuse of software components is an effective strategy for developers to reduce implementation costs; likewise, developers can improve the quality of new products by employing software components that have demonstrated their effectiveness in previous products. As a result, software researchers have increased efforts to provide environments that will support reuse activities, from packaging of components or experiences to identifying and integrating software modules. However, consider the case where a potentially reusable module has been identified, but exhibits slightly different structure on its interfaces than is required by the new application design; current systems require that this module should be transformed to meet the design's needs.

In contrast, our idea is that it may often be more appropriate to partially adapt the design to meet the interfaces defined by an existing module. That is, it may be valuable to have some mechanism for adapting the context of use to meet the needs of reusable modules. There are several reasons why this would be a useful capability to add to existing reuse systems. First, transformations external to the module can be generated directly and automatically, whereas alterations of a source program itself may not be so easily transformed by automatic means. This is undesirable, since having programmers transform implementations manually may introduce needless error. Besides, since the problem is with the interconnection and not with the modules' functionality, it makes more sense to adapt the interfaces to conform to a particular connection than to manipulate the source code. Further, there is no reason to overload an underlying configuration management system with many slight variants of essentially the same module, especially when prototyping: by changing a module's source code, all results from previously run test cases or verification proofs are invalidated. Program correctness will have to be reverified, or test cases rerun, to ensure that the module still performs the intended function. Finally, developers do not always have the option of changing a source code — access to the module source code is often denied for wholly untechnical reasons.

This situation — where developers have a module that is semantically correct but contains structural differences on the interfaces — is likely to become much more common as reuse systems grow in scale. As has been known for a long time, an important way that modules can be made more widely applicable (reusable) is to expand the domain of types on to which the module's interfaces can be validly applied. Using our approach, a single module can be stored in the reuse library, and, during subsequent use of the module, the accessors for that module to operate on specific structures can be introduced automatically based on the new context of use.

With the advent of mixed-language and mixed-architecture programming, the representation of shared data structures must often be coerced to meet another language's (or host architecture's) needs when the variables are accessed. Yet it is difficult to anticipate all possible future uses of a module when it is being added to a reuse system, hence it is difficult to build into that code all the possible coercion routines that could ultimately be required. Instead, it is desirable to have means for separately adapting the module based on its context of use.

Perhaps the most pressing motivation for external adaptation of module implementations is found in a new type of reuse environment under development in a broad effort at the University of Maryland [2]. The fundamental concept in this project is division of the development process into two parts: one process deals directly with applications (the *Application Project*), and the other specifically deals with organizing reuse activities (the *Experience Factory*.) These units operate concurrently and somewhat independently, each according to its own process model. During project development, experience is passed from the Application Project to the Experience Factory, where it is processed and passed back to the Application Project upon request. Experience can be passed in a variety of forms, such as data, lessons learned, and product parts. Since management of experience is a very different task from development, segregating an Experience Factory shields reuse activities from the shorter-term concerns of development managers.

This 'factory' approach to software development entails being able to study previously developed products to identify modules that can be extracted, packaged, and stored in the experience base for use in new projects. Because of the dual process models directing development, it becomes much less likely that programmers will be able to *anticipate* the structure of interfaces when operating on a module: the data structures or order of parameters cannot be entered to match the definition of a known resource (as is currently the case in other programming environments.) In fact, it may only be by accident that the data structures of the execution environment happen to match the structures on which the previous program operates. Programmers will be faced with the task of adapting that module for use in the new context, and, in operating on that type, risk unintended side effects in the alterations. It is therefore desirable to have a mechanism for adapting that module's interface without having to actually manipulate the source code directly.

2. INTERFACE ADAPTATION

To illustrate this situation, consider the following example. The calling module contains a database of employee records, each record containing all of the pertinent data concerning an employee, including some personal information. The module calls an envelope printing routine that requires a record consisting of only the sex, name, and address of the employee. (The trimmed record is not only practical, in the sense of transferring less data, but also necessary, when the original record contains classified information that cannot be released.):

```
ACTUAL:   Employee:{     Name :STR;
                         Address :STR[4];
                         Sex :STR;
                         Age :INT;
                         SocNum :INT;
                         Salary :FLOAT
          }

FORMAL:   Addressee:  {  Sex :INT;
                         Name :STR;
                         Address :STR[4]
          }
```

These modules cannot be linked due to syntactic differences in their respective interface patterns. Not only does the record structure expected by the called module contain fewer fields, but the order of the fields has changed and the **sex** data field is now represented by an integer. Clearly some data manipulation is required.

One alternative might be to augment the code generators in such a way that the arguments are pushed into the call frame in the correct format. Unfortunately, this requires considerable programming, since this must be done to all of the translation processors being used. In addition, the task can be quite complex if the module is used in two or more different contexts. Of course, this method assumes that one has access to the source code of all the language processors.

Another alternative is to implement an intermediate module that accepts the actual interface pattern and produces an argument list that syntactically matches the formal interface pattern. This method, however, partially violates the transparency of the module interconnection. In addition, it is an ad hoc approach to a simple, common problem that can easily be automated. This automation, in fact, is our approach.

2.1. Coercion of Interface Patterns

Before one can specify a coercion, one needs to know the pattern for both the source and targeted interfaces. In joining two modules using NIMBLE, the programmer is given both an *annotated* description of the actual interface pattern and an *unannotated* description of the formal interface pattern. These interface patterns are described in terms of our NIMBLE notation, to be discussed below. By "annotation", we mean that separate components of the interface pattern are labeled so we may refer to them individually when constructing a map from the actual list of parameters to the formal interface pattern. The unannotated parameter list describes the number, order, and type of arguments that the invoked module is expecting; the annotated parameter list describes the number, order, and type of arguments that the calling module is transmitting.

For the sake of consistency, these interface descriptions must match the corresponding declarations in the modules' source code. One way programmers can obtain these patterns is

to simply transcribe them from the source. However, programmers can be notoriously poor translators, so we usually employ automatic techniques for extracting the interface patterns. Systems such as our NEWYACC translator can easily extract just this information from source codes [8]. If source codes are unavailable, the programmer must reproduce his own interface descriptions from program documentation.

The unannotated parameter list, describing the formal interface pattern, is displayed as a list of one or more argument types separated by semicolons:

$$
\begin{array}{rcl}
\textit{arg-list} & ::= & \textit{arg} \mid \textit{arg} \, ; \, \textit{arg-list} \\
\textit{arg} & ::= & \textit{primitive} \mid \textit{structured} \mid \textit{matrix} \mid \textit{pointer} \\
\textit{primitive} & ::= & \textbf{BOOL} \mid \textbf{INT} \mid \textbf{FLOAT} \mid \textbf{STR} \\
\textit{structured} & ::= & \{ \, \textit{arg-list} \, \} \\
\textit{matrix} & ::= & \textit{arg} \, [\, \textit{index-list} \,] \\
\textit{index-list} & ::= & \textit{number} \mid \textit{number} \, , \, \textit{index-list} \\
\textit{pointer} & ::= & \uparrow \textit{arg}
\end{array}
$$

Pointers to data are treated as just another set of data types. In the next section we will discuss the impact pointers have on interface manipulations.

The annotated parameter list, describing the actual interface pattern, is denoted by a list of one or more *labeled* arguments separated by semicolons. The format is similar to that described above, except that each argument is uniquely labeled. Argument components are also labeled, so that the programmer may access individual structure components. In the cases that the programmer is providing the annotated pattern, one may suggestively choose labels for any of the arguments or components, as long as the labels are unique. Our system will systematically annotate the remaining arguments. Throughout this paper, we will use our system-provided labels in all examples, unless otherwise noted.

Consider the following parameter lists:
```
ACTUAL:   a:INT;b:{a:INT;b:BOOL[10]};
          c:{a:INT;b:STR}[20]
FORMAL:   FLOAT;INT;{INT;BOOL[10]};{INT;STR}
```
The calling module is transmitting three parametric arguments: an integer, a structured argument (composed of an integer followed by an array of ten booleans), followed by an array of twenty structures (each composed of an integer followed by a string). The formal pattern specifies the interface pattern expected by the invoked module: a floating-point number, followed by an integer, followed by a structure (composed of an integer and an array of ten booleans), followed another structure (composed of an integer and a string). These parametric interfaces cannot be connected as is.

With the descriptions of these two interface patterns available, the programmer can then use NIMBLE to create a new actual interface pattern. The annotated actual parameter list is provided so that the programmer can pick and choose from arguments in the original pattern. The unannotated formal interface pattern is really only used as a guide to the programmer in creating the map, since the new pattern must be equivalent to the formal parameter list. For the above example, a new actual parameter list could be constructed that *would* match the formal interface pattern: one of the actual integer parameters could be coerced into a floating-point argument to match the first formal parameter; any of the actual integers would match the second formal parameter; the third formal parameter is equivalent to the second actual parameter; and the fourth formal parametric requirement could be satisfied by any of the array elements of the last actual parameter. Nimble is responsible for checking whether the programmer-designed specification satisfies the formal pattern. Once a map has been constructed by the programmer, and its consistency checked, the Nimble translator will generate an operational specification for transforming the original actual interface pattern into the programmer-defined interface pattern. This operational specification can then be further translated for use in a variety of execution environments, as will be discussed in the next section.

Before proceeding with the notation, we need to define a few terms. Two parameter lists are considered to be *structurally equivalent* if there exists a bijection between the lists such that (1) a primitive actual parameter only maps onto a formal parameter of the same primitive type, and (2) a composite actual parameter only maps onto a composite formal parameter, such that their elements are inductively structurally equivalent. If the bijection is order-preserving, such that the ith actual argument maps onto the ith formal argument, then the mapping is an *isomorphism* and the parameter lists are said to be *syntactically equivalent*. We define the notion of *semantically equivalent* parameter lists to be lists that convey the same information, i.e. the same data values, though not necessarily in the same format or order. Henceforth, we use the general term *equivalence* to mean *syntactic equivalence*; we will continue to fully specify *semantic equivalence*.)

Most Nimble specifications are based on the arguments from the original actual parameter list. To access an argument, one references the associated label. If one were to specify an integer argument in the above example, the programmer could use one of the following annotations referring to the actual parameter list:

a   - 1st argument.
b.a   - 1st component of 2nd actual parameter.
c[0].a   - 1st component of the first array element of last actual parameter.
c[1].a   - first component of second array element of last actual parameter.
⋮   ⋮
c[19].a   - first component of last array element of last actual parameter.

Each of the integers listed above would satisfy the *syntactic* requirement of an integer parameter. Which of the 22 actual integers is *semantically* intended must be known and specified by the programmer. Nimble only tests for structural equivalence between interface patterns; semantic errors, such as passing argument a when argument b.a is the value expected, will go unnoticed.

A Nimble specification is very simple; it is a list of Nimble arguments separated by semicolons. Thus, the programmer can reorder the parametric arguments by simply listing their annotations in the desired order.

Example: Reordering

```
ACTUAL:  a:INT;b:FLOAT
FORMAL:  FLOAT;INT
NIMBLE:  b;a
```

The existence or absence of structure is specified with the use of delimiters. Record structure is created by listing the components inside braces; matrix structure is formed by surrounding the array elements by square brackets; by placing a ↑ symbol before an argument, one creates a pointer to the argument. Structure can be relaxed by simply listing an actual argument's components without the associated structure.

Example: Restructuring

```
ACTUAL:  a:INT;b:BOOL[3]
FORMAL:  {INT;BOOL;BOOL;BOOL}
NIMBLE:  {a;b[0];b[1];b[2]}

ACTUAL:  a:INT[3];b:INT[3];c:{a:INT;b:INT};d:INT
FORMAL:  INT[3,3]
NIMBLE:  [a;b;[c.a;c.b;d]]
```

One specifies the coercion of primitive data objects with a function call, where the name of the function is the desired data type and the argument is the labeled actual argument. We provide built-in functions for type conversions among all primitive types.

Example: Primitive Coercion

```
ACTUAL:  a:BOOL;b:FLOAT
FORMAL:  INT;INT
NIMBLE:  INT(a);INT(b)
```

By replacing the function argument with a string data value, one can 'cast' the string into the appropriate primitive data type. Thus, the programmer can create new values whenever the calling module does not provide the required information.

Example: Creation

```
ACTUAL:  a:INT
FORMAL:  INT;BOOL
NIMBLE:  a;BOOL('TRUE')
```

Nimble does not prevent incompatible type coercions. The code is generated to create the new parameter list containing the coerced value. If this value is not a member of the specified type's domain (however that domain is defined by the language and machine on which the invoked module resides), a run-time error will result.

While the above notation is complete, and can describe all possible parametric transformations, it can be cumbersome when dealing with large arrays. Consider the following example:

```
ACTUAL:   a:INT[100]
FORMAL:   INT[50]
```

The actual parameter is an array of one hundred integers, and the invoked module is expecting a vector of fifty integers. But which fifty integers? The first fifty? The last fifty? The components of the array whose index is even? What if we want to specify the diagonal of a 100x100 array, or the submatrix of a multi-dimensional matrix? We have provided a rule that allows the programmer to create matrices by listing the desired elements, but this is simply not feasible where large arrays are concerned.

To simplify such manipulations, we provide a short cut: an EVAL statement, whose format is

```
EVAL ( id , parmlist )
```

The EVAL rule states that the code in module *id* is to be executed with parameters *parm-list*, and the resultant data structure will be passed as a parameter. All EVAL modules used in a particular NIMBLE specification must be declared in an optional declarations section before the specification is given. These declarations include the name of the module to be called in EVAL; the number, order and type of the parameters the module is expecting; and the argument type of the result. NIMBLE checks that the parameter list in the EVAL statement is syntactically equivalent to the interface pattern provided in the declarations section. The resultant type is used when checking that the NIMBLE specification is syntactically equivalent to the formal interface pattern of the invoked module.

The NIMBLE example below exhibits how we can use EVAL to solve our array problem, where module *even* is a simple for-loop that assigns the value of the formal array index i to the value of actual array index 2i.

Example: EVAL

```
ACTUAL:   a:INT[100]
FORMAL:   INT[50]
NIMBLE:   DECLS even :  INT[100] -> INT[50]; END
          EVAL(even, a)
```

In our current implementation, the modules listed in the declaration sections and used in EVAL statements must be provided by the programmer. After some performance analysis, one could provide a library of commonly used coercion modules [12]. The reuse of these modules is as profitable as the reusability of the program modules whose interconnection is made possible by NIMBLE.

We stress that the use of the EVAL statement is not a "catch-all" for situations that cannot be handled by the restructuring symbols and casting functions that comprise the NIMBLE

notation. We provide the EVAL statement because we realize that it is impractical to use the simple notation when dealing with large matrices; it is feature of *convenience*. Along these lines, we also extended the above notation to allow arithmetic and boolean expressions wherever a primitive was allowed, with the exception of the declaration section of modules used by EVAL. This allows *semantic* coercions of the arguments when needed. For example, if the actual interface pattern contains an array of 10 integers, and the called module is expecting a single integer, the expected integer may be the sum of the array elements rather than a particular array entry. This also provides the means to compute the index of the array element to be passed at run-time. Note that the use of expressions is not necessary for the solution of the parametric coercion problem (a syntactic problem); it simply provides a shorthand notation for simple computations that avoid the overhead associated with the use of EVAL.

If the module being invoked is a *function* (as opposed to a procedure), then NIMBLE is also responsible for coercing the function result, since NIMBLE controls all communication between the modules. We use the reserved word RETURN to separate the parameters from the resultant arguments.

Example: Function Calls

```
ACTUAL:   a:{a:str;b:bool[2,3]}[2] RETURN ↑{int;int}
FORMAL:   bool RETURN a:str
NIMBLE:   a[1].b[0,2] RETURN ↑{int(a);int('0')}
```

The ACTUAL pattern specifies the pattern of the parameters that the calling module is sending and the type of the result that it expects in return. The FORMAL pattern describes the parameters expected by the invoked module and the resultant type of the function. The NIMBLE specification describes the transformation from actual parameters to formal parameters, and the return transformation from the formal result to the actual result. Thus, we annotate the return portion of the FORMAL PATTERN. The above format must be used whenever the invoked module has a return value, since all data transfers between the two modules is managed by the NIMBLE module; this is true even if there is no need to coerce the resultant type.

2.2. Translation

The previous section has detailed the features of our NIMBLE language. There is, however, a great deal of underlying system support needed in order to have the desired translations performed efficiently at execution time. The goal of this section is to describe the context of use for NIMBLE.

To illustrate steps taken by the user, plus what happens in the support system at each stage of translation, we will use our example problem from the introduction. In this problem, a procedure having a record Employee needs to call some procedure whose formal parameter is a record structure of type Addressee. The box included earlier gives the actual and formal interface patterns of the parametric transfer. A mapping between the two procedure interfaces can be created using the NIMBLE notation. For illustrative purposes, we gave the arguments suggestive labels to help demonstrate the prevalence of the coercion problem in programming. As discussed in the earlier section, the programmer can either provide his own labels (if he is entering the interface patterns himself), or accept those that are automatically generated (like those we used in the examples in the previous section).

The user may now specify a transformation on the actual pattern. The map is given in terms of the actual pattern's annotation:

NIMBLE: {INT(Sex) ; Name ; Address}

The effect is to create a new record structure, containing the original Sex field (coerced to an integer value) as well as the actual Name and Address fields. The above pattern is consistent with, and in fact identical to, the desired target pattern.

Having the above NIMBLE mapping prepared in a file (or available via various editing tools within our support system), the user may now invoke the NIMBLE translator, with the mapping provided as input. The translator's output is an operational specification of the execution-time steps necessary to transform the actual parameters into a structure that conforms to the formal interface pattern. This specification is given in a high level "pseudo code," in order to be applicable in many different contexts of use. Hence, further translation is required to execute the coercion module in the given programming environment. One goal may be to generate a separate module to be statically linked 'in between' the two modules. In this case, a set of language-specific translators must be available to accept the pseudo code and generate an appropriate procedure, which may then be compiled and linked into the application. Another situation arises when the modules being joined are to reside on different hosts, and hence not only must the NIMBLE translation be performed but the executables must be set up to effect a remote procedure call (RPC). In this case, the support system may elect to link the NIMBLE map into the RPC stubs; it may compile and package the map as a separate tool in the program graph; or, in toolbus-based systems, it may provide the operational specification to a separate tool which is set up to interpret the code.

In general, the pseudo-code generated by NIMBLE must provide relatively few primitive operations in order to simplify the translation schemes to the various underlying support systems. We defined a simple functional language for this purpose: a function to retrieve the value of an argument from the actual parameter list, functions to perform coercion of primitive data types, the EVAL function described above, and a function to append arguments to the *transformed* parameter list actually sent to the invoked module.

The operators of our pseudo-code language are:

```
Value( index );            Int2Str( value );
Eval( function , value-list );    Float2Boolean( value );
Send( value );                    Float2Int( value );
Boolean2Int( value );             Float2Str( value );
Boolean2Float( value );           Str2Boolean( value );
Boolean2Str( value );             Str2Int( value );
Int2Boolean( value );             Str2Float( value );
Int2Float( value );
```

Since our language is functional, all the operations listed above except for the send operation return a value. Fortunately, they all return the same value type: *value*, which we define to be a data string in the format defined by the underlying support system. In many systems, this format may be a sequence of bits in binary; only the type information associated with the sequence can give the data any *real* value, i.e., a base 10 integer value. Thus, though it may seem as if functions Send, Value, and Eval are multi-valued functions, in reality they are only binary string manipulations.

Each operator assumes that a 'packet' of parameters destined for the target interface has been initialized; the operators construct a new packet by either accessing actual parameters in original packet or creating data elements, and then adding them to the new packet in the desired order. The order of the Send operations determines the order of the values in the data packet. Hence the concatenation of the arguments of the Send functions will comprise the structure of the data message to be sent. In the case that a datum must be selected from the source interface, an *index* is calculated (based on the label of the argument referenced and the actual interface pattern) to identify precisely which data element is to be accessed from the parameter packet. Alternately, a datum may be created, in which case the initializing *value* (encoded in a string) is coerced into the appropriate primitive type using one of the Str2xxx functions, and the resultant value is appended to the new data packet.

The *index* provides half of the information necessary for the NIMBLE run-time environment to correctly access the raw data in one data packet for packaging into another packet. This *index* is a sequence of integers which uniquely identifies one logical component of an annotated interface pattern. Starting with the entire source interface structure, the first integer i selects the i'th argument of the structure; the second integer j selects the j'th component of that i'th argument; etc. This selection method is based directly on the annotation scheme as described in the previous section, and all that we have done here is replace the textual labels with an integer identifier.

However, the above indexing scheme may be insufficient for locating the exact offset of a datum in a raw source packet. The reason is that the size of a representation of some primitive data objects can not be known until run-time, e.g., a string datum which is passed on a run-time stack. In order to correctly unwind the representation and extract a particular datum, the run-time agent must know the type of elements in the packet being sent by the calling module. Hence, the actual interface pattern is provided at the beginning of the pseudo-code source for use by later translators.

The formal interface pattern is also provided, so that variable declarations are possible in the cases where we wish to produce source code.

The most basic of the functions is simply Value(*index*), which selects the *index*'th datum from the source message and returns its value. If that element being selected must be coerced along the way, then any of the xxx2xxx casting operators listed above would be used. If a separate *function* must be applied (in effect, a more elaborate or a semantic coercion), then the Eval() function will execute the appropriate module, and return the resultant value to be appended to the packet.

For our example, the pseudo-code generated would be:

```
{STR;STR[4];INT;INT;INT;FLOAT}
{BOOL;STR;STR[4]}
Send(Str2Int(Value(3)));
    ...Corresponds to Sex field and its coercion.
Send(Value(1));
             ...Corresponds to Name field.
Send(Value(2));
    ...Corresponds to Address vector of strings.
```

The first line is the structural pattern of the source interface; it may be unrecognizable since it is no longer annotated. The second line is the interface pattern expected by the invoked module. The remaining lines describe the steps needed to extract the required information from the original parameter packet and create the new actual parameter list.

2.3. Context of Use

To complete the preprocessing given a single language domain, the NIMBLE pseudo-code needs to be translated into an application language source. The easiest way to do this is to treat the program statements as blocks of assignment statements, one program statement for each parameter sent to the invoked module. Based on this operational specification as well as the source interface patterns, the code generated for our example problem would be translated into the C program shown in Figure 1.

This implementation relies on the library routine Str2Int, a coercion routine which would reside in a host library and be linked into the application like most system calls. This program is suitable for use in an environment where all procedures are to be linked and executed in the same process space; a different program would be generated were this to be used in a distributed or other type of environment.

Note the extensive aliasing which may occur: the procedure initiating the call will only know the name of the 'real' procedure to be called, not the intermediate NIMBLE procedure. The linkage editor is responsible for insuring that the actual calls performed will be first to the xlate routine above (or its equivalent, depending on the environment), and also for binding the xlate_inner call to the target procedure. Designers have a great deal of flexibility in how the coercion routine is installed, but the use of NIMBLE in this environment does rely on the existence of a suitably enhanced linkage editor, i.e., one extended to allow this form of aliased bindings. This requirement is satisfied (almost by definition) by most reasonable module interconnection languages (MILs) and related facilities. The system we use for this capability is the POLYLITH software interconnection system [9, 10]. The sequence of steps taken by a user to produce the above example is shown in Figure 2.

However, an alternative to the above compiler-oriented, single process space execution environment is to incorporate the NIMBLE pseudo-code directly into the structural specification which is typically managed by the Module Interconnection Language (MIL) in toolbus-based systems such as POLYLITH. At execution time, an interpreter is used to process the pseudo-code specification and perform the required parametric coercion. This approach is especially effective in prototyping environments. NIMBLE can facilitate the direct (re)use of library modules with a minimal investment in 'pipe fitting.' The sequence of steps a user would take in order to obtain this effect in an interpretive environment is analogous to that shown in Figure 2.

A unique use of the NIMBLE tool is one of data conversion of host files. The NIMBLE pseudo-code can be translated directly into a standalone tool which can be applied directly to data files. This is useful when a large file of data must be transformed in more elaborate ways than can be effected by tools such as, for instance in the Unix domain, *sed* [6] or *awk* [1]. Used in conjunction with a heterogeneous interconnection system such as POLYLITH, NIMBLE can be used to transform data files across different system architectures.

The question of how well we have chosen our set of primitive data types is an important one. Even for a 'simple' datum of type *integer* there are many, and often inconsistent, assumptions made about semantics. The host architecture's binary encoding scheme, the range of values possible, and behavior of operations on elements of the type are all potential sources of error, should our NIMBLE processors deal with the data differently than do the object codes for an application.

In the context of use where all procedures have been implemented in the same language domain and are linked into the same process space, the correspondence between NIMBLE's semantics for a type and the application language's semantics does not need to be strong. This is because the names of primitive types in NIMBLE end up acting simply as place holders for the declarations of that application language. The post-processor, after all, is expected to simply generate a source code in the same language of interest. This fact even makes it easy to add new primitive types, as long as the implementor is able to correctly provide datum size information to the appropriate post-processor.

For other execution environments (e.g., mixed language programming), a support system such as POLYLITH is necessary. In this situation, the NIMBLE type names again act as place

```
struct Employee {                    xlate( a )
    char *Name;                      struct Employee a;
    char *Address[4];                {
    char *Sex;                           int nimble_i;
    int Age;                             struct Addressee b;
    int SocNum;                          b.Sex = Str2Int(a.Sex);
    float Salary; };                     b.Name = a.Name;
struct Addressee {                       for(nimble_i=0;nimble_i<4;nimble_i++){
    int Sex;                                 b.Address[nimble_i] = a.Address[nimble_i];
    char *Name;                          }
    char *Address[4];                    xlate_inner( b );
};                                   }
```

Figure 1: Code automatically generated for user in the example.

holders, but for abstract data types rather than for predefined language types. The interconnection system is then responsible for providing representation functions at the point of the call to map the elements from the host and language specific representation to a 'standard' representation, and for providing inverse representation functions to map the formal arguments from the 'standard' representation to the specific representation expected by the procedure. NIMBLE merely coerces parameters within the 'standard' representation, without concern or knowledge of the specific data representation used by either the source or the destination module. This approach also makes distribution of the two procedures transparent; the call can be turned into an RPC with no change to the procedure implementation themselves. Techniques of this type are described by Purtilo in [11].

In each of the execution environments described above, pointers are handled 'as can be expected' depending upon the context. When all transmitted data is in the same process space, then the NIMBLE place holders for pointer data can be installed in a translated call consistently. When the call crosses process boundaries, then the pointer will only be correct if the underlying execution environment supports the additional address translation needed for non-local referencing. Few systems provide this capability. However, it is important to note that even without this capability, NIMBLE will allow correct dereferencing of pointers at the point of the call should the user's map direct that referenced data be accessed to build an immediate object for transmission to the non-local service (as long as the resultant coercion module lies in the same process space as the invoking module). However, the success of mapping from a data object to a referenced object does depend on the address translation capabilities of the underlying environment.

Finally there is the question of how well NIMBLE translation routines support the calling conventions of the application language domains involved. Our original conception of NIMBLE concentrated on the interconnection of distributed modules, and thus we initially unwittingly constrained our parameter passing conventions to pass-by-value. If the parametric translation module created by NIMBLE is to be linked into the executables of the interconnected modules, then pass-by-reference and pass-by-value/result conventions can

also be supported, as long as (1) the formal interface pattern specifies the parameter passing convention used for each parameter, and (2) the language in which the NIMBLE translation module is written supports the same parameter passing conventions as the language used to write the invoked procedure. The first requirement can be satisfied by annotating each argument in the formal interface pattern with the desired method of parameter passing (recall that the formal pattern was previously unannotated). To satisfy the second requirement, a set of language-specific NIMBLE translators is provided. Fortunately, as was described above, the actual interface manipulation is written in a high level pseudo-code which is easily translated into an appropriate programming language. Ensuring that the created NIMBLE module accepts each actual parameter with the same passing convention as the formal module is enough to guarantee the semantics of the different parameter passing techniques in a single address space environment.

Unfortunately, there are situations involving pointers where, when a user specifies that immediate data be created for transmission to the callee, the post-processor may allocate temporary storage to hold the intermediate values constructed by NIMBLE. Should a pointer to this storage be imprudently returned as the value of some other parameter in the pattern, then a 'core leak' can be established with disastrous consequences: the calling routine would have pointers to storage which the run-time environment might then reallocate for other uses. This type of error can really be classified as a heap management problem, and in many ways is a difficulty independent of any use of NIMBLE.

3. CONCLUSION

We have described a simple language which allows designers to describe how parameters should be transformed and coerced when passed in a procedure call. NIMBLE has been implemented in C and runs on most any 4.2BSD and 4.3BSD Unix systems. Both the current implementation and the ideas behind it are applicable when interfacing components written in a wide variety of application languages. Our system may be used 'stand alone' or in concert with a software interconnection system, although we have found that

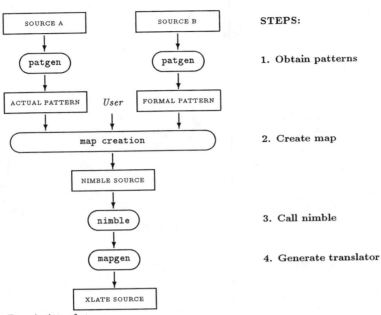

STEPS:

1. Obtain patterns

2. Create map

3. Call nimble

4. Generate translator

Description of steps:

1. Either user or support system invokes `patgen`, a filter created via `newyacc`, to extract the interface patterns for named procedures in a given application language. Alternately, the user can directly enter the pattern.

2. The user creates a desired map based on the two patterns. This step can be performed using normal text editors, or with a Suntools-based editor designed specifically to assist in this step.

3. The user invokes `nimble` to create the operational specification for this map. Equivalence checking between the formal pattern and the range of the map is performed here.

4. The user invokes one of a set of post-processors to generate a language-specific translation routine. Either the user or the support system must notify the interconnection system so that bindings of the call in A to B wil go through the translator.

Figure 2: Sample sequence of steps for preparing a translation with Nimble.

the latter environment allows us to get the most utility from NIMBLE. As such, NIMBLE has become an important resource in the POLYLITH development environment, which in turn supports NIMBLE by organizing all the fragments of information needed for NIMBLE to function.

Related module interconnection language research has focused more closely on semantic correspondence of interfaces, e.g. [7]. However, there has been very little related work on this intermediate 'syntactic' level. One data restructuring system called "CONVERT" was described in [12] — expressed using our terminology, this was really an investigation into what functions one could want to have around to use via in an EVAL operation. It did not deal with transformations on interface patterns. Of more importance to us is the work on SIDL, an interface definition language developed at the Software Productivity Consortium [4, 5]. NIMBLE must check that the range of a user-defined map is 'equal' to the formal interface. In our initial implementation the

'equivalence checker' we used is a strong checker: type and structure must directly correspond. But there are many situations where this level of checking can be relaxed safely, e.g., the primitive datum `integer` may be sent in a message to another machine which represents it with more significant bits, even if the converse is not true. Likewise, the equivalence checking can be tolerant in situations where there are mismatches in primitive types but where there are also known coercion routines to correctly translate. SIDL contains a more elaborate system for checking the compatibility of interfaces, which can help us extend our system's applicability. Finally, other data transformation work has been performed in the database community. The PAL language (PRECI Algebraic Language) was developed to integrate information stored in different databases [3]. Although some of the data integration problems that PAL solves are similar to our coercion problem (type differences, missing data and structural differences), their solutions could not be adapted to the contexts of use which require substantial data transfer during invocation.

The economic advantage of reusing software rather than reimplementing it is highly sought after. Most investigations in this line focus on ways to adapt software (or design specifications) to meet a new context of use. NIMBLE demonstrates that it is easy and valuable to also be able to adapt the context of use to meet the needs of our existing modules.

REFERENCES

[1] Aho, A., B. Kernigan and P. Weinberger. Awk- A pattern scanning and processing language. *AT&T Bell Laboratories*, (second edition) 1978.

[2] Basili, V. Software development: a paradigm for the future. Keynote address at COMPSAC '89, *appears in COMPSAC proceedings.*

[3] Deen, S., R. Amin and M. Taylor. Data Integration in Distributed Databases. **IEEE Transactions on Software Engineering**, vol. 13, (July 1987), pp. 860-864.

[4] Jeffords, R. The SIDL type system. *Software Productivity Consortium*, SPC-TR-88-005, 1988.

[5] Jeffords, R., and S. O'Malley. SIDL: Strongly-typed interface definition language. *Software Productivity Consortium*, SPC-TR-87-009, 1987.

[6] McMahon, L. SED- A non-interactive text editor. *AT&T Bell Laboratories*, 1978.

[7] Perry, D. The Inscape environment. *Proceedings of 11th Intl Conf on Software Engineering*, (May 1989), pp. 2-12.

[8] Purtilo, J., and J. Callahan. Parse tree annotations. **Communications of the ACM**, (December 1989), pp. 1467-1477.

[9] Purtilo, J. Polylith: an environment to support management of tool interfaces. *Proceedings of ACM SIGPLAN Symposium on Language Issues in Programming Environments*, (July 1985), pp. 12-18.

[10] Purtilo, J. On specifying an environment. *Proceedings of the IEEE's Ninth International Computer Software and Applications Conference*, (October 1985), pp. 456-463.

[11] Purtilo, J. Software interconnection technology, UMCP CSD TR-2139, submitted for publication.

[12] Shu, N., B. Housel and V. Lum. CONVERT: A high level translation definition language for data conversion. **Communications of the ACM**, vol. 18, (October 1975), pp. 557-567.

LAZY EVALUATION IN LOGIC PROGRAMMING

Sanjai Narain
RAND Corporation
1700 Main Street
Santa Monica, CA 90406
narain@rand.org

ABSTRACT

This paper presents a method of bringing the concept of lazy evaluation to logic programming in a rigorous yet efficient manner. Its main advantage over previous methods is its considerable efficiency, both from a theoretical as well as implementation point of view. It is based upon making the SLD-resolution rule of inference directly simulate the behavior of a lazy rewriting interpreter satisfying strong computational properties. Thereby, it yields a powerful system in which one can program with functions, relations, non-determinism, lazy evaluation and combinations of these all within a single logical framework.

Our method can also be viewed as contributing to the design and implementation of lazy rewriting. It introduces lazy, non-deterministic rewriting. It proposes a new method of shrinking the search space of reductions to a single branch. It allows a very simple yet efficient implementation in Prolog, so programming of many low-level tasks involved in usual implementations of lazy rewriting is avoided altogether.

Keywords: Lazy evaluation, rewriting, logic programming, functional programming.

1.0 INTRODUCTION

Lazy evaluation is a method of computing which ensures that a computation step is performed only when necessary. The precise meaning of this method depends upon the computational framework in use. For example, in the framework of rewriting e.g. [Hoffmann & O'Donnell 1982, Huet & Levy 1979] lazy evaluation reduces a subterm only when necessary to reduce the whole term. An important advantage of it is that it allows programming with the powerful concept of infinite structures. For example, consider the following rewrite rules:

```
infinite_ones=>[1|infinite_ones].
head([U|V])=>U.
```

where the first rule computes an infinite list of 1s and the second computes the head of a list. Here [] is the empty list and [U|V] the list with head U and tail V. Given the term head(infinite_ones), lazy evaluation will reduce infinite_ones to [1|infinite_ones]. Now, as head([1|infinite_ones]) can be reduced as a whole to 1, infinite_ones is not further reduced. The answer is com-

puted as 1. In contrast, eager evaluation will not compute this answer as it would compute infinite_ones to completion and, of course, never terminate.

More interesting infinite structures naturally arises in representations of processes, e.g. [Kahn & MacQueen 1977, Shapiro 1987], simulation, e.g. oscillating systems give rise to an infinite list of events, real analysis, e.g. Taylor or Fourier series, or graphics, e.g. the works of art by M.C. Escher. Even when only finite structures are involved, lazy evaluation can yield termination more quickly than eager evaluation. In fact, for rewriting, lazy evaluation has been shown to be optimal e.g. [Vuillemin 1974, Hoffmann & O'Donnell 1982, Huet & Levy 1979, Berry & Levy 1979]. This means that normal forms (values) of terms can be determined in a minimum number of reduction steps.

Logic programming is the use of statements of logic as computer programs. Note that as the lambda calculus is a logic, programming in it is also logic programming. See e.g. [Robinson 1987, Darlington et al. 1986]. However, in this paper, we focus on logic programming *proper*, i.e. Horn clauses with the SLD-resolution rule of inference [Kowalski 1979]. The importance of Horn clauses is their *procedural interpretation* [Kowalski 1979] by which clauses can be regarded as procedures in a conventional programming language and SLD-resolution as an interpreter for these. The procedural intepretation allows algorithms to be designed using powerful concepts from logic such as relations, unification, non-determinism, sets or partially instantiated structures. Furthermore, intuitions and proof techniques of logic can be utilized to prove properties of programs. Many important applications of logic programming, via an approximation to it in the form of the language Prolog, are known e.g. [Warren & van Caneghem 1987]. These are in areas such as databases, natural language analysis, symbolic algebra, compiler construction, or crime prevention e.g. [FBI 1988].

Clearly, if the concept of lazy evaluation could be brought to logic programming, then in view of the above discussion, a quite powerful programming system could result. This paper presents a rigorous and efficient method of doing this. It is based, not upon generalizing logic programming to exhibit laziness, but upon extracting laziness out of logic programming itself. This is done by making SLD-resolution *directly* simulate the behavior of a lazy rewriting interpreter satisfying strong computational properties. Thus, it achieves considerable efficiency, both from a theoretical as well as implementation point of view. Applications of the system are discussed in [Narain 1989, Parker 1989, Chau & Parker 1989, Livezey & Muntz 1989].

Our method can also be viewed as contributing to the design and implementation of lazy rewriting. It suggests a combination of lazy evaluation and non-determinism which yields interesting programming possibilities. See Section 6.1 or [Narain 1989]. Restriction (e) of Section 3.0 is a novel device for shrinking the search space of reduction to a single branch. Implementations of lazy rewriting usually require accomplishment of a large number of low-level tasks such as pattern matching, dynamic construction of terms, simultaneous reduction of copies of terms, garbage collection, or tail-recursion optimization. For efficiency, these need to be programmed in a low-level language, so the implementation can be quite complex. However, we are able to make Prolog accomplish such tasks for us in a natural and efficient manner. Thus our implementation is very simple.

The structure of our method is as follows: an expressive, non-deterministic rewriting system F* and a lazy interpreter for it are defined and shown to satisfy strong computational properties. These are regarding reduction-completeness, confluence, elimination of search during reduction, and optimal lengths of reduction. It is then shown how F* can be compiled into Horn clauses in such a way that when SLD-resolution interprets these it directly simulates the behavior of the lazy F* interpreter. For example, the above rewrite rules form an F* program and are compiled to:

(a)   reduce(1,1).
(b)   reduce([U|V],[U|V].
(c)   reduce(infinite_ones,Z) if reduce([1|infinite_ones],Z).
(d)   reduce(head(X),Z) if reduce(X,[U|V]),reduce(U,Z).

These form a ready-to-execute logic program. To find the value of head(infinite_ones) we can type the query reduce(head(infinite_ones),Z). The SLD-resolution inference starting at it is:

    reduce(head(infinite_ones),Z)
        |
By (d) reduce(infinite_ones,[U|V]),reduce(U,Z).
        |
By (c) reduce([1|infinite_ones],[U|V]),reduce(U,Z).
        |
By (b) reduce(1,Z)
        |
By (a)   □

The final answer is computed as Z=1. Note that the inference steps exactly simulate the lazy reduction above.

The result of compilation of an F* program is to add to logic programming a primitive (reduce) for lazily simplifying F* terms. As in the above example, this primitive is at the same "logical level" as other logic programs so its properties can be studied using the same tools employed for studying other logic programs. For deterministic F* programs, such as the one above, it can be regarded as a statement about equality, but with good computational properties. For the above clauses, replace "reduce" with "equal". Thus, it can be freely called from other logic programs and yields a basis for programming with relations, functions, non-determinism, lazy evaluation and combinations of these all within the single framework of logic programming. LOG(F) is defined to be a logic programming system augmented with an F* compiler.

An essential feature of the compilation is that, for the most part, Prolog can be used in place of SLD-resolution. Thus, F* terms can be lazily simplified at approximately the speed of Prolog. As current industrial-strength Prologs are rated at over 100K logical inferences per second our implementation is efficient enough for practical programming.

Section 2.0 defines F* and a lazy interpreter for it and shows that it is reduction-complete. Section 3.0 defines DF*, a deterministic subset of F* and shows that it is confluent, directed, and optimal. Section 4.0 presents a simple algorithm for compiling F* into Horn clauses. Section 5.0 shows that F* compares favorably in performance with Prolog. Section 6.0 discusses applications of LOG(F). Section 7.0 discusses relationship of our approach with previous ones. For brevity, only proof sketches are provided. Full proofs can be obtained in [Narain 1988a, 1988b].

2.0 DEFINITION OF F*

This section defines a first-order rewrite rule system F*, and a lazy reduction strategy for it called select. Most first-order functional programs can be easily expressed in F*. However, one can also write non-deterministic programs. The main result proved is that F* is reduction-complete, in that if a term can be simplified, it can be simplified purely by use of select. Thus its significance is the same as that of the normal-order reduction theorem for lambda calculus. *F* is intended for reduction of only ground terms.*

Function symbols are partitioned, *in advance*, into constructors and non-constructors. For example, 0, 1, 2, 3.1415,..., true, false, [] are 0-ary constructor symbols and | a 2-ary constructor symbol. It is intended that data consist only of constructors whereas partially evaluated terms consist of both constructors and non-constructors.

A **term** is either a variable, or an expression of the form f(t1,..tn) where f is an n-ary function symbol, and each ti is a term. Sometimes, **term** will be used to denote both ground and non-ground terms, but ambiguity would be resolvable from context. A ground term E is said to **match** another term F, with substitution α if E=Fα.

A **reduction rule** is of the form LHS=>RHS, where LHS and RHS are terms, satisfying the following restrictions:

(a) LHS is of the form f(L1,..,Lm), f an m-ary non-constructor function symbol, and each Li either a variable, or a term of the form c(X1,..,Xn), c an n-ary constructor symbol, and each Xi a *variable*.

(b) A variable occurs at most once in LHS. This constraint is called left-linearity.

(c) All variables of RHS occur in LHS.

Note that reduction rules with left-hand-sides of arbitrary depth can easily be expressed in terms of rules with left-hand-sides of depth at most two, as required by (a). For example, fib(s(s(X)))=>plus(fib(X),fib(s(X))) can be expressed as fib(s(A))=>g(A), g(s(X))=>plus(fib(X),fib(s(X))). An **F* program** is a set of reduction rules.

Let P be an F* program and E and E1 be ground terms. We say $E=>_p E1$ if there is a rule LHS=>RHS in P such that E matches LHS with substitution σ and E1 is RHSσ. Where E,F,G,H, are ground terms, let F be the result of replacing an occurrence of G in E by H. Then we say **F=E[G/H]**. Let P be an F* program and E a ground term. Let G be a subterm of E such that $G=>_p H$. Let E1=E[G/H]. Then we say that $E->_p E1$. $-*>_p$ is the reflexive-transitive closure of $->_p$. The subscript P is dropped if clear from context.

A ground term is said to be in **simplified form**, or simplified, if it is of the form c(t1,..,tn) where c is an n-ary constructor symbol, n>=0, and each ti is a ground term. F is called a simplified form of E if E-*>F and F is in simplified form. Simplified forms are analogous to head normal forms in the lambda calculus, and can be used to represent finite approximations to infinite structures. For example, [0|intfrom(s(0))] is a simplified form, and is a finite approximation to [0,s(0),s(s(0)),..]. See below for a definition of intfrom.

A ground term is said to be in **normal form** if each function symbol in it is a constructor symbol. F is called a normal form of E if E-*>F and F is in normal form. Note that this notion of normal form is different from the usual one which is based upon non-reducibility. Our more "declarative" definition simplifies proofs without loss of generality. Also, normal forms are obtained by repeatedly obtaining simplified forms. An example of an F* program is:

```
append([],X)=>X
append([U|V],W)=>[U|append(V,W)]
intfrom(N)=>[N|intfrom(s(N))].
perm([])=>[].
perm([U|V])=>insert(U,perm(V)).
insert(U,X)=>[U|X].
insert(U,[A|B])=>[A|insert(U,B)].
```

The first two rules concatenate lists, the third computes the infinite list of integers starting at N while the last four compute permutations of a list. Note that there is no restriction that F* programs be *Noetherian* or even *confluent*. In particular, infinite structures can be freely defined and manipulated in F*. Also, programs can be non-deterministic in that terms can possess more than one normal form. For example, perm([1,2,3]) possesses as normal forms each of the six permutations of [1,2,3].

Let P be an F* program. A **reduction** in P is a, possibly infinite, sequence E1,E2,E3... such that for each i, $Ei->_p Ei+1$. A **successful reduction** in P is a reduction E0,..,En, n>=0, in P, such that En is simplified.

Let P be an F* program. We now define a reduction strategy, **select$_p$** for P. Informally, given a ground term E it will select that subterm of E whose reduction is necessary in order that some => rule in P apply to the whole of E. *In this, is implicit its laziness.* The relation select$_p$, whose second argument is the subterm selected from E, is defined by the following pseudo-Horn clauses:

select$_p$(E,E) if $E=>_p X$.
select$_p$(E,X) if
    E=f(T1,..,Ti,..,Tn), and
    there is a rule f(L1,..,Li,..,Ln)=>RHS in P, and
    Ti does not match Li, and
    select$_p$(Ti,X).

The first rule states that if E is the given ground term, and there exists another term X such that E=>X, then E itself can be selected from E. In the second rule, E=f(T1,..,Tn), and there is some rule f(L1,..,Ln)=>RHS, such that for some i, Ti in T1,..,Tn does not match Li in L1,..,Ln. In order to reduce E by this rule, it is necessary to reduce Ti. Thus, a term in Ti must be recursively selected for reduction. This rule is a schema, so that an instance of it is assumed written for each 1=<i=<n, and each non-constructor function symbol f.

For example, where P is the set of reduction rules which appear above we have: (a) if E=insert(1,perm([])), select(E,E) by first rule for insert, (b) if E=insert(1,perm([])), select(E,perm([])) by second rule for insert, (c) if E=insert(1,[2,3]), select(E,E) by first, and second rules for insert. (d) if E=[1|append([],[])] then select is undefined for E.

Note that select is non-deterministic in that given E, there can be more than one F such that select(E,F). Furthermore, as selected terms can match the head of more than one rule, there can be more than one reduction computed by select. For example, we have the two reductions computed by select:

perm([1,2]),insert(1,perm([2])),[1|perm([2])].

perm([1,2]),insert(1,perm([2])), insert(1,insert(2,perm([]))), insert(1,[2|perm([])]), [1,2|perm([])].

Let P be an F* program and E,G,H be ground terms. Suppose select$_p$(E,G) and G=>$_p$H. Let E1 be the result of replacing G by H in E. Then we say that E reduces to E1 in an **N-step** in P. The prefix N in N-step is intended to connote normal order. Let P be an F* program. An **N-reduction** in P is a reduction E1,E2,.... in P such that for each i, Ei reduces to Ei+1 in an N-step in P.

Note that if a term E is already simplified, e.g. E=[1|append([],[])], then select is undefined for E. Thus, an N-reduction ending at E cannot be extended further. If we wish to compute normal forms of E, we need a reduction strategy more general than select. It turns out that this can be based upon repeated application of select. Specifically, where P is an F* program, we define a reduction strategy **select-r$_P$**, where r stands for repeated or recursive, by the following pseudo-Horn clauses:

select-r$_p$(E,F) if select$_p$(E,F).
select-r$_p$(c(T1,..,Ti,..,Tm),F) if
  c is a constructor symbol, and select-r$_p$(Ti,F).

Thus, select-r is like select except that if a ground term is in simplified form, it recursively calls select on one of the arguments of the outermost constructor symbol. So, its repeated use can yield normal-forms of ground terms. Again, the second rule is a schema so that an instance of it is assumed written for each 1=<i=<m, and each constructor symbol c.

Let P be an F* program and E,G,H be ground terms. Suppose select-r$_p$(E,G) and G=>$_p$H. Let E1 be the result of replacing G by H in E. Then we say that E reduces to E1 in an **NR-step** in P. NR is intended to connote normal-repeated. Let P be an F* program. An **NR-reduction** in P is a reduction E1,E2,.... in P such that for each i, Ei reduces to Ei+1 in an NR-step in P.

2.1 Reduction-completeness of F*

Theorem 1. Reduction-completeness for simplified forms. Let P be an F* program and D0 a ground term. Let D0,D1,..,Dn be a successful reduction in P. Then there is a successful N-reduction D0,E1,..,Em in P, such that Em-*>Dn.

Proof Sketch: We first define R$_p$(G,H,A,B). Let P be an F* program. Where G,H,A,B are ground terms, R$_p$(G,H,A,B) holds if (a) G=>H, and (b) B is identical with A except that zero or more occurrences of G in A are *simultaneously* replaced by H. Note that A and G can be identical. Again, if P is clear from context, the subscript P is dropped.

We first prove a lemma which states that if for terms E1,F1,F2,G,H, R(G,H,E1,F1), and F1 reduces to F2 in an N-step, then there is an N-reduction E1,..,E2 such that

R(G,H,E2,F2). To prove the theorem, we proceed by induction on the length n of D0,D1,..,Dn, and repeatedly apply this lemma. **QED.**

For example, perm([1,2]) is reducible to the normal form [1,2]. An N-reduction starting at it is perm([1,2]),insert(1,perm([2])), insert(1,insert(2,perm([]))), insert(1,[2|perm([])]), [1,2|perm([])]. Clearly, the last term reduces to [1,2].

Theorem 2. Reduction-completeness for normal forms. Let P be an F* program and D0 a ground term. Let D0,D1,..,Dn be a reduction in P, where Dn is in normal form. Then there is an NR-reduction D0,E1,..,Em=Dn, in P.

Proof Sketch: Similar to that of Theorem 1.

For example, an NR-reduction starting at perm([1,2]), computing the normal form [1,2] is perm([1,2]), insert(1,perm([2])), insert(1,insert(2,perm([]))), insert(1,[2|perm([])]), [1,2|perm([])], [1,2].

3.0 DETERMINISTIC F* (DF*)

We now present a subset of F* called Deterministic F* (DF*) which satisfies quite strong and desirable computational properties. Specifically, each DF* program satisfies confluence, directedness and optimality. Confluence ensures that each term possesses at most one normal form. Directedness eliminates searching among alternative N- or NR-reductions. It is sufficient to generate *any* N- or NR-reduction for obtaining simplified or normal forms. Optimality ensures that terms are simplified in a minimum number of steps. Clearly, DF* programs can be thought of as equality theories and used for functional programming.

We first motivate the design of DF*. An F* program exhibits two types of non-determinism. First, a term can possess more than one normal form as illustrated by the permutations program. Second, there can be more than one N- or NR-reduction starting at a term, some of which may not terminate at all *even when unique normal forms exist*. For example, with a=>a, a=>[], f([])=>[], there is an infinite N-reduction f(a),f(a),f(a),.... However, there is also a finite N-reduction f(a),f([]),[]. Thus, some searching among alternative N- or NR-reductions may be required to compute simplified, or normal forms.

We now show how to eliminate these two types of non-determinism. A DF* program is an F* program satisfying two additional restrictions:

(d) Let LHS1 and LHS2 be variants of heads of two rules in P, such that LHS1 and LHS2 have no variables in common. Then LHS1 and LHS2 do not unify.

(e) Let f(L1,..,Li,..,Lm)=>RHS be a rule in P, where Li is not a variable. Then in every other rule

221

f(K1,..,Ki,..,Km)=>RHS1 in P, Ki is not a variable.

Note that restrictions (a)-(c) are upon rules while (d) and (e) are upon the entire program. An examination of common, first-order functional programs shows that many of them are already in DF*. For example, the following is a DF* program:

```
partition(U,[],L,R)=>t(L,R).
partition(U,[A|B],L,R)=>
  if(lesseq(A,U),
     partition(U,B,[A|L],R), partition(U,B,L,[A|R])).
if(true,X,Y)=>X.
if(false,X,Y)=>Y.
lesseq(0,s(X))=>false.
lesseq(0,0)=>true.
lesseq(s(X),s(Y))=>lesseq(X,Y).
lesseq(s(X),0)=>false.
```

However, in the following, the first two rules violate (d) (but satisfy (e)), and the next two violate (e) (but satisfy (d)):

```
insert(A,[U|V])=>[A,U|V].
insert(A,[U|V])=>[U|insert(A,V)].

f(X,[])=>[].
f([],[U|V])=>[].
```

Theorem 3. Confluence of DF*. Let P be a DF* program, and M,N,P be ground terms such that M-*>N, and M-*>P. Then there exists term Q such that N-*>Q, and P-*>Q.

Proof: In [Huet 1980] is proved a theorem which states that for a left-linear rewrite rule system R, if for every critical pair <P,Q> in R, P reduces in parallel to Q, then R is confluent. As every DF* program is left-linear, and by restrictions (a) and (d) it contains no critical pairs, it is confluent. **QED.** A direct proof is given in [Narain 1988].

Theorem 4. Directedness for simplified forms. Let P be a DF* program. Let E0 be a term and let E0,..,En be a successful reduction. Then *any* N-reduction starting at E0, if extended far enough, would terminate in a term in simplified form. Moreover, all successful N-reductions starting at E are of equal length, and terminate in the same simplified form.

Proof sketch: Distinct N-reductions can arise for three reasons. First, f(t1,..,tn) can match the heads of two rules with differing right hand sides. Second, without restriction (e) there can be two rules with heads L1 and L2, such that the ith argument in L1 is a variable, whereas the ith argument in L2 is a non-variable. Thus, given f(t1,..,ti,..,tn), two N-reductions can arise, depending upon whether ti is simplified or not. Third, t1,..,tn in f(t1,..,tn) can be simplified in different orders. Restriction (d) eliminates the first reason, and restriction (e) the second. The third is eliminated by a simple induction on lengths of terms. **QED**

Theorem 5. Directedness for normal forms. Let P be a DF* program. Let E0 be a term and let E0,..,En be a reduction where En is in normal form. Then any NR-reduction starting at E0, if extended far enough, would terminate in a normal form. Moreover, all NR-reductions starting at E, and ending in normal forms, are of equal length.

Proof Sketch: Similar to that for Theorem 4.

3.1 Optimality of select for DF*

This section discusses how select is optimal in that it simplifies terms in a minimum number of reduction steps, provided one precaution is observed. During reduction, copies of terms are formed when use is made of rules with more than one occurrence of a variable in their right-hand sides. For example, with f(X)=>g(X,X), g([],[])=>[], a=>[], two copies of a are formed in the second term in the N-reduction f(a),g(a,a),g([],a),g([],[]),[]. If we can arrange that whenever a term is reduced, all copies of it are simultaneously reduced, we can show that leftmost N-reductions compute simplified forms in a minimum number of N-steps. This result holds only for DF*, as for F*, leftmost N-reductions may not terminate, even when terms can be simplified. A leftmost N-reduction is that in which of the terms chosen by select for reduction the leftmost one is always reduced.

The proof of minimality is based upon a formalization of graph-reduction, e.g. [Turner 1979], within the framework of rewriting. A reduction step eliminates one node in a graph. The result is derived by comparing the number of nodes eliminated by a leftmost N-reduction strategy with those by any other strategy. One of the trickiest issues is formalization of allocation of new nodes, i.e. those not previously used in the reduction.

Vuillemin [1974] and Berry & Levy [1979] have derived similar results. However their proofs are not directly applicable to DF*. These were derived only for recursive program schemes, i.e. sets of rewrite rules in which the head of each rule is of the form f(X1,..,Xm), each Xi a *variable*. These do *not* have the complication of pattern matching.

4.0 TRANSLATING F* INTO HORN CLAUSES

We now describe a simple yet efficient implementation of F* using Horn clauses. These can be interpreted by SLD-resolution with a static, left-to-right strategy for proving subgoals. Thus, for the most part, Prolog can be used and F* programs made to run at a speed close to that of Prolog programs of similar length and intellectual complexity. As industrial-strength Prologs are rated at over 100K logical inferences per second, F* can be used for practical programming. A direct implementation of F* in a lower-level language ought to be much faster.

The main idea in the compilation algorithm is as follows:

each rule in an F* program is compiled into a distinct Horn clause, which *simultaneously* embodies two pieces of information. The first is about the logic of the rule i.e. its left- and right-hand-sides. The second is about the behavior of select when it attempts to reduce a term by this rule. As a result, when SLD-resolution interprets these clauses, it directly simulates the behavior of select. When the F* program is in DF*, much more efficient clauses can be generated. *Note that, we do not develop an interpreter in Horn clauses which takes F* programs as input.*

The result of compilation is to add to a logic programming system a primitive for lazily simplifying F* terms. This primitive is at the same "logical level" as other logic programs. When the F* program is in DF*, the primitive can be thought of as statements about equality with good computational properties. Thus it can be called freely from other logic programs and forms a basis for programming with abstractions from both lazy rewriting as well as logic programming.

We do point out that for non-deterministic F* programs, Prolog can sometimes fail to simplify terms even when possible. The heuristics for avoiding this are the same when using Prolog to do logic programming. *However, we stress that for DF* programs, Prolog simplifies terms whenever possible.*

4.1 Compilation algorithm

Let P be an F* program. The compilation of P into Horn clauses proceeds in two steps:

Step 1. For each n-ary constructor symbol c in P, and where X1,..,Xn are distinct variables, generate the clause:

reduce(c(X1,..,Xn),c(X1,..,Xn))

Step 2. For each rule f(L1,..,Lm)=>RHS in P generate the clause:

reduce(f(A1,..,Am),Out):-Q1,Q2,..,Qm,reduce(RHS,Out).

where A1,..,Am,Out,L1,..,Lm, are distinct variables not occurring in the rule, and if Li is a non-variable, Qi is reduce(Ai,Li), otherwise Qi is Ai=Li. In practice, if Li is a variable, Ai is replaced by Li in the head, and Ai=Li is dropped from the body.

Thus, the basic lazy reduction primitive is the binary predicate reduce. It halts with success when its second argument is a simplified form of its first. The query reduce(f(t1,..,tn),Z), t1,..,tn ground, matches the head of a reduce clause for f. If f is already a constructor symbol, the query halts with success. Otherwise, if for any i, Li is a non-variable, Qi attempts to simplify ti to the form of Li. Otherwise Qi leaves ti unreduced. If Q1,..,Qm succeed, then for each i, ti has been reduced to a term matching Li. The corresponding substitution, and instance of RHS are

automatically generated, and this instance is recursively simplified. *Thus, the computation of N-reductions, as described in Section 2.0, is exactly simulated.* Its correctness is proved in [Narain 1988a,b]. For example, the F* program:

perm([])=>[].
perm([A|V])=>insert(U,perm(V)).
insert(U,X)=>[U|X].
insert(U,[A|B])=>[A|insert(U,B)].
interleave([U|V],X)=>[U|interleave(X,V)].
a=>[1|a].
b=>[2|b].

is translated into:

reduce([],[]).
reduce([U|V],[U|V]).

reduce(perm(X),Z):-reduce(X,[]),reduce([],Z).
reduce(perm(X),Z):-
    reduce(X,[FX|RX]),reduce(insert(FX,perm(RX)),Z).
reduce(insert(A,X),Z):-reduce([A|X],Z).
reduce(insert(A,X),Z):-
    reduce(X,[FX|RX]),reduce([FX|insert(A,RX)],Z).
reduce(interleave(X,Y),Z):-
    reduce(X,[U|V]),reduce([U|interleave(Y,V)],Z).
reduce(a,Z):-reduce([1|a],Z).
reduce(b,Z):-reduce([2|b],Z).

Here [],|,1,2,.. are constructor symbols. We assume the presence of rules of the form reduce(X,X) where X is a number. If we now type, in Prolog, reduce(perm([1,2,3]),Z), we obtain Z=[1|perm([2,3])], Z=[2|insert(1,perm([3]))], and Z=[3|insert(1,insert(2,perm([])))]. Note that perm([1,2,3]) is only partially reduced, and *directly* by Prolog, not by some lazy interpreter implemented in Prolog.

If we type reduce(interleave(a,b),Z) we obtain Z=[1|interleave(b,a)], illustrating manipulation of representations of infinite structures.

4.2 Computing and printing normal forms

If there is a method to compute simplified forms of terms, it can be applied repeatedly to compute normal forms of terms. *This is guaranteed by reduction-completeness for normal forms.* In particular, for each m-ary, m>=0, constructor symbol c, and distinct variables X1,..,Xm,T1,..,Tm, we can add the following rule:

nf(E,c(X1,..,Xm)):-
    reduce(E,c(T1,..,Tm)),nf(T1,X1),..,nf(Tm,Xm).

Now, to compute the normal form of a term E, we can execute nf(E,X), where X is a variable. For example, nf(perm([1,2,3]),Z), binds Z to each of the six permutations of [1,2,3].

Clearly, computing normal forms is only sensible when they are finite. If they are not, we can at least print finite elements of them as they are generated. For example, we can print members of an infinite list using p_list(X):-reduce(X,[U|V]),write(U),write(' '),p_list(V). Now, if we type p_list(interleave(a,b)), we obtain 1 2 1 2 1 2...

4.3 Three optimizations

First, if the F* program being compiled is also in DF*, then the reduce clauses obtained from its compilation can be further transformed into a deterministic logic program. This means that for every term E, the Prolog search tree corresponding to the query reduce(E,Z) contains exactly one branch. Thus, there is no overhead of backtracking. Furthermore, tail recursion optimization is auotmatically performed for these programs by Prolog compilers.

Second, the assumption that when a term is reduced, all copies of it are simultaneously reduced, is implemented by exploiting the nature of logical variables. If there is more than one occurrence of a variable in an expression, then if any occurrence is bound to a term, Prolog automatically binds all occurrences to the same term. A logical variable is associated with each term, which is bound to its simplified form whenever it is computed. It is arranged that whenever copies of it are made, all of these share the same logical variable. Now a term is reduced only if its variable is unbound. If it is bound to a term this is directly read-off.

Third, by default, all F* functions are lazily evaluated. However, it is often convenient to eagerly evaluate some functions, e.g. arithmetic functions. Eager functions are defined and evaluated in Prolog. Calls to eager functions in F* programs are easily translated to calls to corresponding Prolog predicates.

5.0 COMPARING F* WITH PROLOG

Programs of similar length, and intellectual complexity were written in both F* and in Prolog, and their performance compared. Times are in Quintus Prolog running on a SUN-3/50 with 4mb main memory.

Time in milliseconds			
	Prolog	F*	Prolog/F*
Quicksort (120 elements)	250	783	0.31
Sieve (First 100 primes)	1904	2717	0.70
All permutations of [1..5]	450	550	0.87
8-Queens (All solutions)	59850	15948	3.75
15-Queens (First solution)	>18^5	30300	>60
Infinite plane: First vector	∞	~ 0	∞

In programs such as the first three, where lazy evaluation does not reduce lengths of computation, F* is slower than Prolog by a small amount. Otherwise, it is faster than Pro-

log by unbounded, even infinite amounts. Furthermore, it would directly benefit from future advances in Prolog implementation.

6.0 APPLICATIONS

As we mentioned in Section 4.0, LOG(F) can be thought of as a means of brining lazy evaluation to Prolog by means of rewriting. Thus, usual examples illustrating lazy evaluation such as Sieve of Eratosthenes, Hamming's problem, or Escher-like drawings can be reproduced effortlessly and efficiently in LOG(F) [Narain 1988a,b]. Here we discuss some unconventional applications of LOG(F) which utilize its unique capabilities.

6.1 Programming generate-and-test algorithms

This subsection illustrates the usefulness of a combination of non-determinism and lazy evaluation. Generate-and-test algorithms typically consist of a generation algorithm which computes objects and a testing algorithm which tests whether these satisfy some given condition. Considerable pruning of the search space of generation can be obtained if generation of objects is interleaved with their testing. If from partial information about objects it can be determined that they cannot satisfy the condition, then their further generation can be suppressed. Often this interleaving has to be explicitly programmed and so resulting algorithms can be quite complicated.

Narain [1989] shows how in F* such interleaving can be automated via lazy evaluation, provided generation is done by interpretation of a non-deterministic F* program. We only show one example here. Consider the following problem: Given a number K, and a set S of positive numbers, generate all those subsets of S, the sum of whose members is equal to K. Clearly, for numbers U1,..,Uk in S, if their sum is greater than K, then generation of all subsets of the form [U1,..,Uk|X] can be suppressed. An F* program to solve it with this optimization is:

```
subset([])=>[].
subset([U|V])=>[U|subset(V)].
subset([U|V])=>subset(V).

sum_eq([],Acc,K)=>if_2(equal(Acc,K),[]).
sum_eq([U|V],Acc,K)=>
    if_2((U+Acc)=<K,[U|sum_eq(V,U+Acc,K)]).

if_2(true,X)=>X.
```

The first three rules compute subsets of a list i.e. the normal forms of subset(S) are each of the subsets of S. The second two rules determine whether Acc plus the sum of elements of a list is equal to K. If so, they return the list itself, otherwise they return nothing, and simply fail. Now, the term sum_eq(subset(S),0,K) possesses as normal forms precisely those subsets of S whose members add up to K.

Due to lazy evaluation whenever a term of the form subset(A) is reduced to the form [U|X] sum_eq is called to check whether U plus the current value of Acc exceeds K. If so, none of the reductions rooted at X are generated. Thus, the above optimization is achieved, only by programming the generation and the testing, not the interleaving.

6.2 Narrowing grammars

In the strict Definite Clause Grammar (DCG) formalism it is not possible to represent the grammar rules (A+)->A, (A+)->(A,A+) where A is a variable. This is because DCGs do not allow non-terminals to be variables. However, Chau & Parker [1989] have shown that such rules can be expressed as rewrite rules of F* and call them a narrowing grammar. They also show that an F*-style interpreter can be used for parsing strings in a lazy manner, and that this framework subsumes DCGs.

6.3 Coupling Prolog with relational databases

Buneman & Nikhil [1981] have shown that lazy evaluation can be used for efficiently processing queries upon large databases. It avoids the need to create large intermediate results as well as the need to translate complex queries into iterative tuple-at-a-time procedures. It does so by ensuring that the amount of data retrieved is controlled *automatically* by the functions which process it. For example, if we just wanted to print the five-day moving average for a company's stock, only the stock data for five days would be retrieved initially. At each subsequent step only one day's stock data would be retrieved.

Very similar ideas have been proposed by Parker et al. [1989] who view a relational database as a stream of the tuples in it. They define stream processing functions in F* and compile them into Prolog. Thereby, they obtain a coupling of Prolog with relational database. An important advantage of it is that data from databases can be manipulated using the rich representational power of Prolog.

6.4 Systems Programming

Kahn [1974] has shown that a set of communicating processes can be represented by a set of mutually recursive function definitions. These definitions can be represented in DF*. By compiling these into a parallel Prolog we obtain a basis for systems programming in a parallel Prolog. The advantage of this approach over concurrent logic programming languages e.g. Concurrent Prolog [Shapiro 1987] is that the same Prolog can be used both for systems programming as well as conventional symbolic programming. This approach is discussed at length in a forthcoming paper.

7.0 RELATIONSHIP WITH PREVIOUS WORK

Many proposals have been advanced to combine equational reasoning with logic programming, e.g. [Robinson 1987, Darlington et al. 1986, Hansson et al. 1982, Barbuti et al. 1982, Reddy 1985, Subrahmanyam & You 1984, Hoelldobler 1987, Gallier & Raatz 1986, Miller & Nadathur 1986, Ait-Kaci et al. 1987, Dershowitz & Plaisted 1987, Goguen & Meseguer 1986, Fribourg 1984, Malachi et al. 1986]. They aim for rules of inference more general than those for equational reasoning or for logic programming. An example of such a rule is SLD-resolution in which syntactic unification is replaced by semantic unification. These rules usually contain an element of lazy evaluation, more general than that for rewriting. Many of these systems are of far reaching consequence. However, the computational problems they involve are quite hard. Furthermore, their practical implementation can require considerable programming effort.

In contrast, we have focussed on bringing to logic programming a restricted, but important, form of lazy evaluation, namely that for rewriting. For it, we are able to derive strong computational properties regarding efficiency such as directedness and optimality. (It is not obvious that these hold for above systems). We have also shown how it can be absorbed within logic programming. Thus, we are able to use the single rule of SLD-resolution for both logic programming as well as lazy rewriting. Furthermore, as Prolog can be used, the implementation is greatly simplified and yet remains efficient enough for practical programming.

A few proposals have been made to obtain lazy evaluation by dynamically determining the order in which subgoals are proved by SLD-resolution e.g. [Clark & McCabe 1982, Shapiro 1987, Naish 1985]. However, processes producing infinite objects are represented by non-terminating goals. As these can never be proved, within the strict framework of logic programming, we are not entitled to infer anything. This approach is also difficult to implement efficiently on sequential machines, although it appears more practical on parallel machines. The logical problem with this approach does not arise with ours as we achieve lazy evaluation via rewriting. Goals can terminate even if they conceptually involve production of infinite structures.

A number of proposals have been made for compiling equality theories into Horn clauses e.g. [Bosco et. al 1988, van Emden & Yukawa 1987]. Yet, most of these are restricted to terminating theories, so infinite structures cannot be defined in these. A significant exception is [Tamaki 1984]. However, his method produces much less efficient code than ours as discussed in [Narain 1988b]. Tamaki also discusses the limitation of his approach in a simple case.

In the Set-Equation Language [Jayaraman & Plaisted 1987] a non-deterministic programming style similar to that of F* can be employed. However, in contrast to F*, SEL programs are restricted to be terminating, so infinite structures cannot be defined.

Properties of F* are as strong as those of systems of Hoffmann & O'Donnell [1982] or of Huet & Levy [1979]. However it differs from these in three main respects. First, it is non-deterministic in the sense that a term can possess more than one normal form. This yields interesting programming possibilities (Section 6.1). The other two are deterministic. Second, F* is constructor-based while the other two are not. Thus, left-hand-sides of F* rules cannot contain non-constructor symbols in argument positions. This limits the expressiveness of F* e.g. it cannot express the SK rules of combinatory logic, at least not directly. However, as O'Donnell [1985] has said, constructor-based systems are sufficiently expressive for functional programming. Third, F* was consciously designed to be subsumed within logic programming. It does not appear straightforward to do the same with the other systems. *This was the principal reason for developing a new rewriting system.*

Finally, we have shown how lazy evaluation can be done efficiently within the eager framework of Prolog. The same can be done in an eager Lisp such as Scheme [Abelson & Sussman 1984] but requires higher-order functions. We have shown how to do it in the less expressive first-order framework.

ACKNOWLEDGEMENTS

I would like to thank D. Parker, R. Muntz, Y. Moschovakis, P. Hudak, H. Ait-Kaci, D. Plaisted, M. O'Donnell, R. Paige, H. Chau, T. Leung and the referees for very helpful comments.

REFERENCES

Abelson, H. & Sussman, G. [1985]. *Structure and interpretation of computer programs*, MIT Press & McGraw Hill.

Ait-Kaci, H., Lincoln, P., Nasr, R. [1987]. Le Fun: Logic, Equations and Functions. *Proceedings of symposium on logic programming*, San Francisco.

Barbuti, R., Bellia, M., Levi, G. [1986]. LEAF: A language which integrates logic, equations, and functions. In *Logic programming: functions, relations and equations* (eds.) D. DeGroot, G. Lindstrom, Prentice Hall, N.J.

Berry, G., Levy, J.-J. [1979]. Minimal and optimal computations of recursive programs. *Journal of the ACM*, vol. 26, no. 1, pp. 148-175.

Bosco, P., Giovannetti, E., Moiso, C. [1988]. Narrowing vs. SLD-resolution. *Theoretical Computer Science*, 59.

Buneman, P. & Nikhil, R. [1981]. A practical functional programming system for databases. *Proceedings of conference on functional programming languages and Computer Architecture*.

Chau, H., Parker, D. [1989]. Narrowing Grammar. *Proceedings of the Sixth International Conference on Logic Programming*, Lisbon, Portugal.

Clark, K.L., McCabe F., Gregory, S. [1982]. IC-Prolog language features. In *Logic Programming*, eds. K.L. Clark and S.-A. Tarnlund, Academic Press.

Darlington, J., Field, A.J., Pull, H. [1986]. The unification of functional and logic languages. *Logic programming: functions, relations and equations* (eds.) D. DeGroot, G. Lindstrom, Prentice Hall, New Jersey.

DeGroot, D., Lindstrom, G. (editors) [1986]. *Logic programming. Functions, relations and equations*. Prentice Hall, N.J.

Dershowitz N. & Plaisted, D. [1987]. Equational Programming. *Machine Intelligence 11*.

FBI [1988]. Invited talk at *Fifth International Conference on Logic Programming*, reported on a large Prolog program to assist in deductive aspects of crime prevention.

Fribourg, L. [1984]. Oriented equational clauses as a programming language. *Journal of Logic Programming* vol 1, pp. 165-177.

Gallier, J.H., Raatz, S. [1986]. SLD-resolution methods for Horn clauses with equality based on E-unification. *Proceedings of 1986 symposium on logic programming*, Salt Lake City, Utah.

Goguen, J.A., Meseguer, J. [1986]. Equality, types and generic modules for logic programming. *Logic programming: functions, relations and equations* (eds.) D. DeGroot, G. Lindstrom, Prentice Hall, New Jersey.

Hansson, A., Haridi, S., Tarnlund, S.-A. [1982]. Properties of a logic programming language. In *Logic Programming*, eds. K.L. Clark and S.-A. Tarnlund, Academic Press.

Henderson, P. [1982]. Purely functional operating systems. In *Functional programming and its applications. An advanced course.* (eds.) J. Darlington, P. Henderson, D.A. Turner.

Henderson, P. [1982]. Functional Geometry. *Proceedings of the ACM Symposium on Lisp and Functional Programming*. Pittsburgh, PA.

Hoffman, C.M., O'Donnell, M.J. [1982]. Programming with equations. *ACM Transactions on programming languages and systems*. January.

Hoelldobler, S. [1987]. Equational logic programming.

Proceedings of Fourth Symposium on logic programming, San Francisco, CA.

Hudak, P. [1989]. The conception, evolution, and application of functional programming languages. To appear in *ACM Computing Surveys.*

Huet, G., Levy, J.-J. [1979]. Call by need computations in non-ambiguous linear term rewriting systems. IRIA technical report 359.

Huet, G. [1980]. Confluent reductions: abstract properties and applications to term rewriting systems. *Journal of the ACM,* 27:797-821.

Jaffar, J., Lassez, J.-L., Maher, M.J. [1984]. A theory of complete logic programs with equality. *Journal of logic programming,* vol. 1, no. 3.

Jayaraman, B., Plaisted, D. [1987]. Functional programming with sets. *Proceedings of second conference on functional programming languages and computer architecture,* Lecture Notes in Computer Science, 274, Springer Verlag.

Kahn, G. [1974]. The semantics of a simple language for parallel processing. *Information Processing,* North Holland, Amsterdam.

Kahn, G., MacQueen, D. [1977]. Coroutines and Networks of Parallel Processes. *Information Processing,* North-Holland, Amsterdam.

Kowalski, R. [1979]. *Logic for Problem Solving,* Elsevier North Holland, New York.

Lindstrom, G. [1985]. Functional programming and the logical variable. *12th Annual Symposium on Principles of Programming Languages.*

Livezey, B., Muntz, R. [1989]. ASPEN: A stream processing environment. *Proceedings of PARLE '89, Lecture Notes in Computer Science, No. 366,* Springer Verlag.

Malachi, Y., Manna, Z. [1986]. Tablog: A new approach to logic programming. In *Logic programming: functions, relations and equations* (eds.) D. DeGroot, G. Lindstrom, Prentice Hall, N.J.

Miller, D.A., Nadathur, G. [1986]. Higher-order logic programming. *Proceedings of third international conference on logic programming.* Lecture notes in computer science 225, (ed.) E. Shapiro, Springer Verlag, New York.

Naish, L. [1985]. Automating control for logic programs. *Journal of Logic Programming,* vol. 2, no. 3, October.

Narain, S. [1986]. A Technique for Doing Lazy Evaluation in Logic. *Journal of Logic Programming,* vol. 3, no. 3, October.

Narain, S. [1988]. LOG(F): An optimal combination of logic programming, rewriting and lazy evaluation. Ph.D. Thesis, Department of Computer Science, University of California, Los Angeles.

Narain, S. [1989]. Optimization by non-deterministic, lazy rewriting. *Proceedings of Rewriting Techniques and Applications Conference,* Chapel Hill, NC.

O'Donnell, M.J. [1985]. *Equational logic as a programming language.* MIT Press, Cambridge, MA.

Parker D., Muntz, R., Chau, L. [1989]. The Tangram stream query processing system, *Proceedings of Fifth International Conference on Data Engineering,.*

Pereira, F.C.N., Warren, D.H.D. [1980]. Definite clause grammars for natural language analysis. A survey of the formalism and a comparison with augmented transition networks. *Artificial Intelligence Journal,* 13, pp. 231-278.

Peyton Jones, S.L. [1987]. *The implementation of functional languages.* Prentice Hall, Englewood Cliffs, NJ.

Reddy, U.S. [1985]. Narrowing as the operational semantics of functional languages. *Proceedings of the 1985 symposium on logic programming,* Boston.

Robinson, J.A. [1987]. Beyond LOGLISP: Combining functional and relational programming in a reduction setting. *Machine Intelligence 11.*

Robinson, J.A., Greene, K.J. [1987]. New Generation Knolwedge Processing, vol. III. RADC-TR-87-165. Rome Air Development Center, Griffis Air Force Base, NY.

Shapiro, E. [1987]. (editor) *Concurrent Prolog,* vols. 1 & 2. MIT Press.

Tamaki, H. [1984]. Semantics of a logic programming language with a reducibility predicate. *Proceedings of IEEE Logic Programming Symposium,* Atlantic City, N.J.

Turner, D. [1979]. A New Implementation Technique for Applicative Languages, *Software Practice and Experience,* 9, pp. 31-49.

van Emden, M.H., Yukawa, K. [1987]. Logic programming with equations. *Journal of Logic Programming,* vol. 4, no. 4.

Vuillemin, J. [1974]. Correct and optimal implementations of recursion in a simple programming language. *Journal of Computer and System Sciences,* 9, pp. 332-354.

Warren, D.H.D., van Caneghem, M. (editors) [1986]. *Logic Programming and its Applications,* Ablex Publishing, N.J.

KSL/Logic: Integration of Logic with Objects

Mamdouh H. Ibrahim   Fred A. Cummins

Electronic Data Systems
Detroit Research and Development
3551 Hamlin Rd., 4th Floor, Auburn Hills, MI 48057

Abstract

KSL/Logic is an integration of logic and object-oriented programming that adds the declarative framework and deductive reasoning of logic programming to the powerful modeling capabilities of the object-oriented paradigm. Predicates, logic expressions, and the generalized search protocol of KSL/Logic are implemented as an integral part of KSL, a reflective, object-oriented programming language. KSL/Logic provides capabilities that go beyond those of Prolog to permit domain-based reasoning, functional arguments, matching of complex object patterns, and object representation of facts. This paper describes the syntax and semantics of KSL/Logic and focuses on the object implementation of its predicate resolution.

1. Introduction

Object-oriented programming and logic programming have both attracted growing interest as programming paradigms because of the advantages they offer for representing and reasoning about complex problems. Polymorphism, encapsulation, and inheritance in object-oriented programming support the development of modular and extensible systems. On the other hand, logic programming provides a declarative framework with pattern matching, variable unification, and backtracking that support deductive reasoning. The integration of these two paradigms can provide capabilities that exceed those of either paradigm alone.

Most of the reported strategies for achieving such integration incorporate object-oriented concepts (classes, inheritance, messages, etc.) into logic or functional programming languages, e.g., SPOOL [4], FOOPLog [6], OOLP+ [5], and Vulcan [11]. However, the underlying languages of these systems only supports unification of syntactic representations and cannot unify user defined complex objects. Also, the use of predicate expressions to model complex real-world applications does not achieve the power and simplicity of representations using objects.

Koschmann [12], addressed the integration with a "bridge" approach which interfaces the object-oriented programming of Loops [1] with the logic programming of Quintus Prolog. This approach requires the two paradigms to remain separate and forces the programmer to be proficient in both languages.

In contrast, Orient84/K [9], [10] integrates logic programming in an object framework. The integration is achieved through the creation of knowledge objects which consist of two separate parts: behavior parts (methods and instance variables) and knowledge-base parts (collections of Prolog-like predicates). In this system, logic facts are represented as local predicates in the knowledge-base parts rather than as part of the object representation of the application. This limits recursive reasoning on objects of different classes and also restricts backtracking to the predicates that appear in the same knowledge-base part.

KSL [7] is a reflective, object-oriented programming language implemented in the EDS/OWL [3] programming environment. It was developed to support the implementation of AI applications using object-oriented representation. KSL is easily extended to support the integration of different programming paradigms. This paper presents KSL/Logic, one such extension, that allows logic programming to be imbedded in an object-oriented framework.

KSL/Logic provides logic programming facilities based on Prolog [2] as an integral part of KSL. To a degree, this is similar to Orient84/K. However, the integration approach of KSL/Logic supports unique features and capabilities that go beyond those provided by Prolog and Orient84/K. Fundamental to this approach is the concept of "domain object". A domain object can incorporate component objects, including objects representing "subdomains" [8].

Through the definition of its class, a domain object determines the predicates that will be applied when reasoning occurs in its domain. This allows domain-based reasoning rather than reasoning under the single-domain assumption of Prolog. Predicate behaviors can be specialized on sub-classes; thus complex problems can be implemented as a number of domains with specialized definitions for the same predicates.

KSL/Logic extends the power of predicate expressions beyond Prolog in two ways. First, arguments of predicate expressions can be procedural expressions (i.e., functions). This allows interleaving predicates and functions as needed for automated reasoning languages [13]. Second, argument values can be complex object structures to be matched. KSL/Logic matching and variable unification for these complex arguments provide a more sophisticated pattern matching capability.

Representation of facts in KSL/Logic provides another advantage over other languages. Facts in KSL/Logic are represented by the states and relationships of objects. This object representation of facts rather than predicate expressions fully exploits the object-oriented paradigm.

The remainder of this paper presents the KSL/Logic language and focuses on its object implementation. The next section describes briefly the object representation of KSL procedural behaviors and the extension which implements the non-procedural predicate behaviors of KSL/Logic. Section 3 presents the syntax and semantics of KSL/Logic expressions. Section 4 presents the object implementation of the predicate resolution mechanism and the extensible search network protocol. Section 5 describes tools implemented to support programming with KSL/Logic. Conclusions and future work are discussed in section 6.

2. KSL/Logic Behaviors

KSL [7] is a class-based, pure object-oriented programming language in which all data are objects and operations are performed by message-sending. The object representation of KSL extends to representation of classes, behaviors (methods and slots), and executable expressions as objects. When a message is sent to a domain object, the message selector and the domain object class are used to identify the behavior object that defines the action required. An *Eval* message is then sent to the behavior object causing its functionality to be applied to the domain object. Behaviors can be defined locally on the domain class or inherited as determined by the class hierarchy relationship.

Most of the procedural programming in KSL is implemented with methods (instances of the *Method* class). The *Eval* behavior of a method sends an *Eval* message to each KSL expression object in the method's

expression list. The *Eval* behaviors of these expression objects implement the functionality of KSL. Figure 1 shows an *Age* method, defined on a *Person* class, with three expression objects in its expression list. The first two are variable assignment expressions which set the values of the local variables *BirthYear* and *BirthMonth*. The nested message expressions *BirthDate*, *Year*, and *Month* are used to compute year and month of birth of the person object that is bound to *Self*, a local parameter.

```
Person.Age Method (Parsing Successful)

  (#Method
    (&Selector Age )
    (&Class Person )
    (&ParmList (#List Self ))
    (&VarList (#List BirthYear BirthMonth))
    (&ExprList (#List

    (Set BirthYear (Year (BirthDate $Self)))
    (Set BirthMonth (Month (BirthDate $Self)))
    (When
       (#List (GreaterThan $BirthMonth $CurrentMonth)
              (Subtract (Subtract $CurrentYear $BirthYear) 1))
       (#List True
              (Subtract $CurrentYear $BirthYear)))
  )))
```

Figure 1. An example of a KSL Method

The third expression in the method's expression list is a *When* key-word expression. Key-word expressions are implemented in a form similar to the message expression, but use reserved symbols in place of message selectors. Relational, logical, and iterative key-word expressions are implemented to simplify coding in KSL. For example, the relational *GreaterThan* key-word expression appears as the conditional statement in the first list of the *When* expression. An appropriate *Subtract* message expression computes the age of the person by subtracting its birth year from a global variable, *CurrentYear*. The computed age is returned by the *Age* Method.

KSL can be easily extended because its executable behaviors are represented as objects that conform to the protocols of the object-oriented paradigm. New executable behavior types can be defined simply by specializing existing behavior classes and defining appropriate *Eval* behaviors. Shown in Figure 2 are two specialized behavior classes defined for KSL/Logic: *PredicateBehavior* and *BuiltInPredicateBehavior*. A *PredicateBehavior* object associated with a class of a domain object will contain in its expression list all of the Horn clauses for that predicate as defined for the associated domain class. The specialized *Eval* behavior defined for the *PredicateBehavior* class will invoke the predicate resolution process described in section 4. This will effect the matching, variable unification, and backtracking functions of the predicate Horn clauses.

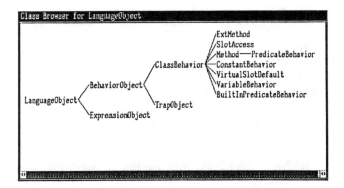

Figure 2. A Class Browser for KSL and KSL/Logic Behaviors

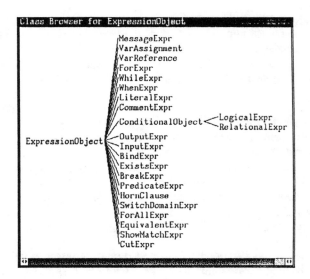

Figure 3. A Class Browser for KSL and KSL/Logic Expressions

Built-in predicates are defined by instances of the *BuiltInPredicatBehavior* class. For example, built-in predicates are implemented for *member* to match or return members of a list, for *is* to compare or assign predicate variable values, for *var* and *nonvar* to determine if a variable is bound, and for *call* to resolve a programmatically constructed predicate expression. All built-in predicates observe a common protocol; each has a specialized class of search node. A prototype instance of this node is attached to the corresponding *BuiltInPredicateBehavior* object for the predicate. These node objects perform the unique functionality of the corresponding built-in predicates.

3. KSL/Logic Expressions

KSL/Logic expressions, like regular KSL expressions, are implemented as objects--instances of specializations of the *ExpressionObject* class. Figure 3 shows the class hierarchy of KSL and KSL/Logic expressions. The syntax of KSL--the external representation of its expressions-- has been extended to express predicate variables, predicate expressions, Horn clauses, plus some additional key-word expressions. This allows KSL and KSL/Logic expressions to be intermixed so that KSL procedural expressions operate as *functions* within the predicate logic expressions of KSL/Logic.

The following paragraphs briefly present the syntactic form of KSL/Logic predicate variables and logic expressions, and provide an informal description of their semantics through discussion of suggestive examples. The notation for describing the syntax of the expressions in the rest of this section uses

<> to delimit the description of an element,
{} to delimit an optional element, and
* to indicate zero or more occurrences of a preceding element.

Predicate Variables:

%*<var-name>*
where <var-name> is a KSL symbol.

In standard KSL, values of local variables cannot be accessed by called procedures. To support variable unification in KSL/Logic, a new class of variables, *PredicateVariable*, was implemented where the variables are designated with a percent sign (%) prefix. These variables can be referenced and accessed by KSL expressions in the same manner as standard KSL variables. The values of these variables, as in Prolog, are generally assigned by the matching mechanism.

Predicate expressions:

(P <selector> <arg-expr>*)
where
<selector> = a name of a predicate--a KSL symbol,
<arg-expr> = an expression that specifies a value or variable to be unified.

Predicate expressions are implemented as key-word expressions. The *Resolve* behavior of these expressions, discussed in section 4, initiates the selection and invocation of the appropriate predicate behaviors through the standard message resolution mechanism. In the example shown in Figure 4, *parent* is a predicate name with predicate variables %A and %B as arguments.

(P parent %A %B)

Figure 4. An Example of a Predicate Expression

Definition of the *parent* predicate is determined by the context in which the expression is resolved; the definition is obtained from the class of the current domain object. Arguments of predicate expressions are evaluated before the resolution is pursued. This allows procedural expressions to appear as arguments with their returned values used in the unification process. Of course, arguments that are unbound predicate variables will have their values determined by the resolution process.

Horn clause expressions:

(HC <consequent> <antecedent>*)
where
<consequent> = a predicate expression to match, and
<antecedent> = an expression that must be true for
                    the Horn clause to succeed.

As in Prolog, predicates are defined by Horn clauses. In KSL/Logic, all of the Horn clauses that define a predicate for a domain class are incorporated in one predicate behavior. Matching and backtracking on Horn clauses are controlled by the evaluation process of their predicate behavior. Figure 5 contrasts a KSL/Logic Horn clause expression with its Prolog counterpart.

```
KSL/Logic:

    (HC (P ancestor %A %C)

        (P parent %A %K) (P ancestor %K %C))

Prolog:

    ancestor (A, C) :-

        parent (A, K) , ancestor (K, C).
```

Figure 5. Examples of a
Horn Clause in KSL/Logic and in Prolog

In KSL/Logic, the list of antecedent expressions is an implicit conjunction which can include both predicate expressions and other KSL expressions. Predicate variables can be referenced in KSL expressions, but they must be bound before the KSL expression is encountered. KSL expressions always "fail" on backtracking.

Figure 6 illustrates the use of the logical and relational expressions (e.g., *And*, *Or*, *LessThan*), message expressions as arguments (e.g., *Debts* messages), and KSL expressions as antecedents (e.g., *Print* message).

```
(HC
 (P getLoan %Person %Amount)
 (Or
    (And
        (P bankLoan %Person (Debts %Person) %Limit)
        (LessThan %Amount %Limit))
    (And
        (P creditUnionLoan %Person (Debts %Person) %Limit)
        (LessThan %Amount %Limit)))
 (Print "Loan available"))
```

Figure 6. Example of a
Horn Clause using KSL and Predicate Expressions

Cut expression:

The KSL/Logic "cut" expression is represented with an exclamation point (!) symbol and appears as an antecedent expression within a Horn clause. The functionality of this expression is equivalent to its Prolog counterpart.

SwitchDomain expression:

(SwitchDomain <new-domain> <p-expr>)
where
<new-domain> = the domain object for which
                     reasoning is to be performed, and
<p-expr>   = the predicate expression to be
                     resolved.

Since the domain of reasoning is implicit for Horn clauses and predicate expressions, the *SwitchDomain* expression is used to direct reasoning to occur in a different domain. It appears as an antecedent expression within a Horn clause and affects only the domain of reasoning of the associated predicate expression.

```
(SwitchDomain (Car $Person1) (P wontStart %Reason) )
```

Figure 7. An Example of a SwitchDomain Expression

In the example shown in Figure 7, the *SwitchDomain* expression directs reasoning to a *Car* object domain which, presumably, has the predicate definitions to resolve the *wontStart* goal.

ForAll expression:

(ForAll <domain> <p-expr> <expr-list> {<cont-cond>})
where
<domain>   = expression that returns the domain of reasoning,
<p-expr>   = predicate expression to be resolved,
<expr-list> = a list of expressions to be executed for each solution returned, and
<cont-cond> = an optional expression that must be true for the matching and backtracking to be initiated and continued. The default is true.

The *ForAll* expression is the principle linkage between procedural KSL code and KSL/Logic. The expressions in the <expr-list> can reference the bindings of variables in the predicate expression for each of the alternative solutions. The optional conditional expression allows the iteration to be terminated before all possible solutions have been pursued. An example is shown in Figure 8.

```
(ForAll $Self (P newmail %QualifiedPerson %Age %Income)
  (#List
    (Print (Name %QualifiedPerson))
    (Print (Address %QualifiedPerson))))
```

Figure 8. An Example of a ForAll Expression

In this example, a successful resolution of the *newmail* predicate behavior will bind a qualified person to the *%QualifiedPerson* variable based on a given age and income. The KSL *Print* messages access the value bound to the *%QualifiedPerson* variable for every successful resolution of the *newmail* predicate. Since the continue condition is omitted, backtracking of the *ForAll* expression continues returning qualified persons until all have been processed. Note that if *newmail* were sent as a message to a domain object, then evaluation of the message would return true if a solution exists and the *%QualifiedPerson* variable would be bound to the first solution found.

4. The Object Implementation of Predicate Resolution

In KSL/Logic, resolution of a predicate expression is performed by invoking the corresponding predicate behavior defined on the class of the domain object. This invocation is accomplished with the standard message resolution mechanism where a predicate name is the

selector, a domain object is the target object, and predicate arguments are the message arguments.

The fundamental difference between predicate behaviors and other KSL behaviors is that the *Eval* of predicate behaviors returns either *False* or a node object capable of performing matching, variable unification, and backtracking, while the *Eval* of other behaviors returns a value as a "result". The returned node object is the root of a search network that is extended and backtracked until a solution is found.

An intermediate node in the search network represents the resolution of a predicate, and its subordinate nodes represent supporting predicate resolutions. Leaf nodes represent either built-in predicates, Horn clauses without antecedent expressions, or KSL expressions that appear as antecedents of a Horn clause. Once the network is constructed, successive *Backtrack* messages operate recursively on the network nodes to return alternative solutions.

A predicate expression to be resolved can appear in a *ForAll* expression or as an antecedent expression in a Horn clause. The process of resolving a predicate expression starts when the expression is sent a *Resolve* message. The *Resolve* behavior will first evaluate the argument expressions to determine the argument values. Next, the predicate behavior that defines the predicate name is invoked. If there is at least one solution, the search node returned contains the appropriate variable bindings and is attached to its parent node if the resolution is part of a larger search.

If the predicate behavior is a *BuiltInPredicateBehavior*, its *Eval* behavior creates a clone of the prototype node stored in the built-in predicate object and sends a *Match* message to it to obtain an initial solution. If the match is not successful, the behavior returns *False*; otherwise, the node is returned to be attached to the search network for later processing of *Backtrack* messages. The *Match* and *Backtrack* behaviors of the specialized node implement the functionality of the built-in predicate.

If the predicate behavior contains Horn clauses, i.e., it is a *PredicateBehavior* object, then the node returned will manage the Horn clause matching and backtracking process for the search. The Horn clauses are taken in the order in which they appear in the *ExpressionList* of the *PredicateBehavior* object.

The arguments of the predicate expression to be resolved must be matched with the corresponding parameters of the consequent expression of the Horn clause. If an argument is an unbound variable reference, the corresponding parameter expression is associated with the variable for later unification (provided that the Horn clause succeeds). If the parameter is a variable reference and the argument is not, then the argument value is assigned to the parameter variable.

When neither the argument nor the parameter are variable references, they must be compared for structure equivalence. The structure matching process will recursively compare the argument structure to the parameter structure. The matching will succeed if, for each component of the structure, one of the following conditions is met:

1) either the argument or the parameter is the symbol *NotSet* (it matches anything),

2) corresponding objects are elementary objects (symbol, string, or numeric) and they are equal,

3) corresponding objects are lists of the same length and their members match,

4) corresponding objects are not lists or elementary objects and they are of the same class, or the class of the argument component is a sub-class of the parameter class. For example, a *Student* object will qualify as a *Person* object if *Student* is a subclass of *Person*.

Once a match on a consequent of a Horn clause has been achieved, the antecedent expressions (the right hand side expressions) of the Horn clause are resolved by sending each a *Resolve* message. If the antecedent expression is a predicate expression, then the resolution is initiated as described above, and the evaluation proceeds to the next antecedent expression upon a successful match.

If the antecedent expression is a KSL procedural expression, it is resolved by sending the expression an *Eval* message to perform an appropriate action and return a value interpreted as true or false. If true, a special KSL node is created and attached to the search network. Logical expressions (*And*, *Or*, and *Not*) that appear as antecedent expressions respond to the *Resolve* message by recursively performing the matching process on its arguments, applying its logical operation to the results.

If a variable reference is used as an antecedent expression, the *Resolve* message is sent to its current value. This allows matching to occur when a variable is assigned a predicate expression as a value.

If a "cut" expression is encountered, a special node is returned that implements the same cut functionality as Prolog.

Any other antecedent KSL object, except the *False* symbol, returns a KSL node in response to the *Resolve* message and it is interpreted as true; a *False* symbol is treated as the built-in *fail* predicate of Prolog.

When an antecedent expression fails, backtracking occurs. An alternative solution is requested by sending the *Backtrack* message to the search node of the preceding antecedent expression. This process is repeated until either all the expressions succeed or all fail. Note that only predicate expressions have alternate solutions; thus KSL expressions can only succeed when matching is progressing down the antecedent list but will always fail when an alternate (backtracking) solution is requested.

When a solution is found, variables from the arguments of the matched predicate expression must be unified before the return. The corresponding parameter expressions are evaluated and the value returned is assigned as the binding of the variable. If, on the other hand, the match fails and cannot succeed with backtracking, then the failing return leaves the argument variables unbound as before the matching process started. Thus when resolution of a predicate expression fails, it does not affect the bindings of variables used in its arguments.

In this implementation, it is important to note that the protocol observed by the search nodes is not limited to predicate resolution or the search algorithms of built-in predicates. It is a generalized search protocol that can incorporate other search techniques as well. For example, specialized nodes could implement searches that incorporate database retrieval.

5. KSL/Logic Programming Tools

The implementation of classes, behaviors, and executable expressions as objects makes KSL a reflective language; it can operate on itself. This quality, along with the object-oriented search network implementation of the predicate resolution, supported the development of powerful programming tools for KSL/Logic.

In addition to the trace and break facilities typical of Prolog implementations, a Horn Clause Editor and Search Tree Browser have been implemented. These tools are specializations of standard KSL facilities and can be invoked from the KSL Debugger tool.

```
Horn Clauses on DMail Domain (Parsing Successful)

(HC (P newmail %QualifiedPerson %Sex %AgeLimit %Income)
    (P member %QualifiedPerson (MailDatabase $Self ))
    (Or (Equal %Sex (Sex %QualifiedPerson))
        (ReallyNotSet (CurrentValue %Sex)))
    (SwitchDomain %QualifiedPerson (P qualify %AgeLimit %Income)))
```

Figure 9a. Horn Clause Editor for DMail Domain

```
Horn Clauses on Person Domain (Parsing Successful)

(HC (P parent %F  %C )
    (P is  %F (Father  %C )))
(HC (P parent %M  %C )
    (P is  %M (Mother  %C )))

(HC (P qualify %AgeLimit %Income )
    (GreaterThanEqual (Age $Self ) %AgeLimit )
    (CheckIncome  $Self %Income ) ! )
(HC (P qualify %AgeLimit %Income )
    (P parent  %P $Self )
    (CheckIncome  %P %Income ) ! )
```

Figure 9b. Horn Clause Editor for Person Domain

Figure 9 illustrates two Horn Clause Editor windows taken from a scaled down version of an example discussed in [8]. The example uses a *newmail* predicate to return person objects satisfying sex, age, and income criteria. The editor presents Horn clauses for the predicates defined on a domain class. Either local predicates or both local and inherited predicates can be displayed. The figure shows local Horn clauses for two domains: *DMail* and *Person*. The Horn Clause Editor is used to add, modify, or delete Horn clauses and when the edited result is saved, the appropriate predicate behaviors are created, modified or deleted.

To facilitate debugging programs written in KSL/Logic, a Search Tree Browser tool is implemented as a special network display reflecting the current tree of predicate invocations. The tree can be observed dynamically as matching and backtracking occur, and the search can be stopped and examined at any point. The display is driven by a generalized form of "active values" implemented in KSL. Procedures to update the display are attached to the predicate resolution nodes. The nodes are mouse sensitive and allow the examination of the search state at any node using pop-up menus. The Horn Clause Editor can also be invoked from this display.

The Search Tree in Figure 10 illustrates the state of the search after resolution of a *newmail* predicate using the Horn clauses illustrated in Figure 9.

6. Conclusions and Future Work

KSL/Logic provides a new degree of integration of logic with objects. This integration provides a superset of Prolog functionality. KSL/Logic predicate arguments can be computational expressions that operate on objects or they can be complex objects, not just lists and predicate expressions. Reasoning in KSL/Logic can occur in multiple domains where predicates can be defined according to the particular domain. This allows complex problems to be partitioned into sub-problems represented by specialized domains providing a more modular architecture and exploiting the advantages of object-oriented programming. The object-oriented implementation of predicate resolution and the search network protocol provide a generalized search mechanism that can be extended to incorporate new search techniques.

The reflective capability of KSL contributed to the KSL/Logic implementation and to the development of its programming tools. The implementation of language expressions as objects allowed new expression types to be defined easily and supported imbedding of KSL procedural expressions in Horn clauses. The language objects also supported the implementation of the Horn Clause Editor and the Search Tree Browser.

Future work should focus on two areas: performance improvement and extensions to backtracking. Procedural KSL can be translated to C and compiled for performance improvement; similar techniques can be applied to predicate behaviors to provide a "compiled

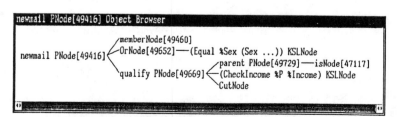

Figure 10. Search Tree Browser

234

search network". Backtracking does not currently back out changes to the object structure of the application model; more comprehensive backtracking facilities should be explored.

Acknowledgments

The authors would like to acknowledge the contributions of Scott Woyak in the design of KSL/Logic and the implementation of its tools.

References

[1] Bobrow, D. G., and Stefik, M. J., *The LOOPS Manual*, Xerox Corp., Palo Alto, CA, 1983.

[2] Clocksin, W. F. and Mellish, C. S., *Programming in Prolog*, Springer-Verlag, 1981.

[3] Cummins, F. A., Bejcek, W. E., Ibrahim, M. H., O'Leary, D. J., and Woyak, S. W., "OWL 3.0 Reference Manual," *Internal Technical Report #AAI-87007*, EDS Research and Development, Troy, MI, August, 1987.

[4] Fukunaga, K. and Hirose, S., "An Experience with a Prolog-based Object-Oriented Language," *Proceedings of OOPSLA '87*, pp. 232-241, 1987.

[5] Dalal, M. and Gangopadhyay, D., "OOLP: A Translation Approach to Object-Oriented Logic Programming," *Proceedings of First International Conference on Deductive and Object-Oriented Databases*, Kyoto, Japan, 1989.

[6] Goguen, J. A. and Meseguer, J., "Unifying Functional, Object-Oriented, and Relational Programming with Logical Semantics," in *Research Directions in Object-Oriented Programming*, B. Shriver and P. Wegner (Eds.), The MIT Press, Cambridge, Massachusetts, 1987.

[7] Ibrahim, M. H. and Cummins, F. A., "KSL: A Reflective Object-Oriented Programming Language," *Proceedings of the International Conference on Computer Languages*, pp. 186-193, 1988.

[8] Ibrahim, M. H. and Cummins, F. A., "Objects with Logic," *Proceedings of the ACM CSC '90*, 1990.

[9] Ishikawa, Y. and Tokoro, M., "A Concurrent Object-Oriented Knowledge Representation Language Orient84/K: Its Features and Implementation," *Proceedings of OOPSLA '87*, pp. 232-241, 1987.

[10] Ishikawa, Y. and Tokoro, M., "Orient84/K: An Object_Oriented Concurrent Programming Language for Knowledge Representation," in *Object-Oriented Concurrent Programming*, A. Yonezawa and M. Tokoro (Eds.), The MIT Press, Cambridge, Massachusetts, 1987.

[11] Kahn, K., Tribble, E. D., Miller, M. S., and Bobrow, D. G., "Objects in Concurrent Logic Programming Languages," *Proceedings of OOPSLA '87*, pp. 232-241, 1987.

[12] Koschmann, T. and Evens, M. W., "Bridging the Gap Between Object-Oriented and Logic Programming," *IEEE Software*, Vol. 5, No. 5, pp. 36-42, July, 1988.

[13] Wos L., Overbeck, R., Lusk, E., and Boyle, J., *Automated Reasoning Introduction and Applications*, Prentice-Hall, Inc. Englewood Cliffs, N.J., 1984.

Implementation and Evaluation of Dynamic Predicates on the Sequential Inference Machine CHI*

A. Atarashi, A. Konagaya, S. Habata, M. Yokota
C&C Systems Research Laboratory
NEC Corporation
4-1-1 Miyazaki Miyamae-ku
Kawasaki 213, Japan.

Abstract

This paper describes the *Dynamic Clause Compilation* technique, which is used to implement Prolog's dynamic predicates. It also reports on the effectiveness of the technique when applied to a practical application program executed on the Sequential Inference Machine CHI.

Dynamic predicates are indispensable in writing practical Prolog application programs. According to the authors' application program analysis, many applications spend more than half of the total execution time in dynamic predicate execution. This means that speeding up dynamic predicates is essential toward improving Prolog application performance.

From this point of view, the authors introduced the *Dynamic Clause Compilation* technique, and implemented it on CHI: As soon as a clause is added to Prolog's database, the clause is compiled into machine instructions. This technique greatly accelerates dynamic predicate execution.

Application program analysis shows that dynamic clause compilation accelerates the application execution speed, up to 5 times faster, than conventional dynamic predicate implementation.

1 Introduction

Dynamic predicates [8] play very important roles in practical application programs written in Prolog. Actually, it is very difficult to write AI applications such as knowledge base systems without dynamic predicates.

In spite of the importance of dynamic predicates, almost no attention has been paid to the dynamic predicate performance. According to the authors' application program analysis, many application programs spend more than half of the total execution time in dynamic predicate execution. This means that various compilation techniques for static predicates do not always contribute to total application performance improvements, and that speeding up dynamic predicates is an important factor in total application performance improvements. In other words, speeding up dynamic predicate is indispensable, in order for Prolog to be a truly practical programming language.

To achieve this goal, the authors introduced the *Dynamic Clause Compilation* technique, and implemented it on the Sequential Inference Machine CHI [6, 3, 5]. When a clause is added to Prolog's database (i.e. `assert`'ed), the clause is compiled into a sequence of machine instructions. This technique remarkably improves dynamic predicate execution speed.

One of the most important issues in the dynamic clause compilation is how to keep source images of clauses, since dynamic predicates require facilities to restore a source image of a clause, and to search for a clause with its source image. The dynamic clause compilation technique realizes the facilities by generating an instruction sequence to restore a source image of a clause, when the clause is `assert`'ed.

Another important issue is the overhead of the dynamic clause compilation. It would be possible that the overhead of the dynamic clause compilation slows down `assert` and overwhelms the performance gains in dynamic predicate execution. However, the authors find that the dynamic clause compilation frequency is much lower than the dynamic predicate execution frequency, and that the performance improvements in dynamic predicate execution supersedes the overhead in dynamic clause compilation.

The organization of this paper is as follows: In Section 2, the authors show how to realize source image restoration in dynamic clause compilation. Section 3 is devoted to the dynamic predicate implementation on CHI, especially internal data structures and special instructions to support dynamic predicate execution. Finally, in Section 4, the authors show the measurement results and performance analysis obtained from executing a practical Prolog application.

2 Source Image Restoration Problem

In order to incorporate dynamic clause compilation, a method must be provided which enables restoring source images for dynamic predicates. This is because some Prolog built-in predicates deal with the source images of dynamic predicates. For example, the built-in predicate `clause` restores a source image of a clause. The built-in predicate `retract` searches for and

---

*This research has been done as a part of the Japanese Fifth Generation Computer Project, promoted by ICOT.

deletes a clause, whose source image matches the argument of `retract` (Fig. 1).

To enable source image restoration and clause search with their source images, three methods have been proposed:

1) **Holding source image**

The object code always holds source image as structured data. This approach is simple, but the restoring process is slow. Object code size also becomes large.

2) **De-compilation from execution code** [1]

The same object code is used for both execution and source image restoration. This approach implements compact object code, fast clause compilation and fast clause image restoration. However, only limited optimizations can be applied at compilation, because certain optimizations might remove information necessary to restore the source image.

3) **Generating code to restore source image**[2]

Code to restore the source image is generated, as well as code for execution. Source image restoration is very fast, and the object code can be freely optimized. However, compilation takes longer and the entire code size becomes large.

The authors once tried a variant of the second method [4]. This method is almost satisfactory, except that it takes only conjunctions (AND-connected goals) of ordinary (not-builtin) predicates into account. Therefore, special execution control predicates, such as cut (`!`), disjunction (`A;B`), if-then-else(`A->B;C`) and so on, cannot be compiled into the corresponding execution control instructions. The problem with regard to cut-operation (`!`), which is one of the most important predicates in Prolog, was serious. Explaining the details would be too specific and is omitted here, but cut implementation on CHI makes it very difficult to adopt the second method.

Therefore, the authors compared the first method and the third method, and decided to adopt the third method, because the authors found that source image restoration speed is important. The problem of the third method is the managing overhead of the code for execution and the code for source image restoration. To solve this problem, the authors merged the code for execution and the code for source image restoration together into one code. The authors also introduced a mode flag, which indicates whether the execution code or the source image restoration code should be executed.

3 Dynamic Predicate Implementation on CHI

This section describes details of dynamic predicate implementation on CHI.

3.1 Dynamic Predicate Execution Mechanism

Figure 2 shows an internal data structure for a dynamic predicate. A functor is a unit of predicate management, and holds clauses for the predicate. In this figure, predicate `f/1` consists of four clauses.

```
f([a]) :- ....
f(_) :- ....
f(a) :- ....
f(b(_)) :- ....
```

The clauses are bi-directionally chained, in order to allow clause addition/deletion at an arbitrary time.

Dynamic predicate execution, including source image restoration, is briefly described below.

Step 1 Switch on the current execution mode flag, at an ordinary predicate call. Switch off the flag at source image restoration.

Step 2 Invoke the entry instruction `itry` of the first clause.

Step 3 Search for a candidate clause. The `itry` traces chained clauses, until it finds a clause, whose indexing key matches the first argument.

Step 4 Execute the execution code of the candidate clause, if the current execution mode flag is on. Otherwise, execute the source image restoration code of the candidate clause.

Step 5 If the candidate execution fails, invoke the `iretry` instruction of the candidate clause. It searches for the next candidate clause and execute the clause, just like `itry` instruction does.

The major difference between dynamic predicate execution and static predicate execution is briefly summarized as follows.

Indexing

Indexing is a technique to avoid redundant clause execution. Static predicates accomplish indexing with hash tables, whereas dynamic predicates carry out indexing with a sequential key search.

In other words, the cost for static predicate indexing is a constant factor, whereas the cost for dynamic predicate indexing is $O(n)$, provided there are n alternatives.

Choice point frame allocation

Static predicates allocate choice point frames only if necessary. Dynamic predicates always allocate choice point frames.

```
?- assert((f(X,Y):-g(X),h(Y))).     % add a clause
yes
?- clause(f(X,Y),Body,_).           % search for a clause
Body = g(X),h(Y)                    % Body is unified with g(X),h(Y)
yes
?- retract((f(X,Y):-g(X),h(Y))).    % delete a clause
yes
```

Figure 1: Source Image Restoration of a Clause

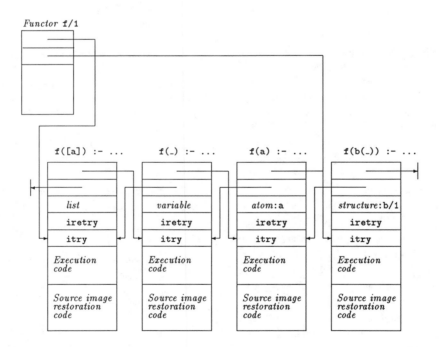

Figure 2: Dynamic Predicate Management

Figure 3: Clause Structure

```
code   previous clause
code   next clause
???    indexing information
inst   retry instruction
inst   entry instruction

       Execution code

       Source image
       restoration
       code
```

concat([X|Y],Z,[X|YZ]) :- concat(Y,Z,YZ).

Execution Code		Source Image Restoration Code	
glis	a0	gstr	a0,concat/3
urvr	a4	urvr	a0
urvr	a5	urvr	a3
grvr	a1,a6	urvr	a4
glis	a2	glis	a0
urvl	a4	urvr	a0
urvr	a7	urvr	a5
prvl	a0,a5	glis	a4
prvl	a1,a6	urvl	a0
prvl	a2,a7	urvr	a6
exec	concat/3	gstr	a1,concat/3
		urvl	a5
		urvl	a4
		urvl	a6
		gcon	a2,'#clause_code'
		prcd	

Figure 4: The concat/3 Code

3.2 Clause Structure

Figure 3 shows the configuration of a clause structure. Important components are explained below.

Indexing Key

The indexing key is the category information for the first argument of the head goal. This key is referred to by entry and retry instructions.

Entry and Retry Instructions

Entry instruction(itry) is the first instruction to be invoked when a dynamic predicate is called. The Retry instruction(iretry) is invoked when a clause fails. Details regarding these instructions are explained in Section 3.3.2.

Execution Code

The execution code is used to execute the clause. It starts from the next address to the entry instruction. The code generation scheme is similar to WAM (Warren Abstract Machine)[9].

Source Image Restoration Code

This code is used to restore source image for a clause. If the clause has the form:

```
Head :- Body.
```

then its source image restoration code is obtained by creating and compiling an imaginary unit clause:

```
clause(Head,Body,Clause).
```

The location of this code is recorded in the operand of the entry instruction.

Figure 4 shows an example of an execution code and a source image restoration code for the second clause of the well known concatenate predicate.

3.3 Instructions to Support Dynamic Predicate Execution

For efficient dynamic predicate execution, the authors have extended the CHI instruction set [3].

3.3.1 Execution Mode Flag

The authors have prepared a flag, which shows the current execution mode. This flag is switched on or switched off at predicate calls. If this flag is on, then the execution code for a clause is executed. If this flag is off, then the source image restoration code for a clause is executed.

On CHI, this flag is assigned to a special hardware register bit. The bit handling can be accomplished in a micro step, in parallel with other micro operations. Therefore, there is no overhead with regards to mode flag handling.

3.3.2 Clause Execution Control Instructions

To control execution over chained clauses, two instructions were introduced, which are extensions to WAM's choice point control instructions try_me_else and retry_me_else, with regards to mode handling and indexing on the first argument.

239

itry

This instruction is invoked upon entry to a dynamic predicate. First, it checks the execution mode flag. In the execution mode (i.e. the mode flag is on), it accomplishes the following steps:

Step 1 Find a candidate clause, whose indexing key matches the first argument.

Step 2 If no such candidate exists, then fail.

Step 3 Otherwise, create a choice point to prepare for failure. The information saved in the choice point frame is the same as that for `try_me_else` instruction, except that the current execution mode flag is also saved.

Step 4 Finally, invoke the execution code for the candidate clause.

Step 5 If the candidate clause execution fails, invoke the `iretry` instruction of the current candidate clause. This instruction tries to find and execute the next candidate clause.

Figure 5 shows a momentary time slot, where the predicate `f/1` is called with the first argument `g(10)`, and `itry` instruction of the first clause is about to finish.

The `itry` instruction first finds a candidate clause, whose indexing key matches the structure `g/1`. In the figure, the second clause `f(g(_)):-...` is the candidate clause.

Then, the `itry` instruction allocates a choice point frame to prepare for failure. The alternative address for the choice point frame points to the retry instruction `iretry` of the candidate clause.

Finally, the `itry` instruction updates the program counter PC, so that the PC points to the start of the execution code for the candidate clause.

In the source mode, `itry` instruction accomplishes the following.

Step 1 Find a candidate clause, such that the index information of the clause matches the first element of the first argument.

Step 2 If no such candidate exists, then fail.

Step 3 Otherwise, create a choice point and invoke the source image restoration code of the candidate clause.

Step 4 If the candidate clause execution fails, then invoke `iretry` instruction of the candidate clause.

Figure 6 shows a momentary time slot, where the source image restoration code of a candidate clause has just succeeded. Registers A_0, A_1 and A_2 are unified with the head goal image for the clause, the body goal image for the clause and the pointer to the code object, respectively.

iretry

This instruction is invoked when clause execution fails. It first restores the control information saved in the current choice point frame, including current execution mode flag status, and accomplishes the following steps in the execution mode.

Step 1 Find a new candidate clause, starting from the clause next to the current candidate clause.

Step 2 If no candidate clause exists, discard the current choice point frame and fail.

Step 3 Otherwise, modify the current choice point frame, so that the `iretry` instruction of the new candidate clause is invoked upon failure. Then, invoke the execution code for the new candidate clause.

Step 4 If the new candidate clause execution fails, invoke the `iretry` instruction of the new candidate clause.

The action for the `iretry` instruction at source restoration mode is easy to infer, and is omitted here.

3.3.3 Source Image Restoration Instructions

The `clause/3` predicate is the core predicate for source image restoration. In fact, almost all source image handling predicates can be implemented with the predicate. For example, the `retract/1` predicate can be roughly implemented as follows:

```
retract((H:-B)) :- !,clause(H,B,R),erase(R).
retract(H) :- clause(H,true,R),erase(R).
```

The authors introduced the `execute_clause` instruction, in order to implement the `clause/3` predicate. When the instruction is invoked, it accomplishes the following.

Step 1 Check if the first argument A_0 is bound to a structure or an atom. If not, raise an error.

Step 2 Switch off the current execution mode flag, to indicate that the source image restoration codes should be executed.

Step 3 Invoke the code, which is held by the functor of the structure A_0. That is, execute the `itry` instruction, which is the first instruction of the code, in the source image restoration mode.

4 Evaluation

This section presents results of evaluating dynamic clause compilation performance, and how the dynamic clause compilation affects a real application program.

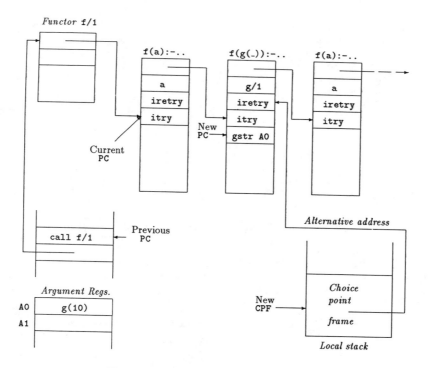

Figure 5: Calling a Dynamic Predicate f/1

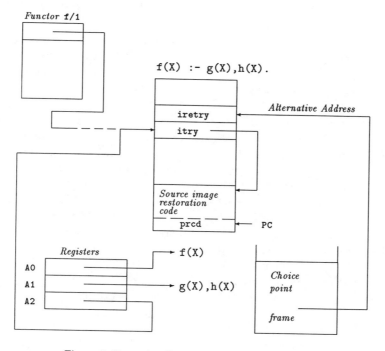

Figure 6: Executing Source Image Restoration Code

Table 1: Time Spent for the Dynamic Clause Compilation

Data	Dcc (msec)	Encode (msec)	Dcc/ Encode
1	1.49	0.17	8.76
2	1.93	0.19	10.16
3	4.14	0.31	13.35
4	2.09	0.25	8.36
5	3.26	0.35	9.31

Table 2: Object Code Size for a Clause

Data	Dcc (words)	Encode (words)	Dcc/ Encode
1	21	12	1.75
2	21	13	1.62
3	38	20	1.90
4	22	17	1.29
5	34	22	1.55

Table 3: Time Spent For a Clause Execution

Data	Dcc (msec)	Decode (msec)	Dcc/ Decode
1	0.036	0.095	0.38
2	0.037	0.110	0.34
3	0.043	0.163	0.26

4.1 Dynamic Clause Compilation Performance

Dynamic clause compilation performance was evaluated, from the view points of compilation speed, object code size and execution speed.

As a comparison, the authors used predicates `encode` and `decode`. These predicates are used in conventional dynamic predicate implementation. The `encode` predicate freezes a term on the global stack into a heap data object. The `decode` predicate melts a heap data object and creates a term on the global stack area.

The authors used the following five simple clauses as sample data.

```
1  foo(a).
2  foo(X,X).
3  foo([X|Y],f(X),g(Y)).
4  foo(X) :- bar(X).
5  foo(X) :- bar(X),baz(X).
```

Table 1 compares the time spent for dynamic clause compilation(Dcc) and `encode`. On average, dynamic clause compilation is 10 times slower than `encode`. One of the reasons that dynamic clause compilation is so slow, is that CHI's dynamic clause compiler is written in Prolog, whereas `encode` is written in low level machine instructions and carefully tuned. Although the dynamic clause compilation performance is not so attractive, there is no reason to be pessimistic about the result, since most important is the total application performance, which is considerably affected by the ratio of dynamic clause compilation frequency to dynamic predicate execution frequency.

Table 2 shows object code size comparison. Dynamic clause compilation requires approximately 60% more memory than `encode`. The authors find that such object code size increase is permissible, because the global stack consumption problem is much more critical, if dynamic predicates are implemented with encode/decode.

A comparison between the clause execution speed and the `decode` speed is shown in Table 3. The authors used only sample clauses 1 to 3, because clauses 4 and 5 have body goals and make correct evaluation difficult. This shows that executing a clause in dynamic clause compilation implementation is more than 3 times faster than encode/decode implementation.

Furthermore, dynamic predicates will run much faster in applications, since indexing cost is very low, when dynamic predicates have several clauses. This is because indexing the clauses is accomplished by `itry` and `iretry` instructions in the dynamic clause compilation method, whereas indexing is carried out by an interpreter in the encode/decode method.

4.2 Dynamic Clause Compilation Effects in Application Program

To prove the effectiveness of the authors' dynamic clause compilation technique, performance of a bibliography information retrieval program [7] was evaluated.

The application consists of 2100 lines of program and 7700 lines of bibliography data. The application uses an inductive inference method, based on the stochastic logic. During program execution, the inductive inference method repeatedly generates, examines and cancels hypotheses. Dynamic predicates are used to represent such hypothesis management.

The flow of this program is as follows: First, the system gives the user 10 bibliographies, according to an initial retrieval command. After that, the user repeats the following three operations, until he is satisfied with the bibliographies that the system gives.

Select bibliographies

The user tells the system which bibliographies are necessary and which are not. This is called *"select* phase".

Calculate a new retrieval command

According to the select phase information, the system performs an inductive inference, to calculate a new retrieval

Table 4: `recorda/z` and `recorded` Frequency

Phase	recorda/z	recorded
Think	388	4268
Find	237	827

command. This is the kernel phase for the system, and the authors call it "*think* phase".

Find new bibliographies

According to the new retrieval command, obtained in the *think* phase, the system newly retrieves 10 bibliographies and gives them to the user. This is called "*find* phase".

Of the three phases explained above, the authors analyzed the *think* and *find* phases, since the *select* phase accomplishes nothing but interaction with the user. All input/output operations were removed during evaluation.

As stated before, this application generates and cancels hypotheses. To represent hypotheses, the application uses `record`, which is a special dynamic predicate, that the system provides. It can be roughly implemented as follows:

```
recorda(X,Y,Z) :- asserta('Functor for record'(X,Y),Z).
recordz(X,Y,Z) :- assertz('Functor for record'(X,Y),Z).
recorded(X,Y,Z) :- clause('Functor for record'(X,Y),_,Z).
```

The difference between records and ordinary dynamic predicates is as follows:

- Adding records is 30% faster than adding clauses to dynamic predicates.

- Object code for records is approximately 30% smaller than objects code for ordinary dynamic predicates.

- Calling records is approximately 30% slower than ordinary predicates.

First, the authors measured how often record handling predicates, such as `recorda`, `recordz` and `recorded` are called in a cycle involving *think* and *find* phases. The result is shown in Table 4. This indicates that the record reference frequency is 8 times higher than the record registration frequency. This is consistent with the authors' assumption that the dynamic predicate execution frequency is higher than the dynamic clause compilation frequency.

Next, the authors measured the time spent for adding records, the object code size for the records and the time spent for calling records, in the cycle involving *think* and *find* phases. Finally, the authors redefined record handling predicates with `encode` and `decode`, to measure the same factors for the same cycle. The results are shown in Tables 5, 6 and 7, respectively.

Table 5: Time Spent for Dynamic Clause Compilation at an Application

Phase	record (msec)	encode (msec)	record/ encode	assert (msec)
Think	1180	196	6.02	1534.0
Find	783	120	6.53	1017.9

Table 6: Total Object Code Size for Clauses at an Application

phase	record (words)	encode (words)	record/ encode	assert (words)
Think	18540	13093	1.42	24102
Find	14508	10857	1.34	18860

In the tables, the `record` field shows the execution time/object code size in the dynamic clause compilation implementation. The `encode` field shows the execution time/object code size in the encode/decode implementation. The `assert` field is provided, to show the estimated value, when ordinary dynamic predicates are used instead of records.

For the time and memory spent for dynamic clause compilation, the result is consistent with the result obtained from simple data. However, if a comparison is made between the result of calling records with that for simple data, it can be easily seen that the record execution speed is much faster. This shows that records have several alternatives, and that `itry` and `iretry` instructions are effective to index clauses.

The total time spent for application execution is shown in Table 8 and Fig. 7. The dynamic clause compilation effectiveness is evident. Dynamic clause compilation greatly contributes to the fast application program execution. This is because the dynamic predicate execution frequency is much higher than dynamic clause compilation frequency, and compiled clauses run very fast, although dynamic clause compilation is not so fast.

5   Conclusion

Dynamic Clause Compilation is presented to accelerate Prolog's dynamic predicates. Its implementation on the Sequential Inference Machine CHI and evaluation results are also described. The measurement results, using a practical Prolog application,

Table 7: Time Spent for Dynamic Predicate Execution at an Application

Phase	record (msec)	decode (msec)	record/ decode	assert (msec)
Think	3760	52803	0.071	2892.3
Find	586	8263	0.071	450.8

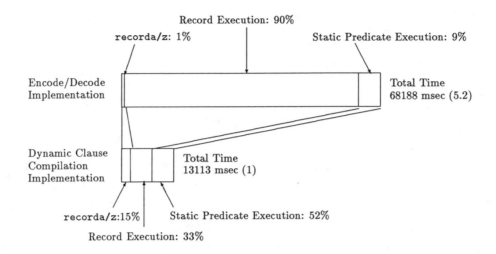

Record Execution: 90%

recorda/z: 1%

Static Predicate Execution: 9%

Encode/Decode Implementation

Total Time 68188 msec (5.2)

Dynamic Clause Compilation Implementation

Total Time 13113 msec (1)

recorda/z:15%

Record Execution: 33%

Static Predicate Execution: 52%

Figure 7: Dynamic Clause Compilation Effects

Table 8: Total Time Spent at an Application Program

phase	record (msec)	encode (msec)	record/ encode	assert (msec)
Think	10899	58958	0.18	10394.3
Find	2214	9230	0.24	2313.7
Total	13113	68188	0.24	12712.0

shows that dynamic predicates run 14 times faster than dynamic predicates in conventional implementation. This result shortens the total application execution time by 1/5, although dynamic clause compilation is 10 times slower than conventional dynamic predicate implementation.

The authors find that Prolog database modification with dynamic predicates is essential in practical Prolog applications, especially in AI applications. Therefore, speeding up dynamic predicates is indispensable. The authors' dynamic clause compilation technique will make a great contribution to practical use of logic programming.

Acknowledgment: The authors would like to thank Dr. Shunichi Uchida (ICOT) for supporting this project, as well as to thank Shinji Yanagida and Satoshi Oyanagi (NSIS) for their efforts in CHI software system implementation and to thank all the members who are engaged in CHI project. They would also like to thank Kazuhiko Ohno (NEC), who was kind enough to allow the authors to use his bibliography retrieval program. Thanks are also expressed to Nobuhiko Koike and Dr. Tatsuo Ishiguro (NEC) for their continuous encouragement, valuable advice and support.

References

[1] Buettner, K.A., "Fast Decompilation of Compiled Prolog Clauses", in *Proc. the Third International Conference on Logic Programming*, London, 1986

[2] Clocksin, W.F., "Implementation Techniques for Prolog Databases", Software — Practice and Experience, Vol. 15(7), 1985

[3] Habata, S., Nazakaki, R., Konagaya, A., Atarashi, A. and Umemura, M., "Co-operative High Performance Sequential Inference Machine: CHI", in *Proc. ICCD'87*, New York, 1987

[4] Konagaya, A., "Implementation and Evaluation of a Fast Prolog Interpreter", in IPC Japan SIG-SYM 46-4, 1988 (in Japanese)

[5] Konagaya, A., Habata, S., Atarashi, A., Yokota, M. "Evaluation of Sequential Inference Machine CHI", in *Logic Programming: Proc. of the North American Conference*, 1989

[6] Nakazaki, R., Konagaya, A., Habata, S., Shimazu, H., Umemura, M., Yamamoto, M., Yokota, M. and Chikayama, T., "Design of a High-speed Prolog Machine (HPM)", in *Proc. of the 12th International Symposium on Computer Architecture*, June 1985

[7] Ohno, K. "Document Retrieval using Inductive Inference Method on Stochastic Logic", in SIG-FAI-8803-2, 1988 (in Japanese)

[8] "Quintus Prolog Reference Manual (Version 10)", Quintus Computer Systems, Inc.,1987

[9] Warren, D.H.D, "AN ABSTRACT PROLOG INSTRUCTION SET", Technical Note 309, SRI International, 1983

The Tahiti Programming Language: Events as First-Class Objects

James Hearne and Debra Jusak
Department of Computer Science
Western Washington University

Abstract

Many problems in computing are naturally conceptualized in terms of computational events, notably in the areas of real-time programming, fault tolerant programming and software development where safety is an issue. More abstractly, events figure in any construct defining the relationship between different threads of control in parallel systems. However, no programming language embodies a fully abstract and consistent facility for representing and managing computational events. Tahiti is an experimental CSP-based language which augments the standard primitive data types with the type Event which enables data objects to be bound to occurrences in the execution of the program itself. This paper describes Tahiti's constructs for representing and managing events without addressing the language's formal semantics or the many implementation issues it arouses.

Introduction

Many problems in computing are naturally conceptualized in terms of computational *events*, i.e., occurrences in the execution of a program itself or in the world to which a program must respond and provide services to. In spite of this, programming languages do not embody a robust mechanism for representing and manipulating computational events. Instead, information about events is typically encoded using semantic primitives drawn from the *state* of the program— the current values of declared data. Tahiti is an experimental programming language implemented in a distributed environment, which attempts to embody a rich and fully orthogonal collection of constructs, including a time logic, for the management of events. This paper sketches informally the ways in which Tahiti departs from conventional, state oriented programming languages. Specifically, it describes the features that Tahiti superimposes onto constructs suitable to a conventional multiprocessing language in the CSP tradition[1, 11, 13]. Formal questions of syntax and semantics as well as the the many novel implementation issues Tahiti arouses are not discussed.

Motivations

A role for event constructs is suggested by quite diverse programming situations, including real-time programming, fault-tolerance and exception handling, and programming where safety is a concern. Computational events also figure prominently in certain unresolved design issues in parallel programming languages that admit non-determinism.

Implicitly, computational events are a persistent element of much programming; for the device we know as *flags* are simply a primitive way of encoding the fact that some programmer-defined event has occurred. Flags are especially conspicuous in real-time programming in which one part of a program communicates with another only through the setting of flags. Indeed, quite elaborate systems of flags are not unusual. For example, in a program organized around a cyclical executive, a given time slice can determine whether a given event has occurred in the most recent cycle by consulting the value of a flag that was set in a different slice. Frequently, flag data will encode not merely the occurrence of an event but such facts as the relative ordering of two events and also whether the flag has been accessed since it was last updated or *vice versa*. As is well known, pressing state information into the service of event management leads to very unwieldy programs. Some efforts to articulate event constructs for real-time programming have been made [4]; indeed, the need to provide such a mechanism is implicit in much real-time language design [22]. No previous effort, however, approaches the design from the point of view of event logic that animates Tahiti.

Events also have a role in the design of constructs for exception handling and fault tolerance. One well-known flaw of exception handling mechanisms (such as those of Ada and PL/1) is that system and programmer defined exceptions are treated inconsistently [16]. Whereas tests for the occurrence of system-defined events are *implicit*, programmer-defined exceptions must be tested for explicitly, thereby cluttering the source code. This conflicts with a major purpose of exception handling mechanisms: to separate code defining normal processing from code responding to exceptional conditons. Since the occurrence of conditions which raise exceptions are themselves computational events, a full mechanism for representing and responding to events will plausibly address this problem in a consistent way.

245

Relatedly, computational events have a place in the area of software safety. In system development where safety is a concern, it is generally possible to identify in advance, usually at the systems engineering level, system states that are hazardous[12]. However, it is difficult to guarantee that software will detect (or avoid causing) such pathological states. A mechanism that efficiently monitors the execution of a program so as to detect and act upon hazardous events, much in the spirit of program annotations [18] would address this problem also.

Most importantly, events also address what amounts to an open question in the design of parallel languages. In any language in which the time order of actions is underdetermined by the semantics of the language it is necessary to allow limited access to *behavioral* predicates which allow one thread of control to determine whether another thread has performed a particular action. Ada, for example, in addition to providing for events in the form of conventional message-passing, allows conditional and timed entry calls. These enable an action in one process—the establishment of a rendezvous—to be conditional on something other than the current values of declared data [1]. In general, wherever parallelism is possible, language designers must define relations between different threads of control by attending to computational events. Typically, this is done by allowing the language designer to determine which events should have a life in the program. Tahiti explores the rival option of providing the most general language for referencing computational events that is consistent with efficiency, typing principles and support for good programming practice. This is distinct from but related to the so-called 'reflective pardigm' under which programs may represent and refer to their own behavior [5, 19, 21].

Event Logic

The view of events and their logic incorporated in Tahiti is essentially that of [8] (elaborated in [9]) adapted to a computational context [3]. Event logic assumes the existence of a set of atomic *event radicals*, just as classical propositional logic assumes the existence of primitive propositions. Event radicals are categorially distinct from propositions, and do not have truth values. Instead of corresponding to situations of affairs, as statements do, event-radicals correspond to kinds of occurrence. For example, event-radical **the-door-closes**—there is no cannonical expression of this idea in ordinary English—corresponds to the many possible occurrences of the event of the door closing just as the statement 'the door is closed' corresponds to the many situations in which the door is closed.

However, event-radicals may be transformed into boolean objects by means of the aspect operators **perf** and **pros**. **Perf**, the 'perfective' operator, transforms an event radical **E** into the statement that the event **E** *has* occurred (at least once). The 'prospective' operator **pros** transforms **E** into the statement that **E** *will* occur.

The opposite transformation is also possible. A proposition **P** proceeded by the 'ingressive' operator '**bcom**' transforms the statement **P** into the event consisting of it coming to be the case that **P**. That is, an occurrence of **bcom P** takes place whenever there is a change in the value of **P** from false to true.

In virtue of these relations, event radicals and aspect operators may be brought into relation with classical logic and event logic is naturally developed as an extension to temporal logic [14, 15].

The Tahiti Language

Type Event

Tahiti accommodates computational events by augmenting the usual collection of predefined types with the type **event**, bestowing on it the same status as any other type. Values of this type are any representable *occurrences* in the execution of the program in which they are defined. Type event thus differs radically from other types for which the values are specifiable in advance of the execution of a program. They are also initially confusing because they do not admit of literal values and are only accessible through attributes which are explained more fully below.

Objects of type event are declared just as any other data item. Thus,

$$e1, e2, e3 : \textbf{event};$$

in the declarative region of a process creates three variable objects that can be bound to any representable execution occurrence. Event objects are always initialized to the distinguished value **noth** which denotes the impossible event, the event which by definition never occurs and which serves as the event analog of the null set. Event variables obtain values other than **noth** through a kind of daemon mechanism called 'whenever clauses' discussed below.

The invocation of event logic into a computing context is not entirely mechanical. The fact that values of type event are computational occurrences does not settle the question as to the descriptive language under which they have a life in programs, since event logic does not determine what computational events can be directly *represented* in a program. It might be reasonable, for example, for an event language to include metalinguistic notions like 'process initiation,' 'process termination' and 'message sent' as distinguishible events in a program execution. Tahiti currently resolves the question of event language design by focusing upon the two categories of event for which a natural language is ready-to-hand. *Semantic events* are events that can be defined in terms of changes in the values of declared data items. *Syntactic events* are defined in terms of source code statements and may be understood as a generalization of flags. These categories refer to methods of definition only; all events are of the same type.

Type event is accessible to subtype discriminations. The declaration,

$$\textbf{subtype } E = \textbf{bcom } (X > 3 \textbf{ and } Y = Z)$$

creates a (semantic) subtype, values of which consist of occurrences of it coming to be the case that X is greater than 3 and Y has the value Z. Though event values are instrinsically dynamic, rules for the specification of subtypes must be expressed in terms of what is known only from state information. This principle rules out, for example, the declaration of a type **E1** consisting of all events which occur after the fifth occurrence of another type **E2**, for this definition must be stated in terms of an attribute, the time of the fifth occurrence of **E2**, that cannot be deduced from state information. A change in the state of a computation is transformed into a computational event by means of the 'ingressive' operator **bcom**. This operator transforms a piece of state information, i.e., a boolean condition, perhaps temporally qualified, into the occurrence of the condition becoming true. For example, the expression

$$\textbf{bcom } (x > 9 \textbf{ and } y = 7)$$

Operator	Meaning
past	*some* previous state
futr	*some* future state
hist	*all* previous states
forv	*all* future states

Table 1: Qualitative Temporal Operators

specifies an event subtype, occurrences of which are defined as *it coming to be the case that $x > 9$ and $y = 7$*. Observe that this event may be aroused under two distinct circumstances, to wit (1) X is bound to a value greater than 9 when Y is updated to 7 or (2) Y is bound to 7 and an update of X changes the expression X > from false to true. It is important to note that although semantic events can be reduced to configurations of state descriptions, events are distinct from states, having for example, attributes such as a real-time stamp and places in the linear ordering of all events of (possibly several) event subtypes.

Temporal Logic and Semantic Events

In order to provide a language for the representation of semantic events, Tahiti embodies a temporal logic of boolean conditions, in terms of which semantic events are defined. Thus, Tahiti permits interrogation of conditions qualified by the temporal operators which access past, present or future states of the executing program. Two categories of temporal operators may be invoked, qualitative and quantitative.

The qualitative temporal operators are the ones classically provided by temporal logic, namely, **past**, **futr**, **hist**, and **forv**. their meanings are given by Table 1.

For example, the statement

$$\textbf{past } x > 9$$

evaluates to true if the condition $x > 9$ evaluated to true at some moment (or state) in the computation previous to the

current state. The statement,

$$\textbf{futr } y = 9$$

evaluates to true if the condition that y = 9 evaluates to true in some future state of the program. (The computational interpretation of this is given below).

Temporal conditions may be joined by boolean connectives and iteratively serve as arguments to temporal operators. Thus,

$$\textbf{past}((\textbf{futr } x > 9) \textbf{ and } y = 3)$$

is a legal Tahiti condition, meaning 'at some previous state of the computation it was the case that y = 3 and at some later state of the computation (relative to that previous state) it was to be the case (or will be the case) that $x > 9$'.

In addition to referring indefinitely to any past or future state of the computation Tahiti also permits the specification of conditions relative to real-times, as described in [10], for which there is ample precedent in languages designed for real-time environments [7]. Syntactically, this is achieved by inserting a number embraced in square brackets between the temporal operator and the boolean condition it qualifies. Thus, the expression

$$\textbf{forv } [5] \, (x > 9)$$

evaluates to true if $x > 9$ evaluates to true for the next 5 seconds. Similarly,

$$\textbf{futr } [5] \, (y = 7 \textbf{ or } 8 < z)$$

evaluates to true if ($y = 7$ or $8 < z$) evaluates to true some time in the next 5 seconds. Bracketed expressions which evaluate to zero are taken to refer to the current state, i.e., an unqualified boolean condition.

Syntactic Events

Syntactic events are defined in terms of source code statements. Event subtypes are declared syntactically by proceeding a sequence of statements embraced in curly brackets ({ }) with an identifier. For example, the following defines a subtype **E**:

$$\textbf{E}: \quad \{ \ x := 47 \ \}$$

With this annotation **E** now defines an event subtype whose occurrences are executions of the defined block of code. Event subtypes are also available for the evaluation of Boolean expressions, an example of which appears below. A limited pattern matching facility is also available, enabling one to define such event types as 'any update of the variable **x**'. Such syntactically defined events are allowed only in connection with sequences of statements in code blocks. The subtype name must have been declared in the same scope as the code on which it is defined.

Definite Descriptions

With the exception of the distinguised event **noth** there can be no literal values of the type event in the usual sense. Tahiti therefore provides a mechanism for constructing definite descriptions of events for purposes of access and assignment. Such descriptions make use of a system of occurrence and subtype attributes, some of which are given in Table 2.

Definite descriptions are expressions which pick out an occurrence by appeal to one or more defining attributes. For example, the assignment,

$$e := (\ (\text{the } x)(\ x = \text{recent of E and pos of } x \text{ in F} = 5)\ )$$

binds the event object **e** to the occurrence which is the most recent of the subtype E and also the fifth occurence of the subtype F. If a definite description does not denote an event that has occurred or if the description does not pick out a

Attribute	Meaning
begin of e	the real-time at which the occurrence e started
end of e	the real-time at which the occurrence e terminated
position of e in E	the position of the occurrence e in ordinal sequence of all occurrences of subtype E
num of E	the number of occurrences of subtype E
n th of E	the nth occurrence of the subtype E.
next of e in E	the next occurrence of subtype E after the occurrence e
previous of e in E	the previous occurrence of subtype E before the occurrence e
recent of E	the most recent occurrence of the subtype E

Table 2: Event and Subtype Attributes

unique occurrence, then the object **e** is bound to the null event, **noth**.

Event Operators

Tahiti provides the two event operators, **perf** and **pros** directly implied by Event Logic. These operators take as arguments event descriptions or event variables and transform them into boolean statements to the effect that an event has or has not occurred at the moment the boolean expression in which they are contained is evaluated. The syntax of such expressions is exemplified by this command:

```
if
    perf ( (the z)
        ( z = recent of E1)
            and
        (z = 2 nth of E2))
then
    y := 1;
end if;
```

which executes the statement **y** := 1 if the most recent occurrence of the subtype **E1** is also the second occurrence of the subtype **E2** and it has occurred in the past.

Event Binding

Since occurrence values are by nature dynamic, an event variable cannot be bound to any value other than **noth** until an event—of the appropriate subtype—takes place. This is accommodated by the declaration of **whenever** clauses. A **whenever** clause is the specification of a daemon which is activated on the occurrence of a defined event, specified by a definite description. For example, the following declaration binds the variable **e** to the occurrence of the event consisting of **x** becoming greater than 3 while **y** = 4:

```
whenever bcom x = 3   process
begin
    print ( x );
end;
```

Figure 1: A *Process* Whenever Declaration

```
whenever bcom x = 3 do
begin
    print ( x );
end;
```

Figure 2: A *Do* Whenever Declaration

```
whenever bcom x > 3 and y = 4 assign e;
```

Whenever daemons may trigger actions other than binding to event variables. They may also initiate the execution of a block of code. Such daemons are of two kinds. *Process* (see Figure 1) daemons execute their associated

block of code in dynamically spawned processes which execute in parallel with the process in which they are declared. *Do* daemons (see Figure 2) by contrast assume control of the process in which they are declared.

Event Scoping

In accordance with the CSP philosophy, all data is by default local to the process in which it is declared. Absent some modification of this restriction, it would be impossible for an event in one process to causally affect the behavior of another process, except through message passing. Since the purpose of Tahiti is to explore event programming, it is necessary to provide a construct which permits a process to enable selective visibility of its own execution events. This is done through a *revelation clause*, modeled on previous constructs for access control mechanisms [2], exemplified thus,

reveal E1 to p1, p2

reveal bcom (x > 2) to p3

This pair of declarations gives processes **p1** and **p2** visibility into occurrences of the named subtype E1 and gives process **p3** visibility into the annonymous subtype consisting of any instance of **x** becoming greater than 2. Visibility enables another process both to query such occurrences and to bind its own event variables to them.

Examples

The introduction to this presentation drew attention to sundry areas in which a facility for event representation and management might have application. This section sketches the natural way to use Tahiti's constructs to address these problems.

Consider the case of a process whose purpose is to divide two real values. The process iteratively receives two values **num** and **denom** *via* messages and sends as a message **num** divided by **denom**. On the exceptional condition that the denominator received by the process is 0, it is to transmit some conventionally large value **val**, rather than the result of the divide operation. A natural encoding of this in Tahiti (which avoids cluttering the main block with a test for the exceptional condition) is given in Figure 3

Flags of the sort characteristic of real-time systems are easily handled through a combination of syntactic and semantic events. Simple flags are constructed by embracing executable code within braces proceeded by an event type name, but the facility is much richer than a simple example can show. It is possible, for example, to query as to whether a certain query has been made. For a process **p1** can embrace the code in which it queries for an event type **E** located in process **p2** within brackets labeled by an event object, thereby creating a new syntactic type. An example is given in Figure 4.

Branching on future or past states or events, is achieved simply by using either a boolean expression qualified by a temporal operator or an event radical qualified by the operator **perf** or **pros**. An example is given in figure 5. In it the assignment **y := 1** is excuted if the boolean **x = 5** evaluates to true sometime in the next five seconds.

The ability to branch on both past and future events (and *a fortiori* past and future states) requires special run-time maneuvering, described in detail elsewhere. The principal devices are as follows. Branching on past events is achieved by selective historical management of event records

```
process divide  =

    num, result, denom : integer;

    substype zerodivide =  bcom ( denom = 0 );

    whenever occr zerodivide do
    begin
        send ( distinguished_value, p );
    end;


begin

loop

    receive ( num, p );

    receive ( denom, p );

    result := num / denom ;

    send ( result, p );

end loop;
```

Figure 3: Exception Handling *via* **Whenever** Clauses

by the Tahiti run-time system. Tahiti's type system and certain normal-form restrictions not described here enable an efficient implementation of this part of the Tahiti system. Though the future and the past are naturally quite symmetrical, the implementation of future conditional computations is quite different from that of past ones. Future conditional events are implemented through a 'branching time' approach to program states. Whenever a future conditional branch is encountered in the course of a computation, a rival process containing the conditionally guarded code, operating on a copy of the current state, is spawned. Both it and its 'double' process execute concurrently until the conditional event occurs or the end of the program is encountered. If the conditional event occurs, the results of the other process are discarded, and the spawned one assumes its role in the computation. Tahiti assumes a rule of 'negation as falure' [6] if the conditional event or state does not occur before the termintation of the program, it is assumed that the future conditional is false.

Status and Future Directions

Tahiti is currently being implemented on a 32 node Intel IPSC/1 machine. Owing to the experimental nature of the language, the compiler now produces IPCS C code which is in turn submitted to the IPCS compiler. Tahiti requires rather elaborate and novel run-time support which is being

```
process p1 =
    reveal E to p2;
        .
        .
        .
    if E: { perf e1 } then
        .
        .
        .
end p1


process p2 =

    whenever p1.E do
        .
        .
        .
    end

begin
        .
        .
        .
end
```

Figure 4: Event Evaluation as an Event

```
if  futr [5] ( x = 5 ) then
    y   := 1
end if
```

Figure 5: Code Branching on a Future Condition

developed as a separate effort.

Following the completion of the current implementation, a number of design modification are clearly anticipated. First, we anticipate elaborations of the basic event language to include 'metalinguistic' and 'supralinguistic' events, events which cannot be specified either semantically or syntactically, as advocated in [20]. These will include both higher level events such as process initiation and termination as well as lower-level references to primitive execution events below the normal level of language semantics, such as transient failures in message passing.

Second, given the logical relations between states and events, orthogonality demands that states be given the same status as computational events along the lines suggested in [17].

Third, we anticipate a diminshed role, or even an elimination, of message passing as a means of synchronized communication between processes. Computational events and messages have clearly overlaping functionality. Message passing performs the dual function of both communication and synchronization. Waiting on events is a form of synchro-nization that allows a programmer to represent processing in the language of the application rather than the language of low-level synchronization primitives. Interestingly, certain classical problems such as the dining philosophers have no natural formulation in Tahiti because the problem they solve is purely one of synchronization, detached from any application. From the point of view of Tahiti, message passing seems a rather primitive communication mechanism. In Tahiti, message passing serves only to communcate data values between separate threads of control. The next major effort in the language will be to seek a construct that serves this purpose which better converges with the semantics of events.

References

[1] Ada^{TM} Reference Manual, ANSI/MIL-STD 1815A.

[2] Paolo Ancilotti, Maurelio Boari and Norma Lijtmaer, 'Language Features for Access Control', IEEE Transactions on Software Engineering, 9, (1), (1983), 16-24.

[3] D.M. Berry, 'Language Design Methods Based on Semantic Principles, Acta Informatica, 15 (1), (1981), 83-98.

[4] Gérard Berry, Sabine Moisan, and Jean-Paul Rigault, "ESTEREL: Towards a synchronous and semantically sound high level language for Real Time applications," Proceedings of the IEEE Symposium on Real-Time Systems, 1983, 30-37.

[5] Yves Caseau, A Model for A Reflective Object Oriented Language, SIGPLAN Notices, 24, 4, April, 1989, 22-24.

[6] K.L. Clark, 'Negation as Failure,' in Gallaire and Minker (eds) Logic and Databases, Plenum Publishing Co. (1978).

[7] B. Dasarathy, 'Timing Constraints of Real-Time Systems: Constructs for Expressing Them, Methods of Validating Them,' IEEE Transactions on Software Engineering, 11 (1), (1985), 80-86.

[8] Antony Galton, The Logic of Aspect: An Axiomatic Approach, Oxford U. Press, 1984.

[9] Antony Galton, 'The Logic of Occurrence' in Galton (ed.) Temporal Logics and Their Applications, Academic Press, 1987.

[10] James Hearne and Geoffrey Matthews, 'A Quantitative Logic of Time,' Technical Report #89-19, Computer Science Department, Western Washington University.

[11] C.A.R. Hoare, 'Communicating Sequential Processes,' *Comm. ACM*, 21 (8)) 666-677 (1978).

[12] Nancy G. Leveson, 'Software Safety: What, Why, and How,' *ACM Computing Surveys*, 18 (2), 1986, 125-164.

[13] *occam*^{TM} *Programming Manual*, Printice-Hall International, (1984)

[14] Amir Pnueli, 'The Temporal Semantics of Concurrent Programs', *Theoretical Computer Science*, 13 (1981), 45-60.

[15] Nicholas Rescher and Alasdair Urquart, *Temporal Logic*, Springer-Verlag (1971).

[16] R.D. Tennent, *Principles of Programming Languages*, Printice Hall, (1980).

[17] R.E. Strom and S. Yemini, 'Type State—A Programming Language Concept for Enhancing Software Reliability', *IEEE Transactions on Software Engineering*, 12 (1) (1986), 151-171.

[18] Terwiliger, R.B. and R.H. Cambell [1988]. PLEASE: Executable Specifications for Incremental Software Development, *Journal of Systems and Software* (to appear)

[19] T. Watanabe and A. Yonezawa, Reflection in an Object-Oriented Concurrent Language, *Proceedings of the ACM Conference on Object-Oriented Programmings, Systems, Languages and Applications*, San Diego, 1988, 306-315.

[20] D.O. Williams, 'Language Requirements for Embedded Systems,' *Computer Standards and Interfaces*, 6 (1), (1987), 51-60.

[21] A. Yonezawa (ed) *ABCL: An Object-Oriented Concurrent System: Theory, Language, Programming, Implementation and Application*, MIT Press, 1989.

[22] S.J. Young, *Real Time Languages*, Elis Horwood, 1982.

Coordination Languages for Open System Design

Paolo Ciancarini
Dipartimento di Informatica
Università di Pisa

ABSTRACT

The concept of "coordination language" has been recently introduced by Carriero and Gelernter to designate a class of programming languages suitable for describing the behavior of "open" systems composed of a dynamic collection of asynchronous, parallel, and communicating agents.

In this paper three coordination languages, Linda, Flat Concurrent Prolog, and DeltaProlog, are discussed with respect to their features for open system design. It is interesting to compare the Linda "coordination model" with the model of logic languages, because both involve forms of communication based on pattern matching .

Although they seem to be equivalent with respect to their expressive power, current implementations of Flat Concurrent Prolog and DeltaProlog miss the efficiency of Linda, for reasons that are discussed in this paper. We have introduced Shared Prolog, a new parallel logic language that is closer to the Linda coordination model.

1. INTRODUCTION

What is an *open system*? We suggest the following definition:

> An open system is a dynamic set of agents both cooperating and conflicting for the use of a dynamic set of services and resources. The agents, the services and the resources are heterogeneous; they operate both in parallel and in concurrency; they communicate; they have some goals (what they would like to do), some duties (what they should do), some rights (what they may do), and some constraints (what they must not do).

Among complex software systems, the class of open systems is one of the most elusive, difficult, and expensive to design, build, and improve. From the point of view of a designer, there is a whole set of questions to which it is difficult to answer: which is the best language to *design* and maybe *implement* an open system? which should be the respective roles and the relations ruling the interaction among the design language, the programming environment, and the underlying *operating system*?

A key sample of open system is *a multiuser software design environment* [6]. This is a system in which a number of agents (programmers and tools) share a number of services that are databases, and compete for resources (CPU time, mass storage space, shared data); the activities of the agents modify the environment itself (compare the concept of *extended database applications* [2]). It is a very expensive and difficult task to build and to consistently modify such systems.

In this paper we are concerned with the problem of defining a programming language to design and possibly efficiently implement open systems. Since real open systems can be very difficult to specify and design, we introduce some toy problems that embed important features. Then we use one of these problems to test and compare three parallel programming languages that incorporate concepts and features useful for open system design: the languages are Linda [12], Flat Concurrent Prolog (FCP) [22], and DeltaProlog (ΔP) [9].

Recently, Linda and FCP were compared in a number of papers with respect to their ability of supporting open system design [4, 5, 23, 24, 16]. In this paper we take into account also the language ΔP since this logic language covers some important aspects that are not covered by FCP. In this way we are able to present an in-deep comparison of the Linda paradigm with respect to the logic programming paradigm.

Although the three languages seem to be comparably equivalent with respect to their expressive power, current implementations of both Flat Concurrent Prolog and DeltaProlog miss the efficiency of Linda, for reasons that are different for the two languages (they are discussed in this paper). We have introduced Shared Prolog, a new logic language that is closer to the Linda coordination model (and hopefully to its efficiency), while it maintains a strong logic flavour [7]. In this paper we show that Shared Prolog can be seen as the logic programming counterpart of Linda.

The paper has the following structure: Section 2 summarizes some key concepts for open system programming languages; Section 3 presents and compares three parallel languages that use some form of pattern matching for communication: they are Linda, Flat Concurrent Prolog, and DeltaProlog. Section 4 introduces Shared Prolog, a parallel logic language based on the Linda model. Section 5 shows how SP has been used in the design of a multiuser software engineering environment.

Section 6 is devoted to draw some final considerations and remarks.

2. OPEN SYSTEM PROGRAMMING

In [16] a number of requirements that should be met by a language for open system programming are enumerated. This paper is an answer to a paper by Carriero and Gelernter [4], that was itself an answer to a paper by Ringwood [21]. Another paper participating to the debate is by Shapiro [24]. The main topic of their debate is language expressiveness for parallel programming and open system design.

The requirements identified in [16] are the following:

Be able to securely encapsulate entities with state;

Be able to dynamically create and connect services;

Be able to not rely on global features;

Be able to define servers that are immune from the misbehavior of others;

Be able to serialize simultaneous events;

Be able to survive hardware failure.

It is interesting to see that the discussion in all the papers is not centred around common programming examples (after all, both the terms "coordination programming" and "open system design language" are brand new!), with a single precise exception: the Dining Philosophers problem. This is because everybody in the computer science community knows the specification of the problem of the Dining Philosophers, introduced long time ago by E.Dijkstra.

However, we feel that the Dining Philosophers (DP) problem does not belong to the most general class of open system programming problems. The DP problem contains no requirements for dynamic creation and connection of new agents or services. Interprocess communications are limited to interaction with the forks. The required scheduling of processes is naive, and no specification of the underlying architecture (and of the related resource allocation problems) is given.

To save the elegance of the Dining Philosophers problem, we can give a number of alternative formulations, each one taking into account at least one of the problems listed above. For instance, one of the reformulations sounds as follows:

The problem of the Restaurant for Dining Philosophers:

A restaurant has one big table with N forks and N seats. Customers are M>N philosophers that can seat if one seat is free. After sitting, a philosopher eats if (s)he can grab two forks, otherwise (s)he thinks. Sometime after sitting a philosopher pays the bill, stands up freeing the seat , and leaves the restaurant.

This problem does not sound very different from the original one (actually, an implicit requirement is that we want to save the work already done, reusing the program

written for the standard Dining Philosophers problem). Alas, it includes a concept of dynamics, since agents (philosophers) can connect to or disconnect from the system, and this makes a lot of difference. The chosen language should support dynamic compositionality of processes. For instance, this is a hard problem for the language CSP, since it lacks of the notion of dynamic creation of processes.

A good source for open system programming problems are games. Practice of games offers a lot of interesting situations that can be used as test for the expressiveness of parallel programming languages. For instance, the problem of safe chess queens is well known [25]. Other interesting problems are the following:

The problem of the distributed network of Poker Players

Build an electronic poker "table", i.e. a computer network to which Poker players can connect and play with maximum trust in the system. The table must shuffle and distribute cards, and obviously collect bets.

The problem of parallel Mastermind

A dynamic set of decoders cooperate in trying to guess a code that is known to a coder. The guesses are stored in a database that is shared by all the decoders. The coder orderly answers to the guesses.

The problem of the Computer Chess Tournament Director

Chess Tournaments Directors seldom use a round robin strategy of coupling players. Normally the couplings are dynamically determined after each round by some standard algorithm (best plays with best). Suppose the algorithm is given (i.e. you can use a program with some definite input - current rating -, and output - a list of pairings). A Computer Chess Tournament Director needs to specify after each round the pairing of N chess machines connected by an electronic network, so that the machines can play without having as interfaces human representatives.

In the paper [18], that introduces an object oriented variant of Linda, the main application proposed for the language is the Japanese game "Janken". Parallel Mastermind has been explored in [8] for a number of parallel logic languages.

The problems described in this section can be solved using a single conventional programming language (e.g. C) extended with low level parallel and communication primitives (e.g. sockets) supported by a conventional operating environment (e.g. Unix on a multiprocessor). However, we are interested in solutions written concisely and safely in some parallel language more high level than C, using communication mechanisms more high level than Remote Procedure Calls or Unix sockets.

Our thesis in this paper is that open system programming consists mainly of explicit scheduling and explicit allocation of resources, and that we should develop and explore languages that can express these concepts. Moreover, we need a new "discipline of programming" for such systems, that should be enforced both by some ad hoc programming language and the related programming environment.

3. COMMUNICATION MECHANISMS BASED ON PATTERN MATCHING

We are going to compare two well known parallel programming languages: Linda and Flat Concurrent Prolog. They are quite different, being the former a set of communication primitives that has been embedded both in imperative languages (e.g. C and Fortran) and in declarative ones (e.g. Lisp), while the latter is a parallel logic language. We take in consideration FCP as main representative of an important family of logic languages comprising also GHC and Parlog. FCP is claimed to be the most expressive of the family [23].

Although Linda and FCP are based on so different computing models, both of them include communication mechanisms based on some variant of pattern matching. FCP uses atomic unification; Linda uses typed pattern matching. A third language that we take into consideration is DeltaProlog, a parallel logic language that has a communication mechanism somewhat analogous to the Linda operations.

3.1. Linda

Linda is a linguistic framework based on an abstract shared memory (the Tuple Space) that is used as general model for specifying interprocess communication [12]. The linguistic framework is composed of four primitives that can be embedded virtually in every programming language:

in(Tuple): reads and consumes a tuple (synchronous).

read(Tuple): reads a tuple without consuming it (synchronous).

out(Tuple): produces a tuple (asynchronous).

eval(Tuple): starts a parallel thread of execution that outputs the Tuple.

These primitives are related to a communication media called the *Tuple Space*, i.e. a set of persistent messages that are produced by a set of parallel programs. The messages can be retrieved in an associative way by typed pattern matching, in terms of any combination of the values of their fields.

Tuples in Linda's TS can be matched against templates in programs. A program can specify within a template one or more *formals*, i.e. holes with a name that will be bound by pattern matching with the corresponding argument of a matching tuple. Typed pattern matching is ruled by the following rules:

1) a tuple and a template must have the same number of arguments;

2) corresponding arguments must have matching types;

3) corresponding data must be equal;

4) there must be no corresponding formals.

The following is the solution to the DP problem [4, 18] for the single philosopher sitting at table with N forks.

```
philo(i)
i: integer;
{
    while (hungry())
    {
        in("sem");
        in(f[i]);
        in(f[(i+1)%N]);
        out("sem");
        eats();
        out(f[i]);
        out(f[(i+1)%N]);
    }
}

waiter(table)
table: tuple_space;
{
    eval(tsc(table));
    table.out("sem");
    for (i=0; i<N; i++)
    {
        table.out(f[i]);
        table.eval(philo(i));
    }
}
```

We introduce a *waiter* procedure to start the philosophers: it is a very simple scheduler. A Linda solution to the RDP problem can capitalize on the above solution using a scheduling loop for M philosophers that eat at a table with N<M seats. All we need is to change the scheduler introducing the concept of free seat:

```
waiter(table)
table: tuple_space;
{
    eval(tsc(table));
    table.out("sem");
    for (k=0; k<N; k++)
    {table.out("free"); table.out(f[k]);};
    while (TRUE)
    {             % choose a philosopher
        j:= choice(M);
        in("free");
        table.eval({    philo(j);
                        out("free");
                   });
    }
}
```

We do need neither to know how it is implemented the philo agent, nor we are using any feature related to the global state of the system. A new philosopher process is connected to the "table" if there is a free place.

Linda's ability of expressing coordination in a very high level way rests on the pattern-matching based communication mechanisms. Tuples are anonymous, and their efficient compilation in a shared address space is the key of Linda power [4].

3.2. Flat Concurrent Prolog (FCP)

In FCP, processes communicate via shared data structures (streams), established when a process creates a new system of processes. FCP models synchronization among processes by imposing some constraints on the unification mechanism [22]. The form of parallelism exploited is an eager evaluation of shared streams.

```
% FCP program for a philosopher [24]
phil(Id,
     [eating(LeftId,done) | Left],
     Right):-
          phil(Id,Left,Right).
phil(Id,
     Left,
     [eating(RightId,done) | Right]):-
          phil(Id,Left,Right).
phil(Id,
     [eating(LId,done)|Left]!,
     [eating(RId,done)|Right]!):-
          phil(Id,Left,Right).
% starting goal
phil(1,F1,F2),phil(2,F2,F3),…,phil(n,Fn,F1).
```

This FCP program relies deeply on atomic unification of logic variables. Two processes (philosophers) sharing a variable (representing a fork) could bind it simultaneously with different messages (provoking a system failure), if atomic unification was not enforced by the FCP language semantics.

If we intend to use the above FCP program for solving the RDP problem, there are at least two solutions. The first one consists of defining a server that elaborates scheduling messages. The message `exits(I)` means that philosopher I is going to leave the table; the message `enters(I)` means that philosopher I is going to join to the table. The server actually is a metainterpreter: it includes in its internal state the original goal, and executes it using the metalevel predicate *eval* [22].

```
% a waiter for dining philosophers
waiter( [exits(I1)|C],
        [phil(I2,L,R)|OtherPs]):-
     I1=I2
     |
     L=R, waiter(C?, OtherPs).
waiter( [exits(I1)|C],
        [phil(I2,L,R)|OtherPs]):-
     I1≠I2
     |
     waiter(    [exits(I1)|C],
                [OtherPs|phil(I2,L,R)]).
waiter( enters(I1)|C],
        [phil(I2,L,M),phil(I3,M,R)|OP]):-
     unknown(M) |
     waiter(C?,[phil(I2,L,M1),
              phil(I1,M1,M2),
              phil(I3,M2,R)|OP])).
waiter(C,Ps):-
     unknown(C) | eval(Ps), waiter(C,Ps).
```

Reuse and modularity are enforced in FCP typically by metalevel programming, since a normal running goal is a sort of monad that is closed with respect its operating environment, apart from its input/output streams.

Suppose that a process has to be connected to an existing set of processes: it is important to have goals as first class objects, and not be compelled to use their representation. The object system can be stopped and restarted within the metalevel system. Metaprogramming is a specification technique rapid and elegant, but also inefficient, and moreover prone to semantic inconsistencies.

However, it is not necessary a metainterpreting server to solve the RDP program. In fact, in FCP it is possible to specify reconfigurating objects [8].

```
% a CP reconfigurating object
object( [connect(NewStream) | OldStream],
        Out):-
     merge(OldStream?, NewStream?, Stream),
     object(Stream?, Out).
object([X | Oldstream], [X | Out]):-
     object(Oldstream?, Out).
object([], []).
```

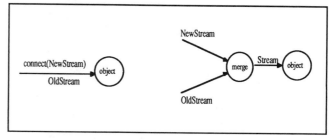

Figure 1 *Behavior of dynamic stream*

As shown in figure 1, when this `object` receives the message `connect(X)`, it reduces to a system composed by two processes, a `merge` which merges X with the old input stream and outputs a stream which is taken as input by an `object` process.

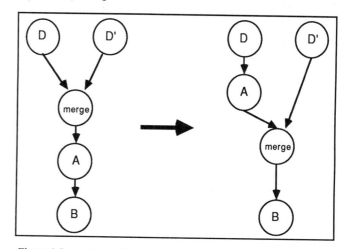

Figure 2 *Dynamic reconfiguration of a network*

Using the technique of reconfigurating objects, we can deeply reconfigure a network of processes, as shown in figure 2. There is an important limitation: two processes can dynamically be linked only if there is a third process that can link both. The design of a dynamic network of philosophers that share a table is so a little complicated. For reasons of space it is not shown in this paper.

3.3. DeltaProlog

DeltaProlog (ΔP) is based on a design choice completely different from the approach followed in FCP [9]. In fact, ΔP extends Prolog: by default, atoms in the body of a rule are sequentially evaluated.

The main difference with respect to a pure Prolog language is given by goals specialized in communication: they are called *event goals*. An event goal is a special Prolog predicate enabling the exchange of values by unification between two parallel processes.

A synchronous event goal of the form T!E should be matched with an event goal of the form T?E. T is the term to be transferred, E is a global name distinguishing this transaction from any other that may be taking place at the same time. Two processes communicating via some event E could have the following goals:

```
process 1                    process 2
..., T1!E, a, b,...           ..., T2?E, c, d, ...
```

They both succeed iff T1 and T2 unify, in which case event E succeeds; afterwards they continue their independent computations. If either unification fails, the corresponding process fails (and backtracks), while the other suspends. So if two complementary event goals are reached but the term unification failed or one of the conditions is not satisfied, the communication does not take place and distributed backtracking is initiated.

```
% Top goal
?- table // philo(0) // ... // philo(4).
```

This top goal specifies six parallel (//) processes: one server for the forks (table) and five philosophers.

```
% program for a philosopher
philo(i):-
    fork(i)!get,
    fork(i+1)!get,
    eat,
    fork(i)!put,
    fork(i+1)!put,
    philo(i).
```

Thanks to backtracking, the rule for philo is very simple. If one of the events fails, the related communication is backtracked: there is no need for a global semaphore. In a centralized solution forks are contained within a monitor.

```
% a monitor
table:-
    fork(I)?get, retract(fork(I)), table
    ::                    % backtrackable choice
    fork(I)?put, assert(fork(I)), table.
```

This solution is quite simple. However, if we try to adapt it to the RDP problem, we find some problems. We must rely on the interpreted evaluation of assert/retract, and on distributed backtracking. Note that backtrackable predicates should include also assert/retract (currently that is not true for standard Prolog implementations). Another drawback is the impossibility of adding new processes to a running goal.

3.4. Discussion

There are many points of contact between Linda and the pair FCP/ΔP. The most striking is the use of some form of communication based on pattern matching.

Linda: typed pattern matching of anonymous tuples.

FCP: atomic unification of named streams.

DeltaProlog: distributed backtracking of named events.

The key of the Linda success seems to be the possibility of efficiently implementing in a distributed environment the tuple space. Analogously, in the parallel logic programming framework the main practical issue with unification and backtracking is if these operations can be efficiently implemented in a distributed environment: currently the answer is negative [24]. In fact, atomic unification is a form of mutual exclusion operation embedded in FCP. The FCP goal

```
?- a(X), b(X)
```

starts two processes sharing a variable X. If a logic language enforces atomic unification, it is impossible that both a and b simultaneously bind X, whichever are the clauses implementing a and b. To implement this feature on a distributed architecture is very expensive.

ΔP is the only concurrent logic language offering "backtrackable invocation" (don't know non determinism) [19]. Of course, the main implementation problem in ΔP is *distributed* backtracking when events goal are to be backtracked. When a process tries to backtrack an event goal, it must inform its partner process so that it too backtracks to the same event. This is necessary to guarantee a complete search in the solution space of the problem. The problem is that the second process, backtracking to the failing event, must backtrack also events activated with the participation of other partners.

FCP goal variables and ΔP events have unique names: these features are important when designing protection rules for open systems. It has been noted that Linda presents many problems in specifying protection rules and capabilities of different agents and services, since the Tuple Space is a global feature, and tuples are anonymous (i.e. every agent can in principle access every tuple). This problem was approached in Linda 3 [13] and in OO-Linda [18]. Linda 3 supports a primitive for structuring the Tuple Space into disjoint multiple hierarchically ordered Tuple Spaces:

tsc(): defines a new tuple space (normally used in the

command `eval(tsc(TS))`.

This new feature, called Nested Tuple Spaces, fills an expressiveness gap in Linda. Shapiro has noted that Nested Tuple Spaces compare closely with FCP shared logic variables (streams) [24].

In the attempt of putting together the strength of FCP (high level communication) and DeltaProlog (Prolog embedding), avoiding their weakness in efficiency, we have introduced Shared Prolog, a logic language that is closely related to the Linda model of communication.

4. SHARED PROLOG:
LOGIC + TUPLE SPACE COMMUNICATIONS

Shared Prolog (SP) is based on the *blackboard procedural interpretation* of logic programming, as opposed to the *process procedural interpretation* of logic programming, which is the basis of FCP [7].

The key idea of the blackboard interpretation consists of embedding Tuple Space communications into a logic framework. A set of logic agents is connected to a shared dynamic knowledge base (in a dynamic knowledge base clauses can be asserted and retracted: this solution is at the basis of Polka [10], a logic language built on the top of Parlog [21]).

An SP program is composed of a blackboard (a logic Tuple Space) and of a set of theories (the logic agents). Both the blackboard and the theories are specified by logic rules. A *blackboard* rule specifies in the head a blackboard name; the body is a (possibly empty) bracketed set of facts (logic tuples that can contain both variables and terms). A *theory* rule specifies in the head a theory name; the body is composed of a set of activation patterns and of a Prolog program.

A *pattern* may be partitioned into a Preactivation and a Postactivation (separated by a vertical bar). The Preactivation is in turn composed of a *Read* guard (a logic goal) and an *In* guard (a set of facts), while the Postactivation is composed of a *Body* (a logic goal) and an *Success* set (a set of facts); optionally can be used also a *Failure* set (a set of facts). This is the syntax for a pattern:

```
Read {In} | Body {Success} ; {Failure}
```

So a pattern consists of five components (the evaluation of the Preactivation has to be performed atomically):

- Read: some conditions to be verified on the blackboard before the theory can be activated; the conditions can be positive, negative, and built-in atomic goals;
- In: a set of facts to be consumed before the theory can be activated;
- Body: the initial goal of the logic program of the theory;
- Success: a set of facts that will be written on the blackboard if the body evaluation successes.

- Failure: a set of facts that will be written on the blackboard if the body evaluation fails.

A formal operational semantics for SP is found in [3].

Now we show the SP solution to the DP problem. In the initial blackboard there are five facts: the forks.

```
% Initial blackboard
board:-
{fork(0),fork(1),fork(2),fork(3),fork(4)}.
```

The computation of an SP program is started by an *initial goal*: in this case we specify a blackboard and a scheduler. They evaluate in parallel.

```
% Initial goal
board ||
philo(0) || philo(1) || philo(2) ||
philo(3) || philo(4)
```

The theory `philo(N)` is specified as follows:

```
% a philosopher
philo(N):-
    not fork(X) ; not fork(Y)
    |
    thinks {}.
◆
    {fork(X), fork(Y)}
    |
    eats {fork(X),fork(Y)}.
with      % knowledge base for this theory
eats:- …
thinks:- …
```

The RDP problem can be naively solved since an SP goal is *compositional*: the system allows to add (delete) at any time a theory to (from) a running goal. A different solution is obtained specifying a scheduler theory; the program looks like the Linda solution shown above.

4.1. Discussion

Compared to FCP, SP avoids radically all the semantic and inefficiency problems deriving from merging streams, allowing however the expression of many kinds of communication. For instance, the following theory implements a server able to communicate with a client that does not know the name of the server [12]. To start the communication, the client deposits in the blackboard a message `connect(client,Any)`. To end the communication the client deposits in the blackboard the atom `terminate(client)`. Initially, for each server i in the blackboard there is an atom `free(server_i)`.

```
% communication with an anonymous server
server:-
    {free(server), connect(U,server)}
    |
    {connected(U,server)}
◆
    connected(U,server)
    {data(U,Data)}
    |
    compute(Data,NewData)
```

```
   {answer(U,NewData)}

♦  not data(U,Data)
   {terminate(U), connected(U,server)}
   |
   {free(server)}
with
compute(Data,NewData):- ...
```

Although SP is inspired by Linda, there are some distinct features. First, tuples in Linda are anonymous, while in SP are logic facts (functor plus arguments) and are accessed via the main functor. Among other things, this allows the use of negative atoms in the Read guard of a pattern, obtaining an interesting bonus in language expressiveness, and moreover it opens the possibility of distribute the blackboard contents. Second, SP uses full logic unification, while Linda uses typed pattern matching. Finally, in Linda you can have read, in, and out spread all over the program, and this gives some semantic problems, while in SP the synchronizations are all symmetrically contained in the patterns (the Preactivation contains all the read/in, the Preactivation all the out). This is not just a nice symmetry, but an important semantic feature, since we found that the SP approach allows a number of compilation-time optimizations.

5. A PROGRAMMING ENVIRONMENT BASED ON SP

Shared Prolog has been used also to specify its own operating environment [6]. Actually, the initial goal of Shared Prolog was the specification of software engineering environments. In our perspective, a *software engineering environment* is specified (and implemented) by a concurrent program that supports the activities of many agents (programmers, tools) that sometimes cooperate and sometimes compete in an open world. A similar approach, in which a declarative programming style is shown to have advantages from a software engineering point of view, is explored in [11]

A prototype of an environment of this kind is SHELL, a Shell Hierarchical Environment based on a Logic Language [1]. SHELL consists of a hierarchy of asynchronous, communicating Prolog agents. They support both the active and the passive components of the environment. In fact, every database and every user are connected to a distinct process. There are shell processes, connected to users, and database processes (blackboards), that contain (shared) objects.

The main computing resources are a project database and a number of agents, i.e. services offered by the environment. The environment consists of a main database dbm, i.e. a blackboard containing the current version of the modules belonging to a software project and of a constellation of user shells which programmers can use to develop and test their own modules.

The environment main task is configuration control. A user can issue to its shell messages like reserve(Mod) and deposit(Mod) to lock or unlock in the database the public version of a module. A user shell inserts messages in the blackboard, where they are handled by a server called mdb_server.

```
% A main database and its server
dbm:- {}. % initial state is empty
mdb_server:-
   not reserved(Mod)
   {reserve(Mod)}
   |
   {reserved(Mod)}.

♦  {release(Mod), reserved(Mod)}
   |
   {}.

♦  {deposit(Mod),
    mod(Mod,Code),reserved(Mod)}
   |
   {mod(Mod,Code)}.

♦  not mod(Mod,_)
   {add_mod(mod(Mod,Code)}
   |
   {mod(Mod,Code)}.
```

It has been easy to enrich this environment with new services (e.g. editors, interpreters and compilers), invoked automatically when some preconditions are verified. For instance, suppose to have the following compilation rule [20], firing whenever a module is edited and saved back in the database.

```
Compile a module:
if not compiled(module)
   and
   for all components of module:
   analyzed(component c)
then compile module
```

Such a rule is directly translated in Shared Prolog. The blackboard contains the following facts: in(M,C) means that the module M contains the component C; analyzed(C) means that the component C has been analyzed by the compiler (and is suitable for linking); compiled(Mod) means that Mod has been compiled.

```
compilation:-
   not compiled(Mod)
   {setof(Comp,
          (in(Mod,Comp),analyzed(Comp)),
          L)}
   |
   do_compile(Mod,L,Result)
   {compiled(Mod,Result)}.
with
do_compile(Mod,L,Result):-...
```

The SP system predicate setof(C,G,L) computes the set L of the terms C satisfying the goal G. The predicate do_compile/2 invokes a standard tool, e.g. a C compiler.

6. CONCLUSIONS

There are three basic aspects that make very beneficial the use of logic programming technology for designing and building open systems.

At a first level, when designing an open system there is the need of shaping and handling both objects contained in shared databases and facts about these objects. First order logic is a powerful data modelling language, that can be used both for designing data and for querying the databases. Linda shares this power, since Tuple Spaces can be easily seen as a shared relational databases.

At a second level it is desirable to easily extend a system building more and more knowledge-based tools. In Prolog it is easy to build planners and "intelligent", knowledge based assistants for problem solving. Deduction and pattern matching mechanisms are embedded into the computational and data model, and there is a set of topics easily solved in a logic framework, as for instance the integration of new tools via meta-interpretation. Linda embeds pattern matching, but not deduction. SP overcomes this problem, and supports distributed AI applications [3].

Finally, there is a third level that is related to the communications mechanisms that should be mostly expressive, because an open system is naturally expressed as a collection of independent cooperating entities that sometimes compete for shared resources.

These are all strong points for a parallel logic language when used as an open system design language. On the negative side, we found that the metainterpretation technique is very commonly used in system programming with logic languages, but gives problems both with efficiency, because it slows execution by a factor of 10 for each level of interpretation, and with semantics [8].

Conversely, Linda maintains both a high level of efficiency being compilable and optimizable on distributed architecture, and a high level of expressiveness in specifying communication mechanisms powerful and intuitive.

Acknowledgements

Part of this paper was written during a visit at the Department of Computer Science of Yale University. A number of discussions with David Gelernter improved this paper.

This work was partially supported by Italian CNR-Progetto Finalizzato Informatica - Calcolo Parallelo.

REFERENCES

[1] V.Ambriola, P.Ciancarini, A.Corradini, M.Danelutto, "SHELL: a Shell Hierarchical Environment based on a Logic Language", TR30-89, Dip. di Informatica, Università di Pisa, 1989.

[2] R.Balzer, "Living in the Next Generation Operating System", *IFIP* 86, 1986, 283-291 (also in *IEEE Software*, 4, 1987).

[3] A.Brogi, P.Ciancarini, "The Concurrent Logic Language Shared Prolog", TR.8-89, Dip. di Informatica, Università di Pisa, 1989.

[4] N.Carriero, D.Gelernter, "Linda in Context", *Comm. ACM*, 32:4, 1989, 444-458.

[5] N.Carriero, D.Gelernter, "Coordination Languages and Their Significance", DCS TR.RR716, Yale University, 1989.

[6] P.Ciancarini, *Specifying and Prototyping Software Development Environments*, (in Italian) PhD Thesis, University of Pisa, 1988.

[7] P.Ciancarini, "Blackboard Programming in Shared Prolog", in D.Gelernter, A.Nicolau, D.Padua, (eds.), Procs. 2nd Workshop on Parallel Languages and Compilers, Research Monograph in Parallel and Distributed Computing, Pitman, 1990.

[8] P.Ciancarini, "System Programming with Logic Languages", TR.31-89, Dipartimento di Informatica, University of Pisa, 1989.

[9] J.Cunha, M.Ferreira, L.M.Pereira, "Programming in DeltaProlog", Proc. 6th Int. Conf. on Logic Programming, MIT Press, 1989, 487-504.

[10] A.Davison, "Blackboard Systems in Polka", *Int. Journal of Parallel Programming*, 16:5, 1987, 401-424.

[11] I.Foster, "Implementation of a Declarative State-Transition System", *Software Practice and Experience*, 19:4, 1989, 351-370.

[12] D.Gelernter, "Generative Communication in Linda", *ACM TOPLAS*, 7:1, 1985, 80-112.

[13] D.Gelernter, "Multiple Tuple Space in Linda", Proc. PARLE, 1989.

[14] B.Huberman (ed.), *The Ecology of Computation*, Elsevier North-Holland, 1988.

[15] K.Kahn, M.Miller, "Language Design and Open Systems", in [14].

[16] K.Kahn, M.Miller, "Comments on 'Linda in Context'", *Comm. ACM*, Technical Correspondence, 10, 1989, 1240-1258, May 1989.

[17] A.Kusalik, "Specification and Initialization of a Logic Computer System", *New Generation Computing*, 4, 1986, 189-209.

[18] A.Matsuoka, S.Kawai, "Using Tuple Space Communication in Distributed Object Oriented Languages", Proc. OOPSLA 88, in *Sigplan Notices*, 23:11, 1988, 276-284.

[19] L.Pereira, L.Monteiro, J.Cunha, J.Apareicio, M.Ferreira, "Delta-Prolog User's Manual", TR Logic Programming and AI Group, Universidade Nova de Lisboa, 1987, pp.20.

[20] P.Feiler, G.Kaiser, "Granularity Issues in a Knowledge-Based Programming Environment", *Information and Software Technology*, 29:10, 1987, 531-539.

[21] G.Ringwood, "Parlog86 and the Dining Logicians", *Comm. ACM*, 31:1, 1988, 10-25.

[22] E.Shapiro, *Concurrent Prolog: Collected Papers*, MIT Press, 1987.

[23] E.Shapiro, "The Family of Concurrent Logic Programming Languages", TR.CS89-08, The Weizmann Institute, 1989, pp. 107.

[24] E.Shapiro, "Embedding Linda and Other Joys of Concurrent Logic Programming", TR.CS89-07, The Weizmann Institute, also in *Comm. ACM*, Technical Correspondence, 10, 1989, 1240-1258.

[25] E.Tick, "Comparing two Parallel Logic Programming Architectures", *IEEE Software*, 6:4, 1989, 71-80.

A "TWO DEGREES OF FREEDOM"
APPROACH FOR PARALLEL PROGRAMMING

J.P.BAHSOUN, L. FERAUD, C.BETOURNE

Laboratoire IRIT   Université PAUL SABATIER
118 route de Narbonne 31062 Toulouse cedex FRANCE

Abstract

In this paper,we present the concept of a Priority Controlled Module PCM which is intended to implement shared objects in a parallelism environment. Next semantics of a PCM is given using a temporal logic. Then, we describe our experience adapting the inheritance mechanisms to the synchronization domain using the concept of a PCM. Because PCM mainly relies on the separation between data abstraction and synchronization, either of them can be thought as a "degree of freedom". Each "degree of freedom" appears as a reusable programming entity and can be implemented using the concept of a "class" occuring in the object oriented languages.

1.INTRODUCTION

Since the early 1970's, the concept of an "object" has been a common paradigm used in the design of many programming languages[20], [27], [29]. In the last decade, the concept of an object has acquired a great importance because of the wide spreading of object oriented languages[11], [30], [22], [1]. Many object oriented languages provide inheritance mechanisms that allow programmers to define new data types as extensions of previously existing types. By supporting incremental modifications, inheritance mechanisms are generally thought to enhance modularity. In this paper, we first describe the concept of a Priority Controlled Module [2], [4] devoted to implement objects shared by processes, secondly we describe our experience adapting the inheritance mechanisms to the synchronization domain using the concept of a PCM.

Parallel programming can be obtained by using different approaches. Our approach was first based on modularity which has been proved to make it easier to develop structured and robust software. As it was pointed out by Grass and Campbell[14], there are three major points in a modular approach of parallelism: resource modularity, concurrency encapsulation, synchronisation modularity.

The approach chosen in designing the concept of a PCM takes into account these requirements for modularity. Resource modularity is reached via data abstraction: PCM is an object of abstract data type involving exportable operations. Concurrency encapsulation is realized by allowing several operations of a PCM to run concurrently. Synchronisation modularity is achieved by the separation of the data abstraction which implements the resource and a local controller called the synchronizer scheduling the accesses. These features are the basis of the "two degrees of freedom" way to program parallelism. The first degree of freedom concerns the implementation of a resource as a representation on which the exportable operations act: it expresses "what is to be done"; the second degree of freedom is the local controller fitting synchronization specifications which implements "when it has to be done"[7]. A PCM is built up according to these two degrees of freedom.The major benefit

of the separation of action ("what") and synchronization ("when") is to allow the reusability of both of them. Thus action and synchronization can be defined as classes of an object oriented language and a particular PCM can be defined by the instantiations of an action class and a synchronization class.

This paper contains an outline of the concept of a PCM in the next section.Then semantics of PCM is given using a temporal logic formalism.In the last section, we discuss the interest of the inheritance mechanism to produce PCM according to either action or synchronization specifications.

2. AN OVERVIEW OF THE PCM

The design of the concept of a PCM was motivated by practical experiments in the field of concurrent programming. When implementing modular solutions to classical synchronization problems, the interest of separating actions and controls appeared clearly. Separating action from synchronization can be reached by implementing the actions as modules scheduled by independent synchronizers such as Hoare's monitors[17]. Though monitor is easy to use and widely applied as a synchronization mechanism in concurrent languages, it may be criticized for several reasons. A first one concerns the reliability of programs: the scheduling of modules by a monitor is not systematic, it greatly depends on the programmer's attention and often leads to a bracketed code without verification of the brackets used :e.g. in the readers and writers problem, the programmer can omit to call "start_read" (resp. "end_read") from the convenient monitor before (resp. after) the execution of read[17]. Secondly, because of mutual exclusion of the operations nested monitor calls may cause deadlocks.
The use of a "signal and continue " statement as it appears in MESA [23] does not avoid the previously described difficulties.

The approach chosen to design the synchronizer of a PCM is closer to path expressions[6] , critical path expressions [19] and Hewitt's serializers[16]: it avoids the above mentioned difficulties by enforcing initial and terminal brackets to operations and it allows the scheduled operations to run concurrently.

A PCM consists mainly of :
-remanent data i.e. data whose values are not lost after a procedure call, such as "static " variables in C or package variables in Ada.
-procedures called operations acting on local data
-a core, called synchronizer, which takes into account all the operations   execution controls.

The only components exportable from a PCM are the operations and their specifications. The operations are executed according to the constraints given by the synchronizer. Parallel execution is possible. The definition of the synchronization behavior rests on the main principle of linguistic distinction between controls related to the intrinsic status of the object and controls determined by an access schedule.For example consider a file accessed by readers and writers [9] according to a FIFO order : a writer may be either delayed because another writer or a reader is working on the file or because the request of the writer conflicts with FIFO order. In order to express access schedules, the concept of a global priority has been introduced : each request in the PCM is qualified by a priority, the set of delayed requests is thoroughly ordered according to the priority. Because of this priority notion, PCM appears as a convenient tool to build up solutions to synchronization problems with an access schedule free from the intrinsic status of the object.The previous variant of the readers and writers problem is implemented by the following PCM (figure 0) where the set of delayed processes is entirely ordered by the variable "rank".

```
RW :Module exports read, write
    ...file representation...
    read:procedure ...read algorithm...
    write:procedure ...write algorithm...
    synchronizer
    writing: boolean =false;   --true if a writer is active
    rc:integer =0;             -- active readers count
    rank:integer = 0;          --orders the requiring processes
    for read:  rank := rank + 1;
      setprio rank when writing  wait ;
       --delayed with priority rank  when a writer
      -- is active or when older processes are waiting
      rc:= rc+ 1;
          next       -- after completion of the operation read
      rc := rc -1
    for write:  rank := rank +1;
          setprio  rank when  writing or rc ≠0  wait;
                   --delayed with priority rank when
                   --the file is occupied or when
                   -- older processes are waiting
      writing := true;
          next       --after completion of the operation write
      writing := false
endsynchronizer
endmodule: RW
```

figure 0

2.1 The synchronizer

The PCM's synchronizer's general structure is as follows:
```
synchronizer
        remanent data; alternatives_list
endsynchronizer
```

The synchronizer is a critical section of the PCM. The remanent data are used in the code of the alternatives, the concept of an alternative is presented in the next subsection.

2.2 Prologue and epilogue

The synchronizer's role is to ensure that the conditions of execution of every operation are consistent with PCM access schedule and its intrinsic status. The synchronizer is composed of alternatives. An alternative, in term, consists of two sequences of

statements respectively called "prologue" and "epilogue". An alternative is bound with each operation. The prologue is executed before the activation of every operation, similarly the epilogue is executed upon completion of every operation. Prologue and epilogue encapsulate every operation execution. The syntax of an alternative is:

for   operation_ident : <prologue>   next <epilogue>

2.3 The wait statement

When a request of a process conflicts with either the PCM's intrinsic status or with its access schedule, the process releases the synchronizer and waits. It will regain possession of the synchronizer once these compatibilities are restored. Process delaying is realized by a specific statement the "wait statement" including:

- a condition expressing the intrinsic status (boolean expression)
- an integer expression representing an access scheduling priority
- a priority queue used to store waiting processes.

The syntax of the "wait statement" is :

setprio <prio> when <condition> wait

The effect of the wait statement is twofold:

- first the priority <prio> is given to the process executing the wait statement.
- second, if the current process priority is not maximum or if <condition> is true the current process is delayed in an internal queue with priority <prio>. When both these conditions are false the wait statement has no effect. The range of priorities is the non negative integers (0 is the highest). Each waiting process and the current process have a priority. Each priority can be modified by performing a wait statement. The set of processes delayed in the synchronizer is totally ordered by the priority. When performing a wait statement, the current process changes its priority to <prio> even if it is not delayed.

2.4 Implicit signaling

Resuming the synchronizer once the current process has been released is performed by an implicit signal mechanism. The synchronizer release occurs in the following cases:

- the current process is delayed in a wait statement
- end of a prologue: an operation may be performed
- end of an epilogue: exit of a PCM.

In all three cases, upon release the synchronizer is repossessed by an internal process whose waiting condition is false and whose priority is maximum. In absence of such an internal process, the synchronizer is given to an external process requesting it.

Examples:
1. A starvation free solution to the readers and writers problem

We will now consider another variant of the concurrent readers and writers problem previously mentioned. In this variant, the priority is given to readers over writers . However, to prevent a possible starvation of writers, we privilege a waiting writer when no readers are waiting. In this solution, a reader is delayed

```
RW:module exports read,write
        ..file representation..
read:procedure ...read algorithm .
write:procedure ..write algorithm .

Synchronizer
ppw =0;    --priority of a privileged writer
pr  =1;    --priority of reader
pw  =2;    --priority of a writer
writing: boolean=false;   --true if write is active
rc : integer= 0;              --active readers count

for read:     setprio pr when writing wait;
              rc:=rc+1;
              next
              rc:=rc-1

for write:    setprio pw  when writing wait;
              setprio ppw when rc≠0 wait;
              writing:=true;
              next
              writing:=false;
end synchronizer
end module: R W
```

figure 1

```
Disk:module exports transfer
        transfer: procedure ... transfer algorithm..
        synchronizer
        cylmax = 255;
        cyl   = 0..cylmax;
        up: boolean:=true;        -- initially the direction is up
        busy: boolean:= false;    -- true if transfer is active
        lb: integer:=0            -- lower bound of the current period
        ub: integer:= 2*cylmax;   -- upper bound
        ct: cyl :=0;                  --current track
        distance :  function (x: cyl) returns integer;
                -- computes the covered distance from the initial
                -- position to  track x
        begin
        if (x<ct) or (x=ct and not up) then  distance:= ub - x
        else distance := lb +x end if
        end;
        for transfer(c:cyl):  --prologue
            setprio distance(c) when busy wait;
            busy := true;
        --possible modifications of  direction and period bounds
            if (c>ct) or (c<ct and up) then
            if up then lb:=lb+2*cylmax else ub:=ub+2*cylmax
            end if;
            up:= not up;
            end if;
            ct:=c;             -- track setting
            next               -- epilogue
                busy:= false
        end synchronizer
        end module: Disk
```

figure 2

when a writer is active or when there is a delayed privileged writer.A writer is confronted with two consecutive wait statements: in the first one, a writer is delayed when another writer is using the file or if there are readers or a privileged writer waiting (these delayed processes have a stronger priority) ; when the synchronizer becomes free and neither readers nor privileged writer are delayed , the writer reaches the second wait statement and becomes privileged, no other process can access the file before it, thus the privileged writer has to wait for the condition "no running readers". The solution is depicted in figure1.

2 . Disk head scheduling

The disk head scheduling using the elevator method[17] is, basically, more a problem of expressing a specific access schedule than a synchronization problem related to the intrinsic status of the disk. In fact, the requested disk operations must be mutually exclusive. However, managing the unsatisfied requests requires the direction of move and the index of the requested track. The latter requirement will be solved using the priority concept of the PCM. The solution uses an array of alternatives. Each alternative is bound to a track and contains an implicit queue for delayed processes requesting this track. The priority value is the total distance scanned by the disk head from the beginning to the requested track. We suppose that the disk head before changing direction goes always to the extremal tracks. The waiting condition is the status of the disk: busy or free.

The disk head moves with period 2*cylmax, cylmax denoting the number of tracks of the disk. Each period is defined by (lb, ub). The lower bound is updated whenever there is a change of the direction of the disk head from up to down; the upper bound is increased whenever, similarly, a change occurs from down to up. These bounds facilitate the computation of the covered distance.

3. Temporal logic semantics of the PCM

3.1 The temporal logic

The temporal logic used is that described in [28]. It is a linear time logic involving the following operators $\Box$ is the necessity operator, $\Diamond$ the eventually operator, o the next operator, Until which is a binary operator. In the formula p Until q , p remains true while q is false, this operator is the weak one ,i.e. p Until q doesn't imply $\Diamond$q. The sequences considered are the interleaving of execution states. In order to deal with events occuring in a PCM, we have defined the operator precedes: "-->". This operator allows to describe accurately every step in the synchronizer, it is moreover necessary to treat access scheduling. "precedes" is defined as follows:

p -> q $\wedge$ ¬(¬p Until q). This relation is defined in [21].

3.2 The control points

The labels occuring in the program can, a priori, be any . However, because the semantics is mainly concerned with the synchronizer's behaviour when control transfers occur, we have defined standard labels called "control points". These labels are supposed to be sufficient to describe the synchronizer's control flow. We will use the following conventions: refering to control point "cp" involving the process i will be denoted cp_i. When the process is implicitly known, the shortened form cp will be used.

For the sake of clarity, we suppose that the wait statements of the synchronizer are ordered and identified by an index thus, **statwait$_k$** will denote the kth wait statement. In a wait statement **cond** and **prio** denote the related condition and priority.

The set of control points considered in this paper is the following:

entry_prolog	entry of a prologue
prolog	execution of a prologue
exit_prolog	leaving a prologue then leaving the synchronizer
entry_epilog	entry of an epilogue
epilog	execution of the epilogue
exit_epilog	leaving an epilogue then leaving the synchronizer
entry	entry_prolog or entry_epilog
body	prolog or epilog
exit	exit_prolog or exit_epilog
statwait$_k$	the kth wait statement
wait$_k$	the atomic statement which causes process delay in the kth wait statement

For a control point **cp**, the next assertions can be used: **at cp, in cp, after cp**. Their intuitive meaning, respectively, is control flow reaches, is in, is after the label **cp**. These immediate assertions are the same as those of the proof lattices of Owicki and Lamport [24]. Every control point **cp** has a single entry and a single exit, that property can be expressed by:

$$\text{at cp} \rightarrow \text{in cp, in cp} \rightarrow \text{in cp Until after cp}$$

3.3 The implementor's properties

In this subsection, we will describe the properties that the implementor has to guarantee to respect the PCM's synchronizer semantics. We will use the following definitions:

(d 0) $\quad A = \{ I \; / \; \text{In body}_I \wedge \neg \; I \in W \}$ is the set of active processes in the synchronizer.

(d 1) $\quad W = \{ I \; / \; \text{In wait}_{k,I} \}$, is the set of processes delayed in the kth wait statement. The process **i** is said internal process if and only if $I \in W \vee I \in A$.

(d 2) $\quad E = \{ I \; / \text{In entry}_I \}$ is the set of processes requiring the synchronizer, they are called "external processes".

(d 3) $\quad \text{MAXPRIO} = \text{Min}(p_I)_{I \in W} \; p_I$ denotes the priority of the delayed process **i**. MAXPRIO (the lowest integer value) is the highest priority of the internal processes. p_i is a private variable of the delayed process **i**.

We denote the condition which enforces processes to wait in a kth wait statement by:

(d 4) $\quad B_{k,I} = (p_I > = \text{MAXPRIO} \vee \text{cond}_k)$. A process **i** is delayed in a wait statement if the priority value of **i** is not maximal or the expression related to the intrinsic status is true.

(d 5) $\quad R = \{ \text{In wait}_{k,I} \wedge \neg \; B_{k,I} \}$ is the set of processes whose waiting condition is false.

3.3.1. Request progressing in the synchronizer

A PCM's operation **op** is called by the following

instruction: **call <PCM.name>.op**

Entry and exit of a synchronizer are atomic: for any processes **i,j**

(I 0)
$$(\neg I \in A \wedge \neg j \in A) \rightarrow$$
$$(\neg I \in A \wedge \neg j \in A) \text{ Until } ((\neg I \in A \wedge j \in A) \vee (I \in A \wedge \neg j \in A))$$

When a process **i** called an operation **op** of a PCM the following assertions hold:

(I 1)
$$\text{at call <PCM.name>.op}_I = \text{at entry\_prolog}_I$$
$$\text{at exit\_epilog}_I = \text{after call <PCM.name>.op}_I$$

Inside the synchronizer, the only way for the request to progress is depicted by the next precedence assertions:

$$\text{In entry\_prolog}_I \; \text{-->} \; \text{In prolog}_I \; \text{-->}$$
$$\text{In exit\_prolog}_I \; \text{-->} \; \text{In op}_I \; \text{-->}$$
$$\text{In entry\_epilog}_I \; \text{-->} \; \text{In epilog}_I \; \text{-->}$$
$$\text{In exit\_epilog}_I$$

A process **i** active in the synchronizer, remains active until it reaches a delay statement or an exit:

(I 2)
$$I \in A \rightarrow I \in A \text{ Until } (\text{ at wait}_I \vee \text{ at exit}_I)$$

The synchronizer remains free until a process crosses the entry or a wait statement:

(I 3)
$$A = \emptyset \rightarrow A = \emptyset \text{ Until (after entry}_I \vee \text{ after wait}_I)$$

3.3.2 The synchronizer's components

Entry:

A process, member of E, will cross the entry when infinitely often both **A** and **R** are empty. This formula guarantees the fairness for processes' entry:

(I 4)
$$I \in E \wedge \Box \Diamond (R = \emptyset \wedge A = \emptyset) \rightarrow \Diamond \text{ after entry}_I$$

The priority of internal ready processes over external ones is stated as:

(I 5)
$$I \in E \rightarrow I \in E \text{ Until } (R = \emptyset \wedge A = \emptyset)$$

The only possibility for a process to gain possession of an idle synchronizer is the entry:

(I 6)
$$(R = \emptyset \wedge A = \emptyset) \rightarrow$$
$$(R = \emptyset \wedge A = \emptyset) \text{ Until after entry}_I$$

The Wait statement:
set <prio> when <cond> wait

This statement can be described by the algorithm:

$$\textbf{statwait}_k: \quad p_l := \textbf{prio};$$
$$\textbf{if } (p_l > \textbf{MAXPRIO} \vee \textbf{cond})$$
$$\textbf{then } \textbf{wait}_k(\neg B_{k,l})$$

$\textbf{wait}_k(\neg B_{k,l})$ is an elementary statement which forces the request to be delayed with priority p_l until B_l will be false.

When infinitely often the synchronizer is idle and a process is ready , this one will cross the wait statement :

$$(1\,7)$$
$$\Box \Diamond (\ \text{in statwait}_{k,l} \wedge l \in R \wedge A = \varnothing) \rightarrow$$
$$\Diamond \ \text{after wait}_{k,l}$$

The relations between "wait" and "statwait" are expressed by:

$$\text{in wait}_l \rightarrow \text{in statwait}_l$$
$$\text{after wait}_l \rightarrow \text{after statwait}_l$$

A delayed process cannot be yet active until its waiting condition B_l will be false and the synchronizer will be free

$$(1\,8)$$
$$\text{in wait}_l \rightarrow \text{in wait}_l \ \text{Until} \ \neg B_l$$

When a delayed process gains possession of synchronizer, its waiting condition must be false:

$$(1\,9)$$
$$\Box(\text{after wait}_{k,l} \rightarrow \neg B_{k,l})$$

The synchronizer's remanent data can only be altered when the body of synchronizer is executed. This fact can be stated as:

$$(1\,10)$$
$$p \rightarrow p \ \text{Until} \ A \neq \varnothing \quad \text{where p is any predicate involving synchronizer's variables.}$$

The priority of a delayed process remains constant as long as the process is blocked. If P_{io} denotes the priority in the wait statement, then:
$$(1\,11)$$
$$\text{in wait}_l \rightarrow ((p_l = p_{lo}) \ \text{Until} \ \neg \ l \in W)$$

Exit
The only property to be assumed is the exit crossing:
$$(1\,12)$$
$$\text{at exit}_l \rightarrow \Diamond \ \text{after exit}_l$$

3.3.3 General consequences

From the previously described implementor's properties, we deduced two main theorems[2] stating respectively that :
- the executions of the synchronizer are mutually exclusive.
- the possession of the synchronizer occurs according to the order induced by the global priority.

4. AN INHERITANCE MECHANISM FOR THE CONCEPT OF A PCM

4.1 FROM OBJECTS TO CLASSES

In the previous sections, we presented the concept of a PCM as the result of applying Grass and Campbell's principles to reach modularity. This approach of parallel programming strongly relies on the concept of an object. At this level of development of PCM, a natural puzzling occurs: what are the features currently lacking which could significantly improve object-based programming? Of course, a lot of answers are possible according to different viewpoints. From the software engineering viewpoint the road to obtain "object-based happiness" [22] is to be continued by taking into account the notion of software reusability. Reusability can be defined "as the ability of a software product to be reused, on the whole or in part, for new applications"[22]. The interest of reusability is based on the observation that many pieces of software are built according common patterns.Taking into account this commonality could avoid to reinvent solutions to previously encountered problems. Reusability can be approached through the separation between the abstract data type and the synchronizer defining a PCM: a particular abstract data type can be coupled with several synchronizers implementing different kinds of controls, symmetrically a given synchronizer may be used to control various abstract data types. This fact can be explained through the following examples:

* Reusability of an abstract data type:

In the well known problem of readers and writers accessing a shared file [9] the implementation of the file and of read and write operations (i.e. the actions) remains constant while different policies are possible: FIFO order, priority to readers avoiding writers starvation. (see figure 3)

* Reusability of a synchronizer:

-the mutual exclusion constraint appears in many concurrent programming problems.Programming a clock entails that the operations "read_clock" and "update" are mutually exclusive; using a buffer needs the same constraint. In both cases, controls related to the operations are the same even when the actions differ. (see figure4)

Implementing the structures obtained by splitting PCM's needs the introduction of new programming concepts which will be compounded according new rules. The concept of a "class", because of its flexibility and its reusability, appears as the convenient linguistic feature.

4.2 THE INHERITANCE MECHANISM

As it was previously stated, the above mentioned examples naturally lead to reconsider the concept of a PCM in the object oriented language framework. According to Meyer [22], the scale of "object-based happiness" has seven steps, PCM can be viewed as belonging to the fourth one : every non-simple type is a module and every high level module is a type.

```
RW :Module exports read, write
       ...file representation...
       read:procedure ...read algorithm...
       write:procedure ...write algorithm...
          :
    end module RW
```

```
synchronizer            --   FIFO order
     writing: boolean =false;  -- true if a writer is active
          rc:integer =0;        --  active readers count
          rank:integer = 0;     --  orders the requiring processes
for read:  rank := rank + 1;
          setprio rank when writing  wait ;
          rc:= rc+ 1;
          next
          rc := rc -1
for write: rank := rank +1;
          setprio rank when writing or rc ≠0 wait;
          next
          writing := false
end synchronizer
```

```
synchronizer -- priority to readers
ppw=0;   --priority of a privileged  writer
pr =1;      --priority of reader
pw =2;     --priority of a writer
writing: boolean=false;   --true if write is active
rc : integer= 0;           --active readers count

for read:  setprio pr when writing wait;
   rc:=rc+1;
   n e x t
   rc:=rc-1

for write: setprio pw   when writing wait;
   setprio ppw when rc≠0 wait;
   writing:=true;
   n e x t
   writing:=false;
end synchronizer
```

figure 3

```
buffer: Module  exports put,get
     x:message ; -- the type message will not be described
     put: procedure (m : in message)  x:= m endprocedure;
     get: procedure ( m :out message)  m:=x endprocedure;
end module
```

```
clock: Module exports read_clock, update
h: integer:= 0;
read_clock:procedure (hour: out integer) hour:=h endprocedure
update: procedure h:=h+1endprocedure
end module
```

```
synchronizer
     mutex:boolean:=false;
     for  op1,op2 : when mutex wait; -- the alternative for op1 and op
               mutex:= true      --   are identical
               next
               mutex := false
end synchronizer
```

figure 4

To reach the next step requires an inheritance mechanism for the concept of a PCM.

We will explain the inheritance mechanism by means of an example : a mail box shared by processes. For the sake of clarity we will use now the classical terminology for object oriented languages: a type will be denoted "class" and its exportable operations will be called "methods".

Basically, in a first step, we consider the action part of the mail box which can be implemented by using the following class which is a pattern to instantiate mail box objects :

```
class mail_box exports put,get
     x:message ; -- the type message will not be described
put: procedure ( m : in message) x:= m endprocedure;
get: procedure ( m : out message) m:=x endprocedure;
 end class
```

The methods of this class are obviously the operations put and get.

At this step, the actions put and get are synchronizationless.Let's suppose we want to build the class of mail boxes where the operations obey a producer consumer scheme. Obtaining this policy for two operations may be implemented according to the following class:

266

```
class prod_cons synchronizes  op1,op2
        empty:boolean:=true;
        for  op1 : when not empty wait;
                        empty:=false
                        next
                        skip
        for op2 : when empty wait;
                empty:= true
                next
                skip
    end  class
```

The class prod_cons_mb can now be defined by inheritance from both previous classes :

```
class prod_cons_mb
        exports put,get inherit mailbox via prod_cons
end  class
```

and some object "mb1" can be straightforwardly created using the implicit method "create" :

```
                mb1 : prod_cons_mb.create
```

The key word **inherit** introduces the ancestor classes, a single one in the above example; the key word **via** stands for the class used to implement synchronization : "mailbox **via** prod_cons" means that the two methods of the class "prod_cons_mb " are bracketed as depicted in the class "prod_cons". The clause **via** specifies an inheritance from class possessing the attribute **synchronizes**.

This use of classes appears as a powerful mean to enhance the " two degrees of freedom" way to program parallelism.The conceptual independence between object representation and synchronization are logically described allowing the programmer to cook easily PCM 's reusing previously existing actions and synchronization pieces of code.
    In the above example, the list of methods of the class "mail_box" exactly matches the list of synchronized operations of "prod_cons" .Of course, reproducing this situation enforces constraints and induces a loss of generality in the inheritance mechanism.We will consider that point in the next subsection.

4.3 MORE ABOUT THE INHERITANCE MECHANISM

From the class "prod_cons_mb" we would like to build new classes either by adding new methods or by imposing others brackets encapsulating the methods. Suppose we first want to display the count of waiting requests for "put" or "get" whenever one of these operations is completed. Obtaining this behaviour can be reached , for example, by prefixing "put" and "get" by a counter incrementation and postfixing them by a decrementation and the display of this counter. The operations on the counter can be viewed as new brackets surrounding the methods. This new bracketing mechanism is strongly independent from the operations it envelops then it can be encapsulated in the following class:

```
class count2 synchronizes op1,op2
    count: integer:=O;
    for op1,op2 :  count:= count+1;
                    next
                count:= count -1;
                display ( count)
end  class
```

(This class has the attribute **synchronizes** although it does not schedule any operation, in this particular case "brackets" would be more accurate.)
    The desired class is then defined as follows:

```
class count_prod_cons_mb
        exports put,get
        inherit mail_box via prod_cons via count2
end  class
```

(see figure 5)

or

```
class count_prod_cons_mb
        exports put,get
        inherit prod_cons_mb via count2
end  class
```

(see figure 6)

The clause "**via** prod_cons **via** count2" introduces two levels of brackets, prod_cons is the most internal from either of them; here the inheritance process is thoroughly explicit. The class count_prod_cons_mb can also be built using the second shortened form; "**inherit** prod_cons_mb **via** count2" specifies that the synchronizer of the class prod_cons_mb is bracketed by count2; in this construct, the inheritance mechanism for the synchronizer is implicit. Nesting bracketed operations was first introduced and implemented in the language LEST [5] devoted to program operating systems. In the current context, it is a workable way for implementing the different levels of control to be crossed when executing a method of a synchronized class. Notice that these levels are thought independently and consequently work independently : each level behaves as a synchronizer depicted in section 2 and is free from the other levels.

We suppose now that we want to control that at most one operation "put" or "get" is active. This behaviour can be easily obtained by nesting the previously described brackets in the reverse order: the internal brackets now are "count2", the external ones are "prod_cons". This mail box class may be implemented as follows:

```
class prod_cons_count_mb
        exports put, get
        inherit mail_box via count2 via prod_cons
end  class
```

Here, the counter "count" increases whenever an operation "put" or "get" becomes active and decreases until zero after its completion.
    We now assume that a mail box belonging to the class "count_prod_cons_mb" is qualified by an internal identification, for example its creation time. Displaying this identification may run concurrently with either "put" or "get" and is not counted as a new execution of an operation, such as "put" or "get", thus this mail box class can be implemented as follows :

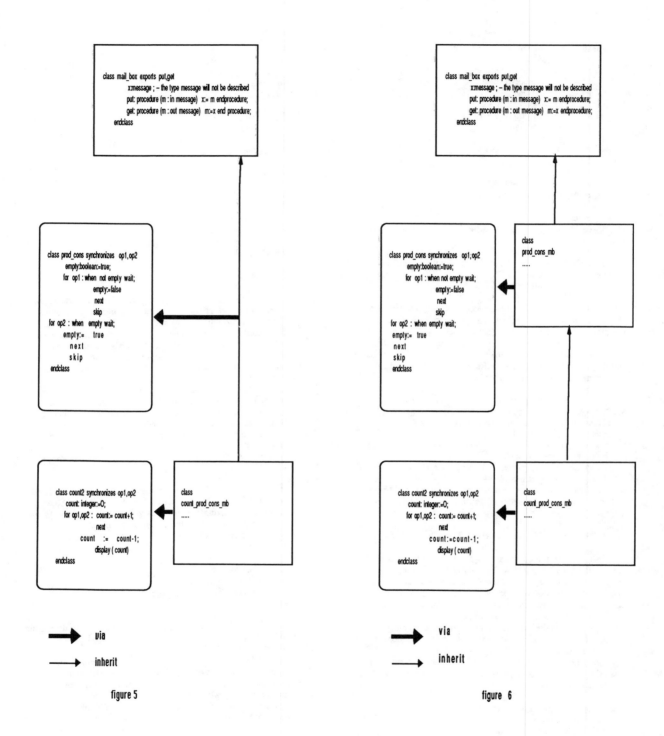

```
class ident_count_prod_cons_mb
      exports put,get,display_ident
      inherit mail_box via prod_cons via count2
identification : string :="$"/clock/"$"
function display_ident returns identification
end class
```

The class ident_count_mutex_mb has three methods, only two of them are really synchronized since they belong to a two level synchronized class; the same class could be obtained using the class "ident" containing the identification mechanism:

```
class ident exports display_ident
identification : string :="$"/clock/"$"
function display_ident returns identification
end class
```

a new definition for "ident_count_mutex_mb" then is possible:

```
class ident_count_mutex_mb
      exports put,get,display_ident
      inherit ident, mail_box via mutex2 via count2
end class
```

5 CONCLUSION

The concept of a PCM seems to be a workable tool to program solutions of synchronization problems, especially when a scheduling policy is involved. In this field, it appears as more flexible than mediators[14]. The concept of a PCM's synchronizer contains the features necessary to express path expressions.While path expressions straightforward define all legal sequences of operations for a resource, synchronizers allow first to split the access to an operation into several steps by means of wait statements, second to introduce any algorithm between two consecutive steps.

The semantics of a PCM can be formally described using a temporal logic; this formalism makes it possible to give the properties that any progammer has to guarantee when implementing a PCM. The semantics presented in the paper was also used to define an original proof system related to the concept of a PCM.In this proof system, programming schemes are given to the PCM user .These schemes guarantee properties such as mutual exclusion, scheduling access... and can be viewed as constraints that, if respected, guarantee the corresponding specifications.The whole proof system is described in [2,4]. The programming schemes induces the reusability of parts of proofs, this fact guided us to transpose this question on the programming language field and mainly influenced the present proposal.

The inherent separation between action and synchronization in the PCM naturally leads to a "two degrees of freedom" approach for parallel programming.Each degree of freedom may be implemented by a specific class.The relations between classes obey an inheritance mechanism.The current proposal treats inheritance from"action class" and inheritance from "synchronization class".The former inheritance consists in making the method list of a class to grow, while the latter relies on nesting synchronizers as brackets pairs, each bracket pair implementing a control step to access a method.This mode of control can be compared with the synchronization mechanism defined in the object oriented language GUIDE [10], where synchronization is restricted to an "activation condition" that must be true before the execution of the controlled operation.

The activation condition is built using internal specific counters related to the execution of the operations: total number of invocations, performed executions count, current pending calls count and so on.It should be noted that internal variables and algorithms are not allowed here and that the concept of a priority is lacking. In this respect the class concept related to PCM seems to be more expressive.

The two degrees of freedom approach presented in this paper is close to the one provided by DRAGOON[10a]. DRAGOON is a programming language that enriches Ada with the typical features of an object oriented language. As in our proposal, a class of DRAGOON may inherit from "action" ancestors and "synchronization" ancestors called "behavioural classes", thus the methods interleaving policy is separated from the functionality of the methods.The main difference between the above construct and DRAGOON concerns the inheritance of synchronization constraints. While "synchronization" classes can be built using any number of ancestors nested as bracketed actions, a class of DRAGOON is only related to one "behavioural class". Moreover, in a behavioural class, synchronization is expressed using merely a precondition involving historic functions when the "synchronization classes" have the expressive power of the PCM's synchronizers.

In the current proposal, the inheritance from several different synchronizers classes is not yet considered. As a consequence the described inheritance mechanism is not complete. The solution of that point is currently under way, it is strongly related to the composition of programming schemes occurring in the above-mentioned proof system.

REFERENCES

[1] P. AMERICA: "Pool-T: a parallel object oriented language". Object oriented computing. The MIT Press. 1987.

[2] J.P.BAHSOUN "Expression de la synchronisation dans un Module Contrôlé par Priorité: Implantation et méthode de preuve". Thèse d'Université. Toulouse 1988.

[3]J.P.BAHSOUN, C.BETOURNE,L.FERAUD "Une expression de la synchronisation et de l'ordonnancement des processus par variables partagées". 6th International Colloquium on Programming.April 1984.LNCS 167 Springer Verlag.pp 13-22

[4] J.P.BAHSOUN,C.BETOURNE,L.FERAUD "Programming and proving synchronizers".Proc. of the 10th Tunisian French Seminar of Computer Science:The rôle of programming languages.Tunis May 1989.pp 217-244

[5]C.BETOURNE,L.FERAUD,J.JOULIA,J.M,RIGAUD."Sur une representation des objets partagés" .RAIRO Informatique/Computer Science vol.14 n°1 1980. pp 77-86

[6] R.H.CAMPBELL,A.N.HABERMANN "The specification of process specification by path expressions.Lecture Notes in Computer Science.Vol16.Springer Verlag 1974. pp 88-102

[7] D.CAROMEL " A general model for concurrent and distributed object oriented programming"SIGPLAN Notices, Feb1989, pp 102-104.

[8] E.M.CLARKE, M.C.BROWNE, E.A.EMERSON, A.P.SISTLA "Using temporal logic for automatic verification of finite state systems". Logics and Models of Concurrent systems.K.APT Editor .NATO ASI Series.Vol 13.1984 pp 3-26

[9]P.J.COURTOIS,F.HEYMANS,D.PARNAS."Concurrent control with readers and writers".CACM Oct.1971.Vol 14. No 10. pp 667-678

[10] D.DECOUCHANT, S.KRAKOWIAK, M.MEYSEMBOURG, M.RIVEILL, X.ROUSSET DE PINA. "A synchronization mechanism for typed objects in a distributed system".Proc. of the ACM SIGPLAN Workshop on object based concurrent programming.San Diego Sept.1989 pp 105-107

[10a] A.Di MAIO,C.CARDIGNO,R.BAYAN, C.DESTOMBES, C.ATKINSON. "DRAGOON: an Ada based object oriented language for concurrent, real time, distibuted systems". Ada Design Choice. Madrid June 1989. Cambridge University Press pp 39-48.

[11] A.GOLBERG,A.ROBSON "SMALLTALK-80:The language and its implementation". Addison-Wesley Publishing Company,Reading 1983.

[12] S.GABBAY,A.PNUELI,S.SHELA,J.STAVI. "On the temporal analysis of fairness".ACM Symposium on programming languages.New York 1980 pp 163-173

[13] S.GRAF,J.SIFAKIS."A logic for the specification and proof of controllable processes of CCS".K.APT Editor.NATO ASI Series Vol.13.1984 pp 370-395

[14]J.E.GRASS,R.H.CAMPBELL"Mediators: a synchronization mechanism".Proc. Principles of distributed systems.IEEE 1986. pp 468-477

[15] B.HAILPERN "Verifying concurrent processes using temporal logic". PhD Thesis LNCS 129 Springer Verlag

[16] C.HEWITT,R.ATKINSON "Specification and proof technique for serializer.IEEE Trans. Software Eng. SE-5.1979.pp 10-13

[17] C.A.R. HOARE Monitors: an operating structured concept. CACM vol.17,16 oct. 1974

[18] A.KARP "Proving failure free of concurrent systems using temporal logic".ACM TOPLAS April 1984. pp 239-253

[19] R.E.LAUER,M.W.SHIELDS "Abstract specifications of resources accessing disciplines : adequacy,starvation, priority and interrupts." SIGPLAN Not.13,12 Dec. 1978 pp

[20] B.LISKOV,S.ZILLES "Programming with abstract data types".SIGPLAN Notices. Vol 9. N°9 April 1974.

[21] Z.MANNA,P.WOLPER. "Synthesis of communicating processes from temporal logic specifications". ACM TOPLAS January 1984. pp 253-281

[22] B.MEYER "Object oriented software construction"Prentice-Hall 1988.

[23] J.G.MITCHELL,W. MAYBURY, R. SWEET "MESA language manual version 5.0" Rep.CSL-79-3 Xerox Palo Alto Research Center Apr. 1979

[24] S.OWICKI,L.LAMPORT. "Proving liveness properties of programs" ACM TOPLAS Jul.198 pp 455-495

[257] A.PNUELI "The temporal logic of programs".Proc. 18th annual symposium on the foundation of Computer Science.IEEE 1977

[26] K.RAMAMRITHAM ,R.KELLER "A specification of synchronizing processes".IEEE TOSE Vol SE-9 n°6 Nov. 1984 pp 722-733

[27] N.WIRTH "MODULA :a language for modular multiprogramming".E.T.H. Zürich March 1976.

[28] WOLPER. Temporal logic can be more expressive 22th on foundations on computer October 1981.

[29] W.A. WULF, R.L. LONDON, M.SHAW "Abstractions and verification in Alphard". Carnegie Mellon University 1975.

[30] A.YONEZAWA, M.TOKORO:"Object-Oriented Concurrent Programming" The MIT Press, 1987.

PARALLELISM IN OBJECT-ORIENTED PROGRAMMING LANGUAGES

Antonio Corradi, Letizia Leonardi

Dipartimento di Elettronica, Informatica e Sistemistica - Universita' di Bologna
2, Viale Risorgimento - 40136 Bologna, ITALY -   E-mail: BOARI@BODEIS.CINECA.IT
This work has been partially financed by the Italy National Research Council within the Italian 'Progetto Finalizzato Sistemi Informatici e Calcolo Parallelo'.

ABSTRACT

The paper discusses parallelism in object-oriented systems. The most appealing way to insert parallelism in an object framework is to associate execution capacity with objects. This approach introduces active objects. The paper describes both synchronous and asynchronous communication between active objects by using examples of existing languages. A second dimension of parallelism comes from accommodating several activities within the same object. The paper describes also the synchronization techniques for the internal activities. The presented examples are written in a highly parallel language, called Parallel Objects. A distinctive characteristic of PO is the possibility of inheritance for the specification of concurrency internal to objects.

1. INTRODUCTION

In the area of object programming languages, designers are still investigating the issue of parallelism. For a discussion of several issues related to object-oriented languages see [25]. Now, several object systems consider the possibility of implanting parallelism into objects with different granularity [28].
In Smalltalk-80 [14] and other languages designed few years ago (such as Loops and InterLisp/Flavors), the process model is independent of the object concepts. This solution lacks of **integration** and **uniformity**. In fact, objects must take into account the presence of processes in execution concurrently even within themselves. We call these proposals *passive-object* systems. In several more recent proposals, objects acquire an **active** role similar to actors in the Actor paradigm [1]. These systems exploit parallelism (*) in two senses.
On the one hand, objects execute independently of each other and communicate by using synchronous and asynchronous protocols. We call this component **inter-object** parallelism.
On the other hand, a single active object can host several **threads of execution** that can run concurrently. Those threads are forced to execute only within the object in which they have been created. We call them **activities** to distinguish them from the processes that can flow and intrude passive objects. We refer to this new type of parallelism as the **intra-object** one.
An *active object-oriented* language can employ either only the first kind of parallelism or both. The two forms of parallelism within an object framework do not interfere. In fact, an object encapsulates its information and in particular it hides its internal

---

(*) In general, processes are usually called concurrent when they give the illusion of going on at the same time because of time multiplexing. Instead, parallelism is currently used to refer to real contemporaneous executions thanks to multiple execution capacity furnished at the architecture level. In the paper, we reason mainly at level of language and therefore independently from the support: concurrency and parallelism are considered as synonym in this framework and, from now on, in the paper.

concurrent behavior from the external world.
Up to now, active object proposals generally prefer to exploit only the first kind of parallelism by following different patterns [28]. Nevertheless, the increasing availability of highly parallel architectures makes also the use of the second component of parallelism reasonable and effective.

In the paper, we present an active object language, **PO** (PO stands for Parallel Objects) [8], in which both components of parallelism are provided. PO pushes further the integration and the uniformity. The concurrency of activities within one object can be specified in several ways. The specification of intra-object concurrency can be reused and freely inherited as the *normal* object behavior.

The paper is organized as follows. The second Section shows communications between objects in several active object languages. The third Section focuses on the granularity of parallelism achievable within a single active object. The fourth Section points out the PO main features in relation with parallelism and its inheritance by the use of some typical examples.

2. OBJECT COMMUNICATION

In object-oriented languages, computation results from **message passing** [13]. The arrival of a message implies that the receiving object will execute a particular action, called generally a **method** or **operation**, connected with the message reception. Therefore, message passing in the object-oriented framework resembles a remote operation request [12]. Objects that send requests play the role of **client**s with regard to the **service**s offered by the called object. A **client-server** relationship is established for the duration of the communication phase.
In general, active objects languages introduce different **modes** of communication that yield different involvements in this relationship. In the following, we analyze these modes: they are considered from the client site perspective and then from the server site. There is a neat separation of client and server policies. The client can adopt more or less synchronous modes. The server schedules requested operations in several ways independently of the communication mode.

2.1 Client Site

2.1.1 Synchronous remote call. In case of synchronous message passing, the client object waits until the server object yields the result of the requested operation. This mode represents a synchronization point for both involved activities, the client and the server one. Its semantics is very similar to the Remote Procedure Call mechanism [19], but embedded within an object framework. In this case, the client-server relationship is tight and connects two objects from the issuing of the request to the return of result. The syntax of this mode of communication is generally the same in all considered languages. This syntax is similar to an operation call in a passive-object language such as Smalltalk [14]. In particular, the PO syntax is:

x request

where

i) **x** is a variable that refers to an object that exports the requested operation in its interface. Object languages adopt a by-reference semantics [17].

ii) **request** includes the operation name and the parameters.

The value of this expression is the result returned by the operation: in an object framework, it is a reference to an object, in its turn. Figure 1 reports a temporal scheme of a synchronous remote call.

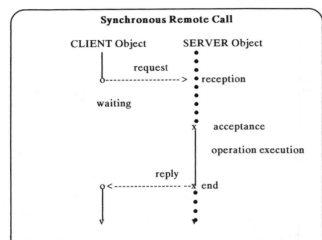

After the reception of a request, the server object must explicitly decide when to accept it. However, one cannot assume a sequentialization of requests at the server site as it happens in a communication between processes (see Section 3). **Figure 1.** Temporal scheme of a synchronous remote call.

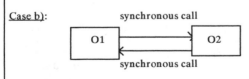

Case a):

O1 calls itself recursively and synchronously.
O1 waits for the answer that cannot arrive. In fact, O1 cannot serve the second request because it can host only one thread of execution.

Case b):

O1 calls O2 by using a synchronous mode of communication.
O2 calls O1 by using a synchronous mode of communication.
O1 and O2 are mutually waiting for an answer from one another.

Figure 2. Deadlock situations.

When a language gives only inter-object parallelism and synchronous mode of communication, e.g. POOL-T [3], it does not completely exploit the potential parallelism of objects. In this case, deadlock situations can arise (see figure 2). The case a) of figure 2 can be solved by dealing differently with the invocations of operations within the same object. The case b) has no general solution,

instead.
For systems that provide inter-object parallelism only, the best solution is to introduce asynchronicity in communications. In fact, a further version of POOL, POOL2 [4], defines asynchronous remote requests to overcome this problem.
Also EDEN [2] and ARGUS [18], for instance, define only synchronous communication, but provide intra-object parallelism.

2.1.2 <u>Other modes of remote operation request</u>. In the following, we sketch other communication modes, alternative to the synchronous one.

Asynchronous Remote Request.
This communication mode allows an object to request an operation of another object without waiting for the reply (figure 3). It is useful when the answer is unimportant and the client only intends to activate a remote service. This kind of communication is similar to asynchronous message passing [21] when the message arrival activates a service procedure at the remote site.

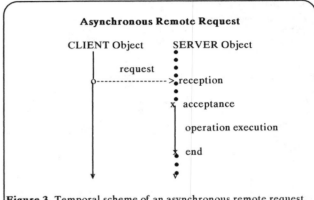

Figure 3. Temporal scheme of an asynchronous remote request.

The asynchronous communication mode allows an object to send multiple requests to different servers. Moreover, this mode better exploits inter-object parallelism.
The client-server relationship in this case is quite loose. The client, after sending the request, it is completely decoupled from the server. The inter-object communication support is in charge of yielding the request to the proper server. This mode of communication implies queuing of requests at the server site. Each active object owns a queue that collects all the sent requests. We assume that multiple messages sent by an object A to an object B maintain at the arrival site the same ordering in which they have been sent (**ordering law**) [27].
Several systems, *ABCL/1* [27], *Concurrent Smalltalk* [26], *Orient84/K* [15] and *PO*, furnish also an asynchronous mode with the described semantics and the corresponding (similar) syntax:

ABCL/1	[x < = **request**] (*)
ConcurrentSmalltalk	**x request&**
Orient84/K	**x request &**
PO	**% x request**

where x and request have the same meaning as before.

Asynchronous Remote Request with future reply.
In this case, a client object O1 can request an operation of another object without waiting for the reply. The request is associated with an intermediate client-related entity. At a future time, O1 can decide to get the reply by using the intermediate entity. If the server

----
(*) In ABCL/1 the syntax for a synchronous remote call is [x < = = request].

object has not delivered the answer yet, O1 waits for it. It is sometimes possible for O1 to verify the presence of the answer, before effectively suspending itself.

With this communication mode, the client-server relationship is more involving and lasts until the client maintains a reference to the intermediate entity.

This mode provides a feature as in the actor communication with continuation. In fact, in Actor languages [1], the continuation is another actor that collects and keeps the answer. In other words, the server actor sends the reply to the continuation. The client actor - when in need of the reply - requests it to the continuation.

In general, object languages that furnish "pure" asynchronous communication give also this other kind of communication, with the following syntax:

ConcurrentSmalltalk	cb <- x request&
ABCL/1	[x < = request $ fv]
Orient84/K	v <- x request &
PO	%%v x request

Although the syntax is similar, there are several differences between the languages depending on:
i) the role of the intermediate entities;
ii) the interaction with the intermediate entities.

The intermediate entity can be either a separate object (*external intermediate entity*) or a data structure internal to the client object (*internal intermediate entity*).

In the first case, this mode is exactly the same as in the message passing with continuation of actors. The latter case implies that the client object is the direct destination of the reply message.

In *ConcurrentSmalltalk*, the intermediate entity is a separate object of a predefined type, called CBox. In the syntax for the asynchronous remote request with future reply

cb <- x request&, (where the symbol <- means assignment)

cb is a variable that refers to a CBox object. A CBox object is automatically created for any communication of this kind. For this reason, it is impossible to reuse the same CBox in another future request.

An operation of "receive" obtains the result from a CBox when it arrives: r <- cb receive.

The *ConcurrentSmalltalk* language defines also operations on CBox objects, such as receiveAnd:, receiveOr:, etc., that allow a client to wait for several results or just for one non-deterministically in the specified set. The functions isReady and notReady can also test whether the CBox already contains the result.

All other object languages considered here, define the client object as the receiver of the reply, since the intermediate entity M is internal to the client object. Figure 4 reports a temporal scheme of an asynchronous remote request with future reply that uses an internal intermediate entity. This figure shows what happens when the client object uses the reply - already arrived - by mean of the internal intermediate entity M.

In *ABCL/1*, the client uses special internal variables, called **future variables**. They refer queue-like special data structures apt to contain the "future" results of computations. Then, the *ABCL/1* syntax of a future communication

[x < = request $ fv]

uses a future variable fv associated with the request.

The same future variable can be used in several communications: it contains all received results. The results are extracted from future variables by using special primitives such as (next-value fv) and (all-values fv). It is possible to test for the presence of the reply with the primitive (ready? fv). In *ABCL/1* it is also possible to use directly an asynchronous mode that specifies a reply destination different from the client object. This mode derives from the Actor model and allows delegation [1].

The syntax of *Orient84/K* is the one for asynchronous requests used in an assignment statement:

v <- x request &

where v is a normal variable that will contain the future reply.

This is possible because any variable possesses a state, ready or notReady. The previous assignment makes the variable v 'notReady'. The system will reset the v state to ready, when the reply arrives. The client can then get the result by using a special primitive **wait (v)**. More complex primitives are furnished to wait either only one result or all results in a specified set.

Also in PO, the programmer uses normal variables to contain future replies. PO calls this kind of communication, marked asynchronous remote request:

%%v x request.

In PO, there is no need of a primitive to obtain the result as in *ABCL/1* or in *Orient84/K*. In fact, any future use of the variable v implies awaiting for the reply (or accepting it, if it has already delivered). The support of PO takes charge of it. Whether a reply is present in the variable v can be tested by using simple equality. In fact, PO variables are initialized to NIL (*). If the test v = NIL is true, the result has not been delivered yet, otherwise it is already present.

The core point w.r.t. the communications with future reply is the possibility of passing the intermediate entities to other objects. There are two cases:

1) When the **intermediate entity** is an **object**, as in *ConcurrentSmalltalk* and in *Actor* languages, no problem arises in passing a reference to it. All objects that have a reference for a such object can independently and consistently ask it for its operations.

2) The **intermediate entity** is referred to by an **internal variable**. In this case, this variable plays two different roles:
i) container of a value (possibly not evaluated yet).
ii) agent able to synchronize the computation in the client.

The passage of one intermediate variable would require the same semantics in all sites that have a reference to it. This, on one hand, contrasts with the normal parameter passing rule that implies that all parameters are evaluated. On the other hand, the "implantation" of results at all sites can be difficult to implement, especially in a distributed system.

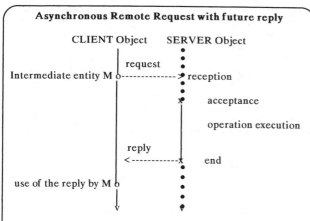

Asynchronous Remote Request with future reply

CLIENT Object   SERVER Object

request

Intermediate entity M ⊶-------------→ reception

acceptance

operation execution

reply

←---------- end

use of the reply by M ⊶

Figure 4. Scheme of an asynchronous remote request with future reply.

(*) In Smalltalk, differently from PO, the value(/object) NIL has two different meanings: i) it is the initial value of any variable, i.e. the value that has any unbound variable; ii) it is the value to indicate "don't care". In PO, this second semantics is obtained by using a distinct primitive value: NULL.

A solution is to pass intermediate variables only when the corresponding reply has arrived. Any attempt to pass a not yet delivered future variable forces a delay in the call, until the reply has arrived.

2.1.3 Other issues related to remote operation requests.

From the area of distributed languages, several other issues have been brought into discussion. On the one hand, the need of communicating to multiple servers. This can be solved by extending the synchronous communication.

On the other hand, the definition of either a **time-out** or/and a (corresponding) **exception handling**.

In fact, the client object could wait indefinitely in case of failure of the server object. This can be avoided if the client can associate a time-out with the invocation. Moreover, an object can associate an exception handling with any request. The object executes the exception handler in correspondence to a specified failure event, for instance, the expiration of the time-out.

Those features are still neglected in many object systems apart from those that have been designed to face fault-tolerance.

ARGUS, for example, leaves to the system the responsibility for the event of failure of the server. The system declares failed the called operation in this case. It is also in charge of assuming reasonable time-outs. The failure event forces the execution of an exception handler associated with the invocation, if it has been provided by the user. PO provides the possibility of associating an operation request with a timeout and handler (see sub-section 3.3):

> x request **timeout: time handler: exceptionoperation**

2.2 Server Site: Several ways of yielding a result

All above mentioned languages allow an object to serve requests independently from the communication mode. POOL2 is the only one where synchronous communication implies the request of an operation that yields a result and asynchronous remote requests are only connected to operations that must not produce results.

The server object has two possibilities to reply:

i) the return of the reply also implies the operation end (the previous figures assumed this situation);

ii) the return of the reply does not mean the end of the operation. The server may continue the operation completely decoupled from the client.

The first possibility is the only one available in a passive object framework with synchronous communication mode [14]. Active object languages, such as *ConcurrentSmalltalk*, *Orient84/K*, *POOL-T* and *PO*, provides also the other choice.

The first two proposals have both the above mentioned possibilities. A syntactic notation distinguishes the two modes of returning a result:

i) terminating return: ^ result;

ii) non-terminating return: ^^ result.

Of course, details must be taken care of: only the first return action has effect in case of multiple use of these notations. In case a server object has already executed a non-terminating return and it come across a terminating return within the same operation, the object only ends the operation. The second reply is never yielded to the client.

In the other two languages, i.e. *POOL-T* and *PO*, there is only one syntax for the return. The return can therefore appear wherever in the operation. In any other case, the end of the operation is marked by the execution of the last statement in the operation code.

3. INTRA-OBJECT PARALLELISM

Active object-based systems, such as *POOL-T*, *ABCL/1*, *Orient84/K* and *ConcurrentSmalltalk*, allow only one thread of execution within any object. This simplifies the object internal behavior and its scheduling because only one activity is in execution at a time, but gives a programmer less expressive power. This may lead to an unneeded proliferation of small parallel objects instead of defining larger objects that encloses a logical and more coordinate semantics. A too large number of objects can make complex the phase of garbage collection.

In the following, we analyze the choices of different active object languages to introduce intra-object parallelism with more or less granularity [10].

Even if only one activity per object is in execution at a time, it is possible to support several concurrent activities. In fact, one activity may be suspended awaiting an event that eventually arrives. Another activity within the same active object may be in execution. Moreover, preemption is introduced to switch object attention from one event to another to handle external and I/O related events. Preemption is also requested when different levels of priority are to be defined. *ABCL/1* defines two different categories of messages and message receptions, ordinary and express, when an object is created. Express messages have priority over normal ones. The arrival of an express message preempts a low priority operation already in execution.

In *Orient84/K*, instead, the user defines operations with priorities. The system handles the suspension of the current activity when a message for a priority operation arrives.

In *PO*, a priority strategy can be expressed as any other policy. In fact, priority is a strategy obtained by tailoring the internal object scheduling via a pre-defined scheduling policy that express it (see sub-section 3.2).

Apart from PO, the expression of greater parallelism is impossible in these systems.

PO, as well as few other systems (ARGUS [18], EDEN [2] and SINA [22]), introduces more activities within the same object. The available capacity of execution of a single CPU is time-multiplexed among all currently ready to be served activities.

To exploit the intra-object parallelism, a language must choose how to generate internal **activities**. Possible choices are:

1) An object **dynamically** generates an internal activity for any incoming request. This activity is destroyed at the operation end. In this case, there is a strict association between a single request and the activity devoted to its service. Languages such as *ARGUS* and *PO* adopt this strategy for intra-object concurrency.

2) An object generates at its creation **several predefined internal activities**. Each of them can serve one operation at a time. The activity provides a service to either only one request type or a set of request types. In the latter case, there is a 1:N connection between a single request and an activity. This choice is implemented by the *EDEN* system. Any request, that cannot be immediately served because there are no free activities, is enqueued and awaits for its service.

3) An internal activity can **spawn a set of sub-activities**. This mechanism is crucial if only the synchronous mode of communication is present [18]. In fact, an object activity can create several sub-activities as its sons. Each of the sons synchronously calls another object and waits for the reply. The parent activity continues its computation. In this way, a language is able to simulate asynchronous remote requests. The language must provide mechanisms to wait for the termination of the son activities.

ARGUS allows an activity to generate sons. The generator activity waits for the completion of its sons. Each son activity can request synchronously an operation. In *Argus*, the sibling sub-activities have no visibility in common, but they may abort each other. As soon as one answer arrives, an activity may kill all other ones. Finally, the father activity can wait for all operation answers or a subset of them. *ABCL/1* not only furnishes asynchronous modes of communication, but also gives the possibility of spawning several activities. Each of them, for example, can make one synchronous call. This possibility is called parallel construct and its syntax is:

> { message-passing ... message-passing }.

The execution of this construct is completed only when all its message-passing components are over.

SINA defines a mechanism to detach one activity. Without this possibility, a *SINA* object can only serve a request at a time. After a detach action, the object is free to serve another request while the detached activity executes in parallel.

Another choice a language must face is the **number of activities** that one object can host in its lifetime. There may be either a limit to the number of activities or no limit may be imposed. In *POOL-T* and *ABCL/1*, only one activity per object is defined at its creation (called *body* in POOL-T). *EDEN* fixes a priori the number of possible activities. These activities are dynamically associated with the requests to which respond. One object of the other languages (*Argus, Orient84/K, ConcurrentSmalltalk, SINA* and *PO*) can create any number of activities in its lifetime.

3.1 Intra-object Synchronization

In case of more activities concurrently present in one object, consistence of the object state must be preserved. The activities internal to the same object can need synchronization. In addition, the need of internal synchronization can arise even if there is only one activity in execution within each object.
We consider **synchronization** as an aspect that depends on:
i) who is in charge of it:
    1) the system may **implicitly** furnish the correct sequentialization;
    2) the user should **explicitly** define it.
ii) When it is specified:
    1) **a priori**. An active object does not generate an activity as long as it potentially conflicts with any existing one;
    2) **a posteriori**. The activities are responsible for synchronizing with each other, after their creation.

POOL-T allows a user to program the body of his/her objects by using an **explicit a priori** scheme of synchronization. A body selects at any time the operation requests it wants to reply to. If a user does not specify a peculiar policy for some objects, the **implicit** default-furnished policy is the FIFO handling of the operation requests.
ABCL/1, *Orient84/K* and *SINA* also provide an **explicit and a priori** scheme of synchronization. These languages define primitives to enable/disable the operations currently accepted by interface. In other words, an object operation can enable or disable other operations to ensure intra-object synchronization.
ARGUS provides an **implicit a posteriori** scenario. Activities that serve operations are generated as soon as the requests reach the object. Within operations, the system provides automatically the correct locking policy to avoid interferences on the state.
EDEN and *ConcurrentSmalltalk* furnish an **explicit and a posteriori** scheme of synchronization. In these cases, object operations use traditional mechanisms (such as monitors or semaphores) to synchronize.
PO makes possible different synchronization schemes. A PO user can take advantage of an **implicit a priori** synchronization scheme by using the policies furnished by the system. Nevertheless, a PO programmer may **explicitly** either insert synchronization primitives in the operations (i.e. **a posteriori**), or **a priori** solve any synchronization problem. In the following, we consider only the latter scheme because it is very innovative. To realize the a priori scheme, each PO object hosts a dedicated activity, the **scheduler**, in charge of monitoring activities. Each object scheduler can solve synchronization before the activation of operations and it may be explicitly user-specified taking advantage of inheritance.

3.2 A Priori Intra-object Scheduling in PO

The PO language defines more powerful and flexible tools than other systems to express a priori internal synchronization [9]. PO allows a programmer to use a priori schemes of synchronization taking advantage of inheritance, i.e. reusing previously defined policies.

In fact, **inheritance** (together with classification) is the basic mechanism to reuse software in object-oriented systems [24], and so it is also used to reuse intra-object synchronization specifications. In particular, in PO there is the possibility of specifying a priori intra-object synchronization at three different levels of abstraction. The **low level** is designed for skillful programmers. It is possible to express any scheduling policy he/she needs. The PO language defines for this level dedicated methods, called **scheduling methods**, that form the code of the object scheduler. In this way, the programmer expresses internal scheduling of objects by using the *same syntax* and the *same classification/inheritance mechanism* used to specify normal operations.
The **high level** allows more naive programmers to take advantage of default scheduling policies furnished by the PO environment. Object-oriented languages are always coupled with an environment with several predefined system classes. The scheduling method that implements the chosen default strategy is defined (installed) in the general class OBJECT, root of the graph of classes, and then is inherited by all objects.
The **third, intermediate level** permits a programmer to use all the available policies expressed as **constraints**. For example a priority constraint allows a user to impose a priority between any two object operations. A special form of inheritance (**composition**) allows the reuse of constraints: their consistency, specially when in composition, can also be checked. All the constraints for an object are automatically translated by the system into scheduling methods.
Inheritance plays a key role in all three levels. The scheduling part of any object is anyway composed of all visible scheduling methods found in the inheritance graph. The scheduling process executes all these methods in an endless loop.

3.3 Intra-object Scheduling details

Figure 5 shows the internal of a PO object. A PO object always contains, apart from its state:
- a queue, called **RequestQ**, that buffers any external message;
- a queue, **ActivationQ**, that collects all the descriptors of the concurrent internal activities;
- a scheduler activity;
- possibly several concurrent activities.

Several primitives are available to operate on the object internal queues. All primitive operations on these queues are given by an object-oriented syntax
In the following examples (Section 4), we use in particular the primitive **isInQueue**, that attempts a matching with an item in a queue searching FIFO. The item (message or activity descriptor) is selected depending on its subfield values; the matching conditions for the subfields are the equality and inequality.

The object scheduler handles the queue RequestQ to deal with the arrived requests. The scheduler decides when to create an activity to serve a request message. In this case, the request is dequeued and the newly created activity is registered in the structure ActivationQ. The scheduler controls also all the activities executing within the object. When an activity completes, it is again the scheduler that handles its termination and then extracts its descriptor from the ActivationQ.
Results of requests are dealt homogeneously with operation requests: they are buffered in the request queue. Then, the object scheduler considers results and pass them to the activities that wait for them.
In case of timeout requests, the scheduler, at the server site, controls expiring deadlines both for still pending requests and for executing activities. In both cases, the server scheduler is in charge of sending the abnormal termination result. There are various strategies to deal with an expiring deadline when the corresponding activity still executes [12]. The simplest one is to let the activity terminate normally and discard its result.

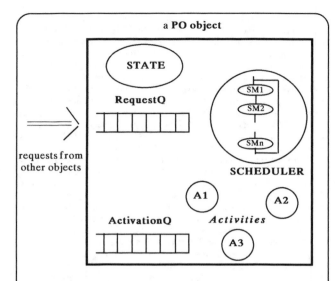

The scheduler activity is expressed in terms of an endless loop of the scheduling methods (in the picture, Scheduling Methods).

Figure 5. Internal structure of an object.

```
2 -->  [2]  -->  [3]  -->  [5]  -->  [7]  -->  [11] ...
3       3        5        7        11              ...
4       5        7        11       13
5       7        11       13       17
6       9        13       17       19
7       11       17       19       23
8       13       19       23       29
9       15       23       29       31
10      17       25       31       37
11      19       29       37       41
12      21       31       41       43
...     ...      ...      ...      ...
```

The flow of integers is reported at any stage

Figure 6. Sieves for five prime number. All even numbers are removed by the first prime number, the "2".

At the client site, the scheduler recognizes this exception and activates the related handler.

The scheduling methods to deal with normal activity termination, returned results and timeouts are predefined and default-furnished to a PO user.

The motivation of a unique arbiter in a parallel environment are strong: the scheduler can freely decide the object concurrency policy and minimizes the interference among other internal activities and without forcing a sequentialization.

4. SOME CASE STUDIES

The case studies to exemplify the *PO* language are:
i) a prime number generator (Sieve of Eratosthenes);
ii) the Fibonacci series;
iii) the management of a directory;
iv) the problem of producers and consumers on a buffer.

4.1 The Sieve of Eratosthenes

This is a typical mathematical problem solved here by using PO. In this solution, we take only advantage of inter-object parallelism, i.e. of the possibility of creating several objects concurrently executing and asynchronously communicating. The solution is based on the dynamic association of one sieve object with any found prime number. A chain of sieves is created. All numbers given by the generator flow through this chain. The propagation of any multiple of a prime number is blocked. When a number reaches the sieve chain end is declared prime and added to the chain.

A solution of this problem is in [5] solved by using POOL-T. The difference between the POOL-T solution and our solution is that at any stage the numbers propagate asynchronously.

In figure 6, we show the situation that arises when the first five prime numbers have been generated. In particular, we report the numbers generated at the beginning and these that go through any stage. Table 1 reports the PO solution.

CLASS: Sieve
    INHERITS_FROM: Object
    INSTANCE_STATE: PrimeNumber <Integer>
                    Next <Sieve>
                        (%% Next Sieve createSieve)
{ variables may be given a type: it is the expected class of belonging. Initial values can be specified by expressions that are evaluated at object creation time. Variables without initial values are set to NIL. The variable Next is set to the next element in the chain. **Note the use of future communication to avoid an infinite creation in the inital phase** }

    INSTANCE_METHODS:
        METHOD: input (pr <Integer>)
{ in case this sieve object contains a prime number, any input number pr is tested for divisibility by it. If the number pr is not divisible by PrimeNumber, it can be a prime number and it must be passed to next sieve. The number pr is sent out via an asynchronous remote request. If a number arrives to a free sieve, i.e. to the current end of the chain, it is a prime }
            (PrimeNumber <> NIL) if ([(pr DIV PrimeNumber) <> 0)
                                    ifTrue ([% Next input (prime)])],
                                    [PrimeNumber <- prime])

        END_METHOD;

    SCHEDULING_PART:
{ methods specified here are executed by the object scheduler of each sieve to allow a correct interleaving of activities. }
        METHOD: scheduling input
{ The primitive isInQueue searches for the first request for the operation *'input'* in the Request Queue. The second expression has the same meaning applied to the Activation Queue. If a request exists and there is no current activation of the input operation, the scheduler dequeues the selected request and creates an activity to serve it }
            Msg <- RequestQ isInQueue (Msg|op <- "input")
            Act <- ActivationQ isInQueue (Act|op <-"input")
            (Msg <> NULL) and (Act = NULL) ifTrue (
                    [RequestQ DEQUEUE (Msg)
                        self EXECUTE (Msg)])
        END_METHOD;
END_CLASS;

Table 1. The class Sieve. The syntax of the scheduling method for input is the same as the normal method input.

The synchronization part of this class of objects can be specified also by using constraints. PO defines, in fact, a constraint with the same semantics described for dealing with the operation input: **Mutex(op)**. Then, one only needs to specify the operation on which to apply this constraint, i.e. in our example: **MutEx (input)**. In fact, only one activity of input can be in execution at a time within a sieve object.

For initializing purpose, we give to the first sieve object the first prime number, i.e. "2". An endless loop generates all the integer numbers. The generator sends each number to the head of the sieve chain asynchronously. The table 2 shows this sieve activation.

Let us remark the importance of the ordering law. Without this assumption, a non prime number that arrives before others could be erroneously declared prime.

```
S <- Sieve createSieve
S input (2);  NewInteger <- 3
[true] whileTrue ( [ % S input (NewInteger)
                     NewInteger <- NewInteger + 1 ])
```

Table 2. Initialization and generation of the solution.

4.2 The Fibonacci Series

The Fibonacci series is another typical problem. In PO, we can effectively take advantage of intra-object parallelism. Several activities can execute concurrently within the same PO object.

A single PO object is capable of calculating simultaneously several Fibonacci numbers. There are two dimensions of concurrency for this object. On the one hand, several requests of Fibonacci numbers sent by external users can be served in parallel by the same object. On the other hand, the activities to solve a single request can be active in parallel within the same object.

Table 3 gives a PO solution to the problem. The solution minimizes the number of objects to deal with a maximally parallel decomposition. Compare the PO solution with others [23], where any stage of the series must be dealt with by a different object.

```
CLASS: FibonacciCalculator
    INHERITS_FROM: Object

    INSTANCE_METHODS:
        METHOD: nthNumber (n, ai_1, ai_2 <Integer>)
            RETURNS: <Integer>
{ If the number n is greater than 3, a new invocation of the method
nthNumber is activated }
        LOCAL_VARIABLES: ai <Integer>
        ai <- ai_1 + ai_2
        (n <= 3) if ( [ ^ ai ],[ ^ self nthNumber (n-1, ai, ai_1) ] )
{ The special variable self expresses a new request sent to the
object itself }
        END_METHOD;

    SCHEDULING_PART:
        METHOD: scheduling nthNumber
{ This method is the automatic translation of the constraint
MaxPar (nthNumber) }
        Msg <- RequestQ isInQueue (Msg|op <- "nthNumber")
        (Msg <> NULL) ifTrue ([ RequestQ DEQUEUE (Msg)
                         self EXECUTE (Msg) ])
        END_METHOD;
END_CLASS;

{ An activation of a FibonacciCalculator }
Fib <- FibonacciCalculator create
n <- Fib nthNumber ( 5, 2, 1)
```

Table 3. The class FibonacciCalculator and its use.

4.3 The Directory Example

With the directory example, we want to point out the possibility of highly parallel scheduling policy when a strict serialization of the operations of an object is not forced by the object semantics. Our solutions show other peculiar characteristics of the PO language, cumbersome to be obtained in other object-oriented parallel languages. This example is reported in [20]. An object DIRECTORY provides the following operations:

1) **dirInsert (key, item)**: it inserts "item" in the directory with "key" as key; it returns either OK or a duplicate key message;
2) **dirDelete (key)**: it deletes the reference with "key" as key from the directory; it returns either OK or a not found indication;
3) **dirLookup (key)** that looks up for the reference with key "key" in the directory; either a reference to the found element or a not found indication is returned;
4) **dirDump** that returns a list of pairs < key, item >: these are the content of the directory.

Usually solutions produce a scheduling that serializes the operations on a directory. Our solutions, instead, considers only a reduced number of dependencies between the operations on a directory [20], not to reduce the potential parallelism. Therefore, we accept that the dirDump operation reports a snapshot of the directory that did never exist. Moreover, a dirLookup operation gives the situation before or after a modification: we do not distinguish between the two possibilities. The only dependency that we

---

```
CLASS: Directory
INHERITS_FROM: Object  ...
SCHEDULING_PART:
        METHOD: scheduling dirInsert
        Msg <- RequestQ isInQueue (Msg|op <- "dirInsert")
        Act1 <- ActivationQ isInQueue (Act1|op <- "dirInsert")
        Act2 <- ActivationQ isInQueue (Act2|op <- "dirDelete")
        ((Msg <> NULL) and (Act1 = NULL) and (Act2 = NULL))
        ifTrue ([ RequestQ DEQUEUE (Msg)
                     self EXECUTE (Msg)])
{ there must not be other concurrent insertions or deletions, to
serve one dirInsert request. That derives from the constraints
MutEx(dirInsert) and MutEx(dirInsert, dirDelete) }
        END_METHOD;

        METHOD: scheduling dirDelete { as in dirInsert request }
        Msg <- RequestQ isInQueue (Msg|op <- "dirInsert")
        Act1 <- ActivationQ isInQueue (Act1|op <- "dirInsert")
        Act2 <- ActivationQ isInQueue (Act2|op <- "dirDelete")
        ((Msg <> NULL) and (Act1 = NULL) and (Act2 = NULL))
        ifTrue ([ RequestQ DEQUEUE (Msg)
                     self EXECUTE (Msg)])
        END_METHOD;

        METHOD: scheduling dirLookup
{ A lookup does not constrain any other operation. That enhances
parallelism, but disrupts serializability. This method is the simple
translation of MaxPar(dirLookup): as soon as a request arrives, an
activity to serve it starts }
        Msg <- RequestQ isInQueue (Msg|op <- "dirLookup")
        (Msg <> NULL) ifTrue ([ RequestQ DEQUEUE (Msg)
                         self EXECUTE (Msg)])
        END_METHOD;

        METHOD: scheduling dirDump {from MaxPar(dirDump) }
        Msg <- RequestQ isInQueue (Msg|op <- "dirDump")
        (Msg <> NULL) ifTrue ([ RequestQ DEQUEUE (Msg)
                         self EXECUTE (Msg)])
        END_METHOD;
END_CLASS;
```
Table 4. Scheduling part of the class Directory - 1st Solution.

take into account is the mutual exclusion of dirInsert operations, dirDelete operations and between the two kinds.

The solution can be specified by PO constraints, as follows:

MaxPar (dirLookup); maximally parallel schedule for lookup and
MaxPar (dirDump);   dump operations
MutEx (dirInsert);   sequential scheduling w.r.t. the
MutEx (dirDelete);   activations of the same method
MutEx (dirInsert, dirDelete); only a type at a time

The above solution limits the directory to accept only one dirInsert and/or dirDelete at a time. Table 4 reports the scheduling part of the directory class automatically derived from the previously defined constraints.

The specifications of the scheduling methods are independent from the normal instance part [6]. A variation of the scheduling part implies only to change the synchronization of the Directory internal activities. Such a separation can usually be achieved by specifying intra-object concurrency via constraints.

In this first solution, we have only considered the possibility of constraining methods in accord with predefined scheduling policies. A skilled programmer may express even a more parallel solution by handling directly the PO low level. In fact, a synchronization dependency between dirInsert and dirDelete is necessary only if there are requests related to the same directory key. Table 5 reports only the new specified scheduling methods for the operations dirInsert and dirDelete.

The new synchronization policy can be easily obtained via modifcation of the expanded scheduling code of Table 4. That code is automatically obtained from the described constraints. The additions a user must write are very confined. The insertions are printed in Italic in Table 5.

CLASS: Directory
INHERITS_FROM: Object   ...

SCHEDULING_PART:
    METHOD: scheduling dirInsert **RETURNS**: < Boolean >
      Msg < - RequestQ isInQueue (Msg | op < - "dirInsert")
      Act1 < - ActivationQ isInQueue (Act1 | op < - "dirInsert",
(1)   *Act1 | parameters | key < - Msg | parameters | key)*
      Act2 < - ActivationQ isInQueue (Act2 | op < - "dirDelete",
      Act2 | parameters | key < - Msg | parameters | key)
      ((Msg < > NULL) and (Act1 = NULL) and (Act2 = NULL))
          ifTrue ([RequestQ DEQUEUE (Msg)
             self EXECUTE (Msg)])
{ to serve a dirInsert request, there must not be other concurrent insertions or deletions, but only for the same key. In particular in **1**, the ActivationQ is searched for an activity that serve a dirInsert and whose key is equal to the key of the message Msg selected in the RequestQ }
    END_METHOD;

    METHOD: scheduling dirDelete **RETURNS**: < Boolean >
      Msg < - RequestQ isInQueue (Msg | op < - "dirInsert")
      Act1 < - ActivationQ isInQueue (Act1 | op < - "dirInsert",
      Act1 | parameters | key < - Msg | parameters | key)
      Act2 < - ActivationQ isInQueue (Act2 | op < - "dirDelete",
      Act2 | parameters | key < - Msg | parameters | key)
      ((Msg < > NULL) and (Act1 = NULL) and (Act2 = NULL))
          ifTrue ([RequestQ DEQUEUE (Msg)
             self EXECUTE (Msg)])
{ The same as in a dirInsert request }
    END_METHOD;
    ...
END_CLASS;

Table 5. Scheduling part of the class Directory - 2nd Solution.

CLASS: InfiniteBuffer
  INHERITS_FROM: Object
  INSTANCE_STATE: buff < Array >
            putIndex, getIndex < Integer > (1)

  INSTANCE_METHODS:
    METHOD: PUT (item)
    buff atPut (putIndex, item); putIndex < - self nextPut
    END_METHOD;

    METHOD: GET **RETURNS**: < Object >
    ^ buff at (getIndex); getIndex < - self nextGet
    END_METHOD;

  PRIVATE_INSTANCE_METHODS:
    METHOD: nextPut (item) **RETURNS**: < Integer >
    ^ putIndex + 1
    END_METHOD;
    METHOD: nextGet **RETURNS**: < Integer >
    ^ getIndex + 1
    END_METHOD;

  SCHEDULING_PART:
  CONSTRAINTS:
  MutEx (PUT)
  MutEx (GET)
  SchedCond (GET, "dim > 0")
END_CLASS;

CLASS: BoundedBuffer
  INHERITS_FROM: InfiniteBuffer
  INSTANCE_STATE: size < Integer > (10)

  PRIVATE_INSTANCE_METHODS:
    METHOD: nextPut (item) **RETURNS**: < Integer >
    (putIndex = size) if ([^ 1], [^ (putIndex + 1)])
    END_METHOD;

    METHOD: nextGet **RETURNS**: < Integer >
    (getIndex = size) if ([^ 1], [^ (getIndex + 1)])
    END_METHOD;

  SCHEDULING_PART:
  SCHEDULING_STATE: dim < Integer > (0)
  CONSTRAINTS:
  SchedCond (PUT, "dim < = size")
END_CLASS;

CLASS: ExtendedBuffer
  INHERITS_FROM: BoundedBuffer

  INSTANCE_METHODS:
    METHOD: GETREAR **RETURNS**: < Object >
    getIndex < - self previousPut; ^ buff at (putIndex)
    END_METHOD;

  PRIVATE_INSTANCE_METHODS:
    METHOD: previousPut (item) **RETURNS**: < Integer >
    (putIndex = 1) if ([^ size], [^ (putIndex - 1)])
    END_METHOD;

  SCHEDULING_PART: **CONSTRAINTS**:
  MutEx (GETREAR)
  MutEx (PUT, GETREAR)
  SchedCond (GETREAR, "dim > 0")
END_CLASS;

Table 6. The classes InfiniteBuffer, BoundedBuffer and Extended-Buffer.

4.4 Buffers

In this example, we want to outline the advantages deriving from inheritance in the specification of intra-object scheduling.

We consider first a class of buffers of infinite dimension. This class defines in the interface two operations: PUT and GET. These operations can be requested by producer and consumer objects. Each infinite buffer handles two indexes, one to put and one to get items. PO allows infinite buffers to be concurrently accessed by producers and consumers. In other words, one activity that serves a request of PUT can execute together with one activity that serves to a GET request. The scheduling must avoid the concurrent execution of more PUT (or GET) operations to prevent mutual exclusion problems on the PUT (or GET) index. Moreover, part of the scheduling strategy is the avoidance of GET when the buffer is empty.

The constraints to solve this synchronization problem are:

MutEx (PUT)
MutEx (GET)
SchedCond (GET, "dim > 0").

The latter constraint states that a GET operation can be executed only if the buffer contains at least an item.

The variable *dim* is private to the object scheduler. To complete the constraint specification, we should add two *postactions* to handle this variable when the PUT or GET activities terminate.

Table 6 reports the complete code for this example.

Then, the specification of a class of buffers of limited dimension, i.e. a class of bounded buffers, can use effectively inheritance: the new class derives from the class of infinite buffers.

Each bounded buffer is handled as a circular buffer. The two indexes, one to put and one to get items, are inherited from the infinite buffer class.

Table 6 reports the code for these two classes. Note that the code for the PUT and GET operations is completely reused. In fact, it is only necessary to respecify the private operations that update the indexes. Again, PO allows bounded buffers to accommodate concurrent activities of PUT and GET. The constraints for this class of objects are completely inherited from its super-class. It is only necessary to add a new constraint to deal with the case of a full buffer:

SchedCond (PUT, "dim < = size").

The new constraint states that a PUT request can only be started if there is enough room in the bounded buffer to accommodate the item.

Specialization of bounded buffer can be further considered. We want to introduce a new class of objects, called extended buffers, that provides an operation to extract items from the rear [16].

We define the new class as a sub-class of the bounded buffer class. See Table 6 for additional details about the added *normal* operation, GETREAR and the corresponding index updating.

The scheduling policy for the new operation GETREAR is mutual exclusion among GETREAR requests and between GETREAR and PUT because they act on the same index. Then, to express the new synchronization policy, we add these constraints:

MutEx (GETREAR)
MutEx (PUT, GETREAR)
SchedCond (GETREAR, "dim > 0").

5. CONCLUSIONS

The paper examines the possible degrees of parallelism within object frameworks. In particular, two components of parallelism have been identified: the inter-object and the intra-object parallelism. The presence of both components is a valuable feature whenever one wants to decompose an application into logical objects in limited number and of 'reasonable' size. No provision of intra-object concurrency can reduce the object size but may force to introduce an otherwise unneeded number of objects. Moreover, that approach can decompose functions closely and logically related on different objects.

The PO language is based on a model that introduces real intra-object parallelism. This language defines enough expressive capacity to design objects derived from a logical decomposition that internally group related functions.

As a peculiar feature, the PO language exploits at any level inheritance: this allows a user to reuse also the specification of parallelism and of synchronization. Intra-object synchronization can be inherited following the usual inheritance rules. A user can exprress intra-object concurrency in PO according to his/her level of expertise.

At the same time, PO allows rapid prototyping of different concurrency policies without varying the rest of objects specification.

A prototype of the PO support has been designed for a SUN architecture using Smalltalk-80 as the support environment [11]. In addition, PO has been used as a guide to solve the problem of mapping objects for massively parallel architectures [7].

REFERENCES

[1] G. Agha, "ACTORS: A Model of Concurrent Computation in Distributed Systems", The MIT Press, 1986.

[2] G.T. Almes *et al.*, "The EDEN system: a technical Review", IEEE Trans. On Software Eng., v.SE-11, n.1 January 1985.

[3] P. America, "POOL-T: A Parallel object-oriented Language", in: 'Object-Oriented Concurrent Programming', The MIT Press, 1987.

[4] P. America, "Definition of POOL2, a parallel object-oriented language", Tech. Rep. No. 0364, Philips Research Laboratories, April 1988.

[5] L. Augusteijn, "POOL-T User Manual", Tech. Rep. n. 0104, Philips Research Laboratories, September 1986.

[6] T. Bloom, "Evaluating Synchronization Mechanisms", Proc. of the 7th Symp. on Operating System Principles, December 1979.

[7] A. Ciampolini, A. Corradi, L. Leonardi, "Parallel Object System Support on Trasputer-based Architectures", Microprocessing and Microprogramming, v. 27, pagg. 339-346, 1989.

[8] A. Corradi and L. Leonardi, "An Environment Based on Parallel Objects: PO", IEEE Phoenix Conference on Computers and Communications, Scottsdale (Arizona), February 1987.

[9] A. Corradi and L. Leonardi, "The Specification of Concurrency: An Object-based Approach", IEEE Phoenix Conference on Computers and Communications, Scottsdale, March 1988.

[10] A. Corradi and L. Leonardi, "PO: An Object Model to Express Parallelism", ACM SigPlan Workshop on Object-based Concurrent Programming, San Diego, ACM SigPlan Notices, v. 24, n. 4, April 1989.

[11] A. Corradi and L. Leonardi, "A Concurrent Prototype in Smalltalk-80", COMPEURO '90, Tel-Aviv (Israel), May 1988.

[12] A. Corradi, L. Leonardi, C. Salati, "Availability by Replication in Embedded Distributed Systems: The CONCORDIA Project", in: 'Achieving Safety and Reliability with Computer Systems', Elsevier Applied Science, 1987.

[13] B.J. Cox, "Message/Object: An Evolutionary Change", IEEE Software, v.1, n.1, January 1984.

[14] A. Goldberg and D. Robson, "Smalltalk-80: the Language and its Implementation", Addison-Wesley, 1983.

[15] Y. Ishikawa and M. Tokoto, "Orient84/K: An Object-Oriented Concurrent Programming Language for Knowledge Representation", in: 'Object-Oriented Concurrent Programming', The MIT Press, 1987.

[16] D.G. Kafura and K.H. Lee, "Inheritance in Actor based Concurrent Object-Oriented Languages", The Computer Journal, v. 32, n. 4, August 1989.

[17] B. Liskov *et al.*, "Abstraction Mechanism in CLU", CACM, v. 20, n.8, August 1977.

[18] B.H. Liskov, "The ARGUS Language and System", Lecture Notes for the 'Course on Distributed Systems', Springer-Verlag, April 1984.

[19] B.J. Nelson, "Remote Procedure Call", Ph.D Thesis, Carnegie Mellon, 1981.

[20] P.M. Schwarz and A.Z. Spector, "Synchronizing shared Abstract Types", ACM Transactions on Computer Systems, v.2, n.3 August 1984.

[21] J.A. Stankovic *et al.*, "A Review of Concurrent Research and Critical Issues in Distributed System Software", Distributed Tech..C. Newsletter, v.7, n.1, March 1985.

[22] A. Tripathi and E. Berge, "An Implementation of the Object Oriented Concurrent Programming Language SINA", Software Practice and Experience, v. 19, n. 3, March 1989.

[23] J. Van Den Bos and C. Laffra, "PROCOL: A Parallel Object Language with Protocols", ACM Conf. Proc. OOPSLA'89, New Orleans, ACM SigPlan Notices, v. 24, n. 10, October 1989.

[24] P. Wegner, "Capital Intensive Software Technology", IEEE Software, v. 1, n. 3, July 1984.

[25] P. Wegner, "Dimensions of Object-Oriented Language Design", OOPSLA'87 Conference Proc., October 1987.

[26] Y. Yokote and M. Tokoto, "Concurrent Programming in ConcurrentSmalltalk", in: 'Object-Oriented Concurrent Programming', The MIT Press, 1987.

[27] A. Yonezawa *et al.*, "Modelling and Programming in an Object-Oriented Concurrent Language ABCL/1", in: 'Object-Oriented Concurrent Programming', The MIT Press, 1987.

[28] A. Yonezawa and M. Tokoro (eds.), "Object-Oriented Concurrent Programming", The MIT Press, 1987.

Incremental Global Optimization for Faster Recompilations[*]

Lori L. Pollock

Dept. of Computer Science
Rice University
Houston, TX 77251
lori@rice.edu

Mary Lou Soffa

Dept. of Computer Science
University of Pittsburgh
Pittsburgh, PA 15260
soffa@cs.pitt.edu

Abstract - Although optimizing compilers have been quite successful in producing excellent code, their use is limited, due to the accompanying long compilation times and the lack of good symbolic debuggers for optimized code. One approach to attaining faster recompilations is to reduce the redundant analysis that is performed for optimization in response to edits, and in particular, small maintenance changes, without affecting the quality of the generated code. Although modular programming with separate compilation aids in eliminating unnecessary recompilation and reoptimization, recent studies have discovered that more efficient code can be generated by collapsing a modular program through procedure inlining. To avoid having to reoptimize the resultant large procedures, this paper presents techniques for incrementally incorporating changes into globally optimized code. The algorithm determines which optimizations are no longer safe after a program change, and also discovers which new optimizations can be performed in order to maintain a high level of optimization. An intermediate representation is incrementally updated to reflect the current optimizations in the program. The techniques developed in this paper have also been exploited to improve on the current techniques for symbolic debugging of optimized code.

1. Introduction

As generating efficient target code continues to be a major requirement of production compilers, sophisticated code optimization has become an integral part of many language translators. Unfortunately, the longer compilation times associated with optimization analysis and code transformations, as well as the problems of symbolically debugging optimized code, discourage programmers from using optimizing compilers. Optimization is often sacrificed for fast compila-

tion and good debugging capabilities by turning off the optimization phase during program development and exploiting optimization only during the final compilation. However, additional bugs are inevitable, making it difficult to predict the "final compilation". As a result, the programmer is left waiting for slower, optimizing compilations more frequently than desired. Maintenance changes cause long waiting periods while the optimizing compiler regenerates the production code for the modified source program. Bugs not detected by the nonoptimizing compiler are sometimes caught by the optimizing compiler through its extensive program analysis.

One approach to reducing the time for recompilation and reoptimization after a change is to develop techniques to effectively support separate compilation and eliminate the need to recompile the entire set of modules when a single module is edited, despite modules optimized using interprocedural information [4]. With the thrust toward modular programming, research has focused on interprocedural issues with the module or procedure as the smallest unit of reanalysis. However, recent studies have found that better code can be generated by procedure inlining, especially with a register allocation scheme that works well on large procedures, rather than compiling the separate procedures, despite optimization that uses interprocedural data flow information [5,9,17]. Coinciding with these studies, compilers often replace call sites in the intermediate program representation by the bodies of the called procedures prior to optimization, which is typically performed on this intermediate representation. Loop unrolling, often performed to increase the opportunities for optimization of loops, also lengthens procedure bodies. Thus, the sizes of the procedures handled by the optimizer are much larger than the procedures in the source program. A change in what appears to be a small procedure in the source program could in fact be a small change in a very large pro-

[*] This work was partially supported by the National Science Foundation under Grant CCR-8618699 to Rice University and CCR-8801104 to the University of Pittsburgh.

cedure from the optimizer's view. Reanalyzing the whole procedure or module for optimization to incorporate a code change could involve a significant amount of redundant analysis.

To make optimizing compilation more palatable for the programmer during program development and maintenance, we advocate a fine grain (i.e., statement level) incremental approach to reoptimization in order to further limit the scope of the optimizer to program changes. The optimizer is *incremental* in that results from previous analyses and transformation are used in an attempt to perform an amount of work proportional to the effect of each program edit. Faster recompilations are achieved by avoiding complete reanalysis of a module in response to a program change. The incremental approach has appeared quite frequently in the literature relating to other facets of compilation [2,6-8,10,16,19]. One of our earlier papers presents algorithms for incrementally incorporating edits into code that is optimized by strictly local optimizations using no information about the flow of data throughout the whole program [12].

However, there has been no previous work on the incremental reoptimization of globally optimized procedures. By gathering information about the flow of data throughout the procedure, global optimization yields better code than locally optimized code which is performed on individual sequential code segments. Accordingly, incremental reoptimization analysis is much more complicated because a single transformation can affect statements in remote segments of the program. Also, in order to incrementally update a program representation that includes global optimizations, the system must incrementally update global data flow information. A number of incremental data flow analysis techniques have recently been proposed [11,15,18,20].

In this paper, we present a technique for incrementally incorporating changes into globally optimized code. In response to program edits, changes in the conditions for safe optimizing transformations are detected using an annotated intermediate representation of the program and the incremental changes in data flow information. The intermediate representation is incrementally updated to reflect the new optimized version of the program. Since the incremental optimizer reanalyzes only the optimizations that are affected by a program change, updates for small changes can be incorporated at a fraction of the time needed for batch reoptimization of an entire procedure. The bulk of the analysis is performed in response to changes rather than in preparation for possible changes. Thus,

analysis is not wasted if, in fact, an edit has no far-reaching effects.

The paper begins in Section 2 by discussing the problems involved in incrementally updating globally optimized code. An overview of our approach to these problems is presented in Section 3. Section 4 describes the annotated intermediate representation used in the incremental analysis. The algorithms that we have developed to perform the incremental reoptimization is presented in Section 5, followed by an analysis of the algorithm in Section 6. Finally, conclusions are discussed in Section 7.

2. Optimization Surgery

In order to preserve the meaning of a source program, each transformation performed by an optimizing compiler should be "safe" in that it does not change the output produced by a program for a given input or cause errors that were not present in the original version of a program. When a program is modified by edits, the conditions for the safety of an optimizing transformation can be altered such that the optimization can no longer be performed without possibly affecting the program semantics. Likewise, there may be optimizations that are safe in the new version, but were not safe in the previous version. These new optimizations need not be performed to maintain correctness, but they must be performed to maintain a high quality of optimized code in response to a series of program changes.

The full effect of a program change involves optimizations directly affected by the user's change and those indirectly affected through the changes in optimizing transformations. The indirect effects of a program edit are caused by the *dependencies* that exist among optimizations in that performing and removing optimizations can create conditions for other optimizations to become safe or unsafe. The following dependencies could exist between any two optimizations α and β:

- *performing* α establishes the safety of β
- *removing* α establishes the safety of β
- *removing* α destroys the safety of β

The dependencies with α and β interchanged could also exist. It should be noted that performing an optimization can never destroy the safety of another optimization because an optimization is never performed on the premise that another optimization will be reversed to make it safe.

Figure 1 presents an example of an *optimization dependency graph*, which is our graphical representation of the full effect of a particular program change on optimizations in terms of the dependency relationships that actually lead to each optimization reversal or creation. Each node (except the root that represents the original edit) represents the creation or reversal of an optimization performed sometime during the incremental update. For example, node 2 (**destroy cs d+e**) in Figure 1 represents the destroyed safety and reversal of the common subexpression optimization of **1: x:=d+e;** and **4: y:=d+e;** to **x:=d+e; y:=x;** by insertion of **d:=m+b**.

A directed edge from node **n** to node **m** in the update dependency graph indicates that the transformation represented by node **m** depends on the prior transformation represented by node **n**. For example, the edge from node 2 (**destroy cs d+e**) to node 3 (**destroy cp y:=x**) indicates that the propagation of the definition of **y** in statement 4 to all of its uses and then the elimination of the copy **y:=x** depends on the common subexpression optimization of **d+e** that created the copy. When the common subexpression is removed in response to the edit, the copy propagation is no longer applicable. The paths leading into a node **n** in the optimization dependency graph depict the dependencies of all prior code changes leading to the optimization change (i.e., creation or reversal) at node **n**. Only the last change along a path to a node actually triggers the new optimization change. The solid edges in Figure 1 indicate the triggering dependencies.

Assuming that optimization changes are detected sequentially, an ordering (i.e., the order in which these changes are detected) is imposed on the optimization reversals and creations in response to an edit. Each node of the optimization dependency graph is labeled by an integer indicating the sequential ordering of the optimization changes imposed by the incremental optimizer. If this sequential ordering of changes is altered, a different optimization dependency graph will result. Since a change can not be caused by a later change, the optimization dependency graph is acyclic (i.e., a directed acyclic graph, or dag).

Another problem in developing an incremental optimizer concerns the mapping from source to target code. Similar to a symbolic debugger, a fine grain incremental compiler must maintain a mapping from source program constructs to the corresponding generated code segments in order to detect statements that are affected by a program edit and then reanalyze only the affected statements. The main task of the incremental optimizer is to update globally optimized code to reflect the changes in the safety of optimizing transformations in response to program changes. How-

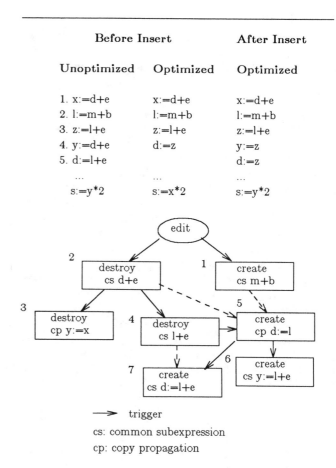

Before Insert		After Insert
Unoptimized	Optimized	Optimized
1. x:=d+e	x:=d+e	x:=d+e
2. l:=m+b	l:=m+b	l:=m+b
3. z:=l+e	z:=l+e	z:=l+e
4. y:=d+e	d:=z	y:=z
5. d:=l+e		d:=z
...	...	...
s:=y*2	s:=x*2	s:=y*2

⟶ trigger

cs: common subexpression

cp: copy propagation

Figure 1. An optimization dependency graph for inserting d:=m+b after statement 2.

ever, its task is complicated by the effect of optimizations on the mapping required by an incremental compiler. Code optimizing transformations complicate this mapping in three ways: (1) Optimizations such as copy propagation and elimination *suspend* the generation of code for portions of source statements. (2) The generated code may be *rearranged* by optimizations such as loop invariant code motion where a computation that is invariant to the loop's execution is moved to a location just prior to the loop entry. (3) A statement may be *replaced* by another statement or sequence of statements. For example, global common subexpression elimination replaces expression evaluations by simple copies. These effects must be considered, and in fact, exploited in the design of an incremental optimizer.

3. An Event Driven Approach

Our approach to incremental reoptimization is to *explicitly* detect which optimizations become unsafe and which new optimizations can be performed in response to a code change. As batch optimization gathers information about the flow of data at different program points and uses this information to determine when an optimizing transformation can be performed safely, an incremental approach to reoptimization must also utilize global data flow information. Our algorithm for incremental reoptimization is actually driven by the *changes* in data flow information. In particular, the optimization dependencies implicitly direct the incremental reoptimization through the changes in data flow information. Both program edits and code transformations from affected optimizations trigger incremental data flow analysis. Likewise, data flow changes trigger the detection of changes in conditions for the safety of optimizing transformations and the incremental update of the intermediate representation. The updates include the incorporation of the new optimizations and the exclusion of the old optimizations that have become unsafe. Only blocks where data flow changes have occurred are considered as candidates for possibly affected optimization.

Data flow changes and an updated program representation are sufficient for detecting new safe optimizations. However, in order to use data flow changes to determine which existing optimizations have become unsafe, a record of each existing optimization is embedded into the intermediate program representation. When an optimization is performed, the intermediate representation is annotated to indicate how the transformation has affected the current code. After detecting conditions that invalidate the safety of an optimization, the record of the optimization is removed from the intermediate representation since it no longer has an effect on the optimized code.

4. Annotated Intermediate Representation

Invoked between semantic analysis and final code generation, an optimizer typically performs its analysis and transformations over a control flow graph representation of the source program. The data dependencies among statements in each sequential code segment (i.e., basic block) can be represented as a directed acyclic graph (i.e., dag). With the goal of improving the generated code, an optimizer transforms this intermediate representation without retaining any information about the individual optimizations that were performed. Figure 2 shows both the flow graph representation and the linearized intermediate code for the optimized version of a small source code segment. We conservatively assume that temporaries and program variables may be used later in the program. The expression **j+10** is folded into the constant **15** and moved outside the loop. The common subexpression evaluation **i+1** is replaced by the value of **n** at labeled statement **12**, and the references to variable **m** are replaced by the constant **15**.

The original expressions and variable references are not retrievable from the optimized intermediate representation. Similarly, the original location of the loop invariant **m:=15** can not be discerned after optimization. Since the incremental reoptimization scheme needs to identify individual optimizations in order to determine whether they remain safe after a program change, we retain the subtrees from the original, unoptimized code and annotate the dag nodes of these subtrees. With these small modifications to the optimizer, our intermediate representation simultaneously represents the unoptimized and optimized program code with an indication of the individual machine independent optimizations responsible for the current form of the optimized code [12]. The optimized code can be generated from this annotated intermediate representation by traversing the control flow graph with a postorder traversal of each dag (depicted in the figures by the integer labels on each dag node), using the annotations to direct the optimization. The unoptimized code can be generated by the same traversal, but using the annotations to regain the effect of the original code.

The annotations to the intermediate representation are dictated by the information required to maintain a complete snapshot of existing optimizations, adequate to determine when optimizations become unsafe due to edits. Thus, the annotations depend on the optimizations being supported by the incremental compiler. However, the information recorded for a transformation can be generalized. Typically, the annotations must represent code that has been *eliminated, relocated,* or *replaced* by optimization. Thus, a variable label for a variable **v** on a dag node is extended to include (1) a field indicating whether the value represented by the node is actually stored to **v** (store) or the store to **v** has been eliminated by optimization (nostore), (2) a field consisting of a pointer to a dag node and an index into the list of labels on that dag node indicating the location of the original store to **v**, and (3) a pointer to references to which the constant value of **v** has been propagated. Since the order in which existing optimizations are affected in response to edits is independent of the order that they were ini-

Source	Unoptimized	Optimized
...	...	...
j := 5;	j = 5	j = 5
i := 0;	i = 0	i = 0
repeat	11: i = i + 1	m = 15
i := i + 1;	m = j + 10	11: i = i + 1
m := j + 10;	n = i + 1	n = i + 1
n := i + 1;	if n > m	if n > 15
if n <= m	goto 12	goto 12
then print(m)	print(m)	print(15)
else print(i+1)	goto 13	goto 13
until (i >= 100);	12: t1 = i + 1	12: t1 = n
...	print(t1)	print(t1)
	13: if i < 100	13: if i < 100
	goto 11	goto 11
	...	...

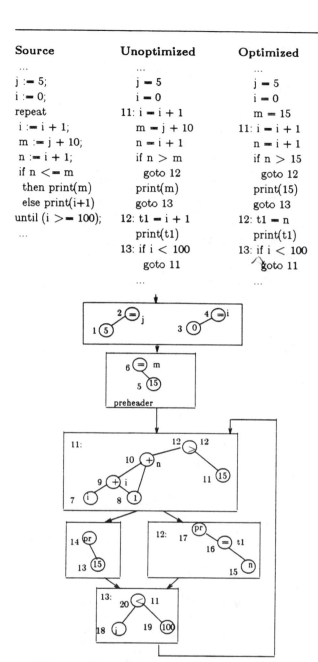

Figure 2. **Intermediate program** representation.

tially performed, no relative timestamp on optimizations is maintained.

Figure 3 depicts the annotated intermediate representation for the segment in Figure 2. The original subtrees for the folded expression **j+10** and eliminated common subexpression **i+1** remain in the intermediate representation with annotations indicating the constant and variable reference to generate during optimized code generation. Each reference to the vari-

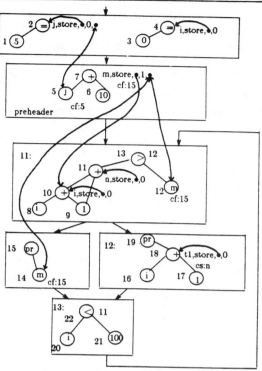

Figure 3. **Annotated intermediate representation.**

able **m**, which has been replaced by the constant **15**, is maintained with the annotation indicating the constant value to emit upon optimized code generation. The node representing the constant definition of **m** includes a pointer to each of its references so the optimization can be removed quickly. The loop invariant statement **m:=j+10** is located in the preheader of the loop, but a pointer to its original location within the loop is retained.

In order to detect affected global optimizations using data flow changes, we maintain current data flow information at each basic block as well as the data flow information that was current when the block was last examined for affected transformations. For a specific data flow problem, the updated GEN, KILL, IN, and OUT sets and the IN and OUT sets in effect before the current change are saved at each basic block. For a basic block **B**, GEN(**B**) contains information about data generated within **B**, while KILL(**B**) contains information about data that is stopped from flowing upon executing **B**. IN(**B**) summarizes the flow of data at the start of **B**, while OUT(**B**) summarizes the flow of data on exit from **B**.

In this paper, we refer to reaching definitions data flow information. Reaching definitions at a point p in a program are the definitions of variables that reach **p** with no intervening redefinition. They can be used in determining the safety of constant folding, copy propagation, and loop invariant code motion.

5. The Incremental Reoptimization Algorithm

Figure 4 presents the algorithm used in incremental reoptimization. Incremental analysis begins by detecting the affected optimizations within the basic block containing the program change. We refer to these optimizations as the locally affected optimizations. The annotated intermediate representation is updated to reflect these transformations. The nonlocalized nature of global optimizations suggests that update for a single global optimization can transform multiple blocks such that intermediate code for several blocks must be updated to completely record the transformation. In order to reduce the frequency of incremental data flow analysis, we detect any additional optimizations within each block transformed by these locally affected optimizations before invoking the incremental data flow analyzer.

The incremental data flow analyzer is then invoked to incrementally update the data flow information throughout the program based on the changes in the GEN and KILL sets at any block transformed by the locally affected optimizations. The incremental reoptimization algorithm is designed to be completely independent of the algorithm used for incremental data flow analysis, so any of the available techniques can be employed [11,15,18,20]. The incremental data flow analyzer returns with a set identifying the blocks where data flow changes have occurred. This set becomes the initial value of the worklist of basic blocks that need to be examined for potentially affected optimizations.

When a block **B** is removed from the worklist, the affected optimizations at **B** are determined based on the changes in the data flow sets IN(**B**) and OUT(**B**). As optimizations are detected as being affected, the annotated intermediate representation is updated. After detecting all of the optimizations affected within a block **B**, the data flow sets that record the previous global data flow information at **B** are updated to the values of the current data flow sets at **B**. The global effects of the transformations are propagated by again invoking the incremental data flow analyzer to update the data flow sets throughout the program. The set of blocks with data flow changes, returned by the incremental data flow analyzer, is added to the current worklist, and the update process continues. Incremental reoptimization terminates when there are no more blocks with global

INPUT: Inserted statement in basic block **B**.
OUTPUT: Updated annotated intermediate representation.
DECLARE *worklist*: basic blocks with altered data flow.

```
BEGIN
  update_locally_affected_optimizations(B);
  worklist := {};
  REPEAT
    IF (worklist is not empty) THEN BEGIN
      Remove a basic block B from worklist;
      update_remote_affected_optimizations(B);
      old_dataflow_sets(B) := current_dataflow_sets(B);
    IFEND;
    FOR each block B with altered GEN(B) or KILL(B)
    DO BEGIN
      Update IN(B) and OUT(B);
      worklist := worklist ⋃ incremental_dataflow(B);
    DOEND;
  UNTIL worklist is empty;
END.
```

Figure 4. Incremental reoptimization algorithm.

data flow changes, reflected by an empty worklist.

5.1. Locally Affected Optimizations

Figure 5 demonstrates the analysis for determining the locally affected optimizations in the block containing the program change. We show the analysis for the effects of inserting a variable definition on global common subexpressions and constant folding. The **remove** and **perform** algorithms for each optimization update the annotated intermediate representation for the transformation and determine any additional local effects of the transformation. The **remove** algorithms remove any trace of the optimizations from the annotated intermediate representation, while the **perform** algorithms record the transformations appropriately. These algorithms also update the corresponding GEN and KILL information and recur to detect and update other locally affected optimizations based on optimization dependencies.

5.2. Remote Affected Optimizations

In Figure 6, we illustrate the detection analysis performed at each basic block where global data flow information has changed. We refer to these blocks as remote blocks. The algorithm is executed for a block **B** when **B** is removed from the worklist for detection of affected optimizations. In particular, we present the analysis for constant folding at a remote block. Affected constant fold optimizations are identified by

286

INPUT: Inserted definition of variable **v** at statement **s**, represented by dag node **n**, in block **B**.
OUTPUT: Updated annotations for common subexpressions (*cs*) and constant folding (*cf*).

BEGIN   {common subexpressions}
IF (there is no prior definition of **v** in **B**) THEN
        FOR EACH expression e in **B** represented by
        a subtree with **n** as a new child node DO
                IF (e is marked later of *cs*) THEN **remove_cs**(e);
                                {constant folds}
FOR EACH parent **p** of **n**
        DO BEGIN
        IF (**p** is marked *cf*) THEN **remove_cf**(p);
        IF (new definition is constant or marked *cf*)
            AND (all other child nodes of **p** are constant,
            single constant definition or marked *cf*)
                THEN **perform_cf**(p);
        DOEND;
END.

Figure 5. Analysis of locally affected optimizations.

examining changes in reaching definitions (defIN(**B**)) entering a block **B** with respect to the leaf nodes of the dag representing **B**.

5.3. Loops and Loop Optimization

Changes in a program's control flow structure can affect the program's loop structure, indirectly affecting loop optimizations through loop creation, destruction, expansion, and contraction. Each natural loop is a single entry, strongly connected region of the flow graph and has an associated back edge, namely an edge $a \rightarrow b$ where b *dominates* a. A node n dominates another node m in the flow graph if every path from the initial node of the flow graph to m passes through n. A loop structure is destroyed when its back edge is destroyed either by deleting the back edge itself or destroying the dominator relation between the head and tail of the back edge. A new loop is created when a back edge is created by either inserting the back edge or creating the necessary dominator relation between the head and tail of an edge.

A loop can be reduced in size without completely destroying the loop structure by deleting an edge with both head and tail inside the loop such that the source of the edge has no more edges leading into the loop and the loop's back edge remains. An existing loop can be expanded when an edge is inserted to create a path of nodes with an ancestor and descendant inside the loop and no edges from outside the loop into any node along

INPUT: Altered reaching definitions (defIN) at a block **B**.
OUTPUT: Updated annotations for constant folding (*cf*).

BEGIN
LET *adddef* = {**d** | def **d** is added to defIN(**B**)};
LET *deletedef* = {**d** | def **d** is deleted from defIN(**B**)};
FOR EACH variable **v** defined in *adddef* $\bigcup$ *deletedef*
    DO BEGIN
    IF (there is a leaf l in **B** labeled by **v**) THEN BEGIN
      IF (there is only 1 definition of **v** in new udIN(**B**))
        THEN BEGIN
        LET **s** := node for a definition of **v** in udIN(**B**);
        IF (**s** is not constant) AND (**s** is not marked *cf*)
            THEN **s** := null;
        ENDIF;
      FOR EACH parent **p** of l
        DO BEGIN
        IF (**p** is marked *cf*)
            AND ((**s** is null) OR (value of **s** $<>$ *cf* value))
                THEN **remove_cf**(p);
        IF (**s** is not null)
            AND (all other child nodes of **p** are constant,
            single constant definition, or marked *cf*)
                    THEN **perform_cf**(p);
        DOEND;
      ENDIF;
    DOEND;
END.

Figure 6. Reoptimization at a remote block.

the new path. Loop contraction and expansion can also be caused by deleting or inserting a back edge that shares a header with another back edge when the associated sets of loop nodes are not a subset or superset of each other.

The analysis for loop structure changes and affected optimizations is illustrated in Figure 7. By examining the dominator relation between the head and tail of each inserted edge, inserted back edges are easily identified. By keeping a record of all existing back edges, deletion of a back edge is easily detected. Changes in dominators are used to detect other destroyed and created back edges. Dominator information is incrementally updated when an edge is inserted or deleted, and the dominators at nodes with dominator changes are examined [3, 13].

When a new back edge is identified, the set of nodes that form the corresponding loop are determined by the node stacking algorithm used in traditional optimizing compilers [1]. The loop's relationship with other loops (i.e., superset, subset, or disjoint) is determined in order to keep a record of the loop nesting

INPUT: Edge e from B_l to B_j and insert versus delete.
OUTPUT: Updated loop structures and optimization.

```
BEGIN
IF (B_j in dominators(B_l)) THEN {changed back edge}
    IF (deletion) THEN delback := {B_l→B_j}
      ELSE addback := {B_l→B_j};
  ELSE BEGIN {changed dominators}
    Incrementally update dominator sets of B_j and successors;
    LET delback := addback := 0;
    FOR EACH block B with altered dominators(B)
      DO BEGIN
        FOR EACH block B_d deleted from dominators(B) DO
          IF (B→B_d) THEN delback := delback ⋃ {B→B_d};
        FOR EACH block B_a added to dominators(B) DO
          IF (B→B_a) THEN addback := addback ⋃ {B→B_a};
      DOEND;
    ENDIF;
FOR EACH edge e in delback DO
  IF (loop l of e has no other back edges unique to l)
    THEN Reverse all optimizations on l and delete l
    ELSE Reverse unsafe optimizations and shrink l;
FOR EACH existing loop l with no structure change DO
  Detect and update any affected loop optimizations on l;
FOR EACH edge e in addback DO BEGIN
  Determine loop l associated with e;
  IF (e is the only back edge unique to l)
    THEN Create new loop l and perform optimization on l
    ELSE Expand loop l and perform new optimizations;
  DOEND;
IF (contract loop by non-back edge deletion)
    THEN Remove any unsafe optimizations and shrink l
  ELSE IF (expand loop by non-back edge insertion)
      THEN Expand l and perform new optimizations;
END.
```

Figure 7. Updating loop structure and optimization.

structure. The loop that corresponds to a destroyed back edge is easily identified by associating each back edge with the set of nodes that comprise the corresponding loop. The sets of added nodes during expansion and deleted nodes during contraction can also be determined by the node stacking algorithm. All loop optimization of destroyed loops is reversed, while the traditional analysis for new loop optimization is performed on new loops. The incremental changes in the loop structure are used to incrementally update optimizations of expanded and contracted loops. We refer the reader elsewhere for the details of the incremental analysis for loop optimization of expanded and contracted loops [13].

6. Analysis of Incremental Reoptimization

In this section, we discuss the correctness, effectiveness, and efficiency of incremental reoptimization. In order to show that the incremental reoptimization algorithm is correct, we show that the following two properties hold: (1) The incremental reoptimization algorithm terminates. (2) The functional equivalence between the optimized and unoptimized code is preserved after a program change is incrementally compiled [13].

Since the incremental scheme is guided primarily by program edits and optimization dependencies (indirectly through data flow changes), incremental optimization may not produce the same optimized code as a multiple pass, batch optimizing compiler. However, it can be shown that the incremental optimization analysis is *complete* in that there are no more optimizations (of the kinds supported by the optimizer) that can be performed on the current code when the algorithm terminates, assuming that there were no more possible optimizations before edit. The proof of this property follows closely to the proof of functional equivalence [13].

Similar to the batch scenario, the order of detection and update of affected optimizations can affect the *quality* of the optimized code. In general, the order of updates is driven by the worklist. However, when detecting the local effects within a basic block, the order of updates can be based on the relative effectiveness of different optimization orders.

Driven by the worklist of basic blocks with data flow changes, incremental reoptimization analysis is performed only at basic blocks where data flow information has changed and at the basic block containing the program edit. This may include blocks where no optimizations are affected since the optimizations within a block may not be affected by the changes in data flowing into the block, but no updates or incremental data flow analysis will be performed when optimizations in a block are unaffected. For each block **B** removed from the worklist, the time accounted to processing **B** is roughly

$$(\alpha + \beta + \gamma) * (number\ of\ blocks\ \mathbf{T})$$

where

T = a block transformed directly by **B**'s optimizations.
α = time to detect affected optimizations at **T**.
β = time to update **T**'s annotations, GEN(**T**), KILL(**T**).
γ = time to globally update IN and OUT sets based on changes to GEN(**T**) and KILL(**T**).

The value α depends on the data flow changes, the existing optimization of **T**, and the opportunity for optimization of **T**. Since it takes constant time to update the annotated intermediate representation and GEN and KILL to reflect an optimization update, the value β is a constant times the number of optimizations affected in **T**. The value of γ depends on the algorithm used for incremental data flow analysis. We expect that the number of blocks transformed directly by a block's affected optimizations (i.e., the number of blocks **T** for a given block **B**) will be small. The number of blocks **B** removed from the worklist throughout incremental update depends on the size of the edit, program structure, and optimizations in the code. Since worst case scenarios are not of practical interest in an incremental setting, it is difficult to assess the actual speedup of recompilation due to incremental reoptimization without empirical studies, which are currently underway.

Control flow changes are the most expensive edits to handle as they can affect the loop structure of the program as well as the flow of many different variables. The incremental update of data flow is more costly, and the number of affected optimizations is potentially greater due to the larger impact of the change. Changes to expressions and variable definitions or uses are incorporated with less effort since the effect on reaching definitions is limited to a single variable and loop structures are unaffected. With the exception of global common subexpressions, the merge, separation, deletion, or insertion of basic blocks has no effect on global optimizations since the flow of data throughout the flow graph remains unchanged.

In addition to improving the quality of the target code, careful ordering of incremental updates can improve the efficiency of incremental reoptimization by avoiding the destruction and reinstatement (or vice versa) of the same optimization. Thus, our *deletion* algorithm begins by identifying whether the deleted statement currently exists in the optimized code, and if so, determines its current form and location. If the deleted statement was previously eliminated by optimization, no further detection is required because deleting a statement that does not exist in the optimized code has no effect. Similarly, if optimization had replaced the statement by a simpler statement, then less analysis is needed to detect the effects of deleting the current, less complex statement. If the statement is moved by an optimization, the effects of deletion are determined according to its current location rather than the original one to avoid unnecessary analysis. Similarly, those optimizations that move, replace, or eliminate an inserted statement are detected early in the *insertion* algorithm.

For incremental reoptimization, the annotated intermediate representation and pertinent data flow information must be available throughout editing. Since this information is not needed during execution unless utilized for symbolic debugging, it need not be readily accessible until the programmer returns to editing and incremental compiling. Since the annotations are designed to record the generalized actions of optimizations, namely elimination, reordering, and replacement, the size of the annotated intermediate representation should not increase in great proportions as new optimizations are supported by the incremental optimizer. Moreover, most of the data flow information and the intermediate representation can be shared by other software tools commonly found in a programming environment.

7. Conclusions

We have presented a technique for reducing the long compilation times typically associated with ambitious optimizing compilers. Based on annotating the intermediate representation typically used during optimization and incrementally processing intermediate code changes, the incremental reoptimization algorithm can be easily incorporated into an incremental compiler.

In a separate paper, we describe how we have exploited the incremental reoptimization analysis, annotated intermediate representation, and data flow information to improve upon the current techniques for symbolic debugging of optimized code [14]. The incremental reoptimization analysis could also be exploited in other contexts. The event driven approach offers an alternative to the traditional multipass optimizer. Additional optimizations could be discovered after an initial optimization pass based on optimization dependencies implicit in the changes in data flow information. Incremental reoptimization analysis could be easily extended to handle optimizations that have been performed exploiting interprocedural data flow information. Edits in one module would result in changes in the interprocedural information at various call sites in other modules. Our incremental reoptimization analysis could interpret these interprocedural changes as local data flow changes at the blocks containing the call sites.

The incremental analysis can be used to provide precise identification of modules that require recompilation in a separate compilation environment which supports interprocedural analysis and optimization.

Current techniques are either approximate or very expensive [4]. These environments also schedule modules for recompilation only when the indicated changes in the interprocedural information cause existing optimization to become unsafe. Using our analysis, conditions permitting additional optimizations can also be detected and thus modules can be earmarked for recompilation in order to maintain highly optimized code. Ideally, the information maintained for incremental optimization analysis could aid in predicting the impact of changes on a module, and this information could be exploited by the recompilation system to make intelligent decisions on whether the module would be more efficiently recompiled at a statement level using incremental reoptimization or completely recompiled.

References

1. Alfred V. Aho, Ravi Sethi, and Jeffrey D. Ullman, *Compilers Principles, Techniques, and Tools*, Addison-Wesley Publishing Company, Reading, MA, 1986.

2. M. P. Bivens, "Incremental generation of high-quality target code," Ph.D. Dissertation, Department of Computer Science, University of Pittsburgh, Pittsburgh, PA, 1987.

3. M. Carroll and B. Ryder, "Incremental data flow analysis via dominator and attribute updates," *Proceedings of the Fifteenth Annual ACM SIGACT/SIGPLAN Symposium on Principles of Programming Languages*, San Diego, CA, January 1988.

4. Keith D. Cooper, Ken Kennedy, and Linda Torczon, "Interprocedural optimization: eliminating unnecessary recompilation," *Proceedings of SIGPLAN '86 Symposium on Compiler Construction*, pp. 58-67, 1986.

5. Jack W. Davidson and Anne M. Holler, "A study of a C function inliner," *Software -- Practice and Experience*, vol. 18, no. 8, pp. 775-790, August 1988.

6. Peter H. Feiler and R. Medina-Mora, "An incremental programming environment," *5th International Conference on Software Engineering*, pp. 44-53, 1981.

7. Ray Ford and Duangkaew Sawamiphakdi, "A greedy concurrent approach to incremental code generation," *Conference Record of the Twelfth Annual ACM Symposium on POPL*, pp. 165-178, 1985.

8. Peter Fritzson, "Preliminary experience from the DICE system, a distributed incremental compiling environment," *Symposium on Practical Software Development Environments*, pp. 113-123, 1984.

9. C. A. Huson, "An in-line subroutine expander for Parafrase," M.S. Thesis, Technical Report UIUCDCS-R-82-1118, University of Illinois at Urbana-Champaign, December 1982.

10. Fahimeh Jalili and Jean H. Gallier, "Building friendly parsers," *Proceedings of ACM Ninth Symposium on Principles of Programming Languages*, pp. 196-206, January 1982.

11. James Keables, Katherine Roberson, and Anneliese von Mayrhauser, "Data flow analysis and its application to software maintenance," *Proceedings of Conference on Software Maintenance*, pp. 335-347, October 1988.

12. L. L. Pollock and M. L. Soffa, "Incremental compilation of locally optimized code," *Conference Record of the Twelfth Annual ACM Symposium on POPL*, pp. 152-164, January 1985.

13. L. L. Pollock, "An approach to incremental compilation of optimized code," Ph.D. Dissertation, Department of Computer Science, University of Pittsburgh, Pittsburgh, PA, 1986.

14. L. L. Pollock and M. L. Soffa, "High-level debugging with the aid of an incremental optimizer," *Proceedings of the 21st Hawaii International Conference on System Sciences*, pp. 524-532, January 1988.

15. L. L. Pollock and M. L. Soffa, "An incremental version of iterative data flow analysis," *IEEE Transactions on Software Engineering*, vol. 15, no. 12, December 1989.

16. T. Reps, T. Teitelbaum, and A. Demers, "Incremental context-dependent analysis for language-based editors," *Transactions on Programming Languages and Systems*, vol. 5, no. 3, pp. 449-477, July 1983.

17. S. Richardson and M. Ganapathi, "Interprocedural analysis versus procedure integration," *Information Processing Letters*, 1989.

18. Barbara Ryder and Marvin Paull, "Incremental Data Flow Analysis," *ACM Transactions on Programming Languages and Systems*, vol. 10, no. 1, pp. 1-50, January 1988.

19. Mayer D. Schwartz, Norman M. Delisle, and Vimal S. Begwami, "Incremental compilation in Magpie," *Proceedings of SIGPLAN '84 Symposium on Compiler Construction*, pp. 122-131, 1984.

20. Frank Kenneth Zadeck, "Incremental data flow analysis in a structured program editor," *Proceedings of SIGPLAN '84 Symposium on Compiler Construction*, pp. 132-143, 1984.

Compiling SIMD Programs for MIMD Architectures

Michael J. Quinn
Department of Computer Science
Oregon State University

Philip J. Hatcher
Department of Computer Science
University of New Hampshire

Abstract

Programming multiple-CPU computers is widely held to be harder than programming sequential computers, but much of the difficulty can be traced to the MIMD programming languages used. SIMD languages provide programmers with a more understandable model of parallel computation. In this paper we summarize the advantages of data parallel languages, a subclass of SIMD languages, and describe how programs written in a data parallel language can be compiled into loosely-synchronous MIMD programs suitable for efficient execution on multicomputers.

1 Introduction

Flynn's [2] taxonomy of computer architectures is the basis for a variety of programmer models of parallel computation. To a programmer, an SIMD (single instruction stream, multiple data stream) computer can be viewed as a single CPU directing the activities of a number of arithmetic processing units, each capable of fetching and manipulating its own local data. In any time unit a single operation is in the same state of execution on multiple processing units, each manipulating different data. Hence this programming model is called *synchronous*.

In contrast, an MIMD (multiple instruction stream, multiple data stream) computer allows the concurrent execution of multiple instruction streams, each manipulating its own data. It is possible for every processor in an MIMD computer to execute a unique program, but it is far more common for every processor to execute the same program. This is known as SPMD (single program, multiple data stream) programming. Although processors may coordinate with each other at synchronization points, the MIMD and SPMD programming models are called *asynchronous*, because between the synchronization points every processor executes instructions at its own pace.

A number of SIMD programming languages have been proposed, including Actus [6], C* [10], Parallel Pascal [8], and Vector C [5]. We believe an SIMD programming language should have the following features: a global name space, which obviates the need for explicit message passing between processing elements; parallel objects, rather than merely parallel scalars; and the ability to make the number of processing elements a function of the problem size, rather than a function of the target machine. We use the term *data parallel* to refer to SIMD languages with all these properties [4]. Of the languages we have listed, only C* fits our definition as a data parallel language.

Earlier work on SIMD programming languages has concentrated on developing compilers for processor arrays or pipelined vector processors [5,6]. Our thesis is that compilers can translate SIMD programs into programs that run efficiently on a wide variety of architectures. In this paper we describe how data parallel programs can be translated into SPMD programs that execute efficiently on multicomputers.

Our work is closely related to recent efforts that translate to multicomputers sequential programs that are augmented with data distribution information [1,9]. We feel that if the language is to contain data mapping constructs, then the language should be explicitly parallel. An SIMD programming model maintains the benefits of using a sequential language (deterministic results, no race conditions, ability to debug on a von Neumann architecture) while allowing the natural expression of inherently parallel operations (such as data reductions). In addition this paper will demonstrate that an SIMD program need not have a strictly synchronous execution. Just as sequential programs can be mapped to asynchronous parallel programs with the same behavior, we map SIMD programs to equivalent asynchronous implementations.

Earlier we presented the design of a C*-to-C compiler based upon a general control flow model [7]. This paper describes a new compiler design based upon a less general control flow model, i.e., one that does not support the goto statement. Experimental results show that the new compiler generates programs with significantly higher efficiency, programs that often rival and sometimes match the speed of hand-coded C programs on a hypercube multicomputer.

Section 2 summarizes the strengths of the data parallel approach to problem solving on parallel computers. Section 3 presents a brief overview of C*, the data parallel language used in our examples. In Section 4 we describe how data parallel programs can be translated into efficient SPMD programs suitable for execution on a hypercube multicomputer. Experimental results appear in Section 5.

2 Strengths of the Data Parallel Model

The data parallel model of computation has a number of inherent strengths. Some of these strengths are common to all SIMD languages, while others are dependent upon the data parallel model's particular attributes.

Several advantages relate to the model's simple control flow. It is easier to determine the state of the system, since all pro-

Application	C	C*	NCUBE C
Matrix multiplication	16	18	85
Prime sieve	23	25	78
Mandelbrot set	31	31	89
Amortization table	31	34	131
Moore's shortest path	48	53	294
Bitonic mergesort	50	51	149
Dijkstra's shortest path	54	71	176
Path consistency	75	85	-
Character thinning	85	78	-
Conjugate gradiant	98	68	-
Fluid flow	182	182	345
Ray tracing	503	517	661

Table 1: Comparison of lines of code needed to program various applications in the sequential language C, the data parallel language C*, and the MIMD parallel C language on the NCUBE. NCUBE C figure reflects node program only.

cessing units are either active or inactive as a universal program counter works through the various control statements. Results of computations are deterministic; the SIMD model, with its single program counter, cannot have race conditions. Building debuggers is straightforward. In fact, programs can be debugged on a von Neumann architecture, if so desired. Because processing elements in a data parallel SIMD program can reference any address in the global name space, programmers can adopt an "I'll say what data I need and let the compiler figure out how to get it" approach.

Because data parallel languages allow any structure, not just scalars, to serve as the unit of parallelism, ordinary C code can be included inside parallel constructs. In this manner each processing element can execute loops based on the values of its local variables, follow pointers to traverse local data structures, etc.

Data parallel SIMD programs are short—usually about the same length as the corresponding sequential C programs. The extra overhead involved in defining the parallel objects is compensated for by the ability to initialize and reference entire data structures in a single statement, rather than in a singly- or multiply-nested for loop as in a sequential programming language. In contrast, a programmer who parallelizes a sequential program using a traditional MIMD programming language usually finds that the parallel program is much longer (see Table 1).

It remains to be seen what proportion of "real world" problems are suitable for this paradigm. After studying Caltech's collection of 84 parallel programs written for a variety of parallel architectures, Fox [3] has concluded that 83% seem amenable to solution via synchronous, loosely-synchronous, or embarrassingly parallel synchronous algorithms, all of which can be implemented as SPMD programs. Given this data, we believe a compiler that translates data parallel programs into SPMD programs will have real utility.

3 The C* Programming Language

In order to express the parallel program segments in this paper, we adopt the conventions of the data parallel programming language C*, developed by Thinking Machines Corporation [10]. C* is a superset of the sequential programming language C. In this section we briefly describe a few important features of C*. For further details, see the paper by Rose and Steele.

All data in C* are divided into two kinds, scalar and parallel, referred to by the keywords mono and poly, respectively. C* allows the programmer to express algorithms as if there were an unbounded number of processors onto which the data can be mapped. Once every piece of parallel data has been mapped to its own processing element, several simple program constructs allow parallel operations to be expressed. The most important of these constructs is an extension of the class type in C++ [11]. A class is an implementation of an abstract data type. Instances of variables of a particular class type are manipulated with that class's member functions. In C* member functions operate on a number of instances of a class in parallel. This "parallel class type" is called a domain.

In C* variables of a domain type are mapped to separate processing elements, and all instances of a domain type may be acted upon in parallel by using that domain's member functions and the selection statement (which is illustrated below). Within parallel code each sequential program statement is performed in parallel for all instances of the specified domain.

The following code segment computes the element-wise maximum of two arrays.

```
domain vector { float a, b, max; } x[100];
< Intervening code >
[domain vector].{
  if (a > b) max = a;
  else max = b;
}
```

The domain type vector defines a domain containing two floating point values named a and b. By declaring x to be a 100-element array of vector, 100 instances of the variable pair are created, one pair per processing element. The selection statement [domain vector] activates every processing element whose instance has domain type vector; i.e., every element of x. Every active processing element executes the statements contained within the selection statement. In this case every processing element evaluates the expression a > b. The universal program counter enters the then clause, and those processing elements for which the expression is true perform the assignment statement max = a. Next the universal program counter enters the else clause, and those processing elements for which the expression is false perform the assignment statement max = b.

C* programs have a single name space, and any expression can contain a reference to any variable in any domain. For example, consider the following code segment, in which every active processing element sets its own value of temp to be the average

of the `temp` values of its predecessor and successor processing
elements:

```
#define N 100
domain rod { float temp; } x[N];
< Intervening code >
[domain rod].{
  int index = this->x;  /* this same as in C++ */
  < Intervening code >
  if ((index > 0) && (index < N-1))
    temp = (x[index-1].temp + x[index+1].temp)/2;
}
```

Each processing element's value of `index` gives its unique position in the domain, a value in the range $0 \ldots N - 1$. All active
processing elements evaluate the right hand side of the assignment statement together, then they all perform the assignment
of values together. Hence an old value cannot be overwritten
before an adjacent processing element has had the opportunity
to read it.

4 The Translation of SIMD Programs Into SPMD Programs

We shall focus on three important issues. The first issue is the
translation of control structures. Because synchronization is relatively expensive on contemporary multicomputers, the compiler must minimize the number of synchronizations required as
the parallel computer works its way through the various control
structures of the data parallel program. The second issue is the
emulation of processing elements. Data parallel programs often
assume a very large number of processing elements. If these programs are to run efficiently on a multicomputer with far fewer
physical processors, then there must be an efficient mechanism
for emulating processing elements on physical processors. The
third issue is message passing optimization. Because message-
passing overhead is often significant on contemporary multicomputers, the compiler must take every opportunity to concatenate
multiple short messages into a single, longer message.

4.1 Minimizing Processor Synchronizations

Any efficient implementation of an algorithm on a multicomputer must simultaneously balance the work among the physical
processors and minimize the number of processor interactions.
In our case, the workload is balanced through an appropriate
mapping of processing elements (e.g., data structures) to physical processors. Automatic mapping of data to processors to
balance the workload and minimize interprocessor communication is beyond the capabilities of contemporary compilers [12],
and we assume the programmer has the means to assist the compiler. Automatic methods of minimizing processor interactions
have been studied with more success, and in the following paragraphs we explain how a SIMD-to-SPMD compiler can perform
this task.

Assuming that we spread processing elements around the
processors of the multicomputer, and that the sequential code is
executed by one additional special-purpose processing element,
the potential communication requirements of an SIMD program
can be traced to those points at which processing elements read
or write values to or from each other. Recall that in the C*
language expressions can refer to values stored in arbitrary processing elements. All variable declarations state, implicitly or
explicitly, which processing element holds the variable being
declared. Therefore, the location of potential communication
points can be reduced to a *type checking* problem, where the
declarations for identifiers appearing in an expression are accessed to determine the meaning of the expression.

We approach the synchronization issue by asking the following question: how much can we loosen the synchronization requirements of the language without affecting the behavior of programs? If a set of processing elements were executing the same
block of code and were only accessing their own local variables,
it would not matter if they synchronized after every statement,
after every other statement, or only at the end of the block.
However, if halfway through the block each processing element
reads a value from its neighbor, the processors must be synchronized prior to accessing their neighbor's memory, in order
to guarantee that the value retrieved by each processor is the
same as it would be under a fully synchronous implementation.
Hence the synchronization points are the points at which we
identify message passing is potentially needed. Synchronization
is incorporated into the message passing primitives.

Parallel looping constructs may require additional synchronization. If the loop body does not require any message passing,
then no synchronization is necessary for the loop. Since the processing elements executing the loop do not interact, it does not
matter if they are executing different iterations of the loop concurrently. Active processing elements only need to synchronize
just before they interact.

If the parallel loop body does require message passing, the
processors must be synchronized every iteration prior to the message passing step. Because our message passing primitives require the active participation of all physical processors, we must
guarantee that if any processing elements are still executing the
loop, all physical processors must be executing at least the message passing primitive required by the loop. In other words, no
processing element can execute the statement after the loop until all processing elements have exited the loop. This constraint
forces all processing elements to communicate each iteration in
order to compute a global logical *OR* of the processing elements'
Boolean loop control values. A processing element can exit the
loop only when the global logical *OR* is *false*. Since this global
OR operation is only required when there is message passing
occurring inside the loop, we bundle the global *OR* operation in
with the required message, allowing us to say that the points at
which messages are being sent are exactly the points at which
the processors perform a barrier synchronization.

Of course, a processing element does not actually execute
the body of the loop after its local loop control value has gone

The C* construct:

```
while (condition) {
    statement_list₁;
    communication;
    statement_list₂;
}
```

is translated into the following C code:

```
temp = TRUE;
do {
    if (temp) {
        temp = condition;
    }
    if (temp) {
        statement_list₁;
    }
    communication;
    gtemp = global_or(temp)
    if (temp) {
        statement_list₂;
    }
} while (gtemp);
```

Figure 1: Translation of C* while loop.

to *false*. Rather, the physical processor on which it resides participates in the message passing and the global *OR* operation. This means that our C* compiler must rewrite the control structure of input programs. Figure 1 illustrates how while loops are rewritten.

The requirement that all physical processors must actively participate in any message passing operation forces our compiler to rewrite all control statements that have inner statements requiring message passing. We must rewrite the statement in order to bring the message passing operations to the surface of the control structure. Figure 2 illustrates how an if statement is handled.

Communication steps buried inside nested control structures are pulled out of each enclosing structure until they reach the outermost level. Figure 3 shows a nested if statement.

The technique just described will not handle arbitrary control flow graphs. For this reason we have not implemented the **goto** statement. We can, however, handle the **break** and **continue** statements.

We want to emphasize that processor synchronizations occur only when processing elements interact. No additional synchronizations are needed to support control flow. This is the primary reason why our new compiler generates more efficient code than our first compiler [7].

The C* construct:

```
if (condition) {
    statement_list₁;
    communication;
    statement_list₂;
}
```

is translated into the following C code:

```
temp = condition;
if (temp) {
    statement_list₁;
}
communication;
if (temp) {
    statement_list₂;
}
```

Figure 2: Translation of simple if statement.

The C* construct:

```
if (condition₁) {
    statement_list₁;
    if (condition₂) {
        statement_list₂;
        communication;
        statement_list₃;
    }
    statement_list₄;
}
```

is translated into the following C code:

```
temp1 = condition₁;
if (temp1) {
    statement_list₁;
}
temp2 = temp1;
if (temp2) {
    temp2 = condition₂;
    statement_list₂;
}
communication;
if (temp2) {
    statement_list₃;
}
if (temp1) {
    statement_list₄;
}
```

Figure 3: Translation of nested if statements.

4.2 Efficiently Emulating Processing Elements

Once the message-passing routines have been brought to the outermost level of the program, emulation of processing elements is straightforward. The compiler puts for loops around the blocks of code that have been delimited by message passing/synchronization steps. Since within the delimited blocks there is no message passing, there is no interaction between processing elements. It makes no difference semantically in which order the processing elements located on a particular physical processor execute.

4.3 Optimizing Message-Passing

A primary goal of the compiler is to minimize the number of messages passed, because message initiation is a relatively expensive operation on a multicomputer. This section discusses a set of message-passing optimizations. We expect to add to this list as we get further experience with C* programs.

One class of messages is eliminated by keeping copies of the sequential code and data on each physical processor. Every physical processor executes the sequential code. Note that this adds nothing to the execution time of the program. If a single physical processor executed the code while the other physical processors sat idle, the execution time would be the same. Because every physical processor has copies of the sequential variables, it can access sequential data by doing a local memory fetch. In other words, assigning the value of a mono variable to a poly variable can be done without any message passing.

By putting a copy of the sequential code and data on each physical processor, we are assuming that mono values are retrieved more often than they are assigned. With our design the retrieval of a mono is free—every physical processor has a local copy of the mono that can be accessed by a processing element without message passing. However, when a processing element stores to a mono variable, the value may have to be broadcast to update all physical processors' copy of the mono. If an analysis of the control flow indicates that all processing elements are active for the store to a mono, and the value being stored is known at compile time to be the same on all processing elements, then the compiler can omit the subsequent broadcast.

The tracking of mono values through a simple data flow analysis can be used to "sequentialize" loop constructs to avoid possible loop synchronizations. For instance, if the loop control variable is initialized to a mono value, the loop termination expression is known to evaluate to the same value on all processing elements, and the loop increment step is the same for all virtual processors, then the compiler knows in advance that all virtual processors will execute the loop the same number of times. No global OR of the loop termination expression value need be done. In addition, no virtual processor emulation of the control portion of the loop structure is required. The for loop that is introduced to emulate virtual processors can be moved inside of the C* loop.

This type of analysis should also be applied to expressions that require message passing. If the compiler determines that all processing elements are requesting the same piece of "non-local" data , then the data should be requested only once by a physical processor and shared among the resident processing elements.

Message-passing expressions should be examined by a common subexpression detection phase of the compiler. Since C* programmers refer to "non-local" values by writing an expression, equivalent expressions should cause the compiler to analyze the intervening code to see if it could affect the value of the expression. If not, then the distant value should only be retrieved once with the expensive message-passing step, and a local copy of the value should be kept for the second reference.

Another optimization is performed by viewing message passing as a possible vector operation. That is, if a block of data (such as a row of a matrix) must be sent to another processor, the whole block can be sent in one message, rather than as a series of shorter messages. The amount of data transferred is essentially identical, but the message-passing overhead is drastically reduced. Since this is a vectorization operation, it can be performed using well-known techniques designed to be used with sequential machines that have vector instructions.

A similar optimization can be performed upon the code generated to support processing elements. Instead of each active processing element sending an individual message, the message bodies of all active processing elements can be gathered together and shipped at once. The motivation once again is to reduce the number of communication steps.

4.4 Summary

To summarize, the compiler must first locate the points at which message passing is required. These points are identical to the synchronization points. Therefore, our message passing primitives also synchronize the processors. Second, the compiler must transform the control structure of the input program to bring message-passing primitives to the outermost level. In order to allow a single physical processor to emulate a number of processing elements, the compiler must insert for loops around the blocks of code that are delimited by the calls to the message passing primitives. Finally, data flow analysis can be used to eliminate some calls on message-passing routines and to combine multiple shorter messages into single, longer messages whenever possible.

5 Experimental Results

To demonstrate the efficiency that can be achieved by SIMD programs executing on a hypercube multicomputer, we present in Figure 4 the speedup achieved by three hand-compiled C* programs. The three programs are: Mandelbrot set calculation, matrix multiplication, and Gaussian elimination. The Mandelbrot program computes the colors of a 128×128 image representing a square of the complex plane centered around the origin and having sides of length 4. The matrix multiplication program multiplies two 128×128 integer matrices. The Gaussian elimination program reduces a dense system of 256 linear equations with 256 unknowns.

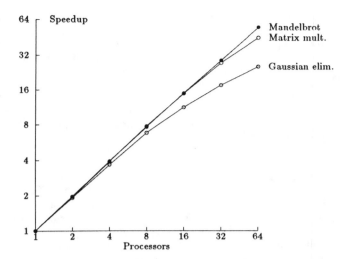

Figure 4: Speedup achieved by three hand-compiled C* programs executing on an NCUBE/seven multicomputer.

The first two programs—Mandelbrot set calculation and matrix multiplication—have a high degree of parallelism and a simple control structure. It is relatively straightforward for the C* compiler to generate code comparable in performance to hand-written C code. The third C* program, Gaussian elimination with partial pivoting, has a good measure of sequentiality to it, and processing elements exchange data frequently. In order to produce efficient target code, a compiler must be able to perform numerous message-passing optimizations. After performing the code optimizations described in the previous section, the resulting Gaussian elimination program is equal in performance to the best known hand-coded C program on the NCUBE.

6 Summary

We have discussed how a compiler can translate data parallel SIMD programs into SPMD-style MIMD programs and have presented evidence that high efficiency is an attainable goal. We are in the process of implementing a C*-to-C compiler for the NCUBE series of hypercube multicomputers. At this time the compiler translates C* programs into SPMD-style C programs, but it does not perform all the message passing optimizations necessary to produce highly efficient C code. Once the optimizing compiler has been completed, we will use it to help us determine which problems seem most suitable for solution via data parallel algorithms.

We do not see data parallel programming as the only solution to the problem of programming MIMD computers, but we do see it as a solution, particularly in the short run. We feel there is a role for an imperative language that is explicitly parallel, yet quite similar to existing sequential languages. An easy-to-learn data parallel language such as C* may help popularize parallel computing.

Acknowledgements This work was supported by National Science Foundation grants DCR-8514493, CCR-8814662, and CCR-8906622.

References

[1] D. Callahan and K. Kennedy. Compiling programs for distributed-memory multiprocessors. *The Journal of Supercomputing*, 2:151–169, 1988.

[2] M. Flynn. Very high-speed computing systems. *Proceedings of the IEEE*, 54(12):1901–1909, December 1966.

[3] G. Fox. What have we learnt from using real parallel machines to solve real problems? In *Third Conference on Hypercube Concurrent Computers and Applications*, pages 897–955, 1988.

[4] W. Hillis and G. Steele Jr. Data parallel algorithms. *Communications of the ACM*, 29(12):1170–1183, December 1986.

[5] K.-C. Li and H. Schwetman. Vector C: a vector processing language. *Journal of Parallel and Distributed Computing*, 2:132–169, 1985.

[6] R. Perrott, D. Crookes, P. Milligan, and W. Martin Purdy. A compiler for an array and vector processing language. *IEEE Transactions on Software Engineering*, 11:471–478, May 1985.

[7] M. Quinn, P. Hatcher, and K. Jourdenais. Compiling C* programs for a hypercube multicomputer. In *SIGPLAN PPEALS 1988, Parallel Programming: Experience with Applications, Languages, and Systems*, pages 57–65, July 1987.

[8] A. Reeves and D. Bergmark. Parallel Pascal and the FPS hypercube supercomputer. In *International Conference on Parallel Processing*, pages 385–388, 1987.

[9] A. Rogers and K. Pingali. Process decomposition through locality of reference. In *SIGPLAN '89 Conference on Programming Language Design and Implementation*, pages 69–80, June 1989.

[10] J. Rose and G. Steele. *C*: An Extended C Language for Data Parallel Programming*. Technical Report PL 87-5, Thinking Machines Corporation, Cambridge, MA, 1986.

[11] B. Stroustrup. *The C++ Programming Language*. Addison-Wesley, Reading, MA, 1986.

[12] M. Wolfe. *Semi-Automatic Domain Decomposition*. Technical Report, Oregon Graduate Center, Beaverton, OR, 1989.

Computation of Interprocedural Definition and Use Dependencies*

Mary Jean Harrold   Mary Lou Soffa

Department of Computer Science
University of Pittsburgh
Pittsburgh, PA 15260

Abstract - The detection of various dependencies that exist among the definitions and uses of variables in a program is necessary in many language processing tools. This work considers the computation of definition-use dependencies that reach across procedure boundaries. In particular, we present efficient techniques to compute interprocedural definition-use and use-definition chains and to incrementally update the chains when a change is made in a procedure. Intraprocedural definition and use information for each procedure is first abstracted and used to construct an interprocedural flow graph. The intraprocedural information is then propagated in two phases throughout the interprocedural flow graph to obtain the complete set of interprocedural reaching definitions and reachable uses. Interprocedural definition-use and use-definition chains are computed from this reaching information. The technique handles the interprocedural effects of the flow of data caused by both reference parameters and global variables, as well as supports separate compilation even in the presence of recursion. The technique has been implemented using a Sun 3/50 Workstation and incorporated into an interprocedural data flow tester.

1. Introduction

An important component of compilation is static analysis, which provides information about the potential flow of data or control throughout a program. Although data flow analysis is traditionally performed in the last two phases of a compiler, namely code optimization and code generation, it has also become an integral part of other language processing tools such as parallelizers, editors, debuggers, anomaly checkers and testers. *Intra*procedural data flow analysis considers the flow of data within a procedure, assuming some initial approximation about reference parameters and global variables at call sites. The current emphasis on modularity has also created a need to consider *inter*procedural analysis

to determine the flow of data across procedure boundaries for use in interprocedural code optimization, generation and parallelization. In order to optimize or parallelize across procedure call sites, information that summarizes the effects that procedure calls have on the data flow of reference parameters and global variables in the calling procedure is usually all that is needed. This summary information typically specifies whether reference parameters and global variables are used, modified or preserved by a call to the procedure.

Although the above summary data flow information is adequate for many applications, it is insufficient for all applications. One such application is data flow testing[6] in which confidence in the correctness of a variable assignment at a point in a program is dependent on whether some test data has caused execution of a sub-path from a definition to points where the variable's value is used. Test data adequacy criteria, based on the data flow in the program, are used to select particular definition-use (def-use) pairs that are identified as the test case requirements for the program. Thus, data flow testing requires the computation of *def-use chains* that contain the locations of all uses of a particular definition of a variable in order to construct the def-use pairs that are used to select paths in the program for testing. Incremental updates to the data flow information require the computation of *use-def chains*, which contain the locations of all possible definitions of a particular use. The computation of definitions and uses that reach across procedure boundaries (i.e., *inter*procedural def-use and use-def chains) is needed for interprocedural data flow testing and its incremental update.

Analysis techniques to compute def-use and use-def chains intraprocedurally are well known [1] and have been used in various tools, including data flow testers. An interprocedural def-use chain for a definition in some procedure **P** consists of the locations of all uses of the definition, taking into account procedures that are reachable from **P** along both call and return sequences. Similarly, an interprocedural use-def chain for a use consists of the locations of all definitions of the use, taking into account procedures that are reachable from **P** along both call and return sequences. Thus, the computation of the

* This work was partially supported by the National Science Foundation under Grant CCR-8801104 to the University of Pittsburgh.

297

interprocedural def-use or use-def chains requires the tracking of definitions and uses of global variables and formal and actual reference parameters that reach across call and return sites.

The modularization that procedures provide makes their separate compilation an attractive feature. When a change is made to a procedure, the ideal is to recompile, and thus, reanalyze, only that procedure. However, a change made in one procedure can have a far reaching effect on the interprocedural definition and use dependencies. One approach to handling this is to reanalyze all of the procedures in a program after a change. A better approach, and the approach used in this work, is to incrementally update the interprocedural information based on intraprocedural changes and thus, limit the reanalysis of procedures.

This paper presents an efficient interprocedural analysis technique that computes interprocedural def-use and use-def chains. The approach taken is modeled after the computation of intraprocedural definition and use dependencies. Individual procedures are first analyzed in any order to abstract the intraprocedural information that is used to construct an *interprocedural flow graph* (IFG). This information is then propagated throughout the program via the IFG while taking into account the calling context of called procedures. In order to be applicable to large programs, the data flow analysis technique supports separate compilation in that procedures are analyzed in isolation of one another. The interprocedural data flow analysis technique computes interprocedural dependencies for recursive procedures even in the presence of separate compilation. The ability to handle recursion makes the data flow analysis technique applicable to a wider range of programs. We also briefly present our technique to incrementally update the interprocedural definition and use information to reflect the effects of an edit in a procedure. Thus, a change in a procedure does not force the reanalysis of the code of any procedure, other than the changed procedure, in order to update the interprocedural definition and use information. [7]

In the remainder of this paper, we focus on the analysis of data dependencies among reference parameters. Related work and the problems of gathering interprocedural definition and use information are discussed in the next section. Section 3 gives an overview of the interprocedural dependency algorithm along with a discussion of the program representation. The technique is then demonstrated using an example. Section 5 presents the details of our algorithm. The incorporation of changes in the data flow information without reanalysis of uneffected procedures is briefly described in Section 6. Concluding remarks are given in Section 7.

2. Background

The problems involved in computing interprocedural data dependencies include accommodating the separate compilation of procedures, handling programs with recursive procedures and ensuring that the data dependencies reflect only def-use pairings for possible control paths through the program. The program in Figure 1 is used to illustrate these difficulties. To assist the reader in tracking the def-use dependencies, each procedure's *control flow graph* is depicted beneath its code. Each node in a control flow graph represents a basic block in the program consisting of statements that are executed sequentially.[1] Edges in the graph represent the flow of control between the basic blocks. To simplify the intraprocedural analysis, each call site is represented by a single basic block. For ease of reference, basic blocks in the flow graphs are numbered consecutively throughout the program and dashed boxes indicate basic blocks containing procedure calls.

In Figure 1, information about the interprocedural flow of data in procedures P1 and P2 is required to determine that the definition of variable X in B_1 may-be-preserved[11] over the call to procedure P1 in B_2 and consequently reaches the use of X in B_3. The analysis to provide this information must also consider the call to procedure P2 from procedure P1. In this case, interprocedural information is being used to determine the local effects of the procedure call on the *calling* procedure. This requires either (1) that the information about called procedures be incorporated at call sites during the analysis of the calling procedure or (2) that an estimate of the information about called procedures be used during initial analysis of the calling procedure and that this information be updated when more accurate data flow information is determined. The problem with the first method is that if procedures are processed in any order or are recursive, incomplete information may be available about called procedures at call sites. Thus, the better approach is to process each procedure individually to abstract the intraprocedural information and then propagate this local information to obtain the interprocedural data flow information.

Tracking of the definition of X in B_1 over procedure calls and returns is required to determine that this definition of X reaches the uses of Y in B_7, B_8, B_{10} and B_{11} in P1 and the uses of Z in B_{12} and B_{13} in P2. In this case, interprocedural information is being used to determine the interprocedural dependencies in the *called* procedures. This requires that the data flow information be propagated throughout the program.

The preservation of the *calling context* of called procedures is important during the computation of the def-use dependencies. Preserving the calling context requires that the tracking of the def-use pairs over the returns from procedures traverses only those paths

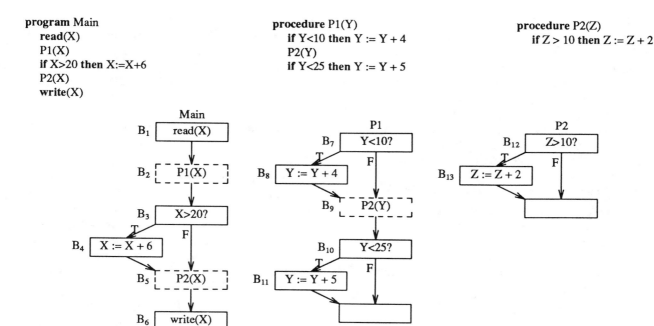

```
program Main                    procedure P1(Y)                    procedure P2(Z)
  read(X)                         if Y<10 then Y := Y + 4            if Z > 10 then Z := Z + 2
  P1(X)                           P2(Y)
  if X>20 then X:=X+6             if Y<25 then Y := Y + 5
  P2(X)
  write(X)
```

Figure 1. Example Program and its Control Flow Graphs

through the program that agree with the call sequence for some possible control path. Consider the definition of X in B_4 that reaches the call to procedure P2 in B_5. Since there is a path through procedure P2 on which Z is not defined, the definition of X in B_4 can reach the end of procedure P2. However, since there are two calls to P2, there are two return paths from procedure P2: one that returns directly to Main and the other that returns indirectly through P1. Ignoring the call sequence suggests that the definition in B_4 has uses in B_3, B_4 and B_6. However, closer inspection of the control paths through the program reveals that this definition reaches the end of P2, and subsequently back into Main, only when it is called directly from Main. Thus, this definition can only reach the use of X in B_6. The calling context must be considered in order to obtain more precise def-use chains.

A number of interprocedural data flow analysis techniques have been developed that are useful for parallelization, optimization and maintenance of programs. None of these techniques compute adequate information to solve the reaching definitions or reachable uses problem that we address. Some of the existing techniques[3, 5, 11, 14] provide summary data flow information for use in determining the local effects of called procedures at call sites. These techniques do not provide information about the locations of interprocedural definitions and uses in other procedures in the program. A technique that processes nonrecursive procedures in reverse invocation order[2] incorporates the abstracted information about called procedures at call sites to obtain the local reaching information. This technique requires

that a procedure be processed only after those that it calls have been processed, which imposes an ordering on the procedure processing. This order restriction results in a penalty when changes are made in a procedure. In addition, recursive procedures cannot be handled with the ordering restriction.

Another related technique[4] uses a graph representation of the program (i.e., the *program summary graph*) to provide flow sensitive interprocedural data flow information that solves the interprocedural KILL, MOD and USE problems. For example, the KILL of each formal parameter in a procedure is a boolean that indicates whether the actual parameter is redefined along all paths by a call to the procedure. Thus, for the program in Example 1, this technique will determine that a variable bound to parameter Y in P1 or parameter Z in P2 is not KILLed by calls to those procedures. However, this technique cannot be used to compute the interprocedural def-use pairs since the program summary graph does not contain information about the locations of the definitions and uses in the program. Further, the algorithms do not handle the preservation of the calling context of called procedures that is required for the computation.

A third technique[8] provides interprocedural slicing of nonrecursive programs using the *system dependence graph* that combines the dependence graphs for each procedure to provide a representation of the program. It also handles the problem of preserving the calling context of called procedures in order to provide more precise slices. The algorithm consists of two phases, each of which visits a subset of the nodes in the graph. It is possible to find the required def-use chains by locating the interprocedural uses and determining a slice for the variables at each of these points. Clearly, this method requires that the slicing algorithm be run for each interprocedural use in the program. Our algorithm also consists of two phases, each of which visits a subset of the nodes in the IFG. However, our technique computes all of the required data dependency information for nonrecursive procedures in one iteration of our algorithm in contrast to the slicing algorithm that requires one iteration for each interprocedural use in the program. In addition, our technique handles recursive procedures.

Finally, use of the *super graph*[12] or in-line substitution to compute the interprocedural def-use and use-def chains is prohibitive for large programs because neither of these techniques support separate compilation of procedures. A further restriction of in-line substitution is that recursive procedures cannot be handled.

3. Overview of the Algorithm

The algorithm to compute the interprocedural def-use and use-def chains for a program is modeled after the iterative data flow technique used at the intraprocedural level: (1) local information about definitions and uses is gathered at points in the program that correspond to regions of code and attached to nodes in the graph representation of the program, (2) with this local information, iterative techniques are used to solve data flow equations for reaching definitions and reachable uses by propagating the local information throughout the graph, and (3) the def-use and use-def chains are computed by associating the local information gathered in (1) with the propagated information determined in (2). At the *intra*procedural level, the regions of code are basic blocks, the definition and use information is gathered at points before and after these blocks, and the graph is a control flow graph. At the *inter*procedural level, the regions represent parts of the program that are of interest interprocedurally (i.e., the procedure control points), the definition and use information is gathered at points before and after these regions, and the graph is an interprocedural flow graph. We present an overview of the algorithm to compute interprocedural def-use chains followed by a discussion of the program representation. The technique to compute interprocedural use-def chains is similar and is thus omitted.

3.1. Steps in the Algorithm

Step 1: Construction of Interprocedural Flow Graph (IFG) subgraphs to abstract control flow information for each procedure in a program. A subgraph is constructed for each procedure. Subgraph nodes represent regions of code associated with points that are of interest interprocedurally and subgraph edges represent the control flow in the procedure. Local information is computed for formal and actual parameters and is attached to appropriate nodes in the subgraph.

Step 2: Construction of an IFG to represent the interprocedural control flow in the program. The subgraphs for the procedures, obtained in step 1, are combined to create the IFG. Edges that represent the bindings of formal and actual parameters in both called and calling procedures are added to get the partial IFG. May-be-preserved information is computed for each procedure using the partially constructed IFG and edges that represent this information are added to complete the construction of the IFG.

Step 3: Propagation throughout the IFG to obtain interprocedural information. The local information at each node is propagated in two phases throughout the IFG. The resulting information consists of the interprocedural definitions that reach (i.e., *reaching definitions*) and the interprocedural uses that can be reached from (i.e., *reachable uses*) the parts of the program represented by the nodes in the IFG.

Step 4: Computation of the interprocedural def-use chains. Interprocedural def-use chains are computed using both the local information computed in step 1 and the propagated interprocedural information computed in step 3.

3.2. Program Representation

A program, composed of a number of procedures, is represented by an *interprocedural flow graph*, or IFG, which based on the program summary graph.[4] The four types of nodes in the IFG that correspond to different regions of code in the program are entry, exit, call and return. Intraprocedural, or local, information is computed about definitions of formal and actual parameters that reach, and uses of formal and actual parameters that can be reached from, these regions and is attached to the appropriate nodes in the graph. For a call node, the region consists of the code from the beginning of a procedure to a call site while the region for an exit node consists of the code for the entire procedure. An entry node represents the code for the entire procedure, and a return node represents the code from a return site to the end of the procedure. At entry and exit points of a procedure, local information is abstracted for formal parameters while at call and return sites, local information is abstracted about actual parameters involved in the call. There is a call node and return node for each actual parameter at a call site and an exit node and entry node for each formal parameter in a procedure.

The computation of the sets of definitions in the procedure that reach the ends of the appropriate regions of code represented by nodes in the IFG, designated the DEF sets for the nodes, is similar to the computation of the generated definition sets for basic blocks in intraprocedural data flow analysis. Thus, the definitions that reach a call site constitute the DEF sets for the call nodes associated with the call site while the definitions that reach the end of the procedure become the DEF sets of the exit node associated with the end of the procedure. A similar situation exists for reachable uses. Information about interprocedural uses that can be reached from the beginning of a procedure and from the return from a procedure is gathered. The computation of the sets of uses, UPEXP, that can be reached from the beginning of regions of code represented by entry and return nodes in the IFG, is similar to the computation of the upwards exposed sets of uses for basic blocks in intraprocedural data flow analysis. The UPEXP sets at entry or return nodes represent the sets of uses that can be reached from the start of, or return from, a procedure respectively. The DEF sets for entry and return nodes and the UPEXP sets for call and exit nodes have no meaning interprocedurally and are given a null value for ease of propagating the data flow.

In an IFG, procedure entry and procedure exit are denoted by $entry_f^P$ and $exit_f^P$ nodes respectively, and both nodes are created for every formal parameter f of every procedure P. Procedure invocation and procedure return are represented by $call_a^{P \rightarrow Q}$ and $return_a^{P \rightarrow Q}$ nodes respectively and both nodes are created for every actual parameter a of every call from procedure P to procedure Q. Since each node represents a single variable, the DEF and UPEXP sets correspond to a single formal or actual parameter. Additionally, the members of these sets are definitions and uses in P. The DEF and UPEXP sets are defined as follows, where a represents an actual parameter, f represents a formal parameter and definitions and uses are contained in P:

$$DEF[n] = \begin{cases} definitions_a \text{ reaching } P \rightarrow Q, \text{ n is } call_a^{P \rightarrow Q} \\ definitions_f \text{ reaching the end of } P, \text{ n is } exit_f^P \\ \phi, \text{ otherwise} \end{cases}$$

$$UPEXP[n] = \begin{cases} uses_f \text{ reachable from } P \text{ start, n is } entry_f^P \\ uses_a \text{ reachable from } P \rightarrow Q \text{ return, n is } return_a^{P \rightarrow Q} \\ \phi, \text{ otherwise} \end{cases}$$

Binding edges in the IFG from call nodes to entry nodes and exit nodes to return nodes correspond to the bindings of formal and actual parameters. Reaching edges from both entry and return nodes to call and exit nodes abstract the control information from the procedure by indicating that a definition that reaches the source of the edge also reaches the sink of the edge. A reaching edge is strictly intraprocedural since it is computed without incorporating the control structure of called procedures at call sites. The computation assumes that there is no use of an actual parameter in the called procedure and that the parameter is redefined in the called procedure. Inter-reaching edges from call nodes to return nodes abstract the control information about the called procedures at call sites. This edge indicates that a definition that reaches the procedure call may-be-

preserved after the return from the procedure. The inter-reaching edges allow the calling context of the called procedures to be preserved during propagation and permit the interprocedural data flow information to be updated incrementally without requiring reanalysis of each affected procedure's flow graph.

4. Example

To illustrate the IFG and the technique, consider the program given in Figure 2, which differs from the program in Figure 1 only in the numbering of statements. We describe the construction of the IFG subgraphs followed by a discussion of the connection of the subgraphs to form the complete IFG. In the IFG subgraphs, circles represent call and return nodes, doubled circles represent entry and exit nodes and dashed lines represent reaching edges. During the first step of the algorithm, the subgraphs *i*, *ii*, and *iii* are constructed for program Main and procedures P1 and P2 respectively. Consider subgraph *ii*, representing procedure P1, where nodes 3, 4, 5 and 6 are created for the call to P2, return from P2, entry to P1 and exit from P1 respectively. Since a definition of an actual parameter associated with formal parameter Y that reaches the beginning of procedure P1 also reaches the call to procedure P2 where it is used as a parameter, reaching edge (5,3) is created. For node 3, inspection of the procedure reveals that the definition of Y in *s6* is the only definition that reaches the call site and thus, DEF[3] is {Y in *s6*}. For simplicity, we use only {*s6*} to unambiguously denote this set.

Next, consider node 6. Since it is assumed that definitions are not preserved over procedure calls, the only definition reaching the end of procedure P1 that can be determined locally is the definition of Y in *s8*. Note that since the associated formal parameter Z may-be-preserved over a call to procedure P2, the definition in *s6* also reaches the end of procedure P1. This information cannot be computed locally and thus, is not part of the DEF set, but it is obtained during the propagation step. The use of Y in *s6* is reachable from the beginning of the procedure and thus, *s6* is in UPEXP[5]. The use of Y in *s8* is reachable from the return from procedure P2, and thus, Y in *s8* is in UPEXP[4]. Finally, the reaching edge (4,6) indicates that there is a path where Y is not redefined from the return from procedure P2 in *s7* to the end of procedure P1.

In the second step, subgraphs *i, ii* and *iii* are connected by adding the binding edges to connect formal and actual parameters. Figure 3 gives the completed IFG. In the main program, nodes 9 and 10 represent the call and return associated with the procedure call in *s2* and nodes 7 and 8 represent the procedure call in *s4*. Edges (3,1) and (2,4) indicate the binding of actual parameter Y in procedure P1 to formal parameter Z in procedure P2. Additional binding edges added during step 2 are: edges (9,5) and (6,10) representing the call to

```
program Main              procedure P1(Y)              procedure P2(Z)
  s1: read(X)               s6: if Y<10 then Y := Y + 4    s9: if Z > 10 then Z := Z + 2
  s2: P1(X)                 s7: P2(Y)
  s3: if X>20 then X:=X+6   s8: if Y<25 then Y := Y + 5
  s4: P2(X)
  s5: write(X)
```

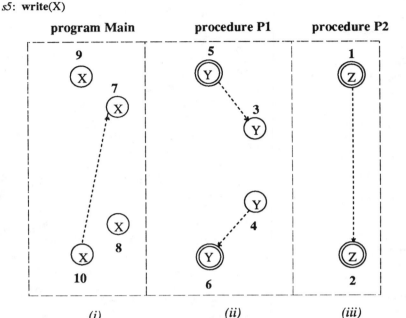

| program Main | procedure P1 | procedure P2 | local data flow information |

node	DEF	UPEXP
1	ϕ	$\{s9\}$
2	$\{s9\}$	ϕ
3	$\{s6\}$	ϕ
4	ϕ	$\{s8\}$
5	ϕ	$\{s6\}$
6	$\{s8\}$	ϕ
7	$\{s3\}$	ϕ
8	ϕ	$\{s5\}$
9	$\{s1\}$	ϕ
10	ϕ	$\{s3\}$

◎ entry/exit nodes

◯ call/return nodes

- - - ▶ reaching edges

(i)   *(ii)*   *(iii)*

Figure 2. Example Program and its IFG Subgraphs

procedure P1 in Main and edges (7,1) and (2,8) representing the call to procedure P2 in Main. An iterative algorithm[4] is used to compute the may-be-preserved information for formal parameters Y and Z represented by nodes 1 and 5 respectively in the graph. Since the results of this analysis indicate that information reaching entry nodes may also reach the exit nodes, the associated formal parameters may-be-preserved over calls to the procedures. Thus, inter-reaching edges are created at the corresponding call sites: inter-reaching edge (9,10) at the call to procedure P1 in Main, inter-reaching edge (7,8) at the call to procedure P2 in Main, and inter-reaching edge (3,4) at the call to procedure P2 in procedure P1. The addition of the binding and inter-reaching edges completes the construction of the IFG.

During the third step of the algorithm, the DEF and UPEXP sets are propagated throughout the IFG to get the definitions that reach, and uses that can be reached from, points in the program. This information is attached to the nodes in the IFG. Consider node 3 in procedure P1 that represents the call to procedure P2. The uses of variables that are bound to Y and can be reached from this point in the program consist of the uses of X in *s3* and *s5*, the use of Y in *s8*, and the uses of Z in *s9*. The use in *s8* is reached over the inter-reaching

edge since Y is preserved over the call to procedure Z, the uses in *s9* are reached over the call to procedure P2, and the uses in *s3* and *s5* are reached over returns to Main. The table included in Figure 3 gives the IN_U and OUT_U set that are computed during the propagation step.

Finally, the interprocedural def-use chains are computed. The def-use chain of the definition of Y in *s6* is the set of uses that can be reached from that point or $\{s3, s5, s8, s9\}$.

5. The Algorithm

The algorithm that computes the four steps for the interprocedural def-use chains is given in Figure 4. In the following sections, the steps in the algorithm are more fully described. Discussion first centers on the analysis of programs with no recursive procedures to illustrate the efficiency of the algorithm. In Section 5.2, the application to recursive procedures is discussed.

5.1. Details of the Algorithm
Step 1: Constructing the IFG Subgraphs

In the first step, each procedure **P** is processed once and its IFG subgraph is constructed. Thus, for each formal parameter **f** in **P**, the $entry_f^P$ and $exit_f^P$ nodes are created. In addition, for each actual parameter **a** at call sites in **P** to procedure **Q**, $call_a^{P \rightarrow Q}$ and $return_a^{P \rightarrow Q}$ nodes

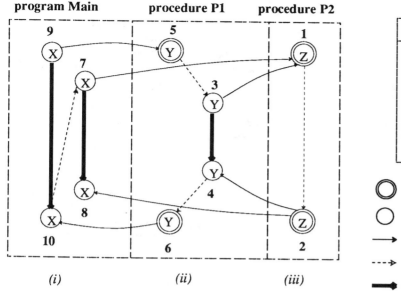

program Main	procedure P1	procedure P2

propagated data flow information

node	IN_U	OUT_U
1-3	{s3,s5,s8,s9}	{s3,s5,s8,s9}
4	{s3,s5,s8,s9}	{s3,s5,s9}
5	{s3,s5,s6,s8,s9}	{s3,s5,s8,s9}
6	{s3,s5,s9}	{s3,s5,s9}
7	{s5,s9}	{s5,s9}
8	{s5}	ϕ
9	{s3,s5,s6,s8,s9}	{s3,s5,s6,s8,s9}
10	{s3,s5,s9}	{s5,s9}

⊚ entry/exit nodes

◯ call/return nodes

⟶ binding edges

--→ reaching edges

⟹ inter-reaching edges

Figure 3. The IFG for Program Main in Figure 2

are created. Intraprocedural data flow analysis is performed on **P** and the local information is abstracted. The local information consists of the DEF and UPEXP sets for regions of code in **P** along with the control information about **P**. The DEF and UPEXP sets are attached to nodes in the IFG subgraph, and the control information is used to construct the reaching edges. In order to compute the DEF and UPEXP sets, basic blocks are added at the beginning (i.e., the *initial* block) and at the end (i.e., the *final* block) of the control flow graph for **P**. During the intraprocedural data flow analysis of **P**, reaching information is gathered at these basic blocks. For $call_a^{P \to Q}$, the DEF set consists of the definitions of **a** in **P** that reach the basic block containing the call to **Q**; for the $exit_f^P$, the DEF set consists of the definitions of **f** in **P** that reach the final block in **P**. The UPEXP set for the $entry_f^P$ consists of the uses of **f** that can be reached from the end of the initial block in **P**; the UPEXP set for the $return_a^{P \to Q}$ consists of the uses of **a** that can be reached from the end of the basic block containing the call to **Q** in **P**.

To compute the control information for **P**, dummy definitions of the formal parameters are added to the initial block and dummy uses of the formal parameters are added to the final block. Dummy definitions and uses of actual parameters are also added to the basic blocks containing the call sites. These dummy definitions and uses facilitate the gathering of the reaching information during the intraprocedural analysis of **P**. For example, if a dummy definition of formal parameter **f** in the initial block reaches the beginning of the final block, a reaching edge is constructed that connects the entry node for **f** with the exit node for **f** in the IFG subgraph for **P**.

Step 2: Constructing the IFG

After all procedures have been processed, the IFG is constructed by creating the appropriate binding edges among actual and formal parameters in the procedures. The inter-reaching edges are obtained by processing the graph using an iterative algorithm[4] to determine whether, for each $entry_f^P$, **f** may-be-preserved. Inter-reaching edges are created for each call-return pair whose associated entry node's may-be-preserved value is *true*. This step results in the completion of the construction of the IFG.

Step 3: Propagating the Local Information

After the first two steps are completed, the IFG, with local information attached to its nodes, is available. The next step is to propagate the local information throughout the IFG to obtain interprocedural use sets for each node in the graph. *Interprocedural reachable use* sets represent the upwards exposed uses of non-local variables located in other procedures that can be reached from the beginning and end of each region of code represented by nodes in the graph. These interprocedural reachable uses are computed by propagating the UPEXP[n] sets backward throughout the graph as far as they can be reached while taking into account the calling context of the called procedures. We use the notation $IN_U[n]$ to refer to the interprocedural reachable use set that can be reached from the beginning of the region of code represented by node **n**; we use the notation $OUT_U[n]$ to refer to the interprocedural reachable use set that can be reached from the end of the region of code represented by node **n**.

```
algorithm ComputeChains(G, P)
input       G: an IFG
            P: a collection of procedures
declare     G_i: an IFG subgraph
            NODESET: set of nodes to process
            EDGESET: set of edges to process
            ORDER: order of procedure processing
            DUC: array of def-use chains
begin
/* Step 1: subgraph construction for each procedure */
  for each P_i ∈ P do          /* process each procedure */
    for each formal f do create entry_f^{P_i}, exit_f^{P_i}
      for each actual a at P->Q do create call_a^{P→Q}, return_a^{P→Q}
      Perform intraprocedural data flow analysis on P_i
      Using the intraprocedural data flow information
          Create reaching edges for P_i
          Extract DEF[k] and UPEXP[k], k ∈ G_{P_i}
    endfor
  endfor
/* Step 2: construction of the IFG */
  Create the binding edges among the G_{P_i}
  Determine may-be-preserved information for each entry node
  Create inter-reaching edges
/* Step 3: IFG propagation to obtain global information */
  for each node n in G do          /* initialization */
    IN_U[n] = UPEXP[n]
    OUT_U[n] = φ
  endfor
  NODESET := {entry, call, return nodes in G} /* phase 1 */
  EDGESET := {all edges in G}
  ORDER := reverse invocation on the call graph
  Propagate(NODESET, EDGESET, ORDER)
  NODESET := {all nodes in G}          /* phase 2 */
  EDGESET := {allowable edges in G}
  ORDER := invocation on the call graph
  Propagate(NODESET, EDGESET, ORDER)
/* Step 4: interprocedural def-use chains computation */
  for each P_i ∈ P do
    for each definition interprocedural definition d in P_i do
      DUC[d] := φ
      if d ∈ call_a^{P→Q} then DUC[d]:=DUC[d] ∪ OUT_U[call_a^{P→Q}]
      if d ∈ exit_f^P then DUC[d] := DUC[d] ∪ OUT_U[exit_f^P]
    endfor
  endfor
end
```

Figure 4. Interprocedural Def-Use Chains Algorithm

IN_U and OUT_U for nodes in the IFG are computed in two phases to preserve the calling context of called procedures. Consider UPEXP[10] in Figure 2 that consists of the use of X in *s3*. If UPEXP[10] is propagated backward in the IFG, it would reach, among others, nodes 6, 4, 2, 1 and 7. This would mean that *s3* is reachable from the call site to P2 in *s4*. However, there is no control path through the program for which statement *s3* can be reached from this call site. The problem occurs when the use is propagated over the call binding edge (7,1) since this does not match the return context. To solve this problem, the propagation is performed in two

```
procedure Propagate(N, E, O)
begin
  for each procedure p, processed in O order do
    while data flow changes do
      for each node n of type N do
        for each node s that is a successor over E of n do
          OUT_U[n] = OUT_U[n]∪ IN_U[s]
          IN_U[n] = OUT_U[n] ∪ UPEXP[n]
        endfor
      endfor
    endwhile
  endfor
end   /* Propagate */
```

Figure 5: Local Information Propagation Procedure

phases. We first process only the entry, call and return nodes and therefore propagate the uses that can be reached in called procedures over the call binding edges, the reaching edges and the inter-reaching edges. Next, we propagate the uses that can be reached in calling procedures over the return binding edges, the reaching edges and the inter-reaching edges (i.e., the *allowable edges*.) Propagation must be restricted to these edges to prevent traversal of paths through the IFG that do not represent control paths through the program. Since we saw in the above example that propagation over the call binding edges is a problem, the inter-reaching edges allow the propagation of the uses to the call and entry nodes without traversing the call binding edges.

The interprocedural reachable use problem is formulated as a simple distributive data flow problem[10] whose lattice of solution is 'can be reached'. A use can be reached from a point in the program if there is a path in the IFG, over allowable edges, from the node representing the point to the node where UPEXP[n] contains the use. The greatest fixed point of the following data flow equations captures this fact. In phase one of the propagation, for each **n** that is an entry, a call or a return node,

$$OUT_U[n] = \bigcup_s IN_U[s], \text{ successors s of n}$$
$$IN_U[n] = OUT_U[n] \bigcup UPEXP[n].$$

In phase two of the propagation, for each n, where successors of n are over allowable edges,

$$OUT_U[n] = OUT_U[n]\bigcup_s IN_U[s], \text{ successors s of n}$$
$$IN_U[n] = OUT_U[n] \bigcup UPEXP[n].$$

The sets of data flow equations are used to compute the $IN_U[n]$ and $OUT_U[n]$ sets during the two phase propagation. Due to the edge restriction during phase two, the previous $OUT_U[n]$ is used in the computation of the new $OUT_U[n]$ during this phase. The IFG subgraphs that represent the procedures are processed one at a time in reverse invocation order on the call graph of the program for phase 1 of the propagation. The IFG subgraphs are processed one at a time in invocation order for phase 2. The equations are solved using procedure *Propagate* given in Figure 5. The parameters to *Propagate*, N, E, and O, indicate which nodes, edges and ordering are considered in the propagation. For uniformity in this presentation, the second set of equations is used in *Propagate*.

The algorithm *ComputeChains* in Figure 4 calls *Propagate* in Figure 5 to compute the uses that can be reached in called procedures throughout a program. If no cycles occur in the IFG, then the algorithm effectively orders the nodes so that the data flow information can be correctly computed in one visit to each node.

Cycles can occur in individual subgraphs or in the interconnections of the subgraphs. A cycle may occur in the subgraph for a procedure if a call site is contained in a loop in the program and there is also an inter-reaching edge connecting the call and return nodes. Iteration over the nodes in each subgraph is provided by the *Propagate* algorithm to compute the data flow information.

Cycles can also occur in the interconnections of the subgraphs when the return from one procedure reaches the call to another procedure, resulting in a reaching edge from the return node to the call node. Reaching edge (10,7) in the IFG in Figure 2 is an example of this type of edge. The cycle created by such an edge has to involve both a call binding edge and an exit node. In the first phase of the *ComputeChains* algorithm, an exit node is not considered, and thus the information is stopped from propagating around the cycle. In the second phase, the propagation involves a call binding edge, which is not part of the propagation, and thus the cycle is not traversed. In the latter case, the information from the return nodes needed by the call nodes is propagated over the inter-reaching edges that are added to preserve the calling context of called procedures. Thus, iteration is needed within subgraphs but not across subgraph boundaries (i.e., the entire IFG).

Step 4: Computation of the Def-Use Chains

After the reachable uses have been computed for each node in the IFG, this information is used with local DEF sets to compute the interprocedural def-use chains. This is accomplished by considering DEF sets for call and exit nodes associated with each procedure. If **d** is a definition in DEF[n] where n is either a call or return node, then the interprocedural def-use chain of **d** consists of the elements in $OUT_U[n]$. If **d** is in DEF[n] for more than one n associated with the procedure, then the interprocedural def-use chain is the union of the OUT_U sets for all n where DEF[n] contains **d**.

5.2. Handling Programs with Recursion

Programs containing recursive procedures can be processed with the same procedure *ComputeChains* by modifying the algorithm to eliminate the procedure ordering and altering the *Propagate* procedure to accommodate iteration over the procedures. This iteration is necessary since the presence of recursive procedures causes cycles in the IFG which cannot be handled in one iteration using the procedure ordering described above.

5.3. Complexity Analysis

The IFG inherits its space requirements from the program summary graph whose size is proportional to the length of the program.[4] The time complexity of the algorithm is determined by considering each of the four steps. In the first step, the creation of the graph requires one visit to each of **n** nodes in the IFG. The last step in the algorithm is performed by considering the definitions in each DEF set and combining the appropriate OUT_U sets to get the interprocedural def-use chains. This step also requires one visit to each node during the computation. In step two, the preserved information that is required for the inter-reaching edges is computed. For programs with no recursion, this computation is linear in the number of nodes in the IFG.[4] The propagation of the local information throughout the graph is accomplished in step three. If no recursion is present, then the *Propagate* algorithm visits each procedure one time to compute the interprocedural information. Processing a procedure may require iteration throughout the subgraph to accommodate the connectiveness of the subgraph due to loops in the procedure. The worst case for nonrecursive programs requires visiting $\frac{n^2}{p}$ nodes where **p** is the number of procedures in the program. For programs with recursive procedures, iteration throughout the subgraphs may be required for steps two and three. For step two, the processing may visit each node **p** times. In step three, **p** iterations may be required to obtain the IN and OUT sets using the iterative version of the *Propagate* algorithm. The worst case requires visiting $p\frac{n^2}{p}$ nodes for recursive programs. Thus, the *ComputeChains* algorithm is $O(n^2)$.

6. Incremental Updates

One of the important features of our technique is that it can be used to provide incremental updates to the interprocedural def-use dependencies. Thus, when a change is made to a program, the changed procedure is reanalyzed using either incremental [9, 13, 14] or non-incremental techniques,[1] and the interprocedural data flow information is updated to reflect the change. Modifications in a program can cause either structural or non-structural changes in the IFG. For example, adding a use causes a non-structural change while adding a definition that affects the reachability of a variable creates a structural change.

For non-structural changes and some structural changes, the local sets at each node are first updated using intraprocedural data flow analysis. Changes are then propagated to the IN and OUT sets for the reachable nodes in the IFG, which are *immediately* updated with the changed information (accounting for the calling context of called procedures). Thus, for these changes, only those nodes whose IN_U and OUT_U sets are altered by the change, are visited. For other structural changes, a two phase propagation phase is required whereby information at each node is updated in the first pass, based on the changes. The reachability of the nodes is then taken into account by a second propagation pass. Both the immediate and two phase propagations are similar to that developed for incremental intraprocedural data flow analysis.[13]

7. Conclusions

In this paper, techniques to compute and incrementally update interprocedural definition and use dependencies for a program are presented. A graph structure that abstracts data flow information for each procedure under consideration is utilized for the efficient propagation of the definition-use information. The technique handles recursion by iterating the information over the program using the graph. When a program does not contain recursion, only one iteration over the complete IFG is required. The intraprocedural data flow analysis is performed on a procedure's code without requiring information from other procedures and thus, the interprocedural data flow analysis technique supports separate compilation. The information can be incrementally updated when an edit is made in a procedure and thus, avoid a costly, unnecessary, complete reanalysis. Although definition-use information for reference parameters is the major focus in this presentation, global variables can also be represented by nodes the graph and the information about globals can then be propagated in a fashion similar to that presented for reference parameters.

The technique is especially useful for extending the concept of data flow testing to include testing interprocedural interactions. A prototype of our interprocedural dependency algorithm has been implemented in C using a Sun 3/50 Workstation. It has also been incorporated into an implementation of an interprocedural tester.[7]

Acknowledgement: The authors thank Barbara Ryder for her helpful suggestions and comments in the writing of this paper.

References

1. A. V. Aho, R. Sethi, and J. D. Ullman, in *Compilers, Principles, Techniques, and Tools*, Addison-Wesley Publishing Company, Massachusetts, 1986.

2. F. E. Allen, ''Interprocedural data flow analysis,'' in *IFIP Information Processing 74*, North-Holland Publishing Company, 1974.

3. J. M. Barth, ''A practical interprocedural data flow analysis algorithm,'' *CACM*, vol. 21, no. 9, pp. 724-736, September 1978.

4. D. Callahan, ''The program summary graph and flow-sensitive interprocedural data flow analysis,'' *Proceedings of the SIGPLAN'88 Conference on Programming Language Design and Implementation*, pp. 47-56, June 1988.

5. K. D. Cooper and K. Kennedy, ''Interprocedural side-effect analysis in linear time,'' *Proceedings of SIGPLAN '88 Conference on Programming Language Design and Implementation*, pp. 57-66, 1988.

6. P. G. Frankl and E. J. Weyuker, ''An applicable family of data flow testing criteria,'' *IEEE Transactions on Software Engineering*, vol. 14, no. 10, pp. 1483-1498, October 1988.

7. M. J. Harrold and M. L. Soffa, ''Interprocedural data flow testing,'' *Proceedings of the Third Testing, Analysis, and Verification Symposium* , December 1989.

8. S. Horwitz, T. Reps, and D. Binkley, ''Interprocedural slicing using dependence graphs,'' *Proceedings of the SIGPLAN'88 Conference on Programming Language Design and Implementation*, pp. 35-46, June, 1988.

9. J. Keables, K. Roberson, and A. von Mayhauser, ''Data flow analysis and its application to software maintenance,'' *Proceedings of the Conference on Software Maintenance-1988*, pp. 335-347, October 1988.

10. G. Kildall, ''A unified approach to global program optimization,'' *ACM Symposium on Principles of Programming Languages*, 1973.

11. D. B. Lomet, ''Data flow analysis in the presence of procedure calls,'' *IBM Journal of Research and Development*, vol. 21, no. 6, pp. 559-571, November 1977.

12. E. W. Myers, ''A precise inter-procedural data flow algorithm,'' *Conference Record of the Eighth Annual ACM Symposium on Principles of Programming Languages*, pp. 219-230, January 1981.

13. L. L. Pollock and M. L. Soffa, ''An incremental version of iterative data flow analysis,'' *IEEE Transactions on Software Engineering*, vol. SE-15, no. 12 , December 1989.

14. B. G. Ryder and M. C. Paull, ''Incremental data-flow analysis,'' *ACM Transactions on Programming Languages and Systems*, vol. 10, no. 1, pp. 1-50, January 1988.

Author Index

1111